T0178121

Lecture Notes in Computer Science

Lecture Notes in Artificial Intelligence   14125

Founding Editor

Jörg Siekmann

Series Editors

Randy Goebel, *University of Alberta, Edmonton, Canada*
Wolfgang Wahlster, *DFKI, Berlin, Germany*
Zhi-Hua Zhou, *Nanjing University, Nanjing, China*

The series Lecture Notes in Artificial Intelligence (LNAI) was established in 1988 as a topical subseries of LNCS devoted to artificial intelligence.

The series publishes state-of-the-art research results at a high level. As with the LNCS mother series, the mission of the series is to serve the international R & D community by providing an invaluable service, mainly focused on the publication of conference and workshop proceedings and postproceedings.

Leszek Rutkowski · Rafał Scherer ·
Marcin Korytkowski · Witold Pedrycz ·
Ryszard Tadeusiewicz · Jacek M. Zurada
Editors

Artificial Intelligence and Soft Computing

22nd International Conference, ICAISC 2023
Zakopane, Poland, June 18–22, 2023
Proceedings, Part I

 Springer

Editors
Leszek Rutkowski (ID)
Systems Research Institute of the Polish
Academy of Sciences
Warsaw, Poland

Rafał Scherer (ID)
Częstochowa University of Technology
Częstochowa, Poland

Witold Pedrycz (ID)
University of Alberta
Edmonton, AB, Canada

Marcin Korytkowski (ID)
Częstochowa University of Technology
Częstochowa, Poland

Jacek M. Zurada (ID)
University of Louisville
Louisville, KY, USA

Ryszard Tadeusiewicz (ID)
AGH University of Krakow
Kraków, Poland

ISSN 0302-9743   ISSN 1611-3349 (electronic)
Lecture Notes in Artificial Intelligence
ISBN 978-3-031-42504-2   ISBN 978-3-031-42505-9 (eBook)
https://doi.org/10.1007/978-3-031-42505-9

LNCS Sublibrary: SL7 – Artificial Intelligence

This Springer imprint is published by the registered company Springer Nature Switzerland AG
The registered company address is: Gewerbestrasse 11, 6330 Cham, Switzerland

Paper in this product is recyclable.

Preface

This volume constitutes the proceedings of the 22nd International Conference on Artificial Intelligence and Soft Computing, ICAISC 2023, Zakopane, Poland, June 18–22, 2023. The Conference was organized by the Polish Neural Network Society in cooperation with the Department of Intelligent Computer Systems at the Częstochowa University of Technology, the University of Social Sciences in Łódź, and the IEEE Computational Intelligence Society, Poland Chapter. The Conference was held under the auspices of the Committee on Informatics of the Polish Academy of Sciences. At ICAISC 2023 the invited lectures were presented by the following outstanding researchers: Luís A. Alexandre, Aleksander Byrski, Włodzisław Duch, Zbigniew Michalewicz, Witold Pedrycz, Jerzy Stefanowski, Wenying Xu and Shaofu Yang. Previous conferences took place in Kule (1994), Szczyrk (1996), Kule (1997) and Zakopane (1999, 2000, 2002, 2004, 2006, 2008, 2010, 2012, 2013, 2014, 2015, 2016, 2017, 2018, 2019, 2020, 2021 and 2022) and attracted a large number of papers and internationally recognized speakers: Lotfi A. Zadeh, Hojjat Adeli, Rafal Angryk, Igor Aizenberg, Cesare Alippi, Shunichi Amari, Daniel Amit, Plamen Angelov, Sanghamitra Bandyopadhyay, Albert Bifet, Piero P. Bonissone, Jim Bezdek, Zdzisław Bubnicki, Jan Chorowski, Andrzej Cichocki, Swagatam Das, Ewa Dudek-Dyduch, Włodzisław Duch, Adel S. Elmaghraby, Pablo A. Estévez, João Gama, Erol Gelenbe, Jerzy Grzymala-Busse, Martin Hagan, Yoichi Hayashi, Akira Hirose, Kaoru Hirota, Adrian Horzyk, Tingwen Huang, Eyke Hüllermeier, Hisao Ishibuchi, Er Meng Joo, Artur Luczak, Janusz Kacprzyk, Nikola Kasabov, Jim Keller, Laszlo T. Koczy, Tomasz Kopacz, Jacek Koronacki, Zdzislaw Kowalczuk, Adam Krzyzak, Rudolf Kruse, James Tin-Yau Kwok, Soo-Young Lee, Derong Liu, Robert Marks, Ujjwal Maulik, Zbigniew Michalewicz, Evangelia Micheli-Tzanakou, Kaisa Miettinen, Krystian Mikołajczyk, Henning Müller, Christian Napoli, Ngoc Thanh Nguyen, Andrzej Obuchowicz, Erkki Oja, Nikhil R. Pal, Witold Pedrycz, Marios M. Polycarpou, José C. Príncipe, Jagath C. Rajapakse, Šarunas Raudys, Enrique Ruspini, Roman Senkerik, Jörg Siekmann, Andrzej Skowron, Roman Słowiński, Igor Spiridonov, Boris Stilman, Ponnuthurai Nagaratnam Suganthan, Ryszard Tadeusiewicz, Ah-Hwee Tan, Dacheng Tao, Shiro Usui, Thomas Villmann, Fei-Yue Wang, Jun Wang, Bogdan M. Wilamowski, Ronald Y. Yager, Xin Yao, Syozo Yasui, Gary Yen, Ivan Zelinka and Jacek Zurada. The aim of this conference is to build a bridge between traditional artificial intelligence techniques and so-called soft computing techniques. It was pointed out by Lotfi A. Zadeh that "soft computing (SC) is a coalition of methodologies which are oriented toward the conception and design of information/intelligent systems. The principal members of the coalition are: fuzzy logic (FL), neurocomputing (NC), evolutionary computing (EC), probabilistic computing (PC), chaotic computing (CC), and machine learning (ML). The constituent methodologies of SC are, for the most part, complementary and synergistic rather than competitive". These proceedings present both traditional artificial intelligence methods and soft computing techniques. Our goal is to bring together scientists representing both areas of research. The proceedings are divided into three parts:

- Neural Networks and Their Applications
- Evolutionary Algorithms and Their Applications
- Artificial Intelligence in Modeling and Simulation

I would like to thank our participants, invited speakers and reviewers of the papers for their scientific and personal contribution to the Conference. Finally, I thank my co-workers Łukasz Bartczuk, Piotr Dziwiński, Marcin Gabryel, Rafał Grycuk, Marcin Korytkowski and Rafał Scherer, for their enormous efforts to make the Conference a very successful event. Moreover, I would like to appreciate the work of Marcin Korytkowski who was responsible for the Internet submission system.

June 2023   Leszek Rutkowski

Organization

ICAISC Chairpersons

General Chair

Leszek Rutkowski — Systems Research Institute, Polish Academy of Sciences, Poland

Co-chair

Rafał Scherer — Częstochowa University of Technology, Poland

Technical Chair

Marcin Korytkowski — Częstochowa University of Technology, Poland

Financial Chair

Marcin Gabryel — Częstochowa University of Technology, Poland

Area Chairs

Fuzzy Systems

Witold Pedrycz — University of Alberta, Canada

Evolutionary Algorithms

Zbigniew Michalewicz — Complexica, Australia

Neural Networks

Jinde Cao — Southeast University, China

Computer Vision

Dacheng Tao   University of Sydney, Australia

Machine Learning

Nikhil R. Pal   Indian Statistical Institute, India

Artificial Intelligence with Applications

Janusz Kacprzyk   Systems Research Institute, Polish Academy of
                                          Sciences, Poland

International Liaison

Jacek Zurada   University of Louisville, USA

ICAISC Program Committee

Hojjat Adeli	Ohio State University, USA
Cesare Alippi	Polytechnic University of Milan, Italy
Rafal A. Angryk	Georgia State University, USA
Robert Babuska	Delft University of Technology, The Netherlands
James C. Bezdek	University of Melbourne, Australia
Bernadette Bouchon-Meunier	Sorbonne University & LIP6, France
Aleksander Byrski	AGH University of Krakow, Poland
Juan Luis Castro	University of Granada, Spain
Yen-Wei Chen	Ritsumeikan University, Japan
Andrzej Cichocki	Systems Research Institute, Polish Academy of Sciences, Poland
Krzysztof Cios	Virginia Commonwealth University, USA
Ian Cloete	Stellenbosch University, South Africa
Oscar Cordón	University of Granada, Spain
Bernard De Baets	Ghent University, Belgium
Włodzisław Duch	Nicolaus Copernicus University, Poland
Meng Joo Er	Dalian Maritime University, China
Pablo Estevez	University of Chile, Chile
Tom Gedeon	Curtin University, Australia
Erol Gelenbe	Institute of Theoretical and Applied Informatics, Polish Academy of Sciences, Poland
Hani Hagras	University of Essex, UK
Saman Halgamuge	University of Melbourne, Australia

Yoichi Hayashi	Meiji University, Japan
Tim Hendtlass	Swinburne University of Technology, Australia
Francisco Herrera	Granada University, Spain
Kaoru Hirota	Tokyo Institute of Technology, Japan
Hisao Ishibuchi	Southern University of Science and Technology, China
Ivan Izonin	Lviv Polytechnic National University, Ukraine
Mo Jamshidi	University of Texas, USA
Nikola Kasabov	Auckland University of Technology, New Zealand
Okyay Kaynak	Bogazici University, Turkey
James M. Keller	University of Missouri, USA
Etienne Kerre	Ghent University, Belgium
Frank Klawonn	Ostfalia University of Applied Sciences, Germany
Robert Kozma	University of Memphis, USA
László Kóczy	Budapest University of Technology and Economics, Hungary
József Korbicz	University of Zielona Góra, Poland
Rudolf Kruse	University of Magdeburg, Germany
Adam Krzyzak	Concordia University, Canada
Věra Kůrková	Czech Academy of Sciences, Czech Republic
Ivan Laktionov	Dnipro University of Technology, Ukraine
Soo-Young Lee	Korea Advanced Institute of Science and Technology, South Korea
Simon M. Lucas	Queen Mary University of London, UK
Luis Magdalena	Technical University of Madrid, Spain
Jerry M. Mendel	University of Southern California, USA
Radko Mesiar	Slovak University of Technology in Bratislava, Slovakia
Zbigniew Michalewicz	Complexica, Australia
Kazumi Nakamatsu	University of Hyogo, Japan
Detlef D. Nauck	British Telecom, UK
Ngoc Thanh Nguyen	Wrocław University of Science and Technology, Poland
Witold Pedrycz	University of Alberta, Canada
Leonid Perlovsky	Northeastern University, USA
Marios M. Polycarpou	University of Cyprus, Cyprus
Danil Prokhorov	Toyota Tech Center, USA
Vincenzo Piuri	University of Milan, Italy
Sarunas Raudys	Vilnius University, Lithuania
Marek Reformat	University of Alberta, Canada
Imre J. Rudas	Obuda University, Hungary
Norihide Sano	Shizuoka Sangyo University, Japan

Rudy Setiono	National University of Singapore, Singapore
Jennie Si	Arizona State University, USA
Peter Sincak	Technical University of Kosice, Slovakia
Andrzej Skowron	Systems Research Institute, Polish Academy of Sciences, Poland
Roman Słowiński	Poznań University of Technology, Poland
Pilar Sobrevilla	Barcelona Tech, Spain
Janusz Starzyk	Ohio University, USA
Jerzy Stefanowski	Poznań University of Technology, Poland
Vitomir Štruc	University of Ljubljana, Slovenia
Ron Sun	Rensselaer Polytechnic Institute, USA
Johan Suykens	KU Leuven, Belgium
Ryszard Tadeusiewicz	AGH University of Science and Technology, Poland
Hideyuki Takagi	Kyushu University, Japan
Vicenç Torra	Umeå University, Sweden
Burhan Turksen	University of Toronto, Canada
Shiro Usui	RIKEN Brain Science Institute, Japan
Roman Vorobel	National Academy of Sciences of Ukraine, Ukraine
Deliang Wang	Ohio State University, USA
Jun Wang	City University of Hong Kong, China
Lipo Wang	Nanyang Technological University, Singapore
Bernard Widrow	Stanford University, USA
Kay C. Wiese	Simon Fraser University, Canada
Bogdan M. Wilamowski	Auburn University, USA
Donald C. Wunsch	Missouri University of Science and Technology, USA
Ronald R. Yager	Iona College, USA
Xin-She Yang	Middlesex University London, UK
Gary Yen	Oklahoma State University, USA
Sławomir Zadrożny	Systems Research Institute, Polish Academy of Sciences, Poland

ICAISC Organizing Committee

Rafał Scherer
Łukasz Bartczuk
Piotr Dziwiński
Marcin Gabryel (Finance Chair)
Rafał Grycuk
Marcin Korytkowski (Databases and Internet Submissions)

Contents – Part I

Evolutionary Algorithms and Their Applications

Artificial Intelligence in Modeling and Simulation

Contents – Part II

Various Problems of Artificial Intelligence

Bioinformatics, Biometrics and Medical Applications

Data Mining and Pattern Classification

Neural Networks and Their Applications

A Novel Approach to the GQR Algorithm for Neural Networks Training

Jarosław Bilski$^{(\boxtimes)}$ ⓘ and Bartosz Kowalczyk ⓘ

Department of Computational Intelligence, Częstochowa University of Technology,
Częstochowa, Poland
{Jaroslaw.Bilski,Bartosz.Kowalczyk}@pcz.pl

Abstract. In this paper, a novel approach to the GQR algorithm is presented. The idea revolves around batch training for the feedforward neural networks. The core of this paper contains a mathematical explanation for the batch approach, which can be utilized in the GQR algorithm. The final section of the article contains several simulations. They prove the novel approach to be superior to the original GQR algorithm.

Keywords: batch training · neural networks · QR decomposition · Givens rotation

1 Introduction

Artificial intelligence and its applications are the most common research areas in Computer Science [15, 20, 26]. Thanks to highly developed techniques of artificial intelligence, they can be used in many fields [9, 10, 12, 13, 18, 19, 21, 22, 24, 27]. As hardware capabilities of computational devices are limited, the researchers should pursuit various training optimization techniques. In most cases neural network training consist of several phases. First sample presentation, then gradient calculation, finally weight update performed by the training algorithm. The last stage can be the most expensive from the computational perspective. Many researchers are looking for new training algorithms [1, 2, 5, 6, 11, 14, 17, 23] and the possibility of accelerating or paralleling existing ones [3, 4, 7, 8, 25]. In order to reduce this problem the batch training has been introduced. The batch size determines how many samples are processed to compute gradients before the weight update phase. In this paper the batch training has been utilized in the GQR algorithm [6].

2 Givens Rotations Basics

One of a few elementary orthogonal transformation methods is the Givens rotations. The most common practice is to limit rotation around a single plain,

This work has been supported by the Polish National Science Center under Grant 2017/27/B/ST6/02852.

stretched between two unit vectors $span\{e_p, e_q\}(1 \leq p < q \leq n)$. Each rotation is described by the following matrix [16].

$$
\mathbf{G}_{pq} = \begin{bmatrix} 1 & & & \cdots & & & 0 \\ & \ddots & & & & & \\ & & c & \cdots & s & & \\ & \vdots & \vdots & \ddots & \vdots & \vdots & \\ & & -s & \cdots & c & & \\ & & & & & \ddots & \\ 0 & & & \cdots & & & 1 \end{bmatrix} \begin{matrix} \\ \\ p \\ \\ q \\ \\ \end{matrix} \tag{1}
$$
$$
\quad p \quad q
$$

Matrices $\mathbf{G}_{pq}$ are called rotation matrices or simply rotations. By definition, those matrices differ from Identity matrix only in terms of four elements $g_{pp} = g_{qq} = c$ and $g_{pq} = -g_{qp} = s$, where

$$
c^2 + s^2 = 1, \tag{2}
$$

which obviously leads to equation $\mathbf{G}_{pq}^T \mathbf{G}_{pq} = \mathbf{I}$ and the proof that matrix $\mathbf{G}_{pq}$ is an orthogonal matrix. The rotation is performed by orthogonal transformation given in Eq. (3)

$$
\mathbf{a} \rightarrow \bar{\mathbf{a}} = \mathbf{G}_{pq} \mathbf{a}. \tag{3}
$$

Knowing the rotation matrix (1) it is easy to notice that only two elements of vector $\mathbf{a}$ will be changed during this transformation. Due to this property, it is possible to compute the values of c and s, so the a_q will be replaced with 0 after being rotated. Let us consider

$$
\bar{a}_q = -sa_p + ca_q = 0. \tag{4}
$$

Both parameters c and s of the rotation matrix have to be calculated by following Eq. (5).

$$
c = \frac{a_p}{\rho}, \qquad s = \frac{a_q}{\rho}, \tag{5}
$$

where

$$
\rho = \sqrt{a_p^2 + a_q^2}. \tag{6}
$$

3 The Givens Rotation in a QR Decomposition

The QR decomposition method assumes that any non-singular matrix regular by columns can be depicted by the product of the upper triangle and orthogonal matrices.

$$
\mathbf{A} = \mathbf{QR}, \tag{7}
$$

where $\mathbf{Q}^T \mathbf{Q} = \mathbf{I}$, $\mathbf{Q}^T = \mathbf{Q}^{-1}$ and $r_{ij} = 0$ for $i > j$. The presented process of the QR decomposition is called the Givens orthogonalization [16]. According to Eqs. (4) and (5), for any vector $\mathbf{a} \in \mathbb{R}^m$, there exists a sequence of Givens rotations $\mathbf{G}_{12}, \mathbf{G}_{13}, \ldots, \mathbf{G}_{1m}$ that can be given as a product of each other

$$\mathbf{G}_1 = \mathbf{G}_{12} \ldots \mathbf{G}_{1,m-1} \mathbf{G}_{1m}. \tag{8}$$

Matrix $\mathbf{G}_1$ is able to perform multiple rotations at once and transform vector $\mathbf{a}$ to the pattern given by the following equation

$$\bar{\mathbf{a}} = \mathbf{G}_1 \mathbf{a} = e_1 \rho = [\rho, 0, \ldots, 0]^T, \; \rho = \pm \|\mathbf{a}\|_2 \tag{9}$$

Rotation matrix (8) is also able to transform the whole matrix. Let $\mathbf{A}$ be a non-singular matrix regular by columns and let $\mathbf{A} \in \mathbb{R}^{m,n}$. The multiplication of matrix

$$\mathbf{A} = \mathbf{A}_1 = \mathbf{M}_1 = \begin{bmatrix} \mathbf{a}_1 & \mathbf{B}_1 \end{bmatrix} \tag{10}$$

by matrix (8) gives the Eq. (11)

$$\mathbf{A}_2 = \mathbf{G}_1 \mathbf{A}_1 = \bar{\mathbf{G}}_1 \mathbf{M}_1 = \begin{bmatrix} \bar{\mathbf{a}}_1 & \bar{\mathbf{B}}_1 \end{bmatrix} = \begin{bmatrix} \rho_1 & \bar{\mathbf{B}}_1 \\ \mathbf{0} & \end{bmatrix} = \begin{bmatrix} r_{11} & r_{12} \cdots r_{1n} \\ \mathbf{0} & \mathbf{M}_2 \end{bmatrix}. \tag{11}$$

Now the left column of matrix $\mathbf{A}$ equals as shown in Eq. (9). The first row of matrix $\mathbf{A}$ is also already rotated as desired in the final upper-triangle form. In the next steps new sequences of rotations need to be performed

$$\mathbf{G}_k = \mathbf{G}_{k,k+1} \ldots \mathbf{G}_{k,m-1} \mathbf{G}_{km} \quad (k = 1, \ldots, m-1). \tag{12}$$

Realizing analogous transformations of matrix $\mathbf{M}_k$, each time the input matrix is one step closer to the desired upper-triangle form

$$\mathbf{A}_{k+1} = \bar{\mathbf{G}}_k \mathbf{M}_k = \begin{bmatrix} \bar{\mathbf{a}}_k & \bar{\mathbf{B}}_k \end{bmatrix} = \begin{bmatrix} \rho_k & \bar{\mathbf{B}}_k \\ \mathbf{0} & \end{bmatrix} = \begin{bmatrix} r_{kk} & r_{k,k+1} \cdots r_{k,n} \\ \mathbf{0} & \mathbf{M}_{k+1} \end{bmatrix}, \tag{13}$$

where

$$\mathbf{G}_k = \begin{bmatrix} \mathbf{I}_{k-1} & \mathbf{0} \\ \mathbf{0} & \bar{\mathbf{G}}_k \end{bmatrix}. \tag{14}$$

After $m - 1$ steps the input matrix is fully transformed into the upper-triangle form

$$\mathbf{R} = \mathbf{G}_{m-1} \ldots \mathbf{G}_1 \mathbf{A}_1 = \mathbf{G}_{m-1,m} \ldots \mathbf{G}_{23} \ldots \mathbf{G}_{2m} \mathbf{G}_{12} \ldots \mathbf{G}_{1m} \mathbf{A}_1 = \mathbf{Q}^T \mathbf{A} \tag{15}$$

Orthogonal matrix $\mathbf{Q}$ can be retrieved from respective rotations

$$\mathbf{Q} = \mathbf{G}_1^T \ldots \mathbf{G}_{m-1}^T = \mathbf{G}_{1m}^T \ldots \mathbf{G}_{12}^T \mathbf{G}_{2m}^T \ldots \mathbf{G}_{23}^T \ldots \mathbf{G}_{m-1,m}^T \tag{16}$$

The full QR decomposition has been accomplished by the Givens rotations as given in Eq. (7).

4   Neural Network Learning with a QR Decomposition

This paper presents training of a multilayer Neural Network with any differentiable activation function [2]. The purpose of the learning process is to minimize batch modified loss function expressed by the formula given below

$$
\begin{aligned}
J(n) &= \sum_{t=1}^{n} \lambda^{n-t} \sum_{m=1}^{M} \sum_{j=1}^{N_L} \varepsilon_j^{(L)\,2}(t,m) \\
&= \sum_{t=1}^{n} \lambda^{n-t} \sum_{m=1}^{M} \sum_{j=1}^{N_L} \left[d_j^{(L)}(t,m) - f\left(\mathbf{x}^{(L)\,T}(t,m)\,\mathbf{w}_j^{(L)}(n) \right) \right]^2
\end{aligned}
\tag{17}
$$

where M is the batch size. The next equations show how to formulate an entry point for the Givens algorithm. In the first step the gradient of loss function expressed by Eq. (17) is computed and equated to $\mathbf{0}$.

$$
\begin{aligned}
\frac{\partial J(n)}{\partial \mathbf{w}_i^{(l)}(n)} &= 2 \sum_{t=1}^{n} \lambda^{n-t} \sum_{m=1}^{M} \sum_{j=1}^{N_L} \frac{\partial \varepsilon_j^{(L)}(t,m)}{\partial \mathbf{w}_i^{(l)}(n)} \varepsilon_j^{(L)}(t,m) \\
&= -2 \sum_{t=1}^{n} \lambda^{n-t} \sum_{m=1}^{M} \sum_{j=1}^{N_L} \frac{\partial y_j^{(L)}(t,m)}{\partial \mathbf{w}_i^{(l)}(n)} \varepsilon_j^{(L)}(t,m) = \mathbf{0}
\end{aligned}
\tag{18}
$$

Equation (18) needs to be transformed

$$
\begin{aligned}
&\sum_{t=1}^{n} \lambda^{n-t} \sum_{m=1}^{M} \sum_{j=1}^{N_L} \frac{\partial y_j^{(L)}(t,m)}{\partial s_j^{(L)}(t,m)} \sum_{p=1}^{N_{L-1}} \frac{\partial s_j^{(L)}(t,m)}{\partial y_p^{(L-1)}(t,m)} \frac{\partial y_p^{(L-1)}(t,m)}{\partial \mathbf{w}_i^{(l)}(n)} \varepsilon_j^{(L)}(t,m) \\
&= \sum_{t=1}^{n} \lambda^{n-t} \sum_{m=1}^{M} \sum_{p=1}^{N_{L-1}} \frac{\partial y_p^{(L-1)}(t,m)}{\partial \mathbf{w}_i^{(l)}(n)} \sum_{j=1}^{N_L} \frac{\partial y_j^{(L)}(t,m)}{\partial s_j^{(L)}(t,m)} w_{jp}^{(L)} \varepsilon_j^{(L)}(t,m) \\
&= \sum_{t=1}^{n} \lambda^{n-t} \sum_{m=1}^{M} \sum_{p=1}^{N_{L-1}} \frac{\partial y_p^{(L-1)}(t,m)}{\partial \mathbf{w}_i^{(l)}(n)} \varepsilon_p^{(L-1)}(t,m) \\
&= \sum_{t=1}^{n} \lambda^{n-t} \sum_{m=1}^{M} \sum_{q=1}^{N_l} \frac{\partial y_q^{(l)}(t,m)}{\partial \mathbf{w}_i^{(l)}(n)} \varepsilon_q^{(l)}(t,m) = \mathbf{0},
\end{aligned}
\tag{19}
$$

where $\varepsilon_p^{(l)}(t)$ is the error value in each layer calculated from the last to the first layer according to Eq. (20)

$$
\varepsilon_p^{(l)}(t) = \sum_{j=1}^{N_{l+1}} \frac{\partial y_j^{(l+1)}(t)}{\partial s_j^{(l+1)}(t)} w_{jp}^{(l+1)}(n) \varepsilon_j^{(l+1)}(t).
\tag{20}
$$

After additional transformations, one obtains

$$
\begin{aligned}
&\sum_{t=1}^{n} \lambda^{n-t} \sum_{m=1}^{M} \sum_{q=1}^{N_l} \frac{\partial y_q^{(l)}(t,m)}{\partial \mathbf{w}_i^{(l)}(n)} \varepsilon_q^{(l)}(t,m) \\
&= \sum_{t=1}^{n} \lambda^{n-t} \sum_{m=1}^{M} \sum_{q=1}^{N_l} \frac{\partial y_q^{(l)}(t,m)}{\partial s_q^{(l)}(t,m)} \frac{\partial s_q^{(l)}(t,m)}{\partial \mathbf{w}_i^{(l)}(n)} \varepsilon_q^{(l)}(t,m) \\
&= \sum_{j=1}^{n} \lambda^{n-j} \sum_{m=1}^{M} \frac{\partial y_i^{(l)}(t,m)}{\partial s_i^{(l)}(t,m)} \mathbf{y}^{(l-1)\,T}(t,m) \varepsilon_i^{(l)}(t,m) \\
&= \sum_{t=1}^{n} \lambda^{n-t} \sum_{m=1}^{M} \frac{\partial y_i^{(l)}(t,m)}{\partial s_i^{(l)}(t,m)} \mathbf{y}^{(l-1)\,T}(t,m) \left[d_i^{(l)}(t,m) - y_i^{(l)}(t,m) \right] = \mathbf{0}
\end{aligned}
\tag{21}
$$

Finally, the result of transformations (21) is linearized

$$f\left(b_i^{(l)}(t,m)\right) \approx f\left(s_i^{(l)}(t,m)\right) + f'\left(s_i^{(l)}(t,m)\right)\left(b_i^{(l)}(t,m) - s_i^{(l)}(t,m)\right) \quad (22)$$

and the following normal equation is obtained

$$\sum_{t=1}^{n} \lambda^{n-t} \sum_{m=1}^{M} f'^2\left(s_i^{(l)}(t,m)\right)\left[b_i^{(l)}(t,m) - \mathbf{x}^{(l)T}(t,m)\mathbf{w}_i^{(l)}(n)\right]\mathbf{x}^{(l)T}(t,m) = \mathbf{0}$$

$$(23)$$

Equation (23) in a vector form is a start point for the Givens algorithm

$$\mathbf{A}_i^{(l)}(n)\,\mathbf{w}_i^{(l)}(n) = \mathbf{h}_i^{(l)}(n), \quad (24)$$

where

$$\mathbf{A}_i^{(l)}(n) = \sum_{t=1}^{n} \lambda^{n-t} \sum_{m=1}^{M} f'^2\left(s_i^{(l)}(t,m)\right)\mathbf{x}^{(l)}(t,m)\mathbf{x}^{(l)T}(t,m) \quad (25)$$

$$\mathbf{h}_i^{(l)}(n) = \sum_{t=1}^{n} \lambda^{n-t} \sum_{m=1}^{M} f'^2\left(s_i^{(l)}(t,m)\right)b_i^{(l)}(t,m)\mathbf{x}^{(l)}(t,m) \quad (26)$$

For simplicity the following substitution is performed

$$\mathbf{z}_i^{(l)}(t,m) = f'\left(s_i^{(l)}(t,m)\right)\mathbf{x}^{(l)}(t,m) \quad (27)$$

Then, equations (25) and (26) are transformed to formulas (28) and (29) respectively

$$\mathbf{A}_i^{(l)}(n) = \sum_{t=1}^{n} \lambda^{n-t} \sum_{m=1}^{M} \mathbf{z}_i^{(l)}(t,m)\mathbf{z}_i^{(l)T}(t,m) \quad (28)$$

$$\mathbf{h}_i^{(l)}(n) = \sum_{t=1}^{n} \lambda^{n-t} \sum_{m=1}^{M} f'\left(s_i^{(l)}(t,m)\right)b_i^{(l)}(t,m)\mathbf{z}_i^{(l)}(t,m) \quad (29)$$

where

$$b_i^{(l)}(t,m) = \begin{cases} b_i^{(L)}(t,m) = f^{-1}\left(d_i^{(L)}(t,m)\right) & for\ l = L \\ s_i^{(l)}(t,m) + e_i^{(l)}(t,m) & for\ l = 1\dots L-1, \end{cases} \quad (30)$$

$$e_i^{(k)}(t,m) = \sum_{j=1}^{N_{k+1}} f'\left(s_i^{(k)}(t,m)\right)w_{ji}^{(k+1)}(t,m)e_j^{(k+1)}(t,m) \quad for\ k = 1\dots L-1$$

$$(31)$$

To solve Eq. (24), the QR decomposition was used. It should be emphasized that subsequent calculations using matrix A are carried out after taking into account all data from the batch. After completion, Eq. (24) should be left-sided multiplied by $\mathbf{Q}^T$

$$\mathbf{Q}_i^{(l)T}(n)\,\mathbf{A}_i^{(l)}(n)\,\mathbf{w}_i^{(l)}(n) = \mathbf{Q}_i^{(l)T}(n)\,\mathbf{h}_i^{(l)}(n)\,, \tag{32}$$

$$\mathbf{R}_i^{(l)}(n)\,\mathbf{w}_i^{(l)}(n) = \mathbf{Q}_i^{(l)T}(n)\,\mathbf{h}_i^{(l)}(n)\,. \tag{33}$$

Obviously, vector $\mathbf{h}$ is rotated along with matrix $\mathbf{A}$. As the result of the QR decomposition, matrix $\mathbf{R}$ is the upper-triangle and its inversion is not expensive. Finally, the weights of neurons in each layer can be adjusted according to the following equations

$$\hat{\mathbf{w}}_i^{(l)}(n) = \mathbf{R}_i^{(l)-1}(n)\,\mathbf{Q}_i^{(l)T}(n)\,\mathbf{h}_i^{(l)}(n)\,, \tag{34}$$

$$\mathbf{w}_i^{(l)}(n) = (1-\eta)\,\mathbf{w}_i^{(l)}(n-1) + \eta\,\hat{\mathbf{w}}_i^{(l)}(n)\,. \tag{35}$$

5   Research and Results

The proposed approach has been tested in three scenarios along with various networks topology. Each benchmark was initially researched in terms of optimal set of hyperparameters. In order to gather valuable statistics each scenario was retried 100 times.

5.1   The Two Spirals Benchmark

The two spirals benchmark consist of 96 samples. Each has two inputs and a single output. This classification test expects neural network to classify points to one of the two spirals—upper or the lower one. In this benchmark the fully connected feedforward neural network with 3 hidden layers, 5 neurons each has been used (FCMLP-2-5-5-5-1). The algorithm's hyperparameters that were used to produce the presented results are $\eta = 0.03$ and $\lambda = 0.99$. Each training lasted for 100 epochs. Table 1 holds the results.

Table 1. The two spirals benchmark results.

Batch size	SR [%]	Time avg. [ms]	MSE
1	97	302.996	0.0665743
8	92	164.391	0.0732619
16	91	151.333	2.18839
32	98	146.292	0.173447
64	98	144.526	0.232894

5.2   The Concrete Benchmark

The concrete benchmark consist of 1030 samples. Each has eight inputs and a single output. This regression test expects neural network to guess the concrete compressive strength. In this benchmark the fully connected feedforward neural network with 2 hidden layers, 8 neurons each has been used (FCMLP-8-8-8-1). The algorithm's hyperparameters that were used to produce the presented results are $\eta = 0.009$ and $\lambda = 0.99$. Each training lasted for 30 epochs. Table 2 holds the results.

Table 2. The concrete benchmark results.

Batch size	SR [%]	Time avg. [ms]	MSE
1	100	1636.5	0.0079282
8	100	579.948	0.0100526
16	100	504.569	0.0114892
32	100	465.12	0.0139548
64	100	444.38	0.0167566

5.3   The Abalone Benchmark

The abalone benchmark consist of 4177 samples. Each has eight inputs and a single output. This classification test expects neural network to guess the age of the abalone, which is a sea creature. In this benchmark the classic feedforward neural network with 2 hidden layers, 4 neurons each has been used (MLP-8-4-4-1). The algorithm's hyperparameters that were used to produce the presented results are $\eta = 0.009$ and $\lambda = 0.99$. Each training lasted for 30 epochs. Table 3 holds the results.

Table 3. The abalone benchmark results.

Batch size	SR [%]	Time avg. [ms]	MSE
1	100	1726.43	0.0110602
8	100	1219.96	0.0109243
16	100	1163.44	0.0110326
32	100	1132.12	0.0113131
64	100	1119.42	0.0115741

6   Conclusion

In this paper the novel batch approach for the GQR algorithm was presented. As it turns out during the experiments, utilization of the batches significantly reduces the training time. Each concluded experiment with batch size bigger than 1 turn out to be supreme to the standard GQR algorithm, which performs weights update for every sample. However, too big batch size can lead to MSE increase. This hyperparameter should be set by the trial and error. For most cases batch size of 32 samples seems to be a good starting point.

As showed in this paper, the batch approach is the right way of optimizing training time in complex algorithms. In the near future we plan to research similar approach for other RLS [2] and GQR based algorithms and the Levenberg-Marquardt [8] algorithm.

References

1. Bilski, J., Kowalczyk, B., Marchlewska, A., Żurada, J.M.: Local Levenberg-Marquardt algorithm for learning feedforwad neural networks. J. Artif. Intell. Soft Comput. Res. **10**(4), 299–316 (2020)
2. Bilski, J., Rutkowski, L.: A fast training algorithm for neural networks. IEEE Trans. Circ. Syst. Part II **45**(6), 749–753 (1998)
3. Bilski, J., Smolag, J.: Parallel architectures for learning the RTRN and Elman dynamic neural network. IEEE Trans. Parallel Distrib. Syst. **26**(9), 2561–2570 (2015)
4. Bilski, J., Wilamowski, B.M.: Parallel Levenberg-Marquardt algorithm without error backpropagation. In: Rutkowski, L., Korytkowski, M., Scherer, R., Tadeusiewicz, R., Zadeh, L.A., Zurada, J.M. (eds.) ICAISC 2017. LNCS (LNAI), vol. 10245, pp. 25–39. Springer, Cham (2017). https://doi.org/10.1007/978-3-319-59063-9_3
5. Bilski, J., Kowalczyk, B., Kisiel-Dorohinicki, M., Siwocha, A., Żurada, J.: Towards a very fast feedforward multilayer neural networks training algorithm (2022)
6. Bilski, J., Kowalczyk, B., Marjanski, A., Gandor, M., Żurada, J.: A novel fast feedforward neural networks training algorithm. J. Artif. Intell. Soft Comput. Res. **11**(4), 287–306 (2021)
7. Bilski, J., Rutkowski, L., Smolag, J., Tao, D.: A novel method for speed training acceleration of recurrent neural networks. Inf. Sci. **553**, 266–279 (2021)
8. Bilski, J., Smolag, J., Kowalczyk, B., Grzanek, K., Izonin, I.: Fast computational approach to the Levenberg-Marquardt algorithm for training feedforward neural networks. J. Artif. Intell. Soft Comput. Res. **12**(2), 45–61 (2023)
9. Bougueroua, N., Mazouzi, S., Belaoued, M., Seddari, N., Derhab, A., Bouras, A.: A survey on multi-agent based collaborative intrusion detection systems. J. Artif. Intell. Soft Comput. Res. **11**(2), 111–142 (2021)
10. Cierniak, R., et al.: A new statistical reconstruction method for the computed tomography using an x-ray tube with flying focal spot. J. Artif. Intell. Soft Comput. Res. **11**(4), 243–266 (2021)
11. Duchi, J., Hazan, E., Singer, Y.: Adaptive subgradient methods for online learning and stochastic optimization. J. Mach. Learn. Res. **12**, 2121–2159 (2011)
12. Gabryel, M., Grzanek, K., Hayashi, Y.: Browser fingerprint coding methods increasing the effectiveness of user identification in the web traffic. J. Artif. Intell. Soft Comput. Res. **10**(4), 243–253 (2020)
13. Gabryel, M., Lada, D., Filutowicz, Z., Patora-Wysocka, Z., Kisiel-Dorohinicki, M., Chen, G.Y.: Detecting anomalies in advertising web traffic with the use of the variational autoencoder. J. Artif. Intell. Soft Comput. Res. **12**(4), 255–256 (2022)

14. Hagan, M.T., Menhaj, M.B.: Training feedforward networks with the Marquardt algorithm. IEEE Trans. Neural Networks **5**, 989–993 (1994)
15. Hinton, G., Sejnowski, T.J.: Unsupervised Learning: Foundations of Neural Computation. The MIT Press, Cambridge (1999)
16. Kiełbasiński, A., Schwetlick, H.: Numeryczna Algebra Liniowa: Wprowadzenie do Obliczeń Zautomatyzowanych. Wydawnictwa Naukowo-Techniczne, Warszawa (1992)
17. Kingma, D.P., Ba, J.: Adam: a method for stochastic optimization (2014)
18. Niksa-Rynkiewicz, T., Szewczuk-Krypa, N., Witkowska, A., Cpalka, K., Zalasinski, M., Cader, A.: Monitoring regenerative heat exchanger in steam power plant by making use of the recurrent neural network. J. Artif. Intell. Soft Comput. Res. **11**(2), 143–155 (2021)
19. Pérez-Pons, M.E., Parra-Dominguez, J., Omatu, S., Herrera-Viedma, E., Corchado, J.M.: Machine learning and traditional econometric models: a systematic mapping study. J. Artif. Intell. Soft Comput. Res. **12**(2), 79–100 (2022)
20. Werbos, J.: Beyond Regression: New Tools for Prediction and Analysis in the Behavioral Sciences. Harvard University (1974)
21. Woldan, P., Duda, P., Cader, A., Laktionov, I.: A new approach to image-based recommender systems with the application of heatmaps maps. J. Artif. Intell. Soft Comput. Res. **12**(2), 63–72 (2023)
22. Zalasinski, M., et al.: Evolutionary algorithm for selecting dynamic signatures partitioning approach (2022)
23. Zeiler, M.: ADADELTA: an adaptive learning rate method (2012)
24. Zhao, X., Song, M., Liu, A., Wang, Y., Wang, T., Cao, J.: Data-driven temporal-spatial model for the prediction of AQI in Nanjing. J. Artif. Intell. Soft Comput. Res. **10**(4), 255–270 (2020)
25. El Zini, J., Rizk, Y., Awad, M.: An optimized parallel implementation of non-iteratively trained recurrent neural networks. J. Artif. Intell. Soft Comput. Res. **11**(1), 33–50 (2021)
26. Żurada, J.M.: Introduction to Artificial Neural Systems. West (1992)
27. Łapa, K., Cpałka, K., Kisiel-Dorohinicki, M., Paszkowski, J., Dębski, M., Le, V.-H.: Multi-population-based algorithm with an exchange of training plans based on population evaluation (2022)

On Speeding up the Levenberg-Marquardt Learning Algorithm

Jarosław Bilski[✉][iD], Barosz Kowalczyk[iD], and Jacek Smoląg[iD]

Department of Computational Intelligence, Częstochowa University of Technology, Częstochowa, Poland
{Jaroslaw.Bilski,Barosz.Kowalczyk,Jacek.Smolag}@pcz.pl

Abstract. A new approach to the practical realizations of calculations to the Levenberg-Marquardt learning algorithm is presented. The proposed solutions aim to effectively reduce the high computational load of the LM algorithm. The detailed application of proposed methods in the process of learning neural networks is explicitly discussed. Experimental results have been obtained for all proposed methods and they confirm a very good performance of them.

Keywords: neural network learning algorithm · Levenberg-Marquardt learning algorithm · parallel computations · approximation · classification

1 Introduction

Currently, many scientists present the results of research on artificial feedforward neural networks see. e.g. [4, 13, 14, 16, 33, 34, 37, 49, 51, 55]. A popular approach to training feedforward neural networks is the use of gradient methods, see e.g. [20, 35, 50]. In many cases, neural network learning algorithms are simulated on serial computers [23, 36, 39, 40, 42, 46, 47]. The use of serial computers for algorithms with high computational complexity results in a significant extension of the learning time. The Levenberg Marquart (LM) algorithm [2, 25, 32] is one of the most effective learning algorithms, unfortunately, it requires a lot of calculations. For large networks and many learning samples, the computational load of the algorithms makes them impractical. Therefore, new methods that significantly reduce real computation time are so important. One way to solve this problem is, for example, to use dedicated high-performance parallel structures, see e.g. [3, 6–13, 15, 26, 44, 45, 54]. This paper shows a new approach to the practical realizations of calculations to the Levenberg-Marquardt learning algorithm. The results of the study of a new computational approach to the LM algorithm are shown in the papers last part.

A sample structure of the feedforward neural network is shown in Fig. 1. This sample network has L layers, N_l neurons in each $l - th$ layer, and N_L outputs.

This work has been supported by the Polish National Science Center under Grant 2017/27/B/ST6/02852.

L. Rutkowski et al. (Eds.): ICAISC 2023, LNAI 14125, pp. 12–22, 2023.
https://doi.org/10.1007/978-3-031-42505-9_2

The input vector contains N_0 input values. The Eq. (1) describes the recall phase of the network

$$s_i^{(l)}(t) = \sum_{j=0}^{N_{l-1}} w_{ij}^{(l)}(t) x_j^{(l)}(t),$$

$$y_i^{(l)}(t) = f(s_i^{(l)}(t)). \tag{1}$$

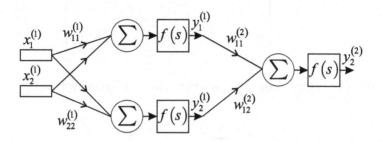

Fig. 1. Sample feedforward neural network.

The Levenberg-Marquard method [25,32] is used to train the feedforward neural network. The following loss function is minimized

$$E\left(\mathbf{w}\left(n\right)\right) = \frac{1}{2}\sum_{t=1}^{Q}\sum_{r=1}^{N_L}\varepsilon_r^{(L)^2}(t) = \frac{1}{2}\sum_{t=1}^{Q}\sum_{r=1}^{N_L}\left(y_r^{(L)}(t) - d_r^{(L)}(t)\right)^2 \tag{2}$$

where $\varepsilon_i^{(L)}$ is defined as

$$\varepsilon_r^{(L)}(t) = \varepsilon_r^{(Lr)}(t) = y_r^{(L)}(t) - d_r^{(L)}(t) \tag{3}$$

and $d_r^{(L)}(t)$ is the $r-th$ desired output in the $t-th$ probe, Q is the number of training data.

The LM algorithm is derived from the Newton method and is based on the first three elements of the Taylor series expansion of the loss function. A change of weights is carried out by

$$\Delta\left(\mathbf{w}(n)\right) = -\left[\nabla^2 \mathbf{E}\left(\mathbf{w}(n)\right)\right]^{-1}\nabla \mathbf{E}\left(\mathbf{w}(n)\right) \tag{4}$$

and requires the calculation of the gradient vector

$$\nabla \mathbf{E}\left(\mathbf{w}(n)\right) = \mathbf{J}^T\left(\mathbf{w}(n)\right)\varepsilon\left(\mathbf{w}(n)\right) \tag{5}$$

and the Hessian matrix

$$\nabla^2 \mathbf{E}\left(\mathbf{w}(n)\right) = \mathbf{J}^T\left(\mathbf{w}(n)\right)\mathbf{J}\left(\mathbf{w}(n)\right) + \mathbf{S}\left(\mathbf{w}(n)\right) \tag{6}$$

where $\mathbf{J}\left(\mathbf{w(n)}\right)$ in (5) and (6) is the Jacobian matrix given by

$$
\mathbf{J}(\mathbf{w}\left(n\right)) =
\begin{bmatrix}
\dfrac{\partial \varepsilon_1^{(L)}(1)}{\partial w_{10}^{(1)}} & \cdots & \dfrac{\partial \varepsilon_1^{(L)}(1)}{\partial w_{ij}^{(k)}} & \cdots & \dfrac{\partial \varepsilon_1^{(L)}(1)}{\partial w_{N_L N_{L-1}}^{(L)}} \\[2ex]
\vdots & \cdots & \vdots & \cdots & \vdots \\[2ex]
\dfrac{\partial \varepsilon_{N_L}^{(L)}(1)}{\partial w_{10}^{(1)}} & \cdots & \dfrac{\partial \varepsilon_{N_L}^{(L)}(1)}{\partial w_{ij}^{(k)}} & \cdots & \dfrac{\partial \varepsilon_{N_L}^{(L)}(1)}{\partial w_{N_L N_{L-1}}^{(L)}} \\[2ex]
\vdots & \cdots & \vdots & \cdots & \vdots \\[2ex]
\dfrac{\partial \varepsilon_{N_L}^{(L)}(Q)}{\partial w_{10}^{(1)}} & \cdots & \dfrac{\partial \varepsilon_{N_L}^{(L)}(Q)}{\partial w_{ij}^{(k)}} & \cdots & \dfrac{\partial \varepsilon_{N_L}^{(L)}(Q)}{\partial w_{N_L N_{L-1}}^{(L)}}
\end{bmatrix}.
\tag{7}
$$

In the hidden layers the errors $\varepsilon_i^{(lr)}$ are calculated in the following way

$$
\varepsilon_i^{(lr)}(t) \overset{\triangle}{=} \sum_{m=1}^{N_{l+1}} \delta_i^{(l+1,r)}(t)\, w_{mi}^{(l+1)},
\tag{8}
$$

$$
\delta_i^{(lr)}(t) = \varepsilon_i^{(lr)}(t)\, f'\left(s_i^{(lr)}(t)\right).
\tag{9}
$$

From this, the elements of the Jacobian matrix can be calculated for each weight

$$
\frac{\partial \varepsilon_r^{(L)}(t)}{w_{ij}^{(l)}} = \delta_i^{(lr)}(t)\, x_j^{(l)}(t).
\tag{10}
$$

It's easy to see that derivatives (10) are calculated similarly to the classic backpropagation method, except that each time there is only one error given to the output. In this algorithm, the weights of the entire network are treated as a single vector and their derivatives create the Jacobian matrix $\mathbf{J}$.

The $\mathbf{S}\left(\mathbf{w}(n)\right)$ matrix (6) is shown by the formula

$$
\mathbf{S}\left(\mathbf{w}(n)\right) = \sum_{t=1}^{Q} \sum_{r=1}^{N_L} \varepsilon_r^{(L)}(t) \nabla^2 \varepsilon_r^{(L)}(t).
\tag{11}
$$

In the Gauss-Newton method it is assumed that $\mathbf{S}\left(\mathbf{w}(n)\right) \approx 0$ and that Eq. (4) takes the form

$$
\Delta\left(\mathbf{w}(n)\right) = -\left[\mathbf{J}^T\left(\mathbf{w}(n)\right)\mathbf{J}\left(\mathbf{w}(n)\right)\right]^{-1}\mathbf{J}^T\left(\mathbf{w}(n)\right)\varepsilon\left(\mathbf{w}(n)\right).
\tag{12}
$$

In the Levenberg-Marquardt method it is assumed that $\mathbf{S}\left(\mathbf{w}(n)\right) = \mu\mathbf{I}$ and that Eq. (4) takes the form

$$
\Delta\left(\mathbf{w}(n)\right) = -\left[\mathbf{J}^T\left(\mathbf{w}(n)\right)\mathbf{J}\left(\mathbf{w}(n)\right) + \mu\mathbf{I}\right]^{-1}\mathbf{J}^T\left(\mathbf{w}(n)\right)\varepsilon\left(\mathbf{w}(n)\right).
\tag{13}
$$

By substitution

$$
\begin{aligned}
\mathbf{A}\left(n\right) &= -\left[\mathbf{J}^T\left(\mathbf{w}(n)\right)\mathbf{J}\left(\mathbf{w}(n)\right) + \mu\mathbf{I}\right] \\
\mathbf{h}\left(n\right) &= \mathbf{J}^T\left(\mathbf{w}(n)\right)\varepsilon\left(\mathbf{w}(n)\right)
\end{aligned}
\tag{14}
$$

the Eq. (13) is as follows

$$\Delta\left(\mathbf{w}(n)\right) = \mathbf{A}(n)^{-1}\mathbf{h}\left(n\right). \tag{15}$$

The Eq. (15) is solved by QR factorization

$$\mathbf{Q}^{T}\left(n\right)\mathbf{A}\left(n\right)\Delta\left(\mathbf{w}(n)\right) = \mathbf{Q}^{T}\left(n\right)\mathbf{h}\left(n\right), \tag{16}$$

$$\mathbf{R}\left(n\right)\Delta\left(\mathbf{w}(n)\right) = \mathbf{Q}^{T}\left(n\right)\mathbf{h}\left(n\right). \tag{17}$$

This paper used the Givens rotations for the QR factorization. The operation of the LM algorithm is described in the following 5 steps:

1. The calculation of the network outputs and errors for all input data, and the loss function.
2. Calculation of the Jacobian matrix by the backpropagation method for each error separately.
3. The calculation of weight increments $\Delta\left(\mathbf{w}(n)\right)$ using the QR factorization.
4. The loss function (2) is calculated again for new weights $\mathbf{w}(n) + \Delta\left(\mathbf{w}(n)\right)$. If the loss function is less than the one previously calculated in step 1, then μ should be reduced β times, the new weight vector is approved and the algorithm goes to Step 1. Otherwise, the μ value is increased β times and the algorithm repeats step 3.
5. The algorithm finishes when the loss function falls below a preset value or the gradient falls below a preset value.

2 The New Methodologies of Calculations of the Levenberg-Marquardt Learning Algorithm

The section presents practical ways of implementing the calculations of the LM algorithm. The main purpose of the modification is to shorten the real running time of the algorithm. The efficiency of the proposed solutions has been presented in relation to the classical LM algorithm implemented serially.

The following sections describe variants of the calculations of the LM algorithm that allow for shortening the calculation time. They all take advantage of the properties of modern processors.

2.1 The LM Transposed

The classical LM algorithm computes the Jacobian matrix $\mathbf{J}$ Eq. (7), and then it computes the matrix $\mathbf{A}$. It is unnecessary to compute the transposed Jacobian matrix $\mathbf{J}^{T}$. The elements of matrix $\mathbf{A}$ are determined by calculating the dot products of the corresponding columns of the Jacobian matrix $\mathbf{J}$. In the proposed variant, instead of calculating the Jacobian matrix $\mathbf{J}$, a transposed Jacobian matrix $\mathbf{J}^{T}$ Eq. (18) is determined. As a result, the elements of matrix $\mathbf{A}$ are determined by calculating the dot products of rows, not columns. This approach takes advantage of the fact that processors read data placed sequentially in memory faster than data placed in different places. Such a case is a matrix, the elements of the rows are placed sequentially, and the elements of the columns are in different places of memory.

$$
\mathbf{J}^T\left(\mathbf{w}\left(n\right)\right) =
\begin{bmatrix}
\dfrac{\partial \varepsilon_1^{(L)}(1)}{\partial w_{10}^{(1)}} & \cdots & \dfrac{\partial \varepsilon_{N_L}^{(L)}(1)}{\partial w_{10}^{(1)}} & \cdots & \dfrac{\partial \varepsilon_{N_L}^{(L)}(Q)}{\partial w_{10}^{(1)}} \\
\vdots & \cdots & \vdots & \cdots & \vdots \\
\dfrac{\partial \varepsilon_1^{(L)}(1)}{\partial w_{ij}^{(k)}} & \cdots & \dfrac{\partial \varepsilon_{N_L}^{(L)}(1)}{\partial w_{ij}^{(k)}} & \cdots & \dfrac{\partial \varepsilon_{N_L}^{(L)}(Q)}{\partial w_{ij}^{(k)}} \\
\vdots & \cdots & \vdots & \cdots & \vdots \\
\dfrac{\partial \varepsilon_1^{(L)}(1)}{\partial w_{N_L N_{L-1}}^{(L)}} & \cdots & \dfrac{\partial \varepsilon_{N_L}^{(L)}(1)}{\partial w_{N_L N_{L-1}}^{(L)}} & \cdots & \dfrac{\partial \varepsilon_{N_L}^{(L)}(Q)}{\partial w_{N_L N_{L-1}}^{(L)}}
\end{bmatrix}.
\tag{18}
$$

2.2   The Mini-Batch LM

In another variant, the Jacobian matrix $\mathbf{J}$ is divided into fragments called mini-batches containing M training data each $\mathbf{J}_i$, see Eq. (19). The mini-batches are determined sequentially, and the dot products of the mini-batch columns are accumulated in the elements of matrix $\mathbf{A}$. The sum of the partial dot products of the mini-batch columns is equal to the dot product of the columns of the entire Jacobian matrix. This approach results in a much smaller memory size required to store a single mini-batch matrix $\mathbf{J}_i$ than for the entire Jacobian matrix $\mathbf{J}$. Modern processors have a multilevel cache. The presented solution allows fitting the minibatch matrix $\mathbf{J}_i$ in the cache of a given level, which is unattainable for the entire Jacobian matrix $\mathbf{J}$ in the case of a large number of training samples Q. Since the cache memory is much more efficient than the main memory, one should expect an acceleration of the LM algorithm.

$$
\mathbf{J}_i(\mathbf{w}\left(n\right)) =
\begin{bmatrix}
\dfrac{\partial \varepsilon_1^{(L)}(iM+1)}{\partial w_{10}^{(1)}} & \cdots & \dfrac{\partial \varepsilon_1^{(L)}(iM+1)}{\partial w_{ij}^{(k)}} & \cdots & \dfrac{\partial \varepsilon_1^{(L)}(iM+1)}{\partial w_{N_L N_{L-1}}^{(L)}} \\
\vdots & \cdots & \vdots & \cdots & \vdots \\
\dfrac{\partial \varepsilon_{N_L}^{(L)}(iM+1)}{\partial w_{10}^{(1)}} & \cdots & \dfrac{\partial \varepsilon_{N_L}^{(L)}(iM+1)}{\partial w_{ij}^{(k)}} & \cdots & \dfrac{\partial \varepsilon_{N_L}^{(L)}(iM+1)}{\partial w_{N_L N_{L-1}}^{(L)}} \\
\vdots & \cdots & \vdots & \cdots & \vdots \\
\dfrac{\partial \varepsilon_{N_L}^{(L)}((i+1)M)}{\partial w_{10}^{(1)}} & \cdots & \dfrac{\partial \varepsilon_{N_L}^{(L)}((i+1)M)}{\partial w_{ij}^{(k)}} & \cdots & \dfrac{\partial \varepsilon_{N_L}^{(L)}((i+1)M)}{\partial w_{N_L N_{L-1}}^{(L)}}
\end{bmatrix}.
\tag{19}
$$

2.3   The Mini-Batch LM Transposed

The variant presented here is a combination of the previous two. This time the transposed Jacobian matrix $\mathbf{J}^T$ is divided into mini-batches $\mathbf{J}_i^T$, see Eq. (20). However, if the mini-batch array fits in the processor's cache, the gain from the sequential distributions of data in the main memory may be small.

$$
\mathbf{J}_i^T\left(\mathbf{w}\left(n\right)\right) = \begin{bmatrix}
\dfrac{\partial \varepsilon_1^{(L)}(iM+1)}{\partial w_{10}^{(1)}} & \cdots & \dfrac{\partial \varepsilon_{N_L}^{(L)}(iM+1)}{\partial w_{10}^{(1)}} & \cdots & \dfrac{\partial \varepsilon_{N_L}^{(L)}((i+1)M)}{\partial w_{10}^{(1)}} \\[2ex]
\vdots & \cdots & \vdots & \cdots & \vdots \\[1ex]
\dfrac{\partial \varepsilon_1^{(L)}(iM+1)}{\partial w_{ij}^{(k)}} & \cdots & \dfrac{\partial \varepsilon_{N_L}^{(L)}(iM+1)}{\partial w_{ij}^{(k)}} & \cdots & \dfrac{\partial \varepsilon_{N_L}^{(L)}((i+1)M)}{\partial w_{ij}^{(k)}} \\[2ex]
\vdots & \cdots & \vdots & \cdots & \vdots \\[1ex]
\dfrac{\partial \varepsilon_1^{(L)}(iM+1)}{\partial w_{N_L N_{L-1}}^{(L)}} & \cdots & \dfrac{\partial \varepsilon_{N_L}^{(L)}(iM+1)}{\partial w_{N_L N_{L-1}}^{(L)}} & \cdots & \dfrac{\partial \varepsilon_{N_L}^{(L)}((i+1)M)}{\partial w_{N_L N_{L-1}}^{(L)}}
\end{bmatrix}.
\tag{20}
$$

2.4   The Parallel LM

The last variant consists of the use of parallel calculations using multi-core processors. It is easy to see that some of the steps of the LM algorithm can be easily parallelized (calculation of network output, errors, Jacobian, gradient, $\mathbf{A}$ and $\mathbf{h}$ matrices). The next stages are possible to be parallelized, but unfortunately with lower efficiency (inverting matrix $\mathbf{A}$, determining weight corrections). Of course, certain pieces of code must run in series. As a result, the acceleration of the algorithm will always be less than the number of cores/threads used. This parallel variant can be effectively applied both to the classical LM algorithm and to all computational variants presented above.

3   Experimental Results

The proposed solutions were tested and compared with the classical variant of the Levenberg-Marquardt learning algorithm. The multilayer perceptron was selected for the experiments. The network has eight inputs, two hidden layers of four neurons, and one output (MLP-8-4-4-1). The hyperbolic tangent was used as the activation function.

The network in each experiment was trained with the Abalone training set. The Abalone training set contains 4177 training data, each with 8 inputs and a single output. The neural networks are trained to detect the age of the sea snail called *abalone* based on its physical properties. The training is finished if the average network error is fallen below a certain threshold (0.012) within a given epoch.

The efficiency of the proposed computational methods was measured in the average training time in milliseconds. The obtained results were presented for the best combination of training parameters. In all cases, the initial weights were randomly selected from the range $[-0.5, 0.5]$. The number of epochs was limited to 10. Each training session was repeated 100 times.

Table 1 shows the results obtained for all proposed variants of training with the LM algorithm. All experiments are based on a single-thread calculation. The table for the individual computational variants shows the sizes of the Jacobian

Table 1. Training results for the for single-threaded calculations.

Variant of algorithm	Jacobian/Mini-bath Matrix size	Mini-batch size	Average training time [ms]	Acceleration [%]
LM Classic	[4177] × [61]	n/a	969,078	n/a
LM Transposed	[61] × [4177]	n/a	743,183	23,3
MBLM	[8] × [61]	8	731,859	24,5
MBLM	[32] × [61]	32	720,062	25,7
MBLM	[128] × [61]	128	731,989	24,5
MBLM Transpozed	[61] × [8]	8	703,905	27,4
MBLM Transpozed	[61] × [32]	32	701,999	27,6
MBLM Transpozed	[61] × [128]	128	729,195	24,8

matrix, the number of samples in the mini-batch, the average training time, and the acceleration relative to the classic LM algorithm. The obtained acceleration was compared with the classic LM algorithm and they turned out to be close. In all variants, an acceleration of 25% (±2%) was obtained. A slight advantage was obtained by the variant using transposed mini-batch matrices. However, keep in mind that if the mini-batch size is too large, it will not fit into the cache of the appropriate level and the profit will be lost.

Table 2 summarizes the accelerations achieved during parallel (multi-thread) calculations. The results given in [%] determine the acceleration depending on the number of threads used in relation to variants counted on a single thread. Accelerations achieved are respectively 57% for 4 threads and 90% for 32 threads. It is clear that above 16 threads the acceleration increases very slowly. This is due to the occurrence of serially counted fragments of the algorithm code. The proposed solutions show a significant reduction in the actual calculation time.

Table 2. Training results for the for multi-threaded calculations.

Variant of algorithm	Acceleration [%]				
	4 threads	8 threads	16 threads	32 threads	128 threads
LM Classic	62,5	80,7	89,8	91,5	92,7
LM Transpozed	57,5	78,1	88,4	89,4	90,2
MBLM	57,6	78,1	88,3	89,4	90,2
MBLM	57,1	77,8	88,2	89,2	89,9
MBLM	58,0	78,2	88,3	89,5	90,3
MBLM Transpozed	57,1	77,8	88,2	89,2	89,9
MBLM Transpozed	57,1	77,8	88,2	89,1	89,9
MBLM Transpozed	57,8	78,1	88,3	89,4	90,2

It should also be remembered that the accelerations obtained in the first three variants are combined with the acceleration resulting from parallelization. As a result, maximum acceleration reaches 92.6%.

4   Conclusion

In this paper, the new computational approaches to the Levenberg-Marquardt learning algorithm for a feedforward neural network is proposed. A multilayer perceptron neural network was selected to verify the proposed solutions. The networks were trained with an Abalone training set. To assess the effectiveness of the proposed solutions, their computational efficiency was compared in relation to the classical learning of the Levenberg-Marquardt algorithm. The conducted experiments showed a significant reduction in the real learning time. For all proposed methods, calculation times have been reduced from 23.3% to 92.6%. It has been observed that the performance of the proposed solution is promising.

A proposed computational approach can be used for other advanced learning algorithms of feedforward neural networks, see e.g. [4,9]. In future research, it is possible to design the proposed methodology to learn other structures including probabilistic neural networks [38] and various fuzzy [1,17,21–24,27,29,43,48,52, 53], and neuro-fuzzy structures [18,19,28,31,41].

References

1. Bartczuk, Ł., Przybył, A., Cpałka, K.: A new approach to nonlinear modelling of dynamic systems based on fuzzy rules. Int. J. Appl. Math. Comput. Sci. (AMCS) **26**(3), 603–621 (2016)
2. Bilski, J., Kowalczyk, B., Smoląg, J., Grzanek, K., Izonin, I.: Fast computational approach to the Levenberg-Marquardt algorithm for training feedforward neural networks. J. Artif. Intell. Soft Comput. Res. **12**(2), 45–61 (2023)
3. Bilski, J., Litwiński, S., Smoląg, J.: Parallel realisation of QR algorithm for neural networks learning. In: Rutkowski, L., Siekmann, J.H., Tadeusiewicz, R., Zadeh, L.A. (eds.) ICAISC 2004. LNCS (LNAI), vol. 3070, pp. 158–165. Springer, Heidelberg (2004). https://doi.org/10.1007/978-3-540-24844-6_19
4. Bilski, J.: The UD RLS algorithm for training the feedforward neural networks. Int. J. Appl. Math. Comput. Sci. **15**(1), 101–109 (2005)
5. Bilski, J., Smoląg, J.: Parallel realisation of the recurrent RTRN neural network learning. In: Rutkowski, L., Tadeusiewicz, R., Zadeh, L.A., Zurada, J.M. (eds.) ICAISC 2008. LNCS (LNAI), vol. 5097, pp. 11–16. Springer, Heidelberg (2008). https://doi.org/10.1007/978-3-540-69731-2_2
6. Bilski, J., Smoląg, J.: Parallel realisation of the recurrent Elman neural network learning. In: Rutkowski, L., Scherer, R., Tadeusiewicz, R., Zadeh, L.A., Zurada, J.M. (eds.) ICAISC 2010. LNCS (LNAI), vol. 6114, pp. 19–25. Springer, Heidelberg (2010). https://doi.org/10.1007/978-3-642-13232-2_3
7. Bilski, J., Smoląg, J.: Parallel realisation of the recurrent multi layer perceptron learning. In: Rutkowski, L., Korytkowski, M., Scherer, R., Tadeusiewicz, R., Zadeh, L.A., Zurada, J.M. (eds.) ICAISC 2012. LNCS (LNAI), vol. 7267, pp. 12–20. Springer, Heidelberg (2012). https://doi.org/10.1007/978-3-642-29347-4_2

8. Bilski, J., Smoląg, J.: Parallel approach to learning of the recurrent Jordan neural network. In: Rutkowski, L., Korytkowski, M., Scherer, R., Tadeusiewicz, R., Zadeh, L.A., Zurada, J.M. (eds.) ICAISC 2013. LNCS (LNAI), vol. 7894, pp. 32–40. Springer, Heidelberg (2013). https://doi.org/10.1007/978-3-642-38658-9_3

9. Bilski, J.: Parallel Structures for Feedforward and Dynamical Neural Networks. AOW EXIT (2013). (in Polish)

10. Bilski, J., Smoląg, J., Galushkin, A.I.: The parallel approach to the conjugate gradient learning algorithm for the feedforward neural networks. In: Rutkowski, L., Korytkowski, M., Scherer, R., Tadeusiewicz, R., Zadeh, L.A., Zurada, J.M. (eds.) ICAISC 2014. LNCS (LNAI), vol. 8467, pp. 12–21. Springer, Cham (2014). https://doi.org/10.1007/978-3-319-07173-2_2

11. Bilski, J., Smoląg, J.: Parallel architectures for learning the RTRN and Elman dynamic neural networks. IEEE Trans. Parallel Distrib. Syst. **26**(9), 2561–2570 (2014). https://doi.org/10.1109/TPDS.2014.2357019

12. Bilski, J., Kowalczyk, B., Marchlewska, A., Żurada, J.M.: Local Levenberg-Marquardt algorithm for learning feedforward neural networks. J. Artif. Intell. Soft Comput. Res. **10**(4), 299–316 (2020). https://doi.org/10.2478/jaiscr-2020-0020

13. Bilski, J., Kowalczyk, B., Marjański, A., Gandor, M., Żurada, J.M.: A novel fast feedforward neural networks training algorithm. J. Artif. Intell. Soft Comput. Res. **11**(4), 287–306 (2021). https://doi.org/10.2478/jaiscr-2021-0017

14. Bilski, J., Kowalczyk, B., Kisiel-Dorohinicki, M., Siwocha, A., Żurada, J.M.: Towards a very fast feedforward multilayer neural networks training algorithm. J. Artif. Intell. Soft Comput. Res. **12**(3), 181–195 (2022). https://doi.org/10.2478/jaiscr-2022-0012

15. Bilski, J., Rutkowski, L., Smoląg, J., Tao, D.: A novel method for speed training acceleration of recurrent neural networks. Inf. Sci. **553**, 266–279 (2021). https://doi.org/10.1016/j.ins.2020.10.025

16. Chu, J.L., Krzyżak, A.: The recognition of partially occluded objects with support vector machines, convolutional neural networks, and deep belief networks. J. Artif. Intell. Soft Comput. Res. **4**(1), 5–19 (2014)

17. Cpałka, K., Rutkowski, L.: Flexible Takagi-Sugeno fuzzy systems. In: Proceedings of the International Joint Conference on Neural Networks, Montreal, pp. 1764–1769 (2005)

18. Cpałka, K., Łapa, K., Przybył, A., Zalasiński, M.: A new method for designing neuro-fuzzy systems for nonlinear modelling with interpretability aspects. Neurocomputing **135**, 203–217 (2014)

19. Cpałka, K., Rebrova, O., Nowicki, R., et al.: On design of flexible neuro-fuzzy systems for nonlinear modelling. Int. J. Gen. Syst. **42**(6), Special Issue: SI, 706–720 (2013)

20. Fahlman, S.: Faster learning variations on backpropagation: an empirical study. In: Proceedings of Connectionist Models Summer School, Los Atos (1988)

21. Dziwiński, P., Przybył, A., Trippner, P., Paszkowski, J., Havashi, Y.: Hardware implementation of a Takagi-Sugeno neuro-fuzzy system optimized by a population algorithm. J. Artif. Intell. Soft Comput. Res. **11**(3), 243–266 (2021). https://doi.org/10.2478/jaiscr-2021-0015

22. Gabryel, M., Przybyszewski, K.: Methods of searching for similar device fingerprints using changes in unstable parameters. In: Rutkowski, L., Scherer, R., Korytkowski, M., Pedrycz, W., Tadeusiewicz, R., Zurada, J.M. (eds.) ICAISC 2020. LNCS (LNAI), vol. 12416, pp. 325–335. Springer, Cham (2020). https://doi.org/10.1007/978-3-030-61534-5_29

23. Gabryel, M., Scherer, M.M., Sułkowski, Ł, Damaševičius, R.: Decision making support system for managing advertisers by Ad fraud detection. J. Artif. Intell. Soft Comput. Res. **11**, 331–339 (2021)
24. Gabryel, M., Kocić, M.: Application of a neural network to generate the hash code for a device fingerprint. In: Rutkowski, L., Scherer, R., Korytkowski, M., Pedrycz, W., Tadeusiewicz, R., Zurada, J.M. (eds.) ICAISC 2021. LNCS (LNAI), vol. 12855, pp. 456–463. Springer, Cham (2021). https://doi.org/10.1007/978-3-030-87897-9_40
25. Hagan, M.T., Menhaj, M.B.: Training feedforward networks with the Marquardt algorithm. IEEE Trans. Neural Networks **5**(6), 989–993 (1994)
26. Kopczyński, M., Grzes, T.: Hardware rough set processor parallel architecture in FPGA for finding core in big datasets. J. Artif. Intell. Soft Comput. Res. **11**(2), 99–110 (2021)
27. Korytkowski, M., Rutkowski, L., Scherer, R.: From ensemble of fuzzy classifiers to single fuzzy rule base classifier. LNAI **5097**, 265–272 (2008)
28. Korytkowski, M., Scherer, R.: Negative correlation learning of neuro-fuzzy system. LNAI **6113**, 114–119 (2010)
29. Kordos, M., Blachnik, M., Scherer, R.: Fuzzy clustering decomposition of genetic algorithm-based instance selection for regression problems. Inf. Sci. **587**, 23–40 (2021)
30. Łapa, K., Przybył, A., Cpałka, K.: A new approach to designing interpretable models of dynamic systems. In: Rutkowski, L., Korytkowski, M., Scherer, R., Tadeusiewicz, R., Zadeh, L.A., Zurada, J.M. (eds.) ICAISC 2013. LNCS (LNAI), vol. 7895, pp. 523–534. Springer, Heidelberg (2013). https://doi.org/10.1007/978-3-642-38610-7_48
31. Łapa, K., Zalasiński, M., Cpałka, K.: A new method for designing and complexity reduction of neuro-fuzzy systems for nonlinear modelling. In: Rutkowski, L., Korytkowski, M., Scherer, R., Tadeusiewicz, R., Zadeh, L.A., Zurada, J.M. (eds.) ICAISC 2013. LNCS (LNAI), vol. 7894, pp. 329–344. Springer, Heidelberg (2013). https://doi.org/10.1007/978-3-642-38658-9_30
32. Marqardt, D.: An algorithm for last-squares estimation of nonlinear parameters. J. Soc. Ind. Appl. Math. **11**, 431–441 (1963)
33. Niksa-Rynkiewicz, T., Szewczuk-Krypa, N., Witkowska, A., Cpałka, K., Zalasiński, M., Cader, A.: Monitoring regenerative heat exchanger in steam power plant by making use of the recurrent neural network. J. Artif. Intell. Soft Comput. Res. **11**(2), 143–155 (2021). https://doi.org/10.2478/jaiscr-2021-0009
34. Patan, K., Patan, M.: Optimal training strategies for locally recurrent neural networks. J. Artif. Intell. Soft Comput. Res. **1**(2), 103–114 (2011)
35. Riedmiller, M., Braun, H.: A direct method for faster backpropagation learning: the RPROP algorithm. In: IEEE International Conference on Neural Networks, San Francisco (1993)
36. Romaszewski, M., Gawron, P., Opozda, S.: Dimensionality reduction of dynamic mesh animations using HO-SVD. J. Artif. Intell. Soft Comput. Res. **3**(3), 277–289 (2013)
37. Rumelhart, D.E., Hinton, G.E., Williams, R.J.: Learning internal representations by error propagation. In: Rumelhart, D.E., McCelland, J. (eds.) Parallel Distributed Processing, vol. 1, Chapter 8. The MIT Press, Cambridge, Massachusetts, (1986)
38. Rutkowski, L.: Multiple Fourier series procedures for extraction of nonlinear regressions from noisy data. IEEE Trans. Signal Process. **41**(10), 3062–3065 (1993)

39. Rutkowski, L.: Identification of MISO nonlinear regressions in the presence of a wide class of disturbances. IEEE Trans. Inf. Theory **37**(1), 214–216 (1991)
40. Rutkowski, L., Jaworski, M., Pietruczuk, L., Duda, P.: Decision trees for mining data streams based on the gaussian approximation. IEEE Trans. Knowl. Data Eng. **26**(1), 108–119 (2014)
41. Rutkowski, L., Przybył, A., Cpałka, K., Er, M.J.: Online speed profile generation for industrial machine tool based on neuro-fuzzy approach. In: Rutkowski, L., Scherer, R., Tadeusiewicz, R., Zadeh, L.A., Zurada, J.M. (eds.) ICAISC 2010. LNCS (LNAI), vol. 6114, pp. 645–650. Springer, Heidelberg (2010). https://doi.org/10.1007/978-3-642-13232-2_79
42. Rutkowski, L., Rafajlowicz, E.: On optimal global rate of convergence of some nonparametric identification procedures. IEEE Trans. Autom. Control **34**(10), 1089–1091 (1989)
43. Rutkowski, T., Łapa, K., Jaworski, M., Nielek, R., Rutkowska, D.: On explainable flexible fuzzy recommender and its performance evaluation using the Akaike information criterion. In: Gedeon, T., Wong, K.W., Lee, M. (eds.) ICONIP 2019. CCIS, vol. 1142, pp. 717–724. Springer, Cham (2019). https://doi.org/10.1007/978-3-030-36808-1_78
44. Smolag, J., Bilski, J.: A systolic array for fast learning of neural networks. In: Proceedings of V Conference on Neural Networks and Soft Computing, Zakopane, pp. 754–758 (2000)
45. Smolag, J., Rutkowski, L., Bilski, J.: Systolic array for neural networks. In: Proceedings of IV Conference on Neural Networks and Their Applications, Zakopane, pp. 487–497 (1999)
46. Starczewski, A.: A clustering method based on the modified RS validity index. In: Rutkowski, L., Korytkowski, M., Scherer, R., Tadeusiewicz, R., Zadeh, L.A., Zurada, J.M. (eds.) ICAISC 2013. LNCS (LNAI), vol. 7895, pp. 242–250. Springer, Heidelberg (2013). https://doi.org/10.1007/978-3-642-38610-7_23
47. Starczewski, J.T.: Advanced Concepts in Fuzzy Logic and Systems with Membership Uncertainty, vol. 284. Studies in Fuzziness and Soft Computing. Springer, Cham (2013). https://doi.org/10.1007/978-3-642-29520-1
48. Starczewski, J.T., Goetzen, P., Napoli, Ch.: Triangular fuzzy-rough set based fuzzification of fuzzy rule-based systems. J. Artif. Intell. Soft Comput. Res. **10**(4), 271–285 (2020)
49. Tadeusiewicz, R.: Neural Networks. AOW RM (1993). (in Polish)
50. Werbos, J.: Backpropagation through time: what it does and how to do it. In: Proceedings of the IEEE, vol. 78, no. 10 (1990)
51. Wilamowski, B.M., Yo, H.: Neural network learning without backpropagation. IEEE Trans. Neural Networks **21**(11), 1793–1803 (2010)
52. Zalasiński, M., Cpałka, K.: New approach for the on-line signature verification based on method of horizontal partitioning. In: Rutkowski, L., Korytkowski, M., Scherer, R., Tadeusiewicz, R., Zadeh, L.A., Zurada, J.M. (eds.) ICAISC 2013. LNCS (LNAI), vol. 7895, pp. 342–350. Springer, Heidelberg (2013). https://doi.org/10.1007/978-3-642-38610-7_32
53. Zalasiński, M., Łapa, K., Cpałka, K.: Prediction of values of the dynamic signature features. Expert Syst. Appl. **104**, 86–96 (2018)
54. El Zini, J., Rizk, Y., Awad, M.: An optimized parallel implementation of non-iteratively trained recurrent neural networks. J. Artif. Intell. Soft Comput. Res. **11**(1), 33–50 (2021). https://doi.org/10.2478/jaiscr-2021-0003
55. Sun, Z., Zhao, Z., Scherer, R., Wei, W., Woźniak, M.: An overview of capsule neural networks. J. Internet Technol. **23**(1), 33–44 (2022)

Reinforcement Learning with Brain-Inspired Modulation Improves Adaptation to Environmental Changes

Eric Chalmers[1]([⊠]) and Artur Luczak[2]

[1] Mount Royal University, Calgary, AB T3E 6K6, Canada
echalmers@mtroyal.ca
[2] University of Lethbridge, Lethbridge, AB T1K 3M4, Canada
luczak@uleth.ca

Abstract. Developments in reinforcement learning (RL) have allowed algorithms to achieve impressive performance in complex, but largely static problems. In contrast, biological learning seems to value efficient adaptation to a constantly changing world. Here we build on a recently proposed model of neuronal learning that suggests neurons predict their own future activity to optimize their energy balance. That work proposed a neuronal learning rule that uses presynaptic input to modulate prediction error. Here we argue that an analogous RL rule would use action probability to modulate reward prediction error. We show that this modulation makes the agent more sensitive to negative experiences, and more careful in forming preferences: features that facilitate adaptation to change. We embed the proposed rule in both tabular and deep-Q-network RL algorithms, and find that it outperforms conventional algorithms in simple but highly-dynamic tasks. It also exhibits a "paradox of choice" effect that has been observed in humans. The new rule may encapsulate a core principle of biological intelligence; an important component of human-like learning and adaptation - with both its benefits and trade-offs.

Keywords: Reinforcement Learning · adaptation · lifelong learning · brain-inspired computing

1 Introduction

"Most work in biological systems has focused on simple learning problems. . . where flexibility and ongoing learning are important, similar to real-world learning problems. In contrast, most work in artificial agents has focused on learning a single complex problem in a static environment." (Neftci and Averbeck) [22]

Real-world environments are constantly changing, and the ability to flexibly adapt to these changes is imperative. But current A.I. does not always demonstrate this ability to the same degree as animals. Here, building on a recent model

© The Author(s), under exclusive license to Springer Nature Switzerland AG 2023
L. Rutkowski et al. (Eds.): ICAISC 2023, LNAI 14125, pp. 23–34, 2023.
https://doi.org/10.1007/978-3-031-42505-9_3

of neuronal learning [20], we propose a reinforcement learning rule that demonstrates more realistic flexibility - including both its benefits and its trade-offs. We test the new reinforcement learning rule in multi-armed bandit tasks and a task inspired by the Wisconsin Card Sorting Test - a psychological test used to assess patients' ability to adapt to changing reward structures. We demonstrate that the new rule improves performance in dynamic decision-making tasks with few to moderate numbers of choices (probably like the routine decision-making faced by animals day-to-day), and that this comes at the expense of performance when selecting between many choices - a paradox-of-choice effect that has been observed in humans. We also discuss some connections between the new rule and several other paradigms from across machine learning.

2   A New Reinforcement Learning Rule

2.1   Basic Building Blocks of Reinforcement Learning

A reinforcement learning agent must be able to estimate the value V of executing action a while in state s - though during the early stages of learning its estimates may not be very good. The agent must learn from each new experience in the environment; improving the efficacy of its value estimates for the future. Suppose at time t the agent is in state s_t, executes action a_t, and then finds itself in the new state s_{t+1} with reward r. The actual, experienced value of this event can be formulated as reward r_t plus the predicted value of being in the new state s_{t+1}:

$$V\left(s_t, a_t\right)_{actual} = r_t + \gamma V\left(s_{t+1}\right) \tag{1}$$

Here γ is a discount factor applied to expected future rewards ($\gamma \epsilon$ [0, 1]). The "temporal difference error" δ expresses the difference between actual and predicted values:

$$\delta_t = V_{actual} - V = r_t + \gamma V\left(s_{t+1}\right) - V\left(s_t, a_t\right) \tag{2}$$

The temporal difference error is a measure of the agent's surprise at the recent experience, and is a useful mechanism for learning. In the canonical Q-learning algorithm, for example, the agent maintains a table of value estimates that are updated proportional to δ, and according to a learning rate parameter α:

$$V\left(s_t, a_t\right) \leftarrow V\left(s_t, a_t\right) + \alpha \delta_t \tag{3}$$

The agent selects actions for execution according to a policy π. For the purpose of this paper, let us assume π is a softmax function that calculates the probability of selecting action a out of the set of actions A, based on current value estimates, and according to a temperature parameter τ:

$$\pi\left(s, a\right) = P\left(a_t = a | s_t = s\right) = \frac{e^{V(s,a)/\tau}}{\sum_{b \epsilon A} e^{V(s,b)/\tau}} \tag{4}$$

Thus the learning process consists of iteratively using value estimates to select actions, and using the observed results to improve the value estimates.

2.2   The New Rule

Building on the Contrastive Hebbian Learning rule [1,3] Scellier and Bengio proposed "Equilibrium Propagation" (EP) as a new, more biologically plausible model for learning in artificial neural networks [24]. EP envisions the network as a dynamical system that learns in two phases. First is the "free phase", in which an input is applied, and the network is allowed to equilibrate. In the second or "weakly clamped" phase, output neurons are soft-clamped or nudged toward a target value. Weights are then updated according to the rule:

$$\Delta W_{ij} \propto \left[u_i^c u_j^c - u_i^f u_j^f \right] \tag{5}$$

where i and j are the indices of neurons on either side of the weight/synapse (note that EP assumes symmetric connections between neurons), u^c is the neuron's squashed clamped-phase activation, and u^f is the neuron's squashed free-phase activation. Luczak, et al. [20] showed that free-phase activity can be well predicted based on past activity, and proposed the following alternative rule:

$$\Delta W_{ij} \propto u_i^c (u_j^c - \tilde{u}_j^f) \tag{6}$$

where the tilde indicates the neuron's prediction of its own free-phase equilibrium given the input. They showed that this rule can explain learning without requiring two distinct phases, as free-phase activity can be predicted in advance.

Importantly, the rule arises naturally as a result of a neuron acting to optimize its own energy balance, and hints at an explanation for consciousness [19], suggesting that it may encapsulate some principle of general intelligence. This motivates our current exploration of an analogous reinforcement learning rule. Examining this new rule, we see the update consists of the prediction error term $(\tilde{u_j^c} - u_j^f)$, modulated by the presynaptic activation u_i^c. Here we abstract the basic form of this rule to produce a rule applicable to reinforcement learning. The prediction error term is easy to place in a reinforcement learning context: it is analogous to the temporal difference error δ. But if we want to formulate a reinforcement learning rule corresponding to the neuronal one, we need a scaling or modulating factor analogous to the presynaptic activation. Since the presynaptic activation is the input to the neuron and the cause of its resulting activity, a natural analog could be $\pi(s_t, a_t)$; the input to the agent's environment and the cause of the resulting experience. We can then formulate a reinforcement learning rule as a modulation of δ by $\pi(s_t, a_t)$:

$$\Delta V(s_t, a_t) \propto \pi_t(s_t, a_t)\delta_t = \pi_t(s_t, a_t) \left[r + \gamma V(s_{t+1}) - V(s_t, a_t) \right] \tag{7}$$

The analogy between the neuronal learning rule and the new RL rule is illustrated in Fig. 1.

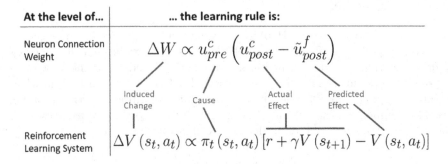

Fig. 1. We abstract the biologically-plausible neuronal learning rule of Luczak et al. to create an analogous rule for reinforcement learning. To calculate a weight update, the prediction error is modulated by the presynaptic input that caused the neuron's activity. In other words, a cause is used to modulate the error in predicting the effect. For an analogous reinforcement learning rule, updates are calculated by using action probability (the cause of the agent's experience) to modulate reward prediction error (the error in predicting the effect of that action)

2.3   Effect of the New Rule

Scaling the temporal difference error by $\pi(s_t, a_t)$ has two effects:

1. **It magnifies the agent's reactions to negative experiences.** If an action that was thought to be valuable (i.e. π is large) brings a negative out-come, the scaled (negative) reward-prediction error will be large. This will depress the perceived value of that action, creating an immediate aversion to it.
2. **It slows down the development of an action preference** - making the agent somewhat more careful in selecting actions. If the agent is unlikely to take an action, the scaled reward prediction error will be small - even if the experience was rewarding. Thus, the agent needs a lot of "convincing" that an un-likely action is desirable.

Thus, modulating the temporal difference error by the action probability $\pi(s_t, a_t)$ in this way biases the agent's learning somewhat toward negative experiences. We hypothesize this will allow the agent to adapt to environmental changes: when a previously rewarding action is no longer rewarded, the agent will quickly suppress its perceived value and carefully search for a new preference.

3   Experiments

3.1   Experiment 1 - Changing Multi-armed Bandit

A changing, n-armed bandit experiment was designed to test the new rule's ability to adapt to changes. Multi-armed bandits are a simple experiment often used to illustrate learning algorithms' performance [30]. The bandit was given one high-reward arm with $p_{reward} = 0.9$ and one no-reward arm with $p_{reward} = 0$. The rest of the arms had random reward probabilities $p_{reward} \sim U(0.25, 0.75)$. The agent receives a +1 reward when the arm it samples is rewarded, and a −1 reward otherwise. The reward probabilities are periodically rotated in such a way that all reward probabilities change, and the arm that was previously high-reward becomes no-reward.

The new rule was implemented in a tabular reinforcement learning agent by modifying the classical Q-learning algorithm to use Eq. 7 as its update rule. This algorithm maintains a table of the perceived values of each action and updates the relevant value after each experience. We also implemented a variety of standard bandit-solving algorithms for comparison: a conventional Q-learning algorithm [27] and an Upper Confidence Bound (UCB) algorithm [2]. All these algorithms are memoryless and so cannot learn the pattern to the reward probabilities' rotation: they perceive each change as a random, unexpected, and complete change to the reward landscape. For reference, we also included a UCB algorithm which has the advantage of being automatically reset each time the rewards change - note the other algorithms are not informed of changes this way; they must figure it out themselves. Thus, this "perfectly-informed" UCB algorithm represents a performance cap that the other algorithms are not expected to reach.

In our experiments each algorithm was allowed to select the best values for learning rate $\alpha\epsilon[0, 2]$ and softmax temperature $\tau\epsilon\{0.5, 1, 2\}$. Note that α is conventionally set to be (much) less than 1, but a large value of α can also produce a quick response to environmental changes, so here we allow each algorithm to select α as high as 2. The parameter searches and the experiments themselves were performed on different bandit instances. The cumulative reward for a 7-armed bandit with changes every 100 steps is shown in Fig. 2.

We note that the conventional Q learning algorithm achieved quick reaction to reward changes by self-selecting a large learning rate α (usually somewhere between 0.7 and 1.5). But this large α also causes the algorithm to switch to a new arm very quickly when it finds a chance reward at that arm - sometimes it switches too quickly and selects a sub-optimal arm, and cumulative reward suffers as a result. The new algorithm, on the other hand, scales reward-prediction-error down when the probability of selecting that arm is low, and so spends more time convincing itself that a new arm is desirable. This longer time spent identifying the new high-reward arm yields more reward overall, as shown in Fig. 2.

To quantify this extra time taken to develop a new arm preference, we first ran a 10-period moving average on the probabilities of selecting each arm. When the maximum probability of any arm except the previously high-reward arm exceeded 50%, we considered the agent to have developed a new preference for that arm. Time-to-preference as the number of bandit arms increases is shown in Fig. 3.

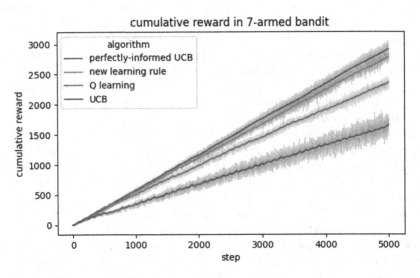

Fig. 2. Cumulative reward obtained on a 7-armed bandit with reward probabilities that change every 100 steps. The "perfectly-informed UCB" algorithm is reset (informed) when the reward probabilities change, and so represents a cap on possible performance. The new learning rule is *not* given this information, yet it performs almost as well. The shaded area is the 95% confidence interval of the mean over 10 repetitions.

3.2 Experiment 2 - Task Inspired by the Wisconsin Card Sorting Test

The Wisconsin Card Sorting Test is a neuropsychological test used to assess patients' ability to adapt to a changing set of rules [4], and has historically been used to identify brain injury and neurodegenerative disease [21]. The test presents patients with cards that can be matched based on several features, such as color, shape, number, etc. The patients are not told the correct matching criteria, but are rewarded when they make a match correctly. The rewarded matching criteria changes periodically throughout the test: healthy patients can generally adapt quickly when the rule changes, while patients with prefrontal cortex damage cannot.

Here we simulate a similar test using a multiclass classification task. Normally distributed clusters of points are created in n-dimensional space and assigned to

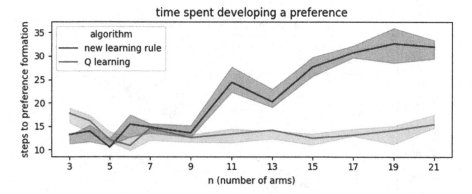

Fig. 3. Time (steps) taken to develop a preference for a new arm after each change, for varying numbers of bandit arms. See text for description of how "preferences" were detected. The new rule is more careful in evaluating options, and this helps it to identify the optimal arm when the number of choices is small. The shaded area represents the 95% confidence interval of the mean over 20 repetitions.

each of k classes. The agent is rewarded when it correctly matches a randomly-drawn point to its current class, but the classes are periodically scrambled (such that all the points previously assigned to class "0" now belong to class "2", for example).

For this test we use a deep Q network based on the new rule in Eq. 7. The network is a perceptron with one hidden layer of 20 neurons, and tanh squashing functions. We use separate policy and value networks that synchronize every 5 trials, and a replay buffer of the last 10 trials. The same network is also instantiated with a conventional update rule for comparison. Figure 4 shows the new rule allowing the network to adapt to each change, while the conventional deep Q network adapts less effectively. Here the classification rule is changed every 100 steps.

3.3 The Paradox of Choice

As humans we often take for granted our ability to change: to update our beliefs in response to new information, or to change a strategy when necessary. But our gift for quick adaptation in everyday situations comes with a trade-off: less-than-optimal performance in situations with many choices. Psychologist Barry Schwartz calls this "the paradox of choice" [25]: As the number of choices increases, our ability to select a satisfying option decreases and our preferences become weaker [9].

Our experiments show a similar paradox-of-choice effect, illustrated in Fig. 5. The new rule creates a bias toward negative experiences that - when the reward landscape changes - quickly depresses perceived value of the previously high-reward arm, and also makes the agent more careful in choosing a new preferred arm. This is an advantage when the number of arms is small, but can become

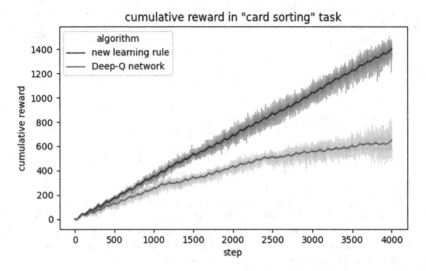

Fig. 4. Cumulative reward obtained in the 4-class version of the task inspired by the Wisconsin Card-Sorting Test, with classes being shuffled every 100 steps. The shaded area is the 95% confidence interval of the mean over 10 repetitions.

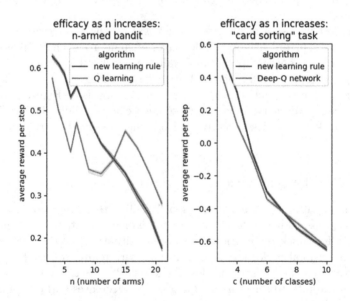

Fig. 5. Average reward-per-step obtained in the n-armed bandit task (left) and "card sorting" task (right). The new rule provides an advantage over conventional learning when the number of choices is small, with the trade-off of a disadvantage when the number of choices is large. This trade-off is likely favorable for many real-world situations, and similar to the "paradox of choice" effect observed in humans.

a disadvantage if there are many arms. In large-n cases, the agent takes too long evaluating new arms and sometimes fails to select one in time. Thus the same effects of the new rule that allow effective adaptation to environmental changes involving few choices, hinder it when the number of choices becomes large. This trade-off likely works heavily in favor of biological agents in the natural world, who rarely have to select between many attractive options, but must continuously adapt to simple though potentially dramatic environmental changes (e.g. the animal discovers that its favorite watering hole now has an alligator in it, and so reverts to a different water source).

4   Discussion

The new rule demonstrates some features of human-like learning. Humans are known to increase decision-making time as the number of options increases, in a relationship known as Hick's law [15]. Our new rule exhibits similar increasing decision time in Fig. 3, while the conventional learning algorithm does not. A paradox-of-choice effect is also observed in Fig. 5, where the new rule outperforms conventional learning until the number of choices becomes large. Humans exhibit this trade-off as well, where "selections made from large assortments can lead to weaker preferences" [9] though it should be noted that the relationship between number of choices and the choice overload effect in humans is complex [10]. The new rule is derived from a recently proposed neuronal predictive learning rule, and thus may encapsulate some basic principles of learning and intelligence that exist at both the neuronal and system levels. We hope this paper will add to the important conversation around A.I. that can adapt to the constant environmental changes of the real world.

The topics of adaptability and continuous learning represent a growing research field [6,14,17,18], and paradigms for detecting and responding to environmental change do exist in the machine learning literature. For example, model-based reinforcement-learning approaches maintain an internal model of the world, with which new experiences can be compared to detect environmental changes. Previous work has stored world models and switched between them when recent experiences indicated an environmental change [7,8], adapted time series change-point algorithms to detect environmental changes [23], and used consciousness-inspired approaches to improve the generalization of a model to a new task [32]. However, these approaches require maintenance of a world model, which can be costly. Ultimately the quick, model-free effect of our rule could work well in conjunction with the more complex goal-oriented-planning effect of a model-based approach: the brain employs both model-free and model-based mechanisms [26], and the combination likely holds promise for A.I. as well.

Another related approach is transfer-learning or meta-reinforcement learning, which aims to accelerate learning in new tasks from a previously experienced family. One meta-RL approach [5] uses a particular recurrent (memory-equipped) network architecture that learns general features of a task family through backpropagation, allowing the recurrent dynamics to quickly tune into details of a new task from the family, in what is thought to be a brain-like mechanism [29]. Meta-RL is currently an active research field [11,13,28]. This general approach could be seen as adaptation through knowledge transfer, though unfortunately the network must be informed (reset) each time the task changes. Again, the quick memory-free effect provided by our rule could work well in conjunction with such transfer-learning methods, resulting in more human-like learning.

The idea of modulating a prediction error appears elsewhere in machine learning literature, and modulating the error in different ways or by different signals produces different effects. Here we have shown that modulating reward prediction error by action probability creates a human-like adaptation-to-change effect, including improved performance in simple but dynamic tasks, as well as a paradox-of-choice effect. Conversely, the Inverse Propensity Score Estimation (IPSE) approach used in counterfactual learning uses the inverse of the probability as a modulating factor [12,16]. This can have the effect of de-biasing learning from data collected in a population that differs from a target population. However, during online learning of dynamic tasks it would result in slower adaptation; opposite to our rule. We could also consider REINFORCE-style reinforcement learning algorithms, which modulate a prediction error by a "characteristic eligibility" term that expresses the gradient of the action probability with respect to the parameter being updated [31]. This quickly makes rewarding actions more likely - in static environments where the gradient has consistent meaning. Our rule, on the other hand, demonstrates a similar learning effect in dynamic tasks. Making predictions is a central operation of the brain, and it is likely that neural circuits modulate prediction errors in many ways to get the right effect at the right time, creating what we know as human-like learning.

Among the various effects that can be obtained by modulating prediction errors in different ways, we believe the one proposed here deserves special future study for two reasons. First, the ability to cope gracefully in dynamic situations is still relatively understudied (high-profile successes of machine learning are typically in static environments like games). Second, since this new RL rule is derived from a biologically plausible neuronal learning rule, it creates a link between neuron learning and system-level learning which could shed light on universal principles of learning and intelligence.

5   Code

See https://github.com/echalmers/modulated_td_error for code accompanying this paper. Experiments described in this paper used this code and were executed on commodity hardware without a GPU.

Acknowledgements. This work was supported by Compute Canada, the Natural Sciences and Engineering Research Council of Canada (NSERC), and the Canadian Institutes of Health Research (CIHR) grants to Artur Luczak.

References

1. Almeida, L.B.: A learning rule for asynchronous perceptrons with feedback in a combinatorial environment. In: Artificial Neural Networks: Concept Learning, pp. 102–111. IEEE Press, January 1990
2. Auer, P.: Using confidence bounds for exploitation-exploration trade-offs. J. Mach. Learn. Res. **3**(Nov), 397–422 (2002)
3. Baldi, P., Pineda, F.: Contrastive learning and neural oscillations. Neural Comput. **3**(4), 526–545 (1991). https://doi.org/10.1162/neco.1991.3.4.526
4. Berg, E.A.: A simple objective technique for measuring flexibility in thinking. J. Gen. Psychol. **39**(1), 15–22 (1948). https://doi.org/10.1080/00221309.1948.9918159
5. Botvinick, M., Ritter, S., Wang, J.X., Kurth-Nelson, Z., Blundell, C., Hassabis, D.: Reinforcement learning, fast and slow. Trends Cogn. Sci. **23**(5), 408–422 (2019). https://doi.org/10.1016/j.tics.2019.02.006
6. Caccia, M., et al.: Online Fast Adaptation and Knowledge Accumulation (OSAKA): a new approach to continual learning. In: Advances in Neural Information Processing Systems, vol. 33, pp. 16532–16545. Curran Associates, Inc. (2020)
7. Chalmers, E., Contreras, E.B., Robertson, B., Luczak, A., Gruber, A.: Context-switching and adaptation: brain-inspired mechanisms for handling environmental changes. In: 2016 International Joint Conference on Neural Networks (IJCNN), pp. 3522–3529, July 2016
8. Chalmers, E., Luczak, A., Gruber, A.J.: Computational properties of the hippocampus increase the efficiency of goal-directed foraging through hierarchical reinforcement learning. Front. Comput. Neurosci. **10**, 128 (2016)
9. Chernev, A.: When more is less and less is more: the role of ideal point availability and assortment in consumer choice. J. Consum. Res. **30**(2), 170–183 (2003). https://doi.org/10.1086/376808
10. Chernev, A., Böckenholt, U., Goodman, J.: Choice overload: a conceptual review and meta-analysis. J. Consum. Psychol. **25**(2), 333–358 (2015). https://doi.org/10.1016/j.jcps.2014.08.002
11. Dorfman, R., Shenfeld, I., Tamar, A.: Offline meta reinforcement learning – identifiability challenges and effective data collection strategies. In: Advances in Neural Information Processing Systems, vol. 34, pp. 4607–4618. Curran Associates, Inc. (2021)
12. Dudik, M., Langford, J., Li, L.: Doubly robust policy evaluation and learning, May 2011. https://doi.org/10.48550/arXiv.1103.4601
13. Fallah, A., Georgiev, K., Mokhtari, A., Ozdaglar, A.: On the convergence theory of debiased model-agnostic meta-reinforcement learning. In: Advances in Neural Information Processing Systems, vol. 34, pp. 3096–3107. Curran Associates, Inc. (2021)
14. Harrison, J., Sharma, A., Finn, C., Pavone, M.: Continuous meta-learning without tasks. In: Advances in Neural Information Processing Systems, vol. 33, pp. 17571–17581. Curran Associates, Inc. (2020)
15. Hick, W.E.: On the rate of gain of information. Q. J. Exp. Psychol. **4**(1), 11–26 (1952). https://doi.org/10.1080/17470215208416600
16. Horvitz, D.G., Thompson, D.J.: A generalization of sampling without replacement from a finite universe. J. Am. Stat. Assoc. **47**(260), 663–685 (1952). https://doi.org/10.1080/01621459.1952.10483446

17. Kwon, J., Efroni, Y., Caramanis, C., Mannor, S.: Reinforcement learning in reward-mixing MDPs. In: Advances in Neural Information Processing Systems, vol. 34, pp. 2253–2264. Curran Associates, Inc. (2021)
18. Liu, H., Long, M., Wang, J., Wang, Y.: Learning to adapt to evolving domains. In: Advances in Neural Information Processing Systems, vol. 33, pp. 22338–22348. Curran Associates, Inc. (2020)
19. Luczak, A., Kubo, Y.: Predictive neuronal adaptation as a basis for consciousness. Front. Syst. Neurosci. **15**, 767461 (2021). https://doi.org/10.3389/fnsys.2021.767461
20. Luczak, A., McNaughton, B.L., Kubo, Y.: Neurons learn by predicting future activity. Nat. Mach. Intell. **4**(1), 62–72 (2022). https://doi.org/10.1038/s42256-021-00430-y
21. Milner, B.: Effects of different brain lesions on card sorting: the role of the frontal lobes. Arch. Neurol. **9**(1), 90–100 (1963). https://doi.org/10.1001/archneur.1963.00460070100010
22. Neftci, E.O., Averbeck, B.B.: Reinforcement learning in artificial and biological systems. Nat. Mach. Intell. **1**(3), 133–143 (2019). https://doi.org/10.1038/s42256-019-0025-4
23. Padakandla, S., Prabuchandran, K.J., Bhatnagar, S.: Reinforcement learning algorithm for non-stationary environments. Appl. Intell. **50**(11), 3590–3606 (2020). https://doi.org/10.1007/s10489-020-01758-5
24. Scellier, B., Bengio, Y.: Equilibrium propagation: bridging the gap between energy-based models and backpropagation. Front. Comput. Neurosci. **11**, 24 (2017)
25. Schwartz, B., Kliban, K.: The Paradox of Choice: Why More Is Less. Brilliance Audio, Grand Rapids, Mich., unabridged edition, April 2014
26. Steinke, A., Lange, F., Kopp, B.: Parallel model-based and model-free reinforcement learning for card sorting performance. Sci. Rep. **10**(1), 15464 (2020). https://doi.org/10.1038/s41598-020-72407-7
27. Sutton, R.S., Barto, A.G.: Reinforcement Learning: An Introduction, 2nd edn. A Bradford Book, Cambridge (1998)
28. Tang, Y., Kozuno, T., Rowland, M., Munos, R., Valko, M.: Unifying gradient estimators for meta-reinforcement learning via off-policy evaluation. In: Advances in Neural Information Processing Systems, vol. 34, pp. 5303–5315. Curran Associates, Inc. (2021)
29. Wang, J.X.: Prefrontal cortex as a meta-reinforcement learning system. Nat. Neurosci. **21**(6), 860–868 (2018). https://doi.org/10.1038/s41593-018-0147-8
30. Wang, J.X., et al.: Learning to reinforcement learn, January 2017
31. Williams, R.J.: Simple statistical gradient-following algorithms for connectionist reinforcement learning. Mach. Learn. **8**(3), 229–256 (1992). https://doi.org/10.1007/BF00992696
32. Zhao, M., Liu, Z., Luan, S., Zhang, S., Precup, D., Bengio, Y.: A consciousness-inspired planning agent for model-based reinforcement learning. In: Advances in Neural Information Processing Systems, vol. 34, pp. 1569–1581. Curran Associates, Inc. (2021)

Multi-Agent Deep Q-Network in Voxel-Based Automated Electrical Routing

Tizian Dagner[✉], Rafael Parzeller, and Selin Kesler

Siemens AG, Otto-Hahn-Ring 6, 81739 Munich, Germany
{tizian.dagner,rafael.parzeller,selin.kesler}@siemens.com

Abstract. Many industries are facing the challenge of increasing the number of cables in their products. All of these cable paths must be planned in a time-consuming, repetitive, and error-prone process. Instead of manually defining all waypoints for a broad range of cables, automation can provide globally optimized and valid paths for accelerated product development. To establish automated electrical routing, an industrial-oriented application is directly integrated into existing 3D CAD workflows. The purpose of this research is to investigate the applicability and performance of Reinforcement Learning in identifying optimal paths in a three-dimensional space. Therefore, information is directly extracted from 3D CAD, and results are immediately returned to CAD. Handing over the crucial task of routing to a Multi-Agent Deep Q-Network (MADQN) promises a scalable solution for various environments of different sizes and levels of complexity. Minimizing the total cable lengths while considering cable and environment-specific constraints is formulated as a shortest-path problem in three-dimensional space in order to make it solvable for the developed approach. To reduce the complexity based on the application domain, the agents' accessible space is decreased to a maximum distance from the initial 3D CAD geometry. This paper provides a detailed explanation of the developed approach, which is compared to established methods in electrical routing such as the A* algorithm.

Keywords: Electrical Routing · Shortest Path · Deep Q-Network · Multi-Agent Reinforcement Learning · Voxel

1 Introduction

A variety of industries are characterized by increasing electrification of their products in order to offer diverse data communication and additional features. The associated, accelerating individualization of these products goes hand in hand with a rising number of electrical components and their connections in the severely limited mechanical installation space. The increasing complexity of cable routing is a direct result, which occurs already in the early stages of virtual product development for mechanical components in 3D CAD. As part of

L. Rutkowski et al. (Eds.): ICAISC 2023, LNAI 14125, pp. 35–45, 2023.
https://doi.org/10.1007/978-3-031-42505-9_4

a planning process in virtual wiring, identifying the best cable paths considering boundary conditions and mutual influence refers to a time-critical task. The error-prone process of ideal path identification is currently based on a manual, repetitive, and time-consuming definition of all waypoints per single connection. In particular, the iterative wiring approach limits the identification of ideal cable harnesses due to the multiple mutual influences between the individual connections and results in a high rework effort even for small mechanical changes. Due to a rising number of product variants and decreasing batch sizes, economical automation of the virtual wiring is required. Ongoing developments and advances in the field of artificial intelligence (AI) offer the possibility to solve complex optimization problems increasingly better than is feasible in the current state [6]. Especially the inclusion of the variety of boundary conditions and their dependencies within a holistic end-to-end automation process counteracts the existing drawbacks when defining the wiring process as an optimization problem.

This paper presents an approach for an automated electrical routing algorithm based on a Multi-Agent Deep Q-Network (MADQN) that interacts with a transformed voxel environment representing the mechanical product. Section 2 includes the state of the art, describing the fundamentals of a Deep Q-Network (DQN) and existing approaches to automating the routing process. The novel automated electrical routing-method is then presented in Sect. 3 describing the system model as well as the algorithm. This is followed by the evaluation. Finally, Sect. 5 concludes this paper and gives an overview of future research.

2   State of the Art

2.1   Electrical Routing Problem in 3D Environments

Existing limitations in the current work processes of electrical routing in 3D CAD are mainly based on a manual and iterative way of working. In essence, this restricts the holistic consideration of all individual connections $i \in \mathcal{N}$. The underlying problem can be described as a shortest-path problem in three-dimensional space under constraints C. It is consequently classified as an NP-hard optimization problem [9]. Each cable K_i is characterized by an individual starting and target point as well as specific diameters D and admissible bending radii $C_{bend}(K_i)$. At this point, the permissible bending radius is equivalent to a boolean query of whether $r_{min}(K_i) \leq r_{allowed}(K_i)$ [9]. For a valid definition of a cable path, various constraints must be fulfilled. In particular, the freedom of collisions $C_{collision}(K_i)$ is to be mentioned here. This includes collisions with surrounding geometries $C_{collision}^{geometry}(K_i)$ from the 3D CAD as well as geometric overlap with other cables $C_{collision}^{cable}(K_i)$. In this context, the trade-off between path optimality and computation time has to be taken into account when the scalability of the solution approach is considered. Due to the often huge solution space, an efficient procedure is ought to achieve an approximate solution to the optimization problem. Each is defined as the minimization of the total length L_{total} of all cables K_i subject to constraints $C(K_i)$, as shown in Eq. 1 [9].

$$\arg\min f(x) \tag{1}$$

$$f(x) = \sum_{i}^{N} f_i(x) = \sum_{i}^{N} L_{total}(\tau_{\pi_\theta}^i) + C(K_i) \tag{2}$$

$$\text{subject to } C(K_i) \geq 0 \tag{3}$$

$\tau_{\pi_\theta}^i$ denotes the trajectory τ of the cable i through the environment applying the policy π_θ. $C(K_i)$ refers to all required constraint functions to account for each design rule that has to be satisfied when planning the cable path of a cable K_i, e.g., the cable-specific bending radius $C_{bend}(K_i)$ or collisions $C_{collision}(K_i)$. As the optimization of L_{total} is often subject to several local minima in iteratively solving the problem, approaches for globally optimizing L_{total} are crucial for industrial applications.

2.2 Deep Q-Network - DQN

The presented approach aims to solve the electrical routing problem in a three-dimensional voxel structure using Multi-Agent DQN (MADQN). In this scenario, the agent is represented by a single cable K_i to be routed, interacting with the environment - the transformed 3D CAD model. In a wiring process with multiple cables, each cable has its own agent - in the context of this paper, this is defined as a multi-agent [5]. The agent is told the current state s of the immediate surrounding environment in the learning process, analogous to the basic Reinforcement Learning model. Accordingly, the agent reacts with the action a, which is selected based on the present policy π and state s. The value of this state-action pair can be defined by the Q-function $Q(s, a)$. In the DQN approach, an artificial neural network is used to approximate the Q-function [7]. During the training process, the neural network's adjustable parameters θ are constantly updated to converge in the direction of the targeted optimization goal $min(L_{total})$, represented by the reward r [7].

Using the centralized training and centralized execution (CTCE) method results in a collectively used policy π for all single agents K_i [3,8]. As a result, the agents become less specialized, but the policy π can be used for new agents with divergent start and target points, resulting in neural network generalization. The opposite method of distributed training and decentralized execution (DTDE) allows for greater specialization in single cable challenges. However, two fundamental problems with DTDE approaches arise. Recent research indicates that distributed training schemes scale poorly with the number of agents due to the added sample complexity to the learning problem [3]. In addition, the use of existing policies by new agents is limited since a selection of the most appropriate policy π_i for the new agent K_i is required first. Using the ability to estimate Q-values with a neural network in the DQN enables the applicability of this method to large environments. The existence of the DQN's replay buffer, particularly in terms of sensitivity to rare geometric features, is a promising method for use in automated routing in 3D space.

3   Electrical Routing Approach

In this chapter, the underlying problem is described as a finite-horizon Markov Game (MG) within a partially observable, deterministic environment. For solving the 3D cable routing problem with multiple cables K subject to constraints $C(K_i)$ a MADQN is proposed. To decrease the state space with reference to the application domain, a reduction of the available movement area is integrated. This approach is based on the concept of an attraction area in a voxel environment [1,2].

3.1   System Model

The underlying problem is declared as a shortest path problem in 3D space under constraints $C(K_i)$. The objective is to minimize the distance to be covered between the starting point of cable $P_S(K_i)$ and the target point $P_T(K_i)$ without causing collisions with the geometry or falling below the cable-specific bending radius. As shown in Eqs. 4 - 6, this results in the associated optimization objective of the shortest path $S_{opt}^{K_i}(P_S, P_T)$ of cable K_i represented as a NURBS-curve given the constraints $C(K_i)$.

$$\pi_\theta^* = \arg\min_{\pi_\theta} f(x) = \arg\min_{\pi_\theta} \sum_i^N L_i(\tau_{\pi_\theta}^i) + C(K_i) \tag{4}$$

$$C(x) = \sum_i^n N_{i,k}(x) f_i(x) P_i \tag{5}$$

$$\text{subject to } \kappa_{min}(C(x)) \geq C_{bend}(K_i) \tag{6}$$

$$\text{and}$$

$$d_{surface}(C(x)) \geq 0 \tag{7}$$

In Eq. 5, $f_i(x)$ is the curve at location $x \in S$ within the state space S. $N_{j,p}(x)$ is the basis function polynomial for control point P_i, and n is the number of control points. $d_{surface}$ in Eq. 7 is the distance from the point x on the cable path to the nearest point on the surface s, and the minimum is taken over all points on the surface s. $\kappa_{min}(C(x))$ refers to the minimum curvature of the NURBS-curve, which is required to maintain the cable-specific bending radius $C_{bend}(K_i)$. As the environment is represented as a voxel space S^v and calculation of $d_{surface}$ can be computationally expensive in case of arbitrarily shaped obstacles, the inequality constraint for collision $C_{collision}(K_i)$ can be simplified to $C_{collision}(K_i) = 0$. By counting all included voxel values being part of the cable path $\sum_i^N f_i(x)$, $C_{collision}(K_i)$ can be calculated efficiently. A finite-horizon Markov Game (MG) with a partially observable and deterministic environment represents the system. The action space $a \in \mathcal{A}$ for the discrete environment S^v is described in Eq. 8.

$$\mathcal{A} = \{(a_x, a_y, a_z) | \; a_x, a_y, a_z \in \{-1, 0, 1\}\}. \tag{8}$$

The state is divided into sub-parts $\mathscr{O}_i$, each of which describes the associated observation of the i-th cable. Each individual observation $\mathscr{O}_i$ includes the agent's current position inside the geometry, all surrounding 26 voxel values as a cube, its previous 4 actions a_i, the Euclidean distance to the target point, and the current timestep. The observation $\mathscr{O}_i$ of the environment transmitted to agent i is agent-specific and does not contain any further information about other agents, except they are within the observed cube. The adjacent neighbour voxels also refer to the action space A. It is enhanced with an action for remaining in the previous position. As detailed in Eq. 9, the instantaneous reward r_i for each cable consists of several parts designed to improve the paths.

$$r(P_t^v(K_i), a_i, P_{t+1}^v(K_i)) = \begin{cases} 0, \text{if } P_{t+1}^v(K_i) \equiv P_T^v(K_i) \\ -10, \text{if } P_{t+1}^v(K_i) \in \mathcal{S}_{object} \\ -10, \text{if } P_{t+1}^v(K_i) \notin \mathcal{S}_{space} \\ -1 + d(a_i), \text{otherwise} \end{cases} \tag{9}$$

Reaching the target position $P_T(K_i)$ of agent i causes a reward of 0. During the process of closing in the direction of the target position P_T, the agent is rewarded inside a defined target point area based on the Euclidean distance $\|P_t^v(K_i), P_T^v(K_i)\|$. The Euclidian distance is then multiplied by the distance to the target in voxel. This corresponds to the transferred attraction area to the target point [1]. The reward within the target point area increases towards the target point at intervals of the defined voxel size. In contrast, the agent is penalized when trying to move to an occupied position $\mathcal{S}_{object}$ or leaving the entire geometry $\mathcal{S}_{space}$ with $r_i = -10$. Forcing the agent to move in the direction of the target point $P_T(K_i)$ is included based on the action trajectory $d(a_i)$ and a reward of $r_i = -1$ in case of moving into the opposite direction.

3.2   Multi-agent Deep Q-Network

The proposed approach for automating the electrical routing process inside 3D CAD applies a MADQN with neural network parameters θ based on a POMG due to the size of the state space in the voxel environment. As a consequence, the transferred observation $\mathscr{O}_i$ is unique per agent K_i, and $\mathscr{O} = \{\mathscr{O}_1, \ldots, \mathscr{O}_N\}$ represents the collection of observations for all agents. When applying the MADQN in a CTCE, the centralized executor $\pi : \mathscr{O} \rightarrow P(\mathscr{U})$ models the joint policy that maps the collection of distributed observations to a set of distributions over individual actions. This allows the straightforward application of single-agent training methods to multi-agent problems [3]. In this context, π_i refers to the policy of the agent, $\mathscr{O}_i$ denotes the individual observation space, and $P(\mathscr{U}_i)$ refers to the distribution over actions. As a consequence, the joint action-value function is expressed by Eq. 10.

$$Q^\pi(\mathscr{O}_1, \ldots, \mathscr{O}_n, \mathscr{U}_1, \ldots, \mathscr{U}_n) = \sum_{i=1}^N Q_i^\pi(\mathscr{O}_i, \mathscr{U}_i) \tag{10}$$

where $\mathscr{O}_i$ is denoted as the individual partial observation, and $\mathscr{U}_i$ refers to the subsequent action. For the contrarian method DTDE to be applied, each of the agents a_i has an associated policy $\pi_i : \mathscr{O}_i \rightarrow P(\mathscr{U}_i)$ that maps local observations to a distribution over individual actions. Since no information is shared between agents explicitly, there is only an exchange of information within the common policy π [3]. The only information shared is the identified existence of an agent that occurs inside the observation cube of another. As the optimization objective of the routing process is defined as minimizing the total cable length L_{total}, the scenario can be assumed as cooperative. However, the actions of the individual agents representing the cables are assumed to be approximately independent of both CTCE and DTDE. Accordingly, it is possible to approximate the overall probability $p(s, a, \theta)$ of the combined actions $p(\mathscr{O}_i, \mathscr{U}_i, \theta)$ as shown in Eq. 11.

$$p(s, a, \theta) \approx \prod_{i=1}^{N} p(\mathscr{O}_i, \mathscr{U}_i, \theta) \tag{11}$$

3.3   Electrical Routing Environment/Framework

Since the state-action space in CTCE grows exponentially, the possible motion space of the agent is limited in this approach according to the application domain. The static environment, available for interaction is based on converting the 3D geometry into voxels. Further development of an attraction area is derived from the application domain restricting the available state space [1]. For this, the 3D CAD geometry is transformed into voxels in a sequential process in the first step. According to the application domain, a maximum allowable distance d_{max} is assumed between the cables to be planned and the geometry. This arises from the necessity of clamping as well as the physical characteristics and slackness of the cables. It also supports the goal of shrinking the state-action space in CTCE [2]. Figure 1 details the reduction of available movement space of agents.

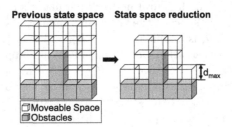

Fig. 1. State-Space reduction in voxel environment

In contrast to previous approaches, only the available moveable space of the agent is stored in a sparse matrix. It must be taken into account that, depending on the defined voxel size, geometric information may be lost during the transformation process. Thus, as the size of a single voxel increase, entire components such as thin-walled cable ducts can be missed. Consequently, these would no longer attend in the path identification, leading to inadmissible cable paths.

4 Validation

The following section investigates the numerical performance of the proposed approaches, applying CTCE and DTDE to the routing task in 3D CAD. The results are compared to the established method of the A* algorithm. Two major features of the method are evaluated: State space reduction for more efficient identification of the best-fitting cable paths and the applicability of a Multi-Agent DQN in this routing environment. For validating the developed approach, a 3D CAD model of a common industrial robot is used [4]. The learning of the MADQN is performed on a general-purpose system (Intel®Core(TM) i9-10980XE CPU @ 3.00 GHz, 97.918 MB, Python 3.8) without the usage of an external GPU. All environments are trained within less than 3 h. For each simulation of the A* an average of over 10 runs is determined.

4.1 Routing Environment

As an example, an industrial robot is used as the routing environment, which is assumed to be static for the present validation [4]. This is available as a 3D CAD model. The loss-free transformation here depends on the selected size of a single voxel. Due to the cable diameters and the necessary granularity of the example, a voxel size of 2 mm is chosen. The initial transfer of the 3D geometry from CAD (Fig. 2(a)) into a voxel environment (Fig. 2(b)) illustrates the discretization of the environment.

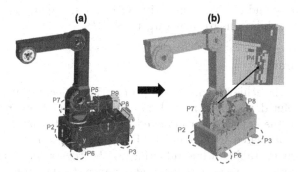

Fig. 2. Representation of the environment: 3D CAD environment with the defined Connection Points (a) and the environment transformed into voxel (b)

Within the environment, there are nine electrical connection points (P), whose coordinates are shown in Table 2. The associated electrical connections result from Table 1. Within the validation, all connections are assumed to have a cable diameter $D(K_i)$ of 2 mm, with the allowable bending radius of the cables set at $3 \times D(K_i)$. For cable movement within the geometry, an allowed maximum distance d_{max} to the robot is defined as 8 mm, which is equivalent to a 4 voxel layer surrounding the geometry.

Table 1. Start and target points

Cable ID	Start Point	Target Point
Cable 1	P3	P6
Cable 2	P2	P7
Cable 3	P5	P9
Cable 4	P4	P8
Cable 5	P3	P1

Table 2. CAD coordinates in the test environment

ConnectionPoint	X	Y	Z
P1	-190.00	-80.00	4.00
P2	30.00	-80.00	4.00
P3	-190.00	80.00	4.00
P4	-76.74	24.00	167.75
P5	-76.74	-18.00	167.75
P6	30.00	80.00	4.00
P7	49.25	0.00	161.75
P8	-177.25	11.50	118.55
P9	-177.50	-11.50	118.55

This results in a smaller movement space for the agents K when using the state space reduction. In the applied case of a voxel size of 2mm and d_{max} of 8 mm, the possible state space is reduced by 95%. The percentage reduction depends strongly on the chosen voxel size. While the reduction for a 4mm voxel is approx. 90%, it is only 57% for a 16mm voxel. It should be noted in this context that excessively large voxels may result in geometric information loss. Furthermore, the size of the surrounding covering has to be chosen according to the cables to be laid and their quantity. Otherwise, the agents K_i might be unable to ensure valid paths to their target point P_T.

4.2 Cable Routing

In order to check the achievement of the optimization objective by the MADQN, five cables are defined, which are routed simultaneously in the environment using the MADQN. In the environment depicted in Fig. 2, both approaches are used to validate the contrasted CTCE and DTDE. Both methods must identify π_θ^* for all K_i shown in Table 1 while adhering to the constraints $C(K_i)$. During the learning process, the respective residual distances to the target point d_T are broken down per cable K_i for direct comparison. Figure 3a shows a CTCE using the target point area, while Fig. 3b contrasts the integration of a DTDE.

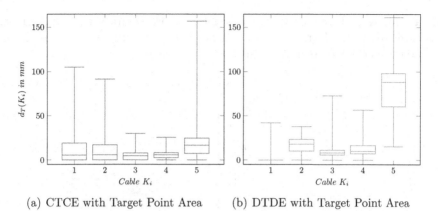

(a) CTCE with Target Point Area   (b) DTDE with Target Point Area

Fig. 3. Comparision of $d_T(K_i)$ for CTCE and DTDE

As illustrated in Fig. 3 not both of the approaches achieve valid pathways for all 5 cables K_i throughout the learning process of 1000 iterations l. As a result, CTCE can plan all 5 cable paths to the target point P_T, whereas DTDE is unable to generate a feasible solution for K_5. It is evident that in both scenarios, K_5 yields the largest scatter of results. This can be related to the fact that analogous to Table 1, it is one of the longer and more complex connections due to the geometry. It is worth highlighting that the interquartile range (IQR) for K_1 is significantly smaller in the DTDE, whereas all other IQRs in CTCE are smaller. This is contrasted with the larger range of values in the upper whisker for K_1, K_2, and K_5 in CTCE. In summary, it can be seen that CTCE with a smaller average IQR gives more stable results, and both the upper quartile and the median value have a smaller value for 4 out of 5 cables. The distinction is especially clear for K_5, where DTDE only achieves a minium value of 15.38 for $d_T(K_5)$, whereas CTCE achieves a nearly equal median of 16.79. Additionally, CTCE reaches a smaller or equal d_T both in absolute terms and as a percentage of the total distance between P_S and P_T.

Given the minimization objective L_{total}, the developed approach is to be validated against an A*-algorithm in Fig. 4a. The achieved individual cable lengths are calculated per cable K_i and their total length L_{total} is compared. All results shown have been obtained taking into account the mutual influence of the individual connections K. As A* and DTDE have not found a valid solution for K_5, for L_{total}, the achieved length $L(K_5)$ of CTCE is assumed. In the evaluation, it becomes clear that the A* generates the shortest, valid paths for the cables $K_1 - K_4$. However, no path is found for K_5 as the algorithm enters a local minimum and does not exit it within the limited computation time per iteration. All three methods produce the same numerical and visual results for K_1, identifying the optimal path with a length of 218.22 in each case. In the case of K_2, however, the result deviation between CTCE and A* can reach up to 13.7%. For cables K_3 and K_4, CTCE shows deviations of 4.2% and 16.79%. In case of DTDE, the divergence is more than 76.45% compared to A*. Of note is the identification of the path for K_5, where only CTCE was able to reach the target point $P_T(K_5)$. This is related to the fact, that DTDE is not able to identify a shorter path for any cable in the same amount of time.

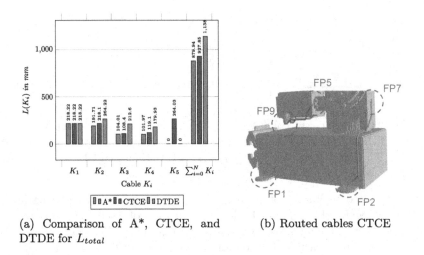

(a) Comparison of A*, CTCE, and DTDE for L_{total}

(b) Routed cables CTCE

Fig. 4. Validation Results

To ensure overall comparability, a path of $L(K_5) = 264.03\ mm$ is assumed for the comparison of L_{total} for all approaches. This results in a 5.44% deviation from the A* on the CTCE's part, while the DTDE result is 29.43% worse than the heuristic. For CTCE as shown in Fig. 4b, these deviations are mainly due to the paths for K_2 (-13.76%) and K_4 (-16.79%). This suggests that the basic solving ability of a MADQN is fundamentally given in the present scenario, but the accuracy of the result needs to be improved. A decisive advantage compared to the heuristic approach is the global and simultaneous consideration of the problem, as well as the possible generalization for geometrically similar 3D CAD objects.

5   Conclusion and Outlook

The presented approach uses a MADQN in CTCE and DTDE to solve the task of virtual wiring in 3D CAD. For this purpose, the problem is initially defined as an optimization problem, and it is shown how this can be formulated as a POMG. Since there is a mutual influence of the individual electrical connections, the task is to be solved cooperatively in order to achieve a minimum total cable length L_{total} under consideration of the given boundary conditions $C(K_i)$. In this context, the approach compares the use of a common neural network for all agents K and individual networks per agent without sharing additional information about the other cables. The approach was validated in an exemplary 3D

CAD geometry and ranked based on different criteria. The geometry of a robot used for this purpose was converted to voxels and the state space constrained by a surrounding hull (Fig. 1, 2). It is also contrasted with a commonly used A* algorithm for comparability. The evaluation results in Fig. 3 show that the CTCE achieves shorter paths for the individual cables during the learning process and performs more consistently concerning the IQR. However, neither approach finds a valid path to the target point $d_T(K_i)$ for all cables simultaneously. The evaluation shows that the use of a Multi-Agent Reinforcement Learning algorithm in automated 3D CAD routing is feasible and provides valid results for a limited number of cables in static environments. While these are 5.44% worse than an A* algorithm in the applied approach, they offer the opportunity to better account for the mutual influence of the connections as they are not planned iteratively. Future work will concentrate on agent communication and the scalability of solution approaches. Furthermore, it is also necessary to examine the possible application of other RL algorithms.

References

1. Asmara, A.: Pipe routing framework for detailed ship design (2013)
2. Denk, M., Bickel, S., Steck, P., Götz, S., Völkl, H., Wartzack, S.: Generating digital twins for path-planning of autonomous robots and drones using constrained homotopic shrinking for 2d and 3d environment modeling. Applied Sci. **13**(1) (2023). https://doi.org/10.3390/app13010105
3. Gronauer, S., Diepold, K.: Multi-agent deep reinforcement learning: a survey. Artif. Intell. Rev. **55**(2), 895–943 (2022). https://doi.org/10.1007/s10462-021-09996-w
4. igus ®GmbH: robolink rl-dc. www.igus.de/product/13631?artNr=RL-D-RBT-3322-BF
5. Lohse, O., Haag, A., Dagner, T.: Enhancing monte-carlo tree search with multi-agent deep q-network in open shop scheduling, pp. 1210–1215 (Nov 2022). https://doi.org/10.1109/WCMEIM56910.2022.10021570
6. Lohse, O., Pütz, N., Hörmann, K.: Implementing an online scheduling approach for production with multi agent proximal policy optimization (MAPPO). In: Dolgui, A., Bernard, A., Lemoine, D., von Cieminski, G., Romero, D. (eds.) APMS 2021. IAICT, vol. 634, pp. 586–595. Springer, Cham (2021). https://doi.org/10.1007/978-3-030-85914-5_62
7. Mnih, V., et al.: Playing atari with deep reinforcement learning (2013). https://doi.org/10.48550/ARXIV.1312.5602
8. Weiß, G.: Distributed reinforcement learning. In: Steels, L. (ed.) The Biology and Technology of Intelligent Autonomous Agents, pp. 415–428. Springer, Heidelberg (1995). https://doi.org/10.1007/978-3-642-79629-6_18
9. Zhu, Z.: Automatic 3D Routing for the Physical Design of Electrical Wiring Interconnection Systems for Aircraft. Ph.D. thesis (Dec 2016). https://doi.org/10.4233/uuid:2ca107b4-202d-4638-a044-d45649b89275

The Analysis of Optimizers in Training Artificial Neural Networks Using the Streaming Approach

Piotr Duda[1]([✉]) [ID], Mateusz Wojtulewicz [2][ID], and Leszek Rutkowski[2,3] [ID]

[1] Department of Computational Intelligence, Czestochowa University of Technology, Czestochowa, Poland
`piotr.duda@pcz.pl`
[2] Institute of Computer Science, AGH University of Science and Technology, Cracow, Poland
[3] System Research Institute of the Polish Academy of Sciences, Warsaw, Poland

Abstract. One of the major challenges in modern artificial neural network training methods is reducing the learning time. To address this issue, a promising approach involves the continuous selection of the most crucial elements from the training set, utilizing data stream analysis. However, transitioning to this new learning paradigm raises several questions. In this study, we explore the significance of employing different optimizers for training neural networks using the streaming method. Experimental results are presented based on a detailed analysis of a convolutional neural network trained on the MNIST dataset.

Keywords: Deep learning · Data stream mining · Boosting algorithm

1 Motivation and Background

The remarkable advancements made by machine learning algorithms, particularly neural networks, are closely tied to their ability to learn increasingly intricate models. Among these advancements, the development of deep learning techniques holds significant importance as they enable the training of networks comprising multiple layers, sometimes even dozens of layers. Consequently, complex tasks like natural language processing and image analysis can now be automated. However, these achievements do not come without a cost. To achieve satisfactory results, it is imperative to gather and process vast amounts of training data. This, in turn, demands considerable time, which directly impacts the production costs associated with these models. Therefore, it has become more crucial than ever to employ techniques that ensure the swiftest convergence of networks.

One of the factors that affects the speed of network convergence is the selection of an appropriate optimizer, which refers to a method used to update the network weights during training. Various optimizers have been extensively discussed in the literature:

L. Rutkowski et al. (Eds.): ICAISC 2023, LNAI 14125, pp. 46–55, 2023.
https://doi.org/10.1007/978-3-031-42505-9_5

SGD - Stochastic Gradient Descent serves as the fundamental weight update method, where the magnitude of weight changes is determined solely by the gradient of the loss function and the chosen learning rate.

Adagrad (Adaptive Gradient) [5] is a method where each updated parameter possesses its own learning rate, which is adjusted based on the parameter's performance summarized throughout the entire learning process.

Adadelta [25], an improvement upon Adagrad, calculates the learning rates for each parameter by considering not only the gradient's value within a specific time window but also Exponentially Weighted Averages over the gradient.

RMSprop (Root Mean Square Propagation) [24], an alternative approach to adjusting the learning rate individually for each parameter, involves dividing the learning rate by the square root of the weighted sum of squared gradients from previous iterations. The importance of subsequent iterations is controlled by the forgetting factor.

Adam, (Adaptive Moment Estimation) [18] currently the most popular optimizer, combines the concepts of Adadelta and RMSprop. It determines the learning rate based on both gradient changes and the squares of their values.

AdaMax [18] is a variation of the Adam optimizer, where the learning rate adjustment is determined by the larger value between Exponentially Weighted Averages over the gradient and the absolute value of the gradient in a given iteration.

Regardless of the chosen optimizer, neural networks are trained using a common approach. During each iteration, the training data is divided into mini-batches, and the loss function values are calculated to update the weights. This iterative process is referred to as an epoch, and the approach is known as the epoch-based approach. In this method, all the data is utilized an equal number of times.

An alternative approach has been proposed in [6]. This method involves evaluating the training set elements based on their suitability for learning. Subsequently, elements are randomly selected for the mini-batch, with a higher probability of selecting elements that are deemed more useful. Consequently, a data stream is formed, where the frequency of occurrence for a particular element may vary over time, depending on the current state of the network's learning process. The concept behind this method is that the network primarily learns from the most valuable elements, thus minimizing the time required for effective learning.

The BBATDD algorithm introduced in [6] appears to be a promising approach that has the potential to revolutionize the learning process of neural networks. Nevertheless, there are numerous issues associated with this algorithm that necessitate additional research and investigation. Consequently, in this study, our focus is to analyze the significance of the optimizer employed in training networks using the stream approach.

The rest of the paper is organized as follows. In Sect. 2, current papers addressing the solutions and alternatives for the long time comsumig learning process are presented. Section 3 provides details of the BBATDD algorithm. Section 4 contains the results of experimental simulations, and Sect. 5 contains conclusions and proposals for further work.

2   Related Works

In this section, we will provide an overview of recently proposed methods aimed at addressing the challenges associated with the time-consuming learning of deep neural networks. The section is divided into two parts, with the first part focusing on methods dedicated to traditional neural network learning, and the second part discussing alternative approaches.

In [23], the authors address the problem of optimal network construction by investigating the placement of dropout layers in neural networks specifically designed for regression tasks. The focus of their study lies in Bayesian neural networks, which have the capability to quantify model uncertainty. They state that the best results are achieved when dropout layers are positioned after and between the residual blocks within the network architecture. Some analysis about convolutional neural network structures can be find in [26]. In [10], the significance of the training set in the learning process of neural networks is investigated. The authors specifically examine the impact of a particular image augmentation technique called Mixup on the training of a network designed for image segmentation. Mixup is an augmentation method that generates new objects by performing linear combinations of input images. The authors explore the effects of employing Mixup during the training phase and assess its influence on the network's ability to generalize the acquired knowledge. Through their analysis, the authors confirm the importance of training data in enhancing the network's generalization capabilities. More abou augmentation techniques can be found in [20]. The paper [4] examines the application possibilities of modern neural networks in addressing security-related issues. The authors specifically focus on the problem of intrusion detection and propose an ensemble approach using autoencoders instead of a single model. The proposed approaches, Autoencoder Enhanced Stacked Neural Network and Sparse Autoencoder Stacked Neural Network, demonstrate improved recall rates for the minority class and lower recall rates for the majority class. Transfer learning is regarded as a highly promising technique for accelerating network learning. It enables the adaptation of pre-trained networks to tackle different problems, particularly when data availability is limited. In [15], the authors examine this issue and propose a Progressive Transfer Learning method tailored for medical images. More on this can be found in [16]. In the paper [2], the authors propose a novel algorithm called SGQR, which combines Givens Rotations and QR decomposition methods to accelerate network learning. The effectiveness of the SGQR algorithm is evaluated through experiments conducted on six benchmarks encompassing approximation, regression, and classification tasks. The experimental results demonstrate the superiority of the proposed algorithm over other popular methods for three different network topologies. Another approach to this topic can be found in [3] and [9].

Stream data mining (SDM) is a field of study dedicated to the efficient analysis of massive datasets. Its primary focus is on processing large, and potentially infinite, data streams. SDM algorithms are designed to handle incoming data from the stream promptly, allowing for the timely processing of information while freeing up resources for new data. However, integrating stream processing methodologies with deep neural networks poses significant challenges due to their inherent characteristics. In the paper [21], the authors apply streaming methodologies to probabilistic neural networks for classification, regression, and density estimation tasks in a time-varying environment. Similar considerations were investigated in papers such as [7,8], and summarized in [22]. The application of data stream methodologies to training Restricted Boltzmann machines was proposed in [12] and further studied in [11,13], and [14]. The application of autoencoders for anomaly pattern detection was explored in [17]. Furthermore, the use of deep clustering networks in streaming environments is considered in [1].

3   Methodology and Experiment Setup

To assess the efficacy of optimizers, this study examines both epoch-based classical learning methods and stream methods as described in [6]. The concept of stream learning involves continuously selecting new data from the training set $(T = \{(X_i, y_i)|i = 1,\ldots,N, X_i \in \mathbf{R}^d\})$, aggregating them into batches, and utilizing them for network training. The sampling process is designed to prioritize data that elicits greater deviations in network responses from expected values. To achieve this, individual element weights are computed using three methods outlined in [6]. All of them are considered in this paper. These weights (v_i), derived from the formulas below, are subsequently normalized to establish a probability mass function for the elements in the training set $(T^S = \{(X_i, y_i, v_i)|(X_i, y_i) \in T, v_i \in (0,1)\}.)$. For further details on the methodology, please refer to [6] and Algorithm 1. To evaluate the effectiveness of optimizers, a convolutional network comprising 5 layers is trained. The initial two layers are convolutional layers with 32 and 64 filters, respectively. These layers employ 3×3 kernels. Following that, a MaxPooling layer with a 2×2 kernel is utilized. The network concludes with two fully-connected layers, one with 128 neurons and the other with 10 neurons. The learning criterion employed is the cross-entropy loss function. Additionally, Dropout with parameters 0.25 and 0.5 is applied after layers 3 and 4, respectively. The network was trained using the MNIST dataset [19], which is a widely-used collection of gray-scale images depicting handwritten numbers. The dataset comprises 60,000 training samples and 10,000 test samples. Each sample is assigned to one of the 10 classes corresponding to the different digits. The network with identical initial weight values was compared using both the epoch-based approach (MB) and three variations of the streaming-based approach: OWC, LB, and NLB. The significance of individual elements was determined according to Eqs. (1)–(3), which describe the respective approaches.

$$OWC \qquad v_i = \begin{cases} \Psi, & f(X_i) \neq c_i \\ v_i, & \text{otherwise.} \end{cases} \tag{1}$$

$$LB \qquad v_i = L(X_i)/M_i, \tag{2}$$

$$NLB \qquad v_i = tanh(L(X_i))/M_i, \tag{3}$$

where Ψ is some pre-define positive number, M_i expresses the number of times a given element has already been drawn into the batch, and L is the value of the loss function for the considered element.

The Boosting Based Training Algorithm with a Drift Detector, called here BBTADD algorithm, is as follows.

Input: S - data stream, M - batch size, λ - CuSum parameters

1   Collect a new batch B from the stream S;
2   **for** *every data element in B* **do**
3   Increase counter of drawn of the current element;
4   Train the network on current element;
5   Compute loss function for a current element;
6   Update v_i according to (1), (2) or (3)

7   **for** *every data element in B* **do**
8   Divide each v_i by their sum

9   **for** *every data element in T* **do**
10   Divide each v_i by their sum

11 Compute loss function on a validation set;
12 Update CuSum algorithm;
13 **if** *concept drift is detected* **then**
14   Reinitialize v_i values

15 *Return to line 1*

Algorithm 1: The BBATDD algorithm.

4   Experimental Results

A set of the most popular optimizers, including vanilla SGD, AdaGrad, AdaDelta, RMSProp, Adam, and AdaMax, were chosen for testing. The experiments were conducted using various learning rates, but for brevity, only the results for the learning rates $lr = 0.05$ and $lr = 0.01$ are presented, due to editorial constraints. Figures 1 and 2 depict the evolution of the loss function value computed on the test set as successive training batches were analyzed. Figure 1 displays the results for the SGD, AdaGrad, and AdaDelta optimizers, while Fig. 2 presents the results for the RMSProp, Adam, and AdaMax optimizers.

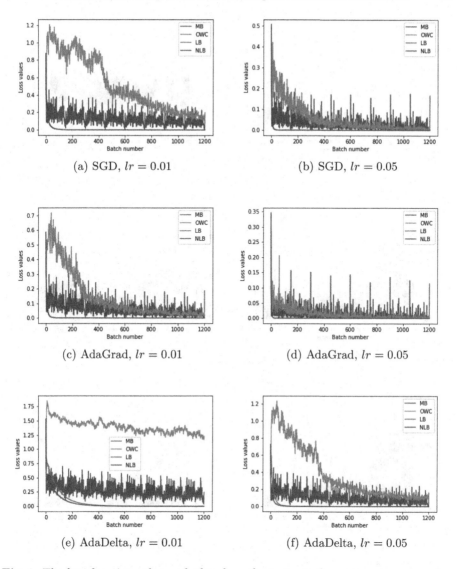

Fig. 1. The loss function values calculated on the test set after processing successive batches with SGD, AdaGrad and AdaDelta optimizers and different learning rate (lr) values.

The experiments were performed on a PC equipped with 64 GB of RAM, an Intel i9-7900X 3.3 GHz 3.31 GHz CPU, and an nVidia GeForce GTX 1080 Ti GPU.

The analysis of the results confirms the findings observed in paper [6]. Irrespective of the optimizer chosen, the OWC method consistently yielded the poorest results. While it occasionally outperformed the MB method in terms of final accuracy, it fell notably short in comparison to the LB and NLB meth-

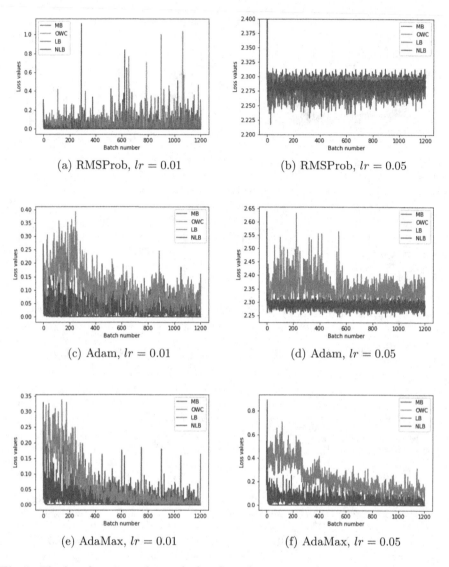

Fig. 2. The loss function values calculated on the test set after processing successive batches with RMSProb, Adam and AdaMax optimizers and different learning rate (lr) values.

ods in terms of quality. The LB and NLB methods consistently outperformed the other approaches when using SGD, AdaGrad, and AdaDelta optimizers. In the remaining cases, they also demonstrated better performance, although the results obtained exhibited greater variability. It is important to note that when using a learning rate of 0.05 with the RMSProp and Adam optimizers, the network did not effectively learn, as evidenced by the final value of the loss function remaining greater than 2. This indicates that the chosen learning rate may be too high for these specific optimizers, leading to suboptimal learning outcomes.

These observations are indeed supported by the statistics presented in Table 1. The table presents valuable information on the average value of the loss function throughout the learning process, the final value obtained after the last batch, and the variance to assess result variability. All values have been rounded to the fourth decimal place for clarity. The table specifically highlights the performance of the MB (Mini-Batch) and LB (Learned Batch) methods, showcasing the difference in results between epoch-based and streaming-based approaches. The best results are indicated using bold font for easy identification.

Table 1. Average loss function value, final loss function value, and variance in loss function values for MB and LB approaches with different optimizers.

	SGD	AdaGrad	AdaDelta	RMSProp	Adam	AdaMax
MB						
Mean	0.1268	0.0622	0.2766	0.0413	0.0356	0.0258
Final	0.196	0.1868	0.2465	0.1997	0.1592	0.1628
Variance	0.005	0.0024	0.014	0.0049	0.0012	0.001
LB						
Mean	0.0057	0.0028	0.067	0.0132	0.0051	**0.0011**
Final	**0.0**	**0.0**	0.0003	0.0712	**0.0**	**0.0**
Variance	0.0014	0.0006	0.0234	0.0011	0.0004	**0.0002**

5   Conclusions

This paper analyzes the significance of using optimizers in training convolutional neural networks with the streaming method. To achieve this, the network's performance trained using the classic minibatch method is compared with three stream learning approaches.

The experimental analysis reveals that the OWC method performs the poorest, regardless of the chosen optimizer. In contrast, the LB and NLB stream methods consistently deliver superior results compared to the epochal approach. The selection of the learning rate has a notable influence on the final outcome, as evident in cases such as Adam and RMSProp, where the network learns with a learning rate of 0.05. However, it should be noted that, in such the case, the network fails to learn for all approaches. The AdaMax optimizer demonstrates the best results overall.

The streaming approach to learning neural networks still raises several challenges that require further research. There is a potential for significant advancements by introducing novel techniques to determine the importance of training data. While the current optimizers perform effectively in the streaming approach, the opportunity exists to propose new methods that are specifically tailored to this innovative approach.

References

1. Ashfahani, A., Pratama, M.: Unsupervised continual learning in streaming environments. IEEE Trans. Neural Netw. Learn. Syst. (2022)
2. Bilski, J., Kowalczyk, B., Kisiel-Dorohinicki, M., Siwocha, A., Żurada, J.: Towards a very fast feedforward multilayer neural networks training algorithm. J. Artif. Intell. Soft Comput. Res. **12**(3), 181–195 (2022)
3. Bilski, J., Kowalczyk, B., Marjański, A., Gandor, M., Zurada, J.: A novel fast feedforward neural networks training algorithm. J. Artif. Intell. Soft Comput. Res. **11**(4), 287–306 (2021)
4. Brunner, C., Kő, A., Fodor, S.: An autoencoder-enhanced stacking neural network model for increasing the performance of intrusion detection. J. Artif. Intell. Soft Comput. Res. **12**(2), 149–163 (2022)
5. Duchi, J., Hazan, E., Singer, Y.: Adaptive subgradient methods for online learning and stochastic optimization. J. Mach. Learn. Res. **12**(7), 1–39 (2011)
6. Duda, P., Jaworski, M., Cader, A., Wang, L.: On training deep neural networks using a streaming approach. J. Artif. Intell. Soft Comput. Res. **10**(1), 15–26 (2020)
7. Duda, P., Jaworski, M., Rutkowski, L.: Knowledge discovery in data streams with the orthogonal series-based generalized regression neural networks. Inf. Sci. **460**, 497–518 (2018)
8. Duda, P., Rutkowski, L., Jaworski, M., Rutkowska, D.: On the parzen kernel-based probability density function learning procedures over time-varying streaming data with applications to pattern classification. IEEE Trans. Cybern. **50**(4), 1683–1696 (2018)
9. Gülcü, Ş: Training of the feed forward artificial neural networks using dragonfly algorithm. Appl. Soft Comput. **124**, 109023 (2022)
10. Isaksson, L.J., et al.: Mixup (sample pairing) can improve the performance of deep segmentation networks. J. Artif. Intell. Soft Comput. Res. **12**(1), 29–39 (2022)
11. Jaworski, M., Duda, P., Rutkowska, D., Rutkowski, L.: On handling missing values in data stream mining algorithms based on the restricted boltzmann machine. In: Gedeon, T., Wong, K.W., Lee, M. (eds.) ICONIP 2019. CCIS, vol. 1143, pp. 347–354. Springer, Cham (2019). https://doi.org/10.1007/978-3-030-36802-9_37
12. Jaworski, M., Duda, P., Rutkowski, L.: On applying the restricted Boltzmann machine to active concept drift detection. In: 2017 IEEE Symposium Series on Computational Intelligence (SSCI), pp. 1–8. IEEE (2017)
13. Jaworski, M., Duda, P., Rutkowski, L.: Concept drift detection in streams of labelled data using the restricted Boltzmann machine. In: 2018 International Joint Conference on Neural Networks (IJCNN), pp. 1–7. IEEE (2018)
14. Jaworski, M., Rutkowski, L., Duda, P., Cader, A.: Resource-aware data stream mining using the restricted boltzmann machine. In: Rutkowski, L., Scherer, R., Korytkowski, M., Pedrycz, W., Tadeusiewicz, R., Zurada, J.M. (eds.) ICAISC 2019. LNCS (LNAI), vol. 11509, pp. 384–396. Springer, Cham (2019). https://doi.org/10.1007/978-3-030-20915-5_35

15. Karam, C., Zini, J.E., Awad, M., Saade, C., Naffaa, L., Amine, M.E.: A progressive and cross-domain deep transfer learning framework for wrist fracture detection. J. Artif. Intell. Soft Comput. Res. **12**(2), 101–120 (2021). https://doi.org/10.2478/jaiscr-2022-0007

16. Kim, H.E., Cosa-Linan, A., Santhanam, N., Jannesari, M., Maros, M.E., Ganslandt, T.: Transfer learning for medical image classification: a literature review. BMC Med. Imaging **22**(1), 69 (2022)

17. Kim, T., Park, C.H.: Anomaly pattern detection in streaming data based on the transformation to multiple binary-valued data streams. J. Artif. Intell. Soft Comput. Res. **12**(1), 19–27 (2022)

18. Kingma, D.P., Ba, J.: Adam: a method for stochastic optimization. arXiv preprint arXiv:1412.6980 (2014)

19. LeCun, Y., Cortes, C.: The mnist database of handwritten digits (2005)

20. Maharana, K., Mondal, S., Nemade, B.: A review: data pre-processing and data augmentation techniques. In: Global Transitions Proceedings (2022)

21. Rutkowska, D., et al.: The L2 convergence of stream data mining algorithms based on probabilistic neural networks. Inf. Sci. **631**, 346–368 (2023)

22. Rutkowski, L., Jaworski, M., Duda, P.: Stream Data Mining: Algorithms and Their Probabilistic Properties. SBD, vol. 56. Springer, Cham (2020). https://doi.org/10.1007/978-3-030-13962-9

23. Shi, L., Copot, C., Vanlanduit, S.: Evaluating dropout placements in bayesian regression resnet. J. Artif. Intell. Soft Comput. Res. **12**(1), 61–73 (2022)

24. Tieleman, T., Hinton, G., et al.: Lecture 6.5-rmsprop: divide the gradient by a running average of its recent magnitude. COURSERA: Neural Netw. Mach. Learn. **4**(2), 26–31 (2012)

25. Zeiler, M.D.: Adadelta: an adaptive learning rate method. arXiv preprint arXiv:1212.5701 (2012)

26. Zhou, W., Wang, H., Wan, Z.: Ore image classification based on improved CNN. Comput. Electr. Eng. **99**, 107819 (2022)

Training Neural Tensor Networks with Corrupted Relations

Tristan Falck and Duncan Coulter[✉]

Kingsway Campus, University of Johannesburg, Auckland Park,
Johannesburg 2092, South Africa
`dcoulter@uj.ac.za`

Abstract. We present two new objective functions through which neural tensor networks – machine learning models designed to learn relations between entities – might be trained, and hypothesize that our novel objectives may bolster the neural tensor network's performance through so-called negative learning. We illustrate that our new training objectives can show more stable training behaviour than the original training objective, and that they can result in better behaviour from the model on a selected problem. We also show that our training objectives may be less extensible into more complex problem domains than the original, however.

Keywords: Neural Tensor Networks · Objective Functions

1 Introduction

Neural tensor networks, first introduced by Socher et al. in 2013, are machine learning models intended to induce relationships between entities [4,7,11]. The original neural tensor network model was evaluated on the Wordnet [5] and Freebase [2] corpora, respectively, and achieved results which outperformed other contemporary models at the time [4,11].

The original neural tensor network model learned a max-margin contrastive objective [11]. That is, the model had to achieve the suppression of incorrect relation calculations as well as the expected amplification of correct relation calculations; the neural tensor network could only satisfy the objective function provided that correct outputs were close to 1.0 and incorrect outputs were close to 0.0. To achieve this focus on negative behavior, Socher et al. made use of so-called "corrupted triplets": entity-relation-entity tuples where the second entity was chosen specifically such that the constituent relation was impossible [7,11].

As with the original research, we train neural tensor networks through an objective function which focuses both on positive and negative behavior. However, we penalize incorrect behaviour through corrupting *relations* as opposed to entities. We hypothesize that our presented training schemes may make use of *negative learning*: inferring that some relation between two entities cannot hold by transitively learning that another relation does.

© The Author(s), under exclusive license to Springer Nature Switzerland AG 2023
L. Rutkowski et al. (Eds.): ICAISC 2023, LNAI 14125, pp. 56–67, 2023.
https://doi.org/10.1007/978-3-031-42505-9_6

Section 2 describes neural tensor networks as well as their original training objective, and Sect. 3 outlines notable utilizations and extensions of the model. Section 4 introduces and elaborates on our two new objective functions. Section 4.2 outlines our hypothesis of negative learning, and Sect. 4.4 illustrates that our training objectives may result in entirely different memory-complexity behaviour than that of the original. Section 5 covers which experiments we employed to compare each of the training objectives, and Sects. 6 and 7 divulge the results and analyses, respectively. We show that our new training objectives may result in better behaviour on a simple problem domain, and also provide an example where our training objectives perform worse than the original.

2   Neural Tensor Networks

Socher et al. introduced neural tensor networks in 2013 and illustrated that the model could outperform contemporary relational learners such as the Hadamard and Bilinear models, among others, when evaluated on the Wordnet and Freebase corpora, respectively [4,11]. The key task of the neural tensor network model in the context of a knowledge base such as Wordnet is knowledge completion – inferring new relations within the given corpus based on exposure to existing relations.

A neural tensor network model ingests an (e_1, R, e_2) triplet, where $e_1 = (e_{1_1}, e_{1_2}, ..., e_{1_d})$ and $e_2 = (e_{2_1}, e_{2_2}, ..., e_{2_d})$ are vector-representations of entities and R indicates the relationship to be considered between them. The model outputs a scalar value which is interpreted as the confidence of the model in the validity of that triplet [9,11], i.e. whether the model believes e_1 and e_2 are likely to share the relation R.

For each relation R to be considered, the neural tensor network possesses the following five groups of parameters: $u_R \in \mathbb{R}^k$, $W_R \in \mathbb{R}^{d \times d \times k}$, $V_R \in \mathbb{R}^{k \times 2d}$ and $b_R \in \mathbb{R}^k$ [7,11], where k is a hyperparameter and d is the dimensionality of e_1 and e_2. As mentioned, the neural tensor network model possesses these groups of parameters independently for each different relation to be considered. That is, u_R, W_R, V_R, b_R each "belong" to the relation R. The total set of parameters utilized by the neural tensor network, therefore, is $\Omega = \{\mathbf{u}, \mathbf{W}, \mathbf{V}, \mathbf{b}\}$ where $\mathbf{u} = \{u_{R_1}, u_{R_2}, ...\}$, $\mathbf{W} = \{W_{R_1}, W_{R_2}, ...\}$, $\mathbf{V} = \{V_{R_1}, V_{R_2}, ...\}$ and $\mathbf{b} = \{b_{R_1}, b_{R_2}, ...\}$ for each relation R to be considered. The presented parameters compose the neural tensor network as presented by Eq. 1 [4,7,9,11], where we use N to represent the model as a function of e_1, R and e_2 (note that tanh is assumed to be vectorized).

$$N(e_1, R, e_2) = u_R^T \tanh(e_1^T W_R^{[1:k]} e_2 + V_R \begin{bmatrix} e_1 \\ e_2 \end{bmatrix} + b_R) \tag{1}$$

Training Objective. As with standard neural networks, neural tensor networks are trained through having the presented internal parameters adjusted through an optimization algorithm in correspondence with their performance on a training corpus [3,6,8,11]. The original implementation of the neural tensor network by Socher et al. made use of the L-BFGS optimization algorithm to train the model [11].

The model learned a max-margin contrastive objective which closely resembled the hinge learning function [10] with the margin hyperparameter having been omitted (some later works with neural tensor networks would reintroduce this margin value [7]). This is to say that the training objective could only be satisfied by the neural tensor network provided correct relation calculations had high confidence and incorrect calculations had low confidence [7,11]. The negative examples required by the objective were constituted by so-called *corrupted triplets* [11] – (e_1, R, e_c) tuples where e_1 could not possibly share the relation R with e_c. For each correct relation (e_1, R, e_2), C corrupted triplets (e_1, R, e_c) are created to be used in conjunction with the original triplet to train the neural tensor network [11]. For I correct training triplets $(e_1^{(i)}, R^{(i)}, e_2^{(i)})$ as indexed by $i \in \{1, 2, ..., I\}$ each corresponding to C corrupted triplets as indexed by $c \in \{1, 2, ..., C\}$, the original training objective J as parameterized by $\mathbf{\Omega}$ (without regularization) is defined in Eq. 2 as adapted from that presented in [11].

$$J(\mathbf{\Omega}) = \sum_{i=1}^{I} \sum_{c=1}^{C} max(0, 1 - N(e_1^{(i)}, R^{(i)}, e_2^{(i)}) + N(e_1^{(i)}, R^{(i)}, e_c)) \qquad (2)$$

The original research made use of L_2 regularization to constrain the complexity of the neural tensor network's resultant hypothesis [11], however we do not implement any regularization for our experimentation.

3   Related Work

Li et al., 2021 analysed neural tensor networks through the lens of Taylor series, having aimed to provide a mathematical explanation of their functionality alongside a link to other neural models [4]. The researchers illustrated that neural tensor networks may be expressed through Taylor polynomials given certain preconditions, and introduced so-called Taylor neural network slices to guide the structure of neural tensor networks [4].

Qiu and Huang, 2015 illustrated how neural tensor networks may be made constituent to larger deep learning architectures. The research extended neural tensor network models into the context of collaborative question answering by applying them to encoded and convolved language [7]. A neural tensor network model was trained to identify the correspondence between matching embedded questions and answers, where both the network's parameters as well as those of the convolutional layers were trainable under the same objective [7]. The consequent so-called convolutional neural tensor network system illustrated how neural tensor networks may be used as a more robust measure of affinity between complex embeddings than traditional similarity metrics.

Serafini and Garcez, 2016 extended the applicability of neural tensor networks from knowledge completion to neurosymbolic learning through their original implementation of the so-called logic tensor network model [9]; a generalized version of the neural tensor network model was used to identify the grounding, or truth-value, of a real-valued logical predicate. The neural tensor network used possessed the interesting trait of only considering the single entity $\mathbf{v}$, which was substituted both for e_1 and e_2, while the parameters of the model corresponded to different predicates as opposed to relations [9].

4   Training Through Corrupted Relations

4.1   New Training Objective Variants

This research presents two variants on a new training objective function, K, used in lieu of that expressed in Eq. 2. The variants on the new training objective are presented in Eq. 3 and 4, respectively. As with J, c indexes corrupted entities, however it is the *relation* which is corrupted as opposed to the second entity. Each of the presented variants of K are more comparable to mean square error objective function often used in machine learning and deep learning applications [6,8] than the original objective J.

$$K_1(\mathbf{\Omega}) = \sum_{i=0}^{I}([N(e_1^{(i)}, R^{(i)}, e_2^{(i)}) - 1]^2 + \sum_{c=0}^{C}[N(e_1^{(i)}, R_c, e_2^{(i)})]^2) \qquad (3)$$

$$K_2(\mathbf{\Omega}) = \sum_{i=0}^{I}\sum_{c=0}^{C}[N(e_1^{(i)}, R^{(i)}, e_2^{(i)}) - 1]^2 + [N(e_1^{(i)}, R_c, e_2^{(i)})]^2 \qquad (4)$$

4.2   Key Hypothesized Advantage of K: Negative Learning

The most significant difference between the variants of K and the original objective J is K's corruption of *relations* as opposed to entities. Intuitively, J, K_1 and K_2 all try to maximize the neural tensor network's confidences for correct triplets and minimize the confidences for incorrect triplets. However, that K relies on corrupting relations as opposed to entities changes the behaviour of the training process as follows:

- For some arbitrary corrupted triplet (e_1, R, e_c), J will teach the parameters corresponding to R that e_1 and e_c do not share relation R.
- For some arbitrary corrupted triplet (e_1, R_c, e_2), K_1 and K_2 will teach the parameters corresponding to R_c that e_1 and e_2 do not share the relation R_c.

The difference in training procedures in subtle, but important. In the case of K, e_1 and e_2 *do* share the relation R for the corrupted triplet (e_1, R_c, e_2); the entities *are* related, and it may be hypothesised that the parameters for R_c could loosely perceive the relation R between e_1 and e_2, thereby reinforcing that

R_c is invalid between the entities. We refer to the hypothesized induction that R_c cannot hold by inferring that R does as *negative learning*. Obviously, both this hypothesized behaviour as well as the novel training algorithms themselves may only be realized if it is impossible for e_1 and e_2 to share both R as well as R_c between them for some arbitrary relation R.

4.3   Difference Between K_1 and K_2

Originally, only K_1 was to be tested, however it was hypothesized that this would result in the model perceiving the corrupted triplets as more important than the correct triplets. For an arbitrary correct triplet (e_1, R, e_c), the corresponding loss as calculated through K_1 would be constituted once by the model's performance on that triplet and C times through its performance on the corresponding corrupted triplets. Intuitively, the corrupted triplets would be more important to the neural tensor network than the triplet itself by a factor of C, as they make up most of the loss.

J implicitly accounts for this problem by including the model's performance on the correct triplet in every term constituting the objective function; despite there being C corrupted triplets per correct triplet, each correct triplet still appears C times (see Eq. 2). This balances the scales between the correct and corrupted triplets, so to speak. K_2 serves an adjustment of K_1 which aims to capture this balancing of importance between the correct and corrupted triplets: by including the correct term in the corrupted summation (see Eq. 4), the loss caused by the model's performance on the correct triplet is amplified by a factor of C.

4.4   Difference in Memory Complexity Between J and K

The training objectives J and K also express different behaviour in terms of memory complexity under certain assumptions. In order to generate corrupted triplets for J, K_1 or K_2, some degree of knowledge about the training corpus beyond only which entities share which relations must be presented. For J, it must be known that e_1 and the corresponding corrupted e_c do not share the relation R, and for K_1 and K_2, it must be known that e_1 and the corresponding e_2 do not share the corrupted relation R_c.

When recovering corrupted triplets in the case of K, it is already known that e_1 and e_2 share the relation R. Hence, under the assumption that the relations between entities are mutually exclusive – that is, that two entities may only share a single relation between them – the additional knowledge required by K_1 and K_2 diminishes to the set of relations which may occur within the corpus (which must be known regardless, since there is a parameter set $\{u_R, W_R, V_R, b_R\}$ for each relation R).

To illustrate why the knowledge requirement of K_1 and K_2 diminishes under the assumption of mutual exclusivity between relations, observe that generating a corrupted triplet for an arbitrary correct triplet (e_1, R, e_2) entails randomly selecting a relation from $\{R_c \mid R_c \in \{R_1, R_2, ...\}, R_c \neq R\}$ without knowing anything else about e_1 and e_2. An example of a problem domain wherein mutual exclusivity between relations is implicit are confidence intervals between two given entities, for instance. Figure 1 illustrates a comparison between J and K in terms of their memory complexity under the assumption of mutually exclusive relations.

For the same reduction in required knowledge to occur for the original training objective J, the assumption that e_1 may share the relation R *only* with e_2 must hold. Under this assumption, a corrupted triplet corresponding to (e_1, R, e_2) could be recovered through randomly selecting an entity e_c from $\{e_c \mid e_c \in \{e_2^{(1)}, e_2^{(2)}, ..., e_2^{(I)}\}, e_c \neq e_2\}$.

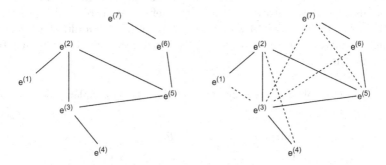

Fig. 1. An example of the knowledge required by the variants of K (left) and that required by J (right) for a problem domain where the assumption of mutually exclusive relations is held (assume $C = 1$). Solid lines represent relations between entities, and dashed lines represent external knowledge required by the algorithm. In this case, J would need to know that a given relation *does not* hold between certain entities. For instance, it must be known that $e^{(2)}$ and $e^{(4)}$ *do not* (dashed line) share the relation held between $e^{(2)}$ and $e^{(3)}$ (solid line). For this use case, the memory complexity of K would likely be preferable.

5   Experiments

Each of the experiments we conducted entailed comparing the performances of J, K_1 and K_2, respectively. We made use of two toy problem domains: scalar product intervals and vector correlations (each of which will be elaborated on in this section). To optimize the neural tensor network across each of the training algorithms for each of the given problems, we made use of the mini-batch gradient descent optimization algorithm. Batches of size 32 and an α-value of 0.1 were employed across 250 epochs per training procedure. We also experimented with differential evolution as a derivative-free optimization alternative, however none of the training objectives achieved any kind of convergence thereunder.

Both of the toy problems met the assumption of mutually exclusive relations, and therefore corrupted triplets for some correct triplet (e_1, R, e_2) for K_1

and K_2 were generated through randomly selecting relations from the full set while ignoring R. In order to generate corrupted triplets for J, entries from $\{e_2^{(1)}, e_2^{(2)}, ..., e_2^{(I)}\}$ were randomly chosen until the calculated relation between e_1 and the chosen e_c was not R.

5.1 Scalar Product Intervals

The first problem domain through which we evaluated the training objectives entailed learning which of five intervals the scalar product between two arbitrary three-dimensional vectors (entities) would fall into. We experimented with numerous delineations between the intervals for this problem with negligible changes to the results for the experimental parameters outlined in Sect. 5. Thus, the intervals of a representative example are defined in Table 1. As an example, the entities $e_1 = (1.0, 0.5, 0.3)$ and $e_2 = (0.3, -1.2, 0.2)$ would share the relation "high negative", since $e_1 \cdot e_2 = -0.24$ which falls into the fourth interval presented in Table 1.

Table 1. The intervals and corresponding relations for the scalar product problem domain.

Interval	R
$0.7 \leq e_1 \cdot e_2$	high positive
$0.2 \leq e_1 \cdot e_2 < 0.7$	low positive
$-0.2 \leq e_1 \cdot e_2 < 0.2$	roughly equal
$-0.7 \leq e_1 \cdot e_2 < -0.2$	high negative
$e_1 \cdot e_2 < -0.7$	low negative

2500 pairs of random vectors $e_1, e_2 \in (-3, 3)$ were generated and the correct relations outlined by Table 1 were recovered by calculating each of the scalar products between them. The set was generated such that each relation was equally represented. 80% of the corpus was used for training while the remaining 20% was used for evaluation. The neural tensor network itself had the hyperparameters $k = 3$ and $C = 3$ for this problem, respectively.

5.2 Vector Correlation

The second experiment was significantly more difficult than the scalar product problem, including ten possible relations as opposed to the previous five. For this problem, the neural tensor network had to learn into which of the ten confidence levels the Pearson correlation ρ between two three-dimensional, centered vectors would fall. The correlation intervals and corresponding relations[1] are shown in Table 2, and the equation for calculating the Pearson correlation[1] ρ is given by

---

[1] Note that the formula for calculating the Pearson correlation as presented in [1] includes the centering of the input vectors. We center the vectors prior to calculating the coefficients, which adjusts the formula.

Eq. 5, as having been adapted from that presented in [1]. The neural tensor network itself had the hyperparameters $k = 3$ and $C = 6$ for this problem, respectively.

$$\rho(e_1, e_2) = \frac{e_1 \cdot e_2}{||e_1|| \cdot ||e_2||} \tag{5}$$

Table 2. The intervals and corresponding relations for the vector correlation problem. The presented intervals do not account for 'perfect correlation' and 'no correlation', as would be present in a more statistically rigorous implementation. Note that the formula for the Pearson correlation ρ is expressed in Eq. 5.

Interval	R
$0.8 \leq \rho(e_1, e_2) < 1.0$	very strong positive correlation
$0.6 \leq \rho(e_1, e_2) < 0.8$	strong positive correlation
$0.4 \leq \rho(e_1, e_2) < 0.6$	moderate positive correlation
$0.2 \leq \rho(e_1, e_2) < 0.4$	weak positive correlation
$0.0 \leq \rho(e_1, e_2) < 0.2$	very weak positive correlation
$-0.2 \leq \rho(e_1, e_2) < 0.0$	very weak negative correlation
$-0.4 \leq \rho(e_1, e_2) < -0.2$	weak negative correlation
$-0.6 \leq \rho(e_1, e_2) < -0.4$	moderate negative correlation
$-0.8 \leq \rho(e_1, e_2) < -0.6$	strong negative correlation
$-1.0 \leq \rho(e_1, e_2) < -0.8$	very strong negative correlation

6   Results

Scalar Product Intervals Problem. All of the presented training objectives performed well on the scalar product interval problem, with each regularly achieving above 90%. K_2 generally resulted in the strongest behavior from the neural tensor network for this problem, followed by K_1 and lastly by J. Notwithstanding, all the algorithms achieved strong testing accuracy for this problem domain. The accuracies displayed by each of the algorithms are illustrated by Table 3. Empirically, the training process for the variants of K were significantly more stable than J, as illustrated by Fig. 2, which shows the average loss per epoch for each of the training algorithms for the scalar product problem.

Vector Correlation Problem. The vector correlation problem proved significantly more difficult for each of the training objectives, with the highest accuracy having been achieved being approximately 50%. Despite its training loss being the best – at least ostensibly – K_1 performed the worst on this problem both in terms of training and testing accuracies. The resultant performances of J and

Table 3. The training and testing accuracies across J, K_1 and K_2 for the scalar product problem domain.

Training Objective	Training Accuracy	Testing Accuracy
J	92.5%	92.4%
K_1	97.3%	93.6%
K_2	98.6%	95.6%

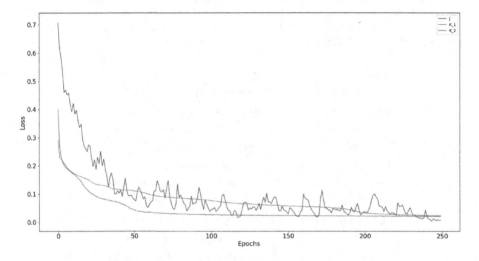

Fig. 2. The average loss per epoch per training algorithm for the scalar product interval problem.

K_2 were close, however J tended to outperform both variants of K with regards to training and testing accuracy. The training and testing accuracies of each of the training objectives are shown by Table 4. As with the scalar product interval problem, both variants of K showed empirically more stable behaviour than J, as illustrated by Fig. 3 which shows their average loss per epoch for the vector correlation problem.

7   Analysis

7.1   Comparing J and K

Section 4.2 outlined the hypothesis of negative learning through K: for some correct triplet (e_1, R, e_2), the parameters corresponding to some R_c could infer that their relation *could not hold* between e_1 and e_2 by transitively learning that R *does* hold between them. This would constitute the 'edge' that K_1 and K_2 have over J, since such transitive learning will not necessarily occur through the latter training objective.

Both variants of K significantly outperformed J on the scalar product interval problem, which could possibly indicate that this hypothesized negative learning occurred. However, that the variants of K outperformed J does not necessarily indicate the hypothesis to be true.

All the given training objectives struggled significantly on the vector correlation problem, having achieved at most 50% training accuracy and even lower testing accuracy. Aside from coming to approximate the formula for ρ given by Eq. 5, it is possible that any information retrievable from the vectors was not sufficient to infer the correlation between them; for a vector whose dimensionality is at least 3, any one of an infinite amount of vectors constituting a cone around the original would provide the same correlation. Notwithstanding, J significantly outperformed K_1 and tended to slightly outperform K_2. This could possibly indicate that K_1 and – to a lesser extent – K_2 are not as extensible into more complex problem domains as J.

Across both problems, the training behaviour for K_1 and K_2 were significantly more stable than that of J. As illustrated by Figs. 2 and 3, respectively, the training loss of the variants of K showed significantly less noise than that of J. This could be seen as an advantage of K over J, and may imply that K converges both more quickly and more predictably than J, at least for the presented problem domains.

7.2   Comparing the Variants of K

K_2's consistently better performance than that of K_1 seems to indicate that balanced weighting between the impacts of the correct and corrupted triplets, respectively, was of material importance. It could be hypothesized that K_1's inability to balance the impact of the correct and corrupted triplets on its overall loss calculation accounted for the strange behaviour observed on the vector correlation problem: that the algorithm showed the lowest loss per epoch while also achieving the worst accuracy during deployment may indicate that it was focusing more on suppressing incorrect outputs than recovering an appropriate hypothesis about the data. Notwithstanding, K_1's lower loss than K_2 over their training could also possibly be explained by K_1 being inherently lower than K_2: K_2 multiplies the loss for some correct triplet (e_1, R, e_2) by C, whereas K_1 only counts the loss for that triplet once.

Table 4. The training and testing accuracies across J, K_1 and K_2 for the vector correlation problem domain.

Training Objective	Training Accuracy	Testing Accuracy
J	49.0%	49.8%
K_1	37.8%	35.6%
K_2	54.2%	48.4%

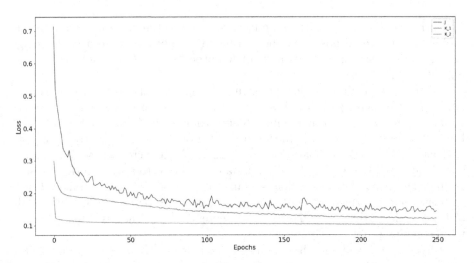

Fig. 3. The average loss per epoch per training algorithm for the vector correlation problem.

8 Conclusion and Future Work

We have presented the training algorithms K_1 and K_2, respectively, which train neural tensor networks through corrupting relations between entities as opposed to corrupting the entities themselves as with the original training objective J. We showed how K might produce entirely different memory-complexity behaviour than J which may make it better suited to problem domains where the assumption of mutually exclusive relations is satisfied.

We hypothesized that the variants of K could bolster the model's performance through our so-called negative learning, as presented in Sect. 4.2. Although we cannot necessarily attribute the efficacy of K to our hypothesized negative learning, the variants of K were shown to be highly stable during training and capable of outperforming the original objective on selected a selected problem domain (scalar product intervals). Given J's better performance on the vector correlation problem, it is possible that K is less extensible into more complex problem domains than J.

When the experimental parameters of 250 epochs and 2500 training examples were used for the scalar product problem, the variants of K outperformed J consistently, allowing us to make use of the representative intervals outlined in Table 1. Notwithstanding, the objective functions displayed far more nuanced performance across the tested interval delineations provided the epochs and number of training examples were significantly lessened; empirically, K would still outperform J provided the intervals were 'tight', such as having the 'roughly equal' band correspond to $[-0.1, 0.1)$. On the other hand, J would become more competitive and often outperform K if the intervals were wider. Neither J nor K were obviously better or worse than one another under these conditions of fewer epoch/examples, and thus we propose further research into the objectives under these circumstances.

Another clear next step for evaluating the efficacy of K_1 and K_2 would be applying them to large complex knowledge-completion problems such as Wordnet and Freebase, as was done with the original neural tensor network model. Additionally, experiments specifically designed to test the presence of negative learning within K_1 and K_2 should be employed; such experiments would indicate whether the efficacy of K could be attributed to negative learning or some other property of the training algorithms.

References

1. Benesty, J., Chen, J., Huang, Y., Cohen, I.: Pearson correlation coefficient. In: Noise Reduction in Speech Processing, pp. 1–4. Springer, Heidelberg (2009). https://doi.org/10.1007/978-3-642-00296-0_5

2. Bollacker, K., Evans, C., Paritosh, P., Sturge, T., Taylor, J.: Freebase: a collaboratively created graph database for structuring human knowledge. In: Proceedings of the 2008 ACM SIGMOD International Conference on Management of Data, pp. 1247–1250 (2008)

3. Engelbrecht, A.P.: Computational Intelligence: An Introduction. John Wiley & Sons, Hoboken (2007)

4. Li, W., Zhu, L., Cambria, E.: Taylor's theorem: a new perspective for neural tensor networks. Knowl.-Based Syst. **228**, 107258 (2021)

5. Miller, G.A.: Wordnet: a lexical database for English. Commun. ACM **38**(11), 39–41 (1995)

6. Nielsen, M.A.: Neural Networks and Deep Learning, vol. 25. Determination press, San Francisco (2015)

7. Qiu, X., Huang, X.: Convolutional neural tensor network architecture for community-based question answering. In: Twenty-Fourth International Joint Conference on Artificial Intelligence (2015)

8. Russell, S.J., Norvig, P.: Artificial Intelligence a Modern Approach, 4th edn. Pearson Education Inc., Boston (2020)

9. Serafini, L., Garcez, A.D.: Logic tensor networks: deep learning and logical reasoning from data and knowledge. arXiv preprint arXiv:1606.04422 (2016)

10. Shah, A., Sra, S., Chellappa, R., Cherian, A.: Max-margin contrastive learning. In: Proceedings of the AAAI Conference on Artificial Intelligence, vol. 36, pp. 8220–8230 (2022)

11. Socher, R., Chen, D., Manning, C.D., Ng, A.: Reasoning with neural tensor networks for knowledge base completion. Adv. Neural Inf. Process. Syst. **26**, 1–10 (2013)

Application of Monte Carlo Algorithms with Neural Network-Based Intermediate Area to the Thousand Card Game

Łukasz Gałka$^{(\boxtimes)}$, Paweł Karczmarek , and Dariusz Czerwinski

Lublin University of Technology, Lublin, Poland
l.galka@pollub.pl

Abstract. Modern techniques of artificial intelligence used in computer games allow to obtain very realistic and effective artificial agents controlling the game on the part of computer players. The main goal of this study is to create modern artificial intelligence algorithms based on neural networks and algorithms based on the Monte Carlo method to control players in the popular card game called Thousand. We propose two approaches based on neural networks trained on the basis of the Monte Carlo algorithm and the recursive Monte Carlo algorithm. Statistical approaches are characterized by high response times. Hence, an attempt is made to implement solutions that maintain high efficiency with a shorter operating time and, consequently, reduced requirements for computing complexity. The research showed no significant differences in the Monte Carlo approaches and the corresponding neural network methods. In the case of recursive method invocation, the effectiveness increased compared to the base methods.

Keywords: Artificial intelligence · card games · Monte Carlo methods · neural networks

1 Introduction

Artificial intelligence (AI) is one of the most studied areas of modern computer science. The researchers widely analyze AI algorithms and its applications to solve real problems of decision-making, prognosis, and retrieving information. One of the most challenging issues of such methods is to rival and compete with human intelligence, in particular in controlling the artificial agents in computer games. One can note interesting kinds of game genres with imperfect information such as card games.

Achieving high performance for artificial agents remains a challenge. In this case, the Monte Carlo method is widely applied [1]. Namely, many random samples and simulations bring a solution for difficult and complicated plays and moves. Nevertheless, such a strategy is strongly related to a number of simulations that need to be considered for the proper decision-making process [2]. It has a great impact on the algorithm complexity and makes the calculation

L. Rutkowski et al. (Eds.): ICAISC 2023, LNAI 14125, pp. 68–77, 2023.
https://doi.org/10.1007/978-3-031-42505-9_7

expensive. Furthermore, in the literature one can find recursive Monte Carlo modeling, where the final decision is based on multiple nested invocation of the simple Monte Carlo approach [3]. It makes the simulation extremely computationally expensive and, in some cases, impossible to perform due to time restrictions. Recursive Monte Carlo simulation allows to increase the efficiency of the algorithm. It is a great desire to invent a new technique that reduces its complexity.

Therefore, the main goal of this study is to propose a novel, innovative method to reduce the complexity of Monte Carlo-based approaches. Namely, we introduce an intermediate region for invocation of the Monte Carlo approach by weaving an artificial neural network (ANN) into the simulation process. This strategy allows to replace nested and computationally complex Monte Carlo method calls through an ANN. It implies that fast simulations of not only single levels of recursion but also higher ones become possible. Moreover, we have implemented our solution for the Thousand card game with imperfect information. We investigate our proposal results in terms of efficiency and time complexity.

The paper is structured as follows. Section 2 presents the related work. Section 3 describes general scheme of the process and prepared components. The results of numerical experiments are presented in Sect. 4. Finally, Sect. 5 is devoted to conclusions and future work directions.

2   Related Work

Various techniques for creating AI in computer games are applied. In the literature, there are attempts to outclass humans by computer algorithms. One of the important and challenging games are imperfect information card games. The large number of different combinations of moves and the predictions of the players' cards cause great complexity when trying to make the optimal play decision [4]. Therefore, building a decision tree covering all possible states is actually impossible. The first attempts to solve the problem are based on conducting random simulations of plays (Monte Carlo method, MC) and determining the most effective possible move [1]. Nevertheless, there are games with imperfect information, where the uncertainty of other players' movements and states must be approximated or predicted in some manner. Performing multiple simulations may indicate the most likely outcome of a particular card throw [5]. However, special attention should be paid to the time of performing such an operation. With a large number of moves, obtaining the result may be delayed. Therefore, scientists introduced an indirect method to reduce the reaction time of the algorithm - namely, Monte Carlo Tree Search (MCTS), where a decision tree is formed based on the MC method [6]. The MCTS is built around the player's most promising moves. It implements heuristics thanks to which the growth of the decision tree goes towards the best moves. The MCTS works very well for games with a very large number of next move branches [7]. The method requires computationally expensive prior tree training. Search space sampling is reduced to the most promising throws.

The second important aspect of creating intelligence in card games are solutions based on artificial neural networks (ANN), particularly deep neural networks [8]. It is worth paying attention to the effectiveness of this type of solutions in games such as Poker or Bridge. The preparation of a strategy introducing ANN to control the game of computer players allows to obtain a model that describes the game quite well. Training of such prepared approaches is usually associated with the variety of plays and their correct assessment. Nevertheless, the success of ANN is associated with the appropriate preparation of the network structure and, in the next step, with exhaustive training. As a result, a fairly fast and effective agent control algorithm can be obtained [9].

On the other hand, the reinforcement learning is an important branch [10]. In this approach, the emphasis is on the preparation of an appropriate environment that allows for automatic collection of information about the best moves. The model interacts with the environment taking into account a certain policy. It needs to be highlighted that the data collected from the environment is used to train the solution. This process is repeated until a satisfactory model is obtained. Also in this case, we can mention successful attempts to apply it in card games [11].

Finally, it is also worth presenting genetic and nature-inspired algorithms used in card games [12]. In the literature one can note gameplay strategy prepared in such manner. Evolutionary algorithms play an important role here. Introducing a few stages and their revisions shows interesting results [13]. Namely, stages such as selection, crossover, and mutation bring solution to very complicated problems, specifically in field of card games.

Another important aspect for this article is to inspect the available methods that will reduce the computational complexity of Monte Carlo-based algorithms. Successful attempts can be noted in the literature. Namely, the Monte Carlo algorithm can be well approximated by ANN [14]. In addition, this solution can also be applied to nested, recursive calls to the Monte Carlo algorithm [15]. However, the main problem with the preparation of the training data is related to the long simulation time of the recursive method [16]. Moreover, invoking multiple levels of recursion, i.e. more than one, becomes infeasible in a reasonable amount of time. Hence the new idea arose to imitate recursive Monte Carlo method calls through the ANN models prepared earlier. More precisely, the recursive method can use ANN instead of invoking a MC simulation. We have implemented such a mechanism for the game Thousand. In [17] authors create agents for such game. However, our idea of combination of ANN and Monte Carlo recursive calls is used for the first time.

3   General Scheme of the Process

The main goal of the research is to prepare and analyze algorithms based on the Monte Carlo method in order to increase the speed of their operation. Additionally, the efficiency of the methods is assessed. Efficiency is defined as the number of points scored by the player in a full round. Therefore, for research purposes an application is prepared that implements the gameplay in Thousand as a finite state machine [18]. This machine is presented in Fig. 1(a) which illustrates successive states and transitions between them. Each state is implemented as an independent module. After fulfilling the appropriate condition, transitions between states are performed. The game starts at the entry point and in an idle state. In particular, we propose an approach based on the Monte Carlo method. This method determines the best moves by repeatedly sampling random moves for players. In the first stage, the game table is copied. Cards that the opponents have are drawn randomly between them. Random algorithms for all players are set on the copied table. The entire hand is then played for each card that may be thrown in that hand. This process is repeated a given number of times. The Monte Carlo algorithm selects the card that will statistically produce the best results when thrown. In order to prepare the game algorithms, a reduced version of the game table is proposed.

It is well known fact that Monte Carlo calculations require a relatively large amount of computing power and are time-consuming. In order to improve the parameters of the game algorithm, a neural network can be effectively used to imitate the behavior of the Monte Carlo method. The structure of such network is shown in Fig. 1(b).

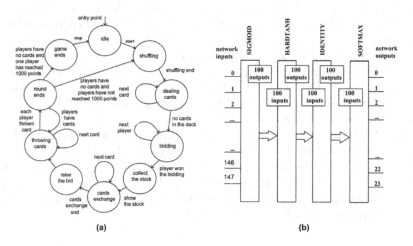

Fig. 1. (a) Finite state machine and (b) used neural network architecture for Thousand game.

This concept is based on a neural network with error back propagation algorithm. The network is selected in such a manner that the number of layers and neurons is as small as possible, so that the network has a fast response. In addition, various combinations of activation functions, number of layers, and number of neurons were tested. A network with the best accuracy parameter on the validation set were selected. The network consists of four layers with different activation functions: Sigmoid, Hardtanh, Identity, and SoftMax. The first layer has 148 inputs. The network output layer has 24 outputs. The connections of the neurons of the adjacent layers are realized as each neuron with each other from the next layer. The outputs represent the probabilities of card selection from the available 24 cards (each output represents one of the 24 cards). The inputs no. 1–24, 25–48, 49–72, 73–96, 97–120, 121–144, 145–148 represent the cards that can be thrown by the current player according to the rules of the game, the cards that the current player has but cannot throw, the card that the next player has thrown, the card that was thrown by the preceding player, the cards that have been collected on the game table, the cards that the opponents own, the registered trump, respectively. Each of the discussed sets of inputs has 24 inputs, where 1 is given if the appropriate card is present, and 0 otherwise.

The improvement of Monte Carlo method efficiency is achieved by replacing random algorithm with nested Monte Carlo method calls. Similarly, such technique is applied in our proposal. As it is reported in the next section, the response time of the neural network is constant. Therefore, it is possible to run multiple recursions of the Monte Carlo method with a constant response time of the algorithm. The underlying Monte Carlo method is labeled RMC-0. A network trained to simulate the underlying method is labeled ANN-0. The intermediate region is a replacement of RMC-0 calls with ANN-0 calls. First-level recursion uses a nested Monte Carlo method call. In the case of using an intermediate region, the method for calculations uses a neural network (ANN-0) trained to simulate a nested call. The multiple N-level recursion (RMC-N) algorithm uses the Monte Carlo method for calculations and an appropriately prepared algorithm based on the N-1 level neural network (ANN-N-1). The intermediate regions are the replacements of RMC-N with ANN-N. In order to obtain the final versions of the algorithm, training data should be prepared for each level of recursion and network training should be conducted.

The ANN-0 network training is carried out on the generated data with the Monte Carlo algorithm. The process is running until the highest accuracy is achieved on the validation set, in order to not over-train the network. The ANN-1 network training is carried out on the generated data with the recursive Monte Carlo algorithm. However, in this case we run Monte Carlo simulation that uses ANN-0 instead of a nested Monte Carlo call.

4   Numerical Experiments

All measurements and activities were conducted on a laptop with an Intel Core i7 10750H processor, 32 GB of RAM, GeForce GTX 1660 Ti graphics card and Ubuntu 20.04 LTS operating system. The test application was implemented in Java. For reliable results, all calculations were performed on a single thread.

In order to check the parameters of the solutions, the effectiveness of the methods and their execution times are analyzed. Rounds start with a random player number. Hence, for experimental purposes, in order to be able to clearly indicate the results of the game, the numbering of players was introduced.

The first and second player algorithms are fixed. The points scored by the third player are used as a measure of effectiveness. The version prepared to build solutions contains only the gameplay stage. Stages such as bidding, collecting a stock, raising a stake, and exchanging cards have been removed. In order to compare the effectiveness, random and naive algorithms as well as algorithms based on neural networks are prepared. Namely, a random player always plays a random card that can be played under the given conditions and rules of the game. The naive player, on the other hand, plays cards in such a way as to get the maximum number of points in the round or, in case of a loss, to minimize the lost points. More precisely, the player raises opponents' cards, if acceptable. Otherwise, it throws the card with the lowest possible score.

First, the influence of the samples number of the Monte Carlo algorithm on the effectiveness of the algorithm is examined, as shown in Fig. 2(a). The analyzed data are collected from 1,400 full hands for each value. In addition, the algorithms of the other players are set to a random algorithm. The number of samples is selected to be 50 because from this value we observe the stabilization of the performance, see Fig. 2(a).

After determination of the parameters of the Monte Carlo algorithm, training and validation sets for the analysis of the neural network (ANN-0) can be prepared. We built the training set on a basis of 1.5 million elements while the validation set contains 150,000 elements. We choose the size of the training set based on the training time which we set for maximum of 2 days at 2000 epochs. In addition, we want this set to be as large as possible to avoid overfitting. The size of the validation set is fixed to 10% of the training set size. Here, the accuracy and precision values mean the fit of the trained network to the solution based on the Monte Carlo method. These parameters versus the number of training epochs are shown in Fig. 2(b). We select the network after 1080 training epochs due to the continued lack of improvement in the accuracy parameter.

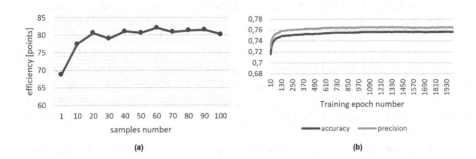

Fig. 2. (a) Monte Carlo efficiency for 1400 full rounds and (b) ANN-0 evaluation.

The similarity of the obtained solution with the base solution can be evaluated. For this purpose, the effectiveness of the third player is tested. All possible combinations of players are considered in this case. We make 1,200 full hands for each analyzed pair of algorithms. The significance of the differences between the Monte Carlo and ANN-0 is checked with the non-parametric U Mann-Whitney test at the significance level of 0.05. The efficiency and test values are presented in Table 1. In each case, the statistical tests show no statistically significant differences between the Monte Carlo method and ANN-0 trained on its basis. Hence, the Monte Carlo method is replaced with the neural network with a very good approximation of effectiveness.

Table 1. Average efficiency of Random, Naive, Monte Carlo, and ANN-0. U-Mann Whitney test results for Monte Carlo and ANN-0 efficiency.

Player #1 algorithm	Player #2 algorithm	Player #3 Random efficiency	Player #3 Naive efficiency	Player #3 Monte Carlo efficiency	Player #3 ANN-0 efficiency	P-value for player #3 efficiency
Random	Random	50.93	67.70	79.96	81.65	0.53
Random	Naive	44.84	61.52	72.33	72.26	0.63
Random	ANN-0	38.02	59.67	68.23	65.33	0.16
Random	ANN-1	40.22	57.85	66.35	65.86	0.97
Naive	Random	42.89	62.47	72.20	74.22	0.33
Naive	Naive	40.09	56.44	67.42	63.87	0.08
Naive	ANN-0	34.96	55.50	60.40	60.48	0.95
Naive	ANN-1	35.24	52.89	59.25	60.02	0.71
ANN-0	Random	38.12	60.40	68.32	67.79	0.74
ANN-0	Naive	35.83	53.68	60.47	60.52	0.72
ANN-0	ANN-0	31.99	52.49	59.25	59.72	0.64
ANN-0	ANN-1	32.38	51.15	56.17	57.94	0.38
ANN-1	Random	37.52	57.02	66.23	66.14	0.96
ANN-1	Naive	35.97	53.46	62.36	60.30	0.24
ANN-1	ANN-0	31.75	51.48	58.93	58.07	0.84
ANN-1	ANN-1	31.48	49.82	57.38	56.55	0.84

The second prepared solution is the recursive Monte Carlo method. Again, we examine the impact of the samples number on the effectiveness. The analyzed data are collected from 1,400 full hands for each value. In this method, the players moves' algorithms are set to the Monte Carlo algorithm with the samples number set to 50. Due to the execution time of this method and no statistically significant difference, the Monte Carlo algorithm can be efficiently replaced with the ANN-0 algorithm. Hence, we have applied this intermediate area (ANN-0) in recursive algorithm. We choose the number of samples after stabilization of the performance to be 50.

After determining the parameters of the recursive Monte Carlo algorithm, training and validation sets for the training of the neural network (ANN-1) are generated on its basis. The experimental conditions are the same as for the previous data. The network after 860 training epochs is selected. In the last step we compare the obtained solution with the recursive Monte Carlo method. The experiment is carried out in the same manner as with the Monte Carlo base solution. The results of the comparison are presented in Table 2. In each case, we observe no statistically significant differences between the recursive Monte

Table 2. Average efficiency of recursive Monte Carlo and ANN-1, U-Mann Whitney test results for those efficiency.

Player #1 algorithm	Player #2 algorithm	Player #3 recursive Monte Carlo efficiency	Player #3 ANN-1 efficiency	P-value for player #3 efficiency
Random	Random	81.43	80.98	0.94
Random	Naive	74.53	75.29	0.44
Random	ANN-0	69.93	68.94	0.88
Random	ANN-1	68.33	66.61	0.27
Naive	Random	72.48	72.94	0.83
Naive	Naive	67.15	67.65	0.56
Naive	ANN-0	63.59	63.32	0.88
Naive	ANN-1	62.48	64.25	0.23
ANN-0	Random	69.58	69.80	0.74
ANN-0	Naive	63.30	63.95	0.79
ANN-0	ANN-0	62.82	62.85	0.79
ANN-0	ANN-1	59.26	59.70	0.74
ANN-1	Random	69.32	68.47	0.88
ANN-1	Naive	62.91	61.97	0.45
ANN-1	ANN-0	58.94	58.52	0.69
ANN-1	ANN-1	59.42	56.74	0.12

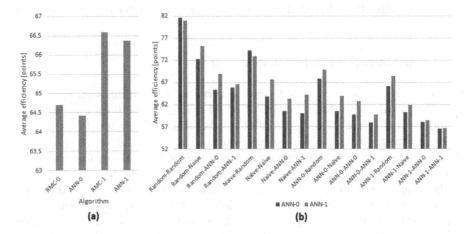

Fig. 3. (a) Average efficiency for prepared algorithms and (b) average efficiency for ANN-0 and ANN-1 and various combination of player #1 and player #2.

Carlo method and the neural network trained on its basis. Additionally, the average values of effectiveness and their difference for the considered algorithms are checked. These values are presented in Table 2. The mean difference for all tested samples is about 0.22. Similarly to the first solution, we can see that the recursive Monte Carlo method is replaced with the neural network with a very good approximation of effectiveness.

Finally, the differences in the prepared solutions based on ANN-0 and ANN-1 networks are checked. We present the average values of effectiveness and their

Table 3. Average reaction times, milliseconds.

Algorithm	Random	Naive	Monte Carlo	ANN-0	Recursive Monte Carlo	ANN-1
Time [ms]	0.0045	0.0050	4.67	0.33	4764.19	0.29

difference for the considered algorithms in the same manner as in the previous comparisons. These values are shown in Fig. 3(b). In the vast majority of cases, we obtained better results for ANN-1 compared to ANN-0.

The mean difference for all tested samples for the algorithms based on ANN is approximately 1.9. For a better presentation of the data, the average efficiencies for the prepared algorithms are presented in Fig. 3(a). It is also worth noting the higher mean effectiveness for ANN-1 solution in comparison with ANN-0.

The second analyzed parameter of the algorithms is the reaction time closely related to the computational complexity of the solutions. The average reaction times of the individual algorithms for 1400 samples each are shown in Table 3. Algorithms utilizing statistical calculations have the longest response times. The Monte Carlo algorithm runs in approximately 5 ms. Moreover, a recursive call of the Monte Carlo method significantly increases the response time which is around 5 s. Algorithms based on neural networks have similar response times of 0.3 ms.

5   Conclusions and Future Work

In this study, we have proposed novel approaches to winning strategy of the Thousand card game. They are based on Monte Carlo methods and artificial neural networks simulating the Monte Carlo results. In the series of comprehensive experiments, we have thoroughly examined various approaches and found their advantages and shortcomings. The use of the recursive Monte Carlo method to train the network gives better results than the use of the base Monte Carlo method and allows for increase in the effectiveness of the algorithm. Additionally, the use of a neural network to simulate statistical algorithms significantly improves the algorithm's response time. It is possible to use the intermediate region to trigger higher-level recursion while keeping the nested simulation execution time constant.

As a future work we are going to examine another classes of deep neural networks as well as to apply the fuzzy rule-based systems based on the information obtained from various player potential behaviors, i.e. points possible to get. Moreover, we are interested in the examining other variants of intermediate areas.

References

1. Yao, J., Zhang, Z., Xia, L., Yang, J., Zhao, Q.: Solving imperfect information Poker games using Monte Carlo search and POMDP models. In: 2020 IEEE 9th Data Driven Control and Learning Systems Conference (DDCLS), pp. 1060–1065. IEEE (2020)

2. Gałka, Ł, Dzieńkowski, M.: Analysis of selected methods of creating artificial intelligence on the example of a popular card game. J. Comput. Sci. Inst. **16**, 233–240 (2020)
3. Bouzy, B., Rimbaud, A., Ventos, V.: Recursive monte carlo search for bridge card play. In: 2020 IEEE Conference on Games (CoG), pp. 229–236. IEEE (2020)
4. Choe, J.S.B., Kim, J.-K.: Enhancing monte carlo tree search for playing hearthstone. In: 2019 IEEE Conference on Games (CoG), pp. 1–7. IEEE (2019)
5. Nishino, J., Nishino, T.: Parallel monte carlo search for imperfect information game daihinmin. In: 2012 Fifth International Symposium on Parallel Architectures, Algorithms and Programming, pp. 3–6. IEEE (2012)
6. Di Palma, S., Lanzi, P.L.: Traditional wisdom and monte carlo tree search face-to-face in the card game scopone. IEEE Trans. Games **10**, 317–332 (2018)
7. Godlewski, K., Sawicki, B.: MCTS based agents for multistage single-player card game. In: 2020 IEEE 21st International Conference on Computational Problems of Electrical Engineering (CPEE), pp. 1–4. IEEE (2020)
8. Justesen, N., Bontrager, P., Togelius, J., Risi, S.: Deep learning for video game playing. IEEE Trans. Games **12**, 1–20 (2019)
9. Dong, L., Wang, Q., He, H.: The algorithm of spiking neural network and application in Poker games. In: Proceedings of the 2020 5th International Conference on Multimedia Systems and Signal Processing, pp. 60–63 (2020)
10. Heinrich, J., Silver, D.: Deep reinforcement learning from self-play in imperfect-information games (2016)
11. Zhang, J., Liu, H.: Reinforcement learning with Monte Carlo sampling in imperfect information problems. In: Xiao, J., Mao, Z.-H., Suzumura, T., Zhang, L.-J. (eds.) ICCC 2018. LNCS, vol. 10971, pp. 55–67. Springer, Cham (2018). https://doi.org/10.1007/978-3-319-94307-7_5
12. García-Sánchez, P., Tonda, A., Fernández-Leiva, A.J., Cotta, C.: Optimizing hearthstone agents using an evolutionary algorithm. Knowl.-Based Syst. **188**, 105032 (2020)
13. Chia, H.-C., Yeh, T.-S., Chiang, T.-C.: Designing card game strategies with genetic programming and Monte-Carlo tree search: a case study of hearthstone. In: 2020 IEEE Symposium Series on Computational Intelligence (SSCI), pp. 2351–2358. IEEE (2020)
14. Grohs, P., Jentzen, A., Salimova, D.: Deep neural network approximations for Monte Carlo algorithms (2019)
15. Cazenave, T.: Nested Monte-Carlo search. In: Twenty-First International Joint Conference on Artificial Intelligence (2009)
16. Furtak, T., Buro, M.: Recursive Monte Carlo search for imperfect information games. In: 2013 IEEE Conference on Computational Intelligence in Games (CIG), pp. 1–8. IEEE (2013)
17. Domańska, A., Ganzha, M., Paprzycki, M.: Teaching bot to play thousand schnapsen. In: Tomar, A., Malik, H., Kumar, P., Iqbal, A. (eds.) Machine Learning, Advances in Computing, Renewable Energy and Communication. LNEE, vol. 768, pp. 645–655. Springer, Singapore (2022). https://doi.org/10.1007/978-981-16-2354-7_57
18. Fathoni, K., Hakkun, R., Nurhadi, H.: Finite state machines for building believable non-playable character in the game of Khalid ibn Al-Walid. In: Journal of Physics: Conference Series, p. 012018. IOP Publishing (2020)

Learning Representations by Crystallized Back-Propagating Errors

Marcus Grum$^{(\boxtimes)}$ (ID)

Potsdam University, 14482 Potsdam, DE, Germany
marcus.grum@uni-potsdam.de

Abstract. With larger artificial neural networks (ANN) and deeper neural architectures, common methods for training ANN, such as back-propagation, are key to learning success. Their role becomes particularly important when interpreting and controlling structures that evolve through machine learning. This work aims to extend previous research on backpropagation-based methods by presenting a modified, full-gradient version of the backpropagation learning algorithm that preserves (or rather crystallizes) selected neural weights while leaving other weights adaptable (or rather fluid). In a design-science-oriented manner, a prototype of a feedforward ANN is demonstrated and refined using the new learning method. The results show that the so-called crystallizing back-propagation increases the control possibilities of neural structures and interpretation chances, while learning can be carried out as usual. Since neural hierarchies are established because of the algorithm, ANN compartments start to function in terms of cognitive levels. This study shows the importance of dealing with ANN in hierarchies through backpropagation and brings in learning methods as novel ways of interacting with ANN. Practitioners will benefit from this interactive process because they can restrict neural learning to specific architectural components of ANN and can focus further development on specific areas of higher cognitive levels without the risk of destroying valuable ANN structures.

Keywords: Artificial neural networks · Backpropagation · Knowledge crystallization · Second-order conditioning · Cognitive levels · NMDL

1 Introduction

Situation. Dozens of attempts have been designed to create self-organizing artificial neural networks (ANN). The primary objective here refers to the autonomous, data-based finding of a powerful synaptic modification rule that will modify weights of an arbitrarily connected ANN, so that an internal structure will be worked out, which is appropriate for a particular task domain [45]. Controlling these attempts of machine learning algorithms becomes particularly essential if ANN become deeper, their architectures get more complex and one aims to interpret internal structures built during the training procedure.

L. Rutkowski et al. (Eds.): ICAISC 2023, LNAI 14125, pp. 78–100, 2023.
https://doi.org/10.1007/978-3-031-42505-9_8

Complication. Nevertheless, numerous hyper-parameters that tune those learning algorithms and the training procedures manually have been identified. Among them, some control the training procedure, such as learning rate, momentum, and rate decay. Others control the ANN architecture, such as the ANN's layer number, layer size, and kind of neural wiring. However, the control of internal structure building by those algorithms is limited.

Motivation. Although one can argue that humans are capable to preserve knowledge at learning procedures [1,2,11], so that humans can learn on-building, more complex knowledge or rather schemata in higher cognitive levels, machine learning does not support the crystallization of neural schemata or rather learning outcomes. If it was possible to control the internal structure building at the training procedure and make learning algorithms crystallize or rather preserve neural schemata without limiting the autonomous finding of powerful synaptic modification rules, one can guide the ANN development and build higher cognitive levels by intention.

Thus, the following research will address the crystallization of knowledge during machine learning or rather ANN training and focuses on the following research question: *"How can neural knowledge, such as previously trained neuronal weights, be crystallized to build on former training performance?"*

Contribution. This research presents a modified, full-gradient version of the backpropagation learning algorithm that preserves (or rather crystallizes) selected neural weights while leaving other weights adaptable (or rather fluid). It does not intend to provide sophisticated empirical proof at numerous task domains and ANN architectures. It rather intends to clarify the basis of such an algorithm. The algorithm shall enable the crystallization of neural schemata as a controlling instrument for on-building research and further enable more ANN-focused, pedagogic valuable training runs.

Structure. The research approach is intended to be design-oriented by the Design-Science-Research Methodology (DSRM) [35]. Thus, the second section provides the foundation of psychological crystallization theories and backpropagation algorithms from which requirements have been derived that need to be reflected by the learning algorithm. The design artifact is then presented in the third section. Its usefulness will be demonstrated with the aid of four example scenarios in section four. It issues ANN refinement by training prolongation of a pre-trained ANN and clarifies how the crystallized backpropagation variant affects internal structure building. This is realized in a comparison with standard backpropagation variants. Section five discusses the suitability of the algorithm design to crystallize neural schemata and carry out autonomous, data-based learning as usual. The insights are concluded in the last section, too.

2   Related Work

2.1   Memory and Overload Theory

Inspired by psychology, human cognition and learning can be described by the memory and overload theory [1,2,11]. Here, human learning is carried out in two phases while each phase is limited by individual kinds of learning burdens and limited capacities. Figure 1 presents an overview and is detailed in the following.

First Phase. The initial learning phase focuses on the acquisition of new knowledge in the working memory and its *fluid systems*. Here, neural schemata are only stored short-term in the form of temporary activation e.g. The learning focus, therefore, lies on the efficient preparation of neural schemata for long-term storage. In working memory, four kinds of fluid systems are available: (1) the phonological loop, which cares about the sound of language, (2) the visuo-spatial sketch pad, which cares about image information, (3) the episodic buffer, which cares about the integration of phonological, visual and spatial information, and (4) the central executive, which manages attention to relevant information and inappropriate actions [1,2,11]. However, learning can be pedagogically supported by dealing with the following four burdens limiting the capacity in accordance with the cognitive load theory [7,51]. (a) The *subjective difficulty*, which can refer to lack of prior knowledge and personal factors, such as worries, fears, or priorities [26]. (b) The *objective difficulties*, which refer to learning tasks requiring too many chunks (adequate entities of information [51]). (c) The *burdens by pedagogical design* describe the preparation of inappropriate learning materials required for the learning tasks. This refers, for instance, to the design of training material, its texts, graphics, and the use of examples. (d) The *free capacities for active operation* can hinder the learning process since the individuals are overwhelmed by competing cognitive operations.

Second Phase. The final learning phase focuses on the stabilization of learned schemata from the short-term memory in the long-term memory and its *crystallizing systems*. Schemata are crystallized when anchoring them, e.g. by repetition or practice, within the current long-term knowledge system. Thus, each fluid system is associated with a corresponding long-term variant crystallizing knowledge in long-term memory. The learning focus, therefore, lies on the efficient integration and crystallization of knowledge, which can be supported by the provision of capacities for storing schemata.

Interim-Conclusion. Regarding the current focus on a learning phase, each phase requires an individual understanding of learning and follows different learning objectives. While knowledge can be considered to be *fluid* in the first learning phase, knowledge is *crystallized* in the second learning phase, so that it is preserved efficiently. This metaphor will guide the crystallized backpropagation design in Sect. 3.

2.2   Backpropagation and Predecessors

Up to today, numerous training procedures have been worked out to create valuable ANN. For instance, ANN have been trained by error-based [5, 36], competitive [3, 40, 43] as well as Hebbian [20, 32, 47] learning algorithms. In this work, error-based learning algorithms are used as tools to modify ANN, so that these satisfy performance requirements for individual tasks. These tasks therefore can be characterized as *supervised learning task* so that a task is specified by giving a desired output vector, which needs to be produced by the ANN's output neurons, for each state vector of the ANN's input neurons (these are used for activating the ANN).

Training Context. Although learning algorithms need to account for different ANN architectures, for simplicity, this work considers the example of feedforward layered networks. Here, one can find a first layer providing input neurons, a last layer providing output neurons and an arbitrary number of intermediate layers providing hidden neurons. Neural weights connect neurons of earlier layers with neurons of later layers. Although connections can skip intermediate layers, they are forbidden from later to earlier layers and among neurons of the same layer. Hence, the learning procedure needs to decide on the circumstances under which hidden layer neurons should be activated so that the entire ANN comes up with the desired input-output behavior. By training the ANN and applying the learning algorithm, neural structures learn internal representations that should be able to produce, for each input vector, an output vector that matches (or is sufficiently close to) the desired output vector.

Backpropagation Routines. The back-propagation algorithm [44, 45], often simply called *backprop*, has received its name because the error is propagated from the back to the front of an ANN. Hence, back-propagation algorithms require the following steps [17]:

1. Input patterns are fed into the ANN and propagated through all layers.
2. The network activation is compared with the intended activation so that an error is derived.
3. The error of the output layer is propagated from the very last layer to the very first layer so that, for each layer, weight adjustments can be derived.
4. Weight adjustments are carried out.

So, these steps will guide the crystallized backpropagation algorithm design in Sect. 3.

Variants Overview. Experiments about the design of gradient procedures were first realized in the 19901990ss ([5, 36]). By now, various improved versions are available, such as PROP [39], Quickprop [10], conjugated gradients [21, 48], and L-BFGS [6]. In LSTM-based ANNs, variants [8] consider a combination of the RTRL approach [41] and the BPTT approach [56] to deal with approximated error gradients and shorten the time between each time step [8, 9].

Second-Order Optimization Variants. Going beyond the previously addressed *first-order optimization techniques*, that use gradient information to construct the next training iteration, advanced variants have derived that provide an addition curvature information of an objective function: for instance, these adaptively estimate the step-length of optimization trajectory in training phase of neural network [52] and so achieve faster training success (e.g. measured by reduced required training iterations, faster convergence, less tuning of hyper-parameters, improved memory allocation, reduced power consumption). Among those variants, one can find for example Newton method [31], conjugate gradient [30], quasi-Newton [49], Gauss-Newton [24], Levenberg-Marqaurdt [55], Approximate greatest descent [12–14] and Hessian-free method [28].

However, since the design of the backpropagation algorithm presented in Sect. 3 should be useful for both first-order and second-order techniques, the following focuses on backpropagation as a well-known first-order optimization method.

Continual Learning. In recent years, numerous methods have been based on backpropagation for proposing continual learning, which means learning from a continuous stream of information and an unspecified fixed number of tasks to be learned [34]. While some methods retrain the whole network and consider a regularization (e.g. [4,25,27,38,59]), some selectively train the network (occasionally by expanding the network to represent new tasks), such as [33,46,57,58,60], and other methods model complementary learning systems (e.g. [23,29,50]).

In principle, these methods can be categorized by the following three: First, methods that retrain the whole network while regularizing to prevent catastrophic forgetting with previously learned tasks. Second, methods that selectively train the network and expand it if necessary to represent new tasks. Third, methods that model complementary learning systems for memory consolidation, e.g. by using memory replay to consolidate internal representations. However, lifelong learning and preserving learned patterns remains a long-standing challenge for machine learning and neural network models since the continual acquisition of incrementally available information from non-stationary data distributions generally leads to catastrophic forgetting or interference [53]. Here, a need for algorithms becomes clear that capture lifelong learning and are capable of avoiding catastrophic forgetting, which the crystallized backpropagation algorithm design in Sect. 3 aims for.

Modular Networks. Specialized training variants have evolved that focus on modular neural networks. These are made up of several ANNs, the so-called modules, that are linked together via an intermediate [42]. Each ANN solves a portion of a learning task, an integrator divides the problem into modules, and finally integrates module outputs to create the system's final output [37]. As these compartments work on different operational levels, one can interpret them to be in a hierarchy.

In principle, for each module, standard backpropagation can be applied, so that a hierarchical mixture of experts is developed manually. Some training variants speak about freezing a certain portion of the parameters at a module and replacing the corresponding multipliers with fixed scalars [22]. Others safely freeze the converged weights and static save their corresponding backward computation [54]. However, the dynamic as well as network-wide handling of errors over a combination of modular neural networks that still participate in backpropagation although they have been frozen, and dealing with learning in hierarchies of modules has not been issued before. Here, an opportunity for algorithms becomes clear that capture dealing with learning in hierarchies of individual neurons, group of neurons or module, which the crystallized backpropagation algorithm design in Sect. 3 aims for.

Research Gap. Although the huge spectrum of algorithms shows the great learning capabilities of ANN - even for temporal patterns because of learning through time - learning algorithms have not considered ANN to be systems within a hierarchical order, such as greater cognitive structures. This accounts for continual learning systems and non-continual learning systems as well as for modular networks or any first-order and second-order optimization method. As algorithmic approaches further have ANN not considered as artificial knowledge carriers, whose neural schemata might be preservable management objects [19], backpropagation algorithms do not enable an interactive controlling of learning procedures in the sense of knowledge management attempts [15]. Thus, users were not able to deal with the corresponding ANN learning burdens by a kind of pedagogic valuable crystallization of preservable ANN sub-structures and they were not supported by crystallized machine learning algorithms, yet. Although the kind of crystallization proposed by this paper is attractive for continual learning, too, because it crystallizes selected ANN structures for preserving them, it needs to be remarked that the kinds of hierarchies and crystallization proposed by the paper are capable to deal with lower cognitive levels and learning burdens. Therefore, the presented experiments focus on building a first hierarchical level of manually crystallized ANN structures for controlling a non-continuous learning system.

3   Designing for Crystallized Backpropagation Mechanism

As required by the four-step procedure of backpropagation procedures in Sect. 2.2, the following specifies relevant steps for the crystallized backpropagation mechanism.

Step 1 - Forward Pass. In the forward pass, the neurons in each layer obtain their states by the input they receive from neurons in earlier layers or bias neurons. The latter ones always have a value of 1.0 so that they are independent of input vectors. However, their weights can be treated just like other weights.

Typically, total input x_j to neuron j is transferred by a linear transfer function of the outputs y_i of the neurons that are connected to j with the weights $w_{j,i}$, so that we have

$$x_j = \sum_i y_i w_{j,i}. \tag{1}$$

The individual neuron output y_j then can be derived by activating its non-linear transfer function, such as sigmoid or tanh functions. Its real-valued output is based on its total input x_j e.g. by

$$y_j = \frac{1}{1 + e^{-x_j}}. \tag{2}$$

Step 2 - Error Determination. The total error E is based on the deviation of activation y produced by an output neuron and the desired output d at that output neuron. Hence, it is defined as

$$E = \frac{1}{2} \sum_c \sum_j (y_{j,c} - d_{j,c})^2. \tag{3}$$

Here, c refers to the index overall input-output dataset entries (cases), j refers to the index over output neurons and the error function is quadratic because it is easily differentiable. However, alternative error functions are possible, too. With the aid of gradient descent methods, E can be minimized by the computation of the partial derivatives of E with respect to each weight of the ANN. For a given dataset entry, the partial derivatives of the error with respect to each weight are computed in two passes - one forward pass described at the first step and one backward pass described next.

Step 3 - Backward Pass. In the backward pass, derivatives are propagated from the last layer back to the first layer. Please remark, the subscript c is suppressed in the following because its working is not depending on whether backpropagation is realized after every case (online learning) or after having seen all cases (batch learning).

However, for each output neuron y_j, computing $\partial E / \partial y_j$ by differentiating Eq. 3 gives

$$\partial E / \partial y_j = y_j - d_j. \tag{4}$$

By applying the chain rule, $\partial E / \partial x_j$ can be computed and gives

$$\partial E / \partial x_j = \partial E / \partial y_j \cdot dy_j / dx_j. \tag{5}$$

When substituting dy_j / dx_j by the differentiation of Eq. 2, we obtain

$$\partial E / \partial x_j = \partial E / \partial y_j \cdot y_j (1 - y_j). \tag{6}$$

Hence, we know how changes in the total input x to an output neuron will affect the error. As this input is based on a linear function of the earlier level neuron activation outputs and we have a linear function on the weights on the connections, the error effect computation because of changed activation outputs and connections is easy. Focusing on a weight $w_{j,i}$, the derivative is

$$\partial E/\partial w_{j,i} = \partial E/\partial x_j \cdot \partial x_j/\partial w_{j,i} = \partial E/\partial x_j \cdot y_i. \tag{7}$$

For the output of the ith neuron, the contribution to $\partial E/\partial y_i$ is resulting from the effect of i on j:

$$\partial E/\partial x_j \cdot \partial x_j/\partial y_i = \partial E/\partial x_j \cdot w_{j,i}. \tag{8}$$

Taking all connections into account that emanate from neuron i, we have

$$\partial E/\partial y_i = \sum_j \partial E/\partial x_j \cdot w_{j,i}. \tag{9}$$

By the Eq. 4–Eq. 9, $\partial E/\partial y$ can be computed for any neuron in the penultimate layer when given all $\partial E/\partial y$ in the last layers. This proceeding can be repeated successively for earlier layers until $\partial E/\partial w$ has been computed for the entire ANN.

Step 4 - Weight Adjustment. Now, the concrete proportion for a weight adjustment can be derived:

$$\triangle w_{j,i}(n) = m \triangle w_{j,i}(n-1) - \alpha \frac{\partial E}{\partial w_{j,i}(n)} \phi_{j,i}. \tag{10}$$

Here, w refers to the weight adjustment of learning iteration n. The constant m refers to the proportion that is considered from former learning iterations ($n-1$) in the sense of momentum. The constant α refers to the learning rate modifying the velocity in which the current gradient is used to modify the velocity of the point in weight space instead of its position (acceleration method).

The focus of crystallized backpropagation procedures refers to the following. In Eq. 10, the fluidity $\phi \in \mathbb{R} \mid 0 \leq \phi \leq 1$ refers to the measure of the flowability or rather a viscosity of neural weights (fluids) and indicates the extent to which connections are crystallized so that neural knowledge is preserved or remains fluid. As this is inspired by the memory and overload theory (cf. Sect. 2.1), by manipulating the weight-specific fluidity, learning burdens and capacities shall become controllable. So far, standard backpropagation algorithms consider the state of having neural weights of perfect fluidity only ($\phi_{j,i} = 1.0$). This work demonstrates crystallized backpropagation by having weights of the perfect state of fluidity ($\phi_{j,i} = 1.0$) and the perfect state of crystallization ($\phi_{j,i} = 0.0$), which are specified manually with the aid of the Neuronal Modeling and Description Language (short: NMDL) [17] in Sect. 4.

However, ϕ might not be designed as a factor. It can be designed as a full-gradient and differentiable version, so that it can be determined by algorithmic learning procedures, such as ANN-based approximations. These might be interpreted as higher cognitive learning processes that affect the ANN of a first activation loop, by

$$\phi_{j,i} = \frac{1}{1 + e^{-x}} \quad , \text{ where } x \text{ refers to second loop ANN output.} \quad (11)$$

This first loop is inspired by the first learning phase from a memory and overload theory perspective (compare with Sect. 2.1), in which fluid knowledge is focused by a first ANN. Building on this first activation loop, on the basis of Eq. 11, a dynamic crystallization can be implemented, which is realized by a second ANN for instance. So, a holistic learning approach can be upgraded from the passive *crystallized backpropagation* to the proactive *crystallizing backpropagation* variant. However, since this second-loop-ANN needs to be trained in addition to the first ANN, and one needs to question adequate dataset and training procedures, here, which adds unnecessary complexity to this paper, the following focuses on a passive approach and will prepare the so-called proactive *double-loop learning* approaches.

Finally, the adjustment of neural weights can be carried out by

$$w_{j,i}^{\text{new}} = w_{j,i}^{\text{old}} + \triangle w_{j,i}. \quad (12)$$

In order to break symmetry, it is recommended to start training with an ANN having small random weights.

4   Demonstration at Industry 4.0 Production Scenarios

The demonstration section applies the research artifact of a crystallized backpropagation and examines if it is useful for overcoming the initial research problem (in accordance with the DSRM [35]). This is realized on the base of a comparison of standard backpropagation procedures and crystallized backpropagation procedures in four experiments. Each experiment refines the same pre-trained ANN (training is prolonged, not continued), so that the effect of the new learning procedure can be examined.

ANN Specification. The pre-trained models were imported from the open-source Concept of Neuronal Modeling (CoNM) model zoo (AGPLv3 license) [16]. They represent a process part of the Industry 4.0 environment [17], in which either a production machine called *Production Machine1* demands transportation in three time steps, or a production worker called *P1* demands the transportation. The Cyber-Physical System called *CPS1* evaluates both demands and instructs its conveyor actuators in time. The corresponding architecture and ANN models can be seen at Fig. 2.

In the figure, as a NMDL NetworkView model, one can recognize individual feedforward weights as directed arcs among brown neurons. Here, the arc's thickness represents the weight's absolute value. Blue arcs represent negative weights and red arcs represent positive weights. Further, dashed rectangular system borders separate ANN sub-components whose inner structure shall be crystallized because their individual performance is appreciated. Hence, these ANN sub-components are connected by black arcs representing absolute values of 1.0 initially. However, the crystallization of internal (or colored) structures only accounts for the novel version of the backpropagation learning algorithm. Traditional backpropagation algorithms will deal with all kinds of weights (blue, red and black arcs) as usual.

Dataset Specification. Further, from the same model zoo, two kinds of datasets have been imported. First, the *XOR dataset* for training and testing. These datasets hold sequences, each holding one moment that corresponds to the two inputs and one output of the xor-truth-table. Second, the *DEFECT dataset* for training and testing. These datasets have been set up with 10 sequences, each holding one moment that corresponds to the *XOR dataset*. It is different from the XOR dataset mentioned in that the second input refers to a random number of either 0.0 or 1.0 not affecting the output at all. So, it can be interpreted as noise or defect input channel disturbing the ANN, which is the reason for calling it *DEFECT dataset* at this work.

Training Specification. The training task has been specified in two ways. First, the initial ANN will be trained by the *standard backpropagation trainer*. Second, the very same ANN will be faced by the *crystallized backpropagation trainer*. Thus, a total of four training and test runs have been carried out for demonstration purposes, which combines the two backpropagation variants and both dataset types as permutations. These are presented in the following sub-sections. However, the four training and testing runs were realized for 100 training iterations. It was assured by testing runs before deploying ANNs to the production environment, that all ANNs trained do satisfy the intended production routines (we call this *behavioral performance*, which is measured in simulation context) leading to successful production outcomes. Therefore, differences in the performance of ANN outputs, which we refer to as *numbered outcome performance*, are omitted from this paper. In any case, they refer only to minor differences and therefore lead to the same behavioral output. Further details about parameter and hyper-parameter design can be found at the public model zoo and corresponding NMDL models [16]. Since multiple runs of experiments have not led to different results, the random seed has not been discussed in detail.

Expectation. Since the second input of the *DEFECT dataset* is interpreted as noise disturbing the ANN, during the course of learning, each ANN operating on this dataset is intended to shrink the influence of the disturbing process step of that input channel. This needs to be independent of the choice of backpropagation algorithm variant. In contrast to this, when being trained on the XOR dataset, the ANNs are intended to preserve the influence of both input channels. This needs to be independent of the choice of backpropagation algorithm variant.

When facing standard backpropagation algorithms, that do not crystallize internal structures of ANN sub-components selected with the aid of NMDL system borders (cf. rectangles of Fig. 2), training will modify any kind of weights (even those that are valuable to be preserved) because they are not controlled. This will be issued in Sub-sect. 4.1. In contrast to this, crystallized backpropagation will preserve internal structures of ANN sub-components selected by the corresponding system borders of Fig. 2 because corresponding weights are crystallized by $\phi = 0.0$. Others remain fluid ($\phi = 1.0$). This will be issued in Sub-sect. 4.2.

Please remark: since the task performance of ANNs presented in the following sub-sections shows negligibly small differences between pre-trained ANNs and ANN outcomes because of the respective backpropagation variants (after all initial task performance of the pre-trained ANN already has been analyzed by [17]), the following focuses on the analysis of weight changes and interpretation at ANN refinement.

4.1   Standard Backpropagation

This sub-section focuses on the two training-dataset combinations that are based on training with standard backpropagation algorithm variants.

Figure 4 shows structural ANN changes that are carried out because of the *standard backpropagation* procedures. As the ANN of Fig. 4a has been refined on XOR dataset and the ANN of Fig. 4b has been refined on DEFECT training and test material, both figures can be analyzed in regard with internal structural changes.

First Learning Task. The weight modifications of the first learning task can be seen in Fig. 4a. Please note the stroke width of the three edges that cross the system borders of ANN sub-components. The interconnecting weights have not been modified much. They refer to the value of 1.0 having only thousands of deviations. Hence, the ANN activation will lead to at least the same total performance, or rather behavior, that already has been accepted before the training refinement. Compared with the ANN in Fig. 5a, one can recognize the changes in inner ANN sub-component weights. This is because standard backpropagation does not crystallize any neural weight and back-propagating errors have led to weight modifications throughout the entire ANN. Hence, the performances of the ANN sub-components have changed and the interpretability of sub-components is reduced.

Second Learning Task. The weight modifications of the second learning task can be seen in Fig. 4b. Please note here the stroke width of the same three edges that have been focused on before.

1. The first input is considered further, which can be seen at the thick weight between the neuron called *Out A Neuron* and the neuron called *Neuron Inp1*. Here, the latter intends to consider the input of 1.0 (that is around the level of 1.0 at the weight mentioned) and the input of 0.0 (that is around the level of 0.0 at the weight mentioned).

2. The influence of the second input is diminished by the ANN. Between the neuron called *Out B Neuron* and *Neuron Inp2*, one can only identify a slight line. Here, the latter neuron intends to consider the input of 1.0 (that is around the level of 0.0 because of the weight mentioned) and the input of 0.0 (that is around the level of 0.0 at the weight mentioned) as well. This is the desired behavior because the second input referred to unusable noise data coming from an inefficient preceding task.

3. The influence of the output is considered further, as a thick edge can be identified between the neuron called *Neuron Outp1* and the neuron called *In C Neuron*. Here, the latter neuron intends to consider the input of 1.0 (that is around the level of 1.0 at the weight mentioned) and its input of 0.0 (that is around the level of 0.0 at the weight mentioned).

Since the standard backpropagation variant does not distinguish crystallized and fluid weights, structural changes of any inner ANN weight can be identified at both Sub-figs. 4a and 4b. This is particularly interesting if training shall adopt an ANN to a certain context. For example, a pre-trained ANN which is able to recognize humans shall get to know a specific person.

4.2   Crystallized Backpropagation

This sub-section focuses on the two training-dataset combinations that are based on training with crystallized backpropagation algorithm variants. Training and testing errors can be found in Fig. 3. Corresponding data and ANN models have been labeled as Neuronal Process Optimization (NPO) experiments.

Figure 5 shows structural ANN changes that are carried out because of the *crystallized backpropagation* procedures. As the ANN of Fig. 5a has been refined on the XOR dataset training and test material and the ANN of Fig. 5b has refined on the DEFECT dataset, both figures can be analyzed in regard with internal structural changes.

Third Learning Task. The weight modifications of the third learning task can be seen in Fig. 5a. Please note the stroke width of the three edges that cross the system borders of ANN sub-components. The interconnecting neuronal weights have not been modified much. They refer to the value of 1.0 having only a thousandth of deviation. Hence, the ANN activation will lead to at least the same total performance level which already has been accepted before the training refinement. Compared with the ANN in Fig. 4a, one can not identify any changes in inner ANN sub-component weights. This is because crystallized backpropagation has preserved selected neural weights. Thus, crystallized back-propagating errors have suppressed corresponding weight modifications. Weight modifications only have been carried out at weights crossing system borders. Hence, the performances of the ANN sub-components have not changed and interpretability of sub-components is controlled.

Fourth Learning Task. The weight modifications of the fourth learning task can be seen in Fig. 5b. Please note here the stroke width of the same three edges that have been focused on before.

1. The first input is considered further, which can be seen at the thick weight between the neuron called *Out A Neuron* and the neuron called *Neuron Inp1*. Here, the latter intends to consider the input of 1.0 (that is around the level of 1.0 at the weight mentioned) and the input of 0.0 (that is around the level of 0.0 at the weight mentioned).
2. The influence of the second input is diminished by the ANN. Between the neuron called *Out B Neuron* and *Neuron Inp2*, one can only identify a slight line. Here, the latter neuron intends to consider the input of 1.0 (that is around the level of 0.0 because of the weight mentioned) and the input of 0.0 (that is around the level of 0.0 at the weight mentioned) as well. This is the desired behavior because the second input referred to unusable noise data coming from an inefficient preceding task.
3. The influence of the output is considered further, as a thick edge can be identified between the neuron called *Neuron Outp1* and the neuron called *In C Neuron*. Here, the latter intends to consider the input of 1.0 (that is around the level of 1.0 at the weight mentioned) and the input of 0.0 (that is around the level of 0.0 at the weight mentioned).

Since the crystallized backpropagation variant is capable to distinguish crystallized and fluid weights, structural changes of any inner ANN sub-component weights can be avoided successfully at both Sub-figs. 5a and 5b. This is particularly interesting if training shall avoid the adaption of an ANN to a certain context because pre-trained representations shall be preserved. For example, a pre-trained ANN which is able to control a production environment shall get to know further scenarios. Since the individual ANN sub-systems presented represent process instances, by this, inefficient tasks can be identified and vanished by learning procedures. The simulated Industry 4.0 production environment applying this can be seen as a video at [18].

5   Summary of All Results and Discussion

Summary. This paper has presented a design for crystallized backpropagation that enables the (I) preservation of neural schemata (or rather time-based activation pattern), (II) a data-based, autonomous weight modification as usual because it is a full-gradient learning algorithm as well as (III) controlled modification of ANN-internal structures during the training procedure. It so extends state-of-the-art of machine learning and provides a new variant of backpropagation. The demonstration has clarified the usefulness of the crystallized backpropagation by four Industry 4.0 production scenarios in refining a pre-trained ANN. It so contributes with further examples and machine learning algorithms for training ANN.

Critical Appraisal. The research question (*"How can neural knowledge, such as previously trained neuronal weights, be crystallized to build on former training performance?"*) can be answered with regard to the design of crystallized backpropagation. Neural schemata can be preserved by the new backpropagation algorithm variant if the effect of back-propagating errors is suppressed by perfect states of crystallization (crystallized back-propagating errors) or rather relativized for neural weight modification (crystallizing back-propagating errors) although errors are still routed through the entire ANN. So, earlier ANN layers can consider the effect of errors propagated from later layers and adapt synaptic connections fluidly (fluid back-propagating errors) while selected neural weights are crystallized efficiently. Hence, the one parts of the ANN that are crystallized perfectly remain the same and can show up former training performance while others can evolve as usual because of the fully gradient-based learning algorithm. With this crystallization mechanism at backpropagation, former training performance can be backed up at crystallized ANN sub-components while others can be controlled to be modifiable and build on that performance by providing new learning capacities at fluid parts. This for instance becomes essential if pre-trained ANN are combined. Further, this crystallization mechanism brings a *second-order conditioning* or *higher-order conditioning* to ANN in which a stimulus is first made meaningful or consequential for an organism through an initial step of learning (this might be trained by a second loop ANN module and is modeled by Eq. 11), and then that stimulus is used as a basis for learning about some new stimulus.

Social Impacts. Today's user interfaces for machine learning are usually designed in a "one size fits all" approach, disregarding the fact that ANN can work at different cognitive levels. As a result, users tend to use ANN as a black box because all ANN sub-structures activated by backpropagation learning algorithms are operating on the same, very bottom cognitive level. Users do not have the control of assigning sub-structures to different (cognitive) levels and controlling backpropagation for these levels. As the crystallized backpropagation variant enables this, it participates in whitening the ANN black box, giving control to users and enabling the interpretation and guided ANN sub-structure training. As the NMDL supports this graphically in a drag-and-drop manner, this supports a low-threshold entry for users, even though additional decisions on crystallization can challenge them.

Limitations and Future Work. The results and insights presented need to be limited in regard with the ANN architectures that have been demonstrated.

Ongoing research should therefore examine further ANN architectures and alternative task domains to demonstrate crystallized backpropagation.

Further, since only perfect states of crystallization and perfect states of fluidity have been demonstrated in this work, further experiments should examine the effect of finer degrees of ϕ. Aside from the use of ϕ as a constant, the functional interpretation ϕ is attractive (cf. Equation 11). For instance, an adaptable variant can be designed, so that a step-wise crystallization is realized. So, later training runs would tend to preserve neural structures. This might lead to the construction of higher cognitive ANN levels. Further, the ANN-based adaptation of ϕ and a crystallized backpropagation through time can unleash a new learning potential of ANN. Here, it is also questionable how the synchronization of ANNs at different cognitive levels can best be designed: Do these have to be trained by the same rate and cycle of activation?

Of course, further forms to crystallize knowledge should be researched because alternatives of neural weight crystallization might be valuable, too. An example can be found in the crystallization of short-term ANN activation.

Appendix

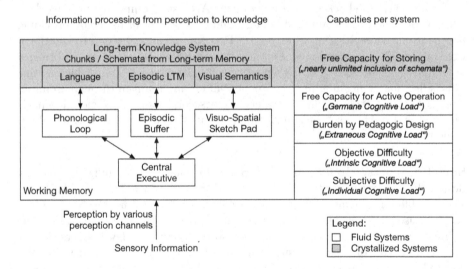

Fig. 1. Memory and overload theory (synthesized from [1, 2, 11]).

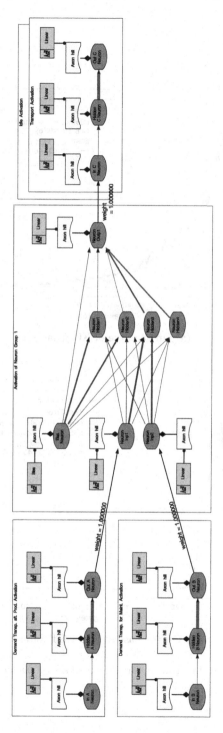

Fig. 2. The initial network architecture for the demonstration of *standard backpropagation* procedures (see Sect. 4.1) and *crystallized backpropagation* procedures (see Sect. 4.2).

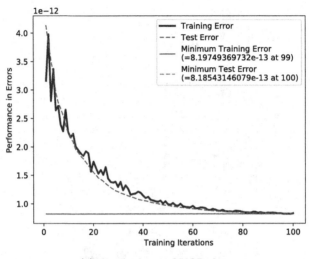

(a) On the base of XOR dataset.

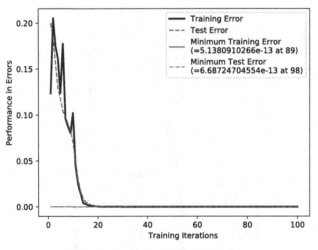

(b) On the base of DEFECT dataset.

Fig. 3. Training and testing course for the *crystallized backpropagation* procedure demonstration.

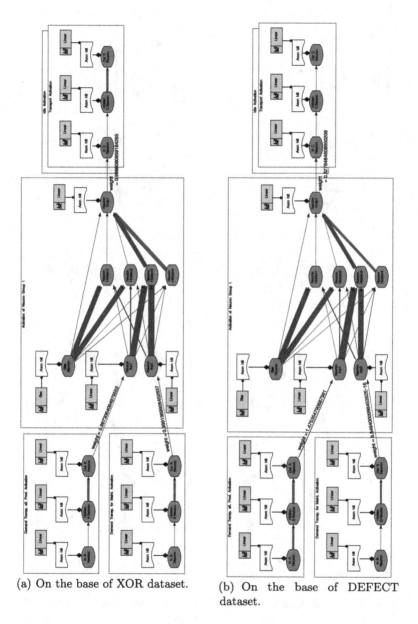

(a) On the base of XOR dataset.

(b) On the base of DEFECT dataset.

Fig. 4. The structural changes by *standard backpropagation* procedures.

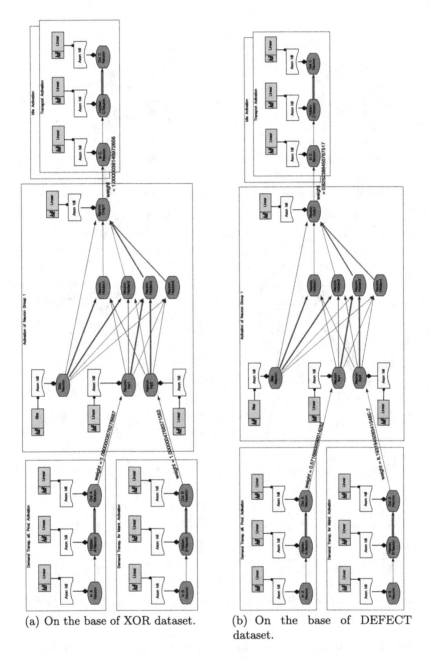

(a) On the base of XOR dataset.   (b) On the base of DEFECT dataset.

Fig. 5. The structural changes by *crystallized backpropagation* procedures.

References

1. Baddeley, A.: Oxford Psychology Series, no. 11. working memory. New York (1986)
2. Baddeley, A., Gathercole, S., Papagno, C.: The phonological loop as a language learning device. Psychol. Rev. **105**(1), 158 (1998)
3. Barlow, H.: Unsupervised learning. Neural Comput. **1**(3), 295–311 (1989). https://doi.org/10.1162/neco.1989.1.3.295
4. Benna, M.K., Fusi, S.: Computational principles of synaptic memory consolidation. Nat. Neurosci. **19**(12), 1697–1708 (2016)
5. Bishop, C.: Neural Networks for Pattern Recognition, p. 1. Oxford University Press, Inc., New York (1995)
6. Byrd, R.H., Lu, P., Nocedal, J., Zhu, C.Y.: A limited memory algorithm for bound constrained optimization. SIAM J. Sci. Comput. **16**(6), 1190–1208 (1995). www.citeseer.ist.psu.edu/byrd94limited.html
7. Clark, R.C., Nguyen, F., Sweller, J., Baddeley, M.: Efficiency in learning: evidence-based guidelines to manage cognitive load. Perf. Improvement **45**(9), 46–47 (2006). https://doi.org/10.1002/pfi.4930450920. www.onlinelibrary.wiley.com/doi/abs/10.1002/pfi.4930450920
8. Eck, D., Schmidhuber, J.: A First Look at Music Composition using LSTM Recurrent Neural Networks. Technical Report No. IDSIA-07-02, p. 1 (2002)
9. Eck, D., Schmidhuber, J.: Learning the long-term structure of the blues. In: Dorronsoro, J.R. (ed.) ICANN 2002. LNCS, vol. 2415, pp. 284–289. Springer, Heidelberg (2002). https://doi.org/10.1007/3-540-46084-5_47
10. Fahlman, S.: Faster learning variations on back-propagation: an empirical study. In: Touretszky, D., Hinton, G., Sejnowski, T. (eds.) Proceedings of the 1988 Connectionist Models Summer School, pp. 38–51. Morgan Kaufmann, San Mateo (1989)
11. Gathercole, S.E.: The development of memory. J. Child Psychol. Psychiat. **39**(1), 3–27 (1998). https://doi.org/10.1111/1469-7610.00301. www.onlinelibrary.wiley.com/doi/abs/10.1111/1469-7610.00301
12. Goh, B.S.: New algorithms for unconstrained optimization problems. In: Proceedings of 1995 American Control Conference - ACC 1995, vol. 3, pp. 2071–2074 (1995). https://doi.org/10.1109/ACC.1995.531260
13. Goh, B.: Approximate greatest descent methods for optimization with equality constraints. J. Optim. Theory Appl. **148**, 505–527 (2011)
14. Goh, B.: Numerical method in optimization as a multi-stage decision control system. In: Latest Advances in Systems Science and Computational Intelligence, pp. 25–30 (2012)
15. Grum, M.: Managing human and artificial knowledge bearers - the creation of a symbiotic knowledge management approach. In: Proceedings of the Tenth BMSD, pp. 182–201 (2020). https://doi.org/10.1007/978-3-030-24854-3_7
16. Grum, M.: NMDL repository (2020). www.github.com/MarcusGrum/CoNM/tree/main/meta-models/nmdl.   www.github.com/MarcusGrum/CoNM/tree/main/meta-models/nmdl, version 1.0.0
17. Grum, M.: Construction of a Concept of Neuronal Modeling. Springer, Heidelberg (2021). https://doi.org/10.1007/978-3-658-35999-7
18. Grum, M.: Towards a concept of neuronal modeling (CoNM) (2021). www.youtu.be/Rasm-lfeZ68. www.youtu.be/Rasm-lfeZ68
19. Grum, M., Gronau, N.: A visionary way to novel process optimizations. In: Shishkov, B. (ed.) BMSD 2017. LNBIP, vol. 309, pp. 1–24. Springer, Cham (2018). https://doi.org/10.1007/978-3-319-78428-1_1

20. Hebb, D.O.: The Organization of Behavior: A Neuropsychological Theory. Wiley, New York (1949)

21. Hestenes, M.R., Stiefel, E.: Methods of conjugate gradients for solving linear systems. J. Res. Natl. Bureau Stand. **49**(6), 409–436 (1952)

22. Isikdogan, L.F., Nayak, B.V., Wu, C., Moreira, J.P., Sushma, R., Michael, G.: Semifreddonets: partially frozen neural networks for efficient computer vision systems. CoRR abs/2006.06888 (2020). www.arxiv.org/abs/2006.06888

23. Kumaran, D., Hassabis, D., McClelland, J.L.: What learning systems do intelligent agents need? complementary learning systems theory updated. Trends Cogn. Sci. **20**(7), 512–534 (2016)

24. LeCun, Y., Bottou, L., Orr, G.B., Müller, K.-R.: Efficient BackProp. In: Orr, G.B., Müller, K.-R. (eds.) Neural Networks: Tricks of the Trade. LNCS, vol. 1524, pp. 9–50. Springer, Heidelberg (1998). https://doi.org/10.1007/3-540-49430-8_2

25. Li, Z., Hoiem, D.: Learning without forgetting. In: Leibe, B., Matas, J., Sebe, N., Welling, M. (eds.) ECCV 2016. LNCS, vol. 9908, pp. 614–629. Springer, Cham (2016). https://doi.org/10.1007/978-3-319-46493-0_37

26. Lufi, D., Okasha, S., Cohen, A.: Test anxiety and its effect on the personality of students with learning disabilities. Learn. Disabil. Q. **27**(3), 176–184 (2004). https://doi.org/10.2307/1593667

27. Maltoni, D., Lomonaco, V.: Continuous learning in single-incremental-task scenarios. arXiv:1806.08568 (2018)

28. Martens, J.: Deep learning via hessian-free optimization. In: Proceedings of the 27th International Conference on International Conference on Machine Learning, ICML 2010, Omnipress, Madison, WI, USA, pp. 735–742 (2010)

29. McClelland, J.L., McNaughton, B.L., O'Reilly, R.C.: Why there are complementary learning systems in the hippocampus and neocortex: insights from the successes and failures of connectionist models of learning and memory. Psychol. Rev. **102**, 419–457 (1995)

30. Møller, M.F.: A scaled conjugate gradient algorithm for fast supervised learning. Neural Netw. **6**(4), 525–533 (1993). https://doi.org/10.1016/S0893-6080(05)80056-5. www.sciencedirect.com/science/article/pii/S0893608005800565

31. Nocedal, J., Wright, S.J.: Numerical Optimization, 2e edn. Springer, New York (2006). https://doi.org/10.1007/0-387-22742-3_18

32. Oja, E.: Simplified neuron model as a principal component analyzer. J. Math. Biol. **15**(3), 267–273 (1982). https://doi.org/10.1007/BF00275687

33. Parisi, G.I., Tani, J., Weber, C., Wermter, S.: Lifelong learning of humans actions with deep neural network self-organization. Neural Netw. **96**, 137–149 (2017)

34. Parisi, G.I., Kemker, R., Part, J.L., Kanan, C., Wermter, S.: Continual lifelong learning with neural networks: a review. CoRR abs/1802.07569 (2018). arxiv.org/abs/1802.07569

35. Peffers, K., et al.: The design science research process: a model for producing and presenting information systems research. In: 1st International Conference on Design Science in Information System and Technology (DESRIST), vol. 24, no. 3, pp. 83–106 (2006)

36. Plaut, D.C., Nowlan, S.J., Hinton, G.E.: Experiments on learning backpropagation. Technical Report CMU-CS-86-126, Carnegie-Mellon University, Pittsburgh, PA, p. 1 (1986)

37. Qiao, J., Meng, X., Li, W., Wilamowski, B.: A novel modular rbf neural network based on a brain-like partition method. Neural Comput. Appl. **32** (2020). https://doi.org/10.1007/s00521-018-3763-z

38. Razavian, A.S., Azizpour, H., Sullivan, J., Carlsson, S.: Cnn features off-the-shelf: an astounding baseline for recognition. In: CVPR 2014, Columbus, OH, vol. 39, no. 1, pp. 806–813 (2014)
39. Riedmiller, M., Braun, H.: A direct adaptive method for faster backpropagation learning: the RPROP algorithm. In: Proceedings of the IEEE International Conference on Neural Networks, San Francisco, CA, pp. 586–591 (1993). www.citeseer.ist.psu.edu/riedmiller93irect.html
40. Ritter, H., Martinetz, T., Schulten, K.: Neuronale Netze: eine Einführung in die Neuroinformatik selbstorganisierender Netzwerke. Reihe künstliche Intelligenz, Addison-Wesley (1991). www.books.google.de/books?id=MfsARQAACAAJ
41. Robinson, A.J., Fallside, F.: The utility driven dynamic error propagation network. Technical Report CUED/F-INFENG/TR.1, Cambridge University Engineering Department, p. 1 (1987)
42. Rojas, R.: Neural Networks - A Systematic Introduction. Springer, Berlin (1996). www.inf.fu-berlin.de/inst/ag-ki/rojas_home/pmwiki/pmwiki.php?n=Books.NeuralNetworksBook
43. Rolls, E., Deco, G.: Computational Neuroscience of Vision. OUP Oxford (2001). www.books.google.de/books?id=SbFpuQAACAAJ
44. Rumelhart, D.E., McClelland, J.L.: Parallel Distributed Processing: Explorations in the Microstructure of Cognition, vol. 1: Foundations. MIT Press (1986)
45. Rumelhart, D.E., Hinton, G.E., Williams, R.J.: Learning representations by back-propagating errors. Nature **323**(6088), 533–536 (1986). https://doi.org/10.1038/323533a0
46. Rusu, A.A., et al.: Progressive neural networks. arXiv:1606.04671 (2016)
47. Sanger, T.D.: Optimal unsupervised learning in a single-layer linear feedforward neural network. Neural Netw. **2**(6), 459–473 (1989). https://doi.org/10.1016/0893-6080(89)90044-0. www.sciencedirect.com/science/article/pii/0893608089900440
48. Shewchuk, J.R.: An introduction to the conjugate gradient method without the agonizing pain. Technical Report, Carnegie Mellon university, Pittsburgh, PA, USA, p. 1 (1994)
49. Sohl-Dickstein, J., Poole, B., Ganguli, S.: An adaptive low dimensional quasi-newton sum of functions optimizer. CoRR abs/1311.2115 (2013). arxiv.org/abs/1311.2115
50. Soltoggio, A.: Short-term plasticity as cause-effect hypothesis testing is distal reward learning. Biol. Cybern. **109**, 75–94 (2015)
51. Sweller, J., van Merrienboer, J.J.G., Paas, F.G.W.C.: Cognitive architecture and instructional design. Educ. Psychol. Rev. **10**(3), 251–296 (1998). https://doi.org/10.1023/A:1022193728205
52. Tan, H.H., Lim, K.H.: Review of second-order optimization techniques in artificial neural networks backpropagation. IOP Conf. Ser. Mater. Sci. Eng. **495**(1), 012003 (2019). https://doi.org/10.1088/1757-899X/495/1/012003
53. van de Ven, G.M., Tolias, A.S.: Three scenarios for continual learning. CoRR abs/1904.07734 (2019). arxiv.org/abs/1904.07734
54. Wang, Y., Sun, D., Chen, K., Lai, F., Chowdhury, M.: Efficient DNN training with knowledge-guided layer freezing. CoRR abs/2201.06227 (2022). arxiv.org/abs/2201.06227
55. Wilamowski, B.M., Yu, H.: Improved computation for Levenberg-Marquardt training. IEEE Trans. Neural Netw. **21**(6), 930–937 (2010). https://doi.org/10.1109/TNN.2010.2045657

56. Williams, R.J., Zipser, D.: Gradient-based learning algorithms for recurrent networks and their computational complexity. In: Chauvin, Y., Rumelhart, D.E. (eds.) Back-Propagation: Theory, Architectures and Applications, pp. 433–486. Lawrence Erlbaum Publishers, Hillsdale (1995). www.citeseer.nj.nec.com/williams95gradientbased.html
57. Xiao, T., Zhang, J., Yang, K., Peng, Y., Zhang, Z.: Error-driven incremental learning in deep convolutional neural network for large-scale image classification. In: Proceedings of the ACM International Conference on Multimedia, Orlando, FL, pp. 177–186 (2014)
58. Yoon, J., Yang, E., Lee, J. Hwang, S.J.: Lifelong learning with dynamically expandable networks. In: ICLR 2018, Vancouver, Canada (2018)
59. Zenke, F., Poole, B., Ganguli, S.: Continual learning through synaptic intelligence. In: ICML 2017, Sydney, Australia (2017)
60. Zhou, G., Sohn, K., Lee, H.: Online incremental feature learning with denoising autoen- coders. In: International Conference on Artificial Intelligence and Statistics, pp. 1453–1461 (2012)

Fuzzy Hyperplane Based K-SVCR Multi-class Classification with Its Applications to Stock Prediction Problem

Pei-Yi Hao[✉]

National Kaohsiung University of Science and Technology, Kaohsiung, Taiwan
haupy@nkust.edu.tw

Abstract. This study incorporates fuzzy set theory into K-SVCR (support vector classification regression for K-class classification) and proposes a novel formulation that is called a fuzzy hyperplane-based support vector classification regression for K-class classification (FH-K-SVCR). The main characteristics of the proposed FH-K-SVCR are that it assigns fuzzy membership degrees to every data vector according to the importance and the parameters for the hyperplane, such as the elements of normal vector and the bias term, are fuzzified variables. The proposed fuzzy hyperplane efficiently captures the ambiguous nature of real-world classification tasks by representing vagueness in the observed data set using fuzzy variables. The fuzzy hyperplane for the proposed FH-K-SVCR model significantly decreases the effect of noise. The experimental results for the real-world stock prediction application show that the proposed FH-K-SVCR model retains the advantages of a K-SVCR which achieves high classification performance in multi-classes classification task, and increases fault tolerance and robustness by using fuzzy set theory.

Keywords: Support Vector Machine · Fuzzy Set Theory · Stock Prediction · Multi-class classification · K-SVCR

1 Introduction

Support vector machines (SVMs) are classic machine learning algorithm that are proposed by Vapnik [1] for binary classification task. In contrast to other machine learning algorithm (such as, artificial neural network) whose goal is to minimize the empirical risk, SVMs implement the principle of structural risk minimization (SRM) and minimizes the upper bound on the real risk. SVM has been successfully employed in wide spectrum of research areas like image classification, face recognition, and text categorization [2]. SVMs are powerful for binary classification problems. For multi-class classification problem in the SVM framework, the following two strategies are typically used. The "one-vs-one" strategy [3] constructs $K(K-1)/2$ binary SVMs classifiers. Each classifier separates two given classes, and the classification model is constructed based on the training samples from the two given classes. The "one-vs-one" strategy may obtain unfavorable classification performance because the information of the remaining

© The Author(s), under exclusive license to Springer Nature Switzerland AG 2023
L. Rutkowski et al. (Eds.): ICAISC 2023, LNAI 14125, pp. 101–111, 2023.
https://doi.org/10.1007/978-3-031-42505-9_9

samples is omitted in the training process of each classifier. The "one-vs-rest" strategy [4] constructs K binary classifiers. Each binary classifier separates one class from the rest classes, and the classification model is constructed based on all of the training samples. The "one-vs-rest" strategy may have class imbalance problem because the number of training samples in one class is much smaller than the number of training samples in the rest classes. Angulo et al. [5] proposed a novel K-SVCR approach that has a ternary output structure $\{-1, 0, +1\}$ for K-class classification problems based on the "one-vs-one-vs-rest" strategy. The K-SVCR constructs $K(K - 1)/2$ classifiers where each classifier is constructed based on all of the training data, which overcomes the class imbalance problems and risk of information loss.

Xu et al. [6] proposed a novel Twin-KSVC approach that combines the advantages of less computational time of the twin SVM and the structural advantage of K-SVCR. Nasiri et al. [7] proposed a least squares version of Twin-KSVC and called it LSTKSVC. Tanveer et al. [8] proposed a least squares version of K-nearest neighbor based weighted Twin-KSVC. Moreover, in many practical applications, the collected training set often contains some outliers. However, original K-SVCR is very sensitive to outliers. Bamakan et al. proposed the Ramp-KSVCR [9] that partially weaken the impact of outliers on the classifiers by utilizing the ε-insensitive ramp loss function. Inspired by K-SVCR and LS-SVM, Ma et al., [10] proposed a robust least squares version of K-SVCR (K-RLSSVCR) which replaces the hinge loss in K-SVCR with a squares ε-insensitive ramp loss.

However, for many practical applications, data points are usually of low quality or corrupted by noise. A traditional K-SVCR considers all training data points to be equally important so it is especially sensitive to abnormal noises or outliers that are far away from their corresponding class in the training data set. Lin and Wang [11] proposed a fuzzy support vector machine (FSVM) for which each training data point is associated with a fuzzy membership. Different memberships indicate different contributions to learning for the classification model. The fuzzy membership function decreases the effect of noise and outliers. Hao [12] proposed a fuzzy hyperplane based SVM (FH-SVM) where the normal vector and bias term within the optimal separating hyperplane are fuzzy sets. Chen et al. [13] proposed an entropy-based fuzzy least squares twin support vector machine for which the fuzzy membership degree for each training sample is calculated using the entropy values for all training data points. Hao et al. [14] proposed a twin version of fuzzy hyperplane based SVM to the application of stock prediction.

Following the line of research in [5] and [12], this study proposes a fuzzy hyperplane version of a K-SVCR that is called a fuzzy hyperplane-based support vector classification regression for K-class classification (FH-K-SVCR). The proposed FH-K-SVCR replaces the crisp hyperplane in K-SVCR with a fuzzy hyperplane in the defining of the one-vs-one-vs-rest decision function in multi-class classification problem. The proposed FH-K-SVCR takes both the advantages of K-SVCR in increasing the classification performance for multi-class classification task and the advantages of FH-SVM in enhancing the fault tolerance and robustness. The fuzzy hyperplane for the proposed FH-K-SVCR addresses uncertainty in the training data set and decreases the effect of noise. Therefore, the proposed FH-K-SVCR is more tolerant of faults and more robust than a traditional K-SVCR classifier if training data points are polluted by noise. The experimental results using real-world stock prediction application verify that the proposed FH-K-SVCR has a comparable classification performance to the stat of the art stock prediction models.

2   Review of Previous Studies

2.1   Support Vector Classification Regression for K-class Classification (K-SVCR)

Given the training set $T = \{(\mathbf{x}_1, y_1), \ldots, (\mathbf{x}_l, y_l)\}$, where $\mathbf{x}_k \in \mathbb{R}^n$ is the training instance, $y_k \in \{1, 2, \ldots, K\}$ is the label of $\mathbf{x}_k$, l and K are the number of samples and classes respectively. K-SVCR, which is a new method of multi-class classification with ternary outputs $\{-1, 0, +1\}$ proposed in [5], evaluates all the training data into a "1-versus-1-versus-rest" structure. For class i and j, the decision function of K-SVCR is

$$f_{ij}(\mathbf{x}_p) = \begin{cases} +1 \ p = 1, \ldots, l_1 \\ -1 \ p = l_1 + 1, \ldots, l_1 + l_2 \\ 0 \ p = l_{12} + 1, \ldots, l \end{cases} \tag{1}$$

where l_1 represents the number of samples in positive class (ith class), l_2 represents the number of samples in negative class (jth class), $l_{12} = l_1 + l_2$ and l_3 represents the number of samples in rest classes. The decision function $f_{ij}(\mathbf{x}_p)$ of K-SVCR can been obtained by solving the following constraint optimization problem:

$$\min_{\mathbf{w},b,\xi,\varphi,\varphi*} \|\mathbf{w}\|^2 + C \sum_{i=1}^{l_{12}} \xi_i + D \sum_{i=l_{12}+1}^{l} (\varphi_i + \varphi_i^*)$$

subject to

$$y_i(\mathbf{w}\cdot\phi(\mathbf{x}_i) + b) \geq 1 - \xi_i, \quad i = 1, \ldots, l_{12}$$
$$\delta - \varphi_i \geq (\mathbf{w}\cdot\phi(\mathbf{x}_i) + b) \geq -\delta + \varphi_i^*, \quad i = l_{12} + 1, \ldots, l \tag{2}$$

where $0 < \delta < 1$ is chosen a priori, $\xi_i, \varphi_i, \varphi_i^* \geq 0$ are stack variables. Using Wolfe's dual formulation of the Lagrangian, we obtain the following dual problem

$$\min_{\gamma} \frac{1}{2}\gamma^T \mathbf{H}\gamma + \mathbf{c}^T \gamma$$

subject to

$$\sum_{i=1}^{l_{12}} \gamma_i = \sum_{i=l_{12}+1}^{l} \gamma_i \sum_{i=l+1}^{l+l_3} \gamma_i$$
$$0 \leq y_i \cdot \gamma_i \leq C, \quad i = 1, \ldots, l_{12},$$
$$0 \leq \gamma_i \leq D, \quad i = l_{12} + 1, \ldots, l + l_{12} \tag{3}$$

2.2 Fuzzy Hyperplane based Support Vector Machine (FH-SVM)

A fuzzy hyperplane-based support vector machine (FH-SVM) determines a fuzzy hyperplane that discriminates positive and negative classes. All parameters for the separating hyperplane, including the bias term b and the components of the normal vector $\mathbf{w}$, are fuzzy variables [12]. To determine the optimal fuzzy hyperplane that divides positive and negative classes with the maximum margin, a FH-SVM uses the following preliminaries.

Preliminary 1 [12]: For arbitrary symmetric triangular fuzzy numbers $A = (m_A, c_A)$ and $B = (m_B, c_B)$, where m represents the center and c represents the width, the partial ordering of fuzzy numbers A and B is defined as follows:

$$A \geq_f B \text{ iff } m_A + c_A \geq m_B + c_B \text{ and } m_A - c_A \geq m_B - c_B. \tag{4}$$

where "$\underset{f}{\geq}$" represents the *fuzzy* larger than relation.

Preliminary 2 [12]: For the fuzzy hyperplane.

$$Y = W_1 x_1 + \cdots + W_n x_n + B = \mathbf{W}^t \mathbf{x} + B, \tag{5}$$

in n-dimensional real space $\mathfrak{R}^n$, $\mathbf{W} = (\mathbf{w}, \mathbf{c})$ represents the fuzzy normal vector and $\mathbf{B} = (b, d)$ represents the fuzzy bias term. The membership function for the fuzzy hyperplane $Y = \mathbf{W}^t \mathbf{x} + B$ is defined as:

$$mem_Y(y) = \begin{cases} 1 - \dfrac{|y - (\mathbf{w}^t \mathbf{x} + b)|}{\mathbf{c}^t |\mathbf{x}| + d} & \mathbf{x} \neq 0 \\ 1 & \mathbf{x} = 0, y = 0 \\ 0 & \mathbf{x} = 0, y \neq 0 \end{cases} \tag{6}$$

where $\mu_Y(y) = 0$ if $\mathbf{c}^t |\mathbf{x}| + d \leq |y - (\mathbf{w}^t \mathbf{x} + b)|$. The training data set is "fuzzy linearly separable" if

$$y_i(\mathbf{W}^t \mathbf{x}_i + B) \underset{f}{\geq} \mathbf{I}_F \tag{7}$$

is satisfied for all data points $\mathbf{x}_i$ in the training data set, where $\mathbf{I}_F$ represents the "fuzzy one", which is also a symmetric triangular fuzzy number whose center is one and whose width is I_w. Using these preliminaries, the FH-SVM determines the optimal fuzzy separating hyperplane by solving the following quadratic programming problem (QPP):

$$\underset{\mathbf{w}, \mathbf{c}, b, d, \xi_{1i}, \xi_{2i}}{\text{minimize}} \frac{1}{2} \mathbf{w}^t \mathbf{w} + C \left(v \left(\frac{1}{2} \mathbf{c}^t \mathbf{c} + d \right) + \frac{1}{N} \sum_{i=1}^{N} \mu_i(\xi_{1i} + \xi_{2i}) \right)$$

subject to

$$y_i(\mathbf{w}^t \mathbf{x}_i + b) + (\mathbf{c}^t |\mathbf{x}_i| + d) \geq 1 + I_w - \xi_{1i}$$
$$y_i(\mathbf{w}^t \mathbf{x}_i + b) - (\mathbf{c}^t |\mathbf{x}_i| + d) \geq 1 - I_w - \xi_{2i}, d \geq 0, \xi_{1i}, \xi_{2i} \geq 0, i = 1, \ldots, N, \tag{8}$$

where $C > 0$ is a regularization parameter and $\mu_i \in (0, 1]$ is the fuzzy membership that indicates the attitude of the training sample $\mathbf{x}_i$ toward its own class.

3 Fuzzy Hyperplane-based Support Vector Classification Regression for K-Class Classification (FH-K-SVCR)

Following the line of research in K-SVCR [5] and FH-SVM [12], this study proposes a fuzzy hyperplane version of a K-SVCR that is called a fuzzy hyperplane-based support vector classification regression for K-class classification (FH-K-SVCR). The proposed FH-K-SVCR replaces the crisp hyperplane in K-SVCR with a fuzzy hyperplane in the defining of the one-vs-one-vs-rest decision function in multi-class classification problem. The proposed FH-K-SVCR takes both the advantages of K-SVCR in increasing the classification performance for multi-class classification task and the advantages of FH-SVM in enhancing the fault tolerance and robustness. The proposed FH-K-SVCR determines the fuzzy normal vector $\mathbf{W} = (\mathbf{w}, \mathbf{c})$ and the fuzzy bias term $B = (b, d)$ such that separates class i and j by in "one-vs-one-vs-rest" manner by solving the following constrained optimization problem:

$$\underset{\mathbf{w},\mathbf{c},b,d,\xi_{1i}\xi_{2i}}{\text{minimize}} \frac{1}{2}\|\mathbf{w}\|^2 + v\left(\frac{1}{2}\|\mathbf{c}\|^2 + d\right) + C\sum_{i=1}^{l_{12}} m_i\xi_i + D\left(\sum_{i=l_{12}+1}^{l} m_i\left(\varphi_i + \varphi_i^*\right)\right)$$

subject to

$$y_i(\mathbf{W}\cdot\phi(\mathbf{x}_i) + \mathbf{B}) \underset{f}{\geq} \mathbf{I_F} - \xi_i, \quad \xi_i \geq 0, \quad i = 1,\ldots,l_{12}$$

$$\delta_\mathbf{F} + \varphi_i \underset{f}{\geq} (\mathbf{W}\cdot\phi(\mathbf{x}_i) + \mathbf{B}) \underset{f}{\geq} -\delta_\mathbf{F} - \varphi_i^*, \quad \varphi_{i'}\varphi_i^* \geq 0, \quad i = l_{12}+1,\ldots,l \quad (9)$$

where "$\underset{f}{\geq}$" represents the *fuzzy* larger than relation, $\mathbf{I}_F$ represents the "fuzzy one", which is also a symmetric triangular fuzzy number whose center is one and whose width is I_d, and δ_F represents a symmetric triangular fuzzy number whose center is $0 < \delta < 1$ (chosen a priori) and whose width is I_δ. According to Preliminaries 1 and 2, the above constrained optimization problem can be re-written as follows:

$$\underset{\mathbf{w},\mathbf{c},d,\xi_{1i},\xi_{2i}}{\text{minimize}} \frac{1}{2}\|\mathbf{w}\|^2 + v\left(\frac{1}{2}\|\mathbf{c}\|^2 + d\right)$$

$$+ C\sum_{i=1}^{l_{12}} m_i(\xi_{1i} + \xi_{2i}) + D\left(\sum_{i=1}^{N} m_i\left(\varphi_{1i} + \varphi_{2i} + \varphi_{1i}^* + \varphi_{2i}^*\right)\right)$$

subject to

$$y_i(\mathbf{w}\cdot\phi(\mathbf{x}_i) + b) + (\mathbf{c}\cdot\phi(\mathbf{x}_i) + d) \geq 1 + I_d - \xi_{1i}, \quad i = 1,\ldots,l_{12}$$

$$y_i(\mathbf{w}\cdot\phi(\mathbf{x}_i) + b) - (\mathbf{c}\cdot\phi(\mathbf{x}_i) + d) \geq 1 - I_d - \xi_{2i}, \quad i = 1,\ldots,l_{12}$$

$$\left(\mathbf{w}\cdot\phi(\mathbf{x}_i) + b\right) + \left(\mathbf{c}\cdot\phi(\mathbf{x}_i) + d\right) \geq -\delta + I_\delta - \varphi_{1i}^*, \quad i = l_{12}+1,\ldots,l$$

$$\left(\mathbf{w}\cdot\phi(\mathbf{x}_i) + b\right) - \left(\mathbf{c}\cdot\phi(\mathbf{x}_i) + d\right) \geq -\delta - I_\delta - \varphi_{1i}^*, \quad i = l_{12}+1,\ldots,l$$

$$(\mathbf{w}\cdot\phi(\mathbf{x}_i) + b) + \left(\mathbf{c}\cdot\phi(\mathbf{x}_i) + d\right) \leq \delta + I_\delta + \varphi_{1i}, \quad i = l_{12}+1,\ldots,l$$

$$\left(\mathbf{w}'\phi(\mathbf{x}_i) + b\right) + \left(\mathbf{c}'\phi(\mathbf{x}_i) + d\right) \leq \delta + I_\delta + \varphi_{1i}, \quad i = l_{12}+1,\ldots,l$$

$$\xi_{1i}, \xi_{2i}, \varphi_{1i}, \varphi_{2i}, \varphi_{1i}^*, \varphi_{2i}^* \geq 0 \quad (10)$$

Minimizing $\|\mathbf{w}\|^2$ is equivalent to maximizing the margin of the fuzzy separating hyperplane. $\frac{1}{2}\|\mathbf{c}\|^2 + d$ measures the vagueness of the model. More vagueness means that the decision boundary is more ambiguous and less vagueness produces a strict boundary. $v > 0$ is the vagueness parameter and $C > 0$ is the regularization parameter and is chosen by the user. The fuzzy membership m_i indicates the attitude of the point x_i toward its own class and $\xi_{1i}, \xi_{2i}, \varphi_{1i}, \varphi_{2i}, \varphi_{1i}^*, \varphi_{2i}^* \geq 0$ are the slack variable that measures the amount by which the fuzzy separable constraint is violated. A smaller value for m_i indicates a decrease in the effect of the slack variable such that the training error for data point x_i is ignored. Using Lagrangian multipliers technique, the optimization problem in Eq. (10) is solved by solving the following dual problem:

$$
\begin{aligned}
\underset{\alpha_{1i}, \alpha_{2i}, \beta_{1i}^*, \beta_{2i}^*, \beta_{1i}, \beta_{2i}}{\text{maximize}} \quad & \frac{-1}{2} \sum_{i=1}^{l_{12}} \sum_{j=1}^{l_{12}} y_i y_j (\alpha_{1i} + \alpha_{2i})(\alpha_{1j} + \alpha_{2j}) k(x_i, x_j) \\
& - \frac{1}{2} \sum_{i=l_{12}+1}^{l} \sum_{j=l_{12}+1}^{l} (\beta_{1i}^* + \beta_{2i}^* - \beta_{1i} - \beta_{2i})(\beta_{1j}^* + \beta_{2j}^* - \beta_{1j} - \beta_{2j}) k(x_i, x_j) \\
& - \sum_{i=1}^{l_{12}} \sum_{j=l_{12}+1}^{l} y_i (\alpha_{1i} + \alpha_{2i})(\beta_{1j}^* + \beta_{2j}^* - \beta_{1j} - \beta_{2j}) k(x_i, x_j) \\
& - \frac{v}{2} \sum_{i=1}^{l_{12}} \sum_{j=1}^{l_{12}} (\alpha_{1i} - \alpha_{2i})(\alpha_{1j} - \alpha_{2j}) k(x_i, x_j) \\
& - \frac{v}{2} \sum_{i=l_{12}+1}^{l} \sum_{j=l_{12}+1}^{l} (\beta_{1i}^* - \beta_{2i}^* - \beta_{1i} + \beta_{2i})(\beta_{1j}^* - \beta_{2j}^* - \beta_{1j} + \beta_{2j}) k(x_i, x_j) \\
& - v \sum_{i=1}^{l_{12}} \sum_{j=l_{12}+1}^{l} (\alpha_{1i} - \alpha_{2i})(\beta_{1j}^* - \beta_{2j}^* - \beta_{1j} + \beta_{2j}) k(x_i, x_j) \\
& - \sum_{i=1}^{l_{12}} \alpha_{1i}(-1 - I_d) - \sum_{i=1}^{l_{12}} \alpha_{2i}(-1 + I_d) - \sum_{i=l_{12}+1}^{l} \beta_{1i}^*(\delta - I_\delta) - \sum_{i=l_{12}+1}^{l} \beta_{2i}^*(\delta + I_\delta) \\
& + \sum_{i=l_{12}+1}^{l} \beta_{1i}(-\delta - I_\delta) + \sum_{i=l_{12}+1}^{l} \beta_{2i}(-\delta + I_\delta)
\end{aligned} \tag{11}
$$

Subject to

$$
\sum_{i=1}^{l_{12}} y_i(\alpha_{1i} + \alpha_{2i}) + \sum_{i=l_{12}+1}^{l} (\beta_{1i}^* + \beta_{2i}^* - \beta_{1i} - \beta_{2i}) = 0
$$

$$
\sum_{i=1}^{l_{12}} (\alpha_{1i} - \alpha_{2i}) + \sum_{i=l_{12}+1}^{l} (\beta_{1i}^* - \beta_{2i}^* - \beta_{1i} + \beta_{2i}) = v
$$

$$
0 \leq \alpha_{1i}, \alpha_{1i} \leq Cm_i, i = 1, \ldots, l_{12}
$$

$$
0 \leq \beta_{1i}^*, \beta_{2i}^*, \beta_{1i}, \beta_{2i} \leq Dm_i, , i = l_{12} + 1, \ldots, l
$$

where $\alpha_{1i}, \alpha_{2i}, \beta_{1i}^*, \beta_{2i}^*, \beta_{1i}, \beta_{2i}$ are non-negative Lagrangian multipliers and $k(x_i, x_j) = \langle \Phi(x_i) \cdot \Phi(x_j) \rangle$ denotes the kernel function. After solving the QPP in Eq. (11) we can obtain the fuzzy normal vector $\mathbf{W} = (\mathbf{w}, \mathbf{c})$ by using the following equations:

$$
\mathbf{w} = \sum_{i=1}^{l_{12}} y_i(\alpha_{1i} + \alpha_{2i})\phi(x_i) + \sum_{i=l_{12}+1}^{l} (\beta_{1i}^* + \beta_{2i}^* - \beta_{1i} - \beta_{2i})\phi(x_i) \tag{12}
$$

$$
\mathbf{c} = \frac{1}{v} \left(\sum_{i=1}^{l_{12}} (\alpha_{1i} - \alpha_{2i})\phi(x_i) + \sum_{i=l_{12}+1}^{l} (\beta_{1i}^* - \beta_{2i}^* - \beta_{1i} + \beta_{2i})\phi(x_i) \right) \tag{13}
$$

While parameters b and d can be determined from the Karush-Kuhn-Tucker (KKT) conditions. For any data point x_i, $Y_i = \mathbf{W}^\cdot \phi(x_i) + \mathbf{B}$ is a symmetric triangular fuzzy number whose center is $\mathbf{w}^\cdot \phi(x_i) + b$ and whose width is $\mathbf{c}^\cdot \phi(x_i) + d$. The proposed FH-K-SVM uses the following fuzzy partial ordering relation to determine the membership level for data point x_i which belongs to the positive class. If $A = (m_A, c_A)$ and $B = (m_B, c_B)$ denote two arbitrary symmetric triangular fuzzy numbers, the membership degree that A is larger than B is calculated using the membership function:

$$R_{\geq B}(A) = R(A, B) = \begin{cases} 1 & \text{if } \alpha > 0 \text{ and } \beta > 0 \\ 0 & \text{if } \alpha < 0 \text{ and } \beta < 0, \\ 0.5\left(1 + \frac{\alpha + \beta}{max(|\alpha|, |\beta|)}\right) & \text{o.w.} \end{cases} \quad (14)$$

where $\alpha = (m_A + c_A) - (m_B + c_B)$ and $\beta = (m_A - c_A) - (m_B - c_B)$. $R_{\geq B}(A) = 0.5$ if $m_A = m_B$, $R_{\geq B}(A) < 0.5$ if $m_A < m_B$ and $R_{\geq B}(A) > 0.5$ if $m_A > m_B$. For class i and j, the fuzzy decision function of the proposed FH-K-SVCR is defined as follows:

$$f_{ij}(\mathbf{x}_p) = \begin{cases} R_{\geq \delta F}(Y_i) \text{ if } \mathbf{w}^\cdot \phi(x_i) + b \geq \delta \\ -R_{\geq Y_i}(-\delta F) \text{ if } \mathbf{w}^\cdot \phi(x_i) + b \leq -\delta \\ min(R_{\geq -\delta F}(Y_i), R_{\geq Y_i}(\delta F)) \text{ otherwise} \end{cases} \quad (15)$$

where δ_F represents a symmetric triangular fuzzy number, whose center is $0 < \delta < 1$ (chosen a priori) and whose width is I_δ. The decision function for the proposed FH-K-SVM returns a value between 0 and 1 for each data point, which defines the degree of membership for data point $\mathbf{x}$ belonging to the positive class. A value of 1 means that the data point is fully a member of the positive class and a value of 0 indicates that data point is not a member of positive class. Values between 0 and 1 mean that data point is a fuzzy member that only partially belong to the positive class.

4 Experiments

Investors must predict stock trends but the stock market's behavior is random, stochastic and influenced by many factors. Daily news carries a sentiment score (negative, neutral or positive) and affects stock market behavior. Many studies predict the next day's stock trend based on daily financial news. For each news item, if the name of the selected stock company appears in the title or content of an item of financial news, this news article is assigned to the corresponding stock.

News items that do not correspond to any stock company are ignored. For each stock, all news items with the same publication timestamp are merged to construct the daily news corpus. This experiment collects the Taiwan stock price time series from the Yahoo Finance website. The stock price time series is aligned to the daily news corpus according to the release date for news. Any trading dates that do not contain any news are deleted. The instances with price movement percentage $\frac{p_d - p_{d-1}}{p_{d-1}} \geq 0.5\%$ are labeled as {rising} class and price movement percentage $\frac{p_d - p_{d-1}}{p_{d-1}} \leq -0.5\%$ are labeled as {falling} class, where p_d denotes the closing price at dth day for the target stock. The instances with price movement percentage between 0.5% and −0.5% are labeled as {flat} class. This

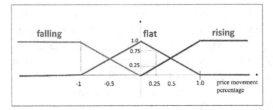

Fig. 1. The fuzzy membership functions that define the fuzzy set for {rising}, {falling}, and {flat} categories.

experiment uses 16 stocks, the majority of which are for semiconductor companies and food companies. This experiment extracts the content, title and publication timestamp for each financial news from the https://www.cnyes.com website for the period of November, 2018 to October, 2019. Each daily news corpus is transformed into a data vector and the sentiment attributes are extracted using the Chinese LIWC (Linguistic Inquiry and Word Count) dictionary [15] and the semantic attributes are extracted using the LDA (latent Dirichlet allocation) hidden topics discovery procedure [16].

Fuzzy theory can be used to solve the stock prediction problem because the meaning of words in the daily news is vague (e.g., large or small). Besides, the boundary that divides rising and falling categories is fuzzy [13]. A stock sample with a +3% stock price rise is more representative of a rising class than a stock sample with a +0.7% stock price rise but a stock sample with a +0.25% price rise may 75% belong to the {flat} class and 25% to the {rising} class. The fuzzy membership value for each stock sample is calculated using the membership function depicted in Fig. 1. This experiment compares the proposed FH-K-SVCR with the state-of-the-art multi-class classification SVM models, including K-SVCR [5], Twin-KSVC [6], LSTKSVC [7], KNN-Twin-KSVC [8], Ramp-KSVCR [9], K-RLSSVCR [10]. A grid search is used to determine the optimal values for the parameters. The classification accuracy rate for each SVM model is calculated using standard ten-fold cross-validation. Table 1 lists the experimental results in terms of the ten-fold cross-validation rates. Table 1 shows that the proposed FH-K-SVCR gives comparable results to state-of-the-art multi-class SVM classifiers. This demonstrates that the ambiguity and imprecision in real-world stock trend classification task is better characterized by the fuzzy hyperplane that is constructed using the proposed FH-K-SVCR.

Table 2 compares the proposed FH-K-SVCR with several state-of-the-art deep leaning methods, including Yun's CNN based stock prediction model [17], Pinheiro's RNN based stock prediction model [18] and Day's DNN based stock prediction model [19]. Table 2 shows that the proposed FH-K-SVCR achieves better classification performance than deep learning (non-fuzzy) algorithms, largely because the proposed FH-K-SVCR assigns a different importance to each training data point during the training process and the fuzzy hyperplane for the proposed FH-K-SVCR reduces the effect of noise.

Table 1. Comparison of the proposed FH-K-SVCR with other multi-class SVM models.

Dataset	K-SVCR	Twin-KSVC	LST-KSVC	KNN-Twin-KSVC	Ramp-KSVCR	K-RL-SSVCR	Our approach
Food stocks	68.46	71.32	69.67	72.85	71.59	72.17	**73.80**
Semiconductor stocks	61.25	64.39	59.98	64.48	63.65	64.23	**66.31**
Average acc ratio	64.855	67.855	64.825	68.665	67.62	68.20	**70.055**

Table 2. Comparison of the proposed FH-K-SVCR with other deep learning models.

Dataset	Yun's CNN model	Pinheiro's RNN model	Day's DNN model	Our approach
Food stocks	71.18	68.57	65.34	**73.80**
Semiconductor stocks	62.79	59.72	57.63	**66.31**
Average acc ratio	66.985	64.145	61.485	70.055

5 Conclusion

This study proposes a fuzzy hyperplane version of a K-SVCR that is called a fuzzy hyperplane-based support vector classification regression for K-class classification (FH-K-SVCR). The proposed FH-K-SVCR replaces the crisp hyperplane in K-SVCR with a fuzzy hyperplane in the defining of the one-vs-one-vs-rest decision function in multi-class classification problem. The proposed FH-K-SVCR takes both the advantages of K-SVCR in increasing the classification performance for multi-class classification task and the advantages of FH-SVM in enhancing the fault tolerance and robustness. Experimental results show that the proposed FH-K-SVCR gives comparable results on stock prediction application. Moreover, decision-making involves a consideration of confidence and risk. In general, the greater the stake that is involved in the decision, the greater is confidence that is required to make the decision to prevent an increase in the risk. The fuzzy hyperplane for the proposed FH-K-SVCR assigns a membership level to an unseen stock sample. This membership level indicates the degree to which the unseen stock sample belongs to the corresponding class and gives an index that quantifies the degree of confidence in the predicted output. Therefore, the proposed FH-K-SVCR is well suited to decision-making applications. In the future, we intend to compare the classification performance of the proposed FH-K-SVCR with more deep learning models on different stock markets.

References

1. Cortes, C., Vapnik, V.: Support-vector networks. Mach. Learn. **20**(3), 273–297 (1995)
2. Khan, N.M., Ksantini, R., Ahmad, I.S., Boufama, B.: A novel SVM model for classification with an application to face recognition. Pattern Recogn. **45**(1), 66–79 (2012)
3. Kressel, U.: Pairwise classification and support vector machines. In: Scholkopf, B., et al. (eds.) Advances in Kernel Methods: Support Vector Learning, pp. 255–268 (1998)
4. Hsu, C.-W., Lin, C.-J.: A comparison of methods for multiclass support vector machines. IEEE Trans. Neural Netw. **13**(2), 415–425 (2002)
5. Angulo, C., Catala, A.: K-SVCR. A multi-class support vector machine. In: L ' opez de M ´ antaras, R., ´ Plaza, E. (eds.) Machine Learning: ECML 2000, LNCS, vol. 1810, pp. 31–38. Springer, Berlin (2000). https://doi.org/10.1007/3-540-45164-1_4
6. Xu, Y., Guo, R., Wang, L.: A twin multi-class classification support vector machine. Cogn. Comput. **5**(4), 580–588 (2013)

7. Nasiri, J.A., Charkari, N.M., Jalili, S.: Least squares twin multi-class classification support vector machine. Pattern Recogn. **48**(3), 984–992 (2015)
8. Tanveer, M., Sharma, A., Suganthan, P.N.: Least squares KNN-based weighted multiclass twin SVM. Neurocomputing (2020)
9. Bamakan, S.M.H., Wang, H., Shi, Y.: Ramp loss K-Support vector classification-regression; a robust and sparse multi-class approach to the intrusion detection problem. Knowl. Based Syst. **126**, 113–126 (2017)
10. Ma, J., Zhou, S., Chen, L., Wang, W., Zhang, Z.: A sparse robust model for large scale multi-class classification based on K-SVCR. Pattern Recogn. Lett. **117**, 16–23 (2019)
11. Lin, C.-F., Wang, S.-D.: Fuzzy support vector machines. IEEE Trans. Neural Networks **13**(2), 464–471 (2002)
12. Hao, P.-Y.: Support vector classification with fuzzy hyperplane. J. Intell. Fuzzy Syst. **30**(3), 1431–1443 (2016)
13. Chen, S., Cao, J., Chen F., Liu, B.: Entropy-based fuzzy least squares twin support vector machine for pattern classification Neural Process. Lett. **51**, 41–66 (2020)
14. Hao, P.-Y., Kung, C.-F., Chang, C.-Y., Ou, J.-B.: Predicting stock price trends based on financial news articles and using a novel twin support vector machine with fuzzy hyperplane. Appl. Soft Comput. **98**, 106806 (2021)
15. Huang, J.-L., et al.: Establishment of a Chinese dictionary of language exploration and word counting. Chin. J. Psychol. **54**(2), 185–201 (2012)
16. Blei, D.M., Ng, A.Y., Jordan, M.I.: Latent Dirichlet allocation. J. Mach. Learn. Res. **3**, 993–1022 (2003)
17. Yun, H., Sim, G., Seok, J.: Stock prices prediction using the title of newspaper articles with Korean natural language processing. In: International Conference on Artificial Intelligence in Information and Communication (2019)
18. Pinheiro, L.D.S., Dras, M.: Stock market prediction with deep learning: a character-based neural language model for event-based trading. In: Proceedings of Australasian Language Technology Association Workshop, pp. 6–15 (2017)
19. Day, M.-Y., Lee, C.-C.: Deep learning for financial sentiment analysis on finance news providers. In: 2016 IEEE/ACM International Conference on Advances in Social Networks Analysis and Mining (ASONAM), pp. 1127–1134 (2016)

Dynamic Hand Gesture Recognition for Human-Robot Collaborative Assembly

Bogdan Kwolek[1(✉)] and Sako Shinji[2]

[1] AGH University of Science and Technology, 30 Mickiewicza,
30-059 Kraków, Poland
bkw@agh.edu.pl
[2] Frontier Research Institute for Information Science, Nagoya Institute
of Technology, Gokiso-cho, Showa-ku Nagoya 466-8555, Japan
sako@msp.nitech.ac.jp

Abstract. In this work, we propose a novel framework for gesture recognition for human-robot collaborative assembly. It permits recognition of dynamic hand gestures and their duration to automate planning the assembly or common human-robot workspaces according to Methods-Time-Measurement recommendations. In the proposed approach the common workspace of a worker and Franka-Emika robot is observed by an overhead RGB camera. A spatio-temporal graph convolutional neural network operating on 3D hand joints extracted by MediaPipe is used to recognize hand motions in manual assembly tasks. It predicts five motion sequences: grasp, move, position, release, and reach. We present experimental results of gesture recognition achieved by a spatio-temporal graph convolutional neural network on real RGB image sequences.

Keywords: Vision-based gesture recognition · spatio-temporal graph neural networks · collaborative robotics · Methods-Time-Measurement

1 Introduction

Hand gestures are an effective method of communication, particularly when communicating with a person who does not understand our spoken language. Vision-based gesture recognition is extremely challenging task not only due to spatio-temporal variations, different realizations of the same gesture but also because of non-rigid, complex articulations of hands. In the recent years, because of range of possible applications, a steady growth of research on hand gesture recognition has been observed [1–4]. Gesture recognition has various applications ranging from sign language recognition [1,5–12], robotics [13] to virtual reality [7,14].

The approaches to recognition of hand gestures can be divided into approaches that utilize glove sensor devices to convert finger and hand motions into data streams, and vision-based ones, which leverage a single or multiple cameras [3]. In general, approaches to gesture recognition based on vision techniques can be divided into static, isolated and continuous [2,3]. Methods intended for

© The Author(s), under exclusive license to Springer Nature Switzerland AG 2023
L. Rutkowski et al. (Eds.): ICAISC 2023, LNAI 14125, pp. 112–121, 2023.
https://doi.org/10.1007/978-3-031-42505-9_10

recognizing static gestures usually operate on single images and usually determine the orientation and shape of fingers and hands while signing digits and alphabets by a performer. In contrast, methods for recognition of dynamic gestures estimate motions of hands and body during signing such gestures. Dynamic gestures are utilized mainly for signing words and sentences. As noticed in [3], the fingerspelling signs can be performed easily by non-expert performers, which makes the acquisition of these signs much easier than dynamic gestures. Li et al. [14] claim that gestures in the interaction process can be distinguished according to varied spatio-temporal operation behaviors, interaction modes, semantics, and interaction ranges.

Due to the significant progress in the field of machine learning in recent years, more and more attention is now being devoted to gesture recognition techniques based on deep neural networks [2]. In [15] a two-stage convolutional neural network (CNN) employing hand color image and its pseudo-depth image has been discussed. A CNN with spatial pyramid pooling for hand gesture recognition has been proposed in [16]. Recently, an accurate method [17] for static hand gesture recognition using a deep CNN has been introduced. For recognition of dynamic gestures a method relying on a 2D convolutional neural network and feature fusion has been proposed in [18].

Deep neural network-based methods require significant repositories of labeled data to train such networks. Manual labeling of images for training deep networks, and in particular image sequences for continuous recognition of dynamic gestures is a tedious and time-consuming process. Thus, in order to reduce costs associated with manual labeling images for sign language recognition a synthetic sign language generator has been proposed in [19]. This tool can be leveraged to synthetically generate sign language datasets from 3D motion capture data. It generates realistic images of body shapes with ground truth 2D/3D poses, depth maps, optical flows, and surface normals. A recently published article [20] compares small sample methods for hand shape recognition.

One of the most meaningful category of human-robot-interaction (HRI) is the collaborative assembly [13]. It aims at assembling by an user a more complex object using sequential subprocesses, where a collaborative robot is supposed to help his/her in their execution. A person and a collaborative robot work on the same task, in the same workspace, at the same time. Sharing the same workspace is a fundamental element in the discussed HRI. So far, only a few non-verbal methods have been developed to support human-machine communication by tracking human posture and skeleton, recognizing hand gestures, detecting gazes and intention recognition. For instance, in a research performed in Toyota Research Institute Europe [21] an artificial cognitive architecture for intention reading in HRI that leverages social cues to disambiguate goals has been developed. This innovative model was validated in an interactive HRI scenario involving a joint game manipulation. In a toy block scenario the manipulation game was performed by a human and a robotic arm. Recently, a neuro-inspired model built on Dynamic Neural Fields for action selection in a human-robot action scenarios has been proposed in [22]. A two-dimensional action execution layer permits representation of the object and action in the same field. In a recently published work [23] a spatial-temporal graph convolutional neural network (ST-GCN) has been used to enable human action recognition for multi-variant assembly in HRI scenarios. The GCN operates on 3D skeleton data extracted by the Kinect sensor. The discussed approach is based on generalized action primitives that were derived from Methods-Time-Measurement (MTM) analysis.

In this work, we propose a novel approach to gesture recognition for human-robot collaborative assembly. The common workspace of a worker and a robot is observed by an overhead RGB camera. A spatio-temporal adaptive graph convolutional neural network operating on 3D hand joints that are extracted by the MediaPipe is used to recognize hand motions in manual assembly tasks. The system classifies motion sequences and estimates their durations. Five motion sequences: grasp, move, position, release, and reach are predicted. They can be then used by the robot to accomplish subsequent sub-tasks or to achieve better workspace planning according to the MTM recommendations.

2   Method

First, we discuss background of the research. Then, in Sect. 2.2 we present the scenario of experiments. Afterwards, we discuss the proposed approach. Finally, we present the spatio-temporal adaptive graph convolutional neural network.

2.1   Background

Assembly time is one of the major estimates of the cost of an assembly. For planning an assembly system or improving the efficiency of an existing assembly line, a quick and reliable method of estimating the time needed to complete a given assembly task is essential. Assembly time is defined as the period of time from starting to finishing an assembly operation. Methods-time measurement is used in industry to describe, analyze, evaluate and plan manual tasks. In the MTM-1 standard five basis motions are considered: grasp, move, position, release, and reach. Reach is the basis motion element involved with movement of the hand or fingers. It is used to describe the movement of the hand or finger to a new destination. Grasp operation is used to describe control on one or many objects with fingers or with hands. It is commonly employed as a prerequisite motion before performing the next basic motion, i.e. grasping an object prior moving it to a new location. Move is used to describe the phase of relocating the object to a new location. Position is in turn usually preceded by a move and is utilized to describe orienting or aligning one object with respect to another. Release is used to describe the phase that ends control of an object by the hand or fingers. MTM-based workplace planning is a time-consuming task since every motion and its duration are usually determined by specialists in planning and ergonomics. Therefore, there is a very high demand for methods that would automate this process.

2.2   Scenario

The aim of this work is to propose and evaluate in a real-world scenario a reliable method for recognizing dynamic hand gestures for human-robot collaborative assembly. For the purposes of evaluating the effectiveness of the proposed approach in such a task, a test stand was built, see Fig. 1. The worker's task is to pick up the objects on the left side of the stand one by one and place them on the right side stand that is closer to the robot's arm. In an alternative scenario, the worker picks object by object from the box and moves object one by one to the stand. The scene is observed by a single overhead camera that is not shown on the picture illustrating this toy task. The aim of the vision system is to continuously classify the hand motions into five classes. In a future work they will be used by the robot to accomplish subsequent sub-tasks or to achieve better workspace planning according to the MTM standard. The Franka–Emika robot will employ a depth camera (Asus Xtion) that is already mounted on the gripper to grasp and then move the objects to new locations.

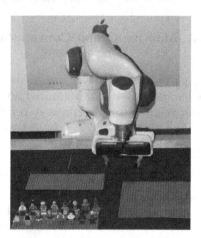

Fig. 1. The robot Franka-Emika from opposite end of the table (common workplace) recognizes motions of the worker's hand using images acquired by an overhead camera (not shown on this illustrative image).

2.3   Proposed Approach

RGB-based 3D hand posture (skeleton) estimation is an inherently ill-posed problem due to the lack of depth information in the 2D input map. MediaPipe Hands is an effective and accurate hand and finger tracking framework [24]. It employs advanced machine learning techniques to infer 21, 3D hand landmarks from a single RGB image. Initially, the palm detector is executed to estimate the hand locations, and afterwards, hand-skeleton finger tracking model performs precise joint localization resulting in 21, 3D hand landmarks per detected hand. A Single shot detection (SSD) is used to detect palms. The algorithm then extrapolates the information from this in order to detect the fingers with a support from a hand landmark model. MediaPipe provides many customizable pre-trained models to estimate and track 3D hand skeletons. In the proposed framework the hand MediaPipe is used to deliver streams of 3D joints locations from RGB image sequences.

The 3D joint streams are fed to a single channel, spatio-temporal Adaptive Graph Convolutional Network [25], which has an attention mechanism and deals with adaptive graphs. In contrast to ST-GCN networks [26] the graph topology in the AGCN network is an optimized parameter and unique for every layer. The residual branch permits increasing the training stability. The ST-AGCN and its extension two-stream (bone and joint) 2 s-AGCN has been developed for human action recognition on skeletal data representing human actions. In such tasks the human skeleton consists of 25 joints. In our approach the ST-AGCN is responsible for predicting hand motions using skeletal data with 21 joints.

2.4 Spatio-Temporal Adaptive Graph Convolutional Neural Network

The adaptive spatial graph convolution layer utilizes both the provided adjacency matrix as well as parameterized and optimized adjacency matrices. The adaptive spatial graph convolution can be expressed as follows:

$$\mathbf{f}_{out} = \sum_{k}^{Kv} \mathbf{W}_k \mathbf{f}_{in}(\mathbf{A}_k + \mathbf{B}_k + \mathbf{C}_k) \tag{1}$$

where K_v denotes the kernel size of the spatial dimension, which is set to 3, $\mathbf{W}_k$ stands for the $C_{out} \times C_{in} \times 1 \times 1$ weight vector of the 1×1 convolution, where C is number of in/out channels, $\mathbf{f}_{in}$ is the input feature vector, $\mathbf{f}_{out}$ is the output feature vector, whereas $\mathbf{A}_k, \mathbf{B}_k, \mathbf{C}_k$ are the adjacency matrices. $\mathbf{A}_k$ represents the physical structure of the human hand in the form of the adjacency matrix, i.e. determines whether there are connections between two graph vertexes. $\mathbf{B}_k$ is a matrix whose elements are parameterized and optimized together with other parameters during the network training. This matrix permits learning new vertex connections. $\mathbf{C}_k$ is a data dependent adjacency matrix, which learns a unique graph for each sample. It is calculated through embedding the input features through a 1×1 convolutional operation and a softmax function. If the number of input channels differs from the number of output channels, a 1×1 convolution is inserted in the residual path. The convolution for the temporal dimension is identical with convolution in ST-GCN [26]. The spatial and temporal GCNs are followed by a batch normalization layer and a ReLU layer.

We implemented a network consisting of seven AGCN blocks with increasing output feature dimensions. It operates on input tensor of size (32,21,3), i.e. (time steps, joints, channels), which after reshaping it to (63,32) is fed to batch normalization layer. The output of batch normalization layer is reshaped to (3,32,21). The last AGCN block is followed by a global average pooling layer, which is in turn followed by a fully connected layer on the output. Every AGCN block is composed of a spatial graph convolution that is followed by a temporal graph convolution with respective kernel sizes. The output sizes of AGCN layers are as follows: (64,32,21), (64,32,21), (64,32,21), (64,32,21), (128,16,21), (128,16,21), and (128,8,21). The temporal stride was set to 1 except the fourth and sixth layers for which the stride was set to 2. The global average pooling layer operates on tensors of size (1,128). The number of neurons in the last layer is equal to six.

3   Experimental Results

At the beginning of this Section we present the dataset. Finally, we present experimental results that were achieved in dynamic hand gesture recognition on real RGB image sequences.

3.1   Dataset

The training dataset consists of 12 videos with total of 54,659 RGB images of size 640×480. Figure 2 depicts sample images illustrating the basic motions: reach, grasp, move, position, and release. In the considered scenario the hand motions always appear in the order mentioned above. Hand gestures were performed by five performers. The videos have been manually labeled, i.e. one of five classes has been assigned to each frame using five MTM-1 basic motions. The images with no hand have been labeled as the sixth class. The gesture categories are distributed as follows: reach – 3,553, grasp – 16,414, move – 5,621, position – 10,669, and release – 17,030. The test set consists of 3 videos with total of 31,190 RGB images. The gesture categories are distributed as follows: reach – 3,911, grasp – 10,140, move – 5,523, position – 4,044, and release – 7,038. The images have been acquired by Logitech HD Pro Webcam C920. On each image 21 $x-$, $y-$ and $z-$ hand joint coordinates have been determined using the MediaPipe Hands Python API. Figure 3 depicts hand skeletons that were extracted by the MediaPipe on images from Fig. 2. The hand joints coordinates together with class labels have been stored as the hand graph dataset with six classes.

3.2   Experimental Evaluation

We implemented, trained and then evaluated neural networks operating on joint streams extracted in advance by the MediaPipe. At the beginning we determined accuracies achieved by an LSTM neural network [27] consisting of 128 hidden nodes in two layers and a fully connected output layer. Afterwards, we implemented a bidirectional LSTM (Bi-LSTM) and a GRU neural network [28]. Finally, we experimented with the AGCN network. The experimental results

Fig. 2. Five basic motions according to MTM: reach, grasp, move, position, and release (from left to right).

Fig. 3. Hand skeletons determined by the MediaPipe on images from Fig. 2.

Table 1. Accuracies and average F1-scores achieved on our dataset for dynamic hand gesture recognition.

	Accuracy [%]	F1-score [%]
LSTM	79.21	77.02
Bi-LSTM	88.99	85.40
GRU	88.65	86.01
AGCN	90.73	88.23

achieved by the above mentioned neural networks are presented in Table 1. As we can observe, the best results have been achieved by the AGCN network. It achieves quite promising results in this challenging task. Figure 4 depicts the confusion matrix that ha been obtained on the test video #2. As can be seen from this plot, the highest number of false predictions was for the position gesture, which was mistakenly recognized as the release gesture and as the move gesture.

3.3   Training Details and Implementation

The experimental evaluations have been performed using Python and AGCN implementation in the PyTorch framework. The AGCN has been trained in 25 epochs, with batch size set to 64. The neural network has been trained using Adam optimizer and plateau learning rate scheduler [29] with an initial learning rate of 1e-4. Taking into account unbalanced number of samples in each class, as in [30], the neural network has been trained using the focal loss. The focal loss copes with class imbalance by down-weighting inliers (easy examples) such that their contribution to the total loss is small even if their amount is big. Through generating horizontally, vertically, and both ways flipped graphs of the original data we augmented the graph data during the training of neural networks. In

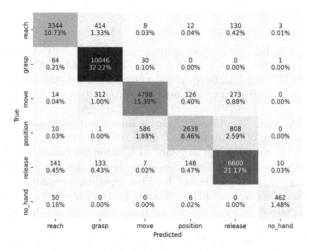

Fig. 4. Confusion matrix on predictions of the AGCN network.

the hand graph we added joints links the fingertips to the base of the right neighbor finger, i.e. the following edges: 4-5, 8-9, 12-13, 16-17, c.f. MediaPipe hand skeleton. The size of the temporal window was set to 32 frames. The 3D joints streams were extracted using the MediaPipe with the minimum detection confidence set to 0.4, whereas the minimum tracking confidence for tracking the landmarks in consecutive images was set to 0.5. All neural networks have been trained on two Nvidia A100 GPUs.

4   Conclusions

The proposed framework permits accurate recognition of dynamic hand gestures on RGB image sequences. It can be useful to automate planning the assembly or common human-robot workspaces according to Methods-Time-Measurement recommendations. In the proposed approach the common worker-robot workspace is observed by an overhead RGB camera. A spatio-temporal adaptive graph convolutional neural network operating on 3D hand joints that are extracted by MediaPipe in advance permits accurate recognition of hand motions in manual assembly tasks. In future work we will investigate whether 2 s-AGCN using both joint and bone streams could improve the performance of gesture prediction. In future research it would be interesting to compare the results achieved by the AGCN, 2 s-AGCN with a multi-scale spatial-temporal GCN as well as with results achieved by a spatio-temporal transformer.

Acknowledgment. This work was supported by Polish National Science Center (NCN) under a research grant 2017/27/B/ST6/01743. This research was also supported in part by NITech Frontier Research Institutes, Invitation Program for International Researchers. Part of this research was done during the first author's stay at Nagoya Institute of Technology, Nagoya, Japan.

References

1. Aloysius, N., Geetha, M.: Understanding vision-based continuous sign language recognition. Multimedia Tools Appli. **79**(31), 22177–22209 (2020)
2. Adeyanju, I., Bello, O., Adegboye, M.: Machine learning methods for sign language recognition: A critical review and analysis. Intell. Syst. with Appl. **12**, 200056 (2021)
3. El-Alfy, E.S., Luqman, H.: A comprehensive survey and taxonomy of sign language research. Eng. Appl. of Artificial Intell. **114**, 105198 (2022)
4. Wadhawan, A., Kumar, P.: Sign language recognition systems: A decade systematic literature review. Archives of Comp. Methods in Eng. **28**(3), 785–813 (2021)
5. Muroi, M., Sogi, N., Kato, N., Fukui, K.: Fingerspelling recognition with two-steps cascade process of spotting and classification. In: Del Bimbo, A., et al. (eds.) ICPR 2021. LNCS, vol. 12666, pp. 728–743. Springer, Cham (2021). https://doi.org/10.1007/978-3-030-68780-9_55
6. Wu, X., Song, G., Zeng, Q., Zhao, Z.: LADS-NET: A deep learning model for dynamic sign language recognition. In: IEEE 5th International Conference on Advance Information Management, Communication, Electronic and Automation Control (IMCEC), vol. 5, pp. 1606–1611 (2022)
7. Fujimoto, T., Kawamura, T., Zempo, K., Puentes, S.: First-person view hand posture estimation and fingerspelling recognition using HoloLens. In: IEEE 11th Global Conference on Consumer Electronics (GCCE), pp. 323–327 (2022)
8. Vu, B., Chen, R., Wong, N.: Classifying sign languages and fingerspellings with convolutional neural networks. Technical Report CS231n: Deep Learning for Computer Vision - Final Proj. Reports & Posters, Dep. of CS, Stanford Univ., Stanford, CA (2022). www.cs231n.stanford.edu/reports/2022/pdfs/23.pdf
9. Wang, S., Wang, K., Yang, T., Li, Y., Fan, D.: Improved 3D-ResNet sign language recognition algorithm with enhanced hand features. Sc. Reports **12**(1), 17812 (2022)
10. Subramanian, B., Olimov, B., Naik, S.M., Kim, S., Park, K.H., Kim, J.: An integrated mediapipe-optimized GRU model for Indian sign language recognition. Sci. Rep. **12**(1), 11964 (2022)
11. Alyami, S., Luqman, H., Hammoudeh, M.: Isolated Arabic sign language recognition using a transformer-based model and landmark keypoints. ACM Trans. Asian Low-Resour. Lang. Inf. Process (2023)
12. Arun Prasath, G., Annapurani, K.: Prediction of sign language recognition based on multi layered CNN. Multimedia Tools Appli. (2023)
13. Semeraro, F., Griffiths, A., Cangelosi, A.: Human-robot collaboration and machine learning: A systematic review of recent research. Robotics Comput.-Integrated Manufact. **79**, 102432 (2023)
14. Li, Y., Huang, J., Tian, F., Wang, H.A., Dai, G.Z.: Gesture interaction in virtual reality. Virtual Reality Intell. Hardware **1**(1), 84–112 (2019)
15. Liu, J., Furusawa, K., Tateyama, T., Iwamoto, Y., Chen, Y.W.: An improved hand gesture recognition with two-stage convolution neural networks using a hand color image and its pseudo-depth image. In: IEEE International Conference on Image Processing (ICIP), pp. 375–379 (2019)
16. Tan, Y.S., Lim, K.M., Tee, C., Lee, C.P., Low, C.Y.: Convolutional neural network with spatial pyramid pooling for hand gesture recognition. Neural Comp. and Appl. **33**(10), 5339–5351 (2021)

17. Babu, U.S., Raganna, A., Vidyasagar, K., Bharati, S., Kumar, G.: Highly accurate static hand gesture recognition model using deep convolutional neural network for human machine interaction. In: IEEE 4th International Conference on Advances in Electronics, Computers and Communications (ICAECC), pp. 1–6 (2022)

18. Yu, J., Qin, M., Zhou, S.: Dynamic gesture recognition based on 2D convolutional neural network and feature fusion. Sci. Rep. **12**(1), 4345 (2022)

19. Miura, T., Sako, S.: SynSLaG: Synthetic sign language generator. In: Proceedings of the 23rd International ACM Conference on Computers and Accessibility, ASSETS 2021, pp. 1–4. ACM (2021)

20. Quiroga, F., et al.: A comparison of small sample methods for handshape recognition. J. Comput. Sci. Technol. **23**(1), 35–44 (2023)

21. Vinanzi, S., Cangelosi, A., Goerick, C.: The role of social cues for goal disambiguation in human-robot cooperation. In: 29th IEEE International Conference on Robot and Human Interactive Communication (RO-MAN), pp. 971–977 (2020)

22. Cunha, A., et al.: Towards collaborative robots as intelligent co-workers in human-robot joint tasks: what to do and who does it? In: 52th International Symposium on Robotics, pp. 1–8 (2020)

23. Koch, J., Buesch, L., Gomse, M., Schueppstuhl, T.: A Methods-Time-Measurement based approach to enable action recognition for multi-variant assembly in human-robot collaboration. Procedia CIRP **106**, 233–238 (2022)

24. Lugaresi, C., et al.: MediaPipe: A framework for building perception pipelines. CoRR abs/ arXiv: 1906.08172 (2019)

25. Shi, L., Zhang, Y., Cheng, J., Lu, H.: Two-stream adaptive graph convolutional networks for skeleton-based action recognition. In: IEEE/CVF Conference on Computer Vision and Pattern Recognition (CVPR), pp. 12018–12027 (2019)

26. Yan, S., Xiong, Y., Lin, D.: Spatial temporal graph convolutional networks for skeleton-based action recognition. In: Proceedings of AAAI Conference on Artificial Intelligence. AAAI Press (2018)

27. Hochreiter, S., Schmidhuber, J.: Long short-term memory. Neural Comput. **9**(8), 1735–1780 (1997)

28. Chung, J., Gulcehre, C., Cho, K., Bengio, Y.: Empirical evaluation of gated recurrent neural networks on sequence modeling. In: NIPS Workshop on Deep Learning (2014)

29. Radford, A., Metz, L., Chintala, S.: Unsupervised representation learning with deep convolutional generative adversarial networks. In: 4th International Conference on Learning Representations, ICLR (2016)

30. Cardoso, D.B., Campos, L.C., Nascimento, E.R.: An action recognition approach with context and multiscale motion awareness. In: 35th Conference on Graphics, Patterns and Images (SIBGRAPI), vol. 1, pp. 73–78 (2022)

Transfer of Knowledge Among Instruments in Automatic Music Transcription

Michał Leś[(⊠)] and Michał Woźniak

Wrocław University of Science and Technology, Wrocław, Poland
{michal.les,michal.wozniak}@pwr.edu.pl

Abstract. Automatic music transcription (AMT) is one of the most challenging tasks in the music information retrieval domain. It is the process of converting an audio recording of music into a symbolic representation containing information about the notes, chords, and rhythm. Current research in this domain focuses on developing new models based on transformer architecture or using methods to perform semi-supervised training, which gives outstanding results, but the computational cost of training such models is enormous. This work shows how to employ easily generated synthesized audio data produced by software synthesizers to train a universal model. It is a good base for further transfer learning to quickly adapt transcription model for other instruments. Achieved results prove that using synthesized data for training may be a good base for pretraining general-purpose models, where the task of transcription is not focused on one instrument.

Keywords: automatic music transcription · transfer learning · music information retrieval · multi-instrumental music transcription

1 Introduction

Automatic music transcription (AMT) is a challenging task in the musical information retrieval domain. It is the process of converting music recordings into symbolic representations such as music sheets or MIDI files. The problem is especially visible for polyphonic music, where multiple frequencies affect each other, giving a result which is hard to estimate using simple algorithms for time-frequency analysis.

Current works often use datasets, which are hard to obtain and maintain. For instruments without any electronic interface, the possibility of gathering an extensive dataset containing real-world recordings with transcription is limited.

This work focuses on discovering the potential of using a model trained on synthesized data for automatic music transcription. These data are easy to generate and could be produced on demand. The intuition behind this idea is related to the possibility of universally recognizing pitch and rhythm by the human ear - it performs similarly no matter the kind of audio source. Synthesized instruments may contain fewer noises than the audio recorded via microphone. However, a

© The Author(s), under exclusive license to Springer Nature Switzerland AG 2023
L. Rutkowski et al. (Eds.): ICAISC 2023, LNAI 14125, pp. 122–133, 2023.
https://doi.org/10.1007/978-3-031-42505-9_11

model trained on such data may focus more on frequency analysis tasks, which is a good base for fine-tuning it to real-world data.

During the presented research, we trained the U-net model with BiLinear LSTM on software-synthesized samples containing timbre from different instruments. We improved the model's performance in the target domain based on real-world recordings that prove that the model trained on synthesized instruments could generalize transcription in note and frame metrics across different datasets after zero-shot transfer. We may use it for quick adaptation to another real-world recording dataset competing with models pre-trained on recordings of the specific instrument.

2   Related Works

This chapter focuses on the description of currently used models for transcription and audio processing methods. Later we describe data representation and metrics used in the existing literature.

Current research often focuses on developing other models [2], and methods [7] to improve standard automatic music transcription metrics or find a way to perform unsupervised [13] or semi-supervised [6] automatic transcription. It may result in analyzing different timbres and instruments less underlined. The importance of timbre in automatic music transcription was presented by Hernandez-Olivan et al. in [12], where they proved that for different instruments, the estimation of source frequency f0 might be a challenging task. In [4], authors demonstrated that neural network-based music transcription depends on audio input representation because different spectrograms may pass different information. Modern deep learning models offer the possibility to perform transcription for multiple instruments together with track separation [9]. Multi-instrument AMT was considered in [18], and results proved that model capable of performing transcription on one instrument is not working well for another instrument, especially when this knowledge is not passed a priori.

After the significant development of machine learning models capable of resolving many problems and approximating complex solutions, it was clear that it may be used for automatic music transcription. Most currently existing solutions are based on image representation of audio recordings in a time-frequency domain called spectrograms. Two kinds of spectrograms are used as input for existing deep learning models to visualize traits of frequencies present in audio recordings - Mel spectrogram and CQT.

Mel spectrogram is based on the result of time-frequency analysis of sound using Short Time Fourier Transform (STFT) [1] and proper alignment using a particular "mel scale", which makes the distance between two pitches equal as the listener perceives it. It is mainly used to maximize transcription accuracy, as frequencies are the essential input to train the model for AMT. Constant Q Transform (CQT) [3] is another method to achieve images containing information about played frequencies. Its properties fit well to analyze the music and expose musical information like timbre, which may be crucial for this research. We decided to use CQT as the primary spectrogram function in our experiments.

MIDI files often represent labels in datasets, which contain all information needed for a musician or software musical instrument to reproduce a similar sound. Usually, it may be represented as a table, where each row contains four parameters:

- value of pitch - it is a general value used to distinguish between different musical tones,
- value of velocity - this value refers to the speed or intensity with which a note or sound is played; it may be often referred to as a measure of how hard a musician strikes a key on a keyboard or plucks a string on a guitar,
- note start - it is the time when the tone is started to be played by an instrument,
- note end - it is time the tone is ended to be played by an instrument.

Timbre is another essential trait of music recordings. The same pitch played by different instruments may result in a different reception of the same tone. It is determined by combining many factors, including a sound's harmonic content, sustain, attack and decay, and how different frequencies are emphasized or de-emphasized. It results in problems with transferring this knowledge because models trained on spectrograms for guitar recordings will not learn the same way of extracting pitch as the model trained on piano recordings.

Another problem with analyzing different timbres is related to available datasets. Only a few datasets contain real recordings, especially for instruments not available in electronic forms, like a piano. Audio data synthesis is present in almost every currently used dataset for AMT [8,11,19] - not only for the generation of new recordings but also for validation of real-world samples. The enormous dataset containing partially generated data is MAESTRO [11], where authors proposed the "Wave2Midi2Wave" approach and created a set of valuable recordings containing traits of real-world ones. There is also some research where authors try to use a semi-supervised approach for transcription to mitigate the problem of small real-world datasets [6] and create the framework for continual learning of different instruments.

Also, currently used metrics for AMT (defined in [15]) are not always enough to measure all aspects of music transcription. Simonetta et al. in [17] proposed another metric, which was correlated with perceptual measures in the outcome of the automatic music transcription model. Due to the lack of timbre generalization capability in the currently existing model, we aim to find a way to create a model which performs well in a new domain (which is related to different instruments) after zero-shot [14] transfer of weights.

3   Proposed Approach

As a base for our experiments, we used part of the model presented as a transcriber in [7] by Cheuck et al. for investigating the spectrogram reconstruction

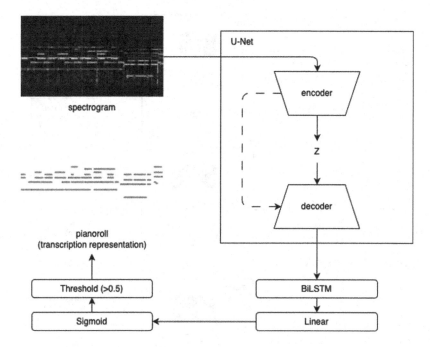

Fig. 1. Architecture of base model used for experiments.

effect. It is composed of U-net [16], BiLSTM and a simple linear layer for classification. We decided to use that model for transcription because of a small number of parameters and relatively good results with the possibility to catch time-series dependencies via bidirectional LSTM. Similar architecture was presented by Hawthorne et al. in [10], but it contained convolutional networks instead of U-net. The exact model configuration is presented in Fig. 1.

We proposed a pipeline presented in Fig. 2 to measure the usefulness of the synthesized data. The data in experiments are randomly sampled during training to extract fixed sequence length from larger tracks, so the original distribution of data should not significantly impact training. For synthesized data generation we used training labels from GuitarSet and MAPS datasets. After audio synthesis, we performed training of the model (resulting in a model trained on Synthesized Instruments - MTOSI) and later used it for fine-tuning to MAPS and GuitarSet data. To compare transfer from MTOSI to transfer from the model trained on each dataset a similar process was performed for the model trained on MAPS dataset and fine-tuned on GuiterSet and vice-versa.

4   Experiment

The experiments were designed to answer the following research questions:

- RQ1: How does the U-net model trained on synthesized data perform on real-world recordings?

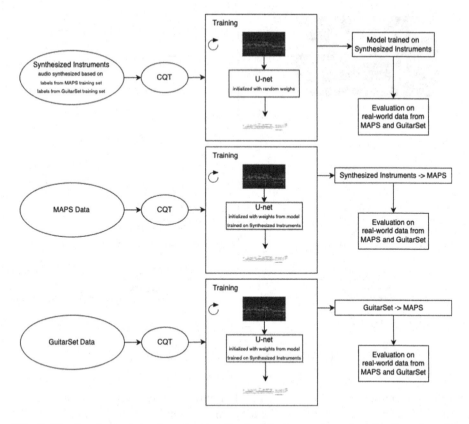

Fig. 2. Pipeline for training based on synthesized instruments and evaluation of results

- RQ2: How does knowledge transfer from the U-net model trained on synthesized data impact training on real-world recordings?
- RQ3: Is the U-net model trained on synthesized data a better candidate for fine-tuning on other instruments than the U-net model trained on real-world piano recordings?

4.1   Setup

Datasets. This section describes types of datasets taken into account with descriptions and conditions used in experiments.

MAPS MAPS [8] is a commonly used dataset for AMT and contains audio recordings with corresponding music notation in MIDI format or text file containing note onset time, note offset time and value of pitch. It consists of 238 music recordings performed in a different environment and in another way. Part of the data was gathered using Diskclavier piano by recording the automatically playing instrument simultaneously by two omnidirectional Schoeps microphones. Some data was generated using a software-based solution (Steinberg's Cubase

SX). It contains music pieces, usual chords, isolated sounds and random sound combinations. For experiments, we used only whole music pieces, which were split into training (80%), validation (10%) and testing (10%) sets. Each recording in MAPS was sampled with a 16 kHz sample rate and transformed into the CQT spectrogram.

GuitarSet. GuitarSet [19] is the most popular dataset containing recordings of guitar annotated semi-unsupervised via a hexaphonic pickup. Authors provide annotations in a convenient JAMS format, which may be easily converted to the pitch value with the corresponding onset and offset time. Additionally, pieces of music were played by different musicians and gathered by different microphones, resulting in seven audio channels. For the experiment, recordings with annotations were split into training (80%), validation (10%), and testing (10%) sets. Each recording was sampled with a 16 kHz sample rate and transformed into the CQT spectrogram.

Synthesized Instruments. This work introduces another type of dataset generated from annotations from other datasets. To achieve the best variety of created samples, we took annotations from MAPS and GuitarSet datasets and created purely synthesized datasets using FluidSynth[1] software and popular soundfont - The Fluid Release 3 General-MIDI Soundfont[2] - used to simulate real instruments. Using this approach, we can generate recordings of many instruments based on existing annotations. For this research, we decided to generate synthesized data from "Acoustic Grand Piano" and "Acoustic Guitar (steel)" MIDI programs of FluidR3_GM soundfont. Split for training, validation and testing was dataset-wise, which means that data from the training set for MAPS and the training set for GuitarSet were present in the training set for SynthesizedInstruments. We are using only randomly chosen fixed-size sequences of each composition for training, so it should not make this model overfit to traits specific to datasets distributions. Achieved recordings contain the clean version of each instrument, which is often not desired in analyzing noisy real-world data recorded by modern microphones. Each recording generated by the software synthesizer was later sampled with a 16 kHz sample rate and transformed into the CQT spectrogram.

Data Processing. Each experiment was focused on training on a specific dataset. We used CQT transform as a spectrogram function for all experiments. We used nnAudio library [5] for spectrogram calculation. To avoid recalculating CQT transform each time, we saved data on disk once it was calculated and loaded it in the subsequent experiments to not perform it again.

Experimental Protocol. Datasets were split into training, validation, and testing sets. We checked the model using the validation set after every ten learning epochs. After training, all datasets were tested using corresponding testing

---

[1] http://www.fluidsynth.org/.

[2] https://member.keymusician.com/Member/FluidR3_GM/index.html.

sets for all available datasets. In the discussion of results, only datasets containing real-world recordings were considered (MAPS and GuitarSet).

Result Analysis. For model evaluation, we used metrics used by other automatic music transcription works available in mir_eval library [15] for Python. Standard metrics used for automatic music transcription are precision (P), recall (R), and F1. They are usually measured in different ways described below:

- frame - it checks if all notes in the small frame (usually 10ms) are in the correct positions. It may favour models generating interrupted outputs, which sounds undesirable, but it is correct in most frames, and recordings with multiple breaks without sound.
- note - a basic metric that checks if the note onset is correct (with small tolerance to start the note sooner or later).
- note with offset - it checks not only note onset but also offset, what makes this metric one of the most challenging because many currently existing models tend to recognize the pitch and the onset time correctly, but the note has improper length or output contains interrupted sound.

Implementation and Reproducibility. Experiments were run on a modern PC with Intel(R) Core(TM) i9-10940X CPU @ 3.30GHz, Nvidia GeForce RTX 3090 and 64 GB of RAM. It is essential to mention that depending on the capability of the target hardware user can adjust the sequence length of the audio recording used for training (327680 in our experiments) and the size of the batch (32 in our experiments). Each training was finished after 2000 epochs. Github repository with code for all experiments is available online[3]

4.2   Results

We evaluated each model on different datasets containing real-world recordings. Afterward, we checked the model's behavior during finetuning on weights of Synthesized Instruments and finetuning performed on the model containing weights trained on corresponding datasets.

In metrics checking the entire frame of output piano roll, the best result for precision and F1 for MAPS dataset was achieved similarly for the model finetuned on MAPS dataset after transfer of weights from the model trained on Synthesized Instruments. The model trained only on MAPS samples has a greater recall value, suggesting that it generates too much output. For the GuitarSet dataset, it appears that using Synthesized Instruments as a base did not improve precision and recall for transcription, but F1 is greater than for any other training. Detailed results for *frame* metrics are presented in Table 1.

In metrics checking the onset of note, the best result for MAPS dataset was achieved for the model finetuned on MAPS dataset after the weight transfer

---

[3] https://github.com/w4k2/automatic_music_transcription.

Table 1. Results for frame metrics

| | Evaluated Datasets | | | | | |
| | MAPS | | | GuitarSet | | |
Model trained on	P	R	F1	P	R	F1
MAPS	0.745	**0.697**	0.718	0.714	0.712	0.703
GuitarSet	0.535	0.375	0.434	**0.900**	0.832	0.863
Synthesized Instruments	0.673	0.362	0.439	0.732	0.394	0.489
Results after transfer from Synthesized Instruments						
Synthesized Instruments − > MAPS	**0.810**	0.656	**0.722**	0.781	0.644	0.692
SynthesizedInstruments − > GuitarSet	0.533	0.412	0.460	0.876	0.873	**0.873**
Results after transfer from GuitarSet						
GuitarSet − > MAPS	0.765	0.656	0.704	0.710	0.698	0.692
Results after transfer from MAPS						
MAPS − > GuitarSet	0.528	0.424	0.466	0.860	**0.884**	0.870

Table 2. Results for note metrics

| | Evaluated Datasets | | | | | |
| | MAPS | | | GuitarSet | | |
Model trained on:	P	R	F1	P	R	F1
MAPS	0.630	0.663	0.642	0.615	0.708	0.646
GuitarSet	0.232	0.234	0.229	**0.795**	0.733	**0.754**
Synthesized Instruments	0.494	0.414	0.423	0.589	0.534	0.537
Results after transfer from Synthesized Instruments						
SynthesizedInstruments − > MAPS	**0.655**	**0.690**	**0.669**	0.678	**0.754**	0.701
SynthesizedInstruments − > GuitarSet	0.215	0.250	0.227	0.751	0.747	0.740
Results after transfer from GuitarSet						
GuitarSet − > MAPS	0.624	0.682	0.648	0.588	0.741	0.642
Results after transfer from MAPS						
MAPS − > GuitarSet	0.242	0.239	0.236	0.767	0.733	0.740

from the model trained on Synthesized Instruments. For GuitarSet dataset, it appears, that using Synthesized Instruments as a base did not improve precision and F1 for transcription, but recall is greater than for any other training. It may suggest that the model creates more outputs based on spectrograms, but it does not improve transcription results. Detailed results for *note* metrics are presented in Table 2.

In metrics checking notes with their corresponding offsets, the best result for MAPS dataset was achieved by the model finetuned on MAPS dataset after the weight transfer from the model trained on Synthesized Instruments. For the GuitarSet dataset, using MAPS model as a base improved recall and F1 for guitar transcription, but precision is a little bit better for the model trained on GuitarSet. Detailed results for *note-with-offset* metrics are presented in Table 3.

Table 3. Results for note-with-offset metrics

| | EVALUATED DATASETS | | | | | |
| | MAPS | | | GUITARSET | | |
Model trained on	P	R	F1	P	R	F1
MAPS	0.406	0.428	0.414	0.246	0.298	0.265
GuitarSet	0.062	0.061	0.060	**0.583**	0.554	0.564
SynthesizedInstruments	0.236	0.191	0.198	0.102	0.104	0.100
RESULTS AFTER TRANSFER FROM SYNTHESIZED INSTRUMENTS						
Synthesized Instruments − > MAPS	**0.423**	**0.445**	**0.432**	0.221	0.260	0.236
SynthesizedInstruments − > GuitarSet	0.063	0.072	0.066	0.547	0.556	0.548
RESULTS AFTER TRANSFER FROM GUITARSET						
GuitarSet − > MAPS	0.392	0.428	0.407	0.236	0.312	0.264
MAPS − > GuitarSet	0.071	0.070	0.069	0.574	**0.566**	**0.566**

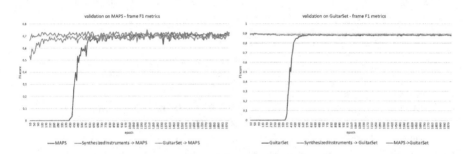

Fig. 3. Validation on target datasets during training of models.

4.3 Time to Achieve Model Convergence

During experiments we noticed, that for finetuning on model trained on SynthesizedInstruments metrics achieved satisfying results significantly faster than on finetuning of piano on weights trained for guitar-only recordings or learning model from random weights. This interesting capability may be used to quickly adapt existing automatic music transcription models for another type of instruments. It is visualized on Fig. 3. It is especially visible for finetuning to MAPS dataset. Learning from randomly initialized weights needed about 600 epochs to achieve good results in measured metrics. When we tried to finetune model trained on Guitarset it needed a similar time to achieve the same results for MAPS metrics as the model trained on Synthesized Instruments. For GuitarSet data we can see, that both pretraining on MAPS and Synthesized Instruments gave similar results from the first epoch. It indicates that model trained on synthesized data is very good candidate to perform transfer and quickly achieve well results for different timbres.

4.4   Lessons Learned

We may claim from the results that the model trained on Synthesized Instruments performed well for MAPS and GuitarSet even after zero-shot transfer. It can perform transcription on real-world recordings without seeing any real-world sample (RQ1 answered). After transfer from Synthesized Instruments, we showed that both GuitarSet and MAPS datasets are easily adjustable to the target domain. The time to achieve satisfying results in MAPS evaluation is significantly better for Synthesized Instruments than for GuitarSet, which gives hope for such a model's usefulness to create adjustable submodels quickly focused on specific instruments (RQ2 answered). Finetuning after initialization with weights trained for Synthesized Instruments on the MAPS achieved the best result for this dataset. Finetunning on GuitarSet real-world recordings of the model learned on MAPS seems to perform better in most cases. It may be related to the fact that the model trained on the MAPS dataset learned to handle microphone-originated noises better. From the results of experiments, a model well-trained on real-world piano recordings may be a better candidate to transfer knowledge to a model focused on other instruments (RQ3 answered). However, GuitarSet is a small dataset, and more experiments with different real-world instrument recordings and samples may be needed to assess the usefulness of the training in the Synthesized Instruments domain.

5   Conclusion

We presented that the synthesized audio data may be a valuable possible source of knowledge to train models for real-world music data. Artificially created different timbres of instruments allow the model to generalize other instrument outputs and perform well on real-world data after zero-shot training. This model cannot directly compete with a model trained on diverse real-world data containing many features related to environmental conditions like different sounds in recording and microphone-specific noises. Transfer of knowledge at the beginning of training allows us to quickly create models with satisfying metrics values, which may be especially useful for problems where the different distributions occur over time. After a long training session, applying knowledge from the model trained on synthesized data may improve existing metrics for more complicated datasets. It may be a good reason for making prototypes for another kind of models focused on resolving automatic music transcription.

Further research may focus on the impact of adding further synthesized instruments to experiment on automatic music transcription generalization and to check the influence of input modification realized by special audio filtering on output. It may be worth reviewing domain-specific spectrogram changes related to different timbres, which could extract special traits specific to each timbre. Finding accurate solutions for spectrogram representation for different instruments is essential to ensure that further research will overcome problems with music transcription generalization.

Acknowledgment. This work is supported by the CEUS-UNISONO programme, which has received funding from the National Science Centre, Poland under grant agreement No. 2020/02/Y/ST6/00037. We would like to thank Jędrzej Kozal for his support during creation of this work.

References

1. Allen, J.: Short term spectral analysis, synthesis, and modification by discrete fourier transform. IEEE Trans. Acoust. Speech Signal Process. **25**(3), 235–238 (1977)
2. Benetos, E., Dixon, S., Duan, Z., Ewert, S.: Automatic music transcription: An overview. IEEE Signal Process. Mag. **36**(1), 20–30 (2018)
3. Brown, J.C.: Calculation of a constant q spectral transform. J. Acoustical Soc. Am. **89**(1), 425–434 (1991)
4. Cheuk, K.W., Agres, K., Herremans, D.: The impact of audio input representations on neural network based music transcription. In: 2020 International Joint Conference on Neural Networks (IJCNN), pp. 1–6. IEEE (2020)
5. Cheuk, K.W., Anderson, H., Agres, K., Herremans, D.: nnaudio: An on-the-fly gpu audio to spectrogram conversion toolbox using 1d convolutional neural networks. IEEE Access **8**, 161981–162003 (2020)
6. Cheuk, K.W., Herremans, D., Su, L.: Reconvat: A semi-supervised automatic music transcription framework for low-resource real-world data. In: Proceedings of the 29th ACM International Conference on Multimedia, pp. 3918–3926 (2021)
7. Cheuk, K.W., Luo, Y.J., Benetos, E., Herremans, D.: The effect of spectrogram reconstruction on automatic music transcription: An alternative approach to improve transcription accuracy. In: 2020 25th International Conference on Pattern Recognition (ICPR), pp. 9091–9098. IEEE (2021)
8. Emiya, V., Bertin, N., David, B., Badeau, R.: Maps-a piano database for multipitch estimation and automatic transcription of music (2010)
9. Gardner, J., Simon, I., Manilow, E., Hawthorne, C., Engel, J.: Mt3: Multi-task multitrack music transcription. arXiv preprint arXiv:2111.03017 (2021)
10. Hawthorne, C., et al.: Onsets and frames: Dual-objective piano transcription. arXiv preprint arXiv:1710.11153 (2017)
11. Hawthorne, C., et al.: Enabling factorized piano music modeling and generation with the maestro dataset. arXiv preprint arXiv:1810.12247 (2018)
12. Hernandez-Olivan, C., Zay Pinilla, I., Hernandez-Lopez, C., Beltran, J.R.: A comparison of deep learning methods for timbre analysis in polyphonic automatic music transcription. Electronics **10**(7), 810 (2021)
13. Maman, B., Bermano, A.H.: Unaligned supervision for automatic music transcription in the wild. In: International Conference on Machine Learning, pp. 14918–14934. PMLR (2022)
14. Radford, A., et al.: Learning transferable visual models from natural language supervision. In: International Conference on Machine Learning, pp. 8748–8763. PMLR (2021)
15. Raffel, C., et al.: Mir_eval: A transparent implementation of common mir metrics. In: ISMIR, pp. 367–372 (2014)
16. Ronneberger, O., Fischer, P., Brox, T.: U-Net: convolutional networks for biomedical image segmentation. In: Navab, N., Hornegger, J., Wells, W.M., Frangi, A.F. (eds.) MICCAI 2015. LNCS, vol. 9351, pp. 234–241. Springer, Cham (2015). https://doi.org/10.1007/978-3-319-24574-4_28

17. Simonetta, F., Avanzini, F., Ntalampiras, S.: A perceptual measure for evaluating the resynthesis of automatic music transcriptions. Multimedia Tools Appli. **81**(22), 32371–32391 (2022)
18. Wu, Y.T., Chen, B., Su, L.: Multi-instrument automatic music transcription with self-attention-based instance segmentation. IEEE/ACM Trans. Audio Speech Lang. Process. **28**, 2796–2809 (2020)
19. Xi, Q., Bittner, R.M., Pauwels, J., Ye, X., Bello, J.P.: Guitarset: A dataset for guitar transcription. In: ISMIR, pp. 453–460 (2018)

The Geometry of Decision Borders Between Affine Space Prototypes for Nearest Prototype Classifiers

M. Mohannazadeh Bakhtiari[1], A. Villmann[2], and T. Villmann[1]([✉])(iD)

[1] Saxon Institute for Computational Intelligence and Machine Learning (SICIM), University of Applied Sciences Mittweida, Mittweida, Germany
thomas.villmann@hs-mittweida.de
[2] Berufliches Schulzentrum Döbeln-Mittweida, Mittweida, DE, Germany

Abstract. In this paper, the geometry of decision border between affine sub-spaces is investigated. Affine sub-spaces are used as prototypes in machine learning approaches such as "Tangent Learning Vector Quantization" and "Tangent Distance Kernel for Support Vector Machines" for classification of data. These models assume that there are class invariant manifolds that can be locally approximated by an affine space of similar dimensions. However, in practice this assumption may not always be true, because the affine spaces compete to provide a suitable local metric that leads to proper decision boundaries for an optimal separation and classification in the feature space. Therefore, considering affine spaces together with the corresponding decision borders is necessary when drawing conclusion about the geometry of the classification problem. An understanding of the type of decision border, between two affine sub-spaces, can be used to modify related learning methods, prevent undesirable scenarios, and gain insights about the geometry of the data set. We will show that the decision borders, that are basically quadratic surfaces, can be affine spaces, Hyper-Cones, or hyperbolic paraboloids embedded in the feature space. Each type of border suggests a relative formation of data points. We will also show when a linear decision border happens.

1 Introduction

Prototype-based learning algorithms, such as Support Vector Machine [12] and Learning Vector Quantization [5,9], are simple interpretable methods for classification of data. However, they often do not achieve the accuracy and performance of state-of-the-art methods, such as deep neural networks. A fundamental problem of prototype-based methods is the linear decision boundaries, defined by the prototypes in the feature space. when classification problem is not linearly separable, a relatively large number of prototypes are required for an acceptable accuracy and performance [6].

Recently, *S. Saralajew and T. Villmann* [7] proposed more complicated prototypes, that are affine prototypes (sub-spaces), rather than vectors. The task

M.M. Bakhtiari—is supported by an ESF PhD grant.

L. Rutkowski et al. (Eds.): ICAISC 2023, LNAI 14125, pp. 134–144, 2023.
https://doi.org/10.1007/978-3-031-42505-9_12

of affine prototypes is to fit or approximate the tangent space of transform-invariant manifolds in the data space [10]. To appreciate the calculation of a tangent vector, the reader is referred to a paper by *Simard et al.* [11]. The decision boundary (border) between two such affine prototypes could be a linear or non-linear manifold. Since each affine prototype creates a local metric, Tangent GLVQ can be compared to Localized Relevance LVQ [3], in which prototypes compete to create optimal decision borders. However, the decision borders have not been investigated for Localized Relevance LVQ and, now, we have a chance to investigate the borders in the context of affine spaces.

In general, the theories in this paper can be used as post-training for troubleshooting and to obtain information about how the data points are relatively distributed. In particular, we would like to study the type of decision boundaries that may arise when using affine prototypes (affine sub-spaces) instead of simple vectors. Destructive situations may be prevented by recognising potential problems. More information can be found in the experiments Sect. 4. Note that the theory, that is developed in this paper, is applicable to similar methods such as Tangent Distance Kernel for Support Vector Machines [2].

When classifying the data using affine prototypes, there is a case when two affine prototypes intersect in the feature space. In this case, there is a chance that the decision boundary is linear. We will show when this happens in Sect. 3 and, also, how to prevent linear borders. If the border is non-linear, then the border is a hyper-cone and it divides the space in more than two sections. For the sake of interpretability and assuming that data points of the same class lie on a continuous manifold, one might be interested to have boundaries that divide the space in only two sections. If the two affine prototypes do not intersect and they are not parallel, then we will prove that the decision border is a Hyperbolic Parabolic surface. In general, by determining the type of decision borders after training phase, we may have some idea about how data points in each section are relatively located. Note that there is an opportunity to extend the work in this paper by considering restricted tangent distances [8] for more flexible decision boundaries.

The remaining of the paper is ordered as follows. The necessary mathematical background is covered in Sect. 2. In Sect. 3, the geometry of the decision boundary between affine spaces, is investigated and potential problem are mentioned. In Sect. 4, previous works about the application of affine spaces are further analyzed. Finally, in Sect. 5, the paper is concluded.

2   Background Mathematics

In this section mathematical notions and notations, that are used in this paper, are briefly noted. We will use capital and lowercase bold letters (such as $\mathbb{M}$ and $\mathbf{x}$) to represent matrices and vectors, respectively. Normal letters (such as x) are reserved for scalars.

A m - dimensional affine prototype is defined by a pair $(\mathbb{W}, \mathbf{w})$, such that $\mathbb{W}$ is a $n \times m$ matrix with orthonormal columns $\mathbf{w}_i$ and $\mathbf{w} \in \mathbb{R}^n$ is the translation of the subspace from the origin. In this paper, we assume that matrix $\mathbb{W}$, that defines the subspace of an affine space, has considerably more rows than columns, because we are assuming that the dimensions m of affine spaces is relatively small compared to the dimensions of the feature space n. The column space $C(\mathbb{W})$ of matrix $\mathbb{W}$ is a subspace in $\mathbb{R}^n$, that is spanned by columns of $\mathbb{W}$. Subspaces $C(\mathbb{W})$ and $C(\mathbb{V})$ may have a non-empty intersection that is a subspace denoted by $C(\mathbb{W}) \cap C(\mathbb{V})$. Subspace $C(\mathbb{W}) - C(\mathbb{V})$ is basically the subspace spanned by columns of $\mathbb{W}$ and not by columns of $\mathbb{V}$.

Given two sub-spaces described by matrices $\mathbb{W}$ and $\mathbb{V}$, we define the mutual degree of freedom of the sub-spaces to be the dimensions of the sub-space $C([\mathbb{W}, \mathbb{V}]) - (C(\mathbb{W}) \cap C(\mathbb{V}))$, where $[\mathbb{W}, \mathbb{V}]$ is the matrix created by the horizontal concatenation of matrices $\mathbb{W}$ and $\mathbb{V}$. It can be proven that the mutual degree of freedom is equal to $2 \cdot Rank([\mathbb{W}, \mathbb{V}]) - Rank(\mathbb{W}) - Rank(\mathbb{V})$. We also define the union matrix $\mathbb{U}(\mathbb{W}, \mathbb{V})$ of matrices $\mathbb{W}$ and $\mathbb{V}$ to be a matrix that spans the sub-space $C([\mathbb{W}, \mathbb{V}])$ and has orthonormal columns.

The Tangent distances of a data point $\varkappa$ to affine prototype $(\mathbb{W}, \mathbb{w})$ is defined as

$$d_T(\varkappa, \mathbb{W}, \mathbb{w}) = \left((\varkappa - \mathbb{w})^T \cdot (I - \mathbb{W}\mathbb{W}^T) \cdot (\varkappa - \mathbb{w})\right)^{\frac{1}{2}} \tag{1}$$

Matrix $I - \mathbb{W}\mathbb{W}^T$ is projection matrix over the complement space of the column space $C(\mathbb{W})$.

A k - dimensional manifold $\mathcal{M}$, embedded in $\mathbb{R}^n$, is a set of points $\varkappa$ such that, for each point $\varkappa$, there is neighborhood of $\varkappa$ that is homeomorphic to an open set in $\mathbb{R}^k$. In this paper, we assume that the manifolds are differentiable as well, such that we can conveniently define local coordinates, whose transformation into one another is a diffeomorphism. The reader is referred to the first chapter of textbook by *Amari* [1] for more information regarding differentiable manifolds.

A n-dimensional quadratic equation $\varkappa^T \cdot \mathbb{M} \cdot \varkappa + \varkappa^T \cdot \mathbb{v} + c = 0$, with $\varkappa \in \mathbb{R}^n$ and a square matrix $\mathbb{M}$, represents the surface of a hypercone if $c = 0$ and $\mathbb{v}$ is the zero vector. If $\mathbb{M}$ is singular and at least one of the elements of $\mathbb{v}$, associated with a zero eigenvalue λ_i of $\mathbb{M}$, is not equal to zero, then the surface is called a Paraboloid. If all the eigenvalues of $\mathbb{M}$ have either the same sign or they are zero, then the paraboloid is an Elliptic paraboloid. Otherwise, it is called a hyperbolic paraboloid. An example of a hyperpolic paraboloid in 3 - dimensional space is a 2 - dimensional quadratic saddle surface. We define the quadratic degree of freedom of a quadratic equation to be the number of non-zero eigenvalues of matrix $\mathbb{M}$.

3   Geometry of Decision Boundary Between Affine Spaces

In this section, we investigate the geometry of the decision boundary between two unrestricted affine prototypes (sub-spaces) in $\mathbb{R}^n$. We first define the general equation for the points that lie on the decision border between two affine prototypes. Then, the general equation is simplified for the case where the two affine prototypes intersect. For this special case, we will show that the decision surface is either a hyper-cone or two intersecting linear surfaces. Furthermore, we will show under which condition the decision boundary of intersecting affine prototypes is non-linear. Note that we would like non-linear boundaries to have better flexibility for classification of data. Since intersecting affine prototypes often give hyper-cones as decision borders and because we often like to have parabolic boundaries (Parabolic surfaces divide the space in two, unlike hyper-cones), we show the condition under which two affine prototypes do not intersect in the feature space. Finally, we show that, given the affine prototypes did not intersect, the decision border would be a Hyperbolic paraboloid. We will further investigate the local curvature of the Hyperbolic Parabolic surfaces for a better geometric imagination of data manifolds.

Based on tangent distance (1), the decision boundary between prototypes $(\mathbb{W}, \mathsf{w})$ and $(\mathbb{V}, \mathsf{v})$ is all $\mathsf{x} \in \mathbb{R}^n$ that satisfy

$$(\mathsf{x} - \mathsf{w})^T \cdot \mathbb{M}_w \cdot (\mathsf{x} - \mathsf{w}) = (\mathsf{x} - \mathsf{v})^T \cdot \mathbb{M}_v \cdot (\mathsf{x} - \mathsf{v}) \tag{2}$$

where $\mathbb{M}_w = I - \mathbb{W}\mathbb{W}^T$ and $\mathbb{M}_v = I - \mathbb{V}\mathbb{V}^T$. Before continuing with the main issues, we would like to establish that the decision borders are undoubtedly the union of $n - 1$ - dimensional manifolds. Given an affine space $(\mathbb{W}, \mathsf{w})$, the tangent distance $d_T(\mathsf{x}, \mathbb{W}, \mathsf{w})$ (1) is a continuous function on $\mathbb{R}^n$. We now define $f(\mathsf{x}) = d_T(\mathsf{x}, \mathbb{W}, \mathsf{w}) - d_T(\mathsf{x}, \mathbb{V}, \mathsf{v})$ which is continuous too (sum of continuous function is continuous). Set of x, that satisfies $f(\mathsf{x}) = 0$, is the boundary between the affine spaces. Topologically, the boundary must divide the space $\mathbb{R}^n$ into at least two sections. In order to do so, the boundary must be a finite union of $n-1$ dimensional continuous manifolds.

If two affine spaces intersect, there exists a vector $\mathsf{l} \in \mathbb{R}^n$ that belongs to the intersection. Without loss of generality, we translate the affine spaces by vector $-\mathsf{l}$ to the origin. Then, the affine spaces are simply linear m-dimensional subspaces defined by matrices $\mathbb{W}$ and $\mathbb{V}$. Now, the set of equidistant points $\bar{\mathsf{x}} = \mathsf{x} - \mathsf{l}$ from the sub-spaces satisfy

$$\bar{\mathsf{x}}^T \cdot \mathbb{M}_w \cdot \bar{\mathsf{x}} = \bar{\mathsf{x}}^T \cdot \mathbb{M}_v \cdot \bar{\mathsf{x}} \tag{3}$$

by taking the right hand side to the left, we get

$$\bar{\mathsf{x}}^T \cdot \mathbb{M}_{wv} \cdot \bar{\mathsf{x}} = 0. \tag{4}$$

where $\mathbb{M}_{wv} = \mathbb{M}_w - \mathbb{M}_v$ is a symmetrical matrix. Also $\mathbb{M}_{wv}$ is neither positive nor negative semi-definite. This can be proven by finding two different x for which $\mathsf{x}^T \cdot \mathbb{M}_{wv} \cdot \mathsf{x}$ has different signs (note that $\mathbb{M}_{wv}$ is the difference of two projection matrices). A consequence is that $\mathbb{M}_{wv}$ always has at least one positive and one negative eigenvalues, given that the affine spaces have the same dimensions and there are two non-zero eigenvalues.

Now, we provide a lemma (without proof) to show that the decision boundary of equation (4) is a hyper-cone.

Lemma 1 *For a symmetric matrix $\mathbb{M}$, there exists a linear transformation $\mathbb{T}$: $\mathsf{x} \to \mathsf{y}$, such that $\mathbb{M} = \mathbb{T}^T \cdot \Lambda \cdot \mathbb{T}$ and $\mathsf{x}^T \cdot \mathbb{M} \cdot \mathsf{x} = \sum_i \lambda_i \cdot y_i^2$. Note that $\mathbb{T}$ is an orthogonal matrix, whose rows contain the eigenvectors of $\mathbb{M}$, λ_i are eigenvalues* of $\mathbb{M}$ corresponding to the i-th eigenvector, and $y = [y_1, \ldots, y_n]^T$ is a coordinate system that is aligned with the eigenvectors.

Using theorem 1, we may change the coordinates system and re-write Eq. (4) as

$$\bar{x}^T \cdot \mathbb{M}_{wv} \cdot \bar{x} = \sum_i \lambda_i \cdot y_i^2 = 0 \tag{5}$$

which is the equation of a hyper-cone in n-dimensional space. The hyper-cone will turn into two intersecting linear sub-spaces if affine prototypes intersect and their mutual degree of freedom (defined in Sect. 2) is 2. We show this using (5) and noting the fact that $\mathbb{M}_{wv}$ has a maximum rank of k, when the mutual degree of freedom of $\mathbb{W}$ and $\mathbb{V}$ is k. If $\mathbb{M}_{wv}$ has rank 2, then it only has two nonzero eigenvalues and the equation of the surface (5) is basically $\lambda_i \cdot y_i^2 + \lambda_j \cdot y_j^2 = 0$ for some i, j. Note that, in this case, λ_i and λ_j have opposite signs, as explained earlier in this section.

In order to avoid hyper-cones, there should be no intersection between affine prototypes. In the next theorem, the condition that should be met to avoid intersection is stated.

Theorem 2 *Affine prototypes* $(\mathbb{W}, w)$ *and* $(\mathbb{V}, v)$ *intersect iff the tangent distance* $d_T(w, \mathbb{U}(\mathbb{W}, \mathbb{V}), v)$ *is equal to zero, where* $\mathbb{U}(\mathbb{W}, \mathbb{V})$ *(defined in Sect. 2) is the union matrix of matrices* $\mathbb{W}$ *and* $\mathbb{V}$.

Proof. A point x in the intersection can be written as

$$x = w + \mathbb{W} \cdot \alpha = v + \mathbb{V} \cdot \beta \tag{6}$$

for m-dimensional vectors α and β. From above, we get

$$\mathbb{W} \cdot \alpha - \mathbb{V} \cdot \beta = v - w \tag{7}$$

The left hand side of above equation is basically the span of $C(\mathbb{W})$ and $C(\mathbb{V})$ together. So, we can write the last equation as

$$[\mathbb{W}, \mathbb{V}] \cdot \gamma = v - w \tag{8}$$

for $\gamma \in \mathbb{R}^{2 \cdot m}$.

there is a γ to satisfy the above equation, only if $v - w$ is in $C([\mathbb{W}, \mathbb{V}])$, which means that the projection of $v - w$ on the subspace $C([\mathbb{W}, \mathbb{V}])$ is the vector itself. Therefore, the tangent distance of $v - w$ to the subspace $C([\mathbb{W}, \mathbb{V}])$ is equal to zero, meaning that $d_T(w, \mathbb{U}(\mathbb{W}, \mathbb{V}), v) = 0$.

If two affine prototypes $(\mathbb{W}, w)$ and $(\mathbb{V}, v)$ do not intersect and their column spaces span different sub-spaces, then there is a high chance the decision boundary between them is non-linear. Here, we show that the border can potentially be either an elliptic or a hyperbolic paraboloid. To show that, we may re-write (2) as below.

$$\varkappa^T \cdot \mathbb{M}_{wv} \cdot \varkappa - 2 \cdot \varkappa^T \cdot (\mathbb{M}_w \cdot \mathsf{w} - \mathbb{M}_v \cdot \mathsf{v}) = \mathsf{v}^T \cdot \mathbb{M}_v \cdot \mathsf{v} - \mathsf{w}^T \cdot \mathbb{M}_w \cdot \mathsf{w} \qquad (9)$$

where $\mathbb{M}_w = I - \mathbb{W} \cdot \mathbb{W}^T$ and $\mathbb{M}_v = I - \mathbb{V} \cdot \mathbb{V}^T$. Now, we use Theorem 1 again to decompose $\mathbb{M}_{wv} = \mathbb{T}^T \cdot \Lambda \cdot \mathbb{T}$ and make the transformation $\mathbb{T} \cdot \varkappa = \mathsf{y}$, with $\mathsf{y} = [y_1, \ldots, y_n]^T$. Then, the above equation becomes

$$\sum_i \lambda_i \cdot y_i^2 - 2 \cdot \mathsf{y}^T \cdot (\mathbb{T} \cdot \mathbb{M}_w \cdot \mathsf{w} - \mathbb{T} \cdot \mathbb{M}_v \cdot \mathsf{v}) = \mathsf{v}^T \cdot \mathbb{M}_v \cdot \mathsf{v} - \mathsf{w}^T \cdot \mathbb{M}_w \cdot \mathsf{w} \qquad (10)$$

The right hand side of above equation is a constant that depends only on the two affine prototypes and not on the specific choice of w and v. Since $\mathbb{M}_{wv}$ is probably singular, many of λ_i in decomposition $\mathbb{M}_{wv} = \mathbb{T}^T \cdot \Lambda \cdot \mathbb{T}$ are zero. Therefore, some of the terms in the sum of the quadratics in (10) will definitely not exist. The non-zero elements of vector $\mathbb{T} \cdot \mathbb{M}_w \cdot \mathsf{w} - \mathbb{T} \cdot \mathbb{M}_v \cdot \mathsf{v}$, that are associated to a zero λ_i, determine the type decision border. We prove that the border is a paraboloid. To prove the claim, we take z_i to be a n-dimensional vector, with 1 at position i and zero elsewhere. Given that the i-th row of $\mathbb{T}$ is the i-th eigenvector $\mathfrak{t}_i$ of matrix $\mathbb{M}_{wv}$, the following inner product is calculated for all i, for which $\lambda_i = 0$

$$z_i^T \cdot (\mathbb{T} \cdot \mathbb{M}_w \cdot \mathsf{w} - \mathbb{T} \cdot \mathbb{M}_v \cdot \mathsf{v}) = \mathfrak{t}_i \cdot \mathbb{M}_w \cdot \mathsf{w} - \mathfrak{t}_i \cdot \mathbb{M}_v \cdot \mathsf{v} \qquad (11)$$

Further, we have already assumed that $\mathbb{M}_{wv} \cdot \mathfrak{t}_i^T = 0$, which gives $\mathfrak{t}_i \cdot \mathbb{M}_w = \mathfrak{t}_i \cdot \mathbb{M}_v$ (because of the symmetry of $\mathbb{M}_w$ and $\mathbb{M}_v$). Hence, we can write (11) as

$$\mathfrak{t}_i \cdot \mathbb{M}_w \cdot \mathsf{w} - \mathfrak{t}_i \cdot \mathbb{M}_v \cdot \mathsf{v} = \mathfrak{t}_i \cdot \mathbb{M}_w \cdot \mathsf{w} - \mathfrak{t}_i \cdot \mathbb{M}_w \cdot \mathsf{v} = \mathfrak{t}_i \cdot \mathbb{M}_w \cdot (\mathsf{w} - \mathsf{v}) \qquad (12)$$

Since we assumed that the dimension of affine prototypes m is much lower than the dimension of the feature space n, there always exists an eigenvector $\mathfrak{t}_i^T$, with $\lambda_i = 0$, such that $\mathfrak{t}_i \cdot \mathbb{M}_w = \mathfrak{t}_i \cdot \mathbb{M}_v \neq 0$. The eigenvector basically lies on the orthogonal complement space of $C([\mathbb{W}, \mathbb{V}])$. We may now write (12) as

$$\mathfrak{t}_i \cdot \mathbb{M}_w \cdot (\mathsf{w} - \mathsf{v}) = \mathfrak{t}_i \cdot (\mathsf{w} - \mathsf{v}) \qquad (13)$$

We know that $\mathfrak{t}_i$, with $\lambda_i = 0$, belongs to the orthogonal complement space of $C([\mathbb{W}, \mathbb{V}])$. Also, based on theorem 2 and assuming that the affine spaces do not intersect, $\mathsf{w} - \mathsf{v}$ has a component in the orthogonal complement space of $C([\mathbb{W}, \mathbb{V}])$. Therefore, there is at least one $\mathfrak{t}_i$, with $\lambda_i = 0$, for which $\mathfrak{t}_i \cdot (\mathsf{w} - \mathsf{v})$ is non-zero. Consequently, the equation (10) is the surface of a high-dimensional paraboloid, as defined in Sect. 2, given that the affine spaces do not intersect.

The next question is whether the decision border is Elliptic or Hyperbolic, given the decision border is a paraboloid. To answer this question, one should investigate the local curvature of the border manifold in hand. We may look at the change in normal vector at each point p on the manifold in the direction of tangent vectors to acquire information about the local curvature. $\mathcal{M}$ is the $n-1$ dimensional manifold of the decision border between spaces $\mathbb{W}$ and $\mathbb{V}$ and $\mathsf{p} \in \mathcal{M}$, meaning that $\mathbb{p}$ satisfies equation (10). The orientation of the tangent space of $\mathcal{M}$ at $\mathbb{p}$ is determined by the normal vector $\mathbb{n}(\mathbb{p}) = \Lambda \cdot \mathbb{p} - (\mathbb{T} \cdot \mathsf{M}_w \mathbb{w} - \mathbb{T} \cdot \mathsf{M}_v \mathbb{v})$. we prove the claim below.

Theorem 3 *If we define* $f(\mathbb{y}) = \sum_i \lambda_i \cdot y_i^2 - \mathbb{y}^T \cdot \mathbb{b} - c$, *where* $\mathbb{b} = 2 \cdot (\mathbb{T} \cdot \mathsf{M}_w \cdot \mathbb{w} - \mathbb{T} \cdot \mathsf{M}_v \cdot \mathbb{v})$ *and* $c = \mathbb{v}^T \cdot \mathsf{M}_v \cdot \mathbb{v} - \mathbb{w}^T \cdot \mathsf{M}_w \cdot \mathbb{w}$, *then vector* $\frac{\partial f}{\partial \mathbb{y}}\big|_{\mathbb{y}=\mathbb{p}} = 2 \cdot \Lambda \cdot \mathbb{p} - \mathbb{b}$ *at point* $\mathbb{p} \in \mathcal{M}$ *is perpendicular to the tangent space* $T(\mathbb{p})$ *at point* $\mathbb{p}$.

Proof. To prove, we assume $\mathbb{e} \in T(\mathbb{p})$ and $\mathbb{p}$ satisfies (10). Then,

$$\lim_{\epsilon \to 0} \frac{(\mathbb{p} + \epsilon \cdot \mathbb{e})^T \cdot \Lambda \cdot (\mathbb{p} + \epsilon \cdot \mathbb{e}) - (\mathbb{p} + \epsilon \cdot \mathbb{e})^T \cdot \mathbb{b} - c}{\epsilon} = 2 \cdot \mathbb{e}^T \cdot \Lambda \cdot \mathbb{y} - \mathbb{e}^T \cdot \mathbb{b} = 0$$

(14)

should be true. This can only mean that $2 \cdot \Lambda \cdot \mathbb{y} - \mathbb{b}$ must be perpendicular to all tangent vectors $\mathbb{e}$ at $\mathbb{p}$.

We now assume a local coordinate system at point $\mathbb{p} \in \mathcal{M}$, defined by the set of mutually perpendicular vectors $\{\mathbb{e}_1, \ldots, \mathbb{e}_{n-1}, \mathbb{e}_n = \mathsf{M} \cdot \mathbb{p}\}$, where $\{\mathbb{e}_1, \ldots, \mathbb{e}_{n-1}\} \in T(\mathbb{p})$.

Starting from $\mathbb{p} \in \mathcal{M}$, we move in the direction of a tangent vector $\mathbb{e} \in T(\mathbb{p})$ and observe the change in the normal vector $\mathbb{n}$. The new point $\mathbb{p} + \epsilon \cdot \mathbb{e}$ is assumed to be on the manifold $\mathcal{M}$, for small ϵ. The normal at $\mathbb{p} + \epsilon \cdot \mathbb{e}$ is $2 \cdot \Lambda \cdot (\mathbb{p} + \epsilon \cdot \mathbb{e}) - \mathbb{b}$. The inner product $\mathbb{e}^T \cdot (2 \cdot \Lambda \cdot (\mathbb{p} + \epsilon \cdot \mathbb{e}) - \mathbb{b})$, between the normal vector at $\mathbb{p} + \epsilon \cdot \mathbb{e}$ and the tangent vector $\mathbb{e}$, shows the direction of curving. If the inner product is negative, then the manifold curves in on the side of the manifold indicated by normal vector $\mathbb{n}(\mathbb{p})$, when moving in $\mathbb{e}$ direction. If the inner product is positive, then the manifold curves to the opposite side of the manifold with respect to the normal vector $\mathbb{n}(\mathbb{p})$, when moving in $\mathbb{e}$ direction. Since $\mathbb{e}^T \cdot (2 \cdot \Lambda \cdot \mathbb{p} - \mathbb{b}) = 0$, the inner product can be simplified to $2 \cdot \epsilon \cdot \mathbb{e}^T \cdot \Lambda \cdot \mathbb{e}$. This means that we can characterize the manifold $\mathcal{M}$ at $\mathbb{p}$ by the signs of $\mathbb{e}_i^T \cdot \Lambda \cdot \mathbb{e}_i$, for all $i = 1, 2, \ldots, n-1$. Since λ_i is an eigenvalue of matrix M and matrix M is neither positive nor negative semi-definite, we state that the decision border between non-intersecting affine prototypes of similar dimensions is a hyperbolic paraboloid.

4   Experiments

We start with a 2-dimensional non-linear toy classification problem for demonstration purposes. Assume that we are given the classification problem that is depicted in Fig. 1. Note that, if we take two one-dimensional affine spaces as prototypes in 2 dimensions, then the prototypes either meet in the space or they are parallel. In both cases, the decision border consists of the vertical line (linear decision borders). Therefore, in this specific example, we take a one-dimensional affine space to represent the purple class and a single-point (vector) prototype to represent the yellow class. After training, the blue line is the affine prototype that represents the purple class in Fig. 1 and the red point is the prototype that represents the yellow class. Note that the square of distances in context of GMLVQ are calculated using the equation $d_\Omega^2(\varkappa, v) = (\varkappa - v)^T \cdot \Omega^T \cdot \Omega \cdot (\varkappa - v)$, where Ω is the local mapping matrix for $\varkappa$, and v is the bias vector of the tangent space. Therefore, the corresponding local Ω-matrices based on GMLVQ are $\Omega_p = \begin{bmatrix} 1 & 0 \\ 0 & 0 \end{bmatrix}$ and $\Omega_y = \begin{bmatrix} 1 & 0 \\ 0 & 1 \end{bmatrix}$ for the purple and the yellow classes, respectively. Also, the bias vectors are $v_p = [0.6, 0]^T$ and $v_y = [0, 0]^T$ for the purple and the yellow classes, respectively. The black parabola is the non-linear decision border between the two prototypes. Note that the classes are completely separated by the decision border and we needed only two prototypes. With normal LVQ, more than two prototypes are required to solve this classification problem.

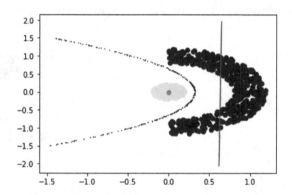

Fig. 1. A 2-D toy problem to visualize non-linear decision border (black parabola) determined by the prototypes: an affine space for the purple class (blue line), and a single-point prototype for the yellow class (red dot), see text for explanation. (Color figure online)

We now move on to higher dimensions to show the capacity of the method. *S. Saralajew et al.* [6] mentioned that MNIST data set is quite flat, meaning that each class can be roughly represented by an affine prototype. However, one should notice that the affine prototypes have been obtained using TGLVQ, that uses a repulsion mechanism for adaptation. This observation raises this question: Do the affine prototypes fairly represent the data manifolds for each class, or they only position themselves so that their decision borders separate the classes effectively. If the latter is the case, then does the dimensions of the affine prototypes give any information about the true dimensions of the data manifolds? To address this problem practically, a toy data-set has been created and analyzed below.

Imagine the data set shown in Fig. 2a. A top view of the same data set is provided in Fig. 2b. The data lies on a 2-dimensional manifold and the problem in not linearly separable. Based on the theories of Tangent GLVQ [7], one will intuitively choose two planes (affine spaces of dimensions two) for the classification of this data set. We will further assume that the planes should roughly

represent their corresponding data with the same label. This leads to the two
planes intersecting in the space and the decision border between them is two
linear planes, which results in maximum 96% classification accuracy. However,
we have already stated that the problem is not linearly separable. Now, let us
imagine that we did not know the dimensions of the manifold and we have chosen the dimensions of the affine spaces to be 1 (two lines). After training using
TGLVQ, the line that represents the purple cluster aligns itself in y axis direction
and represents the purple data acceptably. However, the line that represents the
yellow class roughly goes through the yellow cluster in a perpendicular manner
(directed in z axis). The classification accuracy is 99% now. This experiment
suggests that we may neither know the true dimensions of the manifolds nor the
affine spaces may represent the corresponding data points in the space, even if
the algorithm has classified the data fairly accurately.

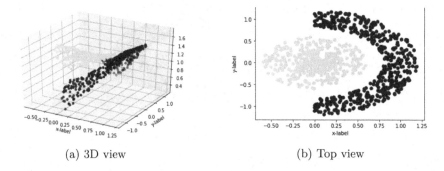

(a) 3D view   (b) Top view

Fig. 2. Toy data set

Now, we would like to compare normal Tangent GLVQ (TGLVQ) [7] and
Tangent LVQ (TLVQ), which is LVQ with affine prototypes and without repulsion mechanism, by applying both to MNIST dataset. TGLVQ, with ten 7-
dimensional affine prototypes, achieves 88.5% accuracy, which performs slightly
better than Generalized Learning Vector Quantization GLVQ [9]. TLVQ achieves
88.5%, 89.5%, and 93.3% accuracy with ten prototypes of dimensions 3, 5, and
7, respectively. It seems that the accuracy of TLVQ will not exceed 95% even
with affine prototypes of dimensions higher than 15. This result supports the
theory that MNIST data set is rather flat, since TLVQ, with only attraction
mechanism, has given better accuracy than TGLVQ, whose affine prototypes
may not confidently represent data manifolds. There is also an indication that
MNIST has class manifold dimensions of maximum 15, because the classification accuracy does no improve with affine prototypes of higher dimensions. For
both TGLVQ and TLVQ, we have approved (using theorem 2) that every two
affine prototypes do not intersect when the classification accuracy is above 85%.
This makes sense because that is roughly the maximum accuracy that a LVQ
method with normal prototypes (linear decision borders) can achieve. We conclude that the decision borders are hyperbolic paraboloids. In Fig. 3, we have

depicted the tangent distance $d_T(w_i, \cup(W_i, W_j), w_j)$ (based on theorem 2) for all pairs of affine prototypes corresponding to digits $i, j \in \{0, \ldots, 9\}$ after applying TLVQ to MNIST. Figure 3 suggest that the affine prototype that represents digit 9 is fairly close to the affine prototype of digits 4 as their mutual value is close to zero. Affine prototypes 3 and 8 are in the same situation. The matrix in Fig. 3 provides valuable information about the affine prototypes that are about to intersect.

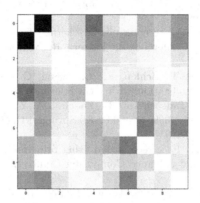

Fig. 3. A measure of closeness of affine prototypes for the MNIST dtata (9 classes - one prototype per class). The lighter a shade of gray is, the closer its value is to zero. (Color figure online)

As a final experiment, we have applied TGLVQ and TLVQ to Olivetti data set that consists of 400 facial images of 40 people. With a random 80% and 20% split of data set into training and test sets, respectively, the models were trained. The tangent spaces, for each class, were initialized at the top m eigen-faces, that were calculated using principal component analysis [4] of faces with the same label. Both TGLVQ and TLVQ show 96.25% accuracy after the initialization phase. TGLVQ achieves 98.75% accuracy after 6000 training steps, while TLVQ remains at the initial accuracy. Calculating $d_T(w_i, \cup(W_i, W_j), w_j)$ for classes i and j shows that most of the affine spaces are actually very close to each other, despite the high accuracy. In case of Olivetti data set, TGLVQ improves the accuracy in comparison to TLVQ, because it pushes affine spaces away from each other to avoid intersection.

5   Conclusion

Affine prototypes can be used for interpretable and effective classification learning of data. We have further investigated the types of decision border between affine prototypes, depending on how the affine spaces are relatively situated, for troubleshooting and to gain insight about the geometry of problems. We have conducted experiments to support the flatness of MNIST data set. We also showed that the affine prototypes do not intersect post training, when Tangent GLVQ or Tangent LVQ is applied to MNIST, to provide optimal decision borders.

References

1. Amari, S.-I., Nagaoka, H.: Methods of Information Geometry, vo;. 191. American Mathematical Soc. (2000)
2. Haasdonk, B., Keysers, D.: Tangent distance kernels for support vector machines. In: 2002 International Conference on Pattern Recognition, vol. 2, pp. 864–868. IEEE (2002)
3. Hammer, B., Villmann, T., Schleif, F.-M., Albani, C., Hermann, W.: Learning vector quantization classification with local relevance determination for medical data. In: Rutkowski, L., Tadeusiewicz, R., Zadeh, L.A., Żurada, J.M. (eds.) ICAISC 2006. LNCS (LNAI), vol. 4029, pp. 603–612. Springer, Heidelberg (2006). https://doi.org/10.1007/11785231_63
4. Kaur, R., Himanshi, E.: Face recognition using principal component analysis. In: 2015 IEEE International Advance Computing Conference (IACC), pp. 585–589. IEEE (2015)
5. Kohonen, T.: Learning vector quantization. In: Self-organizing maps, pp. 175–189. Springer (1995). https://doi.org/10.1007/978-3-642-97610-0_6
6. Saralajew, S., Holdijk, L., Rees, M., Villmann, T.: Robustness of generalized learning vector quantization models against adversarial attacks. In: International Workshop on Self-Organizing Maps, pp. 189–199. Springer (2019) https://doi.org/10.1007/978-3-030-19642-4_19
7. Saralajew, S., Villmann, T.: Adaptive tangent distances in generalized learning vector quantization for transformation and distortion invariant classification learning. In: 2016 International Joint Conference on Neural Networks (IJCNN), pp. 2672–2679. IEEE (2016)
8. Saralajew, S., Villmann, T.: Restricted tangent metrics for local data dissimilarities - mathematical treatment of the corresponding constrained optimization problem. Mach. Learn. Reports 11(MLR-01-2017), submitted (2017). www.techfak.uni-bielefeld.de/˜fschleif/mlr/mlr_01_2017.pdf, ISSN:1865–3960
9. Sato, A., Yamada, K.: Generalized learning vector quantization. In: Advances in Neural Information Processing Systems 8 (1995)
10. Simard, P., LeCun, Y., Denker, J.: Efficient pattern recognition using a new transformation distance. In: Advances in Neural Information Processing Systems 5 (1992)
11. Simard, P., Victorri, B., LeCun, Y., Denker, J.: Tangent prop-a formalism for specifying selected invariances in an adaptive network. In: Advances in Neural Information Processing Systems 4 (1991)
12. Suthaharan, S.: Support vector machine. In: Machine Learning Models and Algorithms for Big Data Classification. ISIS, vol. 36, pp. 207–235. Springer, Boston, MA (2016). https://doi.org/10.1007/978-1-4899-7641-3_9

An Interpretable Two-Layered Neural Network Structure–Based on Component-Wise Reasoning

M. Mohannazadeh Bakhtiari[(✉)] and T. Villmann[iD]

University of Applied Sciences Mittweida, Mittweida, Germany
m.mohannazade@gmail.com, thomas.villmann@hs-mittweida.de

Abstract. The success of deep neural networks have been compromised by their lack of interpretability. On the other hand, most interpretable models do not offer same accuracy as deep neural networks or the former depends on the latter. Inspired by Classification-by-Components networks, in this paper, we present a novel approach into designing a two-layered perceptron network, that offers a level of interpetability. Hence, we use the prediction power of a multi-layer perceptron, while a class of the adapted parameters make fair sense to human. We will visualize the weights, between input layer and the hidden layer, and show that Matching the right objective function with activation function of the output layer, is the key to interpreting the weights and their influence on component-wise classification.

Keywords: neural networks · multi layer perceptron · classification by components · interpretable models · probabilistic classification · convolutional neural networks · feature extraction

1 Introduction

A Multi Layer Perceptron (MLP) frequently has a better accuracy than other classification methods. Yet, one valid argument against MLPs is that they are difficult to interpret [1,2]. Those learning methods that offer interpretability, such as the family of Learning Vector Quantization (LVQ) [3–5], often do not achieve the superior accuracy of MLPs but are often close to that - namely the Matrix-GLVQ (GMLVQ) [6,7].

Thereby, we follow the definition of an interpretable system, which has to be interpretable by design (ante-hoc) whereas explainable systems require additional tools for interpretation [8,9,28]. Molnar [10] emphasises on the reason to provided alongside the decision, so the system can be called interpretable to a certain degree. To deal with the explainability problem of MLPs, a change in traditional MLP-design is required. Z. Chen et al. [12] consider why standard neural networks would potentially end up mixing concepts. Therefore, a careful design

M.M.B. is supported by an ESF PhD grant.

of neural networks can be a large step in having an appropriate interpretable classifier.

There has been attempts to make MLPs explainable. Some train an interpretable network post-hoc to imitate the original network [9,13,14,28]. Such methods need two separate networks and, hence, it is computationally expensive. Also, in case of inconsistency between parallel networks, troubleshooting would be a problem. A method that deploys interpretation as a side, correlated, network is FLINT [11]. FLINT allows the parallel networks to communicate in case of disagreement between the decisions, made by the two networks. Nonetheless, it comes with an extra parallel network, that would increase complexity. There are also other methods to achieve explainability that lack generality, as they use a specific setting for a specific scientific purpose [15–17,28].

In consequence, to make MLPs interpretable it has to be done by design, which requires a specific setting and training for the weights. To prove this claim, we introduce a MLP, such that the outputs of the last hidden layer are the level of detection of a component in the input and the weights between the output layer and the last hidden layer represent scaled correlation values between detection level of components and class hypothesis probabilities. We would call the last hidden layer the "component layer". In case of a two-layered MLP, the weights between input layer and the hidden layer represent members of the feature space and the corresponding features can be visualized. Moreover, in order to maintain the interpretability of information as they pass through layers, it is important to choose suitable activation functions and match it with a suitable local loss function.

The idea of using components for classification has already been proposed by [18], based on the fundamental paper of [19]. The method is called Classification-by-Components (CbC), that relies on Convolutional Neural Networks (CNN) to extract features. Similar to CbC, there are concept-based approaches that have slightly different architectures [20,21]. Nonetheless, the reasoning and components of CbC can be redefined in the framework of our MLP. We use probability theory to connect reasoning parameters to the adaptive weights of MLP. Note that there is a similar work, by M. Nauta at al. [22], that uses CNN and binary trees in neural networks to classify images. However, we have taken a different mathematical approach in this paper.

The contribution of this paper is as follows: 1- The concept of reasoning for the classification of data, that is introduced by S. Saralajew et al. [18], is redefined using the correlation between classes and detected features. Reasoning parameters will be defined according to the new definition. 2- A class of Interpretable Probabilistic Activation (IPA) functions is defined for the output layer. An output layer with IPA functions (unlike Softmax) does not lose information, when processing its input, and it maintains interpretability by allowing the network weights to approach the desired theoretical quantities, that are defined by correlation. Each IPA function is matched with an objective function that facilitates the process. 3- We will show that, under careful considerations and training, the weights of the network tend to a constant multiple of the theoretical correlation coefficients. Hence, the learnt weights are interpretable together with the discovered features.

In the remainder of this paper, we first provide a basic idea of Biederman reasoning [19], that is used in this paper for interpretation, in Sect. 2. In Sect. 3, we introduce a general interpretable architecture for MLPs and the connection between reasoning parameters and network adaptable parameters is explained. To visualize components, two-layered realizations of the interpretable MLP are introduced in Sect. 4. Section 5 contains the experiments on MNIST, Fashion-MNIST, and CIFAR10 data sets. Section 6 concludes the paper.

2   Biederman's Reasoning

The base of interpretation, in this paper, is provided by I. Biederman [19], who argues that human brain decomposes the structure of objects into basic components. The decomposition of an object into basic components helps with object classification. If a component is important to the recognition of an object, then the level of presence or absence of the component in the object is measured to achieve estimation about the nature of the object. Biederman's idea has been mathematically formalized in [18] yielding the CbC model. However, we are interested in a different formulation. We assume a data space $X \subset \mathbb{R}^m$, a set $\mathcal{K} = \{\mathcal{K}_1, \ldots, \mathcal{K}_n\}$ of components $\mathcal{K}_t \in \mathbb{R}^m$ and a set $S = \{1, 2, \ldots, c\}$ of data classes. The components are assumed to be characteristic features of the data. Further, we suppose a detection function $d_t : X \to [-1, 1]$ that determines the level of presence of component $\mathcal{K}_t$ in data $x \in X$. Hence, $d_t(\mathbf{x}) = -1$ means the full absence of component $\mathcal{K}_t$ in object x and $d_t(x) = 1$ means the full presence.

The reasoning quantity $m_{tj}^* \in (-1, 1)$ is introduced as the correlation between detection function $d_t(x)$ and the relative class probability $p(j|x) - p(j)$. Mathematically, the correlation is

$$m_{tj}^* = \frac{1}{\sigma_1 \cdot \sigma_2} \cdot \int_x [p(j|x) - p(j)] \cdot d_t(x) \cdot p(x) \cdot dx \tag{1}$$

where σ_1, σ_2 are standard deviations of $d_t(x)$ and $p(j|x)$, respectively. As a random variable, $d_t(x)$ is assumed to be uniform over $[-1, 1]$, with zero mean. Then, the standard deviation of $d_t(x)$ is $\sigma_1 = \sqrt{\frac{1}{3}}$. The mean of $p(j|x)$ is $p(j) = \int_x p(j|x) \cdot p(x) \cdot dx$. Note that we assumed σ_2 is equal for all classes j.

In (1), the differential definition of class hypothesis probability $p(j|x)$, with respect to the prior probability $p(j)$, makes a relative measure, as opposed to an absolute measure. Hence, m_{tj}^* determines how component $\mathcal{K}_t$ contributes to the classification of an object into class j. The contribution is positive if $p(j|x) > p(j)$, on average, and it is negative if $p(j|x) < p(j)$. Nonetheless, since we assumed the mean of $d_t(x)$ is zero, (1) is equal to

$$m_{tj}^* = \frac{1}{\sigma_1 \cdot \sigma_2} \cdot \int_x p(j|x) \cdot d_t(x) \cdot p(x) \cdot dx \tag{2}$$

We make the following definitions:

1- If $m_{tj}^* > 0$, then component $\mathcal{K}_t$ has "positive reasoning" for class j.

2- If $m_{tj}^* < 0$, then component $\mathcal{K}_t$ has "negative reasoning" for class j.

3- If $m_{tj}^* \approx 0$, then component $\mathcal{K}_t$ has "neutral reasoning" for class j.

According to the above definitions, the presence of component $\mathcal{K}_t$ ($d_t(\varkappa) \approx 1$) strengthens the occurrence probability of class j ($p(j|\varkappa) > p(j)$) iff $\mathcal{K}_t$ has positive reasoning over class j, i.e. $m_{tj}^* > 0$. Presence of component $\mathcal{K}_t$ weakens the occurrence probability of class j ($p(j|\varkappa) < p(j)$) iff $\mathcal{K}_t$ has negative reasoning over class j, i.e. $m_{tj}^* < 0$. Component $\mathcal{K}_t$ is indifferent about probability of class j ($p(j|\varkappa) \approx p(j)$) iff $\mathcal{K}_t$ has neutral reasoning over j, i.e. $m_{tj}^* \approx 0$.

3   An Interpretable Multi Layer Perceptron

Based on the notions and definitions of the previous section, we define a special MLP. Given the training set $T = \{(\varkappa_i, y_i)\}_{i=1}^{\tau}$, where $\varkappa_i \in \mathbb{R}^m$ and $y_i \in S$ and τ is the number of elements in T, the input layer has m nodes. Based on the type of classification task in hand, layers could be implemented between the input layer and component layer to detect features. We call this part of MLP the feature extractor. The last layer of the feature extractor is a hidden layer that is called the component layer and it has a total of n nodes. Each node represents a component $\mathcal{K}_t$, as described in the previous section. The output of a component node $\mathcal{K}_t$ is a detection $d_t(\varkappa)$. The activation function of the component layer is a modified Sigmoid and the output of the component layer is defined as

$$d_t(\varkappa) = 2 \cdot Sg(\mathsf{w}_t^T \cdot \mathsf{h} + b_t) - 1 \tag{3}$$

where $Sg(x) = \frac{1}{1+\exp(-x)}$ is the Sigmoid function. Also, $\mathsf{w}_t = [w_{1t}, \cdots, w_{rt}]^T$ are the weights corresponding to the component $\mathcal{K}_t$ and w_{it} is the weight of arc between the i-th node of the layer before component layer and t-th node of component layer. h is the output of the layer before the component layer, b_t is the bias associated with node t in the component layer. Note that, on the right hand side of (3), h is a function of $\varkappa$.

The output layer has as many nodes as the classes, each of them acting as a probabilistic predictor for a certain class j. A common activation function for classification of probabilistic data is Softmax. Although, Softmax often provides fine accuracies, it compromises interpretability since it is a simple averaging operator that cannot make immediate sense out of previous operations in the context of the interpretable framework, described in Sect. 2. Hence, we should look for a class of interpretable activation functions for output layer. We define an activation function, called "Interpretable Probabilistic Activation" (IPA) function, for the output layer as follows: $f(.)$ is an IPA, if 1- it is differentiable, with non-zero derivatives in the domain of the function, 2- the range of $f(.)$ is $(0,1)$, and 3- it is strictly monotonically increasing. Note that an IPA function is invertible, automatically. A differentiable (non-zero derivatives) and strictly monotonically increasing IPA function $f(.)$ provides a matching local loss function $f^{-1}(.)$, that is differentiable and strictly monotonically increasing. Given $f^{-1}(.)$ is numerically stable and it is tested practically, an IPA function $f(.)$, together with its inverse, will help with interpretation of reasoning parameters and the detected components. This becomes clear later in this section.

The output of component layer and the output layer are related by

$$p(j|\textbf{x}) = f(\sum_t m_{tj} \cdot d_t(\textbf{x})) \tag{4}$$

where m_{tj} is the weight of the arc, connecting the component layer node t to output layer node j. Note that the j-th node of output layer, that corresponds to the class $j \in S$ is denoted by $p(j|\textbf{x})$, which is the probability that the class is j, given data point $\textbf{x}$. We would like to have $p(j|\textbf{x}) + p(\neg j|\textbf{x}) = 1$, for all classes j, rather than $\sum_{j \in S} p(j|\textbf{x}) = 1$ (S is the set of the possible classes). We would like m_{tj} to have the same interpretation as the reasoning quantity m_{tj}^*, as described in Sect. 2. We will show, later in this section, that m_{tj} is a fixed multiple of m_{tj}^*, for all components t and classes j.

The inverse function $f^{-1}(x)$ of IPA activation function $f(x)$ is monotonically increasing. Hence, if the inverse is applied to the predictor (4), we get

$$f^{-1}(p(j|\textbf{x})) = \sum_t m_{tj} \cdot d_t(\textbf{x}) \tag{5}$$

The right hand side of equation (5) is a monotonically increasing function of the probability $p(j|\textbf{x})$ of class j. Therefore, (5) can be explained as follows. If $m_{tj} > 0$, then component $\mathcal{K}_t$ should be detected ($d_t(\textbf{x}) > 0$) to strengthen the possibility of class j happening. If $m_{tj} < 0$, then component $\mathcal{K}_t$ should not be detected ($d_t(\textbf{x}) < 0$) to strengthen the possibility of class j happening. If $m_{tj} \approx 0$, then component $\mathcal{K}_t$ is indifferent regarding class j. The mentioned situations are the definitions of positive, negative, and neutral reasoning, respectively (Sect. 2). Hence, we have successfully integrated reasoning into weights of a MLP. Note that this explanation would have not been easily accessible without an IPA function and its corresponding inverse.

Now we specifically choose Sigmoid function $f(x) = Sg(x)$, as an IPA function. Based on the inverse $f^{-1}(x) = \ln \frac{x}{1-x}$ of the function, the suitable local loss function is the probabilistic contrastive Kullback-Leibler loss [23]. Given, a training pair $(\textbf{x}, y) \in T$, we assume the true probabilities are $q(y|\textbf{x}) = 1$, $q(\neg y|\textbf{x}) = 0$. Hence, the contrastive Kullback-Leibler divergence can be written as below.

$$l(\textbf{x}, y) = -\ln p(y|\textbf{x}) + \ln p(\neg y|\textbf{x}) = -\ln \frac{p(y|\textbf{x})}{1 - p(y|\textbf{x})} \tag{6}$$

Note that the above loss function should not be confused with binary cross-entropy. Also, notice how the above loss function is related to the inverse of the IPA $f(.)$ (5) as below.

$$l(\textbf{x}, y) = -f^{-1}(p(y|\textbf{x})) = -\sum_t m_{ty} \cdot d_t(\textbf{x}) \tag{7}$$

The gradient of above loss, with respect to m_{tj}, is

$$\frac{\partial l}{\partial m_{tj}} = -\delta_{j,y} \cdot d_t(\varkappa) \tag{8}$$

where $\delta_{i,j}$ is 1 if $i = j$ and 0 otherwise.

Here, we show that, given m_{tj} is initialized at zero and the weights of the feature detector are fixed (meaning that the components are fixed), then m_{tj} approaches a multiple γ of the reasoning quantity m_{tj}^* (2), for all components t and classes j. First, the reasoning quantities from (2) is approximated by the training set T.

$$\overline{m_{tj}^*} = \frac{1}{\sigma_1 \cdot \sigma_2} \cdot \frac{1}{\tau} \cdot \sum_{(\varkappa,y)\in T} p(j|\varkappa) \cdot d_t(\varkappa) = \frac{1}{\sigma_1 \cdot \sigma_2} \cdot \frac{1}{\tau} \cdot \sum_{(\varkappa,y)\in T} \delta_{j,y} \cdot d_t(\varkappa) \tag{9}$$

In above equations, in order to get the rightmost expression, we have assumed a one-hot encoding of the labels.

If m_{tj}^z is the value of weight m_{tj} in (4) at learning step z, using the gradient (8), we can estimate $m_{tj}^{N \cdot \tau}$, that is m_{tj} adapted by applying stochastic gradient descent for all elements of the training set $T = \{(\varkappa_i, y_i)\}_{i=1}^{\tau}$ exactly $N \in \mathbb{N}$ times, as

$$m_{tj}^{N \cdot \tau} = m_{tj}^0 + \epsilon \cdot N \cdot \sum_{(\varkappa,y)\in T} \delta_{j,y} \cdot d_t(\varkappa) \tag{10}$$

where $0 < \epsilon \ll 1$ is the learning rate and m_{tj}^0 is the initial value for m_{tj}. Comparing (9) and (10), if we set $m_{tj}^0 = 0$, then $m_{tj}^{N \cdot \tau} = \gamma \cdot m_{tj}^*$, where $\gamma = \epsilon \cdot \sigma_1 \cdot \sigma_2 \cdot \tau \cdot N$.

Although $m_{tj}^{N \cdot \tau}$ is a multiple of the reasoning quantity m_{tj}^*, the order of the final prediction $p(j|\varkappa)$ in (4) will not be different from when m_{tj}^* is used as weights instead of the network weights $m_{tj}^{N \cdot \tau}$, since γ is fixed for all class j and components t and we can factor γ out of the summation in (4). We may also set parameter ϵ, such that $\gamma = 1$, i.e. $\epsilon = \frac{1}{\sigma_1 \cdot \sigma_2 \cdot \tau \cdot N}$. This would cause $m_{tj}^{N \cdot \tau} \approx m_{tj}^*$, however, it is not practical since the learning rate can become too small for training sets with large number of samples.

4   Visualization of Components of the Interpretable Multi Layer Perceptron

In this section, the general interpretable MLP framework, introduced in the previous section, is realized in two ways to facilitate the visualization of components. In both cases, the MLP is a two-layered network.

First, the simplest possible feed-forward two-layered MLP, that meets the requirements of Sect. 3, is introduced, to visualize components. This alternative is called the simple two-layered interpretable MLP. The following relation between the input layer and the output of the component layer is defined.

$$d_t(x) = 2 \cdot Sg(S(w_t, x) + b_t) - 1 \tag{11}$$

with the similarity measure

$$S(w_t, x) = w_t^T \cdot x \tag{12}$$

that is the same as (3), when $h = x$. The hidden layer is basically the component layer and the component w_t belongs to the feature space $\mathbb{R}^m$, so it can be easily visualized. This alternative is often fast, however, it often works well for easy classification tasks and provide fairly interpretable components. However, the accuracy is low for difficult classification tasks.

For more difficult tasks, a more complicated MLP is needed to improve the accuracy. If we have a MLP with more than two-layers, components, associated with detection $d_t(x)$, can be visualized by finding a set of inputs x that maximises the activation $d_t(x)$ [24]. In this paper, however, we have chosen to continue with a two-layered MLP for simplicity. To increase the performance, we use feature extractors, such as Convolutional Neural Networks (CNN) [25,26], as a part of Siamese Neural Network [29,30] with contrastive loss to calculate similarity between a presented sample x and a component w_t. We call this alternative the two-layered interpretable MLP, with feature extractor. The output of the node t of component layer is defined as (11), with the similarity measure $S(w_t, x) = \Omega(w_t)^T \cdot \Omega(x)$, where $\Omega : \mathbb{R}^m \to \mathbb{R}^r$ is a feature extractor that take a sample from input space to a space of r-dimensional appropriate features. After training, the components w_t can be visualized.

5   Experimental Results

In this section, we use the developed interpretable MLP for classification of MNIST, Fashion-MNIST, and CIFAR10 data sets. All the figures have the same structure: The first row includes the components, each labeled alphabetically. The second row shows the reasoning quantities for each class separately. For a class j, the gray-scale reasoning matrix has m_{tj}^* in the first column and $-m_{tj}^*$ in the second column, for the sake of comparison. A white square indicates a value considerably greater than 0 and a black square indicates a value considerably less than 0. The shades of gray are read according to the gray-scale map on the right. Also note that all the components have been augmented, with respect to their exposure and contrast, so the patterns are clearly visible.

5.1   Application of Simple Two-Layered MLP to MNIST

We apply the simple interpretable two-layered MLP to MNIST. For each component $\mathcal{K}_t$ a prototype vector $w_t \in \mathbb{R}^m$ exists in the data space. The detection function of a component $\mathcal{K}_t$ in a data sample x is defined as (11), with similarity (12). In the initial case, we start with exactly one component for each class. Accordingly, $n = 10$ prototypes (components) $w_t \in \mathbb{R}^m$, $t \in \{1, \ldots, c\}$

are randomly initialized. m_{tj} was initialized at 0, for all classes j and components $\mathcal{K}_t$. The weights were adapted all together without a feature extractor for $N \cdot \tau = 10 \times 60000 = 6 \times 10^5$ learning steps, using Adam optimizer, to achieve a classification accuracy of 93%. The result is depicted in Fig. 1. In Fig. 1, all classes are roughly represented by a component. For example j and b represent digits 2 and 9, respectively. On the other hand, component c strongly suggests the absence of class 1. Some components, such as b and e, resemble the digits, that they represent. There are other components, like j, that has discovered edges of objects. Also, some components appear to complicated to be human understandable, such as component d. Then, we reduced the number of components to $n = 9$. We obtained a classification accuracy of 92.5% (6×10^5 learning steps). The result is visualized in Fig. 2. Note that the component c, in Fig. 2 that resembles a mirrored 3, is often discovered by the algorithm as a strong representation of digit 8. Finally, we applied the two-layered MLP to achieve the accuracy 89% ($N \cdot \tau = 6 \times 10^5$ learning steps), with 5 components. This accuracy is higher than the accuracy of GLVQ [3] with 10 prototypes.

5.2 Application of Two-Layered MLP with CNN Feature Extractor to MNIST

The two-layered MLP, with CNN feature extractor, is applied to MNIST data set. The CNN feature extractor consists of two layers with 4 and 16 convolutional filters. Each layer uses tangent hyperbolic activation and average pooling 2 by 2. The Siamese network is trained using contrastive loss with margin 1 [30]. When pairing the data samples for training the Siamese network, the pairs where labelled as 1, if the pairs had the same class, and -1 otherwise. After training, the weights of the Siamese network are fixed. Then, the reasoning parameters m_{tj} and the components w_t are trained with the probabilistic contrastive Kullback-Leibler loss (mentioned in Sect. 3). Starting with 10 components, one may initiate each component with a sample of each class. For 10 components, we report an average accuracy of 96% and the components are visualized in Fig. 3.

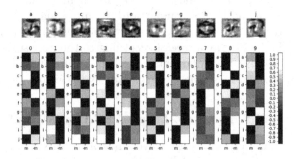

Fig. 1. Visualization of simple MLP with $n = 10$ components applied to MNIST

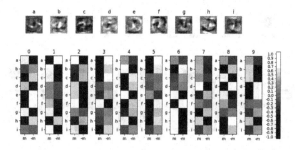

Fig. 2. Visualization of simple MLP with $n = 9$ components applied to MNIST

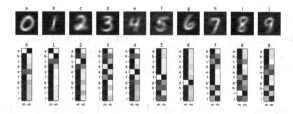

Fig. 3. Visualization of MLP, with feature extractor and 10 components, applied to MNIST

Keeping the same setting as before, for 9 components, we report an average 91.50% classification accuracy.

5.3   Application of Simple Two-Layered MLP to Fashion-MNIST

Fashion-MNIST data set is basically similar to MNIST data set, except that the images belong to clothing items. The 10 possible classes, in the right order, are T-shirt, Trouser, Pullover, Dress, Coat, Sandal, Shirt, Sneaker, Bag, and Ankle Boot. We will refer to each class by an integer from 0 to 9 in the order that has been mentioned. We have noticed that, in case of Fashion-MNIST data set, the CNN components are less human interpretable than when a simple two-layered MLP is used. Therefore, a simple two-layered MLP is applied and the results have been included here. For 6 components, we report an average classification accuracy of 82.5% on the test data set. A sample of the components after training is included in Fig. 4. In Fig. 4, a T-shirt (class 0) is supported by component b. Since component b is missing the long sleeves, it should frequently be absent in Pull-over (class 2) and Coat classes (class 4). About the confusing class of Shirt (class 6), component b stays rather neutral, since a shirt can have either long or short sleeves. The component that considerably differentiates a Pull-over from a Coat is component f. It appears that component f should be absent in a Pull-over, because is contains a zipper (dark line in the middle). Class 8 (Bag) is a tricky class that is supported by components a and c. Component a captures the overall shape of a bag, while component c, which is basically a T-shirt minus a Trouser, roughly highlights the position of the handle of a

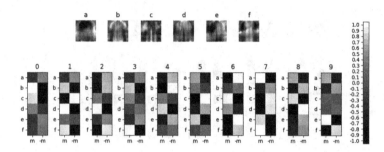

Fig. 4. Visualization of simple two-layered MLP, with 6 components, applied to Fashion-MNIST

bag. About classes Sneaker (7) and Ankle-boot (9), component f supports the Sneaker class, however, because of the dark part above the opening of the sneaker in component f, the component does not support the occurrence of class Ankle-boot. Component f appears to be neutral for classification of Sandal class (5).

5.4 Application of Two-Layered MLP with CNN to CIFAR10

In this section, we report the result of applying the two-layered MLP, with CNN, to CIFAR10 data set. The data points are normalized appropriately. In the Siamese network, the following CNN structure was used: 3 convolutional layers of 5×5 filters. The first, second, and third layers have 32, 64, and 32 filters, respectively. Each convolutional layer is followed by an average pooling layer of size 3×3. Note that, in case of complicated data sets such as CIFAR10, averaging the data samples with the same class will not provide a good representative for the corresponding class. Therefore, we used 10 components, that were initialized with appropriate samples of each class. The final average classification accuracy is 63.5% and the components as well as the reasoning parameters are included in Fig. 5. Unfortunately, the network can hardly distinguish between cats and dogs, since the reasoning parameters for both classes are rather the same. Component a, which is basically a plane, has roughly neutral reasoning for the classification of class "bird", which suggests that if a plane-looking shape is detected, the class may be a bird or it may be something else.

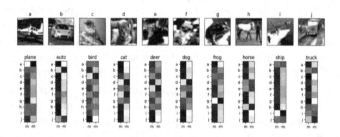

Fig. 5. Visualization of two-layered MLP, with CNN feature extractor and 10 components, applied to CIFAR10

6 Conclusion

This paper develops a novel approach to design interpretable neural networks. If neural networks are designed appropriately, the network weights should estimate a correlation between the detected features and occurrence probability of the classes. If the features are successfully visualized, the reasoning quantities together with the visualized features serve as a level of interpretability for a decision. The method was applied to MNIST, Fashion-MNIST, and CIFAR10 data sets. For MNIST and Fashon-MNIST, we achieved high accuracies, with fairly interpretable components. However, the results of CIFAR10 suggest that the method needs technical improvements to be more effective for difficult data sets.

References

1. Rudin, C.: Stop explaining black box machine learning models for high stakes decisions and use interpretable models instead. Nat. Mach. Intell. **1**(5), 206–215 (2019)
2. Vellido, A.: The importance of interpretability and visualization in machine learning for applications in medicine and health care. Neural Netw. Appli. **32**(24), 18069–18083 (2020)
3. Sato, A., Yamada, K.: Generalized learning vector quantization. In: Advances in Neural Information Processing Systems 8. Proceedings of the 1995 Conference, pp. 423–429 (1996)
4. Seo, S., Obermayer, K.: Soft learning vector quantization. Neural Comput. **15**(7), 1589–1604 (2003)
5. Kohonen, T.: Self-Organizing Maps, 2nd edn. Springer, Berlin, Heidelberg (1995). https://doi.org/10.1007/978-3-642-56927-2
6. Schneider, P., Hammer, B., Biehl, M.: Adaptive relevance matrices in learning vector quantization. Neural Comput. **21**(12), 3532–3561 (2009)
7. Villmann, T., Bohnsack, A., Kaden, M.: Can learning vector quantization be an alternative to SVM and deep learning? J. Artifi. Intell. Soft Comput. Res. **7**(1), 65–81 (2017)
8. Zhang, Y., Tiňo, P., Leonardis, A., Tang, K.: A survey on neural network interpretability. IEEE Trans. Emerging Topics Comput. Intell. (2021)
9. De, T., Giri, P., Mevawala, A., Nemani, R., Deo, A.: Explainable AI: a hybrid approach to generate human-interpretable explanation for deep learning prediction. Procedia Comput. Sci. **168**, 40–48 (2020)
10. Molnar, C.: Interpretable machine learning. http://www.Lulu.com (2020)
11. Parekh, J., Mozharovskyi, P., d'Alché-Buc, F.: A framework to learn with interpretation. In: Advances in Neural Information Processing Systems 34 (2021)
12. Chen, Z., Bei, Y., Rudin, C.: Concept whitening for interpretable image recognition. Nature Mach. Intell. **2**(12), 772–782 (2020)
13. Craven, M., Shavlik, J.: Extracting tree-structured representations of trained networks. Adv. Neural. Inf. Process. Syst. **8**, 24–30 (1995)
14. Bastings, J., Aziz, W., Titov, I.: Interpretable neural predictions with differentiable binary variables. arXiv preprint arXiv:1905.08160 (2019)

15. Liaskos, C., Tsioliaridou, A., Nie, S., Pitsillides, A., Ioannidis, S., Akyildiz, I.: An interpretable neural network for configuring programmable wireless environments. In: 2019 IEEE 20th International Workshop on Signal Processing Advances in Wireless Communications (SPAWC), pp. 1–5 (2019)
16. Yan, Y., Zhu, J., Duda, M., Solarz, E., Sripada, C., Koutra, D.: Groupinn: grouping-based interpretable neural network for classification of limited, noisy brain data. In: Proceedings of the 25th ACM SIGKDD International Conference on Knowledge Discovery & Data Mining, pp. 772–782 (2019)
17. Zhang, Q., Wu, Y.N., Zhu, S.: Interpretable convolutional neural networks. In: Proceedings of the IEEE Conference on Computer Vision and Pattern Recognition, pp. 8827–8836 (2018)
18. Saralajew, S., Holdijk, L., Rees, M., Asan, E., Villmann, T.: Classification-by-components: probabilistic modeling of reasoning over a set of components. In: Advances in Neural Information Processing Systems 32 (2019)
19. Biederman, I.: Recognition-by-components: a theory of human image understanding. Psychol. Rev. **94**(2), 115–147 (1987)
20. Nauta, M., Jutte, A., Provoost, J., Seifert, C.: This looks like that, because... explaining prototypes for interpretable image recognition. In: Joint European Conference on Machine Learning and Knowledge Discovery in Databases, pp. 441–456 (2021)
21. Gautam, S., Höhne, M., Hansen, S., Jenssen, R., Kampffmeyer, M.: This looks more like that: enhancing self-explaining models by prototypical relevance propagation. arXiv preprint arXiv:2108.12204 (2021)
22. Nauta, M., van Bree, R., Seifert, C.: Neural prototype trees for interpretable fine-grained image recognition. In: Proceedings of the IEEE/CVF Conference on Computer Vision and Pattern Recognition, pp. 14933–14943 (2021)
23. Musavishavazi, S., Kaden, M., Villmann, T.: Possibilistic classification learning based on contrastive loss in learning vector quantizer networks. International Conference on Artificial Intelligence and Soft Computing, pp. 156–167 (2021)
24. Nguyen, A., Yosinski, J., Clune, J.: Understanding neural networks via feature visualization: A survey. In: Explainable AI: Interpreting, Explaining And Visualizing Deep Learning, pp. 55–76 (2019)
25. Albawi, S., Mohammed, T.A., Al-Zawi, S.: Understanding of a convolutional neural network. In: 2017 International Conference on Engineering And Technology (ICET), pp. 1–6 (2017)
26. Guo, T., Dong, J., Li, H., Gao, Y.: Simple convolutional neural network on image classification. In: 2017 IEEE 2nd International Conference on Big Data Analysis (ICBDA), pp. 721–724 (2017)
27. Ghiasi-Shirazi, K.: Generalizing the convolution operator in convolutional neural networks. Neural Process. Lett. **50**(3), 2627–2646 (2019)
28. Lisboa, P., et al.: The coming of age of interpretable and explainable machine learning models. In: Proceedings of the 29th European Symposium on Artificial Neural Networks, Computational Intelligence and Machine Learning (ESANN 2021), pp. 547–566 (2021)
29. Davide, C.: Siamese neural networks: An overview. In: Artificial Neural Networks, pp. 73–94. Springer (2021). https://doi.org/10.1007/978-1-0716-0826-5_3
30. Melekhov, I., Kannala, J., Rahtu, E.: Siamese network features for image matching. In: 2016 23rd International Conference on Pattern Recognition (ICPR), pp. 378–383. IEEE (2016)

Viscosity Estimation of Water-PVP Solutions from Droplets Using Artificial Neural Networks and Image Processing

Mohamed Azouz Mrad$^{(\boxtimes)}$ ⓘ, Kristof Csorba, Dorián László Galata,
Zsombor Kristóf Nagy, and Hassan Charaf

Budapest University of Technology and Economics, Budapest Muegyetem rkp. 3,
Budapest 1111, Hungary
mmrad@edu.bme.hu

Abstract. The viscosity of a liquid is the property that measures the liquid internal resistance to flow. Viscosity monitoring is essential for quality control in many industrial areas, such as the chemical, pharmaceutical, and energy-related industries. Capillary viscometers are the most used instrument for measuring viscosity. Still, they are expensive and complex, which represents a challenge in industries where accurate and real-time viscosity knowledge is essential. In this work, we prepared eight solutions with different water and PVP (Polyvinylpyrrolidone) ratios, measured their different viscosity values, and produced videos of their droplets. We aimed to extract the droplets' characteristics using image processing and to use these characteristics to train an Artificial Neural Network model to estimate the viscosity values of the solutions. The proposed model was able to predict the viscosity value of the samples using the characteristics of their droplets with an accuracy of 83.08% on the test dataset.

Keywords: Viscosity · Image Processing · Artificial Neural Networks · OpenCV · Polyvinylpyrrolidone · Viscosity Prediction

1 Introduction

The viscosity of a liquid is the property that measures the liquid internal resistance to flow or shear. Viscosity is a fundamental characteristic parameter of liquids, the monitoring of which is essential for quality control in many industrial areas, such as the pharmaceutical, chemical, and energy-related industries [1]. In the pharmaceutical industry, viscosity significantly impacts the ocular drug absorption and dissolution of Indomethacin [2] and nanoparticles' particle size, drug content, and dissolution profile [3]. Accurate viscosity knowledge is also essential in designing various industrial equipment and chemical processes involving molten salts [4] and in enhanced oil recovery techniques to improve recovery [5]. The measurement of liquids' viscosity is crucial in the industry. Several instruments can be used to measure it: capillary viscometers, orifice viscometers, rotational viscometers, and vibrational and ultrasonic viscometers.

© The Author(s), under exclusive license to Springer Nature Switzerland AG 2023
L. Rutkowski et al. (Eds.): ICAISC 2023, LNAI 14125, pp. 157–166, 2023.
https://doi.org/10.1007/978-3-031-42505-9_14

The capillary viscometer is the most used because of its low cost and simplicity. The capillary method measures the time for a finite volume of liquid to flow through a narrow bore tube under a given pressure [6]. However, these are invasive methods with high costs and prices, making them unsuitable for measuring the viscosity in a continuous manner that allows in-process monitoring and interventions in case of an error, and a need for a cost-effective and time-effective method is essential. A technique that seems convenient for measuring viscosity is using machine learning and image processing algorithms to estimate it based on the droplet characteristics of the liquid. Many researchers have tried to find correlations between liquid viscosity and liquid droplets. A correlation between extensional viscosity and spray droplet sizes of polymer spray solutions was discovered by H. Zhu et al., shown in their paper [7]. Gotaas et al. studied the effect of the viscosity on droplet-droplet collision outcomes [8]. Wang et al. showed that the droplet diameter in vertical gas-liquid annular flows increases logarithmically with increasing liquid viscosity, first rapidly and then slowly [9]. Some researchers also focused on applying image processing techniques for measuring liquid viscosity. Kheloufi et al. measured the fall height of the ball in falling ball viscometers by taking video scenes of the ball during its fall and using it to compute viscosity [10]. Santhosh et al. showed that the viscosity could be accurately estimated using a camera to capture the refracted images of a laser by a tube containing liquid. The images were then processed using thresholding, filtering, and histogram, and an artificial neural network model was used to establish the relationship between these resulting data and the viscosity [11].

Artificial neural networks (ANNs) are suitable for complex and highly nonlinear problems. They have been used widely for their advantages, such as their high accuracy and cost-effectiveness. ANNs were used to estimate the dynamic viscosity of a hybrid nano-lubricant [12], the prediction of Nigerian crude oil viscosity using 32 datasets that include the reservoir temperature, oil and gas gravity, and the solution gas-oil ratio [13]. Esfe et al. showed that an artificial neural network model could predict the dynamic viscosity of ferromagnetic nanofluid with high accuracy [14]. Mrad et al. used an Artificial Neural network model to classify droplets of solutions with different viscosity values [15]. Using Image processing to extract information from videos of droplets with various viscosity values might provide valuable information about the liquids and their viscosity. Using the extracted characteristics of the droplets from the videos to train an Artificial Neural Network model can be a promising alternative to continuously monitor the viscosity of liquids.

In this work, we prepared eight solutions with different water and PVP (Polyvinylpyrrolidone) ratios, measured their viscosity values, and produced videos of their droplets dropping from a syringe pump using a monochrome camera. We aimed to extract the droplets' characteristics from the videos using OpenCV and to use them to train an Artificial Neural Network model to estimate the viscosity of the solutions.

2   Materials and Methods

2.1   Materials

Povidone (PVPK30) was supplied by BASF (Ludwigshafen, Germany). A PVP solution was prepared by adding 37.5 g of PVP to 100 mL of water. Distilled water was used, characterized by a resistance of 20 $\mu S \backslash cm$

2.2   Measurement Setup

We used 1-channel syringe pump SEP-10S PLUS, one transparent rubber tube, a laboratory dropper, Basler acA720-520um USB 3.0 monochrome camera, Pylon Viewer software, PharmaVision Videometry software, LED white light panel, one lab beaker, and eight different laboratory bottles of 500 ml. The materials and the software were provided to us by the Department of Organic Chemistry and Technology at Budapest University of Technology and Economics, Faculty of Chemical Technology and Biotechnology.

2.3   Methods

Experimental Design. Eight liquid samples were prepared for the experiment using the PVP solution and water, with the latter being varied each time to obtain solutions with different viscosity values, as shown in Table 1. The experiment consists of taking videos of the droplets from these different samples in their formation process.

Table 1. The different formulations applied during the samples preparation.

Formulation	Added Water (ml)	PVP Solution (ml)
WaterPVP0 (Water)	300	0
WaterPVP1	300	50
WaterPVP2	125	50
WaterPVP3	66.66	50
WaterPVP4	37.5	50
WaterPVP5	20	50
WaterPVP6	8.33	50
WaterPVP7 (PVP Solution)	0	50

During the experiment, the liquid sample was dispensed at a rate of 20 mL per hour by the automatic syringe pump through the transparent rubber tube to a pipette dropper held by a stand in a fixed perpendicular position to the horizontal plane. A lab beaker was positioned just under the pipette dropper to collect the dropped droplets. A monochrome high-quality recording camera was held fixed using another stand near the dropper. Behind the dropper, a LED panel with strong white illumination was positioned to create a transparent, uniform background and reduce the noise during the image processing. The camera took videos of the droplet formation process from the moment it showed in the dropper until it dropped into the lab beaker. The videos were monitored using PharmaVision Videometry, an internally developed software. The recorded videos were in black and white, with a width of 720 pixels and a height of 540 pixels at 150 frames per second. The resulting videos were detailed and included the most critical steps of the droplet formation process. The experiment can be seen during setup and test in Fig. 1 and Fig. 2. The same experiment was repeated for each of the eight samples. It is crucial to keep a few parameters unchanged during the different experiments. The position of the dropper and the camera, and the infusion rate should remain fixed. The syringe must be washed, and the rubber tube must be emptied from any previous liquid to eliminate any residue that can affect the following measurements. This ensures that the results from the image processing are comparable. Therefore any change to the droplets' characteristics is due exclusively to the viscosity change without any external factor. A total of eight videos were recorded, with each video having a length of 20 min.

Fig. 1. Experimental setup.

Viscosity Measurement. Viscosity values of the different samples were measured using Anton Paar DMA 4500 M viscometer. The values were recorded as shown in Table 2. We measured the rolling time of a steel ball of 1.5 mm diameter through the samples in the capillary tube. The temperature during the measurement was 25.00°C, and the angle of the capillary was −45°.

Image Processing. Image processing aims to help the computer understand the content of an image by processing an input such as a photograph or video

Fig. 2. Experimental setup in test: Droplet in different states

Table 2. Viscosity values of the different samples.

Formulation Number	Viscosity Value mPa · S
$WaterPVP0$ (Water)	0.891
$WaterPVP1$	1.825
$WaterPVP2$	4.306
$WaterPVP3$	7.601
$WaterPVP4$	9.347
$WaterPVP5$	16.51
$WaterPVP6$	33.13
$WaterPVP7$ (PVP Solution)	61.40

frame and providing an output that can be a new image or a set of characteristics of the processed image. In this paper, we used OpenCV, an open-source library of functions that contains a variety of image processing functions, such as image filtering and transformation, object tracking, and feature detection [16]. The Canny algorithm for edges detection was used to detect the droplet edges on the videos [17]. Several characteristics of the droplets were extracted during the image processing:

- **State of the droplet**: The droplets can be seen in three different states on the videos recorded as shown in Fig. 3. Developing state, from the appearance of the droplet until it is completely formed. Before the Detachment state, the droplet is completely formed and in the frame before it detaches from

Fig. 3. A droplet with its edges detected in yellow during its different states: the four droplets from the left show the development phase. Fifth droplet from the left: completely formed droplet in the frame just before the detachment. Last droplet: after detachment.

the dropper. After the detachment state, the droplet is not attached to the dropper and falls until it disappears from the video.

- **Time per droplet**: The time it takes for the droplet to finish the three different states in seconds.
- **Area of the droplet**: The area of the droplet at each frame was extracted in pixels.
- **Perimeter of the droplet**: The perimeter of the droplet at each frame was extracted in pixels.
- **Diameter of the droplet**: The diameter of the droplet at each frame was extracted in pixels.
- **Length of the droplet**: The length of the droplet at each frame was extracted in pixels.
- **Length/Width ratio**: The Length/Width ratio was calculated as independent to the camera distance from the droplet.
- **Y max coordinate**: Before detachment, this feature reflects the maximum length the droplet reached.
- **X and Y coordinates of Center of mass**: Center of mass coordinates of the droplet in pixels.
- **Deltoid Fitting**: A deltoid was fitted inside the droplet in a way that its vertices are the lowest and highest point of the droplet and the two sides of the widest part of the droplet.

Data Analysis. The data collected during the image processing was extracted in eight different excel files. Excel and matplotlib were used to visualize and analyze the data to detect and fix missed and wrong values: the first droplet from each file behaved differently from the other droplets. This is clearly due to the time in which the recording started. The first droplet was removed from all the files to eliminate the noise. Another issue was that some of the droplets did not match the normal chronological states: developing, before detachment, after detachment. The rows that are related to such droplets were deleted.

All the rows from the different excel files with a droplet state "Before detachment" have been concatenated to form a new matrix D_m^n, where $m = 14$ (characteristics of the droplets) and n is the sum of the "Before detachment" rows $n = 181 + 233 + 182 + 269 + 283 + 200 + 184 + 295 = 1827$. Matrix D_m^n has been standardized using the scikit-learn preprocessing method: StandardScaler. StandardScaler fits the data by computing the mean and standard deviation and then centers the data following the equation:

$$Stdr(NS) = (NS - u)/s \qquad (1)$$

where NS is the non-standardized data, u is the mean of the data to be standardized, and s is the standard deviation [18].

Artificial Neural Network. Our goal was to use the extracted characteristics to predict the viscosity values. An Artificial Neural Network (ANN) model was created for this purpose. The model was created using the Python open-source library Keras, a compact, high-level library for deep learning that can run on top of TensorFlow [19]. The model's inputs were the extracted features of the droplets and the targets were the viscosity values. The model used the rectified linear unit activation function ReLU on the model layers. The weights on the models were optimized using the Adam optimizer and Mean Squared Error was used for computing the loss. The number of layers and the number of neurons were optimized based on the prediction accuracy. Regularization term has been varied in order to avoid overfitting. The dataset size was 1827, from which 1018 samples were used for the training (55%), 441 samples were used for validation (25%), and 368 samples were kept for testing (20%). The data used for the training, validating, and testing the model was uniformly selected from the different samples.

Evaluation Measurement. To evaluate the prediction on the model, the approximation error formula was used to calculate the discrepancy between the actual viscosity value and the predicted viscosity value and then a *Accuracyvalue* was used to evaluate the prediction:

$$E = [(PredictedViscsity - RealViscsity)/RealViscsity] * 100 \qquad (2)$$

$$Accuracy = 100 - E \qquad (3)$$

Accuracy is a percentage value which gets higher the closer the predicted value gets to the measured viscosity value, with 100% is a perfect prediction.

Table 3. Model performance on the different test samples

Viscosity	Test Samples	Accuracy %
0.891	37	51.65
1.825	47	78.66
4.306	37	89.47
7.601	54	88.10
9.347	57	76.30
16.51	40	87.73
33.13	37	93.40
61.40	59	94.93
All Test Data	368	83.03

3   Results and Discussion

The number of neurons, layers, epochs, and learning rate on the Artificial Neural Network were varied in order to find the parameters of the model with the best estimation accuracy. The best performing model was designed with three hidden layers each having 14 neurons as shown in Fig. 4. The evolution of the loss over the training is presented in Fig. 5. The ANN model developed was able to estimate the viscosity values with an accuracy of 86.977 % on the training data, 85.706 % on the validation data and 83.087 % on the test data. More precisely the model accuracy was 51.65% on samples with a viscosity value of 0.891, 78.66% on samples with a viscosity value of 1.825 and the accuracy kept improving to reach 94.93% on samples with a viscosity value of 61.40 as shown in Table 3. The proposed model performed significantly better on the samples with higher viscosity values.

```
Model: "sequential"

_____
 Layer (type)                Output Shape              Param #
=================================================================
 dense (Dense)               (None, 14)                210

 dense_1 (Dense)             (None, 14)                210

 dense_2 (Dense)             (None, 14)                210

 dense_3 (Dense)             (None, 1)                 15

=================================================================
Total params: 645
Trainable params: 645
Non-trainable params: 0
```

Fig. 4. Best performing ANN model architecture: Adam optimizer, Relu activation, MLE Loss function

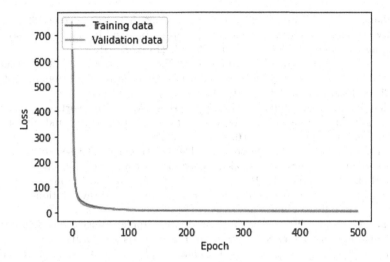

Fig. 5. ANN loss during the training for the model of three hidden layers 14 neurons each on 500 epochs

4   Conclusions

In this work, we prepared eight solutions with different water and PVP ratios, measured their different viscosity values, and produced videos of their droplets. The work aimed to extract the characteristics of the droplets using the image processing library OpenCV and to use the extracted features to estimate the viscosity values of the solutions. An Artificial Neural network model was trained using the droplets' extracted features to predict the solutions' viscosity. The proposed ANN model can estimate the viscosity values with a high accuracy of 83.08% on the test data in the case of the water-PVP solutions. The proposed method is faster and requires minimal human labor, which makes it a great alternative to the classical viscosity measurement techniques.

Acknowledgements. Project no. 2019-1.3.1-KK-2019-00004 has been implemented with the support provided from the National Research, Development and Innovation Fund of Hungary, financed under the 2019-1.3.1-KK funding scheme.

References

1. Viswanath, D.S., Ghosh, T.K., Prasad, D.H., Dutt, N.V., Rani, K.Y.: Viscosity of Liquids: Theory, Estimation, Experiment, and Data. Dordrecht, The Netherlands, Springer Science & Business Media (2007)
2. Toropainen, E., et al.: Biopharmaceutics of topical ophthalmic suspensions: Importance of viscosity and particle size in ocular absorption of indomethacin. Pharmaceutics **13**, 452 (2021)

3. Lokhande, A.B., Mishra, S., Kulkarni, R.D., Naik, J.B.: Influence of different viscosity grade ethylcellulose polymers on encapsulation and in vitro release study of drug loaded nanoparticles. J. Pharm. Res. **7**, 414–420 (2013)

4. Nunes, V.M.; Lourenço, M.J.; Santos, F.J.; Nieto de Castro, C.A. Importance of accurate data on viscosity and thermal conductivity in molten salts applications. J. Chem. Eng. Data **48**, 446–450 (2003)

5. Rashid, B., Bal, A.L., Williams, G.J., Muggeridge, A.H.: Using vorticity to quantify the relative importance of heterogeneity, viscosity ratio, gravity and diffusion on oil recovery. Comput. Geosci. **16**, 409–422 (2012)

6. Brooks, R., Dinsdale, A., Quested, P.: The measurement of viscosity of alloys-a review of methods, data and models. Meas. Sci. Technol. **16**, 354 (2005)

7. Zhu, H., Dexter, R., Fox, R., Reichard, D., Brazee, R., Ozkan, H.: Effects of polymer composition and viscosity on droplet size of recirculated spray solutions. J. Agric. Eng. Res. **67**, 35–45 (1997)

8. Gotaas, C., et al.: Effect of viscosity on droplet-droplet collision outcome: experimental study and numerical comparison. Phys. Fluids **19**, 102106 (2007)

9. Wang, Z., Liu, H., Zhang, Z., Sun, B., Zhang, J., Lou, W.: Research on the effects of liquid viscosity on droplet size in vertical gas-liquid annular flows. Chem. Eng. Sci. **220**, 115621 (2020)

10. Kheloufi, N., Lounis, M.: An optical technique for newtonian fluid viscosity measurement using multiparameter analysis. Appl. Rheol. **24**, 15–22 (2014)

11. Santhosh, K., Shenoy, V.: Analysis of liquid viscosity by image processing techniques. Indian J. Sci. Technol. **9**, 98693 (2016)

12. Afrand, M., et al.: Prediction of dynamic viscosity of a hybrid nano-lubricant by an optimal artificial neural network. Int. Commun. Heat Mass Transf. **76**, 209–214 (2016)

13. Omole, O., Falode, O., Deng, A.D.: Prediction of Nigerian crude oil viscosity using artificial neural network. Pet. Coal **51**, 181–188 (2009)

14. Esfe, M.H., Saedodin, S., Sina, N., Afrand, M., Rostami, S.: Designing an artificial neural network to predict thermal conductivity and dynamic viscosity of ferromagnetic nanofluid. Int. Commun. Heat Mass Transf. **68**, 50–57 (2015)

15. Mrad, M.A., Csorba, K., Galata, D.L., Nagy, Z.K.: Classification of droplets of water-PVP solutions with different viscosity values using artificial neural networks. Processes **10**, 1780 (2022)

16. Naveenkumar, M.; Vadivel, A. OpenCV for computer vision applications. In: Proceedings of the National Conference on Big Data and Cloud Computing (NCBDC'15), Tiruchirappalli, India, 20 March, pp. 52–56 (2015)

17. Sharifi, M., Fathy, M., Mahmoudi, M.T.: A classified and comparative study of edge detection algorithms. In: Proceedings of the International Conference on Information Technology: Coding and Computing, Las Vegas, NV, USA **8–10**, 117–120 (2002)

18. Bisong, E. Introduction to Scikit-learn. In Building Machine Learning and Deep Learning Models on Google Cloud Platform; Springer: New York, NY, USA, pp. 215–229 (2019)

19. Manaswi, N.K.: Understanding and working with Keras. In: Deep Learning with Applications Using Python, pp. 31–43. Apress, Berkeley, CA (2018). https://doi.org/10.1007/978-1-4842-3516-4_2

Pruning Convolutional Filters
via Reinforcement Learning with Entropy
Minimization

Bogdan Muşat[1(✉)] and Răzvan Andonie[1,2]

[1] Department of Electrical Engineering and Computer Science, Transilvania
University of Braşov, Braşov, Romania
bogdan_musat_adrian@yahoo.com

[2] Department of Computer Science, Central Washington University, Ellensburg, USA
razvan.andonie@cwu.edu

Abstract. Structural pruning has become an integral part of neural
network optimization, used to achieve architectural configurations which
can be deployed and run more efficiently on embedded devices. Previous results showed that pruning is possible with minimum performance
loss by utilizing a reinforcement learning agent which makes decisions
about the sparsity level of each neural layer by maximizing as a reward
the accuracy of the network. We introduce a novel information-theoretic
reward function which minimizes the spatial entropy of convolutional
activations. This minimization ultimately acts as a proxy for maintaining accuracy, although these two criteria are not related in any way. Our
method shows that there is another possibility to preserve accuracy without the need to directly optimize it in the agent's reward function. In
our experiments, we were able to reduce the total number of FLOPS of
multiple popular neural network architectures by 5–10×, incurring minimal or no performance drop and being on par with the solution found
by maximizing the accuracy.

Keywords: neural network pruning · reinforcement learning · AutoML

1 Introduction

Modern convolutional neural networks (CNNs) emerged with the publication of
AlexNet [10] in 2012, which paved the way for other architectures like VGG [11],
ResNet [12] and EfficientNet [13]. Although these networks posses a very high
capacity and perform at a super human level, they are often overparametrized
[14], which induces high latency and power consumption on battery powered
devices. Techniques like pruning and quantization [6–8,15,46] have recently
become very popular, since they can generate power-efficient sub-versions of
these overparametrized networks.

While pruning deals with removing unimportant weights from a network by
applying a certain heuristic, quantization operates by using less bits for weights

L. Rutkowski et al. (Eds.): ICAISC 2023, LNAI 14125, pp. 167–180, 2023.
https://doi.org/10.1007/978-3-031-42505-9_15

and activations, thus speeding up overall computations. In our work we only focus on structured pruning, which translates into removing entire filters from a convolutional kernel. For this, we use an automated machine learning (AutoML) framework to select the most suited percentage of structured sparsity for each neural layer [1].

AutoML is a powerful strategy used for many tasks like neural architecture search (NAS), hyperparameter search, data preparation, feature engineering [2,3]. The principle behind it is to automate manual searching tasks and find optimal solutions faster than we can manually do. Recently, AutoML was applied for network compression via pruning [1]. By usage of a reinforcement learning (RL) agent [9], the system can automatically choose the sparsity percentage per layer, and then a magnitude-based pruning heuristic is applied, which removes the top percentage filters with the smallest magnitude. The reward criterion that the agent uses is the accuracy of the network obtained on a randomly chosen subset from the training set or the validation set at the end of the pruning phase.

We discovered that the accuracy of the network is not the only reward criterion that can be used for AutoML network compression. Our central contribution is an information-theoretical reward function (entropy minimization) for the agent, which is completely different than the accuracy used in [9]. We utilize this information-theoretical criterion for network pruning.

Generally, a low entropic value of a system denotes more certainty, while a high entropic value translates into more disorder. In neural networks, the cross-entropy between two probability distributions is very often used as a measure of error between the predicted output of a network and the true class distribution of the target. In contrast, the entropy of neural activations the hidden neural layers is seldom computed or used. This observation offered us the motivation for the current work. As such, we propose to analyze the impact of the entropy of all convolutional layers on network pruning. The question is if such an impact exists and, if true, how to use it for neural pruning. Since an ideal entropy value for the final output of the network is 0 (i.e., to predict the correct class with 100% confidence), our hypothesis is that the entropy of neural activations should be minimized in order to preserve essential information and also reduce uncertainty.

The intriguing result of our work is the discovery of an interesting connection between entropy minimization and structural pruning. This could be related to the structural entropy measure recently introduced in [47], where "structural entropy refers to the level of heterogeneity of nodes in the network, with the premise that nodes that share functionality or attributes are more connected than others".

In practice, we utilize the AutoML framework from [1] to sparsify a neural network and propose as an optimization reward criterion the minimization of the spatial entropy (as defined in [4]) at each convolutional layer. Through our experiments, we empirically show that this minimization acts as a proxy for maintaining accuracy. The novelty of our work consists in discovering that there are other, more principled approaches, to neural network pruning than directly optimize the accuracy of the agent's reward function.

The rest of the paper is structured as follows. Section 2 describes related work. Section 3 introduces the basic notations of spatial entropy, used in this paper. Section 4 details our information-theoretical pruning method. The experimental results are described in Sect. 5 and Sect. 6 concludes with final remarks.

2 Related Work

In this section we summarize relevant previous work related to neural network pruning, AutoML and RL for pruning.

Pruning: The main objective of pruning is the reduction of the total number of floating point operations per second (FLOPS) and parameters by removing redundant weights from the network.

In the context of hardware accelerators, where computational availability might be limited, we argue that the ratio of preserved FLOPS for the same optimized architecture is a better measure of compression than simply counting the number of parameters after pruning, because two networks with the same number of parameters might posses totally different FLOPS counts, and as such the one with less FLOPS for the same should be more desirable. Only when memory space is an issue, a network with less parameters may be preferable.

The first approaches for neural pruning emerged in the '90s with the classical methods of optimal brain damage [31] and optimal brain surgeon [32]. Since then, the importance of pruning was observed in improving training and inference time, better generalization. With the emergence of large deep neural networks, pruning became even more relevant and desirable, since modern network architectures are overparametrized and there is a lot of space for optimization. As such, a large suite of methods for pruning have been proposed in the last years. Comprehensive surveys on neural network pruning can be found in [6,7].

Out of these methods, we highlight a few of them. Frankle *et al.* proposed the lottery ticket hypothesis [33], representing a method to search for subnetworks derived from a randomly initialized network which, if trained from scratch, can attain the same performance as the original network and be sparse at the same time. In [34] the authors argued that the traditional pipeline of pruning: training, pruning, fine-tuning can result in networks with suboptimal performance and what is actually important is the architecture configuration itself resulted from pruning and not the weights that are maintained. As such, they showed that training a pruned network configuration from scratch can result in better accuracy than by fine-tuning it. The fine-tuning procedure is also studied in [36] and they proposed two tricks to improve it. The first one is called weight rewinding which turns back weights which were not pruned to their earlier in time training values and continues retraining them using the original training schedule. The second trick is called learning rate rewinding which trains the final values of the unpruned weights using the same learning rate schedule as weight rewinding. Both tricks were shown to outperform classical fine-tuning. In [35] the authors proposed a method to estimate the contribution of a filter to the final loss and iteratively remove those with smaller scores. To estimate a filter's importance they used two methods based on the first and second order Taylor expansions. [37] introduced "The Rigged Lottery" or RigL which trains sparse networks without the need of a "lucky" initialization. Their method updates the topology of a sparse network during training using parameter magnitudes and infrequent gradient calculations. They obtained better solutions than most dense-to-sparse training algorithms.

AutoML: AutoML has been widely adopted by the community to solve tasks where a huge amount of manual search would be involved. A comprehensive survey on AutoML can be found in [2,3]. We aim to present in the following some of the most important problems associated with AutoML.

Data augmentation has become such an important part of an ML pipeline, that manually searching for strategies is no longer feasible or desirable. As such, methods like AutoAugment [17], RandAugment [25] and Population Based Augmentation [18] have recently emerged in the literature and have been integrated in many training pipelines [26–28]. Such methods are popular because, depending on the input images, they can automatically select between using multiple pre-existing augmentation techniques or choose the best hyperparameters for them.

Another important task is to search for optimal architectures [19–23]. Relevant architectures like EfficientNet B0 [13] and AmoebaNet [29] were found by such techniques. Given the huge search space of neural layers' combinations, human inventiveness and intuition have fallen behind these methods which can exhaustively look up for better solutions. Optimized networks were obtained this way, under specific hardware constraints [30].

AutoML solutions for network pruning were also proposed [1,24]. These methods employ an RL agent to decide which individual weights or filters to drop, or the optimal amount of sparsity for each layer. It is known that some layers need more capacity [6]. Therefore, the uniform distribution approach for sparsity doesn't perform very well, and the sparsity has to be adapted by taking into consideration each layer's constraints.

Reinforcement Learning for Pruning: An important result, the one on which our paper is based on, is by He *et al.* [1]. They used a DDPG agent [9] to choose the percentage of sparsity for each learnable layer, be it either convolutional or fully connected, by maximizing the accuracy of the network after pruning. For pruning convolutional layers, the filters with the lowest total magnitude were marked for sparsification, while for fully connected layers the smallest weights were the ones being discarded. This form of sparsification is considered to be structured, because weights are being dropped respecting a certain structure (i.e., a whole filter), and not being randomly dropped within a filter. This form of structured sparsification is more efficient, as whole filters can be removed from computations, while for the other form of sparsification, called random, some computations within filters have to be performed and others not, complicating the final arithmetic logic.

Another important work that conducts pruning by means of an RL agent is [16]. The important difference compared to the previous work is that pruning is performed during runtime and adapted for the inputs. The assumption here is that some samples need more computational resources to be dealt with and thus the agent decides dynamically how much sparsity the network needs during inference. The main disadvantage is that an additional recurrent neural network (RNN) agent needs to run in order to sample actions during inference, while the previous method finds a fixed sub-network from the original one, which is also used during inference.

3   Background: Spatial Entropy

Our goal is to minimize the spatial entropy of neural convolutional activations using the framework of AMC [1] for structural sparsity. We also want to study whether this minimization can substitute direct accuracy optimization. If this assumption holds true, it might mean that there is a connection between pruning and entropy minimization. In the end, pruning unimportant filters ideally removes useless information.

In [4] the notion of spatial entropy of saliency maps in CNNs was used to study the layer-wise and time-wise evolution of them [4,5]. To compute the spatial entropy, the authors used the aura matrix entropy, initially defined in [38]. In [4] it was noticed that the spatial entropy value decreases when going along the depth of a neural network as the process called semiotic superization takes place. Then, in [5] the authors studied the dynamics of the spatial entropy in time, how it evolves during training, and found a link with fitting and compression present in the information bottleneck framework [39].

To make this paper self-contained, we describe below the mathematical formulations for computing the spatial entropy used in this work. Let us define the joint probability of features at spatial locations (i, j) and $(i + k, j + l)$ to take the value g, respectively g' as:

$$p_{gg'}(k,l) = P(X_{i,j} = g, X_{i+k, j+l} = g') \tag{1}$$

where g and g' are quantized convolutional activation values. In the Experiments section we tested using multiple bin sizes for quantization to verify the robustness of the procedure, and noticed that the proposed minimization produces good solutions for a wide range of bin size values. For each pair (k, l) we define the entropy:

$$H(k, l) = -\sum_{g} \sum_{g'} p_{gg'}(k, l) \log p_{gg'}(k, l) \tag{2}$$

where the summations are over the number of bin sizes. A standardized relative measure of bivariate entropy is [40]:

$$H_R(k, l) = \frac{H(k, l) - H(0)}{H(0)} \in [0, 1] \tag{3}$$

The maximum entropy $H_R(k, l) = 1$ corresponds to the case of two independent variables. $H(0)$ is the univariate entropy, which assumes all features as being independent, and we have $H(k, l) \geq H(0)$.

Based on the relative entropy for (k, l), the Spatial Disorder Entropy (SDE) for an $m \times n$ image $\mathbf{X}$ was defined in [40] as:

$$H_{SDE}(\mathbf{X}) \approx \frac{1}{mn} \sum_{i=1}^{m} \sum_{j=1}^{n} \sum_{k=1}^{m} \sum_{l=1}^{n} H_R(i - k, \, j - l) \tag{4}$$

Since the complexity of SDE computation is high, we decided to use a simplified version - the Aura Matrix Entropy (AME, see [38]), which only considers the second order neighbors from the SDE computation:

$$H_{AME}(\mathbf{X}) \approx \frac{1}{4}\Big(H_R(-1, \, 0) + H_R(0, \, -1) + H_R(1, \, 0) + H_R(0, \, 1) \Big) \tag{5}$$

Putting it all together, starting from a feature map obtained after the application of a convolutional layer, we compute the probabilities $p_{gg'}$ in equation (1), and finally the AME in equation (5), which results in the spatial entropy quantity for a channel. We compute the mean of the spatial entropy values obtained from all the channels to get the final estimate for a particular convolutional activation layer. When computing the mean, we exclude channels which contain only 0 values, which would produce a spatial entropy of 0.

4   Our Method

This section describes our method, which is a modification of the AMC framework [1] for structural pruning. The main difference between our approach and [1] is that our agent's reward function minimizes the spatial entropy of convolutional activations, instead of maximizing the accuracy of the model (see Fig. 1).

The AMC framework is an AutoML tool for pruning which selects the percentage of sparsity for each layer of a neural network (layer by layer), then an algorithm based on L_2 magnitude marks the top percentage filters with lowest magnitude for removal. Since the accuracy of a model is a non-differentiable function for which gradients can not be computed and used during backpropagation, a RL technique has to be used to optimize this criterion, which will be treated as a reward function. Hence, the engine driving the percentage selection for pruning is a DDPG agent [9], trained via an actor critic technique [41], using the accuracy computed on a separate dataset as a reward criterion. The reward function can be computed either on a split from the training dataset or the validation dataset. By pursuing optimal actions (with high reward), the agent will be rewarded correspondingly and encouraged to perform similar actions in the future, while generally discouraging actions with poor reward.

AMC stores inputs and outputs for each layer at the very beginning of optimization by feed-forwarding a batch of input samples (called calibration samples). After pruning using the magnitude-based heuristic, the channels from the

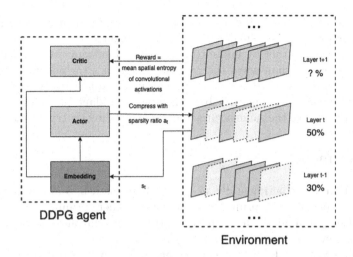

Fig. 1. A DDPG agent is responsible with choosing the amount of sparsity a_t applied to each layer, based on the state of that layer s_t, by considering multiple variables (see the original AMC paper for more details). After the agent decides the amount of sparsity for each layer, the environment computes a reward for the agent. In the original AMC formulation, this reward was the accuracy of the pruned network computed on a validation dataset. In our case, this reward consists in the mean of spatial entropies computed at multiple convolutional layer outputs. The agent's objective is to choose the amount of sparsity for each layer such that this mean entropy is minimized.

inputs of the calibration samples which have the same indexes as the discarded filters will be dropped as well. A least squares regression is applied to adjust the remaining weights to the new inputs and already stored outputs. After the AMC framework finds the best subnetwork configuration which maximizes the given reward function, and the weights have been adjusted as well via the least squares regression, the new network configuration is fine-tuned, as is standard in pruning literature.

Different from the original AMC formulation, we modify the accuracy based reward by introducing a function which minimizes the average of the spatial entropies of convolutional activations. Our goal is to observe if entropy minimization can be used as a criterion in place of directly computing accuracy, establishing thus a potential interesting link between the fields of neural pruning and information theory. Because the framework of AMC tries to constantly increase the amount of reward it receives, and since the mean spatial entropy formulation we use is bounded between 0 and 1 [40], we subtract it from 1 in order to minimize the term. Thus, the optimization problem for the agent becomes finding the amount of sparsity for each layer which would eventually lead to minimize the spatial entropy. In order to compute the mean value (per layer) of the spatial entropy, we use the convolutional outputs from 100 samples, which of course represents only an estimate of the full dataset. Computing the mean spatial entropy using the full dataset would be computationally too costly, and as such resorting to a high smaller sample size is enough.

Our hypothesis is that by minimizing the spatial entropy, we can achieve on par or better results than when the goal is to maximize the accuracy. If this is the case, then we can establish an empirical connection between pruning and information theory, showing that by removing redundant information from a model we can achieve the same accuracy as when we directly try to maximize it.

5   Experiments

In this section we experimentally asses our hypothetical connection between information theory and pruning, verifying whether pruning achieved via AutoML, using minimization of spatial entropy for convolutional activations, can lead to a more compact model with similar accuracy.

For training, we used the deep learning programming framework PyTorch [43] (version 1.10.0) and the public implementation of AMC, modified to our needs.

We started by training a standard VGG-16 [11] on the CIFAR-10 dataset [42]. For that, we trained for 200 epochs using the SGD optimizer with a learning rate of 0.01 and cosine annealing scheduler [44].

In order to establish a baseline to compare our method with, we used the original formulation of the AMC framework and optimize first the network using the accuracy criterion. To achieve a certain level of pruning, AMC pushes up the level of sparsity until only a predefined percentage of the total FLOPS are maintained. The ratio between the number of FLOPS after compression and the number of FLOPS before compression can measure indirectly the amount of sparsity in a network. Table 1 depicts the results for various FLOPS preservation percentages after fine-tuning on the CIFAR-10 dataset. For fine-tuning we used the same training optimizer and hyperparameters as described previously.

Table 1. Accuracy for a VGG-16 network using the original AMC framework for different FLOPS preservation percentage

	Standard VGG-16	VGG-16 with 50% FLOPS	VGG-16 with 20% FLOPS	VGG-16 with 10% FLOPS
Accuracy	93.58%	93.85%	93.26%	92.18%
No. parameters	14728266	4768242	912186	483402

Our intuition is that entropy minimization should be the key in removing redundant information while preserving accuracy. Although, this should be the case, we performed a sanity test to check whether the opposite is also true (i.e., entropy maximization). We first performed some experiments for FLOPS preservation of 50% and noticed that both entropy minimization and maximization achieve comparable accuracy results (before fine-tuning) on the mini validation set used for AMC agent training (Table 2).

Table 2. Accuracy on mini split during AMC agent training for entropy minimization/maximization and FLOPS preservation of 50%

Minimization	Maximization
100%	**99.88%**

Our next experiment used random rewards $\in [0, 1]$ to check whether 50% FLOPS preservation is not a very simple task for the agent. On the mini split dataset used for agent training, we obtained an accuracy of 86%, concluding that even a reward which makes no sense can result in a network with decent performance. Therefore, we decided to use a scenario with 10% preservation ratio in order to better stress test the framework and obtain more relevant results. Table 3 presents the accuracies obtained on CIFAR-10 after fine-tuning two networks obtained via AMC with entropy minimization/maximization and FLOPS preservation of 10%. We notice that with entropy minimization we achieved the same performance as when accuracy is used as a reward. The solution found by this method has $10\times$ less FLOPS and $\approx 38\times$ less parameters than the original VGG-16 network. For entropy maximization the framework produces a solution which has indeed fewer parameters, but uses the same number of FLOPS as the method with entropy minimization. We can see though that the resulting network architecture has a much poorer accuracy performance.

Table 3. Experiments with entropy minimization and maximization and FLOPS preservation of 10%. The accuracies are computed on the CIFAR-10 test set after fine-tuning.

	Minimization	Maximization
Accuracy	**92.36%**	**83.23%**
No. parameters	**386442**	**91290**

In the above experiments, we used a bin size of 256 for quantizing the convolutional activations before computing the spatial entropy. Table 4 shows results for entropy minimization when using various bin sizes. It can be observed that our method is robust against a wide range of values, but the fewer bins results in faster computation - as expected.

Table 4. Accuracy on CIFAR-10 test set after fine-tuning. FLOPS preservation of 10%, different bin size configurations

	32 bins	64 bins	128 bins	256 bins	512 bins
Accuracy	**failed**	**92.43%**	**92.31%**	**92.36%**	**91.97%**
No. parameters	**failed**	**511938**	**619962**	**386442**	**578922**

The authors of [34] discovered that training from scratch a subnetwork configuration found via pruning can produce better results than fine-tuning the preserved weights. We verified this hypothesis with the architectures found by entropy minimization/maximization and noticed that in neither case training from scratch can produce better results (Table 5). In our case, performance is better preserved when the weights are fine-tuned, because the remaining weights are properly adjusted using calibration samples, as described in Sect. 4.

Table 5. Accuracy on CIFAR-10 test set when training a subnetwork from scratch

Acc. maximization 50% FLOPS	Acc. maximization 20% FLOPS	Acc. maximization 10% FLOPS	Entropy minimization 10% FLOPS
92.92%	**92.18%**	**90.99%**	**91.06%**

In order to test the generality of our method for various other architectures, we repeated the same experiments for other popular networks: MobileNetV2 [45] and ResNet50 [12]. The results are depicted in Table 6. Our method is on par with the original AMC framework for various architectures and FLOPS preservation percentages. The only noticeable drop in performance is for ResNet50, which was previously observed to contain less redundancy [46] and was the most difficult to compress, even when using accuracy as a criterion.

Table 6. Accuracy on CIFAR-10 test set with other architectures and various FLOPS preservation percentages

Architecture	Original performance	Accuracy 50% FLOPS	Accuracy 20% FLOPS	Entropy 50% FLOPS	Entropy 20% FLOPS
MobileNetV2	**94.58%**	**94.62%**	**93.59%**	**94.31%**	**93.75%**
ResNet50	**95.21%**	**95.34%**	**95.09%**	**95.27%**	**94.27%**

In our last experiment, we compared our method with other popular pruning methods. We used the ShrinkBench framework proposed in [6] to prune the same VGG16 network that we used in our experiments. From this framework, we selected the two most popular methods used for pruning: Global Magnitude Weight, which places together weights from all the layers and selects the ones with the largest magnitude and Local Magnitude Weight, which selects the weights with the largest magnitudes on a per layer basis. Table 7 shows the results obtained using ShrinkBench. It can be noticed that the accuracies resulted when using this framework are similar to what we obtain using AMC combined with our entropic criterion. One disadvantage of this method is that the type of pruning is unstructured, having the risk that when the network would be deployed to a specialized hardware, it might not reduce computational costs as much as when structured pruning is employed.

Table 7. Accuracy for VGG16 on CIFAR-10 test set using the ShrinkBench framework

Original Accuracy	Global 50% FLOPS	Global 10% FLOPS	Local 50% FLOPS	Local 10% FLOPS
93.58%	**93.78%**	**92.83%**	**93.27%**	**92.34%**

Using an information-theoretical optimization criterion, which aims to minimize entropy, we achieved the same performance as when we optimize directly the accuracy of the model. We were able to reduce the total number of FLOPS of a VGG-16 architecture by $10\times$ and the number of parameters by $\approx 38\times$, while incurring minimal accuracy drop, with similar results for other popular architectures.

6 Conclusions

A standard neural network's output should ideally have a close to zero entropic value in order to confidently predict a class - not necessarily the correct one. Usually, this behavior is achieved by minimization of the cross-entropy between the network's output and the one hot encoding of the true class. This task can be sometimes burdensome, because internal layers of the network are not forced in any way to minimize the final entropy of the output layer.

In our experiments, we explicitly forced the spatial entropy of internal convolutional activations to decrease with the goal to achieve neural pruning. According to our results, using the spatial entropy as an optimization criterion in an AutoML pruning framework, we can achieve good performance for an object recognition task, without directly optimizing the final evaluation metric (accuracy in this case). Because of the overparametrization of a neural network, removing unessential information via entropy minimization helps reduce the model to its relevant (essential) components.

We established an interesting connection between information theory and neural pruning. Our result creates the premises for future applications in neural network pruning. In the future, we aim to explore novel ways in which the entropy can be used for the optimization of neural architectures. One such idea would be to include the entropy measure as a heuristic for selecting the channels to be preserve, instead of using the well known L2 magnitude. Another direction we aim to pursue is whether there is a link between pruning by entropy and semiotic aggregation, as described in [4].

References

1. He, Y., Lin, J., Liu, Z., Wang, H., Li, L., Han, S. AMC: AutoML for Model Compression and Acceleration on Mobile Devices. In: European Conference On Computer Vision (ECCV) (2018). https://doi.org/10.1007/978-3-030-01234-2_48

2. He, X., Zhao, K., Chu, X. AutoML: A survey of the state-of-the-art. Knowl.-Based Syst. **212** 106622 (2021). www.sciencedirect.com/science/article/pii/S0950705120307516

3. Yao, Q., et al.: Taking Human Out of Learning Applications: A Survey on Automated Machine Learning. CoRR. abs/1810.13306 (2018). arxiv.org/abs/1810.13306

4. Muşat, B., Andonie, R.: Semiotic aggregation in deep learning. Entropy **22**(12), 1365 (2020). www.mdpi.com/1099-4300/22/12/1365

5. Musat, B., Andonie, R.: Information bottleneck in deep learning - a semiotic approach. Int. J. Comput. Commun. Contr. **17**(1) (2022). www.univagora.ro/jour/index.php/ijccc/article/view/4650

6. Blalock, D., Ortiz, J., Frankle, J., Guttag, J.: What is the State of Neural Network Pruning? (2020)

7. Gale, T., Elsen, E., Hooker, S.: The State of Sparsity in Deep Neural Networks (2019)

8. Deng, L., Li, G., Han, S., Shi, L., Xie, Y.: Model compression and hardware acceleration for neural networks: a comprehensive survey. Proc. IEEE **108**, 485–532 (2020)

9. Lillicrap, T., et al.: Continuous control with deep reinforcement learning. In: ICLR (2016). www.dblp.uni-trier.de/db/conf/iclr/iclr2016.html#LillicrapHPHETS15

10. Krizhevsky, A., Sutskever, I., Hinton, G.: ImageNet Classification with Deep Convolutional Neural Networks. In: Proceedings of the 25th International Conference on Neural Information Processing Systems - Volume 1, pp. 1097–1105 (2012)

11. Simonyan, K., Zisserman, A.: Very deep convolutional networks for large-scale image recognition. In: 3rd International Conference on Learning Representations, ICLR 2015, San Diego, CA, USA, May 7–9, 2015, Conference Track Proceedings (2015). arxiv.org/abs/1409.1556

12. He, K., Zhang, X., Ren, S., Sun, J.: Deep residual learning for image recognition. In: 2016 IEEE Conference on Computer Vision And Pattern Recognition (CVPR), pp. 770–778 (2016)

13. Tan, M. & Le, Q. EfficientNet: Rethinking Model Scaling for Convolutional Neural Networks. Proceedings Of The 36th International Conference On Machine Learning, ICML: 9–15 June 2019. Long Beach, California, USA (2019)

14. Oymak, S., Soltanolkotabi, M.: Toward moderate overparameterization: global convergence guarantees for training shallow neural networks. IEEE J. Selected Areas Inform. Theor. **1**, 84–105 (2020)

15. Gholami, A., Kim, S., Dong, Z., Yao, Z., Mahoney, M., Keutzer, K.: A Survey of Quantization Methods for Efficient Neural Network Inference. ArXiv. abs/2103.13630 (2022)

16. Lin, J., Rao, Y., Lu, J., Zhou, J.: Runtime Neural Pruning. Adv. Neural Inform. Process. Syst. **30** (2017)

17. Cubuk, E., Zoph, B., Mane, D., Vasudevan, V., Le, Q.: AutoAugment: Learning Augmentation Strategies From Data. In: Proceedings Of The IEEE/CVF Conference on Computer Vision and Pattern Recognition (CVPR) (2019)

18. Ho, D., Liang, E., Chen, X., Stoica, I., Abbeel, P.: Population Based Augmentation: Efficient Learning of Augmentation Policy Schedules. In: Proceedings of the 36th International Conference on Machine Learning, vol. 97 pp. 2731–2741 (2019). www.proceedings.mlr.press/v97/ho19b.html

19. Zoph, B., Le, Q.: Neural Architecture Search with Reinforcement Learning. CoRR. abs/1611.01578 (2016). arxiv.org/abs/1611.01578

20. Pham, H., Guan, M., Zoph, B., Le, Q., Dean, J.: Efficient Neural Architecture Search via Parameters Sharing. In: Proceedings of the 35th International Conference on Machine Learning, vol. 80, pp. 4095–4104 (2018). www.proceedings.mlr. press/v80/pham18a.html

21. Liu, H., Simonyan, K., Yang, Y.: DARTS: Differentiable Architecture Search. CoRR. abs/1806.09055 (2018). arxiv.org/abs/1806.09055

22. Florea, A.-C., Andonie, R.: Weighted random search for hyperparameter optimization. Int. J. Comput. Commun. Contr. **14**, 154–169 (2019)

23. Andonie, R., Florea, A.-C.: Weighted random search for CNN hyperparameter optimization. Int. J. Comput. Commun. Contr. **15**(2) (2020)

24. Huang, Q., Zhou, K., You, S., Neumann, U.: Learning to prune filters in convolutional neural networks. In: 2018 IEEE Winter Conference on Applications of Computer Vision (WACV), pp. 709–718 (2018)

25. Cubuk, E., Zoph, B., Shlens, J., Le, Q.: RandAugment: Practical Automated Data Augmentation with a Reduced Search Space. Advances in Neural Information Processing Systems

26. Khosla, P., et al.: Supervised contrastive learning. Adv. Neural. Inf. Process. Syst. **33**, 18661–18673 (2020)

27. Grill, J., et al.: Bootstrap Your Own Latent - A New Approach to Self-Supervised Learning. In: Advances in Neural Information Processing Systems, vol. 33 pp. 21271–21284 (2020). www.proceedings.neurips.cc/paper/2020/file/ f3ada80d5c4ee70142b17b8192b2958e-Paper.pdf

28. Xie, Q., Luong, M., Hovy, E., Le, Q.: Self-Training With Noisy Student Improves ImageNet Classification. In: Proceedings of the IEEE/CVF Conference on Computer Vision and Pattern Recognition (CVPR) (2020)

29. Real, E., Aggarwal, A., Huang, Y., Le, Q.: Regularized Evolution for Image Classifier Architecture Search (2018). www.arxiv.org/pdf/1802.01548.pdf

30. Cai, H., Zhu, L., Han, S.: ProxylessNAS: Direct Neural Architecture Search on Target Task and Hardware. In: 7th International Conference On Learning Representations, ICLR 2019, New Orleans, LA, USA, May 6–9, 2019. (2019). www. openreview.net/forum?id=HylVB3AqYm

31. LeCun, Y., Denker, J., Solla, S.: Optimal Brain Damage. In: Advances in Neural Information Processing Systems, vol. 2 (1989)

32. Hassibi, B., Stork, D., Wolff, G.: Optimal Brain Surgeon and general network pruning. In: IEEE International Conference on Neural Networks, vol. 1, pp. 293–299 (1993)

33. Frankle, J., Carbin, M.: The lottery ticket hypothesis: finding sparse, trainable neural networks. In: International Conference on Learning Representations (2019)

34. Liu, Z., Sun, M., Zhou, T., Huang, G., Darrell, T.: Rethinking the value of network pruning. In: International Conference on Learning Representations (2019)

35. Molchanov, P., Mallya, A., Tyree, S., Frosio, I., Kautz, J.: Importance estimation for neural network pruning. In: Proceedings of The IEEE/CVF Conference on Computer Vision and Pattern Recognition (CVPR) (2019)

36. Renda, A., Frankle, J., Carbin, M.: Comparing Rewinding and Fine-tuning in Neural Network Pruning. In: International Conference on Learning Representations (2020)

37. Evci, U., Gale, T., Menick, J., Castro, P., Elsen, E.: Rigging the lottery: making all tickets winners. In: Proceedings of The 37th International Conference on Machine Learning, vol. 119 pp. 2943–2952 (2020). www.proceedings.mlr.press/v119/evci20a. html

38. Volden, E., Giraudon, G., Berthod, M.: Modelling image redundancy. In: International Geoscience and Remote Sensing Symposium, IGARSS '95. Quantitative Remote Sensing for Science and Applications, vol. 3, 2148–2150 (1995)
39. Shwartz-Ziv, R., Tishby, N.: Opening the Black Box of Deep Neural Networks via Information. CoRR. abs/1703.00810 (2017). arxiv.org/abs/1703.00810
40. Journel, A.G., Deutsch, C.V.: Entropy and spatial disorder. Math. Geol. **25**(3), 329–355 (1993)
41. Konda, V., Tsitsiklis, J.: Actor-critic algorithms. Adv. Neural Inform. Process. Syst. **12** (1999)
42. Krizhevsky, A.: Learning multiple layers of features from tiny images. University of Toronto, 05 (2012)
43. Paszke, A.: Pytorch: An imperative style, high-performance deep learning library. Adv. Neural Inform. Process. Syst. **32** (2019) H. Wallach, H. Larochelle, A. Beygelzimer, F. d' Alché-Buc, E. Fox, and R. Garnett, Eds. Curran Associates Inc, 2019, pp. 8026–8037. www.papers.nips.cc/paper/9015-pytorch-an-imperative-style-high-performance-deep-learning-library.pdf
44. Loshchilov, I., Hutter, F.: SGDR: stochastic gradient descent with warm restarts. In: 5th International Conference on Learning Representations, ICLR 2017, Toulon, France, April 24–26, 2017, Conference Track Proceedings (2017). www.openreview.net/forum?id=Skq89Scxx
45. Sandler, M., Howard, A., Zhu, M., Zhmoginov, A., Chen, L.: MobileNetV2: Inverted Residuals and Linear Bottlenecks (2018)
46. Wang, Z., Li, C., Wang, X.: Convolutional neural network pruning with structural redundancy reduction. In: 2021 IEEE/CVF Conference on Computer Vision and Pattern Recognition (CVPR), pp. 14908–14917 (2021)
47. Almog, A., Shmueli, E.: Structural entropy: monitoring correlation-based networks over time with application to financial markets. Sci. Rep. **9**, 1–13 (2019)

Unsupervised Representation Learning: Target Regularization for Cross-Domain Sentiment Classification

Michał Perełkiewicz$^{(\boxtimes)}$ ⓘ, Rafał Poświata ⓘ, and Jakub Kierzkowski ⓘ

National Information Processing Institute, Al. Niepodległości 188B, Warsaw, Poland
{mperelkiewicz,rposwiata,jkierzkowski}@opi.org.pl

Abstract. This article proposes an autoencoder-based domain invariant feature representation learning approach to domain adaptation and the cross-domain text classification problem. Finding domain invariant feature representations is a transfer learning method for transmitting knowledge between source and target domain data. Our method aims to avoid the overfitting of an autoencoder model on source domain training data in a trained embedded feature space using a target regularization technique. We hypothesize that when forcing the semantic similarity of target domain representation to source domain representation by adding the source domain similarity penalty to reconstruction loss during autoencoder training, the penalty is greater when the the domain's representations separability is. In this work, we contribute to domain adaptation by demonstrating that a regularization technique based on an auxiliary pretrained domain classification model can be used to build robust, shared domain feature representations. Our model achieves a classification accuracy improvement in standard cross-domain sentiment classification tasks over the baseline model in most cases.

Keywords: Domain Adaptation · Unsupervised Representation Learning · AutoEncoders · Cross-domain Sentiment Classification · Target Regularization

1 Introduction

Supervised machine learning algorithms for classification adapt models to reproduce outputs known from training sets. They are well-studied for various classification tasks in natural language processing and have achieved state-of-the-art results for a wide range of benchmark datasets. However, many supervised learning algorithms work well only under common assumptions. First, the efficacy of supervised machine learning algorithms relies on an abundance of data. In practice, the requirement to collect a large amount of diverse labeled data is often time-consuming and challenging to meet. Moreover, it usually involves expert knowledge and entails high costs.

Another disadvantage of supervised techniques is that they perform well only when the training and the test data is drawn from the same feature space with

© The Author(s), under exclusive license to Springer Nature Switzerland AG 2023
L. Rutkowski et al. (Eds.): ICAISC 2023, LNAI 14125, pp. 181–192, 2023.
https://doi.org/10.1007/978-3-031-42505-9_16

a specific feature distribution; their performance often degrades considerably in the opposite case. This problem affects natural language processing systems that handle a wide range of text data types. This type of system should often provide a similar quality of result regardless of whether it is designed to analyze, for example, formal and informal text, or text that expresses opinions on different kinds of product.

Transfer Learning relaxes the hypothesis that training data must be distributed identically with test data [22]. The transfer learning research problem focuses on extracting and applying knowledge from the data of one domain or knowledge learned while solving one problem, and applying it to the data of another domain to solve another machine learning problem. One of the subfields of transfer learning, domain adaptation, focuses on transferring knowledge from a domain with a specific probability distribution, a *source domain*, to another domain with a different probability distribution, a *target domain*. Among the many methods of transferring knowledge between domains, building a shared domain data representation is one of the most popular [22]. Autoencoder models are commonly used to achieve robust and low-dimensional representations of data [25].

In this article, we consider the problem of cross-domain sentiment classification. We propose a new regularization technique to learn data representation with more close distributions between domains. Our approach comprises two steps. First, we train an auxiliary domain logistic regression model. Then, the model's output is incorporated as a target domain discrepancy penalty for reconstruction loss during autoencoder training. This approach attempts to ensure that the target domain feature space resembles the features of the source domain using a pretrained domain logistic regression model.

We evaluate our method using the Multi-Domain Sentiment Dataset[1], which contains Amazon reviews. Using our method, the results of downstream cross-domain sentiment classification tasks outperform the baseline model in most cases[2]. Our contributions are the proposal of an indirect target regularization technique and proof of the proposed method's efficiency.

The remainder of this article is structured as follows: In Sect. 2, we review related work about domain adaptation approaches in natural language processing—particularly for the cross-domain sentiment classification problem; Sect. 3 presents the proposed domain invariant feature representation learning approach, which uses the target regularization technique, in detail; Sect. 4 describes our experiments; Sect. 5 presents our conclusions.

2   Related Work

A large body of work exists on domain adaptation and cross-domain sentiment analysis. In survey [24], natural language processing domain adaptation research is categorized into model-centric and data-centric groups. The model-centric

---

[1] https://www.cs.jhu.edu/~mdredze/datasets/sentiment/.
[2] The code is available at https://github.com/mmichall/atuda-pytorch.

approach aims to augment the feature space, as well as altering the loss function and the architecture or model parameters [24]. One of the most significant approaches in the model-centric group is the structural correspondence learning (SCL) method proposed in 2006 [5]. It is based on *pivot features*—features that occur frequently in two domains and behave similarly in both. In [4], the authors applied the SCL algorithm to a cross-domain sentiment classification problem, and achieved a significant reduction in relative classification error compared to a supervised baseline. Another feature-centric method is spectral feature alignment [21]. This algorithm is used to align domain-specific words from different domains into unified clusters using domain-independent words. The clusters are then used to reduce the gap between the domain-specific words of the two domains, which can be used to train sentiment classifiers in the target domain accurately. Spectral feature alignment outperforms previous approaches to cross-domain sentiment classification significantly [21]. Ziser et al. extend the concept of the SCL algorithm by incorporating an autoencoder network to learn latent representations to map nonpivots to pivots' features, and using them to augment the training data [32,33]. Some improvements in the pivot-based learning process of deep neural networks in the context of cross-domain sentiment analysis are presented in [34]. The approach of extending pivot features with contextual embeddings has been presented in recent work [2]. Other studies propose training the feature representations and sentiment classifier jointly [18–20].

Autoencoders have formed the basis for a number of cross-domain sentiment classification publications. Using autoencoders to learn unified latent representations from text input data in an unsupervised fashion is a widespread practice [6,7,9–11,30]. Stacked denoising autoencoders (SDAs) learn cross-domain, unified text representations by stacking multiple layers and reconstructing corrupt input text. The trained text representation is then used to train domain independent classifiers. Works [6,7,30] proposed more efficient versions of SDA that introduce scalability to high-dimensional data and add regularization techniques, such as marginalized structured dropout and target regularization techniques, by forcing the reconstruction of text to resemble target domain objects.

The loss-centric group includes methods that manipulate the loss function during training [25]. The seminal method in this category is domain-adversarial neural networks [10]. This kind of adversarial neural network uses a gradient reversal layer to make feature distributions for the source and target domains similar by maximizing the confusion of an auxiliary domain classifier in distinguishing features from the two domains. Another approach uses an adversarial training technique inspired by generative adversarial networks [12] to reduce the approximated Wasserstein distance between domains' representations in Wasserstein generative adversarial networks [1] and Wasserstein distance guided representation learning [28] methods.

Instance weighting methods, another group of loss-centric approaches, propose a training method based on weighting each training instance proportionally to its similarity to the target domain. Work [17] proposes a general instance weighting framework for domain adaptation. The maximum mean discrepancy technique [13] and kernel mean matching [14] correct the difference between the input source and target distributions by reweighting the source instances in such a way that the means of the source and target instances in a reproducing kernel Hilbert space have more similar distributions.

Pseudolabeling techniques based on neural networks have been used with success [26, 27]. These approaches use tri-training methods for unsupervised domain adaptation, and assign pseudolabels to unlabeled samples and trained neural networks as if they were true labels.

Recently, large pretrained models and finetuning methods have been used widely in the domain adaptation of text classifiers. They achieve state-of-the-art results for cross-domain sentiment classification. In 2018, Howard and Ruder [16] proposed universal language model finetuning—an effective transfer learning method for cross-domain text classification tasks. Rietzler et al. finetuned the BERT language model for the aspect–target sentiment classification problem with impressive results. Han et al. [15] proposed a domain-adaptive finetuning of the BERT language model by masked language modeling on text from the target domain to address the problem of cross-domain text classification. The BitFit model [3], which is based on freezing most of the transformer-encoder parameters and training only the task-specific classification layer, achieved promising results.

3   Approach

For the assumptions of the domain adaptation classification problem for text data, we denote the labeled source domain dataset $X_s = \{(x_i^s, y_i^s) : i = 1, ..., n_s\}$, where text representation vector $x_i^s \in \mathbb{R}^m$ and a label $y_i^s \in \{0, 1, ..., l\}$, and the target domain dataset $X_t = \{x_i^t : i = 1, ..., n_t\}$, where text representation vector $x_i^t \in \mathbb{R}^m$. Here, n_s and n_t are the number of instances in X_s and X_t, respectively; l is the number of classes; and m is a length of an example representation vector. For the purpose of evaluation, we used the $Y_t = \{y_i^t : i = 1, ..., n_t\}$ target domain labels dataset. Domain adaptation classification attempts to transfer knowledge learned in a labeled source domain to an unlabeled one. Denoting the set of unlabeled source domain instances as $X_s' = \{x_i^s : i = 1, ..., n_s\}$, the aim of unsupervised representation learning is to create a shared representation of a common set $X = X_s' \cup X_t = \{x_i : i = 1, ..., n\}$, where $n = n_s + n_t = |X|$. We leverage the unsupervised learning method to learn the relationships between features and represent the data using latent features that relate to the original features.

Our approach involves building a shared representation of the X dataset by minimizing the reconstruction loss function of the denoising autoencoder (DAE) model [29] using the novel target regularization method. The target regularization technique is supposed to close the representation of target domain instances to the source domain instances in a shared latent feature space, and to transfer separability features from domain X_s to domain X_t.

Then, the trained shared representation is used to learn a source domain data classifier. To measure the ability of the proposed method of transfer separability knowledge between the source domain X_s and the target domain X_t, we used the trained model to label instances from dataset X_t and measure the accuracy of data classification X_t.

3.1 Denoising AutoEncoder

Autoencoders are neural network models that learn compressed, latent representations of input data. They are trained to reproduce a given input as their output by minimizing reconstruction loss during training in an unsupervised fashion. A trained latent representation includes the most important features of the input data when its dimension is significantly lower than that of the input data. Latent space is often used with downstream tasks, such as classification.

Denoising autoencoders (DAEs) ([29]) attempt to reproduce sentences' input data z_i from the corrupted data $\bar{z}_i \sim C_{z_i}$. The corruption (noising) process of input z_i is performed by setting some of the input values to zero, where C_{z_i} is the conditional probability distribution of a corruption process conditioned on z_i, as a parameter to the density. The purpose of reproducing a corrupted input is to discover the robust representations of the data and obtain a reconstruction distribution $Pr(z_i|\bar{z}_i)$ (which indicates which z_i is most likely, given $\bar{z}_i$), as well as recovering z_i from $\bar{z}_i$. The learning process of a one-layer DAE can be denoted as:

$$h_i = f(W_1 \bar{z}_i + b_1) \tag{1}$$

$$y_i = f(W_2 h_i + b_2) \tag{2}$$

where $z_i \in \mathbb{R}^{m_z}$ is a i-th sentences' input vector representation from a training dataset $Z = \{z_i : i = 1, ..., n_z\}$, n_z is a number of examples in a training set Z, f is a nonlinear activation function, $W_1 \in \mathbb{R}^{k \times m_z}$ and $W_2 \in \mathbb{R}^{m_z \times k}$ are weight matrices, $b_1 \in \mathbb{R}^k$ and $b_2 \in \mathbb{R}^{m_z}$ are bias vectors, and h_i is a middle layer value— a latent representation of z_i; k and m_z are sizes of the hidden layer and input/output layer, respectively.

The basic aim of a DAE model is to make the output y_i as close to the input x_i as possible. In case the inputs and outputs are within the range $[0,1]$, the cross-entropy loss J is often used as a reconstruction loss:

$$j_i = -(z_i \log(y_i) + (1 - z_i) \log(1 - y_i)) \tag{3}$$

$$J = \frac{1}{n_z} \sum_{i=1}^{n_z} j_i \tag{4}$$

As proven in numerous works ([8,9,23,31]) DAE models can be used successfully to train text domain invariant feature representations. The idea behind DAE-based unsupervised representation learning is to train a DAE model on the X dataset—to achieve a shared feature representation $H = \{h_i : i = 1, ..., n\}$ of the two domains simultaneously. The shared representation H is used to learn a downstream classifier on the labeled source examples.

We propose a regularization method for a DAE learning approach. We call it *target regularization* and use it to address the overfitting of the autoencoder on the source domain data and the target domain data independently. The proposed regularization method modifies the reconstruction error in such a way that the target domain data representation comes to resemble the source domain data representation during the training. We want these two domain representations to become less linearly separable in latent space by closing them indirectly.

3.2   Target Regularization

The problem of the similarity of probability distributions for source and target domains has been discussed in several articles ([6,9,23]). To the best of our knowledge, the unsupervised representation learning methods based on autoencoders that have been presented to date are based on closing the probability distributions directly on latent representations. The disadvantage of these methods is that they interfere with a direct manner in terms of domains separability. Our approach incorporates an indirect regularization technique. We change the latent space by manipulating the reconstruction loss (and not the latent representation) indirectly.

The core of the target regularization technique is an auxiliary, pretrained logistic regression model that is trained to distinguish inputs between source and target domains. For the dataset X, we labeled each element on the domain label $L \in \{0, 1\}$ creating labeled dataset $S = \{(x_i, l_i) : i = 1, ..., n\}$, where $x \in X$ and $l \in L$. We assumed values of 1 and 0, respectively, for the source domain and target domain. We then trained the logistic regression model, denoted as:

$$y_{r_i} = \frac{e^{b_r + W_r x_i}}{1 + e^{b_r + W_r x_i}} \tag{5}$$

where $y_{r_i} \in (0, 1)$ is the domain label predicted value for the x_i, W_r is a weight matrix and b_r is a bias vector. To distinguish the original domain (source or target) of instances by minimizing the binary cross-entropy loss J_r:

$$j_{r_i} = -(l_i \log(y_{r_i}) + (1 - l_i) \log(1 - y_{r_i})) \tag{6}$$

$$J_r = \frac{1}{n} \sum_{i=1}^{n} j_{r_i} \tag{7}$$

Then, during the DAE model training, we add the regularization to the reconstruction loss (Eq. 3) as follows:

$$j_{tr_i} = j_i + \alpha j_{r_i} \tag{8}$$

where α is the regularization rate (usually less than 1). As we approximate the data representation of the target domain to the source domain, we assume $l_i = 1$ for all examples x_i, so the reconstruction loss J_{tr} with the target regularization technique is as follows:

$$j_{tr_i} = -(x_i \log(y_i) + (1 - x_i) \log(1 - y_i)) - \alpha \log(y_{r_i}) \tag{9}$$

$$J_{tr} = \frac{1}{n} \sum_{i=1}^{n} j_{tr_i} \tag{10}$$

When the regression model output indicates the high probability of a target class (y_{r_i} is a value close to 1), the regularization penalty j_{r_i} is close to zero and it does not influence the loss to any large extent. Conversely, where the regression model generates a value close to zero, the target regularization penalty is high and influences the final loss to a greater extent. In this situation, the classification is pressurized to modify the latent representation for instances it recognises as source to resemble the target representations. When the DAE model is training with the regularization technique, weights of domain logistic regression model are frozen and are not modifying.

Our thesis is that incorporating the target regularization technique to autoencoders causes those target instance representations to resemble the semantic source data representation by focusing on reconstruction of the most frequent and shared words.

4   Experiments

We conducted unsupervised cross-domain sentiment classification experiments using the Multi-Domain Sentiment Dataset, which contains Amazon reviews of four types of product: books (B), DVDs (D), electronics (E), and kitchen appliances (K).

Our preprocessing corresponded to the setting of [4]. Each review text was transformed into a bag-of-words (BoW) binary vector that encoded the presence or absence of unigrams and bigrams extraced from text data beforehand. As [4] suggests, we limited our preprocessing to the 5000 most frequent terms of the vocabulary of unigrams and bigrams. Reviews with original rating higher than 3 were labeled positive; those with ratings lower than 3 were labeled negative. Each domain (product type) consisted of 2000 labeled inputs and approximately 4000 unlabeled ones (which varied slightly between domains), and the two classes were balanced exactly.

The DAE model was forced to reconstruct whole example text while producing the BoW binary encoded input vector. To "noise" (transform into the zero value) the data, we replaced the 1 value to zero in the input vector with a given probability P_n. Our experiments suggested more robust latent representation for higher values of P_n.[3] For $P_n = 0.7$, we noised 70% of the original vector values. Intuitively, higher values of P_n allowed us to hide some words in the input data and force the DAE model to guess the hidden words based on the remaining, more frequently-occurring words. This approach transformed source data knowledge into target data by learned shared feature representations on data containing examples from source and target domains.

We conducted experiments for each of the 12 pairs of Multi-Domain Sentiment Dataset domains. For each pair, we trained the baseline logistic regression

---

[3] We experimented with $P_n \in \{0.3, 0.5, 0.7, 0.9\}$.

model on BoW vectors; we trained two logistic regression models on pretrained DAE without target regularisation (DAE) and one with (DAE+T_R).

For these experiments, we built autoencoders that contained one hidden layer of size 3000 and input/output layers of size 5000. We chose the sigmoid function as the activation function f so the y_i output values where within the range $(0, 1)$. We conducted test experiments with more hidden, stacked layers with larger sizes, but they failed to improve the results with longer training times. We achieved the best results of our experiments for $P_n = 0.7$ and $\alpha = 0.001$.

4.1   Results

Table 1 presents the results for 12 adaptation tasks on the Multi-Domain Sentiment Dataset. Each adaptation task classifies the sentiment of target domain reviews by the classifier learnt on latent representation of the source domain data. We compare our method with two baselines: a classifier simply learnt on source domain data with BoW representation (BoW) and a classifier learnt on DAE data representation without use of target regularization (DAE). We used support vector machine classifiers for all experiments and present the accuracy of the sentiment classification measure. The rightmost column presents the target domain classification results for the DAE target regularized data representation. We repeated the experiments three times for the DAE and DAE+T_R models for each domain pair, and calculated the average mean and standard deviation for each.

Table 1. The Multi-Domain Sentiment Dataset classification results. The accuracy (%) on target domain data for sentiment classification for each domains pairs. The results of the baselines BoW and DAE, and our proposed method, DAE+T_R

Source → Taget	BoW	DAE	DAE+T_R
B → D	77.8	77.7 ± 0.37	**78.7** ± 0.17
B → E	74.4	75.8 ± 0.69	**76.6** ± 0.26
B → K	76.1	78.2 ± 0.69	**79.5** ± 0.64
K → B	70.6	74.3 ± 0.81	**74.9** ± 0.20
K → E	83.1	84.6 ± 0.26	84.6 ± 0.29
K → D	71.4	75.1 ± 0.75	**76.8** ± 0.23
E → D	69.2	**72.7** ± 1.11	72.2 ± 0.60
E → B	69.5	69.7 ± 0.69	**72.8** ± 0.69
E → K	83.8	84.4 ± 0.12	**84.9** ± 0.59
D → E	72.2	**72.4** ± 0.60	71.7 ± 0.75
D → B	74.6	74.0 ± 1.04	**75.4** ± 0.23
D → K	75.0	78.4 ±0.38	**80.7** ± 1.17
Avg	74.8	76.4 ± 0.63	**77.4** ± 0.40

Our model achieves an improvement in its performance against the baseline model in nine of the twelve cases. The average results of the classification demonstrate the superiority of our target regularization method over the baselines. The average improvement is approximately 2.6% points above the BoW classification and approximately one percentage point above the DAE classification. These results indicate that our hypothesis is a valid one.

For the (K,E) and (D,E) domain pairs, the use of target regularization does not affect the result to any large extent. This result is explained by the fact that the kitchen appliance and electronics domains, as well as the DVD and electronics domains are similar to each other and contain a lot of the same words in similar contexts. This indicates that the use of regularization is unnecessary in the learning of more robust domain representations.

5 Conclusion

We have demonstrated a regularization method that learns a more robust latent representation using DAE for domain data. We have proven that an unsupervised representation learning model based on pretrained domain classifier and AE reconstruction loss modifications can influence the similarity between target and source domain data representations. Using this kind of target regularization we have achieved an improvement compared to the standard DAE representation on a popular dataset. Our work motivates a deeper investigation into regularization techniques and using pretrained domains classifiers in the domain adaptation problem.

References

1. Arjovsky, M., Chintala, S., Bottou, L.: Wasserstein Generative Adversarial Networks. In: Precup, D., Teh, Y.W. (eds.) Proceedings of the 34th International Conference on Machine Learning. Proceedings of Machine Learning Research, vol. 70, pp. 214–223. PMLR (06–11 Aug 2017)
2. Ben-David, E., Rabinovitz, C., Reichart, R.: PERL: Pivot-based Domain Adaptation for Pre-trained Deep Contextualized Embedding Models. CoRR abs/2006.09075 (2020)
3. Ben Zaken, E., Goldberg, Y., Ravfogel, S.: BitFit: Simple Parameter-efficient Fine-tuning for Transformer-based Masked Language-models. In: Proceedings of the 60th Annual Meeting of the Association for Computational Linguistics (Volume 2: Short Papers), pp. 1–9. Association for Computational Linguistics, Dublin, Ireland (May 2022). https://doi.org/10.18653/v1/2022.acl-short.1
4. Blitzer, J., Dredze, M., Pereira, F.: Biographies, Bollywood, Boom-boxes and Blenders: Domain Adaptation for Sentiment Classification. In: Proceedings of the 45th Annual Meeting of the Association of Computational Linguistics, pp. 440–447. Association for Computational Linguistics, Prague, Czech Republic (Jun 2007). www.aclanthology.org/P07-1056
5. Blitzer, J., McDonald, R., Pereira, F.: Domain Adaptation with Structural Correspondence Learning. In: Proceedings of the 2006 Conference on Empirical Methods in Natural Language Processing, pp. 120–128. Association for Computational Linguistics, Sydney, Australia (2006). www.aclanthology.org/W06-1615

6. Chen, M., Xu, Z., Weinberger, K.Q., Sha, F.: Marginalized Denoising Autoencoders for Domain Adaptation. In: Proceedings of the 29th International Conference on International Conference on Machine Learning, pp. 1627–1634. ICML'12, Omnipress, Madison, WI, USA (2012)

7. Clinchant, S., Csurka, G., Chidlovskii, B.: A Domain Adaptation Regularization for Denoising Autoencoders. In: Proceedings of the 54th Annual Meeting of the Association for Computational Linguistics (Volume 2: Short Papers), pp. 26–31. Association for Computational Linguistics, Berlin, Germany (2016). https://doi.org/10.18653/v1/P16-2005, www.aclanthology.org/P16-2005

8. Dong, X., de Melo, G.: A Helping Hand: Transfer Learning for Deep Sentiment Analysis. In: Proceedings of the 56th Annual Meeting of the Association for Computational Linguistics (Volume 1: Long Papers), pp. 2524–2534. Association for Computational Linguistics, Melbourne, Australia (Jul 2018). 10.18653/v1/P18-1235, www.aclanthology.org/P18-1235

9. Ganin, Y., Lempitsky, V.: Unsupervised Domain Adaptation by Backpropagation. In: Proceedings of the 32nd International Conference on International Conference on Machine Learning - Volume 37, p. 1180–1189. ICML'15, JMLR.org (2015)

10. Ganin, Y., et al.: Domain-Adversarial Training of Neural Networks. J. Mach. Learn. Res. **17**(1), 2096–2030 (2016)

11. Glorot, X., Bordes, A., Bengio, Y.: Domain Adaptation for Large-Scale Sentiment Classification: A Deep Learning Approach. In: Proceedings of the 28th International Conference on International Conference on Machine Learning. p. 513–520. ICML'11, Omnipress, Madison, WI, USA (2011)

12. Goodfellow, I., et al.: Generative Adversarial Nets. In: Ghahramani, Z., Welling, M., Cortes, C., Lawrence, N., Weinberger, K. (eds.) Advances in Neural Information Processing Systems, vol. 27. Curran Associates, Inc. (2014)

13. Gretton, A., Borgwardt, K., Rasch, M., Schölkopf, B., Smola, A.: A Kernel Method for the Two-Sample-Problem. In: Schölkopf, B., Platt, J., Hoffman, T. (eds.) Advances in Neural Information Processing Systems, vol. 19. MIT Press (2006)

14. Gretton, A., Smola, A., Huang, J., Schmittfull, M., Borgwardt, K., Schölkopf, B.: Covariate Shift by Kernel Mean Matching. In: Dataset Shift in Machine Learning. The MIT Press (12 2008). https://doi.org/10.7551/mitpress/9780262170055.003.0008

15. Han, X., Eisenstein, J.: Unsupervised Domain Adaptation of Contextualized Embeddings for Sequence Labeling. In: EMNLP (2019)

16. Howard, J., Ruder, S.: Universal Language Model Fine-tuning for Text Classification, pp. 328–339 (2018). https://doi.org/10.18653/v1/P18-1031

17. Jiang, J., Zhai, C.: Instance Weighting for Domain Adaptation in NLP. In: Proceedings of the 45th Annual Meeting of the Association of Computational Linguistics, pp. 264–271. Association for Computational Linguistics, Prague, Czech Republic (2007)

18. Li, Z., Wei, Y., Zhang, Y., Yang, Q.: Hierarchical Attention Transfer Network for Cross-Domain Sentiment Classification. In: Proceedings of the AAAI Conference on Artificial Intelligence, vol. 32 no.(1) (2018). https://doi.org/10.1609/aaai.v32i1.12055, www.ojs.aaai.org/index.php/AAAI/article/view/12055

19. Li, Z., Zhang, Y., Wei, Y., Wu, Y., Yang, Q.: End-to-End Adversarial Memory Network for Cross-domain Sentiment Classification. In: Proceedings of the Twenty-Sixth International Joint Conference on Artificial Intelligence, IJCAI-17, pp. 2237–2243 (2017). https://doi.org/10.24963/ijcai.2017/311

20. Miller, T.: Simplified Neural Unsupervised Domain Adaptation. In: Proceedings of the 2019 Conference of the North American Chapter of the Association for Computational Linguistics: Human Language Technologies, Volume 1 (Long and Short Papers), pp. 414–419. Association for Computational Linguistics, Minneapolis, Minnesota (2019). https://doi.org/10.18653/v1/N19-1039, www.aclanthology.org/N19-1039

21. Pan, S.J., Ni, X., Sun, J.T., Yang, Q., Chen, Z.: Cross-domain sentiment classification via spectral feature alignment. In: Proceedings of the 19th International Conference on World Wide Web. p. 751–760. WWW '10, Association for Computing Machinery, New York, NY, USA (2010). https://doi.org/10.1145/1772690.1772767

22. Pan, S.J., Yang, Q.: A survey on transfer learning. IEEE Trans. Knowl. Data Eng. **22**(10), 1345–1359 (2010). https://doi.org/10.1109/TKDE.2009.191

23. Peng, M., Zhang, Q., Jiang, Y.g., Huang, X.: Cross-domain sentiment classification with target domain specific information. In: Proceedings of the 56th Annual Meeting of the Association for Computational Linguistics (Volume 1: Long Papers), pp. 2505–2513. Association for Computational Linguistics, Melbourne, Australia (Jul 2018). https://doi.org/10.18653/v1/P18-1233, www.aclanthology.org/P18-1233

24. Ramponi, A., Plank, B.: Neural Unsupervised Domain Adaptation in NLP–A Survey. In: Proceedings of the 28th International Conference on Computational Linguistics, pp. 6838–6855. International Committee on Computational Linguistics, Barcelona, Spain (Online) (2020). https://doi.org/10.18653/v1/2020.coling-main.603

25. Ramponi, A., Plank, B.: Neural Unsupervised Domain Adaptation in NLP-A Survey. ArXiv:abs/2006.00632 (2020)

26. Ruder, S., Plank, B.: Strong Baselines for Neural Semi-supervised Learning under Domain Shift. CoRR abs/1804.09530 (2018)

27. Saito, K., Ushiku, Y., Harada, T.: Asymmetric Tri-training for Unsupervised Domain Adaptation. CoRR abs/1702.08400 (2017)

28. Shen, J., Qu, Y., Zhang, W., Yu, Y.: Wasserstein Distance Guided Representation Learning for Domain Adaptation. In: Proceedings of the Thirty-Second AAAI Conference on Artificial Intelligence and Thirtieth Innovative Applications of Artificial Intelligence Conference and Eighth AAAI Symposium on Educational Advances in Artificial Intelligence. AAAI'18/IAAI'18/EAAI'18, AAAI Press (2018)

29. Vincent, P., Larochelle, H., Bengio, Y., Manzagol, P.A.: Extracting and composing robust features with denoising autoencoders. In: Proceedings of the 25th International Conference on Machine Learning, pp. 1096–1103. ICML '08, Association for Computing Machinery, New York, NY, USA (2008). https://doi.org/10.1145/1390156.1390294

30. Yang, Y., Eisenstein, J.: Fast Easy Unsupervised Domain Adaptation with Marginalized Structured Dropout. In: Proceedings of the 52nd Annual Meeting of the Association for Computational Linguistics (Volume 2: Short Papers), pp. 538–544. Association for Computational Linguistics, Baltimore, Maryland (2014). https://doi.org/10.3115/v1/P14-2088, www.aclanthology.org/P14-2088

31. Zhuang, F., Cheng, X., Luo, P., Pan, S.J., He, Q.: Supervised representation learning: Transfer learning with deep autoencoders. In: IJCAI (2015)

32. Ziser, Y., Reichart, R.: Deep pivot-based modeling for cross-language cross-domain transfer with minimal guidance. In: Proceedings of the 2018 Conference on Empirical Methods in Natural Language Processing, pp. 238–249. Association for Computational Linguistics, Brussels, Belgium (Oct-Nov 2018). https://doi.org/10.18653/v1/D18-1022, www.aclanthology.org/D18-1022

33. Ziser, Y., Reichart, R.: Pivot based language modeling for improved neural domain adaptation. In: Proceedings of the 2018 Conference of the North American Chapter of the Association for Computational Linguistics: Human Language Technologies, Volume 1 (Long Papers), pp. 1241–1251. Association for Computational Linguistics, New Orleans, Louisiana (Jun 2018). https://doi.org/10.18653/v1/N18-1112, www.aclanthology.org/N18-1112

34. Ziser, Y., Reichart, R.: Task refinement learning for improved accuracy and stability of unsupervised domain adaptation. In: Proceedings of the 57th Annual Meeting of the Association for Computational Linguistics, pp. 5895–5906. Association for Computational Linguistics, Florence, Italy (2019). https://doi.org/10.18653/v1/P19-1591, www.aclanthology.org/P19-1591

Decentralized Federated Learning Loop with Constrained Trust Mechanism

Dawid Połap[1(✉)], Katarzyna Prokop[1], Gautam Srivastava[2], and Jerry Chun-Wei Lin[3]

[1] Faculty of Applied Mathematics, Silesian University of Technology, Kaszubska 23,44-100 Gliwice, Poland
`Dawid.Polap@polsl.pl, katapro653@student.polsl.pl`
[2] Department of Mathematics and Computer Science, Brandon University, Brandon R7A 6A9, Canada
`SrivastavaG@brandonu.ca`
[3] Western Norway University of Applied Sciences, Bergen, Norway
`JerryLin@ieee.org`

Abstract. Federated learning has made it possible to introduce parallel training of deep neural networks by multiple users. The use of model aggregation contributes to the generalization of it, although there is a possibility of attacks. An example of this is dataset poisoning. Hence, in this research paper, we propose the introduction of a constrained trust mechanism for individual clients. In addition, a decentralized approach makes it possible to increase the effectiveness of the training process by removing the server and reducing the risk of an attack on the transmitting model. The proposed modification of federated learning was subjected to performance tests and compared with other known solutions. The obtained results indicate an increase in safety and accuracy.

Keywords: neural network · federated learning · machine learning · trust mechanism

1 Introduction

The federated learning approach changed the way how machine learning solutions are used [17]. This is especially important in the era of intelligent solutions. The preparation of the product using neural networks was limited to the preparation of the software and training of the network at the modeling/implementation stage. In addition, the basic requirement was to prepare a huge database containing various data used for training. Due to the federated approach, the database is created by software users. Subsequent joining users receives already trained models and only improve them. It should be noted that these are changes with a positive impact on privacy and the continuous improvement of the used artificial intelligence models.

Classic federated learning is known as the centralized approach [2]. All clients train the general model and resend it to the server for aggregation. All models

© The Author(s), under exclusive license to Springer Nature Switzerland AG 2023
L. Rutkowski et al. (Eds.): ICAISC 2023, LNAI 14125, pp. 193–202, 2023.
https://doi.org/10.1007/978-3-031-42505-9_17

are trained on local datasets for creating a new, general model. However, it is worth noting that in the case of poisoning one dataset, the effectiveness of the entire model will be reduced. Such poisoning is possible by changing the labels of images in a database or by modifying the training samples. Particularly, the modification is difficult to detect because it can be a small change of a certain number of important pixels, which may cause classifier training errors. Moreover, adding a specific sequence of pixels to images with different classes may be considered the same class by the classifier. Hence, a very important element of today's research in the field of training neural networks is their security and the ability to detect attacks such as poisoning.

The increase in the security of the federated approach has been achieved by deleting the server and moving the aggregation process to clients. Decentralization is treated as an opportunity to train the network by sharing models just by clients [3]. However, decentralization itself does not contribute to the analysis of the models or the sets themselves. It reduces the latency for the server model. This is due to the possibility of aggregation even when one model has been received.

In this paper, we propose an improvement of decentralized federated learning by trust mechanism, that allows for additional verification of the received models. Each of the obtained models is evaluated and, depending on the possible benefits of the client, a decision on aggregation is made. In addition, we propose a stop condition by analyzing the model exchange loop. The main contribution are:

- adding constrained trust mechanism for validating models in the pre-aggregation phase,
- introducing the client's loop as a stop condition in the federated learning solutions,
- increasing the security level of models involved in federated learning.

2   Related Works

The enormous potential of federated learning has contributed to a wide discussion on practical use as well as improvement. Despite many advantages of the idea itself, federated learning solutions have unresolved issues of insecurity or the stop condition. Recent years have brought many different modifications and ideas to minimize the existing problem. In [13], the decentralized average consensus was introduced to clients because of eliminating the central server. Another idea of consensus is dynamic average one [6]. It is based on treating the client's training as a discrete-time series, then the average model is estimated by the average consensus. The consensus method is important to perform aggregation operations. Moreover, it is a difficult issue in decentralized models. However, there is research that uses also a centralized model with consensus. Consensus is important in a situation when there are many different models and some of them should be selected for aggregation, such a situation was presented in [11], where a fuzzy controller was used for it.

Such systems are quite often implemented through the use of wireless networks [5]. Moreover, there are ideas for improving federated learning by quantum version [8]. The research describes a new version of federated learning by aggregating updates from local calculations to share model parameters. The researchers focused on the analysis of the privacy of the data exchanged through analog transmission schemes over wireless channels. In these solutions, the authors focus on the consensus method as well as the method of data transmission. A popular solution is also the use of encryption algorithms that will additionally secure the data. An example is the use of blockchain and AES and DES algorithms [12]. A similar approach is to use verifiable cipher-based matrix multiplication [18]. Another research is based on creating a participation matrix and trust consensus mechanism [16]. The proposed approach is based on the creation of the mentioned matrix before generating the decryption key. This matrix is used to evaluate each received model. Expert systems are also quite important in this matter [15].

Security, data privacy and consensus are one of the most important issues that scientists work on. However, there should be also discussed the state of the used machine learning in federated learning solutions. Learning transfer is pre-training neural models that need to be reconfigured last layers and retrain. It allows using the already trained network for other problems with retraining [10]. In the case of federated learning, yolo architecture can be used [14]. The authors focused on using this architecture to increase accuracy in IoT solutions. The federated learning approach is very interesting in the case of implementing smart solutions, where many objects can collect their own data and train models. It was shown in medical systems [1], or UAV target recognition [7].

3   Proposed Methodology

In this section, a proposed decentralized federated learning with the ADAM algorithm is presented. Moreover, the additional client's operation for evaluating received models is described.

3.1   Decentralized Federated Learning Loop with Stop Condition

Decentralized federated learning (DFL) assumes that there are K clients and each of them has its own dataset D_k $(k = 1, \ldots, K)$. The number of samples in each dataset can be marked as $n_k = |D_k|$. For each client, the loss function $f(\mathbf{w}, \xi)$ is calculated for a given sample ξ and model $\mathbf{w}$. Based on it, the loss value on the k-th client can be defined as:

$$F_k(\mathbf{w}) = \frac{1}{n_k} \sum_{\xi \in D_k} f(\mathbf{w}, \xi). \tag{1}$$

A global loss function is determined as:

$$F(\mathbf{w}) = \sum_{k=1}^{K} p_k F_k(\mathbf{w}), \tag{2}$$

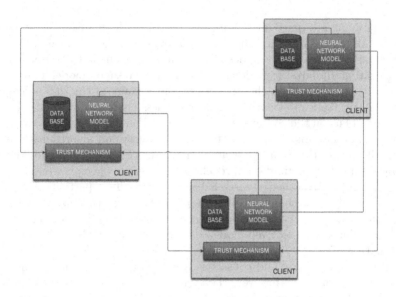

Fig. 1. Decentralized federated learning visualization

where p_k is the weight of the dataset on a given client. Assuming, that each client trains their local model $\mathbf{w^t_{k,i}}$ using ADAM algorithm [9], the mini-batch will be chosen at random from local database D_k and marked as $B^t_{k,i}$ in i-th iteration of the training process. The algorithm assumes calculation first and second moments known as mean m^t_k and variance v^t_k using distribution parameters β_1, β_2. It is formulated as:

$$m^t_k = \beta_1 m^t_k + (1 - \beta_1) g_k \left(\mathbf{w}^t_{k,i}, B^t_{k,i} \right), \tag{3}$$

$$v^t_k = \beta_2 v^t_k + (1 - \beta_2) g^2_k \left(\mathbf{w}^t_{k,i}, B^t_{k,i} \right), \tag{4}$$

where $g_k(\mathbf{w}^t_{k,i}, B^t_{k,i})$ is a local gradient on k-th client calculated as:

$$g_k(\mathbf{w}^t_{k,i}, B^t_{k,i}) = \frac{1}{\left| B^t_{k,i} \right|} \sum_{\xi \in B^t_{k,i}} \nabla f \left(\mathbf{w}^t_{k,i}, \xi \right) \tag{5}$$

Then, the bias correction of the above moments is defined as:

$$\hat{m}^t_k = \frac{m^t_k}{1 - \beta_1}, \tag{6}$$

$$\hat{v}^t_k = \frac{v^t_k}{1 - \beta_2}. \tag{7}$$

Finally, these equations are considered in updating the local model as:

$$\mathbf{w}^{t+1}_{k,i+1} = w^t_{k,i} - \eta^t_i \frac{\hat{m}_t}{\sqrt{\hat{v}_t} + \epsilon}, \tag{8}$$

where η_i^t is a learning rate at i-th iteration of round t and ϵ is a small value to prevent the possibility of dividing by zero.

Traditional federated learning is made by reaching a specific number of rounds in which all clients shared their model with others. In a situation where the accuracy of a specific client is very high – the current model is very good and there is no need to generalize it more. Of course, we are only talking about a single client who will not do aggregation. However, as long as there are other clients, he will share his model upon their request. Federated learning ends when all clients achieve high accuracy on their models. The client will end the aggregation when the local loss of the model will be lower than the receiving models during at least L rounds. It can be modeled as the following condition:

$$\begin{gathered}
\left(F_k^t(\mathbf{w}_k) < F_k^t(\mathbf{w}_r)\right) \wedge \left(F_k^{t-1}(\mathbf{w}_k) < F_k^{t-1}(\mathbf{w}_r)\right) \\
\wedge \ldots \wedge \left(F_k^{t-L-1}(\mathbf{w}_k) < F_k^{t-L-1}(\mathbf{w}_r)\right),
\end{gathered} \tag{9}$$

where $\mathbf{w}_k$ is the current model of k-th client and $\mathbf{w}_r$ is the received model.

Adding a new client after completing DFL can then be done by starting the entire process from the beginning, or training a single client by aggregation with existing models. The proposal is presented in Fig. 1.

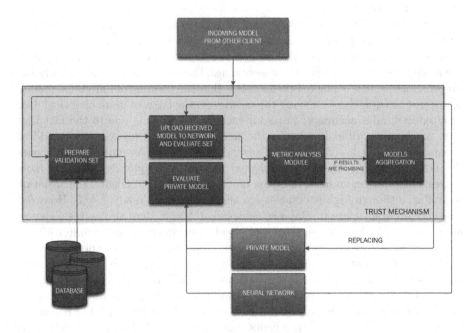

Fig. 2. A visualization of the constrained trust mechanism on client

3.2 The Constrained Trust Mechanism

Received models from other clients can be poisoned, therefore, validation should be considered. For this purpose, the client's operation can be extended by additional validation of incoming models. A simple visualization of this process is shown in Fig. 2. A client randomly selects samples from the database for evaluation of existing and received models. For both evaluations, metric like an accuracy, loss value is calculated and used for evaluation. In the case when obtained results for the received model are better or similar to the current one, aggregation is performed.

4 Experiments

In the conducted experiments, we used FEMNIST (Federated Extended MNIST) [4] which is a dataset prepared for FL development and contains 805263 images split into 64 classes of characters. This dataset is based on 3550 subsets to simulated FL. The evaluation was performed on 20, 40 and 60 clients who were trained as a network composed of 2 convolutional layers (3×3), max pooling (2×2) and fully-connected one with 1024 neurons. Implementation was made in Python, TensorFlow on Intel Core i9-10850K 3.60GHz, 32GB RAM and NVIDIA GeForce RTX 3060.

For all clients, 10 separate tests were performed and all results were averaged. The number of clients and obtained DFL accuracy was presented in Fig. 3 . In the case of 20 clients, the accuracy of models reached almost 81% using the value of the L parameter set to 4. For the lower values, the accuracy was significantly low (approximately 10%). The reason for this is that the training of individual models is stopped too quickly. Analyzing the metrics on the basis of more historical data resulted in similar accuracy values for each $L \geq 4$. This is due to the fact that it is much more difficult to stop the network training process on individual clients. Obtaining lower values for several DFL rounds is much longer, hence the obtained high values of the selected metric (consequently following more aggregation and generalization of the model itself). For 40 clients, the situation is similar, although high accuracies are achieved using already $L = 3$. However, a level of accuracy close to 81% was achieved at $L = 5$. Here we can see a change at the level of higher values. For fewer clients, accuracy was not stable with the higher value of L parameter. A similar situation occurs with 60 clients.

Based on the obtained results during analyzing L parameter, the best results were reached by the application of $L = 4$ and $L = 5$. The proposed stop condition was analyzed using $L = 5$ on all DFL simulation settings. The obtained results are shown in Fig. 4. It is easy to notice that the DFL stop condition is reached in different rounds. The more clients, the learning ended faster. In any case, accuracy over 80% is achieved. However, the number of rounds between different simulation settings is relatively large. For 60 clients, high accuracy was achieved by the 40-th round. More than 50 epochs were needed for a smaller number of clients. The difference between 20 and 40 clients is just 3 rounds. Based on this chart, it can be seen that the last DFL rounds indicate a constant accuracy

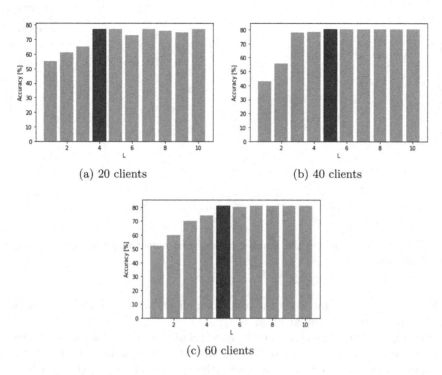

Fig. 3. The impact of L parameter on the stop condition of training

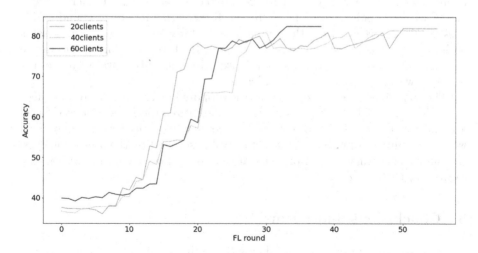

Fig. 4. Reached accuracy during DFL rounds with $L = 4$

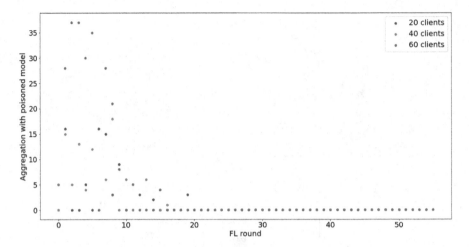

Fig. 5. The graph showing the number of poisoned model aggregation in federated learning round

value. This is a consequence of the remaining clients who train their model, but their metrics are at a similar level.

Subsequent studies focused on the analysis of the mechanism of constrained trust by applying a poisoning attack. In one of the client's datasets, labels were randomly shuffled. Then, in each round, the number of aggregations with this model was counted. Obtained results (see Fig. 5) indicate that in the first 10 iterations, there are many aggregations with poisoning sets. The number of aggregations depends on the number of clients participating in training. With a larger number of clients, more aggregations are counted. However, the number of aggregation with the poisoned model decreases along with subsequent rounds. This is especially noticeable from the 10 iterations. Moreover, the poisoned model is no longer used to generalize the models after 19-th round. This is due to the analysis of metrics, where the use of a poisoned model with private data results in very low accuracy as well as high losses.

The conducted research shows that the proposed mechanism of stopping federated learning enables faster completion of the entire process. As a consequence, a reduction in the number of calculations compared to the classical approach, where the number of rounds is a constant value selected by the user. Moreover, the implemented mechanism of constrained trust allows for an increase in the security of DFL.

5   Conclusions and Future Works

Decentralized federated learning allows the training of many different neural networks on separated devices and sharing models without private data. In this paper, we propose a stop condition based on a metric history of the clients. This allows for minimizing the number of performed DFL rounds and automates the process. The proposal stops training when there is no model improvement several times in a row. At the same time, it is possible to reactivate the client and continue training. In a situation where a given client does not participate in DFL (by training/model aggregation), he still shares his model. Moreover, we presented the mechanism of constrained trust to received models. Such analysis allows increasing protection against poisoning attacks. Based on the conducted research, it was noticed that the proposed solution has great potential in obtaining the automation of the learning process itself. The result shows that with a large number of clients, high accuracy is much faster obtained and reduces the risk of poisoning attacks.

In future work, we plan to focus on extending this research by expanding the constrained trust mechanism and reducing the number of performed calculations.

Acknowledgements. This work is supported by the Rector proquality grant at the Silesian University of Technology, Poland No. 09/010/RGJ22/0067.

References

1. Aich, S., et al.: Protecting personal healthcare record using blockchain & federated learning technologies. In: 2022 24th International Conference on Advanced Communication Technology (ICACT), IEEE, pp. 109–112 (2022)
2. Banabilah, S., Aloqaily, M., Alsayed, E., Malik, N., Jararweh, Y.: Federated learning review: fundamentals, enabling technologies, and future applications. Inform. Process. Manage. **59**(6), 103061 (2022)
3. Barbieri, L., Savazzi, S., Brambilla, M., Nicoli, M.: Decentralized federated learning for extended sensing in 6G connected vehicles. Veh. Comm. **33**, 100396 (2022)
4. Caldas, S., et al.: Leaf: A benchmark for federated settings. arXiv preprint arXiv:1812.01097 (2018)
5. Chen, S., Yu, D., Zou, Y., Yu, J., Cheng, X.: Decentralized wireless federated learning with differential privacy. IEEE Trans. Industr. Inf. **18**(9), 6273–6282 (2022)
6. Chen, Z., Li, D., Zhu, J., Zhang, S.: Dacfl: Dynamic average consensus-based federated learning in decentralized sensors network. Sensors **22**(9), 3317 (2022)
7. Fang, L.l., Hu, H.r., Pu, W., Bi, J.q.: Research on uav target recognition technology based on federated learning. In: 2021 2nd International Conference on Computer Engineering and Intelligent Control (ICCEIC), IEEE, pp. 119–122 (2021)
8. Huang, R., Tan, X., Xu, Q.: Quantum federated learning with decentralized data. IEEE J. Sel. Top. Quant. Electron. **28**(4), 1–10 (2022)
9. Kingma, D.P., Ba, J.: Adam: A method for stochastic optimization. In: ICLR (Poster). (2015)
10. Nguyen, H.C., Nguyen, T.H., Scherer, R., Le, V.H.: Unified end-to-end yolov5-HR-TCM framework for automatic 2d/3d human pose estimation for real-time applications. Sensors **22**(14), 5419 (2022)
11. Połap, D.: Fuzzy consensus with federated learning method in medical systems. IEEE Access **9**, 150383–150392 (2021)
12. Prokop, K., Połap, D., Srivastava, G., Lin, J.C.W.: Blockchain-based federated learning with checksums to increase security in internet of things solutions. J. Ambient Intell. Hum. Comput. 1–10 (2022)

13. Qiu, W., Ai, W., Chen, H., Feng, Q., Tang, G.: Decentralized federated learning for industrial IoT with deep echo state networks. IEEE Trans. Indust. Inform. (2022)
14. Rjoub, G., Wahab, O.A., Bentahar, J., Bataineh, A.S.: Improving autonomous vehicles safety in snow weather using federated YOLO CNN learning. In: Bentahar, J., Awan, I., Younas, M., Grønli, T.-M. (eds.) MobiWIS 2021. LNCS, vol. 12814, pp. 121–134. Springer, Cham (2021). https://doi.org/10.1007/978-3-030-83164-6_10
15. Stateczny, A.: Artificial neural networks for comparative navigation. In: Rutkowski, L., Siekmann, J.H., Tadeusiewicz, R., Zadeh, L.A. (eds.) ICAISC 2004. LNCS (LNAI), vol. 3070, pp. 1187–1192. Springer, Heidelberg (2004). https://doi.org/10.1007/978-3-540-24844-6_186
16. Xu, R., Baracaldo, N., Zhou, Y., Anwar, A., Kadhe, S., Ludwig, H.: Detrust-fl: Privacy-preserving federated learning in decentralized trust setting. In: 2022 IEEE 15th International Conference on Cloud Computing (CLOUD), IEEE, pp. 417–426 (2022)
17. Ye, H., Liang, L., Li, G.Y.: Decentralized federated learning with unreliable communications. IEEE J. Selected Topics Signal Process. 16(3), 487–500 (2022)
18. Zhao, J., Zhu, H., Wang, F., Lu, R., Liu, Z., Li, H.: Pvd-fl: A privacy-preserving and verifiable decentralized federated learning framework. IEEE Trans. Inform. Forensics Security 17, 2059–2073 (2022)

Learning Activation Functions
for Adversarial Attack Resilience
in CNNs

Maghsood Salimi[✉][iD], Mohammad Loni[iD], and Marjan Sirjani[iD]

Malardalen University, Vasteras, Sweden
{maghsood.salimi,mohammad.loni,mmarjan.sirjani}@mdu.se

Abstract. Adversarial attacks on convolutional neural networks (CNNs) have been a serious concern in recent years, as they can cause CNNs to produce inaccurate predictions. Through our analysis of training CNNs with adversarial examples, we discovered that this was primarily caused by naïvely selecting ReLU as the default choice for activation functions. In contrast to the focus of recent works on proposing adversarial training methods, we study the feasibility of an innovative alternative: learning novel activation functions to make CNNs more resilient to adversarial attacks. In this paper, we propose a search framework that combines simulated annealing and late acceptance hill-climbing to find activation functions that are more robust against adversarial attacks in CNN architectures. The proposed search method has superior search convergence compared to commonly used baselines. The proposed method improves the resilience to adversarial attacks by achieving up to 17.1%, 22.8%, and 16.6% higher accuracy against BIM, FGSM, and PGD attacks, respectively, over ResNet-18 trained on the CIFAR-10 dataset.

Keywords: Convolutional Neural Network · Robustness · Adversarial Attack · Activation Function

1 Introduction

In an adversarial attack, malicious inputs are deliberately introduced into a machine learning model to make incorrect predictions [32]. Recent studies demonstrate that adversarial attacks can present a significant threat to various applications, such as computer vision [24], cyber-physical systems [16,39], medical machine learning models [9], and wireless communication [1]. Convolutional Neural Networks (CNNs) have shown their great ability to solve problems in various artificial intelligence fields. However, the vulnerability of CNNs to adversarial attacks has been shown in many studies [16,33,41]. This can be attributed to the activation functions (AFs) of a CNN with adversarial examples as they are never optimized, with the ReLU [34] being the default choice due to its simplicity and mitigating the vanishing gradient problem.

There have been efforts to improve the robustness of CNNs, either by using architecture search [8,13] or adversarial training [7,38]. Nevertheless, no systematic study has been conducted on the impact of learning novel network AFs

© The Author(s), under exclusive license to Springer Nature Switzerland AG 2023
L. Rutkowski et al. (Eds.): ICAISC 2023, LNAI 14125, pp. 203–214, 2023.
https://doi.org/10.1007/978-3-031-42505-9_18

over the robustness of CNNs against perturbed examples. Note that, despite the success of adversarial training methods, they require extensive input datasets, which necessitates resource-intensive data augmentation processes [47].

A natural step, thus, is to ask how the AFs impact the learning process for CNNs against adversarial examples. Our analysis of training CNNs with adversarial examples demonstrated that ReLU reduces trainability due to blocking the gradient flow (Sect. 2). A promising research direction in the field of Automated Machine Learning (AutoML) [17] is to optimize network AFs [2,3,6,10,18,27,37]. However, most of the proposed AF tweaking methods have huge computing demands (up to 2000 GPU hours [2]), resulting in a lack of interest in searching for AFs for various deep learning problems.

In this paper, we introduce an AutoML method that discovers robust AFs against adversarial examples by considering robustness accuracy as the search objective. We leverage a novel search algorithm that employs an ordered sequence of Simulated Annealing (SA) [19] and Late Acceptance Hill-Climbing (LAHC) [5] as the optimization stages. The intuition behind the efficiency of the proposed search method is that SA, as a global search method, practically traps in a local optimum after some search iterations. The LAHC method, on the other hand, starts with a solution augmented by SA and exploits the search space to find the global optimum as quickly as possible.

Unlike [7], our proposed method is a generic optimization approach that does not require data augmentation or adversarial training. Inspired by [27,28], we rely on lower fidelity estimations by training each candidate during the search iterations with fewer epochs, leading to expediting the search procedure.

We demonstrate the effectiveness of our proposed method by achieving up to 17.1%, 22.8%, and 16.6% higher accuracy against BIM, FGSM, and PGD adversarial attacks, respectively, over ResNet-18 trained on CIFAR-10 [20] with ReLU AFs. Additionally, our proposed method improves search efficiency by requiring up to 8.3 GPU days for learning new AFs, which is 9.3× faster than [2]. The proposed method generates similar results with a 4.8% standard deviation, demonstrating the reproducibility of our results.

2   Research Motivation

In this section, we validate the need for new AFs for a CNN under attack, and therefore, propose a robust activation function learning regime. Figure 1 shows the gradient flow for training ResNet-18 with ReLU AFs and new AFs learned by our method. In training ResNet-18 with ReLU, gradient flow is poor, indicating that ReLU potentially increases the information loss during forward propagation when adversarial attacks are present. Additionally, AF optimization is more appropriate for the early layers of the network since the gradient flow for optimized AFs is higher in those layers.

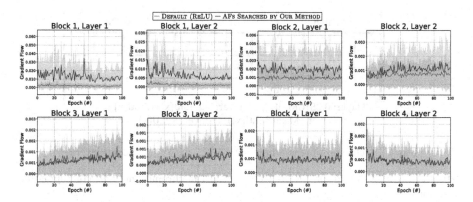

Fig. 1. Showing the gradient flow of the output of the Residual blocks in ResNet-18 with ReLU AF (red) and optimized AFs (blue). (Color figure online)

3   Proposed Method

In general, searching for new AFs is an NP-hard problem with exponential time complexity [27]. Thus, in a reasonable time, polynomial optimization cannot find the optimal solution. In addition, using exhaustive search methods is infeasible in practice, e.g., to exhaustively search an 8000-solution design space, [30] needs 334 GPU days. To this end, we utilize a meta-heuristic search method to deal with the exponential complexity of the AF search problem.

3.1   Search Space

Let us assume we have a CNN model with l hidden layers. The search space is represented by vectors which we call chromosomes. Chromosomes are divided into three parts, each with a length of l. Figure 2 shows an example of a chromosome for a CNN with four hidden layers. The first part of each chromosome is *Switch* which selects the corresponding operation between two AFs. For the sake of simplicity, every possible option for *Switch* is coded into the numbers, as listed in Table 1. As the second and third part of the chromosome, a set of potential candidate AFs is selected where different operations could be applied to them. We consider ReLU, LeakyReLU, Sigmoid, SELU, CELU, Mish, and GELU as the candidate AFs.

The size of the search space depends on various parameters, including the number of layers in the CNN and the number of candidate AFs being considered. The search space size is calculated by the following formula:

$$Search\ Space\ Size = \alpha \times (1 + \beta + (\alpha \times \theta))^l \tag{1}$$

where l is the number of layers, α is the number of candidate AFs, β is the number of possible values for the constant coefficient ($\{0.25, 0.5, 0.75\}$), and θ is the number of possible mathematical operations. According to Table 1, the size of the search space is equal to 7×32^7 for AlexNet with seven hidden layers.

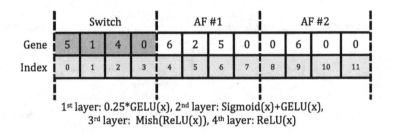

1st layer: 0.25*GELU(x), 2nd layer: Sigmoid(x)+GELU(x),
3rd layer: Mish(ReLU(x)), 4th layer: ReLU(x)

Fig. 2. A chromosome example for a CNN with four hidden layers.

Table 1. Possible values for the *Switch* part of the chromosome and corresponding operations.

Code	Switch	Description
0	$f(x) = g(x)$	Replacing the current AF with another AF selected from the list of candidates
1	$f(x) = g(x) + h(x)$	Accumulating selected AFs, where $g(x)$ comes from *AF #1* and $h(x)$ comes from *AF #2*
2	$f(x) = g(x) - h(x)$	A minus operation is performed on the selected AFs, $g(x)$ and $h(x)$
3	$f(x) = g(x) \times h(x)$	Multiplication of selected AFs, $g(x)$ and $h(x)$
4	$f(x) = g(h(x))$	Composition of selected AFs
5	$f(x) = 0.25 \times g(x)$	A constant value of 0.25 is multiplied by the selected AF $g(x)$ from *AF #1*
6	$f(x) = 0.5 \times g(x)$	A constant value of 0.5 is multiplied by the selected AF $g(x)$ from *AF #1*
7	$f(x) = 0.75 \times g(x)$	A constant value of 0.75 is multiplied by the selected AF $g(x)$ from *AF #1*

Results of applying different operations on two examples AFs, Sigmoid and Tanh, are shown in Fig. 3. Results demonstrate that by applying different operations, newly generated AFs significantly differ from the original ones, indicating the proposed search space is flexible to generate very different outputs.

3.2   Search Strategy

In order to solve different AutoML problems, several studies examined various meta-heuristic search methods, e.g., genetic algorithm [27], Late Acceptance Hill-Climbing (LAHC) and Simulated Annealing (SA) [28], and Particle Swarm Optimization [15]. In this paper, we leverage a multi-stage optimization method comprised of SA [19] and LAHC [5] algorithms.

Simulated Annealing. SA is a meta-heuristic search method that provides LAHC with initial solutions. SA iteratively explores solutions with better *Energy* function values. If a solution with a better *Energy* function is found, the current solution is replaced with the newly generated neighbor, otherwise, the current solution remains unchanged. To avoid becoming trapped in

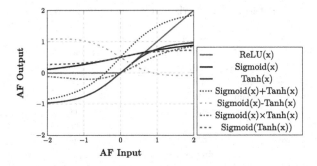

Fig. 3. Generating different mathematical operations using Sigmoid and Tanh.

a local optimum, SA sometimes accepts a bad solution with a probability of $exp(-\Delta/(k \times T))$. k is the Boltzmann's constant and T is the cooling parameter which is decreased with a logarithmic shape based on the predefined maximum (T_{Max}) and minimum temperatures (T_{Min}). SA starts with a high T_{Max} for preventing being prematurely trapped in a local optimum. By approaching T toward T_{Min}, most uphill moves will be rejected. The SA process continues until no further improvements can be made or it will be terminated after a specified number of iterations. Finally, it is worth mentioning that the convergence of SA to global results is guaranteed [12].

Late Acceptance Hill-Climbing. This is a heuristic search method that starts with a near-optimal solution provided by the SA algorithm. LAHC is an extension of the simple hill-climbing algorithm [36], in which a limited number of worse solutions are accepted in hopes of finding a better one later. The *Energy* function of both LAHC and SA algorithms is defined by Eq. 2. In this paper, the *Energy* function and the objective function are used interchangeably.

$$Energy = 100 - Robustness\ Accuracy(\%) \tag{2}$$

Our proposed method has a fast convergence which is due to the single-solution nature of LAHC and SA, while for example, the genetic algorithms are relatively slow due to a population-based optimization [29]. Our experimental results show that our proposed method requires ≈8.3 GPU days on a single NVIDIA ® RTX A4000 for finding the best-performing AF for ResNet-18 trained on CIFAR-10.

4   Experiments

4.1   Experimental Setup

To verify the effectiveness of our proposed method, we use MNIST [23] and CIFAR-10 [20] classification datasets. Our evaluations have been performed on AlexNet and ResNet-18, a variation of ResNet [14], network architectures. To test

Table 2. Summarizing experimental setup.

Search Configuration			
Parameter	MNIST (AlexNet)	CIFAR-10 (AlexNet)	CIFAR-10 (ResNet-18)
Search Epoch (#)	30	100	50
Optimizer	Adam	Adam	Adam
Learning Rate	0.001	0.001	0.001
Train Batch Size	500	512	200
Test Batch Size	250	256	100
Hardware Specification			
GPU			NVIDIA® RTX A4000
GPU Compiler			NVIDIA® NVCC v. 10.1
CO_2 Emission/Day†			1.45 Kg
Training System Memory			64 GB
CPU			Intel® Xeon® W-2245 CPU @ 3.90GHz

† Calculated using the ML CO_2 impact framework: https://mlco2.github.io/impact/ [22]

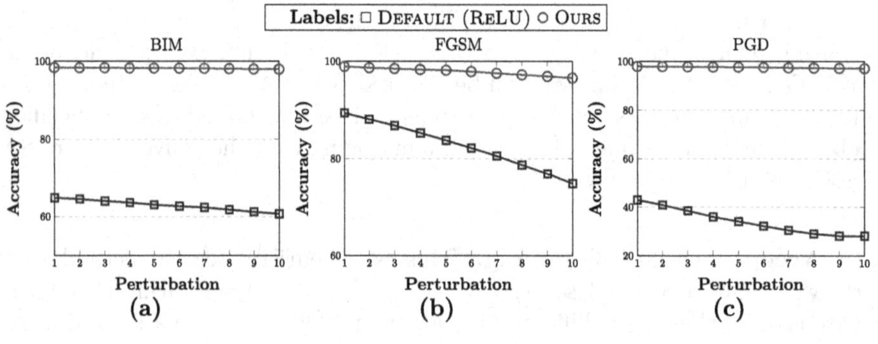

Fig. 4. AlexNet accuracy trained on MNIST with □ ReLU AFs and AFs searched by ○ our proposed method against (a) BIM, (b) FGSM, and (c) PGD. (Color figure online)

the robustness, we consider three popular adversarial attacks, including FGSM [11], PGD [32] and BIM [21]. Table 2 presents the search configuration. Inspired by [27], we trained each candidate with fewer epochs to expedite the search process. The search step takes up to ≈8.3 GPU days on a single NVIDIA® RTX A4000 for ResNet-18 trained on the CIFAR-10 dataset.

4.2 Results on MNIST

Figure 4 shows the results of learning AlexNet AFs on MNIST using our proposed method against three different adversarial attacks including BIM, FGSM, and PGD. AlexNet with ReLU AF is selected as the compression baseline (□). Our proposed method (○) significantly outperforms the default configuration by providing up to 37.3%, 21.8%, and 69.0% higher accuracy over BIM, FGSM, and PGD attacks, respectively.

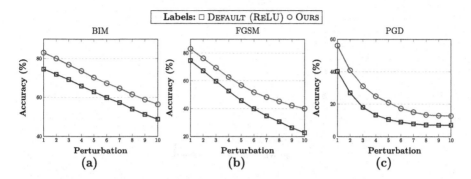

Fig. 5. AlexNet accuracy trained on CIFAR-10 with □ ReLU AFs and AFs searched by ○ our proposed method against (a) BIM, (b) FGSM, and (c) PGD. (Color figure online)

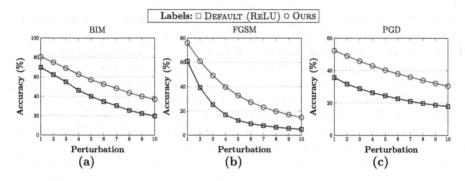

Fig. 6. ResNet-18 accuracy trained on CIFAR-10 with □ ReLU AFs and AFs searched by ○ our proposed method against (a) BIM, (b) FGSM, and (c) PGD. (Color figure online)

4.3 Results on CIFAR-10

Figure 5 shows the results of learning AlexNet AFs trained on CIFAR-10 using our proposed method against three different adversarial attacks including BIM, FGSM, and PGD. AlexNet with ReLU AF is selected as the compression baseline (□). Our proposed method (○) remarkably outperforms the default configuration by providing up to 7.4%, 10.1%, and 15.9% higher accuracy over BIM, FGSM, and PGD attacks, respectively.

Figure 6 shows the results of learning ResNet-18 AFs on CIFAR-10 using our proposed method against three different adversarial attacks including BIM, FGSM, and PGD. ResNet-18 with ReLU AF is selected as the compression baseline (□). Our proposed method (○) significantly outperforms the default configuration by providing up to 18.0%, 23.8%, and 17.3% higher accuracy over BIM, FGSM, and PGD attacks, respectively.

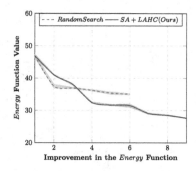

Fig. 7. Comparing the convergence of the proposed method with random search.

4.4 Results of Search Convergence

Figure 7 depicts the *Energy* function (Eq. 2) across search iterations for ResNet-18 trained on CIFAR-10 against the FGSM attack. Our proposed search method finds AFs with a monotonic increase in *Energy*, indicating our proposed method leads to a higher accuracy with fewer search iterations. We also present an empirical evaluation of our method, compared to a random search to show its superior performance. Random search is able to find the optimal architecture in many applications [25, 45]. However, as shown in Fig. 7, our method reached the highest values compared to the random search for the *Energy* function (Eq. 2). Thus, the approach succeeds to find a feasible solution in a reasonable time.

4.5 Analyzing the Discrimination Power of Our Proposed Method

We use the t-distributed stochastic neighbor embedding (t-SNE) method [31] for visualizing the decision boundaries of the original ResNet-18, ResNet-18 with perturbation, and our proposed method for the FGSM attack ($\epsilon = 10/255$) on the CIFAR-10 dataset. Figure 8 illustrates the decision boundaries of classification for each scenario. According to the results, our proposed method has a higher discrimination power than ResNet-18 with perturbation, and our proposed method behaves similarly to the original ResNet-18.

4.6 Reproducibility Statement

Several AutoML papers have problems reproducing their results [26]. We re-ran our proposed method search procedure three more times with different random seeds to verify the reproducibility of our method. Results show that the average of multiple runs converges to AFs with similar results with a standard deviation (STD) of 4.8%. The open-source code is available on GitHub through: https://github.com/RobustInsight/AdversarialAttackResilience.

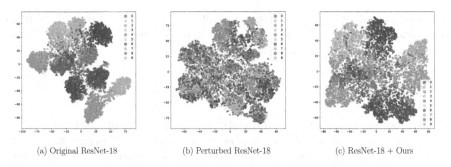

(a) Original ResNet-18   (b) Perturbed ResNet-18   (c) ResNet-18 + Ours

Fig. 8. Visualizing the decision boundary with t-SNE embedding method for (a) original ResNet-18 without perturbation, (b) perturbed ResNet-18, and (c) ResNet-18 with our proposed method optimization.

5 Related Work

To the best of our knowledge, our proposed method is the first automated framework that rapidly learns robust AFs using a multi-stage optimization method. In the past, extensive research has been conducted on improving CNN accuracy. Prior studies are mainly categorized as (i) adversarial training [7,38], (ii) robust optimization [4,40], (iii) architecture modification [8,13], and (iv) AF optimization for adversarial attack resilience in CNNs [42]. In the rest of this section, we briefly discuss state-of-the-art research on AF optimization and compare them with our proposed method.

Studies indicate that AFs are a significant contributor to the vulnerability of neural networks to adversarial examples [46]. Since ReLU is a non-smooth AF, [44] proposed replacing ReLU with its smooth approximations to find harder adversarial examples. A new AF is suggested by [43] that relies on the data and demonstrated its resistance to adversarial attacks. Since ReLU is not smooth and inputs close to zero cause its gradient to abruptly change, the Softplus AF is proposed by [44] whose derivative is continuous and n-times differentiable. Another approach examined the resilience of various layer types within CNNs against adversarial attacks, by considering each layer as a separate nonlinear system and assessing its robustness, utilizing Lyapunov theory. Instead of using non-linear AFs, SPLASH uses piece-wise linear AFs which boosts the robustness of CNNs against adversarial attacks and accuracy as well [42]. The authors in [7] investigated the influence of the shape of AFs on the accuracy and robustness of CNNs by parameterizing various AFs. The approach achieved this by introducing an α parameter to different AFs and examining the effects of altering the α parameter. However, the performance improvement observed is limited as the study only used a restricted set of values and the effect of the α parameter is linear.

These methods have been quite effective, but they suffer from huge computational costs due to the use of reinforcement learning or evolutionary algorithms [27,35,37]. To expedite the learning process of AFs, this work proposes using simulated annealing and late acceptance hill climbing, which can lead to up to 9.3× faster search than [2]. Finally, we make no assumptions about the input dataset, which makes it a more generalized method.

6   Conclusion

The purpose of this study was to investigate how learning activation functions impact the robustness of CNNs against adversarial attacks. Experimental results demonstrate that ReLU is not robust against adversarial attacks, whereas learning network AFs greatly enhances robustness. Overall, our work contributes to the growing body of research on adversarial attack resilience in CNNs and provides a promising approach for designing more robust CNNs.

References

1. Bahramali, A., Nasr, M., Houmansadr, A., Goeckel, D., Towsley, D.: Robust adversarial attacks against DNN-based wireless communication systems. In: Proceedings of the 2021 ACM SIGSAC Conference on Computer and Communications Security, pp. 126–140 (2021)
2. Bingham, G., Macke, W., Miikkulainen, R.: Evolutionary optimization of deep learning activation functions. In: Proceedings of the 2020 Genetic and Evolutionary Computation Conference, pp. 289–296 (2020)
3. Bingham, G., Miikkulainen, R.: Discovering parametric activation functions. arXiv preprint arXiv:2006.03179 (2020)
4. Bradshaw, J., Matthews, A.G.d.G., Ghahramani, Z.: Adversarial examples, uncertainty, and transfer testing robustness in gaussian process hybrid deep networks. arXiv preprint arXiv:1707.02476 (2017)
5. Burke, E.K., Bykov, Y., et al.: A late acceptance strategy in hill-climbing for exam timetabling problems. In: PATAT 2008 Conference, Montreal, Canada, pp. 1–7 (2008)
6. Cui, P., Shabash, B., Wiese, K.C.: EvoDNN-an evolutionary deep neural network with heterogeneous activation functions. In: 2019 IEEE Congress on Evolutionary Computation (CEC), pp. 2362–2369. IEEE (2019)
7. Dai, S., Mahloujifar, S., Mittal, P.: Parameterizing activation functions for adversarial robustness. In: 2022 IEEE Security and Privacy Workshops (SPW), pp. 80–87. IEEE (2022)
8. Devaguptapu, C., Agarwal, D., Mittal, G., Gopalani, P., Balasubramanian, V.N.: On adversarial robustness: a neural architecture search perspective. In: Proceedings of the IEEE/CVF International Conference on Computer Vision, pp. 152–161 (2021)
9. Finlayson, S.G., Bowers, J.D., Ito, J., Zittrain, J.L., Beam, A.L., Kohane, I.S.: Adversarial attacks on medical machine learning. Science **363**(6433), 1287–1289 (2019)
10. Godfrey, L.B., Gashler, M.S.: A continuum among logarithmic, linear, and exponential functions, and its potential to improve generalization in neural networks. In: 2015 7th International Joint Conference on Knowledge Discovery, Knowledge Engineering and Knowledge Management (IC3K). vol. 1, pp. 481–486. IEEE (2015)

11. Goodfellow, I.J., Shlens, J., Szegedy, C.: Explaining and harnessing adversarial examples. arXiv preprint arXiv:1412.6572 (2014)
12. Granville, V., Krivánek, M., Rasson, J.P.: Simulated annealing: a proof of convergence. IEEE Trans. Pattern Anal. Mach. Intell. **16**(6), 652–656 (1994)
13. Guo, M., Yang, Y., Xu, R., Liu, Z., Lin, D.: When NAS meets robustness: in search of robust architectures against adversarial attacks. In: Proceedings of the IEEE/CVF Conference on Computer Vision and Pattern Recognition, pp. 631–640 (2020)
14. He, K., Zhang, X., Ren, S., Sun, J.: Deep residual learning for image recognition. In: Proceedings of the IEEE Conference on Computer Vision and Pattern Recognition, pp. 770–778 (2016)
15. Huang, J., Xue, B., Sun, Y., Zhang, M., Yen, G.G.: Particle swarm optimization for compact neural architecture search for image classification. IEEE Trans. Evol. Comput. 1–1 (2022)
16. Huang, S., Papernot, N., Goodfellow, I., Duan, Y., Abbeel, P.: Adversarial attacks on neural network policies. arXiv preprint arXiv:1702.02284 (2017)
17. Hutter, F., Kotthoff, L., Vanschoren, J. (eds.): Automated Machine Learning. TSSCML, Springer, Cham (2019). https://doi.org/10.1007/978-3-030-05318-5
18. Jin, X., Xu, C., Feng, J., Wei, Y., Xiong, J., Yan, S.: Deep learning with S-shaped rectified linear activation units. In: Proceedings of the AAAI Conference on Artificial Intelligence. vol. 30 (2016)
19. Kirkpatrick, S., Gelatt, C.D., Jr., Vecchi, M.P.: Optimization by simulated annealing. Science **220**(4598), 671–680 (1983)
20. Krizhevsky, A., Nair, V., Hinton, G.: CIFAR-10 and CIFAR-100 datasets. **6**(1), 1 (2009)
21. Kurakin, A., Goodfellow, I.J., Bengio, S.: Adversarial examples in the physical world. In: Artificial Intelligence Safety and Security, pp. 99–112. Chapman and Hall/CRC (2018)
22. Lacoste, A., Luccioni, A., Schmidt, V., Dandres, T.: Quantifying the carbon emissions of machine learning. arXiv preprint arXiv:1910.09700 (2019)
23. LeCun, Y.: The MNIST database of handwritten digits (1998)
24. Lee, M., Kolter, Z.: On physical adversarial patches for object detection. arXiv preprint arXiv:1906.11897 (2019)
25. Li, L., Talwalkar, A.: Random search and reproducibility for neural architecture search. In: Uncertainty in Artificial Intelligence, pp. 367–377. PMLR (2020)
26. Lindauer, M., Hutter, F.: Best practices for scientific research on neural architecture search. J. Mach. Learn. Res. **21**(243), 1–18 (2020)
27. Loni, M., Sinaei, S., Zoljodi, A., Daneshtalab, M., Sjödin, M.: DeepMaker: a multi-objective optimization framework for deep neural networks in embedded systems. Microprocess. Microsyst. **73**, 102989 (2020)
28. Loni, M., et al.: DenseDisp: resource-aware disparity map estimation by compressing siamese neural architecture. In: 2020 IEEE Congress on Evolutionary Computation (CEC), pp. 1–8. IEEE (2020)
29. Loni, M., et al.: FastStereoNet: a fast neural architecture search for improving the inference of disparity estimation on resource-limited platforms. IEEE Trans. Syst. Man Cybern. Syst. **52**(8), 5222–5234 (2021)
30. Loni, M., Zoljodi, A., Sinaei, S., Daneshtalab, M., Sjödin, M.: NeuroPower: Designing Energy Efficient Convolutional Neural Network Architecture for Embedded Systems. In: Tetko, I.V., Kurková, V., Karpov, P., Theis, F. (eds.) ICANN 2019. LNCS, vol. 11727, pp. 208–222. Springer, Cham (2019). https://doi.org/10.1007/978-3-030-30487-4_17

31. Van der Maaten, L., Hinton, G.: Visualizing data using t-SNE. J. Mach. Learn. Res. **9**(11), 2579–2605 (2008)
32. Madry, A., Makelov, A., Schmidt, L., Tsipras, D., Vladu, A.: Towards deep learning models resistant to adversarial attacks. arXiv preprint arXiv:1706.06083 (2017)
33. Moosavi-Dezfooli, S.M., Fawzi, A., Frossard, P.: DeepFool: a simple and accurate method to fool deep neural networks. In: Proceedings of the IEEE Conference on Computer Vision and Pattern Recognition, pp. 2574–2582 (2016)
34. Nair, V., Hinton, G.E.: Rectified linear units improve restricted boltzmann machines. In: Proceedings of the 27th International Conference on Machine Learning (ICML) (2010)
35. Nogami, W., Ikegami, T., Takano, R., Kudoh, T., et al.: Optimizing weight value quantization for CNN inference. In: 2019 International Joint Conference on Neural Networks (IJCNN), pp. 1–8. IEEE (2019)
36. Norvig, P.R., Intelligence, S.A.: A modern approach. Prentice Hall Upper Saddle River, NJ, USA: Rani, M., Nayak, R., & Vyas, OP (2015). An ontology-based adaptive personalized e-learning system, assisted by software agents on cloud storage. Knowledge-Based Systems 90, 33–48 (2002)
37. Ramachandran, P., Zoph, B., Le, Q.V.: Searching for activation functions. arXiv preprint arXiv:1710.05941 (2017)
38. Rebuffi, S.A., Gowal, S., Calian, D.A., Stimberg, F., Wiles, O., Mann, T.: Fixing data augmentation to improve adversarial robustness. arXiv preprint arXiv:2103.01946 (2021)
39. Rosenberg, I., Shabtai, A., Elovici, Y., Rokach, L.: Adversarial machine learning attacks and defense methods in the cyber security domain. ACM Comput. Surv. (CSUR) **54**(5), 1–36 (2021)
40. Strauss, T., Hanselmann, M., Junginger, A., Ulmer, H.: Ensemble methods as a defense to adversarial perturbations against deep neural networks. arXiv preprint arXiv:1709.03423 (2017)
41. Szegedy, C., Zaremba, W., Sutskever, I., Bruna, J., Erhan, D., Goodfellow, I., Fergus, R.: Intriguing properties of neural networks. arXiv preprint arXiv:1312.6199 (2013)
42. Tavakoli, M., Agostinelli, F., Baldi, P.: Splash: learnable activation functions for improving accuracy and adversarial robustness. Neural Netw. **140**, 1–12 (2021)
43. Wang, B., Lin, A.T., Zhu, W., Yin, P., Bertozzi, A.L., Osher, S.J.: Adversarial defense via data dependent activation function and total variation minimization. arXiv preprint arXiv:1809.08516 (2018)
44. Xie, C., Tan, M., Gong, B., Yuille, A., Le, Q.V.: Smooth adversarial training. arXiv preprint arXiv:2006.14536 (2020)
45. Yang, A., Esperança, P.M., Carlucci, F.M.: NAS evaluation is frustratingly hard. arXiv preprint arXiv:1912.12522 (2019)
46. Zantedeschi, V., Nicolae, M.I., Rawat, A.: Efficient defenses against adversarial attacks. In: Proceedings of the 10th ACM Workshop on Artificial Intelligence and Security, pp. 39–49 (2017)
47. Zhang, J., Li, C.: Adversarial examples: opportunities and challenges. IEEE Trans. Neural Netw. Learn. Syst. **31**(7), 2578–2593 (2019)

Federated Learning for Human Activity Recognition on the MHealth Dataset

Sergio Sanchez[1], Javier Machacuay[2], and Mario Quinde[1]([✉]) [iD]

[1] Department of Industrial and Systems Engineering, Universidad de Piura,
Piura, Peru
`sergio.sanchez.f@alum.udep.edu.pe`, `mario.quinde@udep.edu.pe`
[2] Department of Mechanical and Electrical Engineering, Universidad de Piura,
Piura, Peru
`javier.machacuay.v@udep.edu.pe`

Abstract. Human activity recognition (HAR) tasks are essential for developing context-aware features due to their capacity to generate higher-level contexts and personalisable services. The traditional centralised training approach requires clients to share their data with a server that trains the HAR algorithms. This data transfer raises privacy concerns on the clients' side regarding data leaks that can be used to obtain personal data. This research work studies Federated Learning (FL) as a privacy-preserving alternative to developing HAR algorithms. The centralised and FL approaches are implemented to train a Multi-Layer Perceptron neural network using three different activation functions (Tanh, ReLU and Sigmoid). The experiments use the MHealth dataset to train and test the HAR algorithms. The results are analysed to compare the performance of the centralised and FL approaches, the activation functions outcomes, and the communication rounds needed between the server and the clients to reach competitive results for the FL models. The outcomes are positive and encourage further work in using of FL for HAR.

Keywords: Human activity recognition · Federated Learning · Data privacy · Context-Awareness · Artificial Intelligence · Machine Learning

1 Introduction

Human Activity Recognition (HAR) techniques process sensor data to identify human activities as they occur [1]. These signals can be gathered from multimodal wearable sensors (e.g. accelerometers, gyroscope and magnetometers in smartphone and smartwatches) and environmental devices (e.g. cameras, microphones), and are processed through diverse techniques to develop adequate classification algorithms achieving the desired activity of daily living (ADL) identification [8]. Wearable sensors have gained popularity for activity monitoring as they raise less privacy concerns than environmental devices [2], have lower costs, do not need special installations and are perceived as less intrusive [8].

Activity recognition is an active research field because of the benefits it can provide in the development of context-aware reasoning (C-AR) services [8].

L. Rutkowski et al. (Eds.): ICAISC 2023, LNAI 14125, pp. 215–225, 2023.
https://doi.org/10.1007/978-3-031-42505-9_19

HAR systems can provide contextual information for the recognition of human behaviour to develop systems that can be classified under the umbrella term of intelligent environments [2]. An example of using HAR to develop context-aware features supporting cardiac health monitoring can be found in Ref. [12].

One of the main challenges of HAR refers to the privacy concerns brought by the classical centralised approach that is used to develop the algorithms to recognise the desired activities [15]. This approach needs to gather a large amount of data from users' wearable sensors in order to train, test and validate the HAR algorithms. This involves transferring data from the users to the collecting server, which increases the potential risk of personal data leaks. Besides the privacy issue, this centralised approach also implies a communication cost due to the transferring of large amount of data.

This research work uses Federated Learning (FL) to address the privacy issue of sharing and centralising the required data to develop HAR algorithms. FL is a collaborative machine learning scheme addressing the data island issue and focusing specially on preserving data privacy [10]. FL requires multiple clients (e.g. smartphones) to train the prediction models locally and share these models with a server that aggregates them to get a prediction model, which is returned to the clients that train it again. This process is repeated for several communication rounds until a robust and accurate prediction model is obtained and shared with the clients for their prediction tasks. By doing this, the prediction models are exchanged between the server and clients, but the clients' data are never shared.

The Mhealth dataset [4] is used for the simulation of a scenario in which the users registered in the dataset represents the multiple clients of the FL approach. The Mhealth dataset contains training data from 10 users that are labelled for 12 human activities. This research work compares the performance of the FL and the traditional centralised approach using neural networks implementing three different activation functions (Tanh, ReLU and Sigmoid).

The main contribution of this research work is the analysis of each approach performance, the number of communication rounds needed by the FL approach to reach competitive accuracies, all these compared for each activation function used in the FL and traditional model approaches. Future work to continue research on this field is also presented. To the best of our knowledge, this study on the Mhealth dataset has not been reported before and will nourish the debate about the convenience of using FL as an alternative to develop predictive models addressing data privacy issues.

The paper is divided into the following sections to achieve its objectives. Section 2 presents the state-of-the-art of FL and HAR. Section 3 describes the methodology followed for the experiments. Section 4 presents its results. Finally, Sect. 5 and 6 present the discussion and the conclusions, respectively.

2   State-of-the-art

HAR plays a key role in the development of C-AR services enhancing their personalisation to target users' needs better [2]. Context can be defined from a user-centric perspective [3] as *"the information which is directly relevant to characterise a situation of interest to the stakeholders of a system"*. C-AR is then defined as *"the ability of a system to use contextual information in order to tailor its services so that they are more useful to the stakeholders because they directly relate to their preferences and needs"*. HAR supports the creation of contextual information aiding in identifying human behaviour thanks to the technological advances in sensor devices development and in artificial intelligence techniques capable of processing the signals from these sensors [1].

The application of HAR to enhance C-AR systems are diverse. HAR can enhance healthcare systems features [13]. Ref. [9] uses HAR to enhance C-AR services for people with dementia and their healthcarers by recognising wandering behaviour. Ref. [14] is another application example proposing an indoor positioning system aiding in identifying human behaviour to achieve multi-user capabilities in smarthome environments. Despite these benefits, the development of HAR predictive models still has issues to overcome.

The classic training approach requires a server to centralise users' data for training the predictive model that is then sent to the users for their HAR tasks. These data include the sensor data obtained from monitoring the users' activities and the label representing the activity (e.g. walking, running, and so on) performed for each observation. Sharing these data raises concerns in users about potential personal (and even sensitive) data leaks that could be inferred from the shared data. These leaks could expose users' behaviours and their disorders may be inferred from location-based services and sensor data that could lead to discrimination by, for instance, insurance companies [5].

The FL collaborative learning approach is a privacy-oriented alternative because it does not require data transferring from the users to the server. FL is defined as *"a machine learning setting where multiple entities (clients) collaborate in solving a machine learning problem, under the coordination of a central server or service provider. Each client's raw data is stored locally and not exchanged or transferred; instead, focused updates intended for immediate aggregation are used to achieve the learning objective"* [6]. This research studies FL as an alternative to address the privacy issue of developing HAR prediction models.

The use of FL for HAR is an active field. Ref. [12] uses FL to develop a C-AR decision-support system for cardiac health monitoring, using their own generated dataset and machine learning algorithms whose performances are compared to the centralised training approach ones. Ref. [15] uses two models (softmax regression and a deep neural network) to implement FL on the dataset proposed in Ref. [16], compares their performances to the centralised approach ones, and proposes a corrupted data management algorithm. Zhou et al. [18] studies how to overcome the issues of insufficient training data and insecure data sharing for the application of FL in cyber-physical-social systems HAR tasks.

This paper nourishes the debate about using FL as an alternative for HAR tasks to preserve users' personal data. This research work studies the performance of using FL for HAR on the Mhealth dataset, focusing on analysing the number of communication rounds needed to obtain models with competitive performances compared to those obtained using a centralised training approach. This analysis is critically important mainly due to the communication, aggregation and edge-processing requirements of using FL. The paper also analyses the performance of three activation functions (Tanh, ReLU and Sigmoid) implemented in the experiments, adding them to the analysis. To the best of our knowledge, this contribution has not been reported in the literature.

3   Methodology

This section explains the dataset, the experiments setup and the metrics used to evaluate the performances of the centralised and FL approaches.

3.1   The Mhealth Dataset

The Mhealth dataset is made of 10 users' data, whose observations were recorded at 50 Hz. Each observation has their label and 23 independent features. Only 9 independent features are used for this experiment: chest accelerometer (3 axis), lower right arm gyroscope (3 axis) and lower right arm magnetometer (3 axis). This choice was arbitrary and aimed at representing two sensors located at different positions in the users' body, adding complexity to the scenario.

The data is pre-processed to obtain time windows representing small time frames summarised by the mean, range, standard deviation, maximum and minimum for each of the 9 features. These transformations are suggested in the literature [7]. Each time window has then their label and 45 features (5 transformations times the 9 features), and summarises 25 observations with a time window overlapping of 50%, which means that the last 12 observations of time window w_i are the first 12 observations of time window w_{i+1}. Table 1 describes the characteristics of the pre-processed dataset, which is the entry data for the models training and evaluation.

Table 1. Mhealth dataset after the time windows pre-processing

Activity	# of windows (observations)	% of the dataset
Standing still	235	8.95%
Sitting and relaxing	235	8.95%
Lying down	235	8.95%
Walking	235	8.95%
Climbing stairs	235	8.95%
Waist bends forward	219	8.34%
Frontal elevation of arms	219	8.34%
Knees bending (crouching)	227	8.64%
Cycling	235	8.95%
Jogging	235	8.95%
Running	235	8.95%
Jump front & back	81	3.08%

3.2   Experiments Setup

Subject 9 was randomly chosen for the models evaluation. The data of the other 9 users are used to train the centrally-trained models, which are then evaluated with Subject 9. For the FL approach, the same 9 users simulate the 9 clients that train the FL models and send them back to the server for the aggregation. The aggregated models are evaluated with the data of Subject 9. This evaluation is repeated several times to obtain the evaluation metrics for each communication round and, thus, being able to analyse the metrics evolution for each activation function and communication round.

The artificial neural network used for the experiments is the Multi-Layer Perceptron (MLP). The entry layer is made of 45 neurons (one neuron for each entry variable). The hidden layers are made of 64 and 32 neurons, respectively. The output layer is made of 12 nodes associated with the 12 activities to recognise. Figure 1 presents the NN configuration. The hidden layers are programmed with the activation functions to test (Tanh, ReLU and Sigmoid). The output layer uses the activation function Softmax to obtain the probability of each activity.

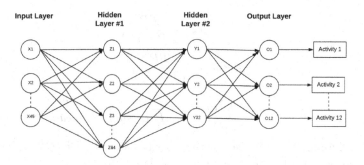

Fig. 1. Multilayer Perceptron (MLP) configuration

For the centralised approach, the data of 9 subjects are merged and used for the training in the server. The model is tested 30 times with different initialisations to analyse its variability. That is, two different seeds are used for each initialisation: one seed to define the initial random weights of the starting model (W_0) and the other for the dataset partition into training (80%) and validation (20%). The hyperparameters for the training are $E = 200$ (epochs) and $B = 32$ (batch size). These hyperparameters are empirically chosen, considering mainly the processing capabilities restrictions.

According to Ref. [17], the nature of the dataset corresponds to a horizontal FL approach in which the clients are different but have the same features. This research work implements a FL approach to train the models using 9 clients. The FL approach is used 30 times with different initialisations to generate 30 models to be tested with the data of Subject 9. That is, two different seeds are used for each initialisation: one seed for the initial random weights of the starting model

(W_0), and the other for the dataset partition into training (80%) and validation (20%). Thirty communication rounds are carried out between each client and the server for each of the 30 different initialisations, in order to improve the global model and analyse the results obtained in the communication rounds.

In the FL approach, the server aggregates the models that were locally trained by the clients. The aggregation can be done using different methods. This research work uses the FedAvg method to aggregate the weights that were previously trained by the clients locally [11]. Thus, the clients received from the server a model whose weights were randomly initialised. The clients train the models locally and send the weights of this trained model back to the server, who aggregates the weights received from the clients (average) to define the weights of the aggregated model. This is considered one communication round. The aggregated model is sent back to the clients to train it again, who send the newly-trained models back to the server for aggregation. This is repeated 30 times (30 communication rounds).

The confusion matrix of the evaluation results allow the calculation of the metrics to analyse the experiment results. Considering HAR an unbalanced classification problem, the metric to use is the *weighted F1-Score (Eq. 3)*.

$$Precision = \frac{TP}{TP + FP} \tag{1}$$

$$Recall = \frac{TP}{TP + FN} \tag{2}$$

$$wF1 - Score_j = \sum_{j=1}^{n}(2 * \Omega_j * \frac{Precision_j * Recall_j}{Precision_j + Recall_j}) \tag{3}$$

where n is the number of classes of the classification problem (12 activities), j is the class whose $wF1 - Score$ is being calculated and Ω_j is the weight of class j (# of class j observations / total of observations).

4   Results

The final wF1-Score is the average of the wF1-Scores of the 30 models obtained from the 30 initialisations. The results are gotten from testing the 30 trained models on the data of Subject 9. Using 30 initialisations aims at reducing the bias of the random initialisations. The results of using the FL approach compared to the CM are presented in Fig. 2-4. The dotted line represents the wF1-Scores cumulative average of the CM testing results. The other lines represent the evolution of the wF1-Scores cumulative average obtained for {5,10,...30} communication rounds (FL approach).

Figures 5–7 present the Box-plot charts comparing the testing results obtained in the 30 different initialisations for the centralised models and the FL models using {5,10,...30} communication rounds. The variation of the centralised model is considerably larger than the one of the FL models.

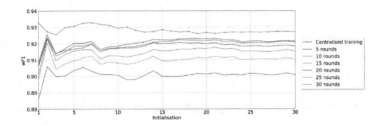

Fig. 2. Centralised and FL models results - Tanh

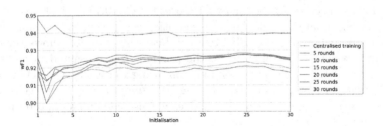

Fig. 3. Centralised and FL models results - ReLU

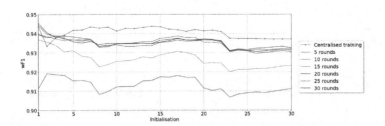

Fig. 4. Centralised and FL models results - Sigmoid

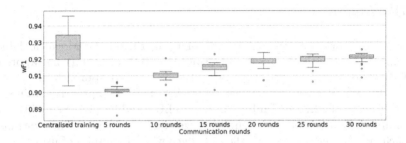

Fig. 5. Box-plot chart for centralised and FL models results - Tanh

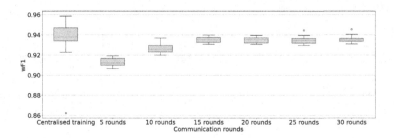

Fig. 6. Box-plot chart for centralised and FL models results - ReLU

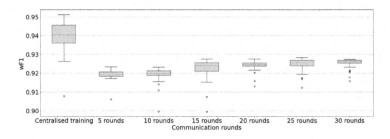

Fig. 7. Box-plot chart for centralised and FL models results - Sigmoid

Table 2 presents the models final wF1-scores after the 30 initialisations. For the FL models, it presents the final wF1-scores for {1–10,15,20,25,30} communication rounds. Equation 4 calculates the variation comparing the communication rounds results, where i is the table row number. The variation shows the wF1-Score improvement (%) compared to the previous row presented in the table. For instance, for the Tanh activation function, using 15 rounds ($i = 11$) improves the wF1-Score in 0.5%, compared to using 10 rounds ($i = 10$). The centralised model ($i = 15$) does not have a Δ as it does not use communication rounds.

$$\Delta = \frac{(wF1_{i+1} - wF1_i)}{wF1_i} \tag{4}$$

5   Discussion

This research work analyses the results of using FL on the Mhealth dataset to compare them with the results of using a centralised traditional approach for HAR. The Avg. wF1-Scores of using the centralised approach are 92.71% (Tanh), 93.70% (ReLU), and 93.95% (Sigmoid). The FL approach obtained an Avg. wF1-Score of 92.14% (Tanh), 93.24% (ReLU), and 92.53% (Sigmoid), after 30 communication rounds between the server and the clients. The centralised approach gets better results, but the difference with the results of using the FL approach with 30 rounds can be considered minimal depending on the C-AR service the HAR algorithm supports.

Table 2. FL models Avg. wF1-Score and variation (Δ) v. centralised model (CM)

Row (i)	Round	Tanh		ReLU		Sigmoid	
		Avg. wF1	Δ	Avg. wF1	Δ	Avg. wF1	Δ
1	1	0.6669	–	0.6907	–	0.7070	
2	2	0.8083	21.20%	0.8282	19.91%	0.8730	23.48%
3	3	0.8780	8.62%	0.8665	4.62%	0.9045	3.61%
4	4	0.8920	1.59%	0.8933	3.09%	0.9123	0.86%
5	5	0.9010	1.01%	0.9111	1.99%	0.9172	0.54%
6	6	0.9048	0.42%	0.9151	0.44%	0.9164	−0.09%
7	7	0.9070	0.24%	0.9205	0.59%	0.9175	0.12%
8	8	0.9083	0.14%	0.9200	−0.05%	0.9180	0.05%
9	9	0.9105	0.24%	0.9241	0.45%	0.9205	0.27%
10	10	0.9106	0.01%	0.9232	−0.10%	0.9192	−0.14%
11	15	0.9155	0.54%	0.9319	0.94%	0.9241	0.53%
12	20	0.9185	0.33%	0.9313	−0.06%	0.9246	0.05%
13	25	0.9210	0.27%	0.9304	−0.10%	0.9254	0.09%
14	30	0.9214	0.04%	0.9324	0.21%	0.9253	−0.01%
15	CM	0.9271	–	0.9370	–	0.9395	–

The communication rounds number is also important to study. A higher number of communication rounds increases the complexity of using FL as it requires more model updates between the server and the clients, a better synchronisation for the model aggregation, more data processing in the clients nodes (edge computing), and so on. However, more communication rounds implies more aggregations that usually lead to more accurate models. FL implementation needs to balance the model scores and the processing and communication requirements of having a higher number of communication rounds.

This paper adds to the discussion on the communication rounds number by showing the results of using up to 30 rounds in the experiments. Figure 2–7 and Table 2 present evidence supporting the fact that using more rounds tends to improving the wF1-Score of the FL models. It is critical to notice that after 5 rounds the Δ per round is less than 1%. Further, after 15 rounds, the Δ every 5 rounds are 0.33% or less. That is, the most relevant wF1-Score improvement occurs within the first 5 rounds. The choice on the rounds number depends on the scenario FL is applied. Predictive algorithms with high scores are desired, especially for health-related tasks. However, the feasibility of involving several clients, using their processing capabilities and coordinating them in the FL collaborative training environment for several rounds is a critical factor to assess.

The traditional centralised approach still presents better results in these experiments, but the FL privacy-preserving property is a critical advantage. Considering a relatively feasible model trained with 5 rounds, the difference (wF1) with the CM is 0.0261 (Tanh), 0.0259 (ReLU) and 0.0223 (Sigmoid). The relevance of these differences depends on the scenario, as well as to the value assigned to the FL privacy-preserving property. In some cases, due to the concern of the training data providers, FL could involve more clients and, thus, get more data to train higher-accuracy algorithms. Depending on the scenario, a centralised approach could not even be considered an option to train these algorithms.

The use of FL for HAR is an active ongoing research field. This research work leads to future work to analysing the performance of FL in other HAR datasets (independently and combined), and other types of FL (vertical and transfer learning). The Mhealth dataset presents a scenario in which the number of clients is considerably less than the number of observations generated by them. It simulates scenarios in which sensors monitor users generating a lot of data (e.g. athletes during a training session). The combination of the Mhealth dataset with other ones will allow, among other options, to test more types of FL in more complex scenarios. Further work also includes studying other neural networks, activation functions, and machine learning techniques, like the ones reported in Ref. [7]. This research work uses FedAvg for the model aggregation step to reduce the rounds number. Other aggregation techniques (e.g. gradient aggregation) reducing the edge-computing requirement shall be studied, as well as the processing times of the local trainings in the clients' nodes.

6   Conclusions

HAR tasks provide contextual data feeding C-AR systems to deliver personalisable and better-targeted features. This research work studies FL as a privacy-preserving alternative training approach to the traditional centralised one. The results show that FL achieves competitive scores, comparing them to those obtained using the traditional centralised approach. FL is used to train and test an MLP using three different activation functions and the Mhealth datasets for the experiments. The outcomes evidence that the best score improvements occur in the first five communication rounds of the FL training for the three activation functions. Although more rounds tend to increase the algorithms' score, analysing the benefits of these variations against the challenges brought by having more rounds is critical to developing feasible HAR algorithms using FL.

References

1. Acampora, G., Cook, D.J., Rashidi, P., Vasilakos, A.V.: A survey on ambient intelligence in healthcare. Proc. IEEE **101**(12), 2470–2494 (2013). https://doi.org/10.1109/JPROC.2013.2262913
2. Augusto, J.C., Callaghan, V., Cook, D., Kameas, A., Satoh, I.: Intelligent environments: a manifesto. Hum. Centric Comput. Inf. Sci. **3**(1), 12 (2013). https://doi.org/10.1186/2192-1962-3-12
3. Augusto, J.C., Muñoz, A.: User preferences in intelligent environments. Appl. Artif. Intell. **33**(12), 1069–1091 (2019). https://doi.org/10.1080/08839514.2019.1661596

4. Banos, O., et al.: Design, implementation and validation of a novel open framework for agile development of mobile health applications. BioMed. Eng. OnLine **14**(2), S6 (2015). https://doi.org/10.1186/1475-925X-14-S2-S6

5. Bettini, C., Riboni, D.: Privacy protection in pervasive systems: state of the art and technical challenges. Pervasive Mob. Comput. **17**, 159–174 (2015). https://doi.org/10.1016/j.pmcj.2014.09.010

6. Bonawitz, K., Kairouz, P., Mcmahan, B., Ramage, D.: Federated learning and privacy. Commun. ACM **65**(4), 90–97 (2022). https://doi.org/10.1145/3500240

7. Ferrari, A., Micucci, D., Mobilio, M., Napoletano, P.: Trends in human activity recognition using smartphones. J. Reliab. Intell. Environ. **7**(3), 189–213 (2021). https://doi.org/10.1007/s40860-021-00147-0

8. Ferrari, A., Micucci, D., Mobilio, M., Napoletano, P.: Deep learning and model personalization in sensor-based human activity recognition. J. Reliab. Intell. Environ. **9**(1), 27–39 (2023). https://doi.org/10.1007/s40860-021-00167-w

9. Giménez Manuel, J.G., Augusto, J.C., Stewart, J.: Anabel: towards empowering people living with dementia in ambient assisted living. Univ. Access Inf. Soc. **21**(2), 457–476 (2022). https://doi.org/10.1007/s10209-020-00760-5

10. Li, L., Fan, Y., Tse, M., Lin, K.Y.: A review of applications in federated learning. Comput. Ind. Eng. **149**, 106854 (2020). https://doi.org/10.1016/j.cie.2020.106854

11. McMahan, H.B., Moore, E., Ramage, D., y Arcas, B.A.: Federated learning of deep networks using model averaging. CoRR abs/1602.05629 (2016), arxiv.org/abs/1602.05629

12. Ogbuabor, G.O., Augusto, J.C., Moseley, R., van Wyk, A.: Context-aware support for cardiac health monitoring using federated machine learning. In: Bramer, M., Ellis, R. (eds.) Artif. Intell. XXXVIII, pp. 267–281. Springer, Cham (2021)

13. Qi, J., Yang, P., Waraich, A., Deng, Z., Zhao, Y., Yang, Y.: Examining sensor-based physical activity recognition and monitoring for healthcare using internet of things: a systematic review. J. Biomed. Inf. **87**, 138–153 (2018). https://doi.org/10.1016/j.jbi.2018.09.002

14. Quinde, M., Giménez-Manuel, J., Oguego, C.L., Augusto, J.C.: Achieving multi-user capabilities through an indoor positioning system based on BLE beacons. In: 2020 16th International Conference on Intelligent Environments (IE), pp. 13–20 (2020). https://doi.org/10.1109/IE49459.2020.9155011

15. Sozinov, K., Vlassov, V., Girdzijauskas, S.: Human activity recognition using federated learning. In: 2018 IEEE International Conference on Parallel & Distributed Processing with Applications, Ubiquitous Computing & Communications, Big Data & Cloud Computing, Social Computing & Networking, Sustainable Computing & Communications, pp. 1103–1111 (2018). https://doi.org/10.1109/BDCloud.2018.00164

16. Stisen, A., et al.: Smart devices are different: assessing and mitigating mobile sensing heterogeneities for activity recognition. In: Proceedings of the 13th ACM Conference on Embedded Networked Sensor Systems, pp. 127–140. SenSys 2015, Association for Computing Machinery, New York, USA (2015). https://doi.org/10.1145/2809695.2809718

17. Yang, Q., Liu, Y., Chen, T., Tong, Y.: Federated machine learning: concept and applications. ACM Trans. Intell. Syst. Technol. **10**(2), 1–19 (2019). https://doi.org/10.1145/3298981

18. Zhou, X., Liang, W., Ma, J., Yan, Z., Wang, K.I.K.: 2D federated learning for personalized human activity recognition in cyber-physical-social systems. IEEE Trans. Netw. Sci. Eng. **9**(6), 3934–3944 (2022). https://doi.org/10.1109/TNSE.2022.3144699

Image Classification Through Graph Neural Networks and Random Walks

William S. M. Silva[1], Priscila T. M. Saito[1,2], and Pedro H. Bugatti[1,2(✉)]

[1] Federal University of Technology - Parana, Curitiba, Brazil
williamsilva.2019@alunos.utfpr.edu.br
[2] Federal University of São Carlos, São Carlos, Brazil
{priscilasaito,pedrobugatti}@ufscar.br

Abstract. Humans can assimilate the context between information from a few perceived data, and this statement applies to the context in images. In machine learning, an image's context can be represented and predicted using graph convolutional networks. In the literature, we saw hierarchies based on fully connected graphs that can simulate the image context. However, this method can be computationally costly and inaccurate, generating erroneous connection structure. This paper introduces a method based on random walks that can better represent the image context with precise connections, optimizing the number of edges and performing better results. We used pre-trained convolutional networks to extract features to introduce the GCN model. We performed two types of hierarchies, fully connected and random walk. We also performed a CNN model (end-to-end) for each literature pre-trained model used. Our method achieved better accuracies against the literature approaches. Moreover, it also considerably decreases the number of edges of the graph.

Keywords: graph neural networks · image analysis · deep learning

1 Introduction

One of the most famous tasks in deep learning study is image classification [13], as object detection and recognition [13,15,23,28]. Convolutional Neural Networks (CNN) can be highly effective in these tasks when the image holds all information at the pixel level [11].

Some context at an object level cannot be detected using the convolutional method in this path. We can use another structure to deal with this task, the graph convolutional network (GCN). In this category, we can use the graph structure to build levels of knowledge, such as hierarchical context reasoning, where image context can be built by a fully connected graph; that is, all objects composed in the image are connected with each other.

However, using this approach, we cannot assure that every object in the image can express the context. Moreover, connecting all the objects can be computationally costly regarding the number of edges (connections). In order to mitigate

L. Rutkowski et al. (Eds.): ICAISC 2023, LNAI 14125, pp. 226–235, 2023.
https://doi.org/10.1007/978-3-031-42505-9_20

this problem, we reduce the number of the graph's edges through the aggregation of graph neural networks and the random walk approach [7,25]. Hence, we can find communities in graph structure by relating each node through weighted edges [26]. To do so, we propose a method based on random walks that can improve the best set of connections for the graph, resulting in a more efficient image context and better classification precision.

2   Background and Related Works

2.1   Convolutional Neural Networks

A CNN extracts features from images, and trains neurons weights [3]. Once the feature is generated, a *ReLU* function introduces non-linearity in the image. Trying to keep it with spatial invariance is applied a pooling method.

As an image comprises a 2-dimensional space, the input to the dense network must be a 1-dimensional array. So a Flattening is performed to cast the 2D array to 1D. The fully connected layer is performed to find more features from the existing images.

With more hidden layers, the more the model can score in a predicted label; the prediction will be compared with a true label of the current image. After that, the weights can be readjusted; this process is denominated linear regression [1,5,21].

2.2   Graph Convolutional Networks

A graph can be represented as $G = (N, E)$ where N is the set of nodes $\{N_0, N_1, ...N_i\}$ and E is the set of edges, just considering an undirected graph. A graph G can represent an image I and describe each node as an object from the image, and relationships can be expressed as semantic or spatial information [10].

Considering that the model can learn a function of signals and features, we can describe the input for the graph as a $N \times D$ feature matrix X, where N is the number of nodes and D is the number of input features, represented in matrix form as an adjacency matrix A [6].

Based on CNNs, GCNs can learn common local and global structural patterns on graphs projecting convolutions and readout functions [27]. In [12], is described two types of GCNs: spatial and spectral. Spatial has convolution as a patch operator, creating a new feature structure based on nodes' neighborhood information. Spectral uses convolution to decompose the graph signal $s \in R^n$ as a scalar for each vertex and then applies a spectral filter on spectral components. In [9,24] was used a model with two layers applied a softmax function for classification with the output values:

$$Z = softmax(\hat{A}ReLU(\hat{A}X\theta^{(0)})\theta^{(1)})$$
(1)

where is defined as $\hat{A} = \hat{D}^{-\frac{1}{2}}\hat{A}\hat{D}^{-\frac{1}{2}}$ and softmax$(x_i) = \frac{1}{Z}\exp(x_i)$ with $Z = \sum_i \exp(x_i)$, defined also the loss function in Eq. 2.

$$L := - \sum_{i \in v_i} \sum_{f=1} Y_{if} \ln Z_{if} \qquad (2)$$

where V_i is the set of indices of labeled vertices and F is the dimension of the output features, being equal to the number of classes, as the final Dense layer in a traditional Convolutional Neural Network.

The label indicator matrix can be expressed as $Y \in R^{|V_i| \times F}$. The definitions cited were created in [9], represented in [12], and illustrated here.

2.3   Random Walk

Random walk is one of the most used methods in graph theory [14]. In [2], the random walk can be calculated as the transition probabilities between vertices and represented with an adjacency matrix. In [7], the authors describe the matrix as connections between nodes, using a graph G, the adjacency matrix can be calculated as $n \times n$, where n is the number of nodes, $A = [A_{ij}]$ with $A_{ij} = 1$ if $i \in T_j$ and $A_{ij} = 0$ otherwise.

Conceptually, we can describe Random Walk road as a speck that starts from a random point and walks x steps in a straight line, then turns through any angle whatever, and walks another x steps in a second straight line. It repeats this process n times [17].

Related to [16,26], it is possible to use random walks based on a distance r to calculate vertex similarities in a graph. With a graph that composes dense subgraphs, it is possible to detect communities by applying a method based on random walks.

3   Proposed Approach

Taking as approach the Random Walk method, which can be applied to compute large networks [19], searching for communities based in a network structured in graph [2,7,16,26].

We assume that a graph convolutional network model can have better accuracy than an end-to-end model, using context images to train the model, as applied in [9], which uses a fully connected graph to link the edges of each node. We took the method as a base to help decrease the connections in a graph and reduce the computational need, taking in that deep learning models can be computationally expensive.

We extracted information from images (bounding box) using a pre-trained model. The values extracted contain image features like borders, the difference between colors, texture, space and other information [3].

3.1   Graph Optimization with Random Walk

Considering an image and all its bounding boxes, we proposed that each image can be a fully connected sub-graph, the complete graph will be the amount of all sub-graphs, and the sub-graphs will not be connected, as explicit in Fig. 1.

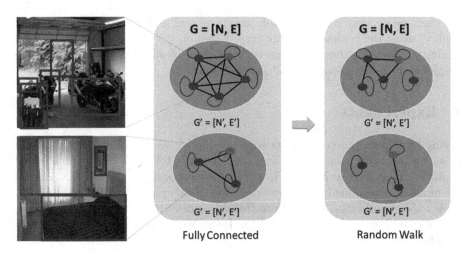

Fig. 1. Illustration of how the network is built. On left we have two images with their bounding boxes; the upper image is from the subclass "garage", and the bottom is from the subclass "bedroom". In the upper image, green, red, and brown are segmented objects defined as motorcycles; blue is a tree, and purple is a chair. In the bottom image, red is a curtain; purple is a frame, and green is a bed. The images had more bounding boxes than the illustration, but we used a smaller size to simulate the build of one graph and its sub-graphs. We built a simulation of how the fully connected sub-graph in the middle. It starts from the bounding boxes and creates connections with every node in the sub-graph, including himself. On the right, we considered the Random Walk method to create the connections of the sub-graph, detecting some communities and optimizing the edges in the network. We considered G as the complete graph and G' as a sub-graph. (Color figure online)

Our Random Walk method will be applied in each sub-graph, trying to detect communities disregarding long-distance connections. We used Euclidean distance D_E, with the feature F_x from one bounding box and F_y from the bounding box connected, to establish the approximation between two nodes, like an edge weight:

$$D_E(F_x, F_y) = \sqrt{(F_x - F_y)^2 * (F_x - F_y)^2} \qquad (3)$$

According to [16], and [26], a random walk seed tends to stand in communities with short distances. The network is built as shown in Fig. 1.

We apply the Random Walk method in the fully connected example of the net. Based on the possible walks that a random seed can give from a node, we can compute a new network, detecting the communities and better connections for the nodes. If we get a random seed as a start point and designate that this node can walk x steps forward or backward, this way, we can calculate the probability of one random node n_x passes in another node n_y, if it is high we assume that those nodes are from the same community, otherwise not.

Then, we computed all the graph structures and performed our random walk method using the community walk trap, based on [19]. We used an image containing all the bounding boxes and the number of steps as input. The entire graph G will be the amount of all subgraphs G'.

4   Experiments

Trying to achieve the best results with our model, we performed a grid search to set up the hyperparameters. We considered [0.5, 0.1, 0.05, 0.01, 0.005, 0.001] as the learning rate, [0.2, 0.3, 0.5, 0.8] as dropout and [16, 32, 64, 128, 256] as the number of neurons in the first layer, and 2,000 epochs.

For the experiments, we used pre-trained models (ResNet50 [8], Xception [4], VGG16 [20], InceptionResNetV2 [22]) in ImageNet [11], to extract features from each bounding box.

4.1   Dataset Description

Due to space limitations to evaluate the GCNs variations, we used the UnRel [18] dataset. The purpose of using this image dataset is that the relationships between the objects are annotated, and the class of each of these relationships is labeled, making it easier to use and pre-process. In Table 1, we described the number of classes, images, and their respective bounding boxes (in total and for the training and testing processes).

Table 1. Description of the Unrel dataset, including the number of classes, images and the number of its respective bounding boxes (in total and for the training and testing sets)

Dataset	Classes	Images	Bounding Boxes	Training	Testing
UnRel	57	822	2156	1725	431

4.2   Results

This section shows the results achieved by each method mentioned so far. To measure the footprint of methods, we used four metrics: the number of edges, the time to build the graph, and the memory space required for the graph.

In Table 2, we show each CNN architecture combined with the GCNFC (Graph Fully Connected) and the GCNRW (Graph Random Walk) their footprints.

Table 2. UNREL dataset footprint results

ResNet50	Edges	Walk	Time (s)	Size (mb)
GCNFC	7054	–	0.31238	0.04109
GCNRW	**5042**	3	**0.27661**	**0.03561**
Xception	Edges	Walk	Time (s)	Size (mb)
GCNFC	7054	–	0.31238	0.04109
GCNRW	**5046**	7	**0.27577**	**0.035563**
VGG16	Edges	Walk	Time (s)	Size (mb)
GCNFC	7054	–	0.31238	0.04109
GCNRW	**5046**	7	**0.27577**	**0.035563**
InceptionV3	Edges	Walk	Time (s)	Size (mb)
GCNFC	7054	–	0.31238	0.04109
GCNRW	**4570**	6	**0.27659**	**0.03401**
InceptionResNetV2	Edges	Walk	Time (s)	Size (mb)
GCNFC	7054	–	0.31238	0.04109
GCNRW	**4604**	1	**0.24632**	**0.03412**

As we can see in Table 2, the random walk method can achieve expressive results if we compare it with the fully connected method. The random walk method used few edges to create the graph; it was built in less time and required less memory. For instance, considering the InceptionV3 architecture, the GNFC generates 7054 edges, while the GCNRW, with a random walk with step 6, comprises only 4570 edges (i.e., a decrease of 35%).

We also performed experiments to obtain quality metrics comparing both graph neural network approaches. Table 3 illustrates these results. According to Table 3, the highest accuracy, obtained from the UnRel dataset, was achieved by the GCNRW (*Random Walk*) topology with the Xception architecture, obtaining an accuracy of 64.16%. The result obtained by the GCNFC topology (*Fully Connected*) was lower than the performance achieved by the GCNRW network, even considering the standard deviation of both networks. Thus, it can be said that, that the GCNRW network had better results than the GCNFC network and used fewer edges to build the graph of connections, considering that the GCNFC network used 7054 edges and the GCNRW network had 5046 edges, with a 28.46% decrease in the number of edges.

It is also possible to note that all the vanilla CNN architectures presented poor results compared to both graph neural networks strategies. For instance, analyzing the ResNet50 architecture, the end-to-end process achieved 12.81% of accuracy, while the GCNFC and the GCNRW reached 64.70% and 63.90%, respectively. This same behavior can be noted considering the other architectures and the considered metrics.

Table 3. Results obtained using the Unrel datasets and considering all metrics

ResNet50	Accuracy	Precision	Recall	F1-Score
CNN	12.81 ± 0.00243	0.0059 ± 0.00368	0.0191 ± 0.00143	0.0057 ± 0.00132
GCN FC	64.90 ± 0.01738	50.37 ± 0.01919	49.25 ± 0.00720	47.46 ± 0.01579
GCN RW	63.90 ± 0.00851	56.20 ± 0.03955	51.52 ± 0.01648	51.18 ± 0.02775
VGG16	Accuracy	Precision	Recall	F1-Score
CNN	29.90 ± 0.01822	20.75 ± 0.053924	18.059 ± 0.02527	16.50 ± 0.03110
GCN FC	58.13 ± 0.01500	46.16 ± 0.00646	44.81 ± 0.01687	43.02 ± 0.00964
GCN RW	61.88 ± 0.02352	50.36 ± 0.03424	49.76 ± 0.02237	47.76 ± 0.02197
InceptionResNetV2	Accuracy	Precision	Recall	F1-Score
CNN	46.00 ± 0.02500	47.04 ± 0.01180	37.55 ± 0.01181	38.72 ± 0.01412
GCN FC	61.07 ± 0.01805	47.49 ± 0.01751	47.69 ± 0.01207	45.12 ± 0.01312
GCN RW	63.64 ± 0.01849	55.30 ± 0.02942	49.83 ± 0.02100	49.73 ± 0.02569
InceptionV3	Accuracy	Precision	Recall	F1-Score
CNN	44.56 ± 0.00677	46.49 ± 0.05692	34.51 ± 0.00480	35.42 ± 0.01450
GCN FC	56.95 ± 0.01125	44.29 ± 0.01873	42.64 ± 0.01121	40.96 ± 0.01644
GCN RW	58.49 ± 0.01407	49.18 ± 0.03646	44.14 ± 0.02076	44.41 ± 0.02695
Xception	Accuracy	Precision	Recall	F1-Score
CNN	49.77 ± 0.01095	50.90 ± 0.04322	42.13 ± 0.03013	43.06 ± 0.01140
GCN FC	61.66 ± 0.01303	46.08 ± 0.01991	46.47 ± 0.00492	43.58 ± 0.01436
GCN RW	64.16 ± 0.03246	51.59 ± 0.05471	50.34 ± 0.02260	48.68 ± 0.03574

Another important metric to analyze the results is the F1-Score since it comprises a harmonic mean between precision and recall. From these metrics, the proposed GCNRW achieved the best results. For example, considering the InceptionV3 architecture, the GCNFC and GCNRW achieved 40.96% and 44.41%, respectively.

Figure 2 shows examples of images classified by the GCNFC and GCNRW. In Fig. 2 (a), both approaches correctly classify the image. However, considering Fig. 2 (c) and (d), the GCNFC cannot reach the correct classification. For instance, in Fig. 2 (c), the correct class was elephant-wear-pants, and the GCNFC classified it as person-hold-plane. This same behavior occurred in Fig. 2 (d); our approach reached the correct classification (i.e., person-inside-tree). In Fig. 2 (b), both approaches failed, however, we can notice that our approach reached a context more similar to the correct classification (dog-wear-pants) when compared to the GCNFC classification (cat-on-the-top-of-dog)

Fig. 2. Example of images classified by the GCNFC and GCNRW

5   Conclusion

In this paper, we proposed aggregating graph convolution networks with random walks to classify images. From our obtained results, we can assure the advantage of our proposed aggregation against state-of-the-art approaches (i.e., end-to-end CNN and fully connected graph neural network).

Our approach achieved better efficacy and efficiency since we reached the best accuracies with fewer graph edges. In future works, we intend to test our approach with other datasets and random walk variations.

References

1. Alexander, S.: Computer Vision and Simulation?: Methods. Technology and Applications, Nova Science Publishers, Inc, Applications and Technology. Computer Science (2016)
2. Bertasius, G., Torresani, L., Yu, S.X., Shi, J.: Convolutional random walk networks for semantic image segmentation. In: The IEEE Conference on Computer Vision and Pattern Recognition, pp. 858–866 (2017)
3. Chary, R.V.R., Lakshmi, D.R., Sunitha, K.V.N.: Feature extraction methods for color image similarity. In: National Conference on Cloud Computing & Big Data, pp. 208–214 (2012)
4. Chollet, F.: Xception: Deep learning with depthwise separable convolutions. CoRR abs/1610.02357 (2016), arxiv.org/abs/1610.02357
5. Dev, D.: Deep Learning with Hadoop. Packt Publishing, Birmingham (2017)
6. Duvenaud, D.K., Maclaurin, D., Iparraguirre, J., Bombarell, R., Hirzel, T., Aspuru-Guzik, A., Adams, R.P.: Convolutional networks on graphs for learning molecular fingerprints. In: Cortes, C., Lawrence, N.D., Lee, D.D., Sugiyama, M., Garnett, R. (eds.) Advances in Neural Information Processing Systems. vol. 28, pp. 2224–2232. Curran Associates, Inc. (2015)
7. Göbel, F., Jagers, A.: Random walks on graphs. Stochast. Process. Appl. **2**(4), 311–336 (1974)
8. He, K., Zhang, X., Ren, S., Sun, J.: Deep Residual Learning for Image Recognition. arXiv e-prints (2015)
9. Kipf, T.N., Welling, M.: Semi-supervised classification with graph convolutional networks. In: 5th International Conference on Learning Representation, pp. 1–14 (2016)
10. Koner, R., Sinhamahapatra, P., Tresp, V.: Relation transformer network. CoRR abs/2004.06193, pp. 1–15 (2020)
11. Krizhevsky, A., Sutskever, I., Hinton, G.E.: ImageNet classification with deep convolutional neural networks. In: Pereira, F., Burges, C.J.C., Bottou, L., Weinberger, K.Q. (eds.) Advances in Neural Information Processing Systems. vol. 25, pp. 1097–1105. Curran Associates, Inc. (2012)
12. Li, Q., Han, Z., Wu, X.M.: Deeper insights into graph convolutional networks for semi-supervised learning. In: Proceedings of the Thirty-Second AAAI Conference on Artificial Intelligence, pp. 1–8. AAAI Press (2018)
13. Liang, M., Hu, X.: Recurrent convolutional neural network for object recognition. In: The IEEE Conference on Computer Vision and Pattern Recognition (CVPR), pp. 3367–3375 (2015)
14. Lovász, L.: Random walks on graphs: a survey. In: Department of Computer Science, Yale University, pp. 1–46 (1993)
15. Maturana, D., Scherer, S.: VoxNet: a 3D convolutional neural network for real-time object recognition. In: 2015 IEEE/RSJ International Conference on Intelligent Robots and Systems (IROS), pp. 922–928 (2015)
16. Okuda, M., Satoh, S., Sato, Y., Kidawara, Y.: Community detection using restrained random-walk similarity. IEEE Trans. Pattern Anal. Mach. Intell. **43**(1), 89–103 (2019)
17. Pearson, K.: The problem of the random walk. Nature **72**(294), 294 (1905)
18. Peyre, J., Laptev, I., Schmid, C., Sivic, J.: Weakly-supervised learning of visual relations. In: International Conference on Computer Vision, pp. 5179–5188 (2017)

19. Pons, P., Latapy, M.: Computing communities in large networks using random walks. In: Computer and Information Sciences, pp. 284–293 (2005)

20. Simonyan, K., Zisserman, A.: Very deep convolutional networks for large-scale image recognition. In: 3rd International Conference on Learning Representations, pp. 1–14 (2015)

21. Sullivan, W.: Deep Learning with Python Illustrated Guide for Beginners and Intermediates: The Future Is Here! Independently Published (2018)

22. Szegedy, C., Ioffe, S., Vanhoucke, V., Alemi, A.: Inception-v4, inception-ResNet and the impact of residual connections on learning. In: Proceedings of the Thirty-First AAAI Conference on Artificial Intelligence, pp. 4278–4284 (2016)

23. Tomè, D., Monti, F., Baroffio, L., Bondi, L., Tagliasacchi, M., Tubaro, S.: Deep convolutional neural networks for pedestrian detection. Sig. Process. Image Commun. **47**, 482–489 (2016)

24. Wang, M., et al.: Deep graph library: Towards efficient and scalable deep learning on graphs (2019)

25. Xia, F., Liu, J., Nie, H., Fu, Y., Wan, L., Kong, X.: Random walks: a review of algorithms and applications. IEEE Trans. Emerg. Top. Comput. Intell. **4**(2), 95–107 (2020)

26. Zhang, W., Kong, F., Yang, L., Chen, Y., Zhang, M.: Hierarchical community detection based on partial matrix convergence using random walks. Tsinghua Sci. Technol. **23**(1), 35–46 (2018)

27. Zhang, Z., Cui, P., Zhu, W.: Deep learning on graphs: a survey. IEEE Trans. Knowl. Data Eng. **34**(01), 249–270 (2018)

28. Zhao, Z., Zheng, P., Xu, S., Wu, X.: Object detection with deep learning: a review. IEEE Trans. Neural Netw. Learn. Syst. **30**(11), 3212–3232 (2019)

Bus Route Classification for Rural Areas Using Graph Convolutional Networks

Timo Stadler[1]($\boxtimes$), Sandra Weikl[1], Simon Wein[2], Peter Georg[3],
Andreas Schäfer[3], and Jan Dünnweber[1]

[1] Faculty of Computer Science and Mathematics, OTH Regensburg,
93040 Regensburg, Germany
timo.stadler@oth-regensburg.de
[2] Department of Psychology, University of Regensburg, 93040 Regensburg, Germany
[3] Department of Physics, University of Regensburg, 93040 Regensburg, Germany

Abstract. In this paper, we present a new approach to determine the estimated time of arrival (ETA) for bus routes using (Deep) Graph Convolutional Networks (DGCNs). In addition, we use the same DGCN to detect detours within a route. In our application, a classification of routes and their underlying graph structure is performed using Graph Learning. Our model leads to a fast prediction and avoids solving the vehicle routing problem (VRP) through expensive computations. Moreover, we describe how to predict travel time for all routes using the same DGCN Model. This method makes it possible not to use a more computationally intensive approximation algorithm when determining long travel times with many intermediate stops, but to use our network for an early estimate of the quality of a route. Long travel times, in our case result from the use of a call-bus system, which must distribute many passengers among several vehicles and can take them to places without a regular stop. For a case study, the rural town of Roding in Bavaria is used. Our training data for this area results from an approximation algorithm that we implemented to optimize routes and generate an archive of routes of varying quality simultaneously.

Keywords: VRP · Graph Learning · Graph Convolutional Networks

1 Introduction

Public transport is playing a more important role than ever before. Modern technologies, like mobile applications, offer many opportunities to make it as accessible and sustainable as possible for both travelers and service providers. With an ever-increasing number of ways to collect, store, process and disseminate large amounts of data, the role of public transport is becoming even more important. Those growing number of options can create benefits for many areas of local public transport and mobility in general.

Especially in rural areas, bus connections are often sparse, although it is precisely there that the distances to be covered, for example, to go shopping, are very long. Therefore, this area in particular can benefit greatly from efficient

© The Author(s), under exclusive license to Springer Nature Switzerland AG 2023
L. Rutkowski et al. (Eds.): ICAISC 2023, LNAI 14125, pp. 236–250, 2023.
https://doi.org/10.1007/978-3-031-42505-9_21

local public transport solutions. This paper deals specifically with improving routes, which are used in a call-bus system with ride-sharing options for rural areas.

The authors of this work cooperate with the bus operators in Roding and help them with the establishment of a new minibus service, where so-called feeders, are being tested for public transport in the Roding area. In the future, public transport in Roding will not operate via fixed routes and stops anymore, but those feeders will pick up passengers at dynamically generated stops near their homes and bring them to their desired destinations. These stops are created using a geometric algorithm that weighs positions according to the number of POIs nearby and population [2]. Especially for rural areas, such dynamic stops and timetables have advantages, as residents have shorter distances to cover and are more flexible in terms of time, for example when they have to attend appointments. The presented research is a step towards improving mobility in rural areas and developing a mobility-on-demand solution for rural areas within the scope of the Bavarian High-Tech and Smart City Initiative [25].

To solve the VRP, an algorithm was developed to find the fastest route for multiple vehicles simultaneously. In this iterative process, the authors came up with the idea of using the individual quality levels of the routes to develop an ETA prediction. For this purpose, graph learning methods are used. The idea is not to replace the exact algorithm with a machine learning model but to give a much faster estimate of the ETA, which does not have to be absolutely reliable. Especially since there are many vehicles in public transport that need to be calculated at the same time, it makes sense to use graph learning to get a quick first estimation.

The use of this system is therefore necessary on the one hand to achieve a speedup in the determination of optimal routes. On the other hand, it can also be beneficial for the individual user. It is often the case that bus drivers take a diversion even though there would be a shorter route. Our system could point out such shortcuts and alternative routes. Moreover, nowadays it is inevitable to deal with real-time data when solving the VRP. Thus, there must be a combination of an information system with the route planning algorithm [21].

As a further step, our neural network model should also estimate the estimated time of arrival (ETA). Since this is a regression, the result must be much more accurate than in our initial use case of classification, which means that a much larger data set must be used. For the implementation of this prediction, a modified model in the form of a Deep Graph Convolutional Network (DGCN) was trained.

These DGCNs can be optimally suited for application to public transport problems. Roads and routes can be represented as graphs with weights assigned to each edge, making it easy to abstract and evaluate a route.

In rural areas, there are far fewer regular bus connections, so a possibility must be created to transport people regardless of time restrictions. Here, too, the use of a GCN is optimal, since it can also store the time characteristics of the rigid bus routes and thus corresponding weak points in the complete timetable can be detected more quickly.

Once a network has been trained, it can be scaled to a larger region or transferred to another region with a similar problem and structure, i.e. the number of parameters is independent of the number of nodes in a network. Our model is therefore not only applicable to the city of our case study but can also be applied to other cities without further adaptation.

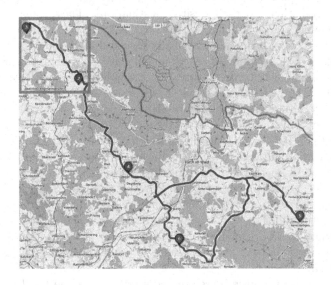

Fig. 1. Map with a diversion around point 6 to be recognized by our GCN.

Figure 1 shows a subroute on the basis of which our graph is created. Pay particular attention to point no. 6, which leads to an extension of the route and is recognized as a necessary diversion because the route from point no. 5 back to the start is via a different route.

In Sect. 2, we will first discuss related work for the classification of routes. Moreover, we show that inference via graph learning is faster than traditional approximation algorithms. This is followed by a description of the general problem to be solved by graph learning in Sect. 3. In Sect. 4 we describe the methods used for our model. In Sect. 5 we give a presentation and evaluation of the results of our (D)GCNs. Section 6 rounds off this paper with an outlook on further improvements that we plan to implement.

2   Related Work

Over the last decades, the VRP has become ever more important [11,18,24]. In parallel the tools have been continuously improved, making it by now possible to plan an optimal route for multiple vehicles in little time.

An early approach was to provide the individual sub-routes in a hierarchical structure based on selection criteria [14]. Here, emphasis is placed on the ranking and sorting of alternatives. The two most widespread selection criteria are still "shortest path" and "least time". For the human navigator, however, a mix of these two route selection criteria is usually an optimal route. For example, a certain route is longer but offers more comfort for the passengers.

In recent years, sensors and devices for wireless communication have also become increasingly affordable, allowing modern route planning to take place in real-time [27]. When classifying systems for route planning, a distinction can be made between systems with different design approaches. For example, there are reactive and predictive systems or static and dynamic systems [27]. With the introduction of our GCN, we want to create a static predictive system, one that can react to changes in the planning of an optimal route at any time through new training using live data.

In order to improve graph learning with knowledge from other areas, some techniques were adopted. Driven by various successful applications in computer vision, recently the interest has emerged to also generalize convolutional neural networks (CNNs) to the non-Euclidean geometry of graphs [4].

Many real-world applications work with data that can be represented in the form of graphs: e.g. social networks, biological or chemical structures, and transport networks [26]. Graph learning refers to a part of machine learning that works with graphs [28]. Due to the diverse and abundant occurrence of data that can be represented as graphs and the possibility of using them to gain new insights, graph learning has gained popularity [16]. GNNs are also used to predict brain activity, help predict disease, or are used to solve a number of optimization problems in wireless networks [22,23,30].

The goal of graph learning is to extract the desired features from a graph. Here, the tasks can be divided into three different layers that can be used. A classification/regression of single attributes of nodes, edges between nodes, or of the complete graph can be performed [6]. In our case of route classification, we are particularly concerned with the classification of a complete graph and the similarity of a graph to other graphs.

Due to the already described versatile occurrence of data in the form of graphs or networks, a number of proposals have been made in recent years for extending neural network models to deal optimally with graphs. Such models exist both based on Recurrent Neural Networks and on Convolutional Neural Networks.

A concept that is similar to Graph Neural Networks is given by Message Passing Neural Networks, as introduced by Gilmer et al. in 2017 [12]. These are also models that propagate information between nodes in a graph. However, we use graphs specifically for representing routes.

Since the data of a Geo Information System (GIS) is also structured as a graph, the idea of using Graph Neural Networks as a tool to solve a VRP as efficiently as possible is obvious. In their survey paper, Jiang et al. compile papers dealing with vehicle speed prediction, traffic prediction, and passenger flow prediction [17]. They also list a variety of different Graph Neural Networks (GNNs), such as GCNs or graph attention networks, which are used to solve traffic forecasting problems. However, the problem of estimating routes or determining ETA has not yet been analyzed by these authors.

A new approach to predicting ETA using GNNs is to use Google Maps data for the analysis. Complex spatiotemporal interactions (such as the start of rush hour) can be predicted [10]. Thus, it can be seen that the optimal planning and classification of routes is an ideal goal for the use of a GCN due to a large number of usable parameters. In our case, all training data are generated by the different phases of our HGS algorithm and there is no need to use artificially corrupted data like in other work.

Our discovery that during the iterations of an approximation algorithm, which continually improves a result valuable training data can be extracted, wherefrom a ML model can be built for rating the quality of unknown sample data is another contribution of this work, which has also applications outside the public transport area.

3   Formulation of the Problem

All routes and stops discussed in this paper are located in the vicinity of the small town of Roding, Bavaria. The town of Roding has about 11500 inhabitants (as of 2008) in an area of $113km^2$. In addition to the town of Roding itself, the complete neighboring region with an area of $674km^2$ is considered. A total of 2000 virtual stops were defined, using our software, within this area to cover it optimally and to have enough points to generate a long desirable route.

We use a hybrid genetic search (HGS) algorithm to solve the resulting special form of the vehicle routing problem for multiple vehicles and passengers simultaneously [3]. This algorithm must be run anew for the calculation of each route or each problem and requires a certain amount of time until the termination criterion is reached. The termination criterion here is either a fixed maximum of iterations or the absence of any improvements after a number of iterations. Routes determined by a Hybrid Genetic Search (HGS) algorithm are used as training data for the graph learning models. This algorithm is used to solve the capacitated vehicle routing problem with pickups and deliveries (CVRPPD) [29].

We use the data that the algorithm uses during route optimization to train the model of a graph learning network. Our model should predict the ETA for each passenger and additionally determine whether the chosen route is good or bad. The approach to use a GCN is intended to cover two areas of application: On the one hand, the algorithm already in use is accelerated by providing the neural network with intermediate results as input and terminating the calculations if it already assumes an optimal route. This leads to an improvement in runtime of up to 90%. On the other hand, the GCN must also function independently and inform the user whether a route he wants to take is optimal or whether it makes sense to choose an alternative route. An example of this would be the choice between a motorway with a higher driving speed and a longer driving distance instead of a country road. This is especially important when used with our call-bus system, where multiple routes are calculated simultaneously and significant time savings can be achieved by identifying non-optimal routes faster.

This algorithm minimizes the cost of a route for a given number of pickup points from which goods, in this case, travelers, are picked up and their destinations (delivery points). This includes minimizing the number of vehicles actually needed and the route length. The results of this algorithm are optimized bus routes with actual and virtual stops in and around the Roding area. An optimal route is defined as the route that takes the least time, so we optimize for the shortest time instead of the shortest distance.

To enable their use as input parameters for the GCN, these routes must be converted into a graph representation. The distances between the respective points correspond to the edges. The graphs are homogeneous, which means they have only one node type and one edge type.

Based on the work of Bruna et al. [5] and Defferard et al. [9], Kipf and Welling [20] have proposed a simple and efficient first-order approximation of the localized spectral graph-filtering. The layer-wise activity in such a multi-layer graph convolutional network (GCN) is thereby obtained by:

$$H^{(l+1)} = \sigma \left(\tilde{D}^{-\frac{1}{2}} \tilde{A} \tilde{D}^{-\frac{1}{2}} H^{(l)} W^{(l)} \right) \tag{1}$$

where $H^{(l)}$ denotes the activation of the previous layer l and $\tilde{A} = A + I_N$ represents the adjacency matrix of a graph $\mathcal{G}$ with added self-connections. Further I_N is the identity matrix, and $\tilde{D}_{ii} = \sum_j \tilde{A}_{ij}$ denotes the degree matrix. The activation function is given by $\sigma(\cdot)$ and $W^{(l)}$ represents a matrix of trainable weights, and for our application we used the ReLU activation function $\text{ReLU}(\cdot) = max(0, \cdot)$. In the first layer the input is given by $H^{(0)} = X$ and the final predictions in layer L are generated using a dense layer with one output neuron. In our proposed application of GCNs, the input features $X \in \mathbb{R}^{N \times F}$ are given by the altitude, location and also distance, and travel time as edge weights between every single node. These features were selected because latitude and longitude describe the stops most accurately and are available for each stop. This also applies to altitude - this was furthermore added as a feature because, for example, fuel consumption, and the willingness of residents and tourists to ascend a significant height to reach a bus stop play a role in the quality of the routes. The distance between two points as an edge feature was added because it best describes the route segments additionally to the required journey time. Other parameters have been omitted so far to keep the model as simple as possible.

The complete network with all layers used is shown in Fig. 2. During learning the weights $W^{(l)}$ are trained using the Adam optimizer [19]. A good trade-off between computational complexity and model accuracy was found using two GCN layers connected in series. They are used for each node to process the local structure information and to collect feature information. In the *mean pooling layer*, the node representations are combined to create a graph representation. This graph representation is then used as input for two successive *fully connected layers*. The fully connected layers are classic feedforward networks in which the

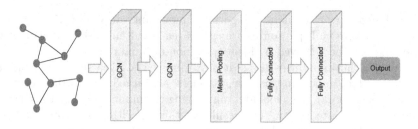

Fig. 2. Structure of the Graph Convolutional Network used

input representations are combined and the prediction result is calculated using the activation function. In the output layer, the sigmoid activation function is used to perform the classification, which is suitable for binary classifications [7]. Binary Cross Entropy is used as a suitable loss function [15].

4   Methods (Implementation)

We used the StellarGraph Machine Learning Library to implement the GCN. This is a library for graph machine learning that is built on the basis of Tensor-Flow and the Keras high-level API [8]. This library is based on the widely used Tensorflow platform and is therefore easy to use.

4.1   Data Collection and Import

Since our training data is generated by an approximation algorithm, we know that arbitrary data that is produced within the first iterations of the procedure is non-optimal and can therefore be labeled as non-optimal solutions for our data set. The calculated solutions from the algorithm are considered optimal solutions, i.e. routes with the lowest travel time. In order to incorporate further geo-information, in the form of elevation data, into the training data of the model we also queried the Google Maps Platform Services [13].

In more detail, the *Directions Advanced API* was used to obtain complete routes with more than 10 stops. The *Directions API* was used to obtain edge features, travel times, and distances between two points on those routes. In total, nearly 1500 queries were made to the Directions Advanced API, and 220,000 queries were made to the Directions API to train our networks.

For each node of the graph, the fields *longitude*, *latitude*, *height* and for each edge the fields *distance* and *travel time* are imported. The request just described was made for all existing and virtual stops. These stops are contained in two CSV files, the virtual stops contain only latitude and longitude, the existing stops also contain information such as the address. These two files represent the pool from which the stops for the route optimization algorithm were chosen.

Z-score normalization is applied to the complete data frame of a node's features. This type of normalization was chosen because the feature distribution is relatively uniform and does not contain any strong extremes.

In each case, the first route of a file is read in as a route of class 0, the last route of a file is the optimal route without detours and corresponds to class 1. The distances between two nodes are normalized to the range of 0 to 1. Unlike the Z-score normalization, this normalization was chosen so that some upward outliers would have less influence.

"Source" and "Target" are keywords reserved by StellarGraph for the start and end nodes of edges; the ID of the nodes is stored here. The mapping of the features to the respective nodes is done by means of these IDs; the line from the feature data frame is searched for that has the ID of the "Source" or "Target" node as its index. "Weight" is also used as a keyword for the weighting of the individual edges.

Therefore, in the following, we also describe routes using these graph-specific terms instead of talking about starts, destinations, and distances.

4.2 Graph Creation

A graph object can be created from the imported data, which can be used for Machine Learning models in StellarGraph. Specifically, an object of the class *StellarDiGraph* is created, i.e. a directed graph, since the route only runs in a certain direction.

In order to be able to carry out the supervised classification, the graphs must be provided with a label that describes their class. In the binary classification of routes, we use the labels 0 and 1 are used for this purpose.

For the journey time prediction, a graph is provided with a label that contains the journey time required for the route in seconds. Those travel times are stored in a CSV file, which contains the file name of the route file as one column and the travel time determined for the optimal route from this file as another column.

The training models applied are graph classification models with Keras. For processing the individual *StellarDiGraph*-instances, these objects have to be converted into a suitable format. For a supervised graph classification, a *PaddedGraphGenerator* is suitable. This is instantiated with the list of StellarDiGraphs. The generator transforms the data into adjacency matrices and arrays for the features that the Keras model can handle.

4.3 Training

Assuming that the data are independent and identically distributed the GCN model is trained with *k-Cross-Validation* and *Early stopping* to avoid overfitting. For each fold, different training and test samples are used for validation. Without early stopping, there would be a danger of overfitting, as the algorithm would adapt too much to the training data, which would lead to a generalization error. The training is stopped at an early stopping value of x if the loss does not decrease over x epochs. The loss was chosen by us as a metric to optimize the model and is therefore observed.

For the binary classification, a data set consisting of 7708 routes was trained. In each case, 3854 data sets belong to class 0 for a route with detours and class 1 for an optimal route. 3610 graphs are trained, the average number of nodes per route is 69.7, the average number of edges is 71.7.

4.4   Implementation of a DGCNN Model

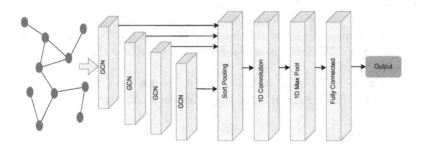

Fig. 3. Model of the Deep Graph Convolutional Neural Network used

To further improve our prediction result and the accuracy of the classification, we extended our model to a Deep Graph Convolutional Neural Network (DGCNN). This model is based on the End-To-End Deep Graph Convolutional Neural Network architecture that is shown in Fig. 3. Unlike the first model, four GCN layers are used here, but their adjacency matrix is $D^{-1}A$ normalized. The last GCN layer is one-dimensional, only this layer is used as input for sorting the nodes in *SortPooling*. The GCN layers and the SortPooling layer are followed by one-dimensional Convolution and Pooling layers to extract local patterns for the sorted node sequence. This is followed by a Fully Connected layer with a dropout of 0.5 until in the last layer with the *Sigmoid Activation* function is used to perform binary classification. Each layer has a size of 32 nodes and the mean training time for this model was $33ms$ per step, which results in a total training time of 2.5 minutes on our machine, which is a 4-GPU A-100 system [1].

The model is trained using data sets with fixed batch sizes for training data and test data. Furthermore, the number of training epochs and the value k, describe to which size the graphs should be scaled.

Since the DGCNN has shown a better performance than the GCN, this model is used for travel time prediction. This improvement in performance can be explained by the fact that the additional layers allow a more complex non-linear function to be learned. The basic model is not changed much, because the learning of the weights for the training data is basically the same, the only difference is that instead of a class a continuous value is output as result. Therefore, the activation function must be changed in the last layer so that the values are not scaled between 0 and 1, but continuous values can also be output above this. In our ongoing experiments, we use the *ReLu* function for this purpose. The loss function must be adapted. In our case, the *Mean Absolute Error* was used.

Table 1. Accuracies for GCN for binary graph classification

GCN	Epochs	Folds	Early Stop	Learning Rate	Batch size	Accuracy
Directed	25	10	25	0.005	64	59.4%
Directed	25	10	25	0.005	128	58.8%
Undirected	50	10	25	0.0005	128	58.5%
Undirected	50	10	25	0.005	128	75.4%
Undirected	50	10	25	0.005	256	72.8%
Undirected	75	10	25	0.005	128	73.7%
Undirected	50	10	25	0.005	512	74.5%
Undirected	50	5	25	0.005	512	65.1%

5   Evaluation

Table 1 shows an overview of different parameterizations with regard to the test accuracies of the dataset. It can be observed that the model performs well with undirected StellarGraph objects, but not with directed StellarDiGraph objects (see lines 1 and 2). The reason for this is the symmetric normalization of the adjacency matrix of the GCN, $D^{-\frac{1}{2}}AD^{-\frac{1}{2}}$, which only performs well for the symmetric adjacency matrix of undirected graphs.

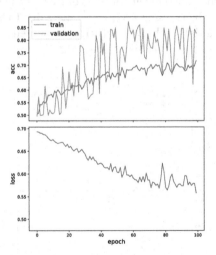

Fig. 4. Accuracy and loss curve for graph classification for the chosen GCN Model

The parameterization with the best accuracy is learning over 50 epochs with 10-fold folded data, a learning rate of 0.005, and a batch size of 128. The table shows only a few exemplary parameterizations, further changes to the existing parameters have also provided similar results in the range above 70% accuracy.

It can be observed that the learning rate for GCN has a large influence on the model's performance - with a value of 0.0005 the model is unreliable and the

Table 2. Accuracies for DGCNN for binary graph classification

DGCNN	Epochs	Learnning rate	Batch size Train|Test	k	Train|Test%	Accuracy
Directed	30	0.001	200|40	35	0.8|0.2	68.4%
Directed	100	0.01	200|40	50	0.8|0.2	50.0%
Directed	100	0.001	400|80	50	0.8|0.2	75.0%
Directed	100	0.001	200|40	67	0.8|0.2	79.6%
Directed	100	0.001	400|80	67	0.8|0.2	80.9%
Directed	50	0.001	400|80	67	0.8|0.2	76.0%
Directed	100	0.005	200|40	50	0.8|0.2	71.8%
Directed	100	0.0001	400|80	67	0.8|0.2	71.3%
Directed	100	0.0005	400|80	67	0.7|0.3	74.7%
Directed	100	0.0005	200|40	67	0.8|0.2	77.2%
Directed	100	0.0005	400|80	67	0.8|0.2	75.48%
Directed	100	0.0005	200|40	67	0.7|0.3	76.3%

loss is high. With a 5-fold convolution of the data set, the model also did not perform as well as with a 10-fold convolution.

For the parameterization of the penultimate line, the curves for the accuracy and the binary entropy loss can be seen in Fig. 4. It can be seen that the values sometimes fluctuate strongly over the epochs; one possible reason for this is that the validation set for the convolution contains outliers. Otherwise, the validation accuracy is higher than the training accuracy. This is due to the fact that dropout is active in the training data, which deactivates some neurons in order to learn. In the validation set, on the other hand, learning takes place with all neurons.

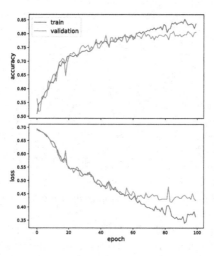

Fig. 5. Accuracy and loss curve for graph classification for the chosen DGCNN Model

A listing of differently parameterized training trials is shown in Table 2. These runs were performed on the same data set as the GCN in the previous chapter, except that these graphs were created as directed graphs, i.e. StellarDiGraphs. The best performance was measured over 100 epochs with a learning rate of 0.001.

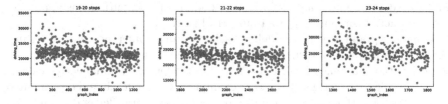

Fig. 6. Distribution of predictions (Green) to actual travel times (Blue) for 19–20, 21–22, and 23–24 stops. (Color figure online)

In addition to this good performance for directed graphs, the accuracy for the individual parameterizations is also similar for undirected graphs, but large fluctuations can be noticed in the graph for an accuracy that is higher than the number of epochs when undirected graphs are used. The two graphs shown in Fig. 5 run with slight fluctuations, but are otherwise similar in their course. From epoch 60 onwards, slight overfitting can be observed, as the test data get a higher loss and a lower accuracy than the training data.

For the best parameterization found so far, the calculated RMSE is 3708.70 s. The distribution of actual to predicted travel times can be seen in Fig. 6. Blue are the actual times, and green the predicted ones. On the x-axis the input graphs are indexed, on the y-axis the travel times in seconds are shown. The division into 3 different graphs with a classification into different groups was chosen because an increase in the number of stops in a route leads to a corresponding jump in the ETA. The model was initially calculated completely for routes with 19–24 stops. In trials, it was found that a GCN trained only with routes up to 19 stops could also make accurate predictions for routes with more stops and vice versa. Thus, our model is arbitrarily scalable to smaller or larger areas. A large generalization of the model can therefore be assumed.

Here we can find more parameters to train the DGCNN with and choose a better-fitting architecture. For a first proof of concept, however, these results confirm that GL is suitable for route classification surprisingly clearly.

For our specific case, this means that our model can decide very quickly whether additional passengers can be picked up and brought to their destination due to the low travel time.

6 Conclusion

In this paper, we presented our Graph Learning model that allows us to decide whether a route of the VRP is optimal, or contains detours. We also presented a first approach based on which ETA prediction is possible. The binary classification of the algorithm achieved an accuracy of 80.9%. This allows us to terminate our long computing HGS algorithm early if the model we trained thinks it has already reached an optimal result. Thus, instead of the previously used rigid termination criteria such as the maximum number of iterations or a certain number of iterations without improvement, the prediction from the DGCNN can be used. An approximate solution method of soft computing was applied to real data, acting supportively to a numerical method.

Using our graph learning models we achieve a mean inference time of $184ms$, which allows us to get a result very quickly and provides the user with decision support without a long wait. In addition, the models are permanently scalable and applicable to similar problems. For example, if the model should be evaluated for a larger area, this can be done at any time. Also, a transfer and application in another rural area with similar characteristics is possible at any time.

It also turned out that our model can be applied to regions with a similar nature of traffic without any changes and still provides good results. Also, an extension of the considered area is possible without making any adjustments.

Especially in the prediction of the ETA based on graph learning, there are still a lot of optimizations possible. Due to the design of our system, it is very easy to increase the dataset with training and test data with minimal effort. The authors are currently trying to obtain further parameters for the nodes and edges between them in the form of live traffic data. In the future, this should be a practical application to provide users with the ETA of their trip. Due to the special version of route planning in the form of the CVRPPD, the user cannot be given the actual journey time here before the journey begins.

Both of these implementations form a basis for further developments in the area of detour detection for routes with dynamic on-demand stops. For example, different quality criteria on the travel time can be used in order to be able to decide reactively in individual cases whether or not there is too much of a detour for a further stop.

Finally, we believe that with this work we have created a system that can support users in their decision-making and provide a reliable termination criterion for rigid algorithms.

References

1. Supermicro Redstone 4-GPU A-100 System. www.supermicro.com/en/Aplus/system/2U/2124/AS-2124GQ-NART.cfm. Accessed 20 Nov 2022
2. Stadler, T., Schrader, J., Dunnweber, J.: A method for the optimized placement of bus stops based on voronoi diagrams. In: Proceedings of the Annual Hawaii International Conference on System Sciences. Hawaii International Conference on System Sciences (2022)
3. Stadler, T., Schrader, J., Dunnweber, J.: A hybrid genetic algorithm for solving the vrp with pickup and delivery in rural areas. In: Proceedings of the Annual Hawaii International Conference on System Sciences. Hawaii International Conference on System Sciences (2023)

4. Bronstein, M.M., Bruna, J., LeCun, Y., Szlam, A.D., Vandergheynst, P.: Geometric deep learning: going beyond euclidean data. IEEE Signal Process. Maga. **34**, 18–42 (2017)
5. Bruna, J., Zaremba, W., Szlam, A., Lecun, Y.: Spectral networks and locally connected networks on graphs. In: International Conference on Learning Representations (ICLR2014). CBLS (2014)
6. Bunke, H.: Recent developments in graph matching. In: Proceedings 15th International Conference on Pattern Recognition, ICPR-2000. IEEE Computer Societ (2000). https://doi.org/10.1109/icpr.2000.906030
7. Daqi, G., Yan, J.: Classification methodologies of multilayer perceptrons with sigmoid activation functions. Pattern Recogn. **38**(10), 1469–1482 (2005)
8. Data61, C.: Stellargraph machine learning library (2018). http://github.com/stellargraph/stellargraph
9. Defferrard, M., Bresson, X., Vandergheynst, P.: Convolutional neural networks on graphs with fast localized spectral filtering. In: NIPS, pp. 3837–3845 (2016)
10. Derrow-Pinion, A., et al.: ETA prediction with graph neural networks in google maps. In: Proceedings of the 30th ACM International Conference on Information & Knowledge Management. ACM (2021). https://doi.org/10.1145/3459637.3481916
11. Gheysens, F., Golden, B., Assad, A.: A comparison of techniques for solving the fleet size and mix vehicle routing problem. Oper. Res. Spektrum **6**(4), 207–216 (1984)
12. Gilmer, J., Schoenholz, S.S., Riley, P.F., Vinyals, O., Dahl, G.E.: Neural message passing for quantum chemistry (2017)
13. Google: Google maps platform - products. http://developers.google.com/%20maps/documentation
14. Hochmair, H.: Towards a classification of route selection criteria for route planning tools. In: Developments in Spatial Data Handling, pp. 481–492. Springer, Heidelberg (2005). https://doi.org/10.1007/3-540-26772-7_37
15. Jadon, S.: A survey of loss functions for semantic segmentation. In: 2020 IEEE Conference on Computational Intelligence in Bioinformatics and Computational Biology (CIBCB), pp. 1–7. IEEE (2020)
16. Jandaghi, Z., Cai, L.: On graph learning with neural networks. In: Nicosia, G., et al. (eds.) LOD 2020. LNCS, vol. 12566, pp. 516–528. Springer, Cham (2020). https://doi.org/10.1007/978-3-030-64580-9_43
17. Jiang, W., Luo, J.: Graph neural network for traffic forecasting: a survey. Expert Syst. Appl **207**, 117921 (2021). https://doi.org/10.1016/j.eswa.2022.117921
18. Karakatič, S., Podgorelec, V.: A survey of genetic algorithms for solving multi depot vehicle routing problem. Appl. Soft Comput. **27**, 519–532 (2015)
19. Kingma, D., Ba, J.: Adam: a method for stochastic optimization (2014)
20. Kipf, T.N., Welling, M.: Semi-supervised classification with graph convolutional networks (2016)
21. Konstantakopoulos, G.D., Gayialis, S.P., Kechagias, E.P.: Vehicle routing problem and related algorithms for logistics distribution: a literature review and classification. Oper. Res. **22**(3), 2033–2062 (2020). https://doi.org/10.1007/s12351-020-00600-7
22. Liao, W., Bak-Jensen, B., Pillai, J.R., Wang, Y., Wang, Y.: A review of graph neural networks and their applications in power systems. J. Mod. Power Syst. Clean Energy **10**, 345–360 (2021)
23. Parisot, S., et al.: Disease prediction using graph convolutional networks: application to autism spectrum disorder and Alzheimer's disease. Med. Image Anal. **48**, 117–130 . https://doi.org/10.1016/j.media.2018.06.001

24. Parragh, S.N., Doerner, K.F., Hartl, R.F.: A survey on pickup and delivery problems. J. für Betriebswirtschaft **58**(1), 21–51 (2008)

25. Preis, A.: Press release no. 148; bavarian hightech-agenda plus. Report from the cabinet meeting (2020)

26. Rafatirad, S., Homayoun, H., Chen, Z., Dinakarrao, S.M.P.: Graph learning. In: Machine Learning for Computer Scientists and Data Analysts, pp. 277–304. Springer, Heidelberg (2022). https://doi.org/10.1007/978-3-030-96756-7_8

27. Schmitt, E., Jula, H.: Vehicle route guidance systems: Classification and comparison. In: 2006 IEEE Intelligent Transportation Systems Conference. IEEE (2006). https://doi.org/10.1109/itsc.2006.1706749

28. Stamile, C., Marzullo, A., Deusebio, E.: Graph Machine Learning. Packt Publishing Limited, Birmingham (2021)

29. Vidal, T.: Hybrid genetic search for the CVRP: open-source implementation and SWAP* neighborhood. Comput. Oper. Res. **140**, 105643 (2022). https://doi.org/10.1016/j.cor.2021.105643

30. Wein, S., Schüller, A., Tomé, A.M., Malloni, W.M., Greenlee, M.W., Lang, E.W.: Forecasting brain activity based on models of spatio-temporal brain dynamics: a comparison of graph neural network architectures (2021)

Expansion Rate Parametrization and K-Fold Based Inference with U-Net Neural Networks for Multiclass Medical Image Segmentation

Roman Statkevych[✉], Yuri Gordienko, and Sergii Stirenko

National Technical University of Ukraine "Igor Sikorsky Kyiv Polytechnic Institute",
Kyiv, Ukraine
statkevich@comsys.kpi.ua

Abstract. In this paper, authors seek a way to improve the performance of state-of-art U-Net models in the context of multiclass segmentation of Human Gastro-Intestinal (GI) Magnetic Resonance Imaging (MRI) by introducing the expansion rate parameter R, which regulates the sizes of layers and allows an increase in the depth of the network while still meeting the model's size limitations and giving better control over model's size. For the inference, a method has been used based on k-fold cross-validation which combines an output of each of the k-models. By combining changes in expansion rate, model depth, and using a proposed inference method, it was possible to boost performance by 6% with larger models and reach comparable results with 2x smaller models.

Keywords: Neural Networks · Image Segmentation · Healthcare Application · U-Net

1 Introduction

Medical image processing for Computer-aided diagnostics of human deceases is one of the popular applications of neural networks. Extensive usage of Graphical Processing Units (GPUs) helped to drastically speed-up training and inference times. However, due to the high pricing of modern GPUs and chip shortage, resources could be very limited. Alternatively, there is a high demand for using neural networks in mobile devices, where size is a constraint that limits the usage of more powerful computational units.

In recent years, multiple efficient network designs were introduced, most notably, the MobileNet family of networks [6], which provided a basic framework and building blocks for other optimal neural networks designs, like EfficientNet [14]. All these networks provided reasonable results compared to classical Neural Networks while having 10–50 times fewer parameters.

For medical segmentation tasks, U-Net [10] is one of the most used network designs, which has a significant amount of different improvements and modifications, for example: 3D-UNet [3] for working with volumetric data, or EffU-Net [2]

© The Author(s), under exclusive license to Springer Nature Switzerland AG 2023
L. Rutkowski et al. (Eds.): ICAISC 2023, LNAI 14125, pp. 251–262, 2023.
https://doi.org/10.1007/978-3-031-42505-9_22

which utilizes building blocks of MobileNet [6]. In the years that followed, dozens of applications utilizing U-Net architecture were introduced: for cell counting [5]; for liver tumor and detection [9]; skull segmentation [7]; kidney glomerulus segmentation [12]. In this paper, we will investigate different known modifications of U-Net architecture for a specific task of multi-class segmentation of the human gastrointestinal tract, and show, that more parameters don't always bring better performance.

It is a logical continuation of our previous research, where an investigation of the influence of different hyper-parameters on the U-Net model's performance was conducted [11] for the task of microscopic image segmentation for detecting kidney glomerulus. Source code of the paper can be found at https://www.kaggle.com/romanstatkevych/expansion-rate-k-fold-inference.

2   Methodology

2.1   Dataset

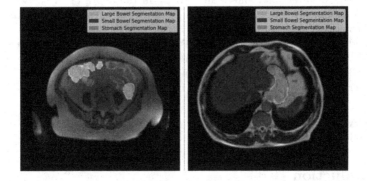

Fig. 1. Example image from the dataset. Segments of different colors represent the Ground-Truth mask of respective classes

As mentioned before, the GI-tract dataset [15] was used for this experiment. It consists of 240 full-MRI scans taken from 85 patients, each scan containing 144 (or 80) slices, having the same height H and width W, giving in a total of $HxWx144$ voxels images (Fig. 1).

The ground-truth mask consists of 3 classes:

– Stomach
– Large bowel
– Small bowel

We split the dataset into a train (80%) and test datasets (20%). As some patients have multiple MRI scans included in the dataset, it was decided to avoid different scans of the same patient appearing in both the test and train datasets, as this might cause high evaluation for these scans in the test dataset due to overfitting.

For k-Fold cross-validation experiment [13], we split the training dataset into 4 folds. Each dataset is randomly reshuffled to overcome selection bias (as we have shown in previous research [11], it is a significant factor)

For testing the method with volumetric data, the entire dataset was split into 75%/25% training/test datasets. All MRI images were arranged into 3D volumes, resized to fit shape $224 \times 224 \times 128$

2.2   Network Architecture

U-Net is one of the most extensively used network architectures for medical image segmentation. It consists of a decoder and an encoder. U-Net accepts a data array with dimensions $W \times H \times C$ (W for width, H for heights, and C for a number of channels. C could be 3 for RGB images, 1 for grayscale). During encoding, the image is split into low-level features, by changing and reshaping intermediate features, while during decoding features are organized in a way that an output layer of the decoder has the same output shape, as an input image, where each pixel contains a vector of scores for each possible class.

Definition 1 (Depth of the encoder/decoder block). *The encoder block's depth d is a number of preceding downsampling layers (or encoder blocks) prior to this block. Respectively, the depth of the decoder block is the number of upsampling layers (or decoder blocks) between this block and the output layer. Encoder and Decoder blocks with the same depth share are connected with the "skip"-connections.*

The decoder and the encoder consist of several blocks. Each encoder blocks E_d yields $W_d \times H_d \times C_d$ array, where d denotes the "depth" of the block. Yielded values are later used in the "lower" encoder block E_{d+1} as input after applying down-sampling logic producing $\frac{1}{2}W_d \times \frac{1}{2}H_d \times 2 \cdot C_d$, and also passed to the corresponding decoder block D_d (so-called "skip connection"). In a classic implementation, [10] encoder block consists of 2 sequential identical 2D Convolution layers (each is followed by ReLU activation layer and Batch Normalization layer). Downsampling is not performed on the last encoder block, instead, its output values are upsampled and passed to a decoder block D_{d-1}. Each decoder block accepts "skip-connection" data, along with upsampled data from the previous decoder block (or last encoded block), and concatenates it (producing an array with dimension $\frac{1}{2}W_d \times \frac{1}{2}H_d \times 3 \cdot C_d$). This data is later processed through 2 2D convolutional blocks (which produce an output with $2 \cdot C_d$ channels), each one followed by ReLU and Batch-Normalization. At last, the output of D_0 is processed through the last 2D Convolution layer with 1×1 kernel, which produces $C \times W \times S$, where S is a class-wise score vector represents to which segmentation class this pixel belongs. For better understanding, U-Net architecture is shown on Fig. 2. Baseline model is chosen to have $W_0 \times H_0 \times C_0 = 256 \times 256 \times 64$, with $C_0 = 64$ as in original paper [10], however. In this paper, we cover several modifications of the original architecture.

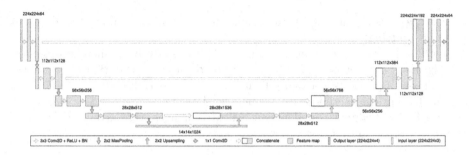

Fig. 2. Baseline U-Net architecture

3D U-Net [3] is a modification of U-Net architecture, designed to work with volumetric data, which has another dimension length, L, along with width W and height H, meaning that input data for 3D U-Net has a shape of $W \times H \times L \times C$. Correspondingly, all convolutional and pooling layers in 3D-UNet have 3D kernels. As a baseline for 3D experiments, first encoder has dimensions $W_0 \times H_0 \times L_0 \times C_0 = 224 \times 224 \times 128 \times 32$.

2.3   U-Net Depth and Expansion Rate

In most of U-Net implementations (including classic one [10]) each $d+1$ encoder or decoder block doubles the width and height of a previous block. In this paper, we decided to investigate this property, by introducing the so-called "expansion rate" and "network depth".

Definition 2 (Expansion rate). *Expansion rate R is a rate, which regulates the number of output channels in the next decoder or encoder so that their output shapes are calculated as $D_{d+1} = E_{d+1} = \frac{1}{2}W_d \times \frac{1}{2}H_d \times R \cdot C_d)$. Classic U-Net [10] has $R = 2$.*

Definition 3 (U-Net model depth). *U-Net model depth δ is the number of encoder blocks in the U-Net model.*

The intuition behind this definition is that changing (reducing) the expansion rate will provide an ability to use deeper networks, by introducing additional encoder/decoder blocks in the network to define deeper features, while keeping the number of the model's parameters the same, or even lower.

2.4   Loss-Function and Evaluation Metrics

For this experiment, we are using binary cross-entropy loss.

$$L = -\frac{1}{N} \sum_{i=1}^{N} y_i \cdot log(p(y_i)) + (1 - y_i) \cdot log(1 - p(y_i)) \tag{1}$$

where y_i is ground-truth data, and $p(y_i)$ is a prediction made by a model.

For evaluation, we use multiple variations of Dice score [4]:

- total Dice-Score - calculated as $DS(G, P)$ (Eq. 2), G and P represent the entire ground truth validation/test dataset and predicted values;
- sample-wise Dice-Score - Eq. 2 calculated for each image from ground-truth G_i and its corresponding prediction P_i and averaged in the end (Eq. 3);
- class-wise Dice-Score - applied to each isolated class k in ground-truth dataset G^k and prediction set P^k (as if in single-class segmentation task)

$$DS(G, P) = \frac{2 \cdot \sum G \times P + \epsilon}{\sum G + \sum P + \epsilon} \tag{2}$$

$$DS_s(G, P) = \frac{1}{N} \sum_{i=1}^{N} DS(G_i, P_i) \tag{3}$$

$$DS_k(G, P, k) = \frac{1}{N} \sum_{i=1}^{N} DS_s(G_i^k, P_i^k) \tag{4}$$

Classic Dice-Score DS is a well-known state-of-art metric. In the original paper, [4], it is used as a measurement of similarity between two sets, consequently, in the evaluation of neural networks, where it is done over a dataset that consists of multiple samples, it is required to treat all the samples from the ground-truth and prediction as one big set of pixels. But it is also possible to calculate the average (as DS_s) and standard deviation of Dice-Score for each specific G_i and P_i, which also helps to evaluate a model's generalization, it is a feature that the original DS lacks. Also, DS poorly describes how a model performs for each of the specific classes in multi-class classification, that's why DS_k was introduced - it calculates a final evaluation metric as an average of Sample-wise Dice-Score DS_s for each separate class k. Understanding this metric might help in model improvement, for example, by using weighted BCE loss to focus on specific classes.

2.5   K-Fold Based Averaged Inference

K-Fold cross validation [13] is a widely used approach to ensure the model's stability of predictions, detect potential problems induced by certain biases, and bolster the overall method's prediction precision. K-fold cross-validation is performed by splitting the training dataset into K subsets, consisting of $\frac{N}{K}$ samples, and training K models, excluding i-th subset from the train set and using it as a validation set for i-th model's evaluation. The results of each fold could be used in various applications, most commonly, best model selection [1] to find the best set of hyper-parameters which would give the most generalized results.

As a part of the proposed method, we decided to utilize each of the K-trained models in a way similar to the ensemble learning [8]: on the inference stage, it is suggested to get the final result of prediction $y(x)$ as an average result of a prediction $y_i(x)$, made by each of the K models (Eq. 5).

$$y(x) = \frac{1}{K} softmax(\sum_{i=1}^{K} y_i(x)) \tag{5}$$

To the best of our knowledge, this specific idea is not mentioned in the literature, however, similar approaches of using outputs of multiple different models (trained on the different datasets, or different hyper-parameters) are widely used in various open-source methods.

2.6   Other Training Parameters

Models were using Adam optimizer with learning rate 10^{-4}. The learning rate is reduced when the validation score didn't increase during 2 epochs. Training is stopped after the validation score didn't improve during the last 4 epochs. Images are loaded with batch size 12.

3   Experimental

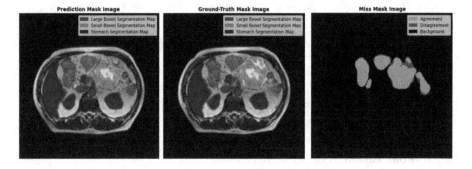

Fig. 3. Prediction results. The image on the top left is a predicted mask, image on the top right is a ground truth

All software for the experimental part of research for testing and training was written in the Kaggle IPython environment, with 16 GB of RAM, Intel(R) Xeon(R) CPU @ 2.00 GHz CPU, and NVIDIA Tesla P100-PCIE-16 GB GPU with 16 GB of video memory. TensorFlow v2.10.0 was used for describing the model architecture and designing training pipelines.

Because of computational complexity, it was decided to run 2 types of experiments:

- train 1 model using first fold to find perspective hyper-parameters for k-fold training, considering best epoch on the validation set;

– train best-performing set of parameters with k-folds (k=4 was chosen), and
validate it with separate test-dataset;

Additionally, 3D-UNet [3] was trained with the validation set to explore
an application of expansion rate to a volumetric input. Due to the extensive
amount of GRAM used for volumetric computations, experiments for 3D-UNet
were taken on a single GPU - NVIDIA A100 video card with 40 GB of video
memory.

In Table 1 results for various combinations of hyper-parameters are shown. R
stands for "expansion rate" (defined above), δ for the model's depths, C_0 for the
width of the initial encoder block. We also provided a number of parameters for
each model, for a better understanding of the model's size and its performance.

We also trained 1 single baseline U-Net model for a comparison with K-Fold
inference results (it marked with ** in the Table 1.

Table 3 shows Dice-Score for each specific isolated class, and the average of
these values (or DS_k which is defined in Eq. 4). This table helps to understand
what class is the easiest to detect for each of the models, and what models are
best performing for each specific class.

For experiments, a model with $R = 2$ and $D = 5$ was taken as a baseline
model [10], which has approximately 31 million parameters. Also, the width of
the first encoder block C_0 was considered (in experiments, 32 and 64 were used).
Tables 1 and 3 only show models which had shown good performance. Both larger
and smaller than baseline models were considered.

Additionally, Fig. 4 shows the performance of each separate k-fold model, and
a total result (marked as a red dot) for each specific model configuration, which
gives an insight into the model's stability of predictions.

Also, additional experiments with 3D-UNet [3] were conducted, and results
are shown in Table 2.

4   Discussion and Future Work

4.1   Effect of K-Fold Inference

K-Fold inference proved to be an effective method of boosting overall performance of the method without changing network architecture. Combining outputs of models trained on a different folds of the dataset improved performance
of plain one-model U-Net by 4.7% (0.733 compared 0.7) for the baseline architecture [10], and pushing it to 6% (0.742) with larger model. As per Fig. 4, all
methods demonstrated significantly better results with K-Fold inference, performing better that any model for a single fold. This might be an evidence that
method helps to address aleatoric uncertainty induced by the dataset, and lead
to a better generalisation, however, further analysis of uncertainty in terms of
Bayesian approach should be conducted.

Idea of this instrument is to utilize all the models, which were trained for
cross-validation, rather than choosing one set of parameters for a single model.

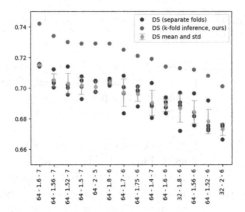

Fig. 4. Comparing each fold's separate results, mean/std, and K-Fold Inference (ours) on the training set (corresponds to DS metric in Table 1) for each set of hyper-parameters. Numbers on X-axis mean C_0 - R - D; 64 - 2 - 5 is the baseline [10]

Although it creates an additonal overhead on computational time and resources to store and run K-models, simplicity of usage is the main advantage of such method.

4.2   Effect of Expansion Rate and Model's Depths

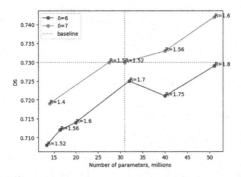

Fig. 5. Dependence of evaluation metric DS (according to Table 1 to a number of parameters, split by parameter δ. Baseline architecture [10] with K-fold inference is shown separately with dashed line

The main intuition of the research was to omit the consideration used in original research [10] that each next encoder has 2x filters. This approach leads to an exponential 2^{δ} growth of a number of parameters with increasing depth δ. For example, the baseline model with $R = 2$ and $\delta = 5$ has 31 million param-eters, while the model with $\delta = 6$ has 125 million parameters, which imposes limitations on the hardware used for execution. By introducing an expansion rate R, additional flexibility allowing control of the model's size was reached as it allows to have deeper models with fewer parameters. Moreover, it allows for reducing the size of a model and increasing its depth simultaneously, allowing it to compensate for the lack of high-level features by introducing more low-level features. As an example shown in 1, $R = 1.4, \delta = 7$ model could reach comparable performance for overall Dice-Score ($DS = 0.719$ compared to $DS = 0.73$ of the baseline), and show the same performance on Sample-wise Dice-Score ($DS_s = 0.849$), while having more than 2 times fewer parameters. Among all of the largest models, $R = 1.6, D = 7$ (having 51 M parameters) has shown improvement in the baseline architecture's result by a margin of 1.01% ($0.742 > 0.73$ for DS, and $0.859 > 0.849$ for DS_s). This model also performed better classification for Stomach and Lower Bowel classes and improved DS_k from 0.877 to 0.884 (provided in Table 3).

An interesting observation is that models with $\delta = 7$ tend to perform better than their counterparts $\delta = 6$, having the same amount of parameter (this could be seen on the Fig. 5). For example, amongst models which have 51 Million parameters, $R = 1.8, \delta = 6$ provided $DS = 0.729$, whilst $R = 1.6, \delta = 7$ have $DS = 0.729$; for 40 Mil parameters models, model $R = 1.56, \delta = 7$ produced $DS = 0.733$, which is more than model $R = 1.75, \delta = 6$ ($DS = 0.729$). These findings are important, as they show that for some tasks increasing the model depth could be prioritized over the widths of layers. Also, models with $\delta = 6$ tend to have bigger standard deviation, which partially explain better performance of $R = 1.7, \delta = 6$ over bigger model $R = 1.75, \delta = 6$.

Regarding 3D-UNet (see Table 2), the baseline model still showed the best performance compared to methods with different expansion rates, but larger depths. However, a smaller model with 15 million parameters showed relatively good performance ($DS = 0.754$, compared to $DS = 0.778$ of the baseline, which has 23 million parameters).

One of the limitations of using the method of increasing depth and decreasing expansion rate is imposed by the size of input data. Due to downsampling logic, each time when downsampling occurs in the encoder block E_d, the dimension of the inputs of the next encoder block is $H_{d+1} \times W_{d+1} = \frac{1}{2}H_d \times \frac{1}{2}W_d$, so the maximum possible depth $D_{max} = log_2(min(W, H))$.

For future work, we should investigate different hyper-parameter modifications, such as Drop-out rate, C_0, δ, as well as various U-Net modifications (combining different backbones and skip connections)

Another promising direction is investigating the usage of 3D versions of U-Net [3]. While 3D models require much more memory and computational resources to process, they allow the processing of entire MRI images within seconds. Another alleged advantage of 3D models, compared to 2D models used in this research, is taking into consideration Z-axis and its interdependence on neighboring images in MRI scans, while in the case of 2D images, all the images from different patients and different projections of the same patient are shuffled and have no prior context.

Table 1. K-Fold (K=4) Inference Experiments results, * depicts baseline architecture [10] with K-Fold inference, ** depicts single-model baseline inference of [10]

C_0	R	δ	params	DS	DS_s
64**	2**	5**	31M	0.70	0.844 (±0.26)
64*	2*	5*	31M	0.73	0.849 (±0.25)
64	1.52	6	13.4M	0.708	0.844 (±0.26)
64	1.4	7	14M	0.719	0.849 (±0.25)
64	1.56	6	16.4M	0.712	0.848 (±0.25)
64	1.6	6	20M	0.714	0.848 (±0.25)
32	1.8	6	20M	0.713	0.849 (±0.25)
64	1.5	7	27.5M	0.73	0.857 (±0.24)
64	1.52	7	31M	0.73	0.856 (±0.24)
64	1.7	6	32.4M	0.725	0.852 (±0.25)
32	2	6	31M	0.702	0.842 (±0.25)
64	1.56	7	40M	0.733	0.859 (±0.24)
64	1.75	6	40M	0.721	0.855 (±0.25)
64	1.8	6	51M	0.729	0.854 (±0.25)
64	1.6	7	51M	**0.742**	**0.859** (±0.24)

Table 2. 3D-U-Net results, * depicts baseline result

C_0	R	δ	params	DS
32*	2*	5*	23M	0.778
32	1.6	6	15M	0.754
32	1.7	6	23M	0.776
32	1.8	6	38M	0.770

4.3   Evaluation Metrics

While DS_s gives more information about the model's generalization than DS, its weakness is that it doesn't address the dataset's imbalance, which means, that if there are two different samples, one of which has only 5% of pixels marked as segments, and the other has 50%, Dice-Score for this specific sample could be the same. Another issue is that for a sample, which only contains a background class, $DS(G_i, P_i) = 1$, so if the dataset consists of a big amount of samples with only a background class, the overall result will be closer to 100%.

Table 3. Per-class Dice-Score with K-fold (K=4) inference (DS_k), * depicts result for baseline architecture [10]

Hyper-parameters			Classes			
C_0	R	δ	Stomach	L.bowel	U.bowel	mean (DS_k)
64*	2*	5*	0.874 ($\pm$0.084)	0.847 ($\pm$0.096)	0.91 ($\pm$0.079)	0.877 ($\pm$0.086)
64	1.56	7	0.88 ($\pm$0.081)	0.855 ($\pm$0.09)	0.908 ($\pm$0.082)	0.881 ($\pm$0.084)
64	1.5	7	0.878 ($\pm$0.078)	0.850 ($\pm$0.091)	0.907 ($\pm$0.079)	0.878 ($\pm$0.082)
64	1.4	7	0.874 ($\pm$0.081)	0.85 ($\pm$0.095)	0.903 ($\pm$0.084)	0.876 ($\pm$0.087)
64	1.52	7	0.877 ($\pm$0.08)	0.852 ($\pm$0.092)	**0.912** ($\pm$0.084)	0.88 ($\pm$0.085)
64	1.6	7	**0.881** ($\pm$0.079)	**0.86** ($\pm$0.086)	0.91 ($\pm$0.08)	**0.884** ($\pm$0.082)
64	1.8	6	0.876 ($\pm$0.082)	0.848 ($\pm$0.095)	0.912 ($\pm$0.083)	0.877 ($\pm$0.087)
64	1.7	6	0.875 ($\pm$0.086)	0.849 ($\pm$0.097)	0.907 ($\pm$0.082)	0.877 ($\pm$0.088)
64	1.75	6	0.876 ($\pm$0.081)	0.85 ($\pm$0.092)	0.907 ($\pm$0.083)	0.878 ($\pm$0.085)
64	1.6	6	0.872 ($\pm$0.083)	0.846 ($\pm$0.093)	0.901 ($\pm$0.084)	0.873 ($\pm$0.087)
64	1.52	6	0.869 ($\pm$0.086)	0.839 ($\pm$0.101)	0.901 ($\pm$0.086)	0.87 ($\pm$0.091)
64	1.56	6	0.87 ($\pm$0.083)	0.844 ($\pm$0.097)	0.9 ($\pm$0.085)	0.871 ($\pm$0.086)
32	2	6	0.866 ($\pm$0.088)	0.839 ($\pm$0.1)	0.899 ($\pm$0.092)	0.868 ($\pm$0.093)
32	1.8	6	0.87 ($\pm$0.08)	0.846 ($\pm$0.096)	0.903 ($\pm$0.086)	0.873 ($\pm$0.087)

5   Conclusions

In this research, K-Fold inference was introduced and the investigation of various combinations of hyper-parameters was conducted. By utilizing K-Fold inference, we have managed to improve results of single baseline U-Net model by 4.7% ($DS = 0.733$ compared to $DS = 0.7$). Additionally, the expansion rate R was defined and its influence on model size and efficiency was reviewed. It was pointed out, that by varying the expansion rate and model's depth, it is possible to reduce the model's size while keeping the model's performance reasonable. For example, a model with 14 million parameters has shown $DS = 0.719$, compared to the baseline model with 31 million parameters $DS = 0.73$. Also, it is possible to introduce deeper models with fewer parameters to still meet the limitation. By utilizing this approach, it was possible to boost the performance of K-fold inference further by 1.01% compared to baseline-architecture ($DS = 0.742$ compared to $DS = 0.733$).

This methodology could be used to develop models with limited computational resources, shed some light on U-Net neural network architecture, and how it behaves with an increase of depth and decrease of the model's width.

Acknowledgement. The work was partially supported by "Knowledge At the Tip of Your fingers: Clinical Knowledge for Humanity" (KATY) project funded from the European Union's Horizon 2020 research and innovation program under grant agreement No. 101017453.

References

1. Arlot, S., Celisse, A.: A survey of cross-validation procedures for model selection (2010)
2. Baheti, B., Innani, S., Gajre, S., Talbar, S.: Eff-UNet: a novel architecture for semantic segmentation in unstructured environment. In: Proceedings of the IEEE/CVF Conference on Computer Vision and Pattern Recognition Workshops, pp. 358–359 (2020)
3. Çiçek, Ö., Abdulkadir, A., Lienkamp, S.S., Brox, T., Ronneberger, O.: 3D U-Net: learning dense volumetric segmentation from sparse annotation. In: Ourselin, S., Joskowicz, L., Sabuncu, M.R., Unal, G., Wells, W. (eds.) MICCAI 2016. LNCS, vol. 9901, pp. 424–432. Springer, Cham (2016). https://doi.org/10.1007/978-3-319-46723-8_49
4. Dice, L.R.: Measures of the amount of ecologic association between species. Ecology **26**(3), 297–302 (1945)
5. Falk, T., et al.: U-Net: deep learning for cell counting, detection, and morphometry. Nat. Methods **16**(1), 67–70 (2019)
6. Howard, A.G., et al.: MobileNets: efficient convolutional neural networks for mobile vision applications. arXiv preprint: arXiv:1704.04861 (2017)
7. Jadon, S.: A survey of loss functions for semantic segmentation. In: 2020 IEEE Conference on Computational Intelligence in Bioinformatics and Computational Biology (CIBCB), pp. 1–7. IEEE (2020)
8. Kuncheva, L.I., Whitaker, C.J.: Measures of diversity in classifier ensembles and their relationship with the ensemble accuracy. Mach. Learn. **51**(2), 181 (2003)
9. Li, X., Chen, H., Qi, X., Dou, Q., Fu, C.W., Heng, P.A.: H-DenseUNet: hybrid densely connected UNet for liver and tumor segmentation from CT volumes. IEEE Trans. Med. Imaging **37**(12), 2663–2674 (2018). https://doi.org/10.1109/TMI.2018.2845918
10. Ronneberger, O., Fischer, P., Brox, T.: U-Net: convolutional networks for biomedical image segmentation. In: Navab, N., Hornegger, J., Wells, W.M., Frangi, A.F. (eds.) MICCAI 2015. LNCS, vol. 9351, pp. 234–241. Springer, Cham (2015). https://doi.org/10.1007/978-3-319-24574-4_28
11. Statkevych, R., Gordienko, Y., Stirenko, S.: Improving U-Net kidney glomerulus segmentation with fine-tuning, dataset randomization and augmentations. In: Hu, Z., Dychka, I., Petoukhov, S., He, M. (eds.) ICCSEEA 2022. Lecture Notes on Data Engineering and Communications Technologies, vol. 134, pp. 488–498. Springer, Cham (2022). https://doi.org/10.1007/978-3-031-04812-8_42
12. Statkevych, R., Stirenko, S., Gordienko, Y.: Human kidney tissue image segmentation by U-Net models. In: IEEE EUROCON 2021–19th International Conference on Smart Technologies, pp. 129–134. IEEE (2021)
13. Stone, M.: Cross-validatory choice and assessment of statistical predictions. J. Roy. Stat. Soc.: Ser. B (Methodological) **36**(2), 111–133 (1974)
14. Tan, M., Le, Q.: EfficientNet: rethinking model scaling for convolutional neural networks. In: International Conference on Machine Learning, pp. 6105–6114. PMLR (2019)
15. UW-Madison: Uw-madison gi tract image segmentation (2022). https://www.kaggle.com/competitions/uw-madison-gi-tract-image-segmentation/overview

Transfer Learning from ImageNet to the Domain of Pigmented Nevi

Grzegorz Surówka[(⊠)] [ID]

Department of Physics, Astronomy and Applied Computer Science, Jagiellonian University,
ul. Łojasiewicza 11, 30-348 Krakow, Poland
grzegorz.surowka@uj.edu.pl

Abstract. The transfer learning method enables the use of a pretrained convolutional network to efficiently model a secondary domain with less data. In this article 18 public convolutional networks of different architecture and depth, pretrained on ImageNet, are tested on three optimizers (Adam, Rmsprop and SGDM), ten learning rate values and two diverse data sets (ISIC 2017 and Melanoma-ML), to choose the best one for the malignant melanoma vs. atypical (but benign) nevi classification. This is important since both types of the pigmented skin lesions can be visually very similar and difficult to distinguish. For the well-known ISIC 2017 data set, we found the best accuracy of 94.36 ± 1.66% for the ResNet 101 convolutional network with the SGDM optimizer and the learning rate of 6e-4. We show our results against the literature on the subject. The best pretrained model(s) can be easily implemented in dermoscopy systems/applications to assist skin/general physicians of all levels of training and experience and patients for premedical self-examination.

Keywords: transfer learning · convolutional networks · computer-aided diagnosis · melanoma

1 Introduction

Machine learning algorithms can be used successfully in medical diagnosis. They have been increasingly applied especially in non-invasive procedures to support pattern recognition, pattern classification, and decision-making tasks. In general, machine learning has the potential to improve the accuracy and efficiency of diagnoses, ultimately leading to better patient outcomes.

1.1 Early Detection of Cutaneous Melanoma

There are cases of cancer in medicine that are trivial to treat in the early stages, but that become fatal as the cancer grows larger. An example is cutaneous melanoma [37]. Due to certain civilization trends (increased UV radiation, nutrition), the lack of appropriate dermatological care (countries with high sun exposure and low population density), or the lack of self-examination habit, many melanoma patients are in a late stage after diagnosis. This results in high mortality, mainly due to metastases to internal organs. The mortality rate from melanoma increases year by year [4].

Early diagnosis and biopsy are a life saving factor. Dermoscopy is the diagnostic standard for pigmented lesions, but its sensitivity is rather poor (60%-100%) depending on the level of experience of the examiners and the diagnostic difficulty of the lesion [40]. Thick (i.e., advanced) melanomas are easy to recognize, but excision does not guarantee a long survival rate. On the other hand, early melanomas are poorly recognized and often confused with atypical nevi. Dysplastic nevi give many false positives and cannot always be treated surgically.

In clinical practice, there are visual metrics that can qualitatively determine the likelihood of melanoma [13]. They include the ABCD(E) rule, the 7-Point Checklist, Menzies, 7FFM, CASH, etc., to mention the most common. Unfortunately, because.

they are based on visual features, their effectiveness is influenced by the maturity of the melanoma lesion and factors such as resolution, lighting, magnification or glare.

Techniques and computer-aided diagnosis (CAD) systems for melanoma have been developed for many years [7]. Different aspects and features have been studied to determine the degree of malignancy [9, 25, 34]. Although no CAD system for melanoma is standardized and validated for clinical use, it is clinically supportive, making decisions to increase the accuracy of diagnosis and reduce the time and cost of treatment.

1.2 Transfer Learning

Convolutional neural networks (CNNs) have grown today into a flagship image analysis tool, which includes, among others, object recognition, scene segmentation, and image classification tasks [33]. CNNs use filtering and pooling methods to extract image features such as edges, corners, blobs, ridges, or more complex objects-of-interest based on texture, shape, etc. at various levels of complexity. Unlike the filters in the computer vision (CV) approach, CNNs learn filters from data to be used for the aforementioned tasks. A typical CNN consists of a number of blocks, each with some convolutional layers, pooling layers, and ReLU-activation (Rectified Linear Unit) layers. Additional fully connected layers (FCs) can be used at the end of all CNN blocks for classification.

CNNs are very effective in many computer vision applications, but deep architectures (often several hundreds of layers) require large amounts of data and a lot of training time. A CNN pretrained on a large and diverse data set can be reused and further developed for a second related task.

There are reports demonstrating successful transfer of the features from ImageNet [22, 29] to other image data sets. The ImageNet database [8, 17], now contains about 10^7 images from 10^4 categories of everyday/computer items, animals, fruit, etc. It is used in the ImageNet Large-Scale Visual Recognition Challenge (ILSVRC).

Our motivation in this article is to study how publicly available CNNs can be pretrained on the ImageNet data set and then adjusted and further trained to the domain of the pigmented skin lesions. We want to find the best CNN topology (from a long list) and parameters that will allow the classification of the melanoma dermoscopy images versus benign nevi. Our goal is not to analyze the theoretical aspects of the concept of transfer learning, but rather to show how a systematic search for an optimal solution in this medical domain can help the medical community to support the diagnosis of melanoma.

2 Material and Methods

Our experiments are based on 18 well-known public convolutional networks: AlexNet [22], ResNet-18/50/101 [14, 41, 47], Inception v1(GoogLeNet) [42, 43] Inception v3 [5, 44], Inception-ResNet v2 [42], VGG-16/19 [39], DarkNet 19/53 [35], SqueezeNet [16], ShuffleNet [48], DenseNet 201 [10], EfficientNet B0 [45], NASNet-Mobile [49], MobileNet v2 [38] and Xception [5]. A description of each of them, even a brief one, is beyond the scope of this article, therefore extensive references are provided. The presented CNNs have implementations within most common ML libraries, such as: PyTorch, TensorFlow/Keras, Matlab, etc., and different/customized versions on GitHub.

Three solvers/optimizers have been tested: Adam (Adaptive Momentum Estimation [21]), SGDM (Stochastic Gradient Descent with Momentum [23]) and RMSPROP (Root Mean Square Propagation [46]).

The weights of the pretrained network have been 'frozen', and for the replaced layers the initial learning rate has been set. Several learning rates have been taken into account: 7e-5, 8e-5, 9e-5, 1e-4, 2e-4, 3e-4, 4e-4, 5e-4, 6e-4, 7e-4.

We used batch normalization for the population and shuffled the data every epoch. The maximum number of epochs was set to 20. Our runtime environment was NVidia GPU 2080 Ti (12GB). Since after augmentation there were almost equal numbers of images in both classes, accuracy was used as a learning metric.

Two different data sets both in size and source of origin have been taken into account:

Data set A [18] is a well-known International Skin Imaging Collaboration (ISIC) database from the 2017 challenge (terms-of-use and licenses are published here: https:// www.isic-archive.com/#!/topWithHeader/tightDarkContentTop/termsOfUse) and contains, respectively, 2000/150/600 (anonymized) training/validation/test examples. They are 1022x767 JPEG-compressed dermoscopy images. There are many metadata fields in this database, the most important of which relate to diagnosis (e.g., angioma, dermatofibroma, melanoma, nevus, etc.), approximate age, sex, location, size of the lesion, and some melanoma related items (class, mitotic index, thickness, ulceration). This information allows an additional selection of the material in terms of classification between melanoma and dysplastic nevi. Ultimately, approximately 87% of the cases have been used from the ISIC database.

Data set B [26] consists of 185 images: 102 cases of malignant melanoma (M) and 83 cases of dysplastic nevus (D). These are 2272x1704 (JPEG) images from a private clinic, but available online. In addition to the histopathological result, no other details are available.

In both repositories, the ground truth about the class of the lesion is based on the declared histopathological examination.

To produce more training data, and also to rebalance the classes (the positive class, melanoma, is usually much smaller than the negative class, benign lesion) we used data augmentation techniques to the minority class by random rotation < 0, 360 > and random uniform scaling (0.5, 2) of the dermoscopy images.

All images were scaled to the appropriate input size for the given network.

Deep learning usually avoids segmentation of lesions or removal of any artifacts/hair. We don't do that either.

Data set A was used in a one-time train/test experiment from the prepared subsets. However, to account for the non-deterministic matrix multiplication on the GPU, $k = 6$ similar experiments were carried out to average the results.

Data set B was used in a $k = 6$ fold cross-validation (C-V) scheme. In this case, the standard deviation accounts for C-V and the non-deterministic matrix multiplication on the GPU.

The batch size for data sets A and B was set to 35 and 26, respectively (GPU burden restrictions). Our experiments concerned the above networks pretrained on the ImageNet data base [8, 17]. To fine-tune the network to a binary classification, the last few layers have been changed: convolution layers (the ReLU activation) and fully connected layers (the sigmoid activation).

3 Results

Tables 1 and 2 show the CNNs pretrained on the ImageNet data set and then trained on data set A or data set B. We were changing the hyperparameters like the optimizers and the learning rate. For data set A the best accuracy of $94.36 \pm 1.66\%$ was achieved for ResNet 101 (Fig. 1) with the SGDM optimizer and the learning rate of 6e-4. For data set B the best accuracy of $84.44 \pm 1.33\%$ was achieved for NASNet-Mobile with the RMSPROP optimizer and the learning rate of 2e-4.

Figure 2 shows training times that are the highest for the Adam optimization and the smallest for SGDM. The amount of time depends strongly on the architecture and can reach a factor of twenty. This shows what performance requirements are placed on the learning environment with different CNNs.

Our results (data set A) show a high level of accuracy (Fig. 1), which is:

1) comparable to the remaining experiments in the field,
2) in principle better than in the domain of plain machine learning (no preprocessing, no fixed features), and, finally,
3) better than the accuracy achieved by experienced/expert physicians.

The article [11] estimates the accuracy of human doctors between 75–84%. This confirms that transfer learning with a CNN can be a valuable tool to support the detection of melanoma, regardless of the individual level of experience of the physician.

However, the diagnostic performance of any CNN CAD system (as well as a doctor's) is inherently related to the data set, even different number of instances accepted for training within this data set, and the setup. These three factors (data set, statistics, network/learning setup) can massively impact the results. The following trends are emerging:

In principle, deeper models lead to better results, but the experimental design beyond the standard adaptation to the classification in question (residual and fully connected blocks, batch normalization, dropouts) and details about the pretrained weights are also crucial.

Table 1. Accuracy (mean ± standard deviation) of transfer learning (threshold = 50%) as a function of the optimizers and the learning rate (lr) for data set A.

CNN	adam		sgdm		rmprop	
	mean	lr	mean	lr	mean	lr
AlexNet	84.91 ± 1.69	9e-05	84.36 ± 1.69	2e-04	83.82 ± 2.31	8e-05
GoogLeNet	86.36 ± 2.33	3e-04	86.36 ± 1.57	7e-04	84.18 ± 1.96	9e-05
Xception	92.73 ± 1.60	2e-04	80.72 ± 1.46	7e-04	92.36 ± 1.90	5e-04
VggNet 16	86.73 ± 2.07	7e-05	86.73 ± 2.01	3e-04	58.73 ± 3.16	8e-05
VggNet 19	83.64 ± 2.84	7e-05	86.37 ± 2.05	3e-04	61.45 ± 3.86	8e-05
DenseNet 201	91.82 ± 1.52	8e-05	90.18 ± 1.99	7e-04	91.27 ± 1.29	8e-05
DarkNet 19	90.36 ± 1.91	7e-05	92.00 ± 1.80	3e-04	87.82 ± 2.81	9e-05
DarkNet 53	88.00 ± 2.07	7e-05	88.00 ± 1.51	2e-04	86.91 ± 1.68	7e-05
SqueezeNet	84.55 ± 2.15	2e-04	83.64 ± 1.56	4e-04	84.55 ± 2.35	1e-04
ResNet 18	89.82 ± 1.46	8e-05	86.00 ± 1.51	6e-04	90.73 ± 1.74	9e-05
ResNet 50	92.55 ± 1.70	1e-04	90.18 ± 1.51	5e-04	92.91 ± 1.74	1e-04
ResNet 101	**93.45 ± 1.65**	8e-05	**94.36 ± 1.66**	6e-04	93.64 ± 1.33	7e-05
Inception v3	91.45 ± 1.39	7e-05	85.82 ± 1.55	7e-04	92.73 ± 1.65	1e-04
InceptionResnet v2	91.09 ± 1.62	2e-04	84.18 ± 1.45	7e-04	91.64 ± 1.46	3e-04
MobileNet v2	88.91 ± 1.94	4e-04	83.09 ± 2.11	7e-04	87.82 ± 2.05	4e-04
NasNet-Mobile	88.00 ± 1.96	6e-04	76.00 ± 2.34	7e-04	86.00 ± 1.51	2e-04
ShuffleNet	88.91 ± 1.77	6e-04	86.73 ± 1.72	6e-04	86.73 ± 2.30	3e-04
EfficientNet-B0	93.27 ± 1.91	7e-04	84.00 ± 1.68	7e-04	**94.18 ± 1.50**	5e-04

AlexNet utilizes large (11x11) and small (5x5) size filters in the early layers and (3x3) in the last layers. Especially large filters are prone to generate artifacts from the learned feature maps.

Inception v1 (GoogLeNet) converges fast but yields worse results, which is the result of the reduced number of parameters (bottleneck layers) and global average pooling. Inception v3 is by 5% better (when referenced to data set A) probably by a deeper hierarchy. It comes with a price for learning time.

Inception-ResNet is very slow to learn and does not meet the required training length. VGG nets are very hierarchical (pyramidal shapes) and usually serve as benchmarks for many applications. Apparently, in the field of pigmented nevi, they perform worse.

The Xception architecture uses the so-called depthwise separable convolutions (DSC) and performs very well (the "extreme Inception architecture"). The original inception blocks are wider and unified to a single dimension (3x3). This makes the network computationally efficient by decoupling spatial and feature map channels.

Table 2. Accuracy (mean ± standard deviation) of transfer learning (threshold = 50%) as a function of the optimizers and the learning rate (lr) for data set B. Cases marked with a dash have failed.

CNN	adam		sgdm		rmprop	
	mean	lr	mean	lr	mean	lr
AlexNet	75.19 ± 1.57	8e-05	77.22 ± 1.58	7e-05	75.74 ± 1.85	8e-05
GoogLeNet	78.15 ± 1.74	1e-04	79.44 ± 1.29	5e-04	78.15 ± 2.06	1e-04
Xception	82.41 ± 1.64	8e-05	78.33 ± 1.39	3e-04	82.04 ± 1.55	4e-04
VggNet 16	77.22 ± 1.42	7e-05	78.89 ± 1.33	1e-04	72.22 ± 0	many
VggNet 19	73.70 ± 1.42	7e-05	79.81 ± 1.23	3e-04	72.22 ± 0	many
DenseNet 201	**82.96 ± 1.11**	1e-04	-	-	-	-
DarkNet 19	81.11 ± 1.76	9e-05	79.26 ± 1.55	9e-05	78.33 ± 1.66	8e-05
DarkNet 53	81.48 ± 1.44	2e-04	**81.30 ± 1.33**	1e-04	80.19 ± 1.80	7e-05
SqueezeNet	76.67 ± 1.33	7e-05	76.85 ± 1.51	1e-04	75.93 ± 1.79	9e-05
ResNet 18	82.41 ± 1.86	2e-04	78.89 ± 1.82	5e-04	80.93 ± 1.39	9e-05
ResNet 50	81.67 ± 1.52	1e-04	79.81 ± 1.65	4e-04	82.59 ± 1.33	8e-05
ResNet 101	81.11 ± 1.52	9e-05	80.93 ± 1.11	6e-04	82.22 ± 1.82	8e-05
Inception v3	80.00 ± 1.72	4e-04	78.70 ± 1.32	4e-04	81.48 ± 1.73	2e-04
InceptionResnet v2	–	–	–	–	–	–
MobileNet v2	79.81 ± 1.49	4e-04	76.30 ± 1.03	7e-04	80.74 ± 1.01	3e-04
NasNet-Mobile	82.22 ± 1.55	1e-04	79.63 ± 1.69	7e-04	**84.44 ± 1.33**	2e-04
ShuffleNet	81.11 ± 1.39	3e-04	78.33 ± 1.66	3e-04	80.00 ± 0.71	5e-04
EfficientNet-B0	82.04 ± 1.19	1e-04	77.59 ± 0.88	6e-04	81.67 ± 1.29	4e-04

DenseNet 201 supports depth-wise and cross-layer data flows and eliminates redundant feature maps. Apparently, this is the reason why it behaves quite well (almost 92% accuracy).

EfficientNet B0 performs very well, but is time consuming and requires a lot of resources. The ResNet 101 architecture has some stacked residual modules, which translates into very good performance (see Fig. 2) and, at the same time, is much deeper than, e.g., AlexNet and VGG. This results in a very good classification accuracy.

The difference in classification efficiency introduced by the optimizers can be as high as 30%. However, overall performance is not readily predictable for individual solutions, as the other two factors (network architecture and learning rate) play a role.

This explains why the fundamentally better Adam optimizer can lose out to the rest.

The more data, the better. This can be best seen from the results of the experiments with data sets A and B. The same but incomplete data set (see Table 2, reference [15] and

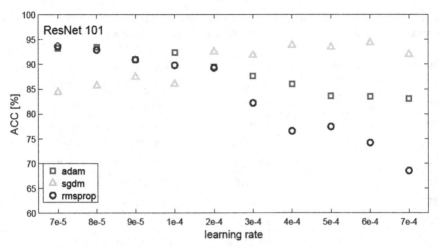

Fig. 1. Accuracy (threshold = 50%) as a function of the optimizer and the learning rate. The best result for data set A is achieved with the ResNet 101 architecture.

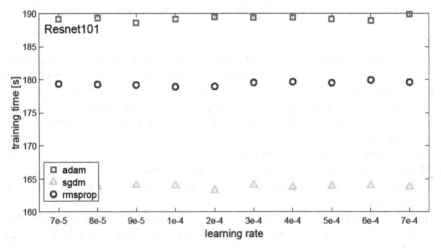

Fig. 2. Data set A: Training time for the ResNet 101 CNN winner in different configurations of optimizers and learning rates.

this work) due to, e.g., different target (sub)classes (benign/displastic, etc.) may degrade performance.

The classification of melanoma versus benign pigmented skin lesions is widely covered in the field literature. However, there are only few transfer learning results, and they usually come from experiments with single or at most a few convolutional networks. There is also no systematic approach to learning conditions, such as optimizers or learning rates. Below, we briefly summarize these attempts and in Table 3 show the achieved accuracy.

Table 3. Accuracy of the transfer learning in the setup of the analyzed deep convolutional networks found in the literature. (IAD = Interactive Atlas of Dermoscopy, ? = not sure)

source	#networks tested	CNN	data set	ACC
[2]	1	ResNet ?	ISIC 2017	85.5%
[6]	4	Caffe	ISIC 201?	93.1%
[12]	1	ResNet-152	Asan	96.0%
[15]	1	AlexNet	ISIC 2017	95.9%
[18]	1	VGG19	IAD	87.2%
[24]	1	VGG16	ISIC 2016	81.3%
[27]	1	VGG16	ISIC 2016	83.5%
[30]	?	ResNet 50	ISIC 2018	93.6%
[32]	4	Inception v3	HAM10000	89.8%
[36]	5	ResNet 50	ISIC 2018	93.5%
this work	18	ResNet 101	ISIC 2017	94.4 ± 1.7%
		NasNet-Mobile	MelanomaML	84.4 ± 1.3%

In [36] they examined: Inception v3, Inception ResNet v2, Mobilenet, Densenet 169 and ResNet 50 networks. The CNN ResNet 50 winner used the batch size of 64 and Adam optimizer for the ISIC 2018 data set (3.000/600 training/testing images).

In [12] Asan, MED-NODE, and atlas site images (19.398 in total) were used, however, approximately ten classes were studied. Finally, it is not clear which of the reported results is obligatory.

The best results of [2] were achieved with a subset of 150 validation images. The article [27] used the Interactive Atlas of Dermoscopy (Atlas) and the ISIC 2016 data set. They report that transferring from very specific tasks, even related ones, is worse than from ImageNet, with fine-tuning.

In [24], they used the VGG16 net and transfer learning from ImageNet on the ISIC 2016 data set in three different ways: (i) training the CNN from scratch and, using the transfer learning paradigm from ImageNet (ii) without and (iii) with fine-tuning of the CNNs architecture. They augmented the data by rescaling, rotations, horizontal shifts, zooming, and horizontal flipping. Method (iii) showed the best accuracy of 81.3%.

The so-called 'dilated convolution' was implemented in [32]. 'Dilated convolution' expands the kernel by inserting zeros between nonzero elements, which makes the field of vision wider but keeps the same computational complexity. They classified seven different skin lesion classes (data set with 10015 600 × 450 dermoscopy images) with four pretrained networks: VGG16, VGG19, MobileNet, and InceptionV3. They employed vertical and horizontal flipping, random width and height shifting, 'zooming' (i.e., scaling), and shearing. Inception v3 yielded the best accuracy of 89.8%.

Work [6] tested two parallel paths combined in late fusion (score averaging): 1) transfer of convolutional neural network features learned from the domain of natural photographs and 2) unsupervised feature learning, using sparse coding, within the domain of dermoscopy images. Two discrimination tasks were examined: a) melanoma versus other lesions and b) melanoma versus atypical lesions only. For task a) they achieved an accuracy of 93.1% and for task b) 73.9%.

The thickness of melanoma is the most important histopathological factor in the prognosis of melanoma, but is less often modeled. One of the works that addressed this problem by transfer learning (from a nonmedical domain) is [18]. They trained the pretrained VGG19 convolutional network on a data set of 244 dermoscopy images of thin/intermediate/thick melanoma cases from the Interactive Atlas of Dermoscopy. The images were cropped for the region-of-interest and corrected for imbalance by the Synthetic Minority Oversampling Technique (SMOTE). The average (over three classes) accuracy for melanoma thickness prediction is 87.2%.

These transfer learning results are collected in Table 3. All the techniques for skin cancer detection from images are summarized in [1, 3, 19, 20, 28, 31].

The (early) diagnosis of melanoma continues to be a medical and CAD challenge. In this work, we have addressed this problem using deep neural networks and transfer learning from the ImageNet database. It is important since a systematic evaluation of transfer learning of melanoma is still lacking. This study is a contribution (18 networks, 3 optimizers, 10 learning rate values, 2 data sets) that may be helpful in this regard. Our best model(s) can be easily implemented in dermoscopy systems or applications running on desktops or even mobile devices. Such systems can assist skin/general doctors of all levels of training and experience and patients for premedical self-examination. As a result, melanoma detection can be much earlier and more accurate than before, helping to reduce the mortality of melanoma.

References

1. Adegun, A., Viriri, S.: Deep learning techniques for skin lesion analysis and melanoma cancer detection: a survey of state-of-the-art. Artif. Intell. Rev. **54**(2), 811–841 (2021)
2. Bi, L., Kim, J., Ahn, E., Feng, D.: Automatic skin lesion analysis using large-scale dermoscopy images and deep residual networks. arXiv:1703.04197 (2017)
3. Brinker, T., et al.: Skin cancer classification using convolutional neural networks: systematic review. J. Med. Internet Res. **20**(10), e11936 (2018)
4. Cancer.net (2022). https://www.cancer.net/cancer-types/melanoma/statistics/. Accessed 30 Jan 2022
5. Chollet, F.: Xception: deep learning with depthwise separable convolutions. arXiv:1610.02357v3 (2017)
6. Codella, N., Cai, J., Abedini, M., Garnavi, R., Halpern, A., Smith, J.R.: Deep learning, sparse coding, and SVM for melanoma recognition in dermoscopy images. In: Zhou, L., Wang, L., Wang, Q., Shi, Y. (eds.) Machine Learning in Medical Imaging. MLMI 2015. Lecture Notes in Computer Science, vol. 9352. Springer, Cham (2015). https://doi.org/10.1007/978-3-319-24888-2_15
7. Dick, V., Sinz, C., Mittlböck, M., Kittler, H., Tschandl, P.: Accuracy of computer-aided diagnosis of melanoma: a meta-analysis. JAMA Dermatol. **155**(11), 1291 (2019). https://doi.org/10.1001/jamadermatol.2019.1375
8. Fei-Fei, L., Deng, J., Li, K.: Imagenet: constructing a large-scale image data-base. J. Vis. **9**(8), 1037 (2009)

9. Ferrante di Ruffano, L., et al.: Computer-assisted diagnosis techniques (dermoscopy and spectroscopy-based) for diagnosing skin cancer in adults. Cochrane Database Syst. Rev. **12**, CD013186 (2018)

10. Gao, H., Liu, Z., Van Der Maaten, L., Weinberger, K.: Densely connected convolutional networks. In: CVPR 1(2), 3 (2017)

11. Haenssle, H., et al.: Man against machine: diagnostic performance of a deep learning convolutional neural network for dermoscopic melanoma recognition in comparison to 58 dermatologists. Ann. Oncol. **29**(8), 1836–1842 (2018)

12. Han, S., Kim, M., Lim, W., Park, G., Park, I., Chang, S.: Classification of the clinical images for benign and malignant cutaneous tumors using a deep learning algorithm. J. Investig. Dermatol. **138**(7), 1529–1538 (2018)

13. Harrington, E.B.C., Wesseling, N., et al.: Diagnosing malignant melanoma in ambulatory care: a systematic review of clinical prediction rules. BMJ Open **7**, e014096 (2017)

14. He, K., Zhang, X., Ren, S.: Deep residual learning for image recognition. In: Proceedings of the IEEE Conference on Computer Vision and Pattern Recognition, pp. 770–778 (2016)

15. Hosny, K., Kassem, M., Foaud, M.: Classification of skin lesions using transfer learning and augmentation with Alex-net. PLoS ONE **14**(5), e0217293 (2019)

16. Iandola, F., Han, S., Moskewicz, M., Ashraf, K., Dally, W., Keutzer, K.: Squeezenet: Alexnet-level accuracy with 50x fewer parameters and 0.5 mb model size. arXiv:1602.07360 (2016)

17. ImageNet (2022). http://www.image-net.org/. Accessed 01 Feb 2022

18. ISIC, https://www.isic-archive.com/topWithHeader/tightContentTop/about/. Accessed 01 Dec 2021

19. Jaworek-Korjakowska, J., Kleczek, P., Gorgon, M.: Melanoma thickness prediction based on convolutional neural network with vgg-19 model transfer learning. In: Proceedings of the IEEE/CVF Conference on Computer Vision and Pattern Recognition Workshops (2019)

20. Kareem, O., Abdulazeez, A., Zeebaree, D.: Skin lesions classification using deep learning techniques: review. Asian J. Res. Comput. Sci. **9**(1), 1–22 (2021)

21. Kassem, M., Hosny, K., Damasevicius, R., Eltoukhy, M.: Machine learning and deep learning methods for skin lesion classification and diagnosis: a systematic review. Diagnostics **11**(8), 1390 (2021)

22. Kingma, D., Ba, J.: Adam: A Method for Stochastic Optimization (2021). https://doi.org/10.48550/arxiv.1412.6980/. Accessed 01 Dec 2021

23. Krizhevsky, A., Sutskever, I., Hinton, G.: ImageNet classification with deep convolutional neural networks. Adv. Neural. Inf. Process. Syst. **25**, 1097–1105 (2012)

24. Liu, T., Gao, Y., Yin, W.: An improved analysis of stochastic gradient descent with momentum. Adv. Neural. Inf. Process. Syst. **30**, 18261–18271 (2020)

25. Lopez, A., Giro-i-Nieto, X., Burdick, J., Marques, O.: Skin lesion classification from dermoscopic images using deep learning techniques. In: 2017 13th IASTED International Conference on Biomedical Engineering (BioMed), pp. 49–54. IEEE (2017)

26. Maiti, A., Chatterjee, B., Ashour, A., Dey, N.: Computer-aided diagnosis of melanoma: a review of existing knowledge and strategies. Curr. Med. Imaging **16**(7), 835–854 (2020)

27. Melanoma ML (2021). https://doi.org/10.17026/dans-zue-zz2y/. Accessed 01 Dec 2021

28. Menegola, A., Fornaciali, M., Pires, R., Bittencourt, F., Avila, S., Valle, E.: Knowledge transfer for melanoma screening with deep learning. In: 2017 IEEE 14th International Symposium on Biomedical Imaging, pp. 297–300 (2017)

29. Naeem, A., Farooq, M.S., Khelifi, A., Abid, A.: Malignant melanoma classification using deep learning: datasets, performance measurements, challenges, and opportunities. IEEE Access **8**, 110575–110597 (2020)

30. Pan, S., Yang, Q.: A survey on transfer learning. IEEE Trans. Knowl. Data Eng. **22**(10), 1345–1359 (2009)

31. Pomponiu, V., Nejati, H., Cheung, N.M.: Deepmole: deep neural networks for skin mole lesion classification. In: 2016 IEEE International Conference on Image Processing, pp. 2623–2627 (2016)
32. Popescu, D., El-Khatib, M., El-Khatib, H., Ichim, L.: New trends in melanoma detection using neural networks: a systematic review. Sensors **22**(2), 496 (2022)
33. Ratul, A., Mozaffari, M., Lee, W.S., Parimbelli, E.: Skin lesions classification using deep learning based on dilated convolution. BioRxiv: 860700 (2020)
34. Rawat, W., Wang, Z.: Deep convolutional neural networks for image classification: a comprehensive review. Neural Comput. **29**, 2352–2449 (2017)
35. Razmjooy, N., et al.: Computer-aided diagnosis of skin cancer: a review. Curr. Med. Imaging **16**(7), 781–793 (2020)
36. Redmon, J.: Darknet: Open source neural networks inc (2013–2016). https://pjreddie.com/darknet/
37. Sagar, A., Jacob, D.: Convolutional neural networks for classifying melanoma images. Biorxiv 2020–05 (2021)
38. Saginala, K., Barsouk, A., Aluru, J., Rawla, P., Barsouk, A.: Epidemiology of melanoma. Med. Sci. **9**(4), 63 (2021)
39. Sandler, M., Howard, A., Zhu, M., Zhmoginov, A., Chen, L.: MobileNetV2: inverted residuals and linear bottlenecks. In: 2018 IEEE/CVF Conference on Computer Vision and Pattern Recognition, pp. 4510–4520 (2018)
40. Simonyan, K., Zisserman, A.: Very deep convolutional networks for large-scale image recognition. arXiv:1409.1556 (2014)
41. Skvara, H., Teban, L., Fiebiger, M., Binder, M., Kittler, H.: Limitations of dermoscopy in the recognition of melanoma. Arch. Dermatol. **141**, 155–160 (2005)
42. Srivastava, R., Greff, K., Schmidhuber, J.: Training very deep networks. In: Advances in neural information processing systems, vol. 28 (2015)
43. Szegedy, C., Ioffe, S., Vanhoucke, V., Alemi, A.: Inception-v4, inception-resNet and the impact of residual connections on learning. In: Thirty-First AAAI Conference on Artificial Intelligence, p. 4 (2017)
44. Szegedy, C., et al.: Going deeper with convolutions. In: Proceedings of the IEEE Conference on Computer Vision and Pattern Recognition, pp. 1–9 (2015)
45. Szegedy, C., Vanhoucke, V., Ioffe, S., Shlens, J., Wojna, Z.: Rethinking the inception architecture for computer vision, Proceedings of the IEEE Conference on Computer Vision and Pattern Recognition pp. 2818–2826 (2016)
46. Tan, M., Le, Q.: EfficientNet: rethinking model scaling for convolutional neural networks. arXiv:1905.1194 (2019)
47. Tieleman, T., Hinton, G.: Lecture 6.5-rmsprop: divide the gradient by a running average of its recent magnitude. COURSERA Neural Netw. Mach. Learn. **4**(2), 26–31 (2012)
48. Veit, A., Wilber, M., Belongie, S.: Residual networks behave like ensembles of relatively shallow networks. In: Advances in neural information processing systems, vol. 29 (2016)
49. Xiangyu, Z., Zhou, X., Lin, M.: ShuffleNet: an extremely efficient convolutional neural network for mobile devices. arXiv:1707.01083v2 (2017)
50. Zoph, B., Vasudevan, V., Shlens, J., Le, Q.: Learning transferable architectures for scalable image recognition. arXiv:1707.070122(6) (2017)

Towards Detecting Freezing of Gait Events Using Wearable Sensors and Genetic Programming

Adane Nega Tarekegn[(✉)] [ID], Faouzi Alaya Cheikh [ID], Muhammad Sajjad [ID], and Mohib Ullah [ID]

Department of Computer Science, Norwegian University of Science and Technology (NTNU), Gjøvik, Norway
adane.n.tarekegn@ntnu.no

Abstract. Freezing of gait (FOG) is one of the most common manifestations of advanced Parkinson's disease. It represents a sudden interruption of walking forward associated with an increased risk of falling and poor quality of life. Evolutionary algorithms, such as genetic programming (GP), have been effectively applied in modelling many real-world application domains and diseases occurrence. In this paper, we explore the application of GP for the early detection of FOG episodes in patients with Parkinson's disease. The study involves the analysis of FOG by exploiting the statistical and time-domain features from wearable sensors, followed by automatic feature selection and model construction using GP. Efforts to use data from wearable sensors suffer from challenges caused by imbalanced class labels, which affect the task of GP model development. Thus, the cost-sensitive approach is incorporated into GP to tackle the imbalanced problem. The standard metrics, such as sensitivity, specificity, and F1-score, were used for testing the final model. With 30 repetitions, the average performance of the GP model has shown promising results in detecting the occurrence of FOG episodes in Parkinson's disease.

Keywords: Freezing of Gait · wearable sensors · Genetic programming · Cost-sensitive learning · Parkinson's diseases · Machine learning

1 Introduction

Predictive models are designed to support medical staff and patients with decisions for screening and diagnosing, early intervention and prevention of diseases, providing patient risk stratification, or making lifestyle changes [1]. Building a clinical predictive model requires data that are representative of a specific population or domain and reliably recorded within the time frame of interest for the prediction. Such models are generally defined as either likelihood of disease or disease group classification, detection or identification of disease cases, the diagnostic or prognostic, likelihood of response or risk of recurrence [2]. This

© The Author(s), under exclusive license to Springer Nature Switzerland AG 2023
L. Rutkowski et al. (Eds.): ICAISC 2023, LNAI 14125, pp. 274–285, 2023.
https://doi.org/10.1007/978-3-031-42505-9_24

study focuses on building a predictive model for detecting freezing of gait (FOG) in Parkinson's disease (PD). PD is a complex and progressive brain disorder, which is characterized by a combination of motor symptoms such as bradykinesia, resting tremor, rigidity, freezing of gait, and non-motor symptoms, such as psychiatric disorders, pain, and fatigue [3]. Among these, FOG is one of the most common and disturbing motor manifestations in the advanced stages of PD. It is a common gait impairment or activity disorder often characterized by the inability to walk and severe difficulty in locomotion with an increased risk of falling. FOG can be defined as a "brief, episodic absence or marked reduction of forward progression of the feet despite having the intention to walk" [4]. The diagnosis and treatment of FOG are challenging for healthcare professionals due to the heterogeneity of the patient, and FOG may not manifest during hospital visits [4]. Wearable technologies based on inertial sensors and machine learning have been widely used for their automatic detection and predictions through different sensor placements on the human body. Such predictions can be important in quantifying the characteristics of gait disorders and freezing events in PD. Despite the promising results with the detection of FOG using machine learning techniques, there are still open issues for improvement in terms of stability and generalization capability to implement real-time FOG detection systems using machine learning techniques and/or evolutionary algorithms.

Evolutionary algorithms, such as genetic programming (GP), have been successful in automatically evolving variable-length computer programs to solve practical problems [5,6]. Unlike Blackbox methods such as neural networks, GP has the advantage of being human-friendly and providing an explicit mathematical formula as its output. However, like other machine learning models, the performance of GP can be highly affected by the presence of imbalanced class labels in the data that may lead to high-false negative rates. The resampling methods, such as under-sampling and over-sampling, are popular approaches for dealing with an imbalanced data problem. However, both approaches can cause either the loss of important information or adding irrelevant classification data that can affect the prediction accuracy for minority examples in the imbalanced dataset [7]. Thus, in this study, cost-sensitive learning in GP (CSGP) is proposed to alleviate the imbalanced problem and predict FOG episodes in PD. The main motivation for using GP over traditional machine learning techniques is twofold. Firstly, GP performs an implicit feature selection automatically, discovering relationships among variables and producing fully explorable models. Secondly, GP can present its result by generating interpretable models in the form of parse trees or mathematical equations, which are relatively easy to explain.

2 Preliminaries and Related Works

2.1 Wearable Sensors-Based FOG Detection

Wearable sensors have been used in the detection and analysis of FOG episodes to characterize their severity and to enable the application of rhythmic auditory cueing. Rhythmic Auditory Stimulation (RAS) is applied to produce a rhythmic ticking sound upon detection of a FOG episode. Several research papers proposed wearable systems based on motion sensors for the detection and treatment of FOG with auditory stimulation [8]. Marc B et al. [9] proposed a wearable system for FOG detection that provides the rhythmic auditory signal. They used accelerometers placed on the ankles to evaluate the frequency components of motion. Authors in [10] proposed a machine learning algorithm for online FOG detection and treatment using a smartphone as a wearable device. They tested several learning methods, including Naive Bayes, k-Nearest Neighbor, Random Forests, decision trees, and others with different sensor locations and temporal windows size to optimize FOG detection accuracy and latency. The results obtained demonstrate the potential of machine learning algorithms. A recent review on the application of machine learning and wearable sensors for FOG detection is presented in [11].

However, there are still challenges to studying FOG events in real life, as FOG events are influenced by several factors, such as the state of the patient's medication (On and Off), the severity of PD and other personal factors. Moreover, datasets are usually imbalanced that require augmentation strategies, more robust and accurate machine-learning methods are also required. This study explores the possible advantages of genetic programming (GP) in the detection and prediction of FOG events in PD.

2.2   Genetic Programming

Genetic programming (GP) is a part of evolutionary algorithms that apply heuristic search principles inspired by natural evolution to the problem of finding an optimal solution through parameter optimization [12]. The term evolution refers to an artificial process analogous to the biological evolution of living organisms in accordance with Darwin's theory of evolution by natural selection [13]. GP can be expressed as a domain-independent approach that genetically breeds a population of computer programs to solve a problem [14]. GP is a search and optimization algorithm that iteratively transforms a population of computer programs into a new generation of programs using various genetic operators. The most commonly used operators are crossover, mutation, and reproduction. The crossover operator recombines randomly chosen subtrees among the parents and creates a new program for the new population. The mutation operator replaces a randomly chosen subtree with a randomly generated tree, while the reproduction operator replicates a selected individual to a new population. GP finds the solution to the problem in the form of programs or functions.

2.3   Highlights of This Article

- This paper proposed the application of cost-sensitive GP (CSGP) and wearable sensors for the detection of FOG events in Parkinson's disease.
- We investigate how well the existing cost-sensitive learning approaches in machine learning perform if they are applied in a GP-based classifier.
- GP performed optimal feature extraction automatically, discovering relationships among variables and generating interpretable models in the form of a

tree-like structure. This shows that GP maintains its substantial advantage over traditional machine learning algorithms.

- Our experimental results highlighted that CSGP successfully performed automatic FOG detection with high efficiency and excellent performance.

3   Methods and Materials

3.1   Dataset Description

In this paper, we used the publicly available Daphnet dataset developed for FOG detection from wearable sensors attached to the leg, thigh, and trunk of PD patients [9]. A total of 10 participants performed three basic walking activities: (1) walking back and forth in a straight line, (2) random walking with a series of initiated stops, (3) walking simulating activities of daily living, such as entering and leaving rooms, and walking to the kitchen. These activities were performed based on two sessions to replicate a normal daily walking routine. During the first session, the wearable system collected all the data and conducted online FOG detection without RAS feedback. In the second session, the same procedure was followed. However, the RAS feedback was activated. The sensors recorded three-dimensional (3D) accelerations at a sampling frequency of 64 Hz and transferred their data to a wearable computer, which was attached to the trunk of the subjects (along with the third sensor) and provided RAS upon the detection of a freezing episode.

3.2   Data Preprocessing

The data collected by the wearable sensors has been cleaned, filtered, and standardized, resulting in a dataset that is consistent and suitable for analysis and model training processes.

- **Signal Filtering:**the triaxial linear accelerations signals are made up of several components, and thus there can be inherent noise components. As a result, the signals were filtered to remove the noise using a median filter and a third-order low-pass Butterworth filter with a 15 Hz cut-off.
- **Normalization:** the aim of normalization is to change the values of features in the dataset to a common scale, without distorting differences in the ranges of values. For this purpose, Min-max normalization was used to transform each acceleration signal into the range between 0 to 1 with mean and standard deviation.
- **Data Segmentation:** Data segmentation is the process of dividing sensor signals into partially overlapping windows. Before training a GP and other machine learning models, raw time-series data recorded from wearable sensors are split into temporal segments. The sliding approach is frequently used and has been demonstrated to be useful for handling flowing data. In this paper, we used a windowing function with a window length of 4 s with an overlap of 0.5 s. A window was labelled as a FOG window if more than 50% of the samples were labelled as FOG.

- **Feature Extraction and Selection:** After segmenting the data, statistical and time-domain features were extracted and used for model development, as suggested by Mazilu et al. [15]. A total of 54 features were obtained and the most relevant ones were automatically selected using an embedded automatic feature selection mechanism in GP. The importance of each feature was based on the number of references in all models generated during the GP iterations. This approach allows the model to focus on the most significant information and improve performance.

3.3 Cost-Sensitive GP

Most machine learning classifiers, including GP, assume that misclassification costs (false negative and false positive) are set balanced [16]. In most of the real-world domains, however, this assumption is not true. Usually, in the medical domain, the proportion of healthy patients is larger than unhealthy patients, i.e., many datasets of medical diagnosis exhibit imbalanced class distribution [17]. In these FOG datasets, 9% of the data was recorded as FOG events, and the remaining 90% of the data was recorded as normal locomotion. When using the GP model in this dataset, a very low sensitivity was observed in the rare class. Consequently, FOG events belonging to the minority class are misclassified more than those belonging to the majority class. Traditionally in GP, classification problems are solved with accuracy as a fitness function. However, when the data of the problem to be solved contains an imbalanced class distribution, only accuracy cannot be a good option since maximizing the accuracy will naturally lead to classifying everything as the majority class and does not give acceptable results. Therefore, one of the techniques to overcome this biasedness and overfitting, and at the same time to build a good classifier for imbalanced data, is cost-sensitive learning. Cost-sensitive learning focuses on providing a higher cost for predicting a specific class, such as any misclassification of a class will penalize (cost more) the classifier. A cost matrix, which is similar to the confusion matrix, describes the cost for misclassification in a particular scenario and gives a higher cost to misclassifying rather than correctly classifying the instance. In this paper, the minority classes are denoted by '+', and the majority classes are denoted by '-'. Let C (i, j) be the cost of misclassifying an instance from 'class i' as 'class j', and C (i, i) denotes the cost of correct classification (zero cost). The cost matrix can be computed as shown in Table 1, where C (-, +) and C (+, -) correspond to the costs associated with a false negative (FN) and a false positive (FP), respectively.

Table 1. Cost Matrix

		Predicted class	
		FOG	No FOG
Actual Class	FOG	C(+,+)	C(-,+)
	No FOG	C(+,-)	C(-,-)

Table 1 shows an example of a cost matrix where classifying a person with 'FOG' as having 'No FOG' will cost the classifier a penalty equal to C(-,+). A penalty cost equals C(+,-) can also be defined for classifying a normal person as having the FOG event. Defining high-cost values gives more importance to that class. Therefore, it helps in building a classifier for imbalanced data and can help in training the classifier to detect the class with a smaller number of instances and avoid the overfitting problem. This paper applies a cost-sensitive approach in GP (CSGP) to build a predictive model for detecting the presence of FOG in patients, capable of minimizing the expected misclassification costs and errors through a fitness function. Therefore, the fitness function can be calculated as shown in equation (3) which aims to choose the classifier with the minimum misclassification cost (total cost):

$$Totalcost = C(-,+) \times FN + C(+,-) \times FP$$

where FP denotes the total number of false positives and FN is the total number of false negatives. FP is the number of instances that were classified as having the FOG, and actually, they have not. FN is the number of instances that have FOG but were classified as not having the FOG event.

3.4 Proposed Model Framework

The model development process follows an approach that is comprised of a combination of two phases, as shown in Fig. 1. The first phase includes data preprocessing and parameter setup. In the beginning, we performed data pre-processing, which includes noise reduction, missing data filling, data normalization, and filtering. Data segmentation is also required to convert multi-dimensional sensor data into sample data in suitable conditions for model training. Then feature extraction and feature selection were applied to each window segment. For GP, the main parameters, such as population size, number of generations, crossover rate, and mutation rate, have been configured. The second phase includes the development of a GP model using cost-sensitive learning based on the preprocessed dataset and GP parameters from phase one. Following this, the sample data are separated into training and test data for model training and evaluation. Finally, the fitness score in terms of accuracy, precision, recall, F1-score, and confusion matrix is used to validate the final model. The overall GP model development framework is evolved using a fitness measure that includes a series of steps.

4 Experimental Settings

In this section, an experimental setup is established for the proposed approach to demonstrate the performance of GP for FOG analysis and detection. To evaluate the generated model, several experiments were performed using HeuristicLab

3.3.16 framework [18] by splitting the datasets into training and testing. Taking into account that the data is imbalanced, stratified sampling is applied in splitting the data in order to preserve the ratio of each class in the training and testing parts. The proportions are 75% and 25% for the training and testing, respectively, where the training set is used to train the model and includes both input data and the corresponding expected output, and the testing set includes only input data that is being used to assess how well GP is trained and to estimate model properties.

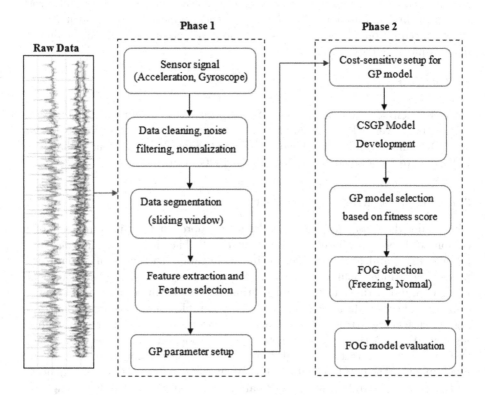

Fig. 1. CSGP model development workflow

4.1   GP Parameter Setup

In GP, setting the control parameters is an important first step to manipulate data and obtain better results. For this, a systematic experimentation process was conducted to tune the parameters of GP using different population sizes (i.e., 100, 330, 500, and 1000). For mutation and crossover rates, GP experimented at 2%, 5%, 10% and 15% for mutation, and 85%, 90%, and 95% for crossover. Due to the stochastic nature of GP, 30 runs were performed in all problems, each with a different random number generator seed. The selection mechanism has been the tournament selection and the maximum tree depth set to the default value. GP requires that further control parameters be specified. In this experiment, the best performance was obtained with the parameter values listed in Table 2.

Table 2. GP Control Parameter Settings

Parameter	Value
Population Size	1000
Maximum number of generations	100
Crossover probability	0.90
Mutation probability	0.15
Selection method	Tournament selection
Termination condition	Max generation
Tree initialization	Ramped half and half
Genetic operators	Crossover, mutation
Elites	1

4.2 Performance Evaluation

In GP, the fitness function defines a measure to calculate the accuracy of a solution by comparing the predicted class labels with the actual class labels. In a binary classification problem, the outcome of classification performance can be represented by a confusion matrix, as shown in Table 3. The predictive model was evaluated using common statistical parameters such as sensitivity, specificity, accuracy, and F1-score, which are based on the true positives (TP), true negatives (TN), false positives (FP), and false negatives (FN). Sensitivity (true positive rate) is the ratio of the proportions of positive patient cases that are accurately predicted divided by the total number of actual positive cases. Specificity (true negative rate) is calculated as the number of negative case predictions divided by the total number of actual negative cases. Accuracy measures the number of all correct predictions divided by the total number of samples. However, the overall accuracy is known to be unsuitable for classification with unbalanced data [19]. Measuring the individual classification accuracy of the minority and majority classes separately using sensitivity and specificity can avoid this learning bias when evaluating model performance in unbalanced class scenarios. The F1-score is used as the harmonic mean of precision and recall [20]. It provides the most reliable evaluation of the model's prediction performance while considering the worst-case prediction scenario for a classifier.

5   Results and Discussions

In analyzing GP for FOG detection, the most fundamental aspect is to know the number of samples that are classified correctly and those which are classified

Table 3. Confusion matrix

	Predicted Positive Class	Predicted Negative Class
Actual Positive Class	True Positive (TP)	False Negative (FN)
Actual Negative Class	False Positive (FP)	True Negative (TN)

incorrectly. In cost-sensitive GP (CSGP), this task is handled by evaluating the quality of the generated model using sensitivity and specificity. The quality of GP is generally called the fitness of a solution candidate. The fitness of the proposed CSGP model was tested using different penalty cost matrices starting from 3 until 13 by representing the penalty cost matrices using the expressions [1:1], [1:3], [1:5], [1:7], [1:9],[1:11] and [1:13]. These costs are increased by +2 and came from extensive experiments with different penalty costs, where 13 was the last penalty cost because sensitivity values increase significantly with larger costs. The results of the CSGP with five different cost matrices on the Daphnet FOG dataset are compared using sensitivity and specificity as fitness functions, as shown in Fig. 2, which shows how the sensitivity of CSGP increases with the different penalty cost matrices, where [1:1] represents the performance of the original data classification.

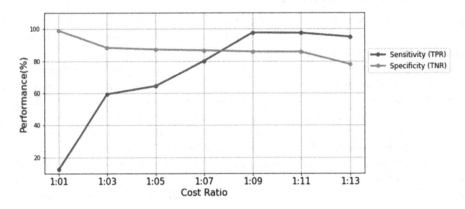

Fig. 2. The performance of CSGP on FOG detection at various penalty costs.

The increase in sensitivity values reflects the high detection of subjects with FOG but also the high misclassification of the normal subjects. It is clear from the figure that the sensitivity fitness function detects more FOG events with higher penalty costs, while specificity relatively drops with higher costs. The sensitivity values start at 13% for the [1:1] penalty cost matrix and reach 97.6% with the [1:9] penalty cost matrix. Then it falls to reach 95% with [1:13] penalty cost matrix. CSGP using the cost penalty matrix of [1:9], achieved the highest performance with a sensitivity value equal to 97.6% and an accuracy value equal to 96%. However, it achieved the lowest specificity of 85.8%. In addition, the population dynamics of CSGP across generations are also evaluated based on mean squared error (MSE). Using MSE on the selected cost matrix, the average fitness of the best solution per generation is calculated based on results stored from 30 runs of GP. Figure 3 shows the median MSE on the five simulations at 100 generations.

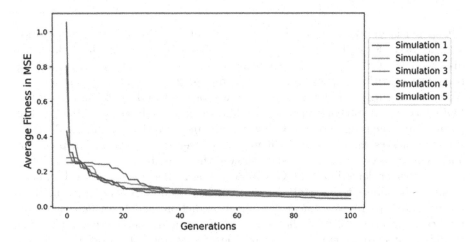

Fig. 3. CSGP evolution plots using mean squared error (MSE).

Table 4. Performance comparison of GP and machine learning techniques

Models	Accuracy	Recall	Precision	F1-Score
GP	96.0	**97.6**	85.8	**98.0**
RF	97.9	81.0	–	0.75
XGB	85.7	85.0	–	92.0
LR	97.0	82.0	–	86.0
DT	81.4	81.0	–	89.00

The median fitness refers to the average of the fitness scores across the entire population. The evolution of the error in average fitness reveals the ability of CSGP to learn the relationship between variables. There is a constant decrease in the test error across generations, indicating that no overfitting is occurring. The final model produced by GP includes the best features selected during the evolutionary process. These variables are the most frequent variables which were the most relevant for the detection of FOG events. Table 4 presents the performance comparison of GP with other benchmark machine learning classifiers, namely random forest (RF), extreme gradient boosting (XGB), logistic regression (LR) and decision tree (DT). The comparison is based on accuracy, recall, precision, and F1-score. Our results showed that GP was able to show competitive performance in the detection of FOG events compared to the traditional machine learning models.

6   Conclusions

This paper is an investigation of genetic programming with a cost-sensitive approach (CSGP) for early detection of freezing of gait (FOG) events in Parkinson's disease (PD). CSGP used various penalty costs for prediction errors ranging from 3 to 13 with a step of 2, and each is represented as a penalty cost matrix. After configuring the different cost matrixes for the CSGP algorithm using the FOG dataset, several experiments with 30 runs were conducted by adjusting the parameters. The proposed approach was evaluated with the well-known GP classification fitness functions, including accuracy, sensitivity, specificity, precision and mean squared error. The results showed that the proposed approach CSGP achieved better detection of FOG episodes using higher penalty costs. From the results, it is evident that CSGP demonstrated substantial potential as a method for the automated development of clinical prediction models for detection and prediction purposes. Overall, the results are encouraging, and further studies can be investigated to extend and optimize the findings for FOG studies and other medical problems using cost-sensitive evolutionary algorithms.

Acknowledgments. This work was supported by European Union through the Horizon 2020 Research and Innovation Programme in the context of the ALAMEDA project under grant agreement No GA 101017558.

References

1. Harrell, F.E.: Multivariable modeling strategies. In: Regression Modeling Strategies. SSS, pp. 63–102. Springer, Cham (2015). https://doi.org/10.1007/978-3-319-19425-7_4

2. Tarekegn, A.N., Ricceri, F., Costa, G., Ferracin, E., Giacobini, M.: Predictive modeling for frailty conditions in elderly people: machine learning approaches. JMIR Med. Informatics. (2020). https://doi.org/10.2196/16678

3. Roca, L.G., Ríos, L.N., Sucarrats, G.M., Medina, H.C., García, D.S.: Parkinson's disease, Kranion (2021). https://doi.org/10.24875/KRANION.M21000002

4. Nutt, J.G., Bloem, B.R., Giladi, N., Hallett, M., Horak, F.B., Nieuwboer, A.: Freezing of gait: moving forward on a mysterious clinical phenomenon. Lancet Neurol. (2011). https://doi.org/10.1016/S1474-4422(11)70143-0

5. Tarekegn, A., Ricceri, F., Costa, G., Ferracin, E., Giacobini, M.: Detection of frailty using genetic programming. In: Hu, T., Lourenço, N., Medvet, E., Divina, F. (eds.) EuroGP 2020. LNCS, vol. 12101, pp. 228–243. Springer, Cham (2020). https://doi.org/10.1007/978-3-030-44094-7_15

6. Tarekegn, A.N., Alemu, T.A., Tegegne, A.K.: A cluster-genetic programming approach for detecting pulmonary tuberculosis. Ethiop. J. Sci. Technol. (2021). https://doi.org/10.4314/ejst.v14i1.5
7. Galar, M., et al.: A review on ensembles for the class imbalance problem: bagging-, boosting-, and hybrid-based approaches. IEEE Trans. Syst. Man, Cybern. Part C Appl. Rev. **42**, 463–484 (2012). https://doi.org/10.1109/TSMCC.2011.2161285
8. Punin, C., et al.: A non-invasive medical device for Parkinson's patients with episodes of freezing of gait. Sensors (Switzerland) (2019). https://doi.org/10.3390/s19030737
9. Bächlin, M., et al.: Wearable assistant for Parkinson's disease patients with the freezing of gait symptom. IEEE Trans. Inf Technol. Biomed. (2010). https://doi.org/10.1109/TITB.2009.2036165
10. Mazilu, S., et al.: Online detection of freezing of gait with smartphones and machine learning techniques. In: 2012 6th International Conference on Pervasive Computing Technologies for Healthcare, PervasiveHealth (2012). https://doi.org/10.4108/icst.pervasivehealth.2012.248680
11. Martínez-Villaseñor, L., Ponce, H., Miralles-Pechuán, L.: A Survey on Freezing of Gait Detection and Prediction in Parkinson's Disease. In: Martínez-Villaseñor, L., Herrera-Alcántara, O., Ponce, H., Castro-Espinoza, F.A. (eds.) MICAI 2020. LNCS (LNAI), vol. 12468, pp. 169–181. Springer, Cham (2020). https://doi.org/10.1007/978-3-030-60884-2_13
12. Lissovoi, A., Oliveto, P.S.: On the time and space complexity of genetic programming for evolving Boolean conjunctions. J. Artif. Intell. Res. **66**, 655–689 (2019). https://doi.org/10.1613/jair.1.11821
13. Darwin, C.: The origin of species, by means of natural selection, or the preservation of favored races in the struggle for life. Crayon **7**, 149–150 (1860). https://doi.org/10.2307/25528056
14. O'Reilly, U.-M.: Genetic programming. In: Proceedings of the Fourteenth International Conference Genetic and Evolutionary Computation Conference Companion - GECCO Companion '12, ACM Press, New York, New York, USA, p. 693 (2012). https://doi.org/10.1145/2330784.2330912
15. Mazilu, S., Calatroni, A., Gazit, E., Roggen, D., Hausdorff, J.M., Tröster, G.: Feature learning for detection and prediction of freezing of gait in Parkinson's disease. In: Perner, P. (ed.) MLDM 2013. LNCS (LNAI), vol. 7988, pp. 144–158. Springer, Heidelberg (2013). https://doi.org/10.1007/978-3-642-39712-7_11
16. Thai-Nghe, N., Gantner, Z., Schmidt-Thieme, L.: Cost-sensitive learning methods for imbalanced data. In: Proceedings of the International Joint Conference Neural Networks (2010). https://doi.org/10.1109/IJCNN.2010.5596486
17. Yildirim, P.: Chronic kidney disease prediction on imbalanced data by multi-layer perceptron: chronic kidney disease prediction. In: Proceedings - International Computer Software Applications Conference (2017). https://doi.org/10.1109/COMPSAC.2017.84
18. Wagner, S., et al.: Architecture and design of the HeuristicLab optimization environment (2014). https://doi.org/10.1007/978-3-319-01436-4_10
19. Bhowan, U., Zhang, M., Johnston, M.: Genetic programming for classification with unbalanced data (2010). https://doi.org/10.1007/978-3-642-12148-7_1
20. Witten, I.H., et al.: Data mining: practical machine learning tools and techniques. Elsevier (2011). https://doi.org/10.1016/C2009-0-19715-5

CNN-LSTM Optimized by Genetic Algorithm in Time Series Forecasting: An Automatic Method to Use Deep Learning

Eder Urbinate$^{(\boxtimes)}$ ⬤, Fernando Itano⬤, and Emilio Del-Moral-Hernandez⬤

Polytechnic School, University of Sao Paulo, Sao Paulo, Brazil
{eder.urbinate,emilio.delmoral}@usp.br, itanofe@lsi.usp.br

Abstract. Time series forecasting is a challenge in several areas and for several applications. A series of tools have emerged to tackle this problem, from classic models to modern models that use machine learning and deep learning. One of these areas of great interest is financial. Specifically, forecasting the prices of stocks and indices can be especially difficult due to the characteristics of this type of series. In this work, we propose a method to automatically develop a deep network using a genetic algorithm to select the hyperparameters. To test the proposed method, we used four datasets, including financial and non-financial time series. In both financial and non-financial datasets, the proposed method with automated hyperparameter selection did better than the models made by other authors using different methods.

Keywords: Genetic Algorithms · Convolutional Neural Networks · Long Short-Term Memory · Time Series Forecasting

1 Introduction

For decades, time series forecasting has been one of the areas of greatest interest in several fields of knowledge, and examples of this have been verified in finance, engineering, medicine, climate, industry, and commerce. For these applications, several different tools have been developed and used, from classical linear models to models that use deep learning.

Deep Neural Networks, such as long short-term memory networks (LSTM) [5], a model built for and widely used in time series forecasting, are capable of capturing short and long-term dependencies at the same time, thus achieving great results in several applications. In addition to LSTM, convolutional neural networks (CNN) were initially proposed by [9], which have convolutional layers, reached the state of the art for various applications with images, and were then adapted to work in one dimension in time series forecasting.

More recently, these two models were combined, generating the deep networks of the CNN-LSTM type with good results in applications such as speech recognition [19], among others, which generate networks capable of filtering features in the convolutional layers while still capturing the time dependence in the

L. Rutkowski et al. (Eds.): ICAISC 2023, LNAI 14125, pp. 286–295, 2023.
https://doi.org/10.1007/978-3-031-42505-9_25

recurrent layers. Due to the size and number of hyperparameters in this type of network, a negative point may be the difficulty in selecting and adapting these hyperparameters to achieve the best results in a given application.

To overcome this difficulty, several evolutionary computation techniques, such as genetic algorithms [12], swarm intelligence, and others, have been used to select a good set of hyperparameters that allow the model to achieve the desired performance.

In this work, we propose using a deep network by combining CNN and LSTM, both automatically optimized by a genetic algorithm (GA). Automatically optimizing CNN-LSTM with GA makes it possible to explore a wide range of possible combinations of hyperparameters in search of the best results without requiring as much time as if this exploration were performed manually. Our main contributions are:

- Proposing a simple and intuitive way to automatically build deep network models using GA to select hyperparameters, maintaining the stability of the evolutionary process;
- Presenting the CNN-LSTM deep learning models developed with this method, capable of outperforming the references models, and analyzing their evolutionary process.

2   Related Works

As mentioned before, time series forecasting is a topic of interest in many areas of knowledge and is very useful in a wide range of applications, including traffic, energy, and electricity, as well as financial series like stock prices, exchange rates, and indices. It is possible to find several articles in the literature that use deep networks for time series forecasting, employing both CNN [8] and LSTM [14], applied to the most diverse areas of knowledge, such as medicine, finance, commerce, and industry.

Over the years, LSTM and others recurrent neural networks (RNN) architectures have remained a baseline for time series forecasting in many applications. For example, [15] shows how recurrent neural networks dominated most of the period from 2005 to 2019 for time series forecasting in financial markets.

CNN gained greater visibility in 2012 due to winning competitions such as the ImageNet Large Scale Visual Recognition Challenge (ILSVRC) [9], considerably exceeding the results of previous years. They have convolutional layers and have reached the state of the art for several years in a row for imaging applications. This application has recently received attention, mainly from the financial community, for stock price prediction [6].

Some works use models with neural networks with convolutional layers and also LSTM layers, here called simply CNN-LSTM, in time series applications, as is the case of [11,18]. These combinations are often able to reach values comparable to the state of the art and often surpass the state of the art in several applications. [2,11] use a hybrid architecture of CNN and LSTM together with the adaptation of the hyperparameters, employing a method using a genetic algorithm, with better results than those of the other methods presented herein.

The increase in complexity and the number of variables in the architectures causes difficulty in selecting and adapting the hyperparameters of the networks. In many cases, the adaptation occurs manually and by brute force, empirically exploring different possibilities and consuming substantial computational power and processing time.

To solve, circumvent, or reduce the difficulties linked to the choice and adaptation of hyperparameters, there are different strategies for choosing hyperparameters and adapting neural networks automatically, such as genetic algorithms [3], particle swarm optimization [4], Random Forest [13,17], among others. It is also possible to find applications of genetic algorithms for CNN networks in other applications, such as images [16], which is the area for which this type of neural network is initially suggested.

In the genetic algorithm, there are different genetic operators, such as crossover and mutation [16], elitism, selection, competition, and evaluation, among others. Here, we address these neural network architectures by combining convolutional and recurrent layers, and adapting hyperparameters with a genetic algorithm. These architectures are described in more detail in the next sections.

3   Methodology

In this section, we describe the methods and experimental apparatus used. One of the objectives is to present a simple methodology for implementing genetic algorithms through a modular interpretation of genes and chromosomes to make the application to other architectures easy and intuitive.

3.1   Deep Networks

CNN is usually interpreted as feature extraction layers, represented by convolutional layers that form the first layers of the network proposed here. The convolutional operators for one-dimensional CNNs that have been adapted to be used for time series forecasting are shown below [10]:

$$\mathbf{h}_t^{l+1} = A((\mathbf{W} * \mathbf{h})(l, t)) \tag{1}$$

$$(\mathbf{W} * \mathbf{h})(l, t) = \sum_{\tau=0}^{k} \mathbf{W}(l, \tau)\mathbf{h}_{t-\tau'}^{l} \tag{2}$$

where $\mathbf{h}_t^l$ is an intermediate state at layer l at time t, * represents the convolution operator, $\mathbf{W}(l, \tau)$ is a fixed filter weight at layer l, kernel size is k, and $A(.)$ is an activation function.

Then, LSTM layers that can be interpreted as sequence learning are placed after convolutional layers. At the end of the network, the fully connected layers with classification layers finish off the proposed model's architecture.

The CNN-LSTM proposed network is presented in Fig. 1, which follows the one presented in [11]. The differential of the model proposed here is the choice of hyperparameters with the evolutionary process presented in detail in the next topics.

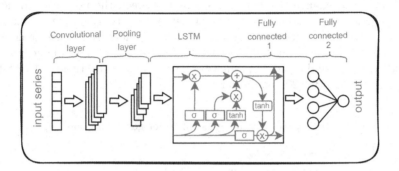

Fig. 1. CNN-LSTM architecture example.

3.2 Genetic Algorithms

We propose a way of building an evolutionary process that is intuitive and easy to implement; it can be implemented in different types of deep or non-deep neural networks and could be interpreted in the context of auto-Machine Learning, since the genetic algorithm chooses the parameters automatically and can work independently of the network architecture chosen.

The process starts by defining the hyperparameters to be optimized; here, they are the filters, kernel size, activation functions, dropout, optimizers, number of epochs, and n time steps of the lookback window, as shown in Table 1. We used a mixed chromosomic representation, so only one gene is needed to represent each hyperparameter. Each gene can assume integer values for categorical and discrete characteristics. This representation is simpler than binary chromosomic representation, avoiding the Hamming Abyss [12]. As proposed by [7], we modified the genetic operators to work with the simplified chromosomic representation.

The fitness function is responsible for measuring the performance of the artificial neural network represented by each individual. We defined it as the root mean square error (RMSE) on the test dataset. The evolutionary process uses the RMSE value to search for a set of hyperparameters that define an artificial neural network with a lower RMSE.

The evolutionary process starts with an initial population of 50 artificial neural networks, with randomly selected hyperparameters. These neural networks are evaluated, and 5% of the ones with the best performance is selected to move on to the next generation (elitism technique). The remaining 95% of the neural networks are selected by using the tournament method with a size equal to two. Then, the crossover operator is applied with the uniform method and 50% probability to exchange the hyperparameters between the two selected neural networks, resulting in two neural networks with potentially different characteristics. Finally, the mutation operator is applied to randomly change some of the hyperparameters with a probability of 10%, better exploring the hyperparameter's search space and avoiding premature populational convergence. This whole process is repeated for 20 generations.

Table 1. Hyperparameters values for genes selection.

Gene	Type	Value
Filters	integer	2, 4, 8, 16, 32, 64, 128, 256, 384, 512
Kernel size	integer	1, 2, 3, 4, 5
Activation Function	categorical	Relu, Selu, Elu
Dropout	discrete	0, 0.001, 0.1
Optimizer	categorical	Adamax, Adadelta, Adam, Adagrad, Ftrl, Nadam, RMSprop, SGD
Epochs	integer	5 to 700
n (time steps window)	integer	1 to 200

3.3   Data-Sets: Non-financial and Financial Series

[2] uses a CNN model with optimization using genetic algorithms with applications in different time series; we selected some of them to test our implementation and compare the results, namely: MONTHLY-SUNSPOTS, LYNX, and VEHICLE Sales.

[11] employs architecture of the CNN-LSTM type, but selects hyperparameters without genetic algorithms; the application is in a financial series, posing an additional difficulty due to the nature of the problem. The series used is the SCI - Shanghai Composite Index (000001). Table 2 details the datasets and the number of parameters for each one.

Since we work with non-normalized data, we have to pre-process the input data so that the learning process occurs faster and without an overflow problem in the values of the neural network approximation. Without this preparation, the learning process is also able to select hyperparameters that can give good prediction values, but the process becomes slow and many individuals in the generations give values at a threshold where the network has been saturated.

Table 2. Description of datasets used.

Dataset	Description	Parameters
Monthly Sunspots	Wolf's Sunspot Numbers between 1700 and 1988	2820
Lynx	Annual number of lynx trapped in Mackenzie River between 1821 and 1934	114
Vehicle Sales	US monthly sales of petroleum and related products (chemical, coal, vehicle) between January 1971 and December 1991	252
SCI	Shanghai Composite Index (000001) - Data from July 1991 to August 2020	7124

We applied a data standardization similar to the one in the [11], known as z-score, whereby the data are normalized for training and are eventually transformed back to the initial proportion for the prediction.

To assess the overfitting of the trained neural network, we split the dataset into train, validation, and test, with proportions of 70%, 20%, and 10% respectively.

The codes were written in Python 3 using the Keras framework and executed in Google Colaboratory https://colab.research.google.com/. The codes are available via GitHub https://github.com/fernandoitano/cnn-lstm-ga.

3.4   Evaluation Metrics

We performed 30 independent runs of the evolutionary process for each dataset to assess the stability of the results. The mean RMSE and the standard deviation of the 30 best neural networks obtained with the repetitions were used to compare the proposed method with the reference articles. Also, a Z-test [1] was conducted to assess the statistical difference between the proposed method and related works.

4   Results

In this section, we present the results from the proposed method and compare them with references models. The reference [2] gives the value in mean squared error (MSE), which was converted to RMSE to make comparison possible.

The Sunspots dataset allows observing that all evolutionary processes come to an end at better values than the comparative article; Fig. 2 shows the evolution of RMSE for generation per run time. Note how the error evolves, but in addition, even the replica with the worst value obtained at the end of the evolutionary process is better than the value of the reference article. The reference article had results between 18,788 and 21,855 with an average of 19,645, while our model had results between 16,003 and 16,641 with an average of 16,317.

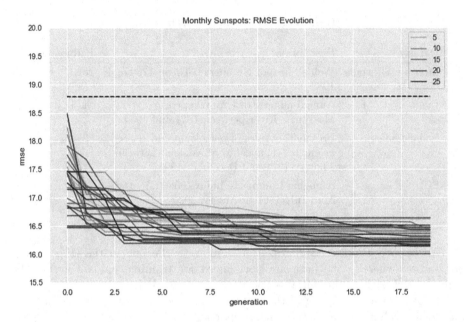

Fig. 2. Evolution of RMSE for generations per run time for Monthly-Sunspots dataset, with the dashed line representing minimum RMSE value from reference article.

For the Vehicle dataset, the model proposed here was also able to consistently outperform the reference article. Again, we achieved better results than the reference article, and our model had an average value of 1.0366 with a standard deviation of 0.7359, compared to the best reference value of 2.9687. The same occurred with the Lynx dataset, whereby our method outperformed the reference article, achieving a mean value of 94.748 with a standard deviation of 48.4975, while the best reference value was 741.862.

The proposed CNN-LSTM model with selection of hyperparameters by genetic algorithm was able to excel the reference article results, even for financial series, where there is an additional difficulty to predict values. For the SCI dataset, the error evolves over the generations, reaching RMSE values at the end of the genetic process in the range of 38.356 to 40.745 with an average value of 39.363. The statistical analysis demonstrated that the proposed model's value is superior to the reference value by obtaining a p-value of 0.001173 in the Z-test, making it superior even at the 1% significance level.

Figure 3 presents the result of how the output predicted by the model was compared to the expected y_test value of the series. The value is noted to be very close to the real value of the series.

Lastly, we show the overall results and how the proposed model compares to the reference articles. Table 3 shows that the results from the proposed model were better in all the scenarios tested, including the financial series. Despite the additional difficulty common to series in the finance universe, the proposed model was able to select models with smaller errors than the reference one.

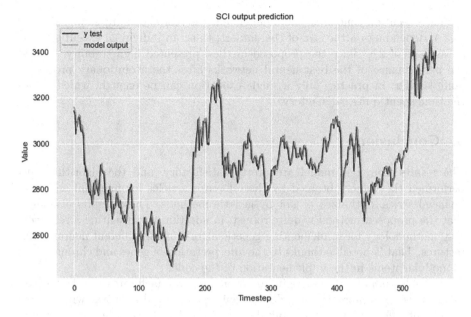

Fig. 3. SCI Dataset: Actual vs Predicted values for test data.

Table 3. Comparison of the RMSE error value between the proposed method and the reference article non-financial and financial datasets.

Dataset	Proposed Method Avg ± Std	Reference article Min	Avg	Max
Monthly Sunspots	16.317 ± 0.157	18.788	19.645	21.855
Lynx	94.748 ± 48.498	741.862	890.628	947.147
Vehicle Sales	1.037 ± 0.736	2.969	3.402	3.728
SCI	39.363 ± 0.584	–	39.688	–

In all cases, our method outperformed both reference articles, in the 4 datasets both in financial and non-financial series and also in relation to the other evolutionary method. Despite the additional difficulty intrinsic to the financial problem, the proposed model also generated statistically better values. Based on the series tested, we can deduce that the CNN-LSTM neural network with the evolutionary process is robust and capable of solving the problem of choosing parameters independently of the user and achieving satisfactory values, even better than other results in the literature.

The proposed method also allows evaluation of the characteristics of the network, both throughout the process and at its end. This analysis showed that the networks generated for the different datasets have quite different hyperparameters from each other. This is another positive aspect of using the proposed method because it generates more adapted networks for each case.

The execution time of the 30 independent runs for each dataset was about 2 to 3 d, depending on the size of the dataset; thus, an individual execution took an average of 2 h. Since the proposed method presented high stability, that is, the performance of the best neural networks after the evolutionary process is quite similar, in practice only a single execution can be enough, which makes the time spent quite satisfactory.

5 Conclusion

The results from our model are pretty satisfactory, and the algorithm out-performed the values obtained by the reference articles for financial and non-financial series, optimized or not by genetic methods. These results also show that the proposed method is quite robust, in addition to presenting a relatively easy methodology for implementing genetic algorithms in different neural architectures. That is possible thanks to the interpretation of genes and chromosomes as modular items in the implementation of the code.

The selection of parameters in an automated way facilitates a task that can be arduous, even more so when dealing with deep neural networks with a large number of different layers and input data; it can reduce the computational exploration time, helping the end user in choosing the hyperparameters quickly and practically.

As future work, we can explore the construction of auto-ML architectures in blocks to let the network choose the general structure by itself, expanding the idea used here, whereby a CNN-LSTM type network was used. In this case, genes could be defined as convolutional blocks, recurrent blocks, and fully-connected blocks, among other possibilities. The evolutionary process could then build individuals with totally different architectures to be compared with each other and expand the tests in financial series, which have an additional difficulty. The proposed method was developed for use with time series of up to tens of thousands of time steps, such as daily financial series with data from several years included in this application; it is also a future work to optimize the method for larger series.

References

1. Casella, G., Berger, R.L.: Statistical inference. Cengage Learning (2021)
2. Cicek, Z.I.E., Ozturk, Z.K.: Optimizing the artificial neural network parameters using a biased random key genetic algorithm for time series forecasting. Appl. Soft Comput. **102**, 107091 (2021)
3. David, O.E., Greental, I.: Genetic algorithms for evolving deep neural networks. In: Proceedings of the Companion Publication of the 2014 Annual Conference on Genetic and Evolutionary Computation, pp. 1451–1452 (2014)
4. Garro, B.A., Vázquez, R.A.: Designing artificial neural networks using particle swarm optimization algorithms. Comput. Intell. Neurosci. 2015 (2015)
5. Hochreiter, S., Schmidhuber, J.: Long short-term memory. Neural Comput. **9**, 1735–1780 (1997). https://doi.org/10.1162/neco.1997.9.8.1735

6. Hu, Z., Zhao, Y., Khushi, M.: A survey of forex and stock price prediction using deep learning. Appl. Syst. Innov. **4**(1) (2021). https://doi.org/10.3390/asi4010009, https://www.mdpi.com/2571-5577/4/1/9

7. Itano, F., de Abreu de Sousa, M.A., Del-Moral-Hernandez, E.: Extending MLP ANN hyper-parameters optimization by using genetic algorithm. In: 2018 International Joint Conference on Neural Networks (IJCNN), pp. 1–8 (2018). https://doi.org/10.1109/IJCNN.2018.8489520

8. Koprinska, I., Wu, D., Wang, Z.: Convolutional neural networks for energy time series forecasting. In: 2018 International Joint Conference on Neural Networks (IJCNN), pp. 1–8. IEEE (2018)

9. Krizhevsky, A., Sutskever, I., Hinton, G.E.: ImageNet classification with deep convolutional neural networks. In: Pereira, F., Burges, C.J.C., Bottou, L., Weinberger, K.Q. (eds.) Advances in Neural Information Processing Systems, vol. 25, pp. 1097–1105. Curran Associates, Inc. (2012)

10. Lim, B., Zohren, S.: Time-series forecasting with deep learning: a survey. Philosophical transactions of the royal society a: mathematical, physical and engineering sciences **379**(2194), 20200209 (2021). https://doi.org/10.1098/rsta.2020.0209

11. Lu, W., Li, J., Li, Y., Sun, A., Wang, J.: A CNN-LSTM-based model to forecast stock prices. Complexity 2020 (2020)

12. Mitchell, M.: An Introduction to Genetic Algorithms. MIT Press, Cambridge (1996)

13. Park, H.J., Kim, Y., Kim, H.Y.: Stock market forecasting using a multi-task approach integrating long short-term memory and the random forest framework. Appl. Soft Comput. **114**, 108106 (2022). https://doi.org/10.1016/j.asoc.2021.108106

14. Sagheer, A., Kotb, M.: Time series forecasting of petroleum production using deep LSTM recurrent networks. Neurocomputing **323**, 203–213 (2019)

15. Sezer, O.B., Gudelek, M.U., Ozbayoglu, A.M.: Financial time series forecasting with deep learning: a systematic literature review: 2005–2019. Appl. Soft Comput. J. (2020). https://doi.org/10.1016/j.asoc.2020.106181

16. Sun, Y., Xue, B., Zhang, M., Yen, G.G., Lv, J.: Automatically designing CNN architectures using the genetic algorithm for image classification. IEEE Trans. Cybernet. **50**(9), 3840–3854 (2020)

17. Wang, S., Aggarwal, C., Liu, H.: Random-forest-inspired neural networks. ACM Trans. Intell. Syst. Technol. (TIST) **9**(6), 1–25 (2018)

18. Wu, J.M.-T., Li, Z., Herencsar, N., Vo, B., Lin, J.C.-W.: A graph-based CNN-LSTM stock price prediction algorithm with leading indicators. Multimedia Syst. **29**, 1751–1770 (2021). https://doi.org/10.1007/s00530-021-00758-w

19. Zhao, J., Mao, X., Chen, L.: Speech emotion recognition using deep 1D & 2D CNN LSTM networks. Biomed. Signal Process. Control **47**, 312–323 (2019). https://doi.org/10.1016/j.bspc.2018.08.035

Authorship Attribution of Literary Texts Using Named Entity Masking and MaxLogit-Based Sequence Classification for Varying Text Lengths

Tomasz Walkowiak[(✉)][iD]

Faculty of Information and Communication Technology,
Wroclaw University of Science and Technology, Wroclaw, Poland
`tomasz.walkowiak@pwr.edu.pl`

Abstract. This paper explores the problem of identifying an author based on text passages of varying length, ranging from 100 to 2,000 words. The study builds on previous research on authorship attribution of Polish literary texts, finding that the TF-IDF with multilayer perceptron outperforms other techniques. The study investigates whether the issue with BERT in authorship attribution can be mitigated by removing named entities from the input data and replacing posteriori probabilities with logits in sequence classification. The results demonstrate that machine learning methods are capable of almost perfect authorship attribution on short texts, and the proposed MaxLogit approach significantly improves results. However, except in the case of short passages up to 400 words, better results are obtained with TF-IDF than with BERT. The study concludes with a discussion of the results and suggestions for future research.

Keywords: stylometry · natural language processing · Polish · BERT · TF-IDF · MaxLogit

1 Introduction

The goal of the multidisciplinary scientific discipline of stylometry [6,14] is to investigate the connection between the statistical characteristics of texts and their meta-characteristics (such as authorship, literary period). The majority of stylometric investigations focus on authorship attribution and English-language texts [12]. Authorship attribution is primarily focused on two categories of texts: literary texts [3,17] and inter-person communication texts (emails, social media posts) [2,8,9].

The paper aims to address the issue of identifying an author of literary texts based on text passages of varying length, ranging from 100 to 2,000 words. The proposed approach involves classifying short text fragments of 100 words and then analyzing the sequence of decisions for each subsequent fragment to make

© The Author(s), under exclusive license to Springer Nature Switzerland AG 2023
L. Rutkowski et al. (Eds.): ICAISC 2023, LNAI 14125, pp. 296–303, 2023.
https://doi.org/10.1007/978-3-031-42505-9_26

a decision for the whole passage. The study is built upon previous research [16] on authorship attribution of Polish literary texts from the late 19th and early 20th centuries, which found that the TF-IDF [15] with the multilayer perceptron [10] outperformed other techniques. Despite being the state-of-the-art in text classification, BERT [5] was found to be ineffective in the analyzed task.

Therefore, we explore whether the problem with BERT in authorship attribution can be mitigated by removing named entities from the input data. Next, we propose replacing posteriori probabilities (used in [16]) with logits in sequence classification.

The paper is structured as follows. Section 2 describes the used corpus and the sequence classification method. The next section shows three group of results: baseline, name entity masking approach and usage of logits in sequence classification. They are followed by a discussion. Finally, conclusions are given.

2   Methods

2.1   Data Set

Following experiments described in [16], we performed our experiments on a collection of 99 Polish novels written by 33 different authors [7]. The novels were split into training and testing sets at random, with a ratio of 2:1. Each novel was then segmented into fragments consisting of 100 words, and the original order of these fragments was retained to enable classification based on consecutive fragments consisting a passage. Notably, the passages in the training set were from different novels than those in the testing set, mimicking a realistic scenario in which a passage from a book is being analyzed without being encountered during the learning phase.

2.2   Classification of Passages

The objective of the paper is to determine the identity of an author using a passage from a book, with the analyzed segments ranging from 100 to 2,000 words in length. The classification process involves the following steps:

- developing a classifier using fragments of fixed length (100 words) as training data;
- applying the classifier to each fragment in the input passage;
- using the classifier outputs (such as posterior probabilities) for each fragment to build the decision for a passage.

2.3   Max Softmax Probability Method

In [16], the authors proposed a sequence classifier that involves identifying the author (class) with the highest sum of posteriori probabilities estimated by the classifier. To implement this, the softmax output $p_c(x_i)$ for each fragment x_i of class c is calculated. The passage classifier for a series of consecutive fragments is then determined using the MSP (maximum of softmax probabilities) rule:

$$\arg\max_c \sum_i p_c(x_i). = \arg\max_c \sum_i \frac{e^{f_c(x_i)}}{\sum_j e^{f_j(x_i)}} \tag{1}$$

where $f_c(x)$ is the unnormalized logits of classifier f on input x. The BERT implantation does not return softmax values, but only raw logits.

3   Experiments and Results

3.1   Baseline

As a first step, we wanted to establish a baseline for further improvements. Therefore, we used two classification methods from [16], i.e., TF-IDF (with 5,000 words from texts) with MLP and the tuned BERT network (with Polbert[1] as the underlying language model). We trained MLP and BERT on a training dataset of 100 word fragments from books. Next, we identified the authorship of test set passages following the method described in Sect. 2.3 Results for passages ranging from 100 to 2,000 words are presented in Fig. 1.

We can observe that the accuracy improves consistently as the length of a passage increases. Additionally, BERT performs better than TF-IDF for shorter passages of up to 700 words, but TF-IDF outperforms BERT for longer texts.

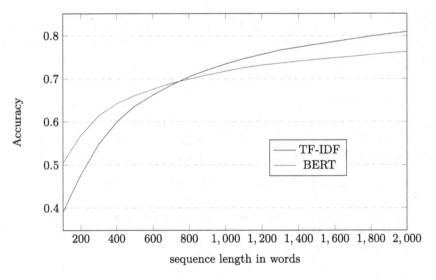

Fig. 1. Results of the baseline methods: accuracy scores for TF-IDF and BERT with MSP sequence classifier, evaluated on passages ranging from 100 to 2,000 words.

---

[1] https://huggingface.co/dkleczek/bert-base-polish-uncased-v1.

3.2 Name Entity Masking

In the second step, we aimed to address the issue of BERT overfitting to data in author attribution tasks, as reported in [16]. We wanted to make the training process more challenging for BERT and prevent the network from memorizing named entities from books. In many cases, the same places and names are mentioned repeatedly throughout a book, and focusing the network on these named entities could make the training easier. However, the names of characters in other books by the same author may differ, making such features misleading for the network. Therefore, we masked all named entities in the books by replacing them with a dedicated token [MASK]. To achieve this, we used Named Entity Recognition for Polish (NER) and the XMLRoberta architecture (as described in [4]). This architecture was trained to detect name entity boundary and fine-grained categorization (82 types were used) [13].

The achieved results are presented in Fig. 2. The solid lines represent the results from the baseline, while the dashed lines represent the results obtained by named entity masking. We can observe that this masking slightly decreases the TF-IDF results, while in the case of BERT, it leads to an increase in accuracy of around 0.02. Consequently, the length of passages for which BERT outperforms TF-IDF has shifted to 900 words. The experiments have demonstrated that named entities are one of the reasons for BERT's overfitting to training data, but there is still room for further improvement.

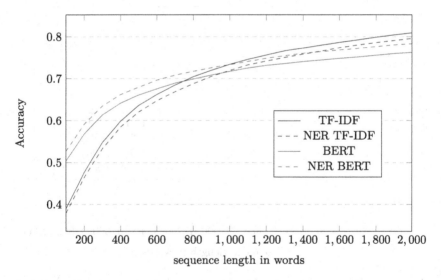

Fig. 2. The results of the NER masking method (dashed lines) compared to the basic methods (solid lines).

3.3   MaxLogit

The Maximum Softmax Probability (MSP) can be interpreted as a classification confidence score. However, due to the normalization used in the softmax function, it can mix two different cases. It can produce small values when the input object's exact class is difficult to determine (as the probability mass can be dispersed among similar classes), or the object is unfamiliar and considered an outlier [11]. Similarly, it can give large values when the object's class is easy to determine, or the object is unfamiliar, but more familiar to a given class than others. To overcome this problem, we propose using the maximum of the sum of unnormalized logit scores for a sequence detection. This approach follows the method used in Out-of-Distribution called MaxLogit [11].

Therefore, the MaxLogit sequence classifier is given by formula:

$$\arg\max_c \sum_i f_c(x_i). \tag{2}$$

The results for the MaxLogit sequence classifier (dashed lines) are presented in Fig. 3. We can observe that MaxLogit improves the accuracy of BERT by approximately 0.02. However, the improvement for TF-IDF is much more significant, at around 0.09. Furthermore, TF-IDF consistently provides better results than BERT for passages longer than 400 words.

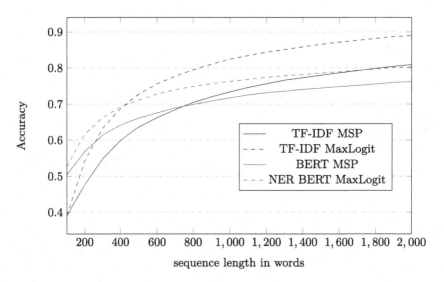

Fig. 3. The results of the MaxLogit based sequence classifier (dashed lines) compared to the baseline methods (solid lines).

3.4 Detail Results

Table 1 shows the accuracy for combination of all methods: TF-IDF/BERT, with or without name entity masking, and MSP/MaxLogit for sequence classification. The best results are marked in bold.

Table 1. Accuracy scores for TF-IDF and BERT with MSP/MaxLogit sequence classifier and with and without NER masking, evaluated on passages ranging from 100 to 2,000 words.

Model	NER	Averaging	100	200	300	500	700	1,000	1,500	2,000
TF-IDF	no	MSP	0.3901	0.4763	0.5486	0.6361	0.6846	0.7337	0.7798	0.8091
	yes	MSP	0.3790	0.4645	0.5337	0.6203	0.6687	0.7193	0.7657	0.7957
	no	MaxLogit	0.3901	0.5430	0.6332	**0.7269**	**0.7769**	**0.8246**	**0.8657**	**0.8900**
	yes	MaxLogit	0.3790	0.5247	0.6102	0.7023	0.7513	0.7970	0.8350	0.8583
BERT	no	MSP	0.5040	0.5679	0.6141	0.6609	0.6892	0.7171	0.7444	0.7624
	yes	MSP	**0.5269**	0.5911	0.6354	0.6793	0.7081	0.7333	0.7644	0.7832
	no	MaxLogit	0.5040	0.5958	0.6401	0.6909	0.7168	0.7436	0.7694	0.7836
	yes	MaxLogit	**0.5269**	**0.6165**	**0.6627**	0.7109	0.7397	0.7626	0.7857	0.8028

4 Conclusion

The authors presented and tested two improvements in the task of identifying the author of a book passage of varying length, i.e., the masking of name entities and the usage of raw logits in sequence classification.

The achieved results demonstrate that machine learning methods are capable of almost perfect authorship attribution on short texts, with accuracy increasing from approximately 53% for 100-word passages to 89% for 2,000-word passages. The proposed MaxLogit approach significantly improves results (by approximately 9% in the case of TF-IDF). However, except in the case of short passages up to 400 words, we were not able to obtain better results for BERT than for TF-IDF.

Future plans include further improving the performance of BERT using metric learning approaches [1], as well as conducting similar analyses on text in English and Spanish.

Acknowledgements. Financed by the European Regional Development Fund as a part of the 2014–2020 Smart Growth Operational Programme, CLARIN - Common Language Resources and Technology Infrastructure, project no. POIR.04.02.00-00C002/19.

References

1. Bellet, A., Habrard, A., Sebban, M.: Metric learning, synthesis lectures on artificial intelligence and machine learning, vol. 9. Morgan & Claypool Publishers (USA), Synthesis Lectures on Artificial Intelligence and Machine Learning, pp. 1–151 (2015). https://doi.org/10.2200/S00626ED1V01Y201501AIM030, https://hal.archives-ouvertes.fr/hal-01121733
2. Calix, K., Connors, M., Levy, D., Manzar, H., McCabe, G., Westcott, S.: Stylometry for e-mail author identification and authentication (2008)
3. Can, M.: Authorship attribution using principal component analysis and competitive neural networks. Math. Comput. Appl. **19**(1), 21–36 (2014)
4. Conneau, A., et al.: Unsupervised cross-lingual representation learning at scale. In: Proceedings of the 58th Annual Meeting of the Association for Computational Linguistics, pp. 8440–8451 (2020). https://doi.org/10.18653/v1/2020.acl-main.747
5. Devlin, J., Chang, M.W., Lee, K., Toutanova, K.: BERT: pre-training of deep bidirectional transformers for language understanding. arXiv preprint arXiv:1810.04805 (2018)
6. Eder, M., Piasecki, M., Walkowiak, T.: Open stylometric system based on multi-level text analysis. Cognitive Studies — Études cognitives 17 (2017). https://doi.org/10.11649/cs.1430
7. Eder, M., Rybicki, J.: Late 19th- and early 20th-century polish novels (2015). http://hdl.handle.net/11321/57, CLARIN-PL digital repository
8. Fabien, M., Villatoro-Tello, E., Motlicek, P., Parida, S.: BertAA : BERT fine-tuning for authorship attribution. In: Proceedings of the 17th International Conference on Natural Language Processing (ICON), pp. 127–137. NLP Association of India (NLPAI), Indian Institute of Technology Patna, Patna, India (2020). https://aclanthology.org/2020.icon-main.16
9. Grivas, A., Krithara, A., Giannakopoulos, G.: Author profiling using stylometric and structural feature groupings. In: Working Notes of CLEF 2015 - Conference and Labs of the Evaluation forum, Toulouse, France, September 8–11, 2015. CEUR Workshop Proceedings, vol. 1391. CEUR-WS.org (2015). http://ceur-ws.org/Vol-1391/68-CR.pdf
10. Hastie, T., Tibshirani, R., Friedman, J.: The Elements of Statistical Learning. SSS, Springer, New York (2009). https://doi.org/10.1007/978-0-387-84858-7
11. Hendrycks, D., et al.: Scaling out-of-distribution detection for real-world settings. In: Chaudhuri, K., Jegelka, S., Song, L., Szepesvari, C., Niu, G., Sabato, S. (eds.) Proceedings of the 39th International Conference on Machine Learning. Proceedings of Machine Learning Research, vol. 162, pp. 8759–8773. PMLR (17–23 Jul 2022). https://proceedings.mlr.press/v162/hendrycks22a.html
12. Juola, P.: Authorship attribution. Found. Trends Inf. Retr. **1**(3), 233–334 (2006). https://doi.org/10.1561/1500000005
13. Marcińczuk, M., Kocoń, J., Oleksy, M.: Liner2 – a generic framework for named entity recognition. In: Proceedings of the 6th Workshop on Balto-Slavic Natural Language Processing, pp. 86–91. Association for Computational Linguistics, Valencia, Spain (2017). https://doi.org/10.18653/v1/W17-1413, https://aclanthology.org/W17-1413
14. Päpcke, S., Weitin, T., Herget, K., Glawion, A., Brandes, U.: Stylometric similarity in literary corpora: Non-authorship clustering and Deutscher Novellenschatz. Digital Scholarship in the Humanities (2022). https://doi.org/10.1093/llc/fqac039, fqac039

15. Salton G, B.C.: Term-weighting approaches in automatic text retrieval. Info. Process. Manage. **24**(5), 513–523 (1988)
16. Walkowiak, T.: Author attribution of literary texts in polish by the sequence averaging. In: Rutkowski, L., Scherer, R., Korytkowski, M., Pedrycz, W., Tadeusiewicz, R., Zurada, J.M. (eds.) Artificial Intelligence and Soft Computing, pp. 367–376. Springer International Publishing, Cham (2023). https://doi.org/10.1007/978-3-031-23480-4_31
17. Walkowiak, T., Piasecki, M.: Stylometry analysis of literary texts in polish. In: Rutkowski, L., Scherer, R., Korytkowski, M., Pedrycz, W., Tadeusiewicz, R., Zurada, J.M. (eds.) Artificial Intelligence and Soft Computing, pp. 777–787. Springer International Publishing, Cham (2018). https://doi.org/10.1007/978-3-319-91262-2_68

Gates Are Not What You Need in RNNs

Ronalds Zakovskis[1]([⊠]) [iD], Andis Draguns[2] [iD], Eliza Gaile[1] [iD], Emils Ozolins[2] [iD], and Karlis Freivalds[3] [iD]

[1] Faculty of Computing, University of Latvia, Riga, Latvia
`ronalds.zakovskis@gmail.com`, `eliiza.gaile@gmail.com`
[2] Institute of Mathematics and Computer Science, University of Latvia, Riga, Latvia
`andis.draguns@lumii.lv`, `ozolinsemils@gmail.com`
[3] Institute of Electronics and Computer Science, Riga, Latvia
`karlis.freivalds@edi.lv`

Abstract. Recurrent neural networks have flourished in many areas. Consequently, we can see new RNN cells being developed continuously, usually by creating or using gates in a new, original way. But what if we told you that gates in RNNs are redundant? In this paper, we propose a new recurrent cell called *Residual Recurrent Unit* (RRU) which beats traditional cells and does not employ a single gate. It is based on the residual shortcut connection, linear transformations, ReLU, and normalization. To evaluate our cell's effectiveness, we compare its performance against the widely-used GRU and LSTM cells and the recently proposed Mogrifier LSTM on several tasks including, polyphonic music modeling, language modeling, and sentiment analysis. Our experiments show that RRU outperforms the traditional gated units on most of these tasks. Also, it has better robustness to parameter selection, allowing immediate application in new tasks without much tuning. We have implemented the RRU in TensorFlow, and the code is made available at https://github.com/LUMII-Syslab/RRU.

Keywords: Recurrent neural networks · Residual neural networks · Gates · Robustness · Deep learning ·

1 Introduction

Recurrent neural networks (RNN) have achieved widespread use in sequence processing tasks such as language modeling, speech and music recognition. RNNs are composed of a single computation cell, called Recurrent Unit which is unrolled along the sequence dimension.

In order to achieve stable training and the ability to store and make use of long-term dependencies, the recurrent units are designed in a special way. The

---

We would like to thank the Faculty of Computing, University of Latvia for covering the costs related to the conference, the IMCS UL Scientific Cloud for the computing power, and Leo Trukšāns for the technical support. This research is funded by the Latvian Council of Science, project No. lzp-2018/1-0327 and lzp-2021/1-0479.

L. Rutkowski et al. (Eds.): ICAISC 2023, LNAI 14125, pp. 304–324, 2023.
https://doi.org/10.1007/978-3-031-42505-9_27

most well-known units are LSTM and GRU, which use a gating mechanism to store and extract information from the recurrent state. Two kinds of gates are used in these units – reset gates and update gates, where each of them is based on modulating the state information with the input information and is implemented by multiplying two values, one of which is often range-limited by the sigmoid function. Gates are considered crucial for the propagation of long-term information [6] and virtually all proposals of Recurrent Units, including numerous recent developments, contain such multiplicative input-state interactions. Recent developments of improved RNN variants contain even more multiplicative interactions [13] that culminate in Mogrifier LSTM, where the input information is modulated through a series of reset gates [17]. They find that about five reset gates achieve the best performance yielding Mogrifier LSTM to be the top-performing RNN cell on several datasets so far.

In contrast, we show that gates are not essential at all to construct a well-performing recurrent unit. To this end, we develop a recurrent cell not containing a single gate (see the visualization in Fig. 1). The proposed cell surpasses not only GRU and LSTM but also the so-far best Mogrifier LSTM on many commonly used benchmark tasks. Our cell is based on a residual ReLU network employing normalization and ReZero [1] recurrent state update. If well-performing recurrent units without gates can be created, perhaps we shouldn't think of gates every time we think of recurrent networks and maybe this insight could help us create strong non-gated networks in the future.

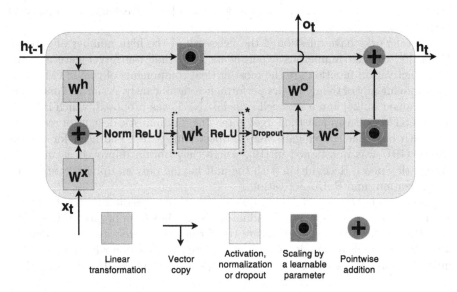

Fig. 1. The structure of the *Residual Recurrent Unit* (RRU) with two state-input linear transformations. The dotted brackets cover the layer which can be used zero or more times, in this case - once.

2 Relation to Prior Work

A great number of RNN cells have been developed. They usually use gates to ensure stable training over many time steps. The most well-known is LSTM [9] which has an extra cell state that can pass information directly forward and three gates (forget, input, and output) that control the data flow. This specific structure has allowed it to become a state-of-the-art cell, still being used extensively to this day. Its success is considered to stem from the 3 gates at its core, and since then, it has been considered that RNN cells need gates for optimal performance.

Following the success of the LSTM, a new cell called GRU [5] was proposed, which is loosely based on LSTM and often referred to as the light version of the LSTM. This cell combines the forget and input gates of an LSTM, resulting in 2 gates total – reset gate and update gate. As a lighter cell, it can be computed faster while the results are often similar.

Based on the marvelous results of LSTM and GRU, many extensions and modifications have been proposed. Phased LSTM [18] introduce a new time gate. Gating also in the depthwise direction is explored in [11,26]. The power of multiplicative interactions, which is the central operation in gates, is explored in [13,25]. The number of gates is brought to the culmination in Mogrifier LSTM, which does input and hidden state modulation by multiple rounds of reset gates [17]. Their results suggest that using about five rounds of reset gates gives the optimal performance and positions Mogrifier LSTM as the currently best RNN cell in WikiText-2, Penn Treebank word-level, and Penn Treebank character-level tasks.

Several works have questioned the necessity of the high number of gates in RNNs. [6], through numerous experiments, find that the forget gate and the output activation function are the most critical components of the LSTM block, and removing any of them impairs performance significantly. A similar conclusion was obtained in [24] and a new cell called JANET was proposed, which is based on the LSTM but uses just the forget gate. The minimalistic designs of recurrent cells with only one forget gate were proposed in [8,28]. The need for a reset gate in GRU was questioned in [19], where they obtain improved accuracy in Automatic Speech Recognition with the unit having only an update gate, Batch Normalization, and ReLU activation.

There has been some tinkering done with using a residual shortcut connection in RNNs. Consequently, a Residual RNN [27] has been proposed. Res-RNN and gRes-RNN were proposed, where the former is a purely residual recurrent network and the latter combines residual shortcut connection with a gate. Their units show improved speed but are not able to unequivocally beat LSTM in terms of accuracy. [12] proposes a Residual LSTM, which is a mix between a regular LSTM and a residual shortcut connection to improve performance in case of many layers. Even with the addition of the residual shortcut connection, it still contains a high number of gates.

3   Residual Recurrent Unit

We propose a new cell that does not contain a single gate but provides a competitive performance. We call this cell the *Residual Recurrent Unit*, RRU for short. The cell consists of a residual shortcut connection and several linear transformations employing Normalization and ReZero [1] recurrent state update. ReZero is a simple zero-initialized parameter that controls how much of the residual branch contributes to the updated state. ReZero helps us make the unit structure gateless, which makes it more simple. As it is initialized as 0, only the previous state is taken into effect at the first few training steps, and the optimal weight for the residual branch emerges during training. ReZero ResNet has been shown to have a non-vanishing gradient yielding stable training for very deep convolutional networks and Transformers [1] and achieving great results. Here we adapt it to replace gates in recurrent networks to see what benefits it could give to recurrent units.

The visualization of our cell can be seen in Fig. 1. RRU takes input x_t at the current time-step t which is a vector of dimension m and the previous state h_{t-1} of dimension n and produces the updated state h_t and the output o_t of dimension p. The calculations done in the RRU, are described as:

$$j_t = \text{ReLU}(\text{Normalize}(W^x x_t + W^h h_{t-1} + b^j)) \tag{1}$$
$$[j_t = \text{ReLU}(W^k j_t + b^k)]^* \tag{2}$$
$$d_t = \text{Dropout}(j_t) \tag{3}$$
$$c_t = W^c d_t + b^c \tag{4}$$
$$h_t = \sigma(S) \odot h_{t-1} + Z \odot c_t \tag{5}$$
$$o_t = W^o d_t + b^o \tag{6}$$

In the above equations, upper case letters depict the learnable parameters. Weight matrices with their respective dimensions are: $W^x \in \mathbb{R}^{m \times g}$; $W^h \in \mathbb{R}^{n \times g}$; $W^k \in \mathbb{R}^{g \times g}$; $W^o \in \mathbb{R}^{g \times p}$; $W^c \in \mathbb{R}^{g \times n}$, where g is the hidden size which we choose to be equal to $q*(m+n)$, and q is the middle layer size multiplier (we typically use values from 0.1 to 8.0). Bias vectors and their dimensions are: $b^j \in \mathbb{R}^g$; $b^k \in \mathbb{R}^g$, $b^o \in \mathbb{R}^p$; $b^c \in \mathbb{R}^n$. There are two learnable scaling factors S and Z of dimension n. The sigmoid function is denoted as σ, $[\cdot]^*$ denotes the use of the equation inside the brackets zero or more times, and $\odot$ denotes scalar multiplication.

The structure of RRU is similar to the ReZero residual network [1]. At first, the previous hidden state h_{t-1} and the input of the current timestep x_t are passed through a linear transformation followed by L2 normalization and ReLU. Then, zero or more linear transformations follow employing ReLU activation. To make the formulas clearer, Eq. 2 has two vectors named j_t, in reality, each layer has its own W^k and B^k. This value is a hyperparameter, for which each dataset has a specific value that works best, usually 1 or 2. Dropout [21] follows, and the result is linearly transformed to get two values - the output of the current timestep o_t and the hidden state candidate c_t. The next hidden state h_t is produced by a weighted sum of the previous state and the candidate. The candidate is scaled by a zero-initialized parameter Z according to the ReZero principle. There is a slight difference from the ReZero paper in that we use a separate scale for each feature map, but ReZero uses a common scaling factor for all maps, see Sect. 6 for evidence that our version works better.

Another difference from the traditional ResNet architecture is that we have introduced a scaling factor S for the residual connection (ResNet has a fixed $S = 1$). Such change is motivated by the need for the recurrent network to forget some of the information from the previous time steps. The scale S is limited to the range $0 - 1$ by the sigmoid function to eliminate unstable behavior in some cases, especially if S has become negative. Since $S < 1$, the cell's memories gradually fade out. Note that is a learnable parameter (for each feature map separately) so the network can choose the rate of forgetting. Such fade-out is not so flexible as a forget gate employed in other cells but the network can compensate for it using the residual branch c. We have observed that the value of S actually changes during training, mainly decreasing for most of the feature maps. This can be explained that the network initially uses the residual connection to provide a stable gradient for training but later learns to rely on the c value more which provides greater control. The value of S is initialized in the way that after the sigmoid, it is uniformly distributed in the range $0 - 1$. This idea is suggested by [7] and relieves us from the need for another hyperparameter that needs to be tuned. We also experimented with a constant initialization of S; that worked similarly but required an adequate constant, usually in the range $0.4 - 0.95$ depending on the dataset (see Sect. 6). The ablation study also shows that S is important in general; for Penn Treebank removing the scaling produces a significantly worse result.

The initial hidden state h_0 is prepared to have all zeros except the first feature map, which is set to $\frac{1}{4}\sqrt{n}$. Initializing with all zeroes causes a blowup due to the employed normalization in the case when zeros are given also as the input values x_t in the first timesteps. Such inputs may occur if the input is padded by zeros from some shorter sequence.

Note that although Eq. 5 resembles the update gate of LSTM, it is not because in the update gate, both of the multiplied values depend on the input or hidden state but in our case, S and Z are learnable parameters – effectively constants after training.

4   Experiments

To test our unit's performance against the chosen competitors (GRU, LSTM, Mogrifier LSTM), we run experiments on language modeling, music modeling, sentiment analysis, and MNIST image classification tasks. These tasks are commonly used for evaluating recurrent networks. All chosen units are equivalent in terms of trainable parameters in our experiments, to ensure a fair comparison.

For polyphonic music modeling, the task is to predict the next note when knowing the previous ones. The model's performance is measured by negative log-likelihood (NLL) loss which sums the negative logarithm of all the correct prediction probabilities. For this task, we chose four datasets that are usually evaluated together - JSB Chorales, Nottingham, MuseData, Piano-midi.de [4]. They are already split into training, validation, and testing portions. For word-level language modeling, we use the Penn Treebank dataset [16]. The aim of this dataset is to predict the next word by knowing the previous ones. The network's performance is measured in perplexity, which is the probability that a word will show up as the next word from the previous context. For character-level language modeling datasets we chose enwik8 [10], text8[1] and Penn Treebank [16]. The aim is to predict the next character from the previous ones. The performance is measured in BPC (bits per character), which is the number of bits used to represent a single character from the text. Although word-level and character-level tasks may seem similar, they evaluate different aspects of the cell. The word-level task has a large vocabulary, so the emphasis is put on evaluating RRU's ability to deal with diverse inputs, but the character-level task has a large window size requiring the cell to remember and process long history.

The goal for the IMDB sentiment analysis dataset [15] is to predict the sentiment of the text as either positive or negative. This dataset is of interest because it is quite different from the previous ones. The performance of the network is measured as the accuracy of the predictions. The challenging part of the dataset is to learn the hidden state in a way that can understand even complicated structures, for example, double negatives, etc.

A frequently used dataset for evaluating recurrent networks is MNIST image classification. RNNs are not well suited for image classification; therefore, it puts every aspect of the network under stress. The aim here is to predict the number that each picture represents by processing a sequence that consists of all the pixels in the picture.

For music modeling and word-level language modeling, we run hyperparameter optimization on each cell, using Bayesian hyperparameter tuning from the HyperOpt library [3]. The optimized hyperparameters include: the number of learnable parameters, dropout rate, learning rate, and some of the most influential hyperparameters specific to each cell; for more detailed configurations see Appendix D. The RRU cell has a built-in dropout, so to get an equitable environment, we added recurrent dropout to GRU, LSTM, and Mogrifier LSTM as described in [20]. For character-level Penn Treebank, we also run optimization, but we only grid search through the different dropout rates from 0.0 to 0.9 – and the best testing result from these runs is shown in the results table. This experiment is further described in Appendix A. For the rest of the datasets, hyperparameter tuning would require computational power exceeding our bud-

---

[1] http://mattmahoney.net/dc/textdata.

Table 1. Evaluation results on each task. The "+/-" notation means that we did a grid search through ten different dropout values to find the one which performs the best. Every metric over the horizontal line is better if it is lower and every metric under it is better if it is higher.

Task	Tuned	RRU	GRU	LSTM	Mogrifier LSTM
Music JSB Chorales (NLL)	+	**7.72**	8.20	8.33	8.18
Music Nottingham (NLL)	+	**2.92**	3.22	3.25	3.28
Music MuseData (NLL)	+	**7.03**	7.31	7.24	7.22
Music Piano-midi.de (NLL)	+	**7.38**	7.58	7.54	7.52
Word-level Penn Treebank (Perplexity)	+	**102.56**	122.21	140.35	126.88
Character-level Penn Treebank (BPC)	+/-	**1.27**	1.28	1.34	1.29
Character-level enwik8 (BPC)	-	1.37	1.53	1.49	**1.36**
Character-level text8 (BPC)	-	**1.35**	1.55	1.44	1.37
Sentiment analysis IMDB (Accuracy)	-	**87.20**	87.04	85.89	86.23
Sequential MNIST (Accuracy)	-	**98.74**	98.36	92.88	98.14
Permuted MNIST (Accuracy)	-	97.67	**98.68**	97.39	97.81

get, so we only run a singular experiment on each cell on as fair a configuration as possible, that is, we try to use the same configuration but sometimes changes to the configuration have to be made, for more details see Appendix D.

Each experiment was done on a single machine with 16 GB RAM and a single NVIDIA T4 GPU, time spent during a single, full training varies from averagely 4 min (JSB Chorales) to averagely 115 h (enwik8). We use RAdam optimizer [14] with gradient clipping. We train each dataset until the validation loss stops decreasing for 3–11 epochs, depending on the dataset.

Results of all of these experiments can be seen in Table 1. RRU is a definite leader giving the best performance on almost all of the datasets. Notably, RRU scores on top for all fully hyperparameter-optimized cases. In the two cases where RRU is outperformed, it still comes close, and it is probable that RRU would achieve the best performance if full hyperparameter optimization were performed for these datasets. We suspect that the RRU could reach a state-of-the-art performance score on specific datasets, but we didn't have the time and resources to spend on tuning to achieve this. Convergence graphs of some of these experiments can be seen in Appendix C, in which RRU usually converges first and with better results.

5   Robustness Against Hyperparameter Choice

One of the main reasons for LSTM's and GRU's wide usage is their robustness against hyperparameter choice; that is, usually, you can use them with some default parameters, and they will give decent results. Such property has been described in several works, one being [23]. We will test the robustness of each cell to the selection of learning rate and learnable parameter count – the two

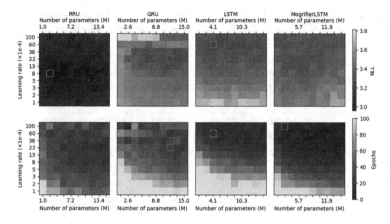

Fig. 2. Robustness against learning rate and parameter count on the Nottingham dataset. The top row gives the testing NLL, and the bottom row shows the number of epochs needed to reach the best NLL. Good results are depicted with blue color, and poor results – with yellow. The red squares correspond to runs where the training failed, and the pink frames show the run with the best NLL. We observe that RRU consistently produces the best NLL across the entire range and achieves that within a small number of epochs. (Color figure online)

most important hyperparameters. We run a grid search on the Nottingham music modeling dataset with a reasonably wide hyperparameter range for all the cells. We plot the validation NLL and the number of epochs needed to reach the best accuracy as heatmaps in Fig. 2. The figure shows that our cell has a much broader range of parameters in which it works well, which also means that our cell can be used successfully without much parameter tuning. Further robustness experiments can be seen in Appendix B.

6 Ablation Study

In this section, we investigate the influence of the key elements in our cell by replacing them with simpler ones to determine whether our cell's structure is optimal. We compare the RRU performance against versions with:

- Removed normalization.
- Using a single scalar multiplier Z for all feature maps as proposed in the ReZero paper [1]. Our cell uses a different multiplier for each map.
- Added ReLU over Eqs. 4 and 6. Such a setup is employed in some ResNet architectures [29,30] and could have more expressive power.
- Residual weight S set as a constant with a scalar value 1 i.e. using an unscaled residual shortcut connection, expressing Eq. 5 as $h_t = h_{t-1} + Z \odot c_t$.
- Residual weight S initialization with a scalar value 0.95 instead of a random one.

Table 2. Ablation study results for all of the datasets. "Character-level Penn Treebank" is denoted as "Character PTB" and "Word-level Penn Treebank" is denoted as "Word PTB" to save space.

Version	Character PTB (BPC)	IMDB (Accuracy)	Sequential MNIST (Accuracy)	Nottingham (NLL)	Word PTB (Perplexity)
RRU	**1.32**	**87.45**	**98.74**	**2.92**	**102.70**
no normalization	**1.32**	87.21	98.03	**2.92**	104.60
single scalar ReZero	**1.32**	87.08	98.45	2.97	104.44
ReLU over c and o_t	1.34	87.17	86.38	3.07	120.76
$S = 1$	2.25	86.78	98.43	3.56	110.74
S initialized with 0.95	1.33	86.71	98.60	2.96	103.09

For these experiments, we have chosen character-level Penn Treebank, IMDB, Sequential MNIST datasets, on which we do a single run, and Nottingham, word-level Penn Treebank, on which we optimize the hyperparameters as described in Sect. 4. For each dataset's configuration see the respective dataset's configuration for RRU in Sect. 4, except for character-level Penn Treebank for which the configuration differs by the dropout rate which isn't tuned, but set as 0.3. The results can be seen in Table 2. We conclude that the current structure of our cell gives the best performance. Interestingly, the considered simplifications produce only slightly worse results, suggesting that the RRU's structure is robust to changes. Although great results can be achieved without normalization, it seems to give the RRU more stability during the training and contributes to robustness (see Appendix B). We notice that our approach of using a different ReZero multiplier for each hidden map gives better performance than using only the singular scalar ReZero parameter. Adding another ReLU over the vectors c_t and o_t does not help. Passing the full state without a scaling factor S decreases performance. Using constant initialization seems to give a similar performance, but in these experiments, the random initialization gave us better results with the added bonus of fewer hyperparameters to tune.

7   Conclusion

By developing a new RNN cell without any gates and showing that it outperforms the gated cells on many tasks, we have demonstrated that gates are not necessary for RNNs. Our proposed RRU cell is robust to parameter selection and can be used in new tasks without much tuning. RRU has roughly the same speed as pure TensorFlow implementations of LSTM or GRU, and we look forward to low-level optimized CUDA RRU implementation that matches the speed of optimized LSTM and GRU implementations. We expect that the insights gained in this work will contribute to further improvements in the designs of recurrent and residual networks.

A   Appendix 1 - Dropout Analysis

While running experiments, we noticed that our cell seems to handle dropout better than the other cells. To test this observation, we ran a grid search on Nottingham and character-level Penn Treebank datasets for each cell through

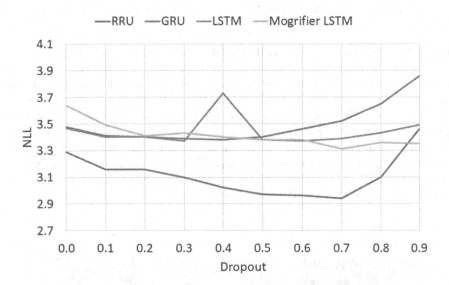

Fig. 3. NLL (lower is better) depending on the dropout rate for each cell on the Nottingham dataset.

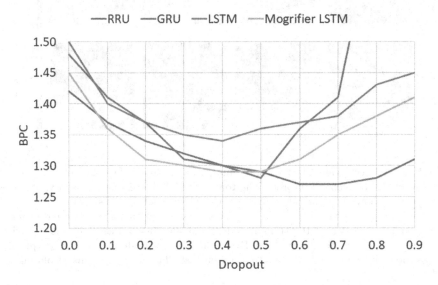

Fig. 4. BPC (lower is better) depending on the dropout rate for each cell on the character-level Penn Treebank dataset.

different dropout rates – from 0.0 to 0.9, for more details of the configurations used see Appendix D. The results from these experiments can be seen in Figs. 3 and 4. From these results, we can see that all cells benefit from dropout, but for RRU, its impact is much more pronounced, and RRU ultimately reaches better final results than the other cells. We can also see that the RRU works best with a dropout rate of around 0.7. Possibly, dropout is better suited for ReLU networks, as is RRU, rather than for gated networks.

B   Appendix 2 - Further Robustness Experiments

In Sect. 5 we tested the robustness of our cell. Here we will do the same experiment on a different dataset, the word-level Penn Treebank, to furthermore test the robustness. We plot the validation perplexity and the number of epochs needed to reach the best accuracy as heatmaps in Fig. 5. The figure shows that our cell has a much broader range of parameters in which it works well, which also means that our cell can be used successfully without much parameter tuning. We also notice that the LSTM and the Mogrifier LSTM had trouble learning anything at all on very small learning rates.

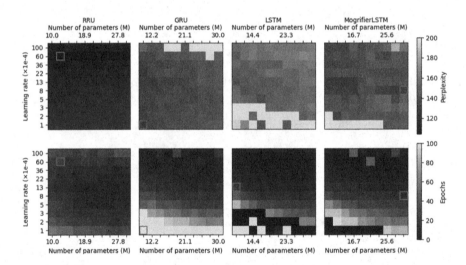

Fig. 5. Robustness against learning rate and parameter count for different cells on the word-level Penn Treebank dataset. The top row gives the testing perplexity, and the bottom row shows the number of epochs needed to reach the best perplexity. Good results are depicted with blue color, and poor results – with yellow. The red squares correspond to runs where the training failed, and the pink frames show the run with the best perplexity. We observe that RRU consistently produces the best perplexity across the entire range and achieves that within a small number of epochs. (Color figure online)

In Sect. 6 we looked at different RRU versions from which we concluded that our version tops the other versions, but we want to show in more detail why normalization is beneficial in the RRU. We will compare the RRU with and without normalization with the robustness tests as described in Sect. 5. We plot the validation loss and the number of epochs needed to reach the best accuracy as heatmaps in Fig. 6 and 7. We observe that RRU with normalization consistently produces the best loss across the entire range and achieves that within a small number of epochs which shows that normalization helps gain a much broader range of parameters in which it works well and helps avoid failed training sessions.

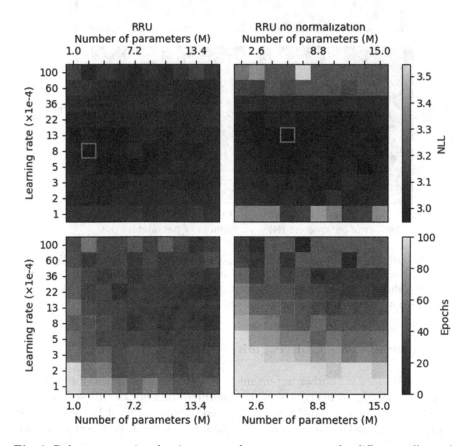

Fig. 6. Robustness against leaning rate and parameter count for different cells on the Nottingham dataset. The top row gives the testing NLL, and the bottom row shows the number of epochs needed to reach the best loss. Color depictions are the same as in Fig. 5. (Color figure online)

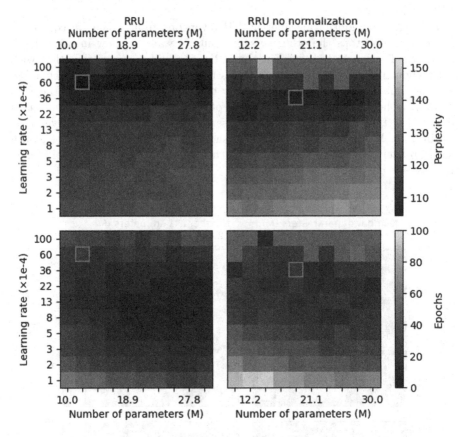

Fig. 7. Robustness against leaning rate and parameter count for different cells on the word-level Penn Treebank dataset. The top row gives the testing perplexity, and the bottom row shows the number of epochs needed to reach the best loss. Color depictions are the same as in Fig. 5. (Color figure online)

C   Appendix 3 - Convergence Speed

Convergence speed is another important factor in neural networks, for that reason, we will display convergence graphs of three datasets in this section, one for each training mode - JSB Chorales (tuned), character-level Penn Treebank (half-tuned) and IMDB (not tuned). The graphs are taken from the experiments done in Sect. 4.

The convergence graph of the JSB Chorales dataset with the best parameters found in tuning for each cell can be seen in Fig. 8. We can observe that RRU in this dataset trains much faster, beating every other cell's best NLL at the 17th epoch, which implies that early stopping could be done.

The convergence graph of the character-level Penn Treebank dataset after half-tuning (going through 10 different dropout values and taking the best one) has been done can be seen in Fig. 9. We see that the RRU beats all the other

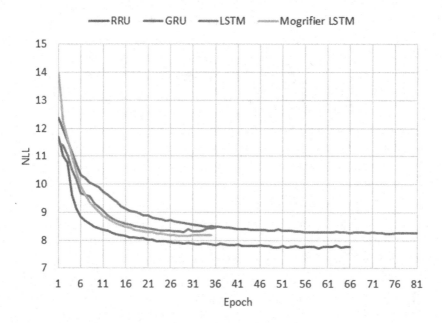

Fig. 8. Validation NLL on JSB Chorales dataset for each epoch and tuned cell.

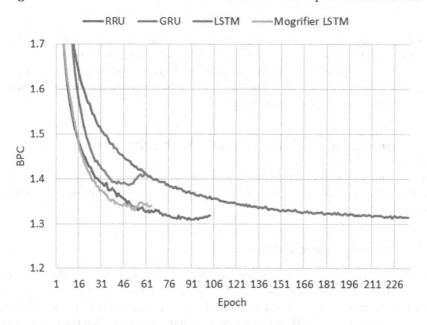

Fig. 9. Validation BPC on character-level Penn Treebank dataset for each epoch and half-tuned cell. In this Figure RRU has a 0.7 dropout, GRU has a 0.5 dropout, LSTM has a 0.4 dropout and Mogrifier LSTM has a 0.5 dropout.

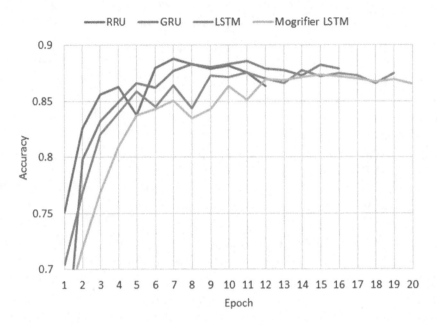

Fig. 10. Validation Accuracy on the IMDB dataset for each epoch and cell.

cells here while doing it in a similar epoch count as others, even when it has a larger dropout rate, which usually increases epoch count tremendously.

The convergence graph of the IMDB dataset can be seen in Fig. 10. In this graph, we once again see that the RRU is capable of reaching its best accuracy first and beating the other cells with it.

D   Appendix 4 - Experiment Configurations

This appendix is intended for the elaboration on the configurations of the experiments that are written in Sect. 4, but for specific configurations, we suggest contacting the author(s).

D.1   Dataset Configurations

Polyphonic music modeling datasets contain sequences of played piano-roll elements (MIDI note numbers between 21 and 108 inclusive), which we represent as a binary mask for each time step, where ones are placed in the positions corresponding to the MIDI notes played at that time step. We trim or pad the sequences to length 200, similarly to how it was done by [22].

Word-level Penn Treebank dataset is already split into training, validation and testing portions. We use a context length of 64 and a vocabulary of 10 thousand, which includes all of the words in the dataset.

Character-level Penn Treebank also is already split into training, validation, and testing portions. However, enwik8 and text8 are not, so we use the standard split for each of them, which is 90% training, 5% validation, and 5% testing. We use a window size of 512 for Penn Treebank and 256 for enwik8 and text8. The training is run in a stateful manner, meaning that we pass the old state forward to the next window (with a 10 % chance of passing a state filled with zeros).

The IMDB dataset consists of 25 thousand training sequences and 25 thousand testing sequences. We take 5 thousand sequences from the end of the training set as a validation set. We trim the sequences to length 500 and use a vocabulary of size 10 thousand created from the most frequently occurring words (there are approximately 25 thousand different words in total) to be able to fit the sequences into our GPU memory.

We use the MNIST image classification dataset in a specific way: we use Sequential MNIST in which we take the image by pixel rows and get a single sequence and Permuted MNIST in which the pixels of each row are randomly permuted according to some fixed permutation, which makes the task harder. Each 28×28 image is transformed into a sequence of 784 elements. The dataset consists of 60 thousand training images and 10 thousand testing images. We reserve 10 thousand images from the training data for validation.

D.2   Main Experiments

All four polyphonic music datasets use the same configuration. We set context size as 200 (as done in [22]), batch size as 16, and the number of layers as 1, for RRU we use 1 ReLU layer and an output size of 64, all of these values we experimentally found to work well. The training stops when there hasn't been a lower NLL for 7 epochs.

For the word-level Penn treebank, we set context size as 64, batch size as 128, number of layers as 2, and embedding size of 64, for RRU we use 1 ReLU layer and output size of 128, all of these values we experimentally found to work well. The training stops when there hasn't been a lower perplexity for 7 epochs.

For polyphonic music modeling and word-level language modeling, we run hyperparameter optimization on each cell, where we tune the learning rate, the dropout rate, and the number of parameters in 100 runs, with ranges as described in Table 3. We also tune the following parameters of the RNN cells: for RRU we tune the middle layer size multiplier q in the range [0.1; 8.0]; for the LSTM we tune the forget bias in the range [-3.0; 3.0]; for the Mogrifier LSTM we tune the feature rounds in the range [5; 6] and the feature rank in the range [40; 90], as these were mentioned as the optimal ranges in the Mogrifier LSTM paper. Optimal values for the tuned parameters for each dataset and cell can be seen in Table 4.

For character-level Penn Treebank we set the number of parameters as 24 million, learning rate as $1e - 3$, we set context size as 512, batch size as 64, the number of layers as 2, and embedding size of 16, for RRU we use 2 ReLU layers, middle layer size multiplier q as 4.0 and output size of 128, for LSTM we set forget bias as 1.0, for Mogrifier LSTM we use 4 feature mask rounds of rank

Table 3. Parameter ranges for main experiments that used tuning. ^{u} means the value is taken from the uniform scale and ^{l} means from the logarithmic scale. If '.' is present in the range, it means it includes float numbers, else the range is only from integers. 'M' means that the value is multiplied by 10^6. These ranges were picked because they seemed sufficient to include all of the optimal values, which were approximately identified in the initial experiments.

Dataset	Learning rate	Dropout rate	Number of parameters
JSB Chorales	$[1e-4; 1e-2]^l$	$[0.0; 0.8]^u$	$[1M-15M]^u$
Nottingham			
MuseData			
Piano-midi.de			
Word-level Penn Treebank			$[10M-30M]^u$

Table 4. Optimal values for the main experiments that used tuning. 'M' means that the value is multiplied by 10^6. "JSB Chorales" is denoted as "JSB", "MuseData" is denoted as "Muse", "Piano-midi.de" is denoted as "Piano" and "Word-level Penn treebank" is denoted as "Word PTB" to save space.

Parameter	JSB	Nottingham	Muse	Piano	Word PTB
RRU					
Learning rate	0.00495	0.00029	0.00030	0.00077	0.00683
Dropout rate	0.79362	0.77186	0.77518	0.71577	0.66035
Number of parameters	6.9M	2.6M	8.6M	5.9M	25.9M
Middle layer size multiplier q	1.76958	7.31994	6.85699	3.68371	6.86655
GRU					
Learning rate	0.00460	0.00454	0.00260	0.00932	0.00012
Dropout rate	0.67605	0.33787	0.64839	0.75069	0.27062
Number of parameters	1.8M	3.4M	1.9M	2.4M	10.0M
LSTM					
Learning rate	0.01000	0.00882	0.00493	0.00727	0.00162
Dropout rate	0.30081	0.20310	0.35383	0.22951	0.10384
Number of parameters	1.3M	1.3M	1.8M	11.9M	14.2M
Forget bias	0.76843	-0.04104	1.85746	0.59993	-2.33114
Mogrifier LSTM					
Learning rate	0.00255	0.00169	0.00135	0.00012	0.00074
Dropout rate	0.47521	0.73808	0.55499	0.77291	0.46872
Number of parameters	1.3M	6.0M	10.3M	2.9M	24.2M
Feature mask rounds	6	5	5	5	5
Feature mask rank	58	48	76	63	74

Table 5. Parameter values for parameters that are the same for each cell in non-tuned main experiments. "Sequential MNIST", and "P-MNIST" are denoted together as "MNISTs" and "text8", and "enwik8" are denoted together as "wiki8s". 'M' means that the value is multiplied by 10^6. [*RRU*] means the parameter is used in the RRU cell (the same denotation is used for the other cells).

Parameter	wiki8s	IMDB	MNISTs
Number of parameters	48M	20M	70K
Context size	256	512	784
Batch size	64	64	64
Number of layers	2	2	2
Embedding size	32	64	–
Breaks after ... epochs with no performance gain	3	5	5
[*RRU*] ReLU layers	2	1	1
[*RRU*] Middle layer size multiplier q	4.0	2.0	2.0
[*RRU*] Output size	128	64	64
[*LSTM*] Forget bias	1.0	1.0	1.0
[*MogrifierLSTM*] Feature mask rounds	6	5	6
[*MogrifierLSTM*] Feature mask rank	79	40	50

Table 6. Parameters that differ between cells on some datasets in non-tuned main experiments. '*' in the "Cell" field means that all cells have the same configuration.

Dataset	Cell	Learning rate	Dropout rate
enwik8	*	1e-3	0.7
text8	RRU	1e-3	0.7
	GRU	1e-4	
	LSTM	1e-3	
	Mogrifier LSTM	1e-3	
IMDB	*	1e-3	0.5
	RRU	1e-3	0.7
Sequential MNIST	GRU	1e-3	0.7
& P-MNIST	LSTM	1e-4	0.7
	Mogrifier LSTM	5e-5	0.5

24, all of these values we experimentally found to work well. The training stops when there hasn't been a lower BPC for 11 epochs. We run this configuration through ten different dropout rates from 0.0 to 0.9 and report the one with the lowest BPC.

The remaining datasets - enwik8, text8, IMDB, Sequential MNIST, and P-MNIST - are run with no tuning. We tried to use the same configuration for each of the cells, but it wasn't always possible, because for some datasets some cells were unable to train with the common configuration. The configuration that was the same for each of the cells can be seen in Table 5 and the slight differences can be seen in Table 6. All of these parameter values were experimentally found to work well. enwik8 number of parameters (48 million) were taken from the Mogrifier LSTM paper and Sequential MNIST, P-MNIST number of parameters (70 thousand) were taken from [2].

D.3   Robustness Experiments

For Nottingham here we use the same configuration as the configuration for Nottingham in the main experiments (Sect. D.2), except no tuning is done, so we set the middle layer size multiplier q as 2 and dropout rate as 0.5. There are 100 runs in total from a full grid search from learning rates $1e-4$, $2e-4$, $3e-4$, $5e-4$, $8e-4$, $13e-4$, $22e-4$, $36e-4$, $6e-3$, $1e-2$ (ten values from $1e-4$ to $1e-2$ in logarithmic scale) - and the number of parameters - 1.0M, 2.6M, 4.1M, 5.7M, 7.2M, 8.8M, 10.3M, 11.9M, 13.4M, 15.0M (ten values from 1.0M to 15.0M in uniform scale).

For word-level Penn Treebank here we use the same configuration as the configuration for word-level Penn Treebank in the main experiments (Sect. D.2), except no tuning is done, so we set middle layer size multiplier q as 2 and dropout rate as 0.5. There are 100 runs in total from a full grid search from learning rates - $1e-4$, $2e-4$, $3e-4$, $5e-4$, $8e-4$, $13e-4$, $22e-4$, $36e-4$, $6e-3$, $1e-2$ (ten values from $1e-4$ to $1e-2$ in logarithmic scale) - and the number of parameters - 10.0M, 12.2M, 14.4M, 16.7M, 18.9M, 21.1M, 23.3M, 25.6M, 27.8M, 30.0M (ten values from 10.0M to 30.0M in uniform scale).

D.4   Dropout Experiments

For Nottingham here we use the same configuration as the configuration for Nottingham in the main experiments (Sect. D.2), except no tuning is done, so we set the number of parameters to 5 million, learning rate as $1e-3$, middle layer size multiplier q as 2.0. We run this configuration through different dropout rates – from 0.0 to 0.9.

For character-level Penn Treebank experiment configuration see character-level Penn Treebank experiment configuration in Sect. D.2.

References

1. Bachlechner, T., Majumder, B.P., Mao, H.H., Cottrell, G.W., McAuley, J.: Rezero is all you need: fast convergence at large depth. arXiv preprint arXiv:2003.04887 (2020)
2. Bai, S., et al.: An empirical evaluation of generic convolutional and recurrent networks for sequence modeling. arXiv preprint arXiv:1803.01271 (2018)
3. Bergstra, J., et al.: Hyperopt: a python library for optimizing the hyperparameters of machine learning algorithms. In: Proceedings of the 12th Python in Science Conference, vol. 13, p. 20. Citeseer (2013)

4. Boulanger-Lewandowski, N., et al.: Modeling temporal dependencies in high-dimensional sequences: application to polyphonic music generation and transcription. arXiv preprint arXiv:1206.6392 (2012)

5. Cho, K., et al.: Learning phrase representations using RNN encoder-decoder for statistical machine translation. arXiv preprint arXiv:1406.1078 (2014)

6. Greff, K., Srivastava, R.K., Koutník, J., Steunebrink, B.R., Schmidhuber, J.: LSTM: a search space odyssey. IEEE Trans. Neural Netw. Learn. Syst. **28**(10), 2222–2232 (2016)

7. Gu, A., et al.: Improving the gating mechanism of recurrent neural networks. In: International Conference on Machine Learning, pp. 3800–3809. PMLR (2020)

8. Heck, J.C., Salem, F.M.: Simplified minimal gated unit variations for recurrent neural networks. In: 2017 IEEE 60th International Midwest Symposium on Circuits and Systems (MWSCAS), pp. 1593–1596. IEEE (2017)

9. Hochreiter, S., Schmidhuber, J.: Long short-term memory. Neural Comput. **9**(8), 1735–1780 (1997)

10. Hutter, M.: The human knowledge compression contest. http://prize.hutter1.net/ 6 (2012)

11. Kalchbrenner, N., Danihelka, I., Graves, A.: Grid long short-term memory. arXiv preprint arXiv:1507.01526 (2015)

12. Kim, J., et al.: Residual LSTM: design of a deep recurrent architecture for distant speech recognition. arXiv preprint arXiv:1701.03360 (2017)

13. Krause, B., Lu, L., Murray, I., Renals, S.: Multiplicative LSTM for sequence modelling. arXiv preprint arXiv:1609.07959 (2016)

14. Liu, L., et al.: On the variance of the adaptive learning rate and beyond. arXiv preprint arXiv:1908.03265 (2019)

15. Maas, A., et al.: Learning word vectors for sentiment analysis. In: Proceedings of the 49th Annual Meeting of the Association for Computational Linguistics: Human Language Technologies, pp. 142–150 (2011)

16. Marcus, M., et al.: Building a large annotated corpus of English: The Penn Treebank (1993)

17. Melis, G., Kočiskỳ, T., Blunsom, P.: Mogrifier LSTM. arXiv preprint arXiv:1909.01792 (2019)

18. Neil, D., Pfeiffer, M., Liu, S.C.: Phased LSTM: accelerating recurrent network training for long or event-based sequences. arXiv preprint arXiv:1610.09513 (2016)

19. Ravanelli, M., et al.: Light gated recurrent units for speech recognition. IEEE Trans. Emerg. Top. Comput. Intell. **2**(2), 92–102 (2018)

20. Semeniuta, S., et al.: Recurrent dropout without memory loss. arXiv preprint arXiv:1603.05118 (2016)

21. Srivastava, N., et al.: Dropout: a simple way to prevent neural networks from overfitting. J. Mach. Learn. Res. **15**(1), 1929–1958 (2014)

22. Subakan, Y.C., Smaragdis, P.: Diagonal RNNs in symbolic music modeling. In: 2017 IEEE Workshop on Applications of Signal Processing to Audio and Acoustics (WASPAA), pp. 354–358. IEEE (2017)

23. Talathi, S.S., Vartak, A.: Improving performance of recurrent neural network with relu nonlinearity. arXiv preprint arXiv:1511.03771 (2015)

24. Van Der Westhuizen, J., Lasenby, J.: The unreasonable effectiveness of the forget gate. arXiv preprint arXiv:1804.04849 (2018)

25. Wu, Y., Zhang, S., Zhang, Y., Bengio, Y., Salakhutdinov, R.: On multiplicative integration with recurrent neural networks. arXiv preprint arXiv:1606.06630 (2016)

26. Yao, K., Cohn, T., Vylomova, K., Duh, K., Dyer, C.: Depth-gated recurrent neural networks. arXiv preprint arXiv:1508.03790 9 (2015)

27. Yue, B., et al.: Residual recurrent neural networks for learning sequential representations. Information **9**(3), 56 (2018)

28. Zhou, G.B., et al.: Minimal gated unit for recurrent neural networks. Int. J. Autom.
Comput. **13**(3), 226–234 (2016)

29. He, Kaiming, Zhang, Xiangyu, Ren, Shaoqing, Sun, Jian: Identity Mappings in
Deep Residual Networks. In: Leibe, Bastian, Matas, Jiri, Sebe, Nicu, Welling, Max
(eds.) ECCV 2016. LNCS, vol. 9908, pp. 630–645. Springer, Cham (2016). https://
doi.org/10.1007/978-3-319-46493-0_38

30. He, K., et al.: Deep residual learning for image recognition. In: Proceedings of
the IEEE Conference on Computer Vision and Pattern Recognition, pp. 770–778
(2016)

Generating Image Captions in Polish Using Transformer Architecture

Michał Żebrowski[✉][iD] and Jacek Komorowski[iD]

Warsaw University of Technology, Warsaw, Poland
michal.zebrowski.mail@gmail.com, jacek.komorowski@pw.edu.pl

Abstract. This paper presents an attention-based method for image captioning. Existing deep-learning methods mainly use recurrent neural networks for producing captions. We present Transformer based image captioning method dubbed CaptFormer. Our method use convolutional neural network for image feature extraction and Transformer for generating image captions. CaptFormer is meant for generating captions in a morphologically rich fusional language, such as Polish. For evaluation of our method, we created a custom multilingual dataset. Our multilingual dataset contains English and machine-translated Polish captions. Images and English captions in our dataset comes from Flick 30K and MS COCO.

Keywords: Image captioning · NLP · Transformer

1 Introduction

Applying deep learning methods to generate image captions is an area of active development. However, most of the methods described in the literature generate captions in English [5,8,18,21]. In this paper, we focus on generating image captions in Polish, which is a morphologically rich fusional language. Image captioning is a task that combines computer vision and neural image processing. In this task, we have an image as an input and our goal is to generate a caption in natural language as an output. Effective image captioning methods have wide practical applicability and can be used in many domains, such as image indexing and retrieval, screen readers to improve the accessibility of image-based content for visually impaired people, or autonomous vehicles.

Image captioning combines computer vision and natural language processing, therefore we are facing issues from both branches of computer science. The image captioning method should be able to understand the scene presented in the image. The scene can contain objects of various types (e.g. people, animals, vehicles, furniture). Each of these objects can interact with each other (e.g. moving, pushing). The scene itself can be presented in varying lighting conditions or seen from different viewpoints. This makes the task more difficult than standard image classification or object segmentation. The image captioning method must be capable to express interactions and relations between objects in a natural

© The Author(s), under exclusive license to Springer Nature Switzerland AG 2023
L. Rutkowski et al. (Eds.): ICAISC 2023, LNAI 14125, pp. 325–336, 2023.
https://doi.org/10.1007/978-3-031-42505-9_28

language. So, the difficulty of this task depends on the target language. Creating captions in a morphologically rich fusional language, like Polish, appears to be much harder than generating text in a positional language like English. In this work, we evaluate the feasibility of creating an image captioning method generating plausible descriptions of images in the Polish language. We also compared the quality of captions generated in a positional language (English) and in a fusional language (Polish).

Our main contribution is an image captioning method, called CaptFormer, suited for the generation of plausible captions in a semantically rich language, such as Polish. Our method combines convolutional neural network and Transformer [16] architecture. Additionally, we created a custom multilingual data set for the image captioning task. The dataset is based on popular English-language image captioning datasets: Flickr 30K [22] and MS COCO [10].

2   Related Work

Modern image captioning methods [2,5,8,18] take their origin in machine translation. Such methods mostly use encoder-decoder deep neural networks. First, the encoder extracts features from an input image. Then, the decoder produces captions based on the features produced by the encoder.

Kiros [8] proposes an encoder-decoder neural network with multimodal space. They build an encoder using a deep convolutional network (CNN) and use a long short-term memory recurrent network (LSTM) for learning a joint image-sentence embedding. The decoder is a structure-content neural language model that disentangles the structure of a sentence from its content, conditioned on representations produced by the encoder.

Vinyals [18] presents a neural image caption generator model, dubbed NIC. NIC encodes the image into a fixed-size feature vector using a convolutional neural network. The output of the encoder is fed to the decoder, which is RNN with LSTM cells. Xu [21] extends this approach, by allowing the decoder to attend to different parts of the input image during the caption generation.

Generating image captions in syntactically rich Polish language deserved relatively little attention. Bartosiewicz [2] proposes an encoder-decoder architecture to generate image captions in Polish. He uses InceptionV3 as the image feature extractor and LSTM network for generating captions. Results of their experimental study show that removing Polish letters from captions reduces the performance of their model. Donahue [5] uses a similar approach for image captioning and extends it for video description in English.

Our method combines convolutional architecture in the encoder part with the Transformer-based [16] approach, which recently dominated the natural language processing field.

3   Image Captioning Method

The method presented in this paper, called CaptFormer, is inspired by recent advances in attention-based neural language models, such as Transformer [16], GPT-2 [13], and attention-based image captioning [21].

Solutions for generating image captions have always been closely related to solutions for machine translation. These tasks are very similar, image captioning can be treated as a translation of an image into a text in the target language. The presented method is a natural step in the evolution of image captioning methods after the invention of the encoder-decoder paradigm [18] and the introduction of the attention mechanism [21]. We improve the decoder part, by replacing the RNN-based network with the Transformer architecture.

The method takes an image as an input and produces a vector that represents next-token probabilities. During inference time, we use beam search [3] to decode next-token probabilities into the natural language text. Beam search is a breadth-first tree search, where only the w most promising paths (candidate captions) at depth t are kept for future examination. In our experiments, we use beam search with a beam size of $w = 5$.

3.1   Network Architecture

Figure 1 shows an architecture of our image captioning method. The network has a typical encoder-decoder structure. The encoder is responsible for extracting features from an input image. The decoder generates the tokens of an image caption. Our model architecture relies on an attention mechanism to draw global dependencies between the input (image) and the output (caption).

Encoder consists of three blocks. First is the convolutional neural network (CNN) feature extractor. In our experiments, we use ResNet-50 [7] architecture pre-trained on ImageNet without fine-tuning. We remove the last two layers from ResNet-50. The input is an RGB image with 224×224 resolution. The CNN feature extractor produces a 7×7 feature map with 2048 channels. Next, we flatten the feature map into a 49-element feature vector with 2048 channels and pass it to the second block. It is a position-wise feed-forward network (FFN) [16] with two linear layers and ReLU non-linearity. Each feature vector element is processed independently by the FFN. We apply dropout [14] to the output of the second layer with the rate of $p_{drop} = 0.1$. As the last encoding step, we use the normalization layer [1].

Decoder largely follows Transformer's decoder [16] design, with modifications proposed in GPT-2 model [13] (moving layer normalization to the input of each sub-block). The decoder consists of $N = 12$ stacked identical layers. Each layer has six sub-layers. The odd (first, third and fifth) sub-layers are responsible for data normalization. A second sub-layer performs masked multi-head attention (with $h = 8$ heads) over the input of the decoder. Masking is required to enforce

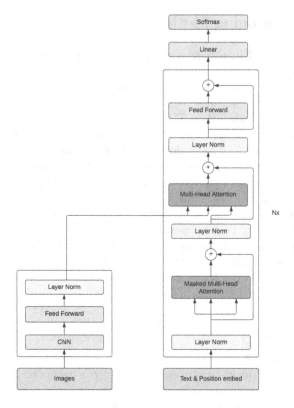

Fig. 1. CaptFormer architecture.

a unidirectional language model, allowing a caption generation from left to right during inference time. A fourth sub-layer performs multi-head attention over the output of the encoder. The sixth sub-layer is a simple, position-wise fully connected feed-forward network (FFN). We apply dropout to the output of even layers with $p_{drop} = 0.1$ rate. We use learned embeddings to convert the tokens to vectors of dimension $d_{decoder}$. To encode the position of each token in sequence (caption), we use learned position embeddings [6]. The input of the decoder is the sum of token embeddings and positional embeddings. Similar to the original Transformer, we use a residual connection [7] around each of the even sub-layer. All sub-layers in the decoder, as well as embedding layers, produce outputs of dimensions $d_{decoder} = 256$.

3.2   Dataset

Due to the lack of sufficiently large Polish datasets for image captioning, we decided to build our own multilingual dataset. Our dataset is based on popular English datasets for image captioning. See Fig. 2 for an exemplary image and Table 1 for its captions in the training set. We choose two popular datasets:

Flickr 30K [22] and MS COCO [10]. Our multilingual dataset contains original English captions and machine-translated Polish versions. Polish translations of captions were obtained using Google Translate.

Fig. 2. An exemplary training set image.

Table 1. Image 2 captions in the training set. Original English captions from MS COCO training set. Polish captions are machine-translated versions of English captions.

Original English caption	Machine translated Polish caption
Two men play Nintendo Wii together in a house.	Dwóch mężczyzn gra razem w domu na Nintendo Wii.
Two men are standing in front of a sofa staring ahead.	Dwóch mężczyzn stoi przed sofą i patrzy przed siebie.
2 men stand in a room holding video game controllers	2 mężczyzn stoi w pokoju z kontrolerami do gier wideo
Two men look bored as they play a game on the Wii	Dwóch mężczyzn wygląda na znudzonych podczas gry na Wii
Two men are standing in the living room and holding wii remotes.	Dwóch mężczyzn stoi w salonie i trzyma piloty wii.

Flickr 30K dataset consists of 31 783 images of everyday activities, events and scenes. All images come from Flickr site. Each image has five different captions obtained via crowdsourcing, resulting in 158 915 captions in total.

MS COCO is a richly-annotated dataset containing around 330 000 images of everyday scenes. MS COCO is used in a variety of tasks, such as image recognition, segmentation or captioning. We used 616 767 crowd-sourced captions for 123 287 images coming from training and validation sets.

Our Multilingual Dataset was created by the following procedure. First, Flickr 30K and MS COCO were merged into one big dataset. Then, we split images into three subsets: training (80%), validation (10%) and testing (10%). Finally, we added machine-translated Polish captions next to the original English captions. We used Google Translate for machine translation. See Tab. 2 for detailed information about our dataset.

Table 2. Data distribution for training, validation and test set.

dataset	number of images	number of captions
training	124 056 (80%)	620 552
validation	15 507 (10%)	77 559
test	15 507 (10%)	77 571

3.3 Network Training

Each batch consists of $n = 32$ (image, caption) pairs. We add on-the-fly data augmentation. First, images are resized to 256×256 resolution and randomly cropped to 224×224 pixels. Then, we apply a random horizontal flip with probability $p = 0.5$. In the end, we apply normalization for each of RGB channels using $mean = [0.485, 0.456, 0.406]$ and $std = [0.229, 0.224, 0.225]$.

Captions are tokenized using Byte-level Byte Pair Encoding (BBPE) tokenization [19] and vocabulary with 50 257 tokens. At the beginning of each caption, we add a special <s> token representing the beginning of the sequence, and </s> token at the end representing the end of the sequence.

After a batch is constructed, we add a special <pad> token to the captions which are shorter than the longest caption in the batch. This ensures all captions in the batch have the same number of tokens (length).

To train our network, we use cross-entropy (1) as a loss function, which is further averaged over all tokens in batch, excluding a special <pad> token. This token was added in order to align the length of image captions in the batch and should be masked in a loss function.

$$CE = -\sum_i^V P^*(i) \log P(i) \tag{1}$$

where V is the length of the vocabulary, $P^*(i)$ is a 1-of-V vector encoding the ground truth, with 1 at the position corresponding to the ground truth token and $P(i)$ is the predicted probability of each token.

The loss function is minimized using a stochastic gradient descent approach. We use Adam optimizer and apply the same learning rate scheduler as proposed in the Transformer [16] paper: the learning rate initially increases during the warm-up phase, and then decreases proportionally to the inverse square root of the step number.

4 Experimental Results

All models were trained for 40 epochs. For all trained models, we saved checkpoints after every epoch. We used the model from the checkpoint with the lowest value of loss function on validation set. In our experiments, we use beam search with a beam size of $w = 5$ for decoding network output. We set the maximum output length during inference to 30 tokens. Early stopping was also possible when the model generated an end of sequence token </s>. Examples of image captioning in Polish with English translation of captions can be seen in Fig. 3.

Ludzie stoją na targu z owocami i warzywami. (Eng. *People are standing at the fruit and vegetable market.*)

Mężczyźni w pomarańczowych kamizelkach odblaskowych pracują na stacji kolejowej. (Eng. *Men in orange reflective vests work at the train station.*)

Snowboardzista w powietrzu na szczycie góry. (Eng. *Snowboarder in the air on top of the mountain.*)

Kobieta leżąca na łóżku z kotem. (Eng. *Woman lying on the bed with a cat.*)

Mężczyzna w okularach gra na akordeonie na chodniku. (Eng. *A man with glasses plays the accordion on the sidewalk.*)

Dwóch rowerzystów w wyścigu. (Eng. *Two cyclists in a race.*)

Fig. 3. Examples of image captioning in Polish with English translations of results.

4.1 Evaluation Metrics

To evaluate, we choose three popular metrics: BLEU [11], ROUGE-L [9] and CIDEr-D [17]. Some of them were created initially for different tasks, but all compare generated (candidate) sentences with reference sentences. To calculate these metrics, we use COCO evaluation server [4]. All reported metrics are multiplied by 100. This is a popular procedure to improve the readability of the results.

BLEU (Bilingual Evaluation Understudy) [11] metric was originally created for evaluation of machine translations. Due to very similar evaluation procedure, BLEU was adopted in image captioning. BLEU score is based on counting co-occurrences of n-grams between reference and candidate sentences. Mostly BLEU-4 is used, but sometime BLEU-1, BLEU-2 and BLEU-3 are also reported.

ROUGE (Recall-Oriented Understudy for Gisting Evaluation) [9] is a set of metrics designed to evaluate text summarization algorithms. ROUGE metrics include: ROUGE-N, ROUGE-L, ROUGE-W, ROUGE-S and their modifications. Instead of n-grams, ROUGE-L uses a measure based on Longest Common Subsequence (LCS). ROUGE-L is defined as F measure. It is calculated from the precision and recall based on LCS.

CIDEr (Consensus-based Image Description Evaluation) [17] is a metric created specially for image captioning. The CIDEr metric measures consensus in image captions by performing a Term Frequency Inverse Document Frequency (TF-IDF) weighting for each n-gram. CIDEr used in evaluation suffers from gaming. To make it more robust from gaming, CIDEr-D add clipping and a length based Gaussian penalty to the CIDEr.

4.2   Evaluation Results

For comparison, we evaluate baseline method. Our baseline is the Soft-Attention based method presented in the article "Show, attend and tell" [21]. Training and testing were performed on a Polish subset of our multilingual dataset. We used the same tokenization and the same data augmentation approach as in our method. Our method achieves better results according to every reported metric. Both methods are implemented using PyTorch [12] and Transformers [20].

Baseline method uses CNN to extract feature vectors, RNN to generate captions, and soft-attention in between. For evaluation, we used the same CNN as in our method. The baseline model performs poorly on the test dataset, achieving only CIDEr-D score of 41.4, ROUGE-L score of 35.5 and BLEU-4 score of 12.5. This is related to the fact that the method sometimes generates not finished captions.

In Table 3 we present comparison between CaptFormer and baseline method [21]. CaptFormer achieved better result than baseline method. CaptFormer yields a CIDEr-D score of 54.2, ROUGE-L score of 40.0 and BLEU-4 score of 16.5.

In Table 4 we present comparison between different decoding strategies: greedy search and beam search. Greedy search iteratively considers the set of

Table 3. Evaluation results of image captioning in Polish.

Method	BLEU-1	BLEU-2	BLEU-3	BLEU-4	ROUGE-L	CIDEr-D
Baseline [21]	46.3	29.6	18.9	12.5	35.5	41.4
CaptFormer	**52.6**	**35.9**	**24.1**	**16.5**	**40.0**	**54.2**

the w best sentences up to time t as candidates to generate sentences of size $t+1$, and keep only the resulting best w of them [18]. We report results achieved using beam search with beam size of $w = 5$. In greedy search, a caption is created from the most promising token at each position. This corresponds to beam search with beam size of $w = 1$. Both strategies were compared on the same model with the same weights. Beam search achieved better results for each metric. Beam search outperforms greedy search by 0.4 ROUGE-L score and 2.4 CIDEr-D score. BLEU score depends on length of n-grams used to calculate BLEU. It starts from 0.9 for BLEU-1 up to 1.5 for longer n-grams (BLEU-2, BLEU-3 and BLEU-4).

Table 4. Results of image captioning using CaptFormer with different decoding strategies.

Decoding	BLEU-1	BLEU-2	BLEU-3	BLEU-4	ROUGE-L	CIDEr-D
Greedy Search	51.5	34.4	22.6	15.0	39.6	51.8
Beam Search	**52.6**	**35.9**	**24.1**	**16.5**	**40.0**	**54.2**

In Table 5 we present comparison between different decoder initialization strategies: pretrained and random initialization. We evaluated a model equivalent to smallest GPT-2 ($h = 8$, $N = 12$, $d_{decoder} = 768$). In pretrained strategy, we took pretrained weights for common layers between CaptFormer and GPT-2. Layers which does not exist in GPT-2 were trained from scratch. We utilize the smallest GPT-2 model pretrained on Polish subset of Oscar corpus [15]. We observed that pretrained version faster achieves satisfying results. It reaches the lowest value of loss function in six epochs. Finally, a randomly initialized model achieved slightly better results.

Table 5. Results of image captioning with different decoder initialization strategies.

Initialization	BLEU-1	BLEU-2	BLEU-3	BLEU-4	ROUGE-L	CIDEr-D
Pretrained	51.9	34.4	22.8	15.3	39.4	51.3
Random	**52.5**	**35.3**	**23.4**	**15.6**	**39.7**	**52.8**

Failure Cases are shown on Fig. 4. Some of the generated captions partially or completely do not correspond to the input image. The proposed method mistook a piece of paper for a laptop, a camera for a telescope, the colors of footballers' clothes or hats of people in the photos. CaptFormer also detected the wrong number of people in the photo and mistook the image of a dancing child for the activity of playing a video game.

Kobieta siedząca na łóżku z laptopem. (Eng. *Woman sitting on the bed with a laptop.*)

Dwóch pływaków w basenie. (Eng. *Two swimmers in the pool.*)

Mężczyzna i kobieta grają w grę wideo. (Eng. *A man and a woman are playing a video game.*)

Mężczyzna w niebieskiej koszuli i czapce bejsbolowej pracuje na dachu samolotu. (Eng. *A man in a blue shirt and baseball cap works on the roof of an airplane.*)

Dwóch piłkarzy, jeden w kolorze zielonym, a drugi w kolorze zielonym, gra w piłkę nożną. (Eng. *Two soccer players, one in green and the other in green, are playing soccer.*)

Mężczyzna w czarnym kapeluszu i czarnej kurtce patrzy przez teleskop. (Eng. *A man in a black hat and black jacket looks through a telescope.*)

Fig. 4. Failure cases, Polish captions with English translations.

Comparison with Captioning in English. In this section, we compare results of image captioning depending on language. For comparison, we evaluate CaptFormer on English language. Training and testing were performed on an English subset of our multilingual dataset. Results are shown in Table 6. Results obtained for English are much better than for Polish. CaptFormer used for image captioning in English yields 88.0 CIDEr-D score, 51.9 ROUGE-L score and 28.5 BLEU-4 score. Result shows, if we want to achieve the same level of image captions, we need much better solutions for fusional languages.

Table 6. Result of image captioning in English and Polish using CaptFormer.

Language	BLEU-1	BLEU-2	BLEU-3	BLEU-4	ROUGE-L	CIDEr-D
English	**69.6**	**52.4**	**38.6**	**28.5**	**51.9**	**88.0**
Polish	52.6	35.9	24.1	16.5	40.0	54.2

5   Conclusions

In this paper, we present CaptFormer, a Transformer based method for image captioning. CaptFormer is an encoder-decoder network. Encoder uses CNN for image feature extraction. Decoder is RNN free text generator. Experiments performed on custom multilingual dataset shows that attention-based solutions overcomes RNN. Experiments shows also that image captioning in Polish is a much harder task than image captioning in English and requires more effective solutions.

References

1. Ba, J.L., Kiros, J.R., Hinton, G.E.: Layer normalization. arXiv preprint arXiv:1607.06450 (2016)
2. Bartosiewicz, M., et al.: Generating image captions in polish-experimental study. In: 2021 14th International Conference on Human System Interaction (HSI), pp. 1–6. IEEE (2021)
3. Boulanger-Lewandowski, N., Bengio, Y., Vincent, P.: Audio chord recognition with recurrent neural networks. In: ISMIR, pp. 335–340. Citeseer (2013)
4. Chen, X., et al.: Microsoft coco captions: data collection and evaluation server. arXiv preprint arXiv:1504.00325 (2015)
5. Donahue, J., et al.: Long-term recurrent convolutional networks for visual recognition and description. In: Proceedings of the IEEE Conference on Computer Vision and Pattern Recognition, pp. 2625–2634 (2015)
6. Gehring, J., Auli, M., Grangier, D., Yarats, D., Dauphin, Y.N.: Convolutional sequence to sequence learning. In: International Conference on Machine Learning, pp. 1243–1252. PMLR (2017)
7. He, K., Zhang, X., Ren, S., Sun, J.: Deep residual learning for image recognition. In: Proceedings of the IEEE Conference on Computer Vision and Pattern Recognition, pp. 770–778 (2016)
8. Kiros, R., Salakhutdinov, R., Zemel, R.S.: Unifying visual-semantic embeddings with multimodal neural language models. arXiv preprint arXiv:1411.2539 (2014)
9. Lin, C.Y.: Rouge: A package for automatic evaluation of summaries. In: Text Summarization Branches Out, pp. 74–81 (2004)
10. Lin, T.-Y., et al.: Microsoft COCO: common objects in context. In: Fleet, D., Pajdla, T., Schiele, B., Tuytelaars, T. (eds.) ECCV 2014. LNCS, vol. 8693, pp. 740–755. Springer, Cham (2014). https://doi.org/10.1007/978-3-319-10602-1_48
11. Papineni, K., Roukos, S., Ward, T., Zhu, W.J.: Bleu: a method for automatic evaluation of machine translation. In: Proceedings of the 40th Annual Meeting of the Association for Computational Linguistics, pp. 311–318 (2002)
12. Paszke, A., et al.: Pytorch: an imperative style, high-performance deep learning library. In: Advances in Neural Information Processing Systems, vol. 32 (2019)
13. Radford, A., Wu, J., Child, R., Luan, D., Amodei, D., Sutskever, I., et al.: Language models are unsupervised multitask learners. OpenAI Blog 1(8), 9 (2019)
14. Srivastava, N., Hinton, G., Krizhevsky, A., Sutskever, I., Salakhutdinov, R.: Dropout: a simple way to prevent neural networks from overfitting. J. Mach. Learn. Res. 15(1), 1929–1958 (2014)

15. Suárez, P.J.O., Romary, L., Sagot, B.: A monolingual approach to contextualized word embeddings for mid-resource languages. arXiv preprint arXiv:2006.06202 (2020)
16. Vaswani, A., et al.: Attention is all you need. In: Advances in Neural Information Processing Systems, vol. 30 (2017)
17. Vedantam, R., Lawrence Zitnick, C., Parikh, D.: Cider: consensus-based image description evaluation. In: Proceedings of the IEEE Conference on Computer Vision and Pattern Recognition, pp. 4566–4575 (2015)
18. Vinyals, O., Toshev, A., Bengio, S., Erhan, D.: Show and tell: a neural image caption generator. In: Proceedings of the IEEE Conference on Computer Vision and Pattern Recognition, pp. 3156–3164 (2015)
19. Wang, C., Cho, K., Gu, J.: Neural machine translation with byte-level subwords. In: Proceedings of the AAAI Conference on Artificial Intelligence, vol. 34, pp. 9154–9160 (2020)
20. Wolf, T., et al.: Transformers: state-of-the-art natural language processing. In: Proceedings of the 2020 Conference on Empirical Methods in Natural Language Processing: System Demonstrations, pp. 38–45 (2020)
21. Xu, K., et al.: Show, attend and tell: neural image caption generation with visual attention. In: International Conference on Machine Learning, pp. 2048–2057. PMLR (2015)
22. Young, P., Lai, A., Hodosh, M., Hockenmaier, J.: From image descriptions to visual denotations: new similarity metrics for semantic inference over event descriptions. Trans. Assoc. Comput. Linguist. **2**, 67–78 (2014)

Evolutionary Algorithms and Their Applications

An Hybrid NSGA-II Algorithm for the Bi-objective Mobile Mammography Unit Routing Problem

Thiago Giachetto de Araujo$^{(\boxtimes)}$, Puca Huachi Vaz Penna[ORCID],
and Marcone Jamilson Freitas Souza[ORCID]

Departamento de Computação, Universidade Federal de Ouro Preto (UFOP),
Campus Universitário, Morro do Cruzeiro, Ouro Preto, MG 35.400-000, Brazil
{thiago.giachetto}@aluno.ufop.edu.br, {puca,marcone}@ufop.edu.br

Abstract. This work deals with the Mobile Mammography Unit Routing Problem in Brazil. The problem is a Multi-depot Open Vehicle Routing Problem variant. In this problem, there are a fixed number of depots, each with a limited number of Mobile Mammography Units (MMUs). Each MMU has a known screening capacity and a set of candidate cities it can serve with known demands for screening. The objective is to define the cities visiting order for each MMU, maximizing the served screening demand and minimizing the total travel distance. We introduce a mathematical programming formulation and two algorithms based on Non-dominated Sorting Genetic Algorithm II (NSGA-II). They differ from each other by the use of a local search. One version has a Local Search as a mutation operator, and the other does not. Both algorithms were tested on benchmark based on real data from Minas Gerais state, Brazil. We used the hypervolume metric to analyze the performance of the proposed algorithms considering different scenarios. The results indicate that using multiple crossover operators and adding a local search as a mutation operator to the algorithm brings better results.

Keywords: Mobile Mammography Unit Routing · Multi-objective Optimization · NSGA-II · Variable Neighborhood Descent · Vehicle Routing

1 Introduction

According to the World Health Organization (WHO), cancer is the leading cause of death in the world. It was responsible for 10 million deaths in 2020. Among all types of cancer, breast cancer is the most common, responsible for 2.26 million new cases in 2020. Nevertheless, it was the fifth in mortality, accounting for 685 thousand deaths in 2020 [8,28]. In Brazil, the reality is the same observed worldwide. Breast cancer has the highest incidence among women and causes the highest mortality (except for non-melanoma skin cancer) [13]. In 2020, it was estimated that 29.7% of cases and 16.5% of deaths in women caused by

L. Rutkowski et al. (Eds.): ICAISC 2023, LNAI 14125, pp. 339–351, 2023.
https://doi.org/10.1007/978-3-031-42505-9_29

cancer were due to breast cancer (when excluding cases of non-melanoma skin cancer) [14].

The Brazilian situation is worsened by the inequality allocation of mammography equipment. The total number of equipment would be sufficient to attend the entire country screening demand. However, the Ministry of Health imposes on women a maximum travel distance of 60 km (or 60 min) to carry out the [26] screening. Consequently, some regions of the country are not served by any mammography unit, and others have more equipment than necessary [1]. Faced with this problem of unbalanced allocation of mammography equipment, several authors have studied this problem. They proposed mathematical formulations and heuristic resolution methods that can help decision-makers allocate equipment in the most efficient way [6,22,23].

Furthermore, to install a mammography unit is necessary a minimum screening demand. Added to the continental dimensions of Brazil, some regions will never be their screening demand completely met. Given this problem, some authors propose using mammography trucks to deal with this residual screening demand [4,22,23]. However, the possibility of using Mobile Mammography Units (MMUs) requires the public manager to make new decisions. For example, how many MMUs are needed to meet all screenings? Which routes will each vehicle take? With this new problem in mind, [20] introduced the Mobile Mammography Unit Routing Problem (MMURP). They treated the problem at two hierarchical levels. At the first level, the objective is to maximize the demand for screenings, and the second is to minimize the total traveled distance by the MMUs.

In this paper, we work with the MMURP as a bi-objective problem, aiming to maximize the demand for screenings and minimize the total traveled distance by the MMUs. The MMURP is a Multi-depot Open Vehicle Routing Problem (MDOVRP) variant. As the vehicle routing problem is NP-hard [16], this work proposes a heuristic for its resolution and uses it to solve the MMURP problem in the state of Minas Gerais, which is the Brazilian state with the largest number of cities and the fourth in area [12]. We run several scenarios that differ from each other by the number of MMUs available in each depot.

The rest of this article is organized as follows. Section 2 introduces the formulation for the MMURP. Section 3 presents the proposed algorithm and its components. Section 4 reports the computational results. Finally, Sect. 5 concludes the paper.

2   Formulation

The MMURP uses the following notation. Let $G = (V, A)$ be a complete and directed graph, where V represents the set of vertices and A the sets of arcs. Let D be the set of m depots and U the set of n candidate cities to be visited. Then, $V = U \cup D = \{1, \ldots, n, n+1, \ldots, n+m\}$, where $U = \{1, \ldots, n\}$ and $D = \{n+1, \ldots, n+m\}$. Each depot $k \in D$ has r_k MMUs, each one with the capacity to perform Q annual screenings. Given two cities $i, j \in V$, the distance between them is given by $c_{ij} \geq 0$. The female population of each city $i \in U$ demands q_i screenings per year. The MMU travel distance between two candidate cities should be lower than $distMax$.

The proposed model adapts the MDOVRP$_{2i-flv}$ formulation for the Multi-depot Open Vehicle Routing Problem (MDOVRP) presented in [15]. A new parcel to the objective function that aims at maximizing the screening demand served was added, and changes in the constraints that require visiting all cities to allow the non-attendance of some of them. Moreover, the number of vehicles per depot and the maximum travel distance allowed between two candidate cities were added. The following are the decision variables:

$x_{ij} = 1$, if a vehicle travels from node $i \in V$ to a node $j \in V$, 0 otherwise.
$w_j = 1$, if the screening demand of city $j \in U$ is served, 0 otherwise.
$u_{ij} > 0$, represents an upper bound on the MMU service capacity available when leaving a node $i \in V$ to $j \in V$.

The mathematical model proposed in this work for the bi-objective MMURP is defined as follows:

$$\min_x \sum_{i \in V} \sum_{j \in V} c_{ij} x_{ij} \tag{1}$$

$$\max_w \sum_{j \in U} q_j w_j \tag{2}$$

subject to:

$$\sum_{i \in V, i \neq j} x_{ij} = w_j, \qquad\qquad \forall j \in U \tag{3}$$

$$\sum_{j \in U} x_{kj} \leq r_k, \qquad\qquad \forall k \in D \tag{4}$$

$$\sum_{j \in U} q_j \cdot w_j \leq \sum_{k \in D} r_k \cdot Q \tag{5}$$

$$c_{ij} \cdot x_{ij} \leq dist_{max}, \qquad\qquad \forall i \in U, j \in V, i \neq j \tag{6}$$

$$\sum_{i \in V, i \neq j} x_{ij} - \sum_{i \in U, i \neq j} x_{ji} \geq 0, \qquad\qquad \forall j \in U \tag{7}$$

$$x_{ij} + x_{ji} \leq 1, \qquad\qquad \forall i, j \in V, i \neq j \tag{8}$$

$$\sum_{j \in V} \sum_{k \in D} x_{jk} = 0 \tag{9}$$

$$\left(\sum_{i \in V, i \neq j} u_{ij} - \sum_{i \in V, i \neq j} u_{ji} \right) - q_j \geq -Q \cdot (1 - w_j), \qquad\qquad \forall j \in U \tag{10}$$

$$(Q - q_i) \cdot x_{ij} \geq u_{ij}, \qquad\qquad \forall i, j \in U \tag{11}$$

$$Q \cdot x_{kj} \geq u_{kj}, \qquad\qquad \forall k \in D, j \in U \tag{12}$$

$$x_{ij} \in \{0, 1\}, \qquad\qquad \forall i, j \in V \tag{13}$$

$$u_{ij} \geq 0, \qquad\qquad \forall i, j \in V \tag{14}$$

$$w_j \in \{0, 1\}, \qquad\qquad \forall j \in U \tag{15}$$

The objective function (1) aims to minimize the total traveled distance, and (2) aims to maximize the total screening demand served. Constraints (3) guarantee that the demand of a city j will be served only if it is visited once. Constraints (4) and (5) establish an upper bound for the number of MMUs leaving each depot and the demand for screenings that can be served. Constraints (6) bounds the maximum travel distance for an MMU between two cities, except for the first city, leaving a depot. Constraints (7) establish that when a location is visited, it can be the end of the route or go to another city, as long as it is not a depot. Constraints (8) forbid the use of the path ij and ji at the same time, and Constraint (9) prevents the return of any vehicle to a depot. Constraints (10) can be divided into two cases: if w_j is equal to 0, they are redundant; if w_j is equal to 1, they require a sufficient capacity to meet the demand at city j. Constraints (11) and (12) are upper bounds for the variables u. Constraints (13) to (15) define the domain of the decision variables.

3   An Hybrid NSGA-II Approach for the MMURP

The Non-dominated Sorting Genetic Algorithm II (NSGA-II) is a population-based meta-heuristic proposed in [7]. The method is an improved version of NSGA [24]. In this new version, the non-dominated sorting algorithm was improved. NSGA-II has an algorithmic complexity of $O(MN^2)$, whereas, in the NSGA, it was $O(MN^3)$ (where M is the number of objectives and N is the population size). Otherwise, NSGA-II is elitist, combining the parents and children of one generation and choosing the best ones for the next generation; and it is no longer necessary to define a sharing parameter to maintain the diversity that is maintained considering the fitness function and a crowded-comparison operator [7].

The NSGA-II used here was implemented as proposed in [7]. The improvements made are inside the *make_new_pop* procedure. Algorithm 1 presents the pseudo-code of the proposed *make_new_pop* procedure. It works with a list of crossover operators (CXL), a crossover probability (p_c), a list of mutation operators (MOL), a mutation probability (p_m), and the size of population (N). These operators are described in Subsect. 3.4.

A new population C and the lists of operators are initialized at lines 2–4. New individuals are added to C, (lines 6–17) while the new population is not full (line 5). With probability pc (line 6), a crossover operator is randomly chosen from the CXL (line 8) and applied to parents p_1 and p_2 (line 9), generating two children c_1 and c_2. For each child, a random mutation operator is chosen from MOL (line 12) and it is applied with probability pm (line 11). At line 13, the child is added to C. Finally, the new population C is returned (line 19).

3.1   Representation

The problem solution, named complete solution, is represented by a list of routes. Each route is denoted by a list, where the first position is the depot, and the others are the candidate cities in the visit order. However, in our algorithm, an

---

Algorithm 1. Algorithm to create a new population

1: **function** MAKE-NEW-POP(P)
2:     $C \leftarrow \emptyset$
3:     Initialize the Crossover Operator List (CXL)
4:     Initialize the Mutation Operator List (MOL)
5:     **while** $|C| \leq |P|$ **do**
6:         $p_1, p_2 \leftarrow choose\_parents(P)$
7:         **if** $random(0, 1) \leq pc$ **then**
8:             Choose randomly a crossover operator $C^\varsigma \in CXL$
9:             $c_1, c_2 \leftarrow C^\varsigma(p_1, p_2)$
10:            **for each** $c \in \{c_1, c_2\}$ **do**
11:                **if** $random(0, 1) \leq pm$ **then**
12:                    Choose randomly a mutation operator $\mathcal{M}^\varsigma \in MOL$
13:                    $c \leftarrow \mathcal{M}^\varsigma(c)$
14:                **end if**
15:                $C \leftarrow C \cup \{c\}$
16:            **end for**
17:        **end if**
18:    **end while**
19:    **return** C
20: **end function**

---

individual is represented as a visiting order, known as a giant tour. The giant tour is a permutation of candidate cities without the use of delimiters (depots).

The procedure to transform a giant tour into a complete solution is called *Split*, which will be presented in Subsect. 3.3. The inverse process, of transforming a complete solution in the giant tour, is called $Split^{-1}$ [19].

Let a complete solution with L different routes, where each route $\mathcal{R}^l = (d_l, i_1^l, i_2^l, \ldots, i_{b_l}^l)$, $\forall l \in L$, $b_l \in \mathbb{N}$, $i_j^l \in N$, $\forall j \in \{1, 2, \ldots, b_l\}$, and $d_l \in D$. A transformed individual is represented as a giant tour given by:

$$g = (i_1^1, i_2^1, \ldots, i_{b_1}^1, i_1^2, i_2^2, \ldots, i_{b_2}^2, \ldots, i_1^L, i_2^L, \ldots, i_{b_L}^L)$$

3.2   Initial Population

The initial population contains one solution given by a greedy constructive heuristic for the traveling salesman problem (TSP) that uses an insertion by the nearest neighbor [3], and the other solutions are random permutations of candidate cities.

3.3   Individual Evaluation

The individuals are evaluated using the Split procedure. This procedure consists of building a route that is not dominated by any other route with the same visiting order. On MMURP, a solution A will be dominated by a solution B, if $dem_B \geq dem_A$ and $dist_B < dist_A$ or $dem_B > dem_A$.

In the MMURP, each depot has a limited number of MMUs, which must be allocated to the routes. As the MMUs in each depot are resources required by other routes, the route construction problem becomes a resource-constrained shortest path problem (RCSPP). To solve this problem, we adapted a multi-label extension of Bellman's algorithm [19]. The label for a path turns a vector $L = (\phi, \pi | a_1, a_2, \ldots, a_p)$, where ϕ is the total distance, π is the screening demand met, and a_k is the number of MMUs of depot k used by this path. The splitting procedure for the MMURP is detailed in Algorithm 2.

Algorithm 2. Splitting algorithm for the MMURP

1: $\Lambda(0) \leftarrow \{(0, 0 | 0, \ldots, 0)\}$
2: **for** $i \leftarrow 1$ *to* n **do**
3:     $\Lambda(i) = \emptyset$
4: **end for**
5: **for** $i \leftarrow 1$ *to* n **do**
6:     **for all** depot d_k **do**
7:         **for all** label $L = (\phi, \pi | a_1, a_2, \ldots, a_p) \in \Lambda(i-1)$ **do**
8:             **if** $a_k + 1 \leq r_k$ **then**
9:                 $tour\_distance \leftarrow c(d_k, T_i)$
10:                $tour\_demand \leftarrow q(T_i)$
11:                $W \leftarrow (\phi + tour\_distance, \pi + tour\_demand | a_1, \ldots, a_k + 1, \ldots, a_p)$
12:                **if** no label in $\Lambda(i)$ dominates W **then**
13:                    delete in $\Lambda(i)$ all labels dominated by W
14:                    $\Lambda(i) \leftarrow \Lambda(i) \cup \{W\}$
15:                **end if**
16:                $j \leftarrow i + 1$
17:                $stop \leftarrow false$
18:                **repeat**
19:                    $tour\_demand \leftarrow tour\_demand + q(T_j)$
20:                    **if** $c(T_{j-1}, T_j) \leq dist_{Max} \wedge (tour\_demand \leq Q)$ **then**
21:                        $tour\_distance \leftarrow tour\_distance + c(T_{j-1}, T_j)$
22:                        $W \leftarrow (\phi + tour\_distance, \pi + tour\_demand | a_1, \ldots, a_p)$
23:                        **if** no label in $\Lambda(j)$ dominates W **then**
24:                            delete in $\Lambda(j)$ all labels dominated by W
25:                            $\Lambda(j) \leftarrow \Lambda(j) \cup \{W\}$
26:                        **end if**
27:                    **else**
28:                        $stop \leftarrow true$
29:                    **end if**
30:                    $j \leftarrow j + 1$
31:                **until** $(j \geq n) \vee (stop = true)$
32:            **end if**
33:        **end for**
34:    **end for**
35: **end for**

Given a sequence of cities T_i, $\forall i \in \{1, \ldots, n\}$ to be served, with size n, the Algorithm 2 creates an auxiliary graph H with $n + 1$ nodes. At each node i, we obtain a set of non-dominated solutions $(\Lambda(i))$, which met the screening demand of the first $i - 1$ cities of the sequence. Many of these solutions are discarded using a dominance rule.

For example, consider that we have 2 depots, with $r = (2, 3)$, and a label $L = (150, 2500|1, 2)$. The label L represents a path with a distance of 150, meets the demand of 2500, and uses 1 and 2 MMUs of each respective depot. L dominates $(160, 2500|1, 2)$ and $(140, 2400|1, 2)$, which have, respectively, a lower total distance or meet a bigger demand with the same number of MMUs. L also dominates $(150, 2500|2, 2)$: the travel distance and demand met are equal, but this uses more MMUs than L. Finally, L is not comparable with $(160, 2500|0, 2)$: the travel distance of L is better but needs more MMUs on depot 1.

Initially, only node 0 has a label, which is equivalent to an empty path (lines 1–4). For each node i of H and each depot d_k, we iterate through each label of non-dominated solutions at node $i - 1$, that is feasible to use one more vehicle from depot d_k (lines 5–8). At lines 9–11, a new route W is started. If W is not dominated by any solution of $\Lambda(i)$ (line 12), all solutions of $\Lambda(i)$ that is dominated by W are removed and W is inserted in $\Lambda(i)$ (lines 13–14). In the lines 16 and 17 the variables j and *stop* are initialized. In the loop from 18 to 31, routes that goes from city T_i to T_j, passing through $T_{i+1}, \ldots, T_{j-1}$ are built. A city j is added to the path until two consecutive cities have a distance greater than $dist_{Max}$ or the route screening demand is greater than Q (line 20). In lines 21–22, a new route W is started. If W is not dominated by any solution of $\Lambda(j)$ (line 23), all solutions of $\Lambda(j)$ that are dominated by W are removed and W is inserted in it (lines 24-25). If the distance between two cities exceeds the maximum distance or the screening demand met exceeds the maximum capacity of an MMU (line 20), the variable *stop* $\leftarrow$ *true* (line 28), which terminates the loop before j reaches n.

3.4   Genetic Operators

The crossover and mutation operators are defined as follows:

Crossover
As we have used the giant tour to represent the individuals and this representation is the same commonly used in TSP, we can take advantage of this, using the same recombination operators of TSP [18]. Thus, in our algorithm, 3 recombination strategies are used, which are chosen at random every time that parents need to be recombined: OX (Order Crossover), CX (Cycle Crossover) and PMX (Partial Mapped Crossover) [11].

Mutation
We use a list of mutation operators (MOL). Every time a mutation operation occurs, an operator is randomly chosen in MOL. The mutations used are 1, 2,

or 3 exchanges between any two positions in the giant tour or a local search in intra-route or inter-route neighborhoods defined at the end of this section.

The local search algorithm used is the Randomized Variable Neighborhood Descent (RVND) [21, 25], which is a VND [10] variant, where the order of use of neighborhoods in the search process is random, rather than predefined, as in VND.

The search performed by VND on a function f uses a predefined set of neighborhoods, $\mathcal{N} = \{\mathcal{N}_1, \mathcal{N}_2, \ldots, |\mathcal{N}|\}$. $\mathcal{N}_j(s)$ is the set of neighboring solutions of s in the jth neighborhood ($\mathcal{N}_j$). If s' is a local optimum concerning the neighborhood $\mathcal{N}_j(s)$, then $f(s') \leq f(s)$ for all $s' \in \mathcal{N}_j(s)$.

VND performs the search with a systematic change of neighborhoods until the current solution cannot be improved. The search starts using the neighborhood $\mathcal{N}_1$ and remains there as long as there is an improvement. If there is no improvement, the neighborhood is replaced by the next one following the pre-established order. The neighborhood is reset to the first one whenever there is an improving solution. The search continues until there are no improvements in any of the neighborhoods. Therefore, the solution returned by the method is a local optimum concerning all neighborhoods.

In RVND, the order in which the neighborhoods are used is random. Every time that a better solution is found, the list of neighborhoods is reset and a new neighborhood is chosen at random. However, the search ends in the same way as VND, when the solution is a local optimum for all neighborhoods [25].

The neighborhoods used to explore the solution space of the problem during the local search accept only feasible solutions and are defined below.

Intra-route neighborhoods: This set of neighborhoods is defined through the following moves:
- **Shift - $\mathcal{N}'^{(1)}$:** a candidate city is removed from its position and reinserted into another in the same route.
- **Swap - $\mathcal{N}'^{(2)}$:** two candidate cities i and j from a route r are swapped.

Inter-route neighborhoods: Five moves define this set of neighborhoods:
- **Shift(1,0) - $\mathcal{N}^{(1)}$:** a candidate city i is transferred from route r_1 to route r_2.
- **Swap(1,1) - $\mathcal{N}^{(2)}$:** a candidate city i of a route r_1 is exchanged with the city j of a route r_2.
- **Shift_Depot - $\mathcal{N}^{(3)}$:** a route r is moved from a depot D_1 to a depot D_2.
- **Swap_Depot - $\mathcal{N}^{(4)}$:** the depot D_1 of a route r_1 is exchanged with the depot D_2 of a route r_2.
- **Insert_Not_Visited - $\mathcal{N}^{(5)}$:** a candidate city not visited i is inserted into a route r.

4 Computational Experiments

The proposed NSGA-II algorithm was implemented in C++ and compiled using GNU c++ 11.3.0 with options -O3 and -march=native. All experiments were performed on a computer with an Intel Core i7-4790 CPU 3.60 GHz x 4 running Ubuntu 22.04.1 operating system. A single thread was used for all tests.

Two versions of the NSGA-II were implemented. The first version (V1) is the full version described in Sect. 3. The second version (V2) differs from the first by not applying local search.

The hypervolume metric was used to evaluate the performance of the two versions of the NSGA-II algorithm. This metric has the characteristic of being strictly monotonic, i.e., a better Pareto front approximation will have a greater hypervolume value, assuming that all points of both fronts dominate the reference point [2]. To calculate the hypervolume, the algorithm proposed in [9] was used, and it is available at https://lopez-ibanez.eu/hypervolume.

In order to normalize the results, we transform the second objective into a minimization problem and sum $maxDem = Q \sum_{k \in D} r_k$, which is the maximum demand that can be met. Thus, the second objective value is always positive and ranges from 0 to $maxDem$. This way, the hypervolume was calculated and normalized by the product of $maxDem$ and $maxDist$. The calculation of $maxDist$ was done by a constructive heuristic, which draws routes with maximum distance, obeying the capacity restrictions of the MMUs.

To evaluate the two versions of the implemented algorithms, 13 instances based on real data were generated[1]. The number of mammography units used was obtained in [27] and it is related to data from the state of Minas Gerais on September/2019. The travel distances between the cities were obtained from the work of [5]. As the data on where each woman did the mammogram is not available, we adapted the models present in the studies [4, 22] to be possible to simulate the assistance provided in different cities in the state of Minas Gerais. We used the number of mammography units present in each municipality and simulated which city with a mammography unit installed covers the cities without one, aiming to maximize the number of served women. We added the constraint that cities with a mammography unit should first meet their own demand and, if they have idle capacity, they will cover a neighboring city; cities can only serve neighbors that are within their health region; and one city can cover a percentage of another city's demand.

Table 1 shows the summary of instance characteristics. The first column brings the instance id, the second column the number of cities, and the third column shows the number of depots. The fourth column shows the maximum service capacity of each MMU, and the fifth column shows the number of MMUs per depot. Columns 6 and 7 bring the reference point used to calculate the hypervolume.

Our hybrid NSGA-II implementation requires a few parameters to be defined in advance. For the experiments, these parameters were determined using the irace [17] tool. To use the irace, it is necessary to define a set of instances and a set of values for each parameter. Table 2 shows the range of values considered by irace and the returned parameter values. Table 3 shows the results obtained in the experiments, where each version of the algorithm ran 30 times. The first column

---

[1] All used instances are available at https://bit.ly/3mxnIbl.

Table 1. Instance characteristics

ID	#cities	#depots	MMU Capacity	#vehicles per depot	Max distance	Max demand
i01	350	2	5069	1, 1	3758	10138
i02	350	2	5069	8, 8	28262	81104
i03	350	2	5069	16, 16	47531	162208
i04	350	2	5069	24, 24	66271	243312
i05	350	2	5069	32, 32	81868	324416
i06	350	2	5069	40, 40	91329	405520
i07	350	2	5069	48, 48	94308	486624
i08	350	2	5069	56, 56	94308	567728
i09	350	2	10138	1, 1	4132	20276
i10	350	2	10138	8, 8	35072	162208
i11	350	2	10138	16, 16	57341	324416
i12	350	2	10138	24, 24	73380	486624
i13	350	2	10138	32, 32	78944	648832

Table 2. Parameter values considered and returned by irace for the hybrid NSGA-II.

Param.	Range	Returned values
N	{25, 30, 35, 40, 45, 50}	50
Gen	{500, 1000, 1500, 2000}	1500
p_m	{0.05, 0.075, 0.10, 0.125, 0.15, 0.20}	0.15
p_c	{0.85, 0.90, 0.95}	0.90
CXL	{{OX}, {CX}, {PMX}, {OX, CX, PMX}}	{OX, CX, PMX}
MXL	{{1 Swap}, {2 Swaps}, {3 Swaps}, {1, 2, 3 Swaps, LS}}	{1, 2, 3 Swaps, LS}

shows the instance id. Columns 2–3 show the values obtained for algorithm V1 and columns 4-5 for algorithm V2. For each algorithm, we have the average value and standard deviation of hypervolume and the average value of execution time for each instance.

Observing the results of Table 3, we can notice that the local search has an important role in providing a better quality set of solutions when using hypervolume as a metric.

Table 3. Results of NSGA-II with LS (V1) and without LS (V2)

ID	V1		V2	
	HV	Time (s)	HV	Time (s)
i01	**0.969 (4.8E-04)**	9.58	0.955 (8.3E-03)	2.89
i02	**0.919 (2.4E-03)**	68.64	0.857 (1.2E-02)	9.88
i03	**0.857 (2.6E-03)**	219.31	0.785 (8.6E-03)	42.79
i04	**0.804 (4.5E-03)**	471.49	0.728 (7.2E-03)	126.92
i05	**0.743 (7.0E-03)**	944.94	0.690 (5.0E-03)	301.56
i06	**0.630 (4.8E-03)**	1432.96	0.619 (4.3E-03)	499.90
i07	0.509 (6.4E-03)	2108.69	**0.509 (3.1E-03)**	593.28
i08	0.405 (1.9E-02)	2318.49	**0.413 (4.5E-03)**	572.47
i09	**0.963 (3.9E-04)**	11.14	0.952 (5.7E-03)	2.89
i10	**0.911 (3.2E-03)**	107.06	0.847 (1.5E-02)	12.70
i11	**0.832 (4.1E-03)**	377.21	0.740 (1.4E-02)	73.89
i12	**0.692 (2.0E-03)**	916.06	0.653 (3.3E-03)	255.33
i13	0.510 (4.8E-03)	1381.72	**0.511 (1.8E-03)**	440.57

5   Conclusions

This paper addressed a variant of the Multi-depot Open Vehicle Routing Problem, the Mobile Mammography Unit Routing Problem (MMURP), with the objectives of maximizing the demand for screenings and minimizing the total travel distance by the MMUs. We introduced a mathematical programming formulation for the problem and developed a hybrid algorithm based on the Non-dominated Sorting Genetic Algorithm II (NSGA-II) for treating it. The NSGA-II uses three crossover operators with a Randomized Variable Neighborhood Descent (RVND) as one of the mutation operators. For testing the hybrid NSGA-II, we used 13 instances based on real data and compared its results with those of a version of NSGA-II without the local search as a mutation operator.

Using the hypervolume metric to compare the sets of non-dominated solutions, on average, the NSGA-II with the local search yielded better results in 10 of 13 instances. On the other hand, the NGSA-II without the local search required less than 30% of the computational time compared to its complete version.

Acknowledgments. The authors are grateful for the support provided by the Universidade Federal de Ouro Preto, and by the Coordenação de Aperfeiçoamento de Pessoal de Nível Superior (CAPES, Finance Code 001), Conselho Nacional de Desenvolvimento Científico e Tecnológico (CNPq, grants 428817/2018-1 and 303266/2019-8), and Fundação de Amparo à Pesquisa do Estado de Minas Gerais (FAPEMIG, grant PPM CEX 676/17).

References

1. Amaral, P., Luz, L., Cardoso, F., Freitas, R.: Spatial distribution of mammography equipment in brazil. Revista Brasileira de Estudos Urbanos e Regionais **19**(2), 326 (2017). https://doi.org/10.22296/2317-1529.2017v19n2p326
2. Audet, C., Bigeon, J., Cartier, D., Le Digabel, S., Salomon, L.: Performance indicators in multiobjective optimization. Eur. J. Oper. Res. **292**(2), 397–422 (2021). https://doi.org/10.1016/j.ejor.2020.11.016
3. Bellmore, M., Nemhauser, G.L.: The traveling salesman problem: a survey. Oper. Res. **16**(3), 538–558 (1968). https://doi.org/10.1287/opre.16.3.538
4. de Campos, M.V.A., de Sá, M.V.S.M., Rosa, P.M., Penna, P.H.V., de Souza, S.R., Souza, M.J.F.: A mixed linear integer programming formulation and a simulated annealing algorithm for the mammography unit location problem. In: ICEIS, pp. 428–439 (2020). https://doi.org/10.5220/0009420704280439
5. de Carvalho, L.R., do Amaral, P.V.M., Mendes, P.S.: Matrizes de distâncias e tempo de deslocamento rodoviário entre os municípios brasileiros : uma atualização metodológica para 2020. Textos para Discussão Cedeplar-UFMG 630, Cedeplar, Universidade Federal de Minas Gerais (2021). https://ideas.repec.org/p/cdp/texdis/td630.html
6. Corrêa, V.H.V., Costa Lima, B.J., Silva-e-Souza, P.H., Penna, P.H.V., Souza, M.J.F.: Localização de mamógrafos: um estudo de caso na rede pública de saúde. In: Anais do Simpósio Brasileiro de Pesquisa Operacional, p. 84874. Rio de Janeiro, Brazil (2018). http://bit.ly/3ZDmusx
7. Deb, K., Pratap, A., Agarwal, S., Meyarivan, T.: A fast and elitist multiobjective genetic algorithm: NSGA-II. IEEE Trans. Evol. Comput. **6**(2), 182–197 (2002). https://doi.org/10.1109/4235.996017
8. Ferlay, J., et al.: International agency for research on cancer (2020). https://gco.iarc.fr/today. Accessed 18 Mar 2023
9. Fonseca, C., Paquete, L., Lopez-Ibanez, M.: An improved dimension-sweep algorithm for the hypervolume indicator. In: 2006 IEEE International Conference on Evolutionary Computation, pp. 1157–1163 (2006). https://doi.org/10.1109/CEC.2006.1688440
10. Hansen, P., Mladenović, N., Todosijević, R., Hanafi, S.: Variable neighborhood search: basics and variants. EURO J. Comput. Opt. **5**(3), 423–454 (2017). https://doi.org/10.1007/s13675-016-0075-x
11. Hussain, A., Muhammad, Y., Nauman Sajid, M., Hussain, I., Mohamd Shoukry, A., Gani, S.: Genetic algorithm for traveling salesman problem with modified cycle crossover operator. Computational Intelligence and Neuroscience 2017, pp. 1–7 (2017). https://doi.org/10.1155/2017/7430125
12. IBGE: Áreas territoriais (2021). https://bit.ly/3Mh1TqO. Accessed 23 Mar 2023
13. INCA: A situação do câncer de mama no brasil: síntese de dados dos sistemas de informação (2019). https://bit.ly/3ocLOZt
14. INCA: Estatísticas de câncer (2022). https://www.inca.gov.br/numeros-de-cancer. Accessed 3 Jul 2022
15. Lalla-Ruiz, E., Mes, M.: Mathematical formulations and improvements for the multi-depot open vehicle routing problem. Optim. Lett. **15**(1), 271–286 (2020). https://doi.org/10.1007/s11590-020-01594-z
16. Lenstra, J.K., Kan, A.R.: Complexity of vehicle routing and scheduling problems. Networks **11**(2), 221–227 (1981). https://doi.org/10.1002/net.3230110211

17. López-Ibáñez, M., Dubois-Lacoste, J., Cáceres, L.P., Birattari, M., Stützle, T.: The Irace package: iterated racing for automatic algorithm configuration. Oper. Res. Perspect. **3**, 43–58 (2016). https://doi.org/10.1016/j.orp.2016.09.002

18. Prins, C.: A simple and effective evolutionary algorithm for the vehicle routing problem. Comput. Oper. Res. **31**(12), 1985–2002 (2004). https://doi.org/10.1016/S0305-0548(03)00158-8

19. Prins, C., Lacomme, P., Prodhon, C.: Order-first split-second methods for vehicle routing problems: a review. Transp. Res. Part C Emer. Technol. **40**, 179–200 (2014). https://doi.org/10.1016/j.trc.2014.01.011

20. Rosa, O.A.S., Rosa, P.M., Penna, P.H.V., Souza, M.J.F.: Um algoritmo construtivo para o problema de roteamento de unidades móveis de mamografia. Simpósio Brasileiro de Pesquisa Operacional (2020). http://bit.ly/3lVa5Ck

21. Souza, M.J.F., Coelho, I.M., Ribas, S., Santos, H.G., Merschmann, L.H.C.: A hybrid heuristic algorithm for the open-pit-mining operational planning problem. Eur. J. Oper. Res. **207**(2), 1041–1051 (2010). https://doi.org/10.1016/j.ejor.2010.05.031

22. Souza, M.J.F., Penna, P.H.V., Moreira de Sá, M.V.S., Rosa, P.M.: A vns-based algorithm for the mammography unit location problem. In: International Conference on Variable Neighborhood Search. pp. 37–52. Springer (2020). DOI: 10.1007/978-3-030-44932-2_3

23. Souza, M., Penna, P., Sá, M., Rosa, P., Monteiro, J., Lisboa, M.: Localização de mamógrafos: formulações e estudo preliminar de caso de Rondônia. In: Anais do LI Simpósio Brasileiro de Pesquisa Operacional, vol. 51, p. 107698. SOBRAPO, Galoá, Limeira (SP) (2019). https://bityli.com/HAEBCtEkv. Accessed 31 Aug 2022

24. Srinivas, N., Deb, K.: Muiltiobjective optimization using nondominated sorting in genetic algorithms. Evol. Comput. **2**(3), 221–248 (1994). https://doi.org/10.1162/evco.1994.2.3.221

25. Subramanian, A., Drummond, L., Bentes, C., Ochi, L., Farias, R.: A parallel heuristic for the vehicle routing problem with simultaneous pickup and delivery. Comput. Oper. Res. **37**(11), 1899–1911 (2010). https://doi.org/10.1016/j.cor.2009.10.011

26. SUS: Série parâmetros sus - volume 1 - caderno 1 - republicado 1 (2017). https://bit.ly/41tfmjD

27. SUS: Cnes - recursos físicos (2019). http://bit.ly/40BKfm9. Accessed 28 Mar 2023

28. WHO: Cancer, February 2022. https://www.who.int/news-room/fact-sheets/detail/cancer. Accessed 18 Mar 2023

Controlled Refresh of the Population in Differential Evolution for Real-World Problems

Petr Bujok[✉][ID], Martin Lacko, and Patrik Kolenovský

University of Ostrava, 30. dubna 22, 70200 Ostrava, Czech Republic
{petr.bujok,martin.lacko,patrik.kolenovsky}@osu.cz

Abstract. In this paper, a new variant of the Differential Evolution (DE) algorithm is proposed to control the diversity of individuals in the population. The proposed approach is based on the failure of individuals in successive generations. The positions of the unsuccessful individuals are refreshed by employing the position parameters of the successful individuals from the population. Two control parameters of the proposed approach are studied to eliminate inappropriate settings. These nine variants of newly designed DE variants are compared with the classic DE algorithm when solving the set of real-world problems CEC 2011. The results show a very promising ability to solve real-world problems when the DE uses the proposed mechanism with the appropriate settings.

Keywords: Differential evolution · Diversity · Experiment · Real-world problems · Statistical comparison

1 Introduction

Differential evolution (DE) is an efficient and popular optimisation algorithm frequently used for more than 20 years. DE was introduced to solve real-valued optimisation problems. The global optimisation problem is defined in the search space Ω that is bounded by its constraints, $\Omega = \prod_{j=1}^{D}[a_j, b_j]$, $a_j < b_j$. Then, the objective function f is defined in all $x \in \Omega$ and the point x^* for $f(x^*) \leq f(x), \forall x \in \Omega$ is the solution of the global optimisation problem.

1.1 Differential Evolution

In 1995, Storn and Price introduced a population-based optimiser called DE, which is from a group of evolutionary algorithms, and where a population is developed by evolutionary operators, mutation, crossover, and selection [8].

The location and diversity level of the population P influences the efficiency of DE when solving various optimisation problems. Higher diversity is represented by a population located in a bigger portion of Ω, and for low diversity, vice versa. Population located in an area with a local minimum means that DE stagnates, and a global solution is not provided.

L. Rutkowski et al. (Eds.): ICAISC 2023, LNAI 14125, pp. 352–362, 2023.
https://doi.org/10.1007/978-3-031-42505-9_30

In this paper, the refreshment of positions of unsuccessful individuals in DE is proposed. The approach brings the ability to avoid stagnation of the classic DE algorithm. The approach is universally applicable to any population-based optimisation method. In this study, the variant of DE/ran/1/bin is employed to eliminate the influence of any adaptation of the DE parameters. The proposed variant is applied experimentally to the set of real-world problems CEC 2011 [5].

The rest of this paper is organised as follows. In Sect. 2, lately, proposed approaches of diversity control in DE are briefly described. Section 3 provides the main idea of the proposed approach to refresh the position of stagnated individuals in DE. The experimental settings and the description of the optimisation problems are provided in Sect. 4. Sections 5 and 6 include a discussion of results and conclusions.

2   Diversity of Population in DE

Evolutionary algorithms are population-based optimisation techniques employing individuals to detect potentially good areas of the search space Ω. The set of individuals (typically called population) is initialised mostly in a random way and covers most of the interesting locations. During the update process of the population (different for each optimisation method), the individuals are gradually located rather in a smaller area. Therefore, the diversity of the population decreases, the algorithm gets stuck, and the global solution is not provided [2].

Scientists try to control the diversity of the population. The most critical aspect of this research field is detecting the most appropriate moment to refresh the population to increase its diversity. The problem is to recognise the proper moment when the population is located in local and global minimum areas.

2.1   Related Works

Castillo et al. introduced a replacement strategy for elite individuals to balance the exploration and exploitation of DE [3], where the DE/rand/1/bin strategy is used. The results of the experiment performed on CEC 2016 and CEC 2017 showed that the proposed DE variant is able to outperform the adaptive variants of jSO, EBOwithCMAR, L-SHADEepsilon, etc.

Cheng et al. proposed a new DE variant with a diversity-based mutation operator [4]. The principle of the newly proposed mutation scheme is to order (rank) individuals in mutation using the diversity of population and function values of individuals. The results achieved on the jDE, SHADE and L-SHADE variants (where the original, rank-based and newly proposed variants are employed) showed the superiority of the proposed DE variant.

Navarro et al. proposed DE employing a moving average approach based on historical function values to control the diversity level [6]. The proposed approach is employed to the classical strategy of DE/best/1/bin, where the Opposition-Based (OBO) mechanism is also used. The results illustrate the superiority of the proposed approach compared to JADE, L-SHADE, etc.

Šenkeřík et al. proposed a chaotic-based random-number generator for the DE algorithm [7]. The authors used adaptive variants of jDE and SHADE, where the standard and proposed number generator methods were compared on the CEC 2015 set and $D = 10$. The authors assessed that a higher diversity level of the population at the beginning of the search process is crucial.

Vázquez et al. introduced a cluster-based diversity control in DE [9]. The proposed approach is used in the classical DE/rand/1/bin strategy where values of F and CR are adapted. The results achieved from the comparison with several adaptive DE variants showed better performance of the newly proposed method.

Yu et al. proposed a variant of DE that controls the size and diversity of the population when solving the problem of estimation of parameters of photovoltaic models [10]. The proposed method employs independent sub-populations of individuals, where the scaling factor F is estimated based on the current diversity level. The proposed algorithm was compared with several adaptive DE variants and provided results that illustrate the superiority of the new approach.

All of the aforementioned approaches focus on adapting the DE parameters. In this paper, the proposed algorithms use fixed population size values and DE control parameters. Moreover, standard DE with the combination of rand/1 mutation and binomial crossover is used as one of the most efficient strategies of DE [1]. The introduced approach enables to refresh of part of the DE population when the individuals stagnate in one position for several generations.

3   Proposed Approach of Refresh the Population

Although the DE algorithm is a very efficient optimiser, it gets stuck in the area of local minima in some problems, similar to other optimisation algorithms. In this paper, a new approach for the refreshment of part of the DE population is proposed. The proposed mechanism is constructed to detect the stagnation of the individuals in the population and refresh its positions controlled by the population parameters determined by the remaining individuals. The proposed approach is very simple because it is used at the end of each generation only if stagnated individuals exist in the population. Two numerical parameters control the mechanism, and its settings are studied in this paper to simplify it for applications. Note that the proposed approach can be applied to any population-based optimisation algorithm. The main goal of the refreshment is to eliminate situations when individuals get stuck in an area of a local solution.

3.1   Select Individuals for Refreshment

During the updating of the population, the number of successive unsuccessfully generated offspring individuals is counted for each individual. When a newly generated solution y_i is not better than the parent individual x_i ($f(y_i) \geq f(x_i)$) the failure counter of the ith individual increases by one, while the better offspring individual ($f(y_i) < f(x_i)$), set the counter at zero (reset).

At the end of each generation, the counter of each individual is compared with a predefined limit called ref_G, which is the input parameter of the proposed approach. The ith individual x_i is selected to be refreshed only if it has a number of unsuccessful offspring higher than ref_G.

3.2   Refreshment of Individuals

The proposed approach enables to refresh of the position of unsuccessful individuals that got stuck for several predefined successive generations. The idea is to replace the old positions of badly reproductive individuals with new, refreshed positions. The new position is generated randomly and controlled by two parameters, the mean value and variance. These parameters are estimated from the current population, represented only by successful individuals.

At first, the population of individuals is randomly initialised, and failure counters for each individual of the population are set to zero values. Then, the process of updating the population is repeated until the predefined stopping condition is not met.

The new individuals are generated using the standard rand/1/bin strategy and evaluated by function value. If the new position is better than the current position, the new position is inserted into the population, and the failure counter of the current individual is set to zero (reset). Otherwise, if the new position is not better than the current position, the old position remains in the population, and the failure counter of the current individual is increased by one. If the failure counter of any individual achieves a predefined number, the centre and diversity of successful individuals are computed. The centre serves to determine a new position for unsuccessful individuals, where the three scenarios of how the new centre of the population will be computed are possible:

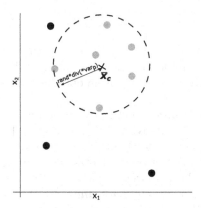

Fig. 1. An illustration of the refreshment approach.

1. If the number of successful individuals in the population is greater than one, then the centre is computed by:

$$\bar{x}_c = \frac{1}{N^*} \sum_{i=1}^{N^*} x_i \tag{1}$$

where x_i is a successful parent individual and N^* is the total number of successful individuals ($N^* \leq N$).

2. If there is only one successful individual in the population, then the centre is represented by the position of the individual:

$$\bar{x}_c = x_i. \tag{2}$$

3. If there are no successful individuals in the population, then 10 % of better individuals are selected from the population according to the failure counter. It means that the individuals who produce better offspring more recently (have a lower count of unsuccessful generations) are selected instead of the individuals producing worse offspring for a longer time.

Further, when the centre is computed, the second parameter needed to refresh the individuals, called diversity, is designed by the standard deviation of the individuals' coordinates from the population:

$$div = \sqrt{\frac{1}{N} \sum_{i=1}^{N} \sum_{j=1}^{D} (x_{ij} - \bar{x}_j)^2}, \quad \bar{x}_j = \frac{1}{N} \sum_{i=1}^{N} x_{ij} \tag{3}$$

where D represents the dimension of the problem, and N is the size of the population. Finally, employing both estimated control features of the population, the new refresh position of the stagnated individual is generated using the rule:

$$new = \bar{x}_c + rand \cdot div \cdot var_p \tag{4}$$

where $rand$ represents a randomly generated number between 0 and 1 from a uniform distribution, $\bar{x}_c$ and div is the centre and the diversity-level of the current population, respectively, and var_p is an optional parameter of the approach to decrease the influence of diversity.

A better illustration of how the proposed refreshment approach produces a new position for unsuccessful individuals is proposed in Fig. 1. The grey bullets represent successful individuals in the population, and the black bullets denote unsuccessful individuals. The cross illustrates the centre of the successful part of individuals, and the dashed circle depicts possible new refreshed positions around the centre with a radius equal to $rand \cdot div \cdot var_p$ (4). It is clear that the greater the diversity of the individuals in the populations (div) and the value of the var_p parameter, the larger the distance of the newly refreshed position from the centre of the population $\bar{x}_c$, and vice versa. Several different values of the var_p parameter are studied in this paper to provide some recommended settings, especially for real-world problems.

4 Experimental Settings

A test suite of 22 real-world problems of the CEC 2011 competition is used [5]. The functions provide various computational complexity with various dimensions of the search space (from $D = 1$ to $D = 240$). For each algorithm and problem, 25 independent runs were performed, limited by the prescribed number of function evaluations $MaxFES = 150000$. The partial results after one-third and two-thirds of MaxFES are also studied. The solution of the problem is represented by a point in the terminal population with the smallest function value.

The classic DE employing the DE/rand/1/bin strategy is used. The DE control parameters are set to $N = 90$, $F = 0.8$, and $CR = 0.5$. DE_c denotes the proposed DE with a refreshment approach. The number of generations, when the number of unsuccessful offspring of individuals is counted, is set to $ref_G = \{10,\ 50,\ 100\}$. The proposed variant of DE with refreshment using the variance-control parameter with a static $var_p = 0.01$ is denoted by the symbol s, and the version using a linearly decreased setting between 0.2 and 0.05 represents the index d. All algorithms are implemented in Matlab 2020b, where statistical analysis is evaluated. All computations were carried out on a standard PC with Windows 7, Intel(R) Core(TM)i7-4700 CPU 3.0 GHz, 16 GB RAM.

5 Results

Nine variants of the proposed DE with the refreshment approach are experimentally compared with the original DE on 22 real-world problems. The median values computed for each problem and algorithm are provided in Table 1. The algorithms that provide the best median (or mean) value are underlined. For a better overview, the total number of the best, second, third, and last positions from the Kruskal-Wallis tests are shown at the bottom of the table. The proposed variant of refreshing DE with $ref_G = 10$ and decreasing var_p provided the best results, followed by the variant with $ref_G = 10$ and fixed $var_p = 0.01$. The original DE provides good results for three real-world problems. It is interesting that the proposed variant of refreshing DE without the parameter var_p (DE_{c10}) is not able to increase the efficiency of the original DE. In fact, it is the worst-performing method in comparison. This fact points out the importance of the var_p parameter.

The comparison of the ten DE variants on all 22 real-world problems using the Friedman test is shown in Table 2. The mean ranks of each method and three particular stages of the search show that the variants of DE_{c50s} and DE_{c100s} performed substantially better compared to other methods (the best method is underlined and bolt, the second is only bolt, and the third is only underlined). It is interesting that overall results are slightly better for DEc with fixed ref_G than for DEc with decreasing ref_G. The proposed DE variants with a refreshing approach and a shorter period of studying failure offspring (DE_{c10d} and DE_{c10s}) perform better than the original DE and the proposed variants without the controlling parameter var_p but the longer studying period achieves better results.

Table 1. Median values of DE variants compared using the Kruskal-Wallis test.

Fun	DE	DEc_{10}	DEc_{50}	DEc_{100}	DEc_{10s}	DEc_{50s}	DEc_{100s}	DEc_{10d}	DEc_{50d}	DEc_{100d}
T01	0.22635	19.7128	7.46757	1.33535	**0**	2.24E-08	1.97E-11	**0**	7.90E-10	7.07E-06
T02	-6.97614	-4.56773	-5.21135	-6.37601	**-10.8247**	-8.73974	-8.02729	-9.6247	-7.94316	-8.08995
T03	1.15E-05	1.15E-05	1.15E-05	1.15E-05	1.15E-05	1.15E-05	1.15E-05	1.15E-05	1.15E-05	1.15E-05
T04	20.8199	20.8199	19.0015	20.8199	**14.7972**	20.8199	20.8199	20.1333	20.8199	20.8199
T05	**-21.1386**	-16.1532	-17.1659	-18.3455	-20.1522	-20.0664	-21.0005	-20.0564	-20.3101	-20.422
T06	**-18.2734**	-13.0127	-14.7408	-15.2626	-17.023	-17.9371	-17.3541	-16.7453	-17.2733	-17.5269
T07	1.72376	1.78696	1.75172	1.74026	1.77462	1.74531	1.74655	**1.71087**	1.78352	1.74948
T08	220	220	220	220	220	220	220	220	220	220
T09	223722	1.50E06	397047	263965	**1606.62**	2122.17	13756.3	1826.27	2056.96	10769.9
T10	-20.7034	-10.3197	-20.8097	-21.0626	-19.9495	-20.8193	-20.99	-20.3467	**-21.4301**	-21.3617
T11.1	9.01E+07	1.84E+08	1.13E+08	9.81E+07	52321.6	52493	135753	52357.8	**52303.2**	95316.2
T11.2	5.55E+06	9.97E+06	6.87E+06	6.19E+06	1.07E+06	1.07E+06	1.10E+06	**1.07E+06**	1.07E+06	1.09E+06
T11.3	**15452.2**	15462.7	15459.2	15454.7	15492.8	15466	15455.3	15496.8	15472.4	15457
T11.4	19391.1	19355.6	19364.2	19422.2	19229.2	19066.4	**19057.5**	19506.6	19370.8	19373.2
T11.5	32958.9	33051.7	32975.8	32986.2	33110.8	32960.4	**32949.2**	33116	33023.4	32971.5
T11.6	137792	141417	137386	136952	143238	136093	**135986**	146917	141307	139932
T11.7	3.37E+06	1.16E+09	4.76E+07	1.28E+07	2.14E+06	**2.11E+06**	2.11E+06	3.13E+06	2.48E+06	2.23E+06
T11.8	3.29E+06	3.50E+07	8.24E+06	4.88E+06	1.01E+06	944575	987483	**943115**	944991	962603
T11.9	4.71E+06	3.63E+07	9.56E+06	6.03E+06	1.60E+06	**1.27E+06**	1.45E+06	1.68E+06	1.43E+06	1.51E+06
T11.10	3.32E+06	3.57E+07	7.20E+06	5.09E+06	951911	943775	989987	**943199**	945837	973427
T12	25.3009	36.392	30.8256	28.0699	34.065	28.6135	26.7919	**16.366**	25.2706	25.5729
T13	20.8968	34.416	20.3376	15.772	33.3497	17.7724	14.7123	19.6011	14.308	**11.1147**
#1st	3	0	0	0	4	2	3	5	2	1
#2nd	2	0	1	1	2	6	2	2	3	1
#3rd	1	0	0	3	2	2	4	2	4	2
#last	1	15	0	0	0	0	0	4	0	0

Table 2. Mean ranks from the Friedman test of median values.

FES	DEc_{50s}	DEc_{100s}	DEc_{50d}	DEc_{100d}	DEc_{10d}	DEc_{10s}	DE	DEc_{100}	DEc_{50}	DEc_{10}
50,000	**3.91**	4.73	4.36	4.59	4.45	**4.27**	6.14	6.14	7.55	8.86
100,000	**4.14**	4.18	4.23	4.77	4.77	4.82	5.34	6.48	7.32	8.95
150,000	**3.86**	4.05	4.50	4.55	4.89	5.25	5.41	6.45	7.23	8.82

Table 3 provides the median values of the reference method that achieves the best mean rank from the Friedman test (DEc_{50s}) and the symbols that represent the results of the Wilcoxon rank-sum tests. If there is a significant difference between the reference and the selected method, the symbols '+' or '−' are used (where a number of symbols illustrate the level of significance), and the symbol '≈' means that there are no differences between the methods. At the bottom of the table, the number of worse ('w'), equal ('eq') and better ('b') results are counted, where the significantly different results represent the last row (symbols with s). The proposed variant of DEc_{50s} provides worse results for problems T05, T11.3, and T12, compared to the original DE. Studying the numbers of worse (w) results of the counterparts, the reference variant is the best performing DE in comparison, followed by the variant of DEc_{100s}. These results mean that the fixed settings of var_p perform rather better compared to decreasing ones.

Table 3. Median values of DEc_{50s} and results of the Wilcoxon tests.

Fun	DEc_{50s}	DE	DEc_{10}	DEc_{50}	DEc_{100}	DEc_{10s}	DEc_{100s}	DEc_{10d}	DEc_{50d}	DEc_{100d}
T01	2.24E–08	≈	– – –	– – –	≈	+++	≈	+++	≈	≈
T02	–8.73974	– – –	– – –	– – –	– – –	+++	–	+++	–	– –
T03	1.15E–05	≈	≈	≈	≈	≈	≈	≈	≈	≈
T04	20.8199	≈	≈	≈	≈	≈	≈	≈	≈	≈
T05	–20.0664	+	– – –	– – –	– – –	≈	≈	≈	≈	≈
T06	–17.9371	≈	– – –	– – –	– – –	–	≈	– –	≈	≈
T07	1.74531	≈	≈	≈	≈	≈	≈	≈	≈	≈
T08	220	≈	≈	≈	≈	≈	≈	≈	≈	≈
T09	2122.17	– – –	– – –	– – –	– – –	+++	– – –	+++	≈	– – –
T10	–20.8193	≈	– – –	≈	+++	– – –	++	– –	+++	+++
T11.1	52493	– – –	– – –	– – –	– – –	≈	– – –	≈	≈	– – –
T11.2	1072760	– – –	– – –	– – –	– – –	– – –	– – –	≈	≈	– – –
T11.3	15466	+++	≈	++	+++	– – –	+++	– – –	≈	++
T11.4	19066.4	– – –	– – –	– – –	– – –	– –	≈	– – –	– – –	– – –
T11.5	32960.4	≈	– – –	≈	–	– – –	≈	– – –	– – –	≈
T11.6	136093	–	– – –	≈	≈	– – –	≈	– – –	– – –	– – –
T11.7	2107580	– – –	– – –	– – –	– – –	≈	≈	– – –	– – –	–
T11.8	944575	– – –	– – –	– – –	– – –	– – –	– – –	≈	≈	– – –
T11.9	1267990	– – –	– – –	– – –	– – –	– – –	– –	– – –	– –	– – –
T11.10	943775	– – –	– – –	– – –	– – –	–	– – –	≈	–	– – –
T12	28.6135	+++	– – –	–	≈	– – –	++	+++	+++	+++
T13	17.7724	– – –	– – –	– – –	+++	– – –	+++	– –	+++	+++
w/eq/b		13/3/6	18/3/1	18/2/2	14/3/5	14/2/6	10/3/9	10/2/10	12/3/7	14/3/5
$w_s/eq_s/b_s$		11/8/3	17/5/0	14/7/1	12/7/3	12/7/3	7/11/4	9/9/4	7/12/3	10/8/4

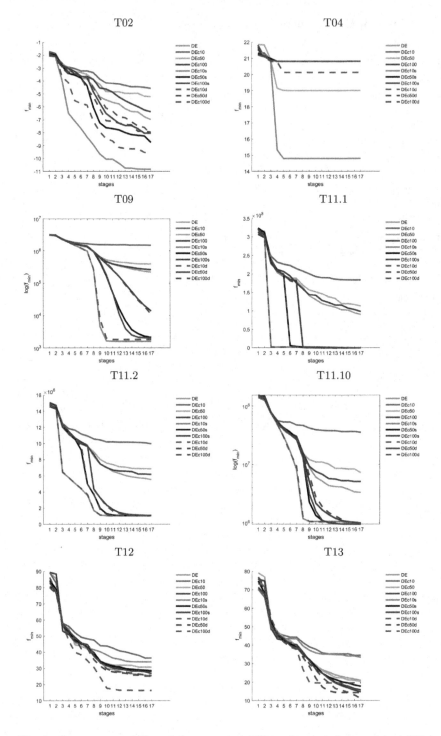

Fig. 2. Convergence ability of the proposed DEc variants and the original DE.

Controlling the diversity in DE population is close-knitted to the convergence of the algorithm. Therefore, Fig. 2 illustrates the convergence curves of the compared methods for some real-world problems. The values are measured in 17 stages of the search process, and median values from 25 runs for each algorithm and problem are calculated. The proposed DE variants using the refreshing approach using the variance-control parameter converged faster and achieved better (lower) objective function values.

6   Conclusion

In this study, a new approach to refresh unsuccessful individuals in the DE population is proposed and applied to the classic DE algorithm. The results of the comparison of real-world problems show that the proposed approach is able to significantly increase the performance of DE. The statistical comparison results in the following conclusions. The number of unsuccessful generations of the individuals is best set to $ref_G = 50$.

Regarding the refreshment formula, using the optional control parameter var_p increases the performance significantly compared to the proposed variants without this parameter. This parameter plays a crucial role in the refreshment approach.

The last experimentally verified setting of the proposed approach was for the optional parameter var_p. The fixed setting of $var_p 0.01$ achieved the best overall results (the Friedman test), and the linearly (dynamically) decreasing setting from 0.2 to 0.05 provided also very promising performance. The short number of unsuccessful generations of the individuals ($ref_G = 10$) provided worse results, compared to longer periods ($ref_G = 50, 100$).

Further development, tuning, and applications of the newly proposed refreshment approach will be studied in future work.

References

1. Bujok, P., Tvrdík, J.: A comparison of various strategies in differential evolution. In: Matoušek, R. (ed.) MENDEL, 17th International Conference on Soft Computing, pp. 48–55. Czech Republic, Brno (2011)
2. Bujok, P., Tvrdík, J., Poláková, R.: Differential evolution with adaptive mechanism of population size according to current population diversity. Swarm Evol. Comput. **50**, 100519 (2019). https://doi.org/10.1016/j.swevo.2019.03.014
3. Castillo, J.C., Segura, C.: Comparison of nature-inspired population-based algorithms on continuous optimisation problems. Swarm Evol. Comput. **50**, 100490 (2019). https://doi.org/10.1016/j.swevo.2019.01.006
4. Cheng, J., Pan, Z., Liang, H., Gao, Z., Gao, J.: Differential evolution algorithm with fitness and diversity ranking-based mutation operator. Swarm Evol. Comput. **61**, 100816 (2021). https://doi.org/10.1016/j.swevo.2020.100816
5. Das, S., Suganthan, P.N.: Problem definitions and evaluation criteria for CEC 2011 competition on testing evolutionary algorithms on real world optimization problems. Jadavpur University, India and Nanyang Technological University, Singapore, Tech. Rep. (2010)

6. Navarro, M.A., et al.: Improving the convergence and diversity in differential evolution through a stock market criterion. In: Jiménez Laredo, J.L., Hidalgo, J.I., Babaagba, K.O. (eds.) EvoApplications 2022. LNCS, vol. 13224, pp. 157–172. Springer, Cham (2022). https://doi.org/10.1007/978-3-031-02462-7_11

7. Senkerik, R., et al.: Population diversity analysis in adaptive differential evolution variants with unconventional randomization schemes. In: Rutkowski, L., Scherer, R., Korytkowski, M., Pedrycz, W., Tadeusiewicz, R., Zurada, J.M. (eds.) ICAISC 2019. LNCS (LNAI), vol. 11508, pp. 506–518. Springer, Cham (2019). https://doi.org/10.1007/978-3-030-20912-4_46

8. Storn, R., Price, K.V.: Differential evolution - a simple and efficient heuristic for global optimization over continuous spaces. J. Global Optim. **11**, 341–359 (1997)

9. Vázquez, G., Segura, C.: Differential evolution with explicit control of diversity for constrained optimization. In: Proceedings of the 2020 Genetic and Evolutionary Computation Conference Companion, pp. 207–208. GECCO 2020, Association for Computing Machinery, New York, NY, USA (2020). https://doi.org/10.1145/3377929.3389978

10. Yu, Y., Wang, K., Zhang, T., Wang, Y., Peng, C., Gao, S.: A population diversity-controlled differential evolution for parameter estimation of solar photovoltaic models. Sustain. Energy Technol. Assess. **51**, 101938 (2022). https://doi.org/10.1016/j.seta.2021.101938

A New Hybrid Particle Swarm Optimization and Evolutionary Algorithm with Self-Adaptation Mechanism

Piotr Dziwiński[(✉)] [iD] and Łukasz Bartczuk[iD]

Department of Intelligent Computer Systems, Częstochowa University of Technology, Częstochowa, Poland
{piotr.dziwinski,lukasz.bartczuk}@pcz.pl

Abstract. Particle Swarm Optimization (PSO) has demonstrated remarkable convergence capabilities in various optimization problems. It is increasingly employed in conjunction with gradient-based methods to enhance the learning process of deep neural networks. However, PSO suffers from a significant drawback, namely the propensity to become trapped in local minima, particularly in challenging multi-modal problems. To address this issue, this study introduces a novel Hybrid Particle Swarm Optimization and Genetic Algorithm with a Self-Adaptation mechanism. Self-adaptation mechanism enables the hybrid algorithm to dynamically adjust its behavior according to the current state of the global best solution search. Initial simulations conducted in this research validate the effectiveness of the proposed approach.

Keywords: hybrid algorithm · particle swarm optimization · genetic algorithm · self-adaptation · deep neural network

1 Introduction

Optimization is a widely used tool in machine learning. It consists in finding the optimal values of the parameters of a specific model to minimize the value of the objective function or to maximize a specific indicator of the quality of the solution (e.g. model quality or simplicity). It is used to construct fuzzy systems, neuro-fuzzy systems [7,8,12,27], decision trees [11] or learning deep neural networks [1,17–20,26]. Standard algorithms for learning deep neural networks such as gradient algorithms with different improvements, for example, novel SGQR algorithm [2], Levenberg-Marquardt [3], SGD [4] or improved Adam optimizer [32] can fail before the search for an optimal solution is completed, getting stuck in a local minimum, especially for difficult, complex problems. During the last decades, many nature-inspired methods have been proposed to overcome this drawback and are used to solve difficult optimization problems. For example: Genetic Algorithms (GA) [21,31], evolutionary algorithms, evolutionary strategies [5,24], differential evolution [6]. Swarm intelligence and evolutionary algorithms are used increasingly for learning deep neural networks [1,20,26].

© The Author(s), under exclusive license to Springer Nature Switzerland AG 2023
L. Rutkowski et al. (Eds.): ICAISC 2023, LNAI 14125, pp. 363–374, 2023.
https://doi.org/10.1007/978-3-031-42505-9_31

The advantage of these methods lies in the better convergence and the ability to avoid local minima, in contrast to the commonly used different versions of gradient methods [2–4]. Recently, solutions combining gradient-based methods with algorithms based on swarm intelligence have gained particular interest [1,20,26]. Researchers manage to obtain very good results in terms of the quality of the obtained solutions as well as the learning time. Particularly noteworthy is the Particle Swarm Optimization Algorithm (PSO), which has recently been increasingly used practically in deep learning. Its greatest advantages are: fast convergence and partial resistance to local minima. Nevertheless, with the wrong choice of algorithm parameters, premature convergence or stagnation can be observed. Shi et al. [28] propose the first important modification of the PSO algorithm by introduce inertia weight w. Trela et al. [29] perform convergence analysis and parameter selection of the PSO. Nickabadi et al. [25] present a novel PSO algorithm that incorporates an adaptive inertia weight. Phong et al. [26] propose the utilization of Heterogeneous Learning Rate in conjunction with PSO for training convolutional neural networks. Dziwiński et al. propose a Hybrid Particle Swarm Optimization and Evolutionary algorithm (HPSO-E) [9], which incorporates mutation and crossover operators from the GA. By introducing new solutions to the population of individuals with a certain probability, the algorithm enhances movement speed and prevents stagnation.

The HPSO-E algorithm was initially proposed in the publication by Dziwiński and Bartczuk [9], incorporating the mutation and crossover operators from the GA [14–16]. In a subsequent study [10], a Multiple Input Single Output (MISO) fuzzy-neural system was employed to regulate the probability of executing the genetic operators based on the outcomes obtained from both algorithms. The parameters of the MISO system and the PSO algorithm underwent a learning process. However, this approach suffered from the necessity of training the fuzzy-neural system and adapting the algorithm parameters for significantly distinct optimization problems. Furthermore, it was observed that different parameter settings were required for the PSO algorithm when employed in conjunction with the GA algorithm. Alternatively, strategies such as comprehensive learning [22] or a multi-population-based approach [23] can be employed to mitigate the issue of local minima trapping.

This article presents a novel approach aimed at addressing the challenge of selecting key parameters for the PSO algorithm across different problem domains. The proposed solution entails the automatic adaptation of parameter values through self-adaptation. Self-adaptation is achieved by incorporating selected algorithm parameters into the solution vector. It is posited that individuals achieving superior results will exhibit movement patterns that are better suited to the current stage of problem-solving, thus implying an improved parameter setting for the algorithm. Furthermore, distinct particles within the algorithm may exhibit varying behavior depending on the current progress. Consequently, the new hybrid algorithm can dynamically adjust the behavior of individuals during operation, thereby enhancing progress, preventing premature convergence, and facilitating escape from local minima.

The subsequent sections of this paper are structured as follows. In Sect. 2, we provide an overview of the fundamental version of the LDPSO algorithm. The previous iteration of the algorithm is outlined in Sect. 3. Section 4 details our proposed approach incorporating the self-adaptation mechanism. The simulation results, as well as a comprehensive analysis of the behavior of the hybrid algorithm, are presented in Sect. 5. Finally, Sect. 6 encompasses the conclusion of our study along with potential avenues for future research.

2   Linear Decrease Particle Swarm Optimization Algorithm

The LDPSO algorithm is a simple method to solve optimization problems in the form:

$$\min_{\mathbf{x} \in \mathbf{R}^D} f(\mathbf{x}), \tag{1}$$

where $f(\mathbf{x})$ is an optimized objective function and $\mathbf{x}$ is a solution of the problem. In this algorithm the solution $\mathbf{x} = [x^1, \ldots, x^D]$ is described as the particle i, $i = 1 \ldots N$, that also contains information about the best local solution $\mathbf{p}_{it} = [p_{it}^1, \ldots, p_{it}^D]$ found so far, and velocity vector $\mathbf{v}_{it} = [v_{it}^1, \ldots, v_{it}^D]$ in the iteration t. Each particle of the swarm moves with the velocity $\mathbf{v}_{it}$ throughout solution space in different directions using the best local solution $\mathbf{p}_{it}$ found by the particle so far and the best global solution $\mathbf{g}_t = [g_t^1, \ldots, g_t^D]$ of the entire swarm. A new velocity $\mathbf{v}_{i(t+1)}$ and position $\mathbf{x}_{i(t+1)}$ of each particle are computed according to Eqs. (2) and (3):

$$v_{i(t+1)}^d = v_{it}^d \cdot w + c_1 \cdot r_1 \cdot (p_{it}^d - x_{it}^d) + c_2 \cdot r_2 \cdot (g_t - x_{it}^d), \tag{2}$$

$$x_{i(t+1)}^d = x_{it}^d + v_{i(t+1)}^d, \tag{3}$$

where w is an inertia weight specifying the change value of the velocity between iteration (t) and $(t+1)$, for $w = 1$, we can obtain the base algorithm introduced by Kennedy and Eberhart [13]), c_1 and c_2 are two acceleration coefficients that scale the influence of the best local and global solutions, r_1 and r_2 are two uniform random values within the range $(0, 1]$. The pseudocode of the PSO algorithm is shown in the Algorithm 1. The inertia weight w is used to control the influence of the speed from the previous steep to speed in the current one.

3   Hybrid Particle Swarm Optimization and Evolutionary Algorithm

The Linear Decreasing Particle Swarm Optimization (LDPSO) algorithm, as discussed in the preceding section, has proven to be a valuable tool in addressing various optimization problems. Nevertheless, one of its prominent shortcomings is its susceptibility to becoming trapped in local optima. Dziwiński and Bartczuk

---

Algorithm 1: Algorithm of particle swarm optimization (PSO)

Data: Population size N, acceleration constant c_1, c_2, inertia weight w

Result: The best solution $\mathbf{g}_{t_{max}}$

1 Initialization;

2 **repeat**

3 $\quad$ Evaluate each particles $ex_{it} = f_{ob}(\mathbf{x}_{it})$;

4 $\quad$ Update the best local solution $\mathbf{p}_{it}$;

5 $\quad$ Update the best global solution $\mathbf{g}_t$;

6 $\quad$ **for** $i \leftarrow 1$ **to** N **do**

7 $\quad\quad$ Compute $\mathbf{v}_{i(t+1)}$ according to equation (2);

8 $\quad\quad$ Compute $\mathbf{x}_{i(t+1)}$ according to equation (3);

9 $\quad\quad$ $t \leftarrow t + 1$;

10 **until** *Terminate condition has not been met*;

---

[9] proposed a new Hybrid Particle Swarm Optimization and Evolutionary algorithm (HPSO-E) which solves partially this disadvantage.

They introduced the mutation and crossover operators from the genetic algorithm to the LDPSO algorithm. The tournament selection method was employed to identify the most promising individuals within the population, and subsequently, the selected individuals were subject to the application of these operators. The best local solutions of selected individuals were mutated and crossed with a certain probability. After applying genetic operators, they introduce new solutions to selected individuals of the population only if they are better (replacement strategy). The key feature of this proposal is that genetic operators did not affect the performance of the LDPSO algorithm if they did not improve the solutions. A comprehensive exposition of the HPSO-E algorithm can be found in the study [9].

The primary drawback of the proposed method lies in the requirement for empirical determination of the parameters associated with the LDPSO algorithm and the genetic algorithm, specifically the utilization probability of the genetic component. The research conducted further reveals that for the LDPSO algorithm to attain maximum convergence, different values for the inertia coefficient are necessary when it collaborates with the genetic algorithm. To address these aforementioned limitations, in this study, we propose the incorporation of a self-adaptation mechanism for key parameters, including the inertia weight and the probability of employing the genetic algorithm. The modification of these algorithmic parameters will automatically tailor the behavior of individual population members to the nature of the problem being solved, as well as the progress made in its resolution. Furthermore, the self-adaptation approach will effectively mitigate two critical shortcomings of the HPSO-E algorithm: premature stagnation and the issue of becoming trapped in local minima. The latter concern is particularly significant in the training of deep neural networks. The details of the proposed solution are elaborated in Sect. 4.

4   HPSO-E with Self-Adaptation Mechanism

In this study, a novel Hybrid Particle Swarm Optimization and Evolutionary algorithm with a Self-Adaptation mechanism (HPSO-ESA) is introduced, featuring the self-adaptation of pivotal parameters, such as the inertia weight and the probability of utilizing a genetic algorithm for preventing premature convergence and the possibility of trapping in the local minima. A proposed approach involves adding these key parameters to the vectors that describe the problem under consideration $\mathbf{x} = [x^1, \ldots, x^D, w, p_e]$. The crucial concern lies in determining the source for these parameters but also influence of these additional parameters on the collective behavior of the population of individuals. The four potential scenarios are possible:

1. The entire population adopts the parameters of the global best solution (HPSO-ESA-G)

$$(w_{it}, p_{eit}) = f_{global}(\mathbf{g}_t), \mathbf{g}_t = [g_t^1, \ldots, g_t^D, w_t, p_{et}]; \qquad (4)$$

2. Individuals employ their local solutions (p_{it}) (HPSO-ESA-L)

$$(w_{it}, p_{eit}) = f_{local}(\mathbf{p}_{it}), \mathbf{p}_{it} = [p_{it}^1, \ldots, p_{it}^D, w_{it}, p_{eit}]; \qquad (5)$$

3. The entire population employs local or global best parameters based on a certain experimentally determined probability (HPSO-ESA-LG)

$$(w_{it}, p_{eit}) = \begin{cases} f_{local}(\mathbf{p}_{it}) \text{ if } lg < rand() \\ f_{global}(\mathbf{g}_t) \text{ } otherwise; \end{cases} \qquad (6)$$

where: lg - is parameter describing the probability of using the local best solution as guide for parameter settings.

4. The entire population adheres to the scenario (3) while also subjecting the probability of selecting a strategy for parameter adaptation to the self-adaptation process. Then the solution vector takes shape

$$\mathbf{x} = [x^1, \ldots, x^D, w, p_e, lg]. \qquad (7)$$

In this work, the first two scenarios are tested. The others require further simulation studies. The remaining parameters of the hybrid algorithm were determined through empirical experimentation and displayed negligible variation across a diverse set of optimization problems. Furthermore, empirical investigations suggest that incorporating a higher number of operational parameters of the hybrid algorithm into the self-adaptation mechanism yields detrimental outcomes for the majority of problems (more varied results are obtained).

5   Simulations

Simulation studies were carried out on a set of 10 widely recognized benchmark functions, as documented in [30]. These experiments were initially conducted

---

Algorithm 2: Hybrid particle swarm optimization evolutionary algorithm with self-adaptation mechanism (HPSO-ESA)

Data: Population size $N = |\mathbf{X}|$, acceleration constant c_1, c_2, inertia weight w, evolutionary operators probability p_e, crossover probability p_c, number of crossover positions n_c, mutation probability p_m, number of mutated positions n_m and tournament size T, global params enable gpe, local params enable lpe;

Result: The best solution $\mathbf{g}_{t_{max}}$

1 Initialize the current position $\mathbf{x}_{it}$, the best local position $\mathbf{p}_{it}$ and the global best solution $\mathbf{g}_t$ randomly in the domain of the problem, $t = 0$;

2 Evaluate each particle $ex_{it} = f_{ob}(\mathbf{x}_{it})$, $ep_{it} = f_{ob}(\mathbf{p}_{it})$, $\mathbf{x}_{it} \in \mathbf{X}_t$;

3 Update the best local solution $\mathbf{p}_{it}$, $\mathbf{p}_{it} \in \mathbf{P}_t$;

4 Update the best global solution $\mathbf{g}_t$;

5 **repeat**

6   **for** $i \leftarrow 1$ **to** N **do**

7   **if** $(gpe = True)$ **then**

8             $(w_{it}, p_{eit}) = f_{global}(\mathbf{g}_t)$;

9   **else**

10   **if** $(lpe = True)$ **then**

11                 $(w_{it}, p_{eit}) = f_{local}(\mathbf{p}_{it})$

12   Compute $\mathbf{v}_{i(t+1)}$ according to equation (2);

13   Compute $\mathbf{x}_{i(t+1)}$ according to equation (3);

14   Evaluate each particle of the main population $ex_{it} = f_{ob}(\mathbf{x}_{it})$;

15   Update the best local solution $\mathbf{p}_{it}$ based on ex_{it};

16   Set the temporal swarm of offspring as empty set $\mathbf{CH}_t = \emptyset$;

17   **for** $i \leftarrow 1$ **to** N **do**

18   **if** $(p_{eit} > r(0,1))$ **then**

19   **if** $(p_m > r(0,1))$ **then**

20   Choose a descendant: $(\mathbf{ch}_m, j) = \text{Tournament}(\mathbf{P}_t, T)$;

21   Mutate($\mathbf{ch}_m$, n_m);

22   Evaluate the particle $ech_m = f_{ob}(\mathbf{ch}_m)$;

23   Insert $(\mathbf{ch}_m, ech_m, j)$ into $\mathbf{CH}_t$;

24   **if** $(p_c > r(0,1))$ **then**

25   Chose a offspring: $(\mathbf{ch}_{c1}, j1) = \text{Tournament}(\mathbf{P}_t, T)$, $(\mathbf{ch}_{c2}, j2) = \text{Tournament}(\mathbf{P}_t, T)$;

26   Crossover($\mathbf{ch}_{c1}$, $\mathbf{ch}_{c2}$, n_c);

27   Evaluate the particle $ech_{c1} = f_{ob}(\mathbf{ch}_{c1})$;

28   Evaluate the particle $ech_{c2} = f_{ob}(\mathbf{ch}_{c2})$;

29   Insert $(\mathbf{ch}_{c1}, ech_{c1}, j1)$ into $\mathbf{CH}_t$;

30   Insert $(\mathbf{ch}_{c2}, ech_{c2}, j2)$ into $\mathbf{CH}_t$;

31   Apply the replacement strategy of $\mathbf{p}_{it}$;

32   Update the best global solution $\mathbf{g}_t$;

33     $t \leftarrow t + 1$;

34 **until** *Terminate condition has not been met;*

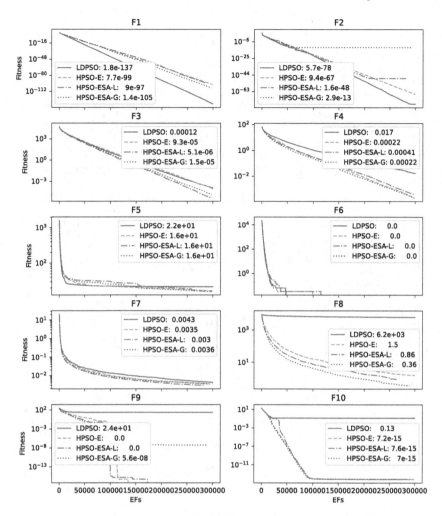

Fig. 1. Progress of the algorithms for different benchmark functions

with a dimensionality of D = 30. The number of objective function evaluations was determined as NEval = D * 10000. The parameters settings for the tested algorithms are presented in the Table 1.

To ensure robustness and reliability of the results, the experiments were repeated 30 times using identical parameter settings for the following algorithms:

1. Linear Decreasing Particle Swarm Optimization (LDPSO) [13];
2. Hybrid Particle Swarm Optimization and Evolutionary algorithm (HPSO-E) [9];
3. Hybrid Particle Swarm Optimization and Evolutionary algorithm with Self-Adaptation mechanism based on Global best (HPSO-ESA-G) - scenario (1);

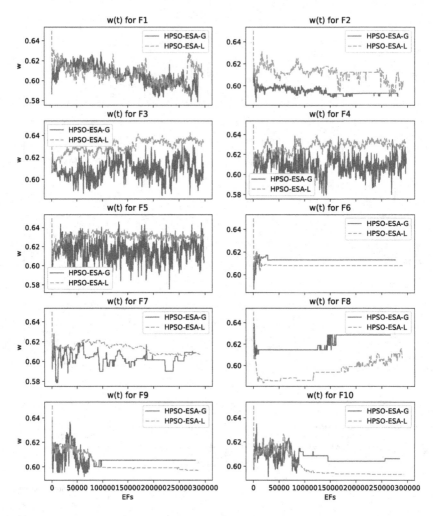

Fig. 2. Changes of the inertia weight w parameter for global and local HPSO-ESA algorithm

4. Hybrid Particle Swarm Optimization and Evolutionary algorithm with Self-Adaptation mechanism based on Local best (HPSO-ESA-L) - scenario (2).

The average progress of the algorithms over 30 repetitions, as a function of the number of evaluations, is depicted in Fig. 1. For the simple unimodal benchmark functions (F1-F3), the self-adaptation mechanism enables comparable results to the LDPSO algorithm, despite the incorporation of genetic operators (mutation and crossover), which are not ideally suited for such problems. In contrast, for the more challenging multimodal problems (F4-F10), the self-adaptation mechanism significantly improves the results, particularly for functions F8-F10, surpassing the performance of the LDPSO algorithm. Furthermore, the HPSO-ESA-G

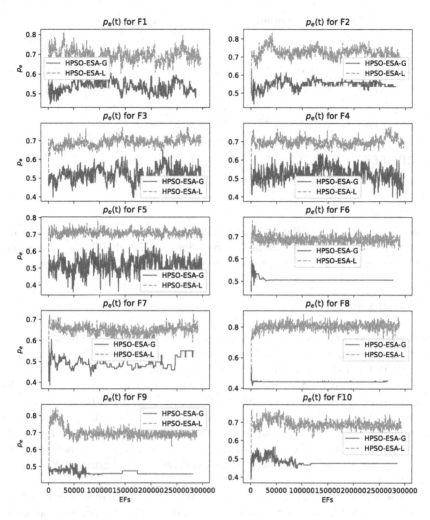

Fig. 3. Changes of the probability of using of the genetic algorithm p_e for global and local HPSO-ESA algorithm

algorithm consistently outperforms the HPSO-E algorithm. Based on these findings, it can be concluded that the self-adaptation mechanism proves more effective for tackling complex multimodal problems. Figure 2 illustrates the variation of the inertia weight (w) as a function of the number of evaluations. The self-adaptation mechanism adjusts the value of w for all benchmark functions, with more dynamic changes observed in the global best update scenario. It should be noted that the plots for the local best update scenario represent the average value of w across all particles, resulting in a seemingly more stable trend.

Table 1. The parameters for all evaluated algorithms

Algorithm	Parameters	Source
LDPSO	w: 0.68, c_1: 1.5, c_2: 1.75	[28]
HPSO-E	w: 0.68, c_1: 1.5, c_2: 1.75,	
	p_e: 0.4, p_m: 0.9, p_c:0.5, n_m: 1, n_c: 15, T: 4	[9]
HPSO-ESA-G	$w \in [0.52, 0.7]$, c_1: 1.5, c_2: 1.75, gpe: True	
	$p_e \in [0.1, 0.9]$:, p_m: 0.9, p_c:0.5, n_m: 1, n_c: 15, T: 4	-
HPSO-ESA-L	$w \in [0.52, 0.7]$, c_1: 1.5, c_2: 1.75, lpe: True	
	$p_e \in [0.1, 0.9]$, p_m: 0.9, p_c:0.5, n_m: 1, n_c: 15, T: 4	-

The changes in the probability of utilizing the genetic operators are depicted in Fig. 3. In general, for all benchmark functions, the probability (p_e) assumes higher values when the algorithm employs the local best update scenario.

6   Conclusions

In this study, we propose a novel hybrid particle swarm optimization and evolutionary algorithm with a self-adaptation mechanism. This approach combines the conventional LDPSO algorithm with the genetic algorithm while introducing a new self-adaptation mechanism. The self-adaptation mechanism enables the adjustment of the inertia weight and the probability of utilizing the genetic component based on the specific problem being solved and the progress made in searching for the optimal solution. Initial simulations conducted on 10 well-known benchmark functions demonstrate that our self-adaptation method yields superior results compared to the previous version of the algorithm [9], underscoring the efficacy of our approach.

Further simulations are required to evaluate the performance of our method on additional benchmark functions, including those with higher dimensionalities. Additionally, key experiments should be conducted to assess the effectiveness of our approach in learning deep neural networks. These future investigations will provide a more comprehensive understanding of the capabilities and potential applications of our proposed hybrid algorithm.

References

1. Albeahdili, H.M., Han, T., Islam, N.E.: Hybrid algorithm for the optimization of training convolutional neural network. Int. J. Adv. Comput. Sci. Appl. **1**(6), 79–85 (2015)
2. Bilski, J., Kowalczyk, B., Kisiel-Dorohinicki, M., Siwocha, A., Żurada, J.M.: Towards a very fast feedforward multilayer neural networks training algorithm. J. Artif. Intell. Soft Comput. Res. **12**(3), 181–195 (2022). https://doi.org/10.2478/jaiscr-2022-0012

3. Bilski, J., Smoląg, J., Kowalczyk, B., Grzanek, K., Izonin, I.: Fast computational approach to the Levenberg-Marquardt algorithm for training feedforward neural networks. J. Artif. Intell. Soft Comput. Res. **13**(2), 45–61 (2023). https://doi.org/10.2478/jaiscr-2023-0006

4. Bottou, L.: Stochastic gradient descent tricks. In: Montavon, G., Orr, G.B., Müller, K.-R. (eds.) Neural Networks: Tricks of the Trade. LNCS, vol. 7700, pp. 421–436. Springer, Heidelberg (2012). https://doi.org/10.1007/978-3-642-35289-8_25

5. Cpałka, K., Rutkowski, L.: Evolutionary learning of flexible neuro-fuzzy systems. In: Proceedings of the 2008 IEEE International Conference on Fuzzy Systems (IEEE World Congress on Computational Intelligence, WCCI 2008), Hong Kong June 1–6, CD, pp. 969–975 (2008)

6. Dawar, D., Ludwig, S.A.: Effect of strategy adaptation on differential evolution in presence and absence of parameter adaptation: an investigation. J. Artif. Intell. Soft Comput. Res. **8**(3), 211–235 (2018)

7. Dziwiński, P., Avedyan, E.D.: A new method of the intelligent modeling of the nonlinear dynamic objects with fuzzy detection of the operating points. In: Rutkowski, L., Korytkowski, M., Scherer, R., Tadeusiewicz, R., Zadeh, L.A., Zurada, J.M. (eds.) ICAISC 2016. LNCS (LNAI), vol. 9693, pp. 293–305. Springer, Cham (2016). https://doi.org/10.1007/978-3-319-39384-1_25

8. Dziwiński, P., Bartczuk, Ł, Tingwen, H.: A method for non-linear modelling based on the capabilities of PSO and GA algorithms. In: Rutkowski, L., Korytkowski, M., Scherer, R., Tadeusiewicz, R., Zadeh, L.A., Zurada, J.M. (eds.) ICAISC 2017. LNCS (LNAI), vol. 10246, pp. 221–232. Springer, Cham (2017). https://doi.org/10.1007/978-3-319-59060-8_21

9. Dziwiński, P., Bartczuk, Ł, Goetzen, P.: A new hybrid particle swarm optimization and evolutionary algorithm. In: Rutkowski, L., Scherer, R., Korytkowski, M., Pedrycz, W., Tadeusiewicz, R., Zurada, J.M. (eds.) ICAISC 2019. LNCS (LNAI), vol. 11508, pp. 432–444. Springer, Cham (2019). https://doi.org/10.1007/978-3-030-20912-4_40

10. Dziwiński, P., Bartczuk, Ł: A new hybrid particle swarm optimization and genetic algorithm method controlled by fuzzy logic. IEEE Trans. Fuzzy Syst. **28**(6), 1140–1154 (2019)

11. Dziwiński, P., Bartczuk, Ł, Przybyszewski, K.: A population based algorithm and fuzzy decision trees for nonlinear modeling. In: Rutkowski, L., Scherer, R., Korytkowski, M., Pedrycz, W., Tadeusiewicz, R., Zurada, J.M. (eds.) ICAISC 2018. LNCS (LNAI), vol. 10842, pp. 516–531. Springer, Cham (2018). https://doi.org/10.1007/978-3-319-91262-2_46

12. Dziwiński, P., PrzybyŁ, A., Trippner, P., Paszkowski, J., Hayashi, Y.: Hardware implementation of a Takagi-Sugeno neuro-fuzzy system optimized by a population algorithm. J. Artif. Intell. Soft Comput. Res. **11**(3), 243–266 (2021)

13. Eberhart, R., Kennedy, J.: A new optimizer using particle swarm theory. In: MHS1995. Proceedings of the Sixth International Symposium on Micro Machine and Human Science 1995, pp. 39–43 (1995)

14. Esmin, A.A.A., Lambert-Torres, G., Alvarenga, G.B.: Hybrid evolutionary algorithm based on PSO and GA mutation. In: 2006 Sixth International Conference on Hybrid Intelligent Systems (HIS2006), p. 57. IEEE (2006)

15. Esmin, A.A., Matwin, S.: HPSOM: a hybrid particle swarm optimization algorithm with genetic mutation. Int. J. Innov. Comput. Inf. Control **9**(5), 1919–1934 (2013)

16. Fang, N., Zhou, J., Zhang, R., Liu, Y., Zhang, Y.: A hybrid of real coded genetic algorithm and artificial fish swarm algorithm for short-term optimal hydrothermal scheduling. Int. J. Electr. Power Energy Syst. **62**, 617–629 (2014)

17. Gabryel, M., Lada, D., Filutowicz, Z., Patora-Wysocka, Z., Kisiel-Dorohinicki, M., Yi Chen, G.: Detecting anomalies in advertising web traffic with the use of the variational autoencoder. J. Artif. Intell. Soft Comput. Res. **12**(4), 255–266 (2022)

18. Gabryel, M., Scherer, M.M., Sułkowski, Ł., Damaševičius, R.: Decision making support system for managing advertisers by ad fraud detection. J. Artif. Intell. Soft Comput. Res. **11**, 331–339 (2021)

19. Gabryel, M., Kocić, M.: Application of a neural network to generate the hash code for a device fingerprint. In: Rutkowski, L., Scherer, R., Korytkowski, M., Pedrycz, W., Tadeusiewicz, R., Zurada, J.M. (eds.) ICAISC 2021. LNCS (LNAI), vol. 12855, pp. 456–463. Springer, Cham (2021). https://doi.org/10.1007/978-3-030-87897-9_40

20. Kan, X., et al.: A novel PSO-based optimized lightweight convolution neural network for movements recognizing from multichannel surface electromyogram. Complexity **2020**, 1–15 (2020)

21. Łapa, K., Cpałka, K., Przybył, A.: Genetic programming algorithm for designing of control systems. Inf. Technol. Control **47**(5), 668–683 (2018)

22. Liang, J.J., Qin, A.K., Suganthan, P.N., Baskar, S.: Comprehensive learning particle swarm optimizer for global optimization of multimodal functions. IEEE Trans. Evol. Comput. **10**(3), 281–295 (2006)

23. Łapa, K., Cpałka, K., Kisiel-Dorohinicki, M., Paszkowski, J., Dębski, M., Le, V.-H.: Multi-population-based algorithm with an exchange of training plans based on population evaluation. J. Artif. Intell. Soft Comput. Res. **12**(4), 239–253 (2022). https://doi.org/10.2478/jaiscr-2022-0016

24. Mizera, M., Nowotarski, P., Byrski, A., Kisiel-Dorohinicki, M.: Fine tuning of agent-based evolutionary computing. J. Artif. Intell. Soft Comput. Res. **9**(2), 81–97 (2019)

25. Nickabadi, A., Ebadzadeh, M.M., Safabakhsh, R.: A novel particle swarm optimization algorithm with adaptive inertia weight. Appl. Soft Comput. **11**(4), 3658–3670 (2011)

26. Phong, N.H., Santos, A., Ribeiro, B.: PSO-Convolutional neural networks with heterogeneous learning rate. IEEE Access **10** 89970–89988 (2022)

27. Rutkowski, T., Romanowski, J., Woldan, P., Staszewski, P., Nielek, R., Rutkowski, L.: A content-based recommendation system using neuro-fuzzy approach. FUZZ-IEEE **2018**, 1–8 (2018)

28. Shi, Y., Eberhart, R.: A modified particle swarm optimizer. In: 1998 IEEE International Conference on Evolutionary Computation Proceedings. IEEE World Congress on Computational Intelligence (Cat. No. 98TH8360), pp. 69–73. IEEE (1998)

29. Trelea, I.C.: The particle swarm optimization algorithm: convergence analysis and parameter selection. Inf. Process. Lett. **85**(6), 317–325 (2003)

30. Wang, L., Yang, B., Orchard, J.: Particle swarm optimization using dynamic tournament topology. Appl. Soft Comput. **48**, 584–596 (2016)

31. Wei, Y., et al.: Vehicle emission computation through microscopic traffic simulation calibrated using genetic algorithm. J. Artif. Intell. Soft Comput. Res. **9**(1), 67–80 (2019)

32. Zhang, Z.: Improved Adam optimizer for deep neural networks. In: 2018 IEEE/ACM 26th International Symposium on Quality of Service (IWQoS). IEEE (2018)

Data Mining Car Configurator Clickstream Data to Identify Potential Consumers: A Genetic Algorithm Approach

Juan Manuel García-Sánchez[1,2]([ORCID]), Xavier Vilasís-Cardona[1][ORCID],
Álvaro García-Piquer[1][ORCID], and Alexandre Lerma-Martín[2]

[1] Research Group of Smart Society, La Salle-Ramon Llull University,
08022 Barcelona, Spain
`juanmanuel.g@salle.url.edu`
[2] SEAT S.A., 08760 Martorell, Spain

Abstract. The Car Configurator (CC) website provided by automotive Original Equipment Manufacturers (OEMs) enables customers to choose from the brand's portfolio of cars without having to list them all. Afterwards, users move to dealership to formalize the purchase. However, the car they acquired might differ from the one they consulted online. Because there is no record from these deviations, CC data is considered noisy and meaningless. This paper investigates the question of whether valuable information can be extracted from CC clickstream data to aid automotive manufacturers in their operations. The data mining technique of genetic algorithms is employed to identify the characteristics that maximize the correlation between clickstream data and car sales. The findings reveal that the genetic algorithm outperforms the benchmark correlation value and that most frequently occurring elements from sales and webpage data may not be the most effective indicators of potential consumers. The proposed methodology can help identify future clients and target marketing efforts.

Keywords: Car Configurator · Clickstream · Sales · Data mining · Genetic algorithm · Correlation · R2 Score · Automotive industry

1   Introduction

The Car Configurator (CC) website is a tool provided by automotive Original Equipment Manufacturers (OEMs) to their customers. It enables them to choose from the brand's portfolio of cars without having to list them all, as highlighted in [10]. The website also provides an estimate of the purchase value and allows customers to book a date with the dealership. This online service is particularly

This work is partially funded by the Department de Recerca i Universitats of the Generalitat de Catalunya under the Industrial Doctorate Grant DI 2019-34.

important during the clients' exploration phase. Research conducted by [9] has demonstrated the significance of the internet as an information search channel, alongside other channels such as word-of-mouth, mass media, and retailers. This behavior has been echoed for the German market in [8]. Future consumers firstly browse online and then visit dealerships to consult and finalize their purchase, so CC webpage becomes a non-transactional one. This transforms the car industry into a *webrooming* business. It means that customers follow *Research Online Purchase Offline* (ROPO) strategy.

Dealerships represent a third party with their own commercial interests. Their influence is evident when customers arrive at the dealership intending to purchase a particular car configuration seen online, but ultimately purchase a different one. This change in choice may be attributed to several factors, such as unavailability or late delivery of the first option or a generous discount offered on the alternative model. Unfortunately, dealerships do not maintain records of these deviations. Consequently, while the CC website is the initial contact point between customers and the car brand, it generates large and particularly noisy data, which automotive OEMs do not consider when developing their operational strategies.

This note outlines a methodology to answer the following research question: **Can Car Configurator clickstream data provide useful insights for automotive manufacturers?** We pursue to find the relevant filters that help to distinguish between web visitors with purchasing interest and those ones doing window shopping. To achieve this objective, data mining techniques will be employed, utilizing genetic algorithms. It will seek to identify the characteristics that maximizes correlation between clickstream data and car sales. This approach has been chosen due to sales records are a critical metric within the automotive industry and are used to develop factory production plans.

The attributes that genetic algorithm explore are: (a) access day of the week; (b) user's geographical location; (c) TRIM; (d) engine and (e) exterior color of the car model. We conduct five trials under the same initial conditions to increase the robustness of the results. Hence, we compare these outcomes to the one obtained from plain clickstream data, used as benchmark line. Finally, the rules derived from the best solution are analyzed. We detail the frequency of the elements chosen in each chromosome attribute as well as the individual fitness of the rules. The findings reveal that the genetic algorithm outperformed the benchmark correlation value, increasing it from 29.42 to an average of 91.21 ± 3.8 R2 Score, and that most frequently occurring elements from sales and webpage data may not be the most effective indicators of potential consumers.

The article is structured in the following way. Firstly, in Sect. 2, we present related works for the research topic. Hence, Sect. 3 describes the dataset provided by the automotive OEM source. Next, the methodology and results of the research are in Sect. 4 and Sect. 5, respectively. The discussion takes place in Sect. 6. Finally, Sect. 7 provides conclusions gained and future research paths.

2   Related Works

The effectiveness of machine learning algorithms is influenced by the selection of features from the dataset. High-dimensional datasets negatively affect the performance of learning algorithms, as they strive to analyze and incorporate all features. To address this issue, feature selection techniques are commonly used as a pre-processing step to analyze and compress large datasets. The main goals of feature selection techniques include reducing the dimensionality of the dataset, among others. A thorough examination of the current advancements in methods for selecting relevant features can be found in [12]. Special mention deserves genetic algorithms. They are a type of optimization algorithm inspired by the process of natural selection. It starts with an initial population of potential solutions, and through a process of selection, crossover, and mutation, evolves the population over multiple generations towards an optimal solution.

This approach has proven competent for a variety of optimization problems in which traditional optimization methods are infeasible or inefficient. Work [5] employed a genetic algorithm to select features and optimize parameters for support vector machines, achieving better model performance on a benchmark dataset. Note [7] developed a genetic algorithm for feature selection that used a greedy approach to select relevant features based on their contribution to a classification task. Book [15] includes a detail guide about optimization of feature selection by means of genetic algorithms in the context of data mining.

There are effort, as well, in the context of using correlation as an assessment metric. It is called correlation-based feature-subset selection (CFS). It has proved its validity in cancer research, as it is explained in note [11]. A gene-search algorithm for analyzing genetic expression data was implemented, which combines a genetic algorithm with correlation-based heuristics for data preprocessing. Nevertheless, it is extented to other uses, such as Integration of data sources to build a Data warehouse, as it is related in paper [13]. It proposes a method for selecting an optimal subset of attributes based on correlation analysis, which identifies redundant attributes that do not significantly contribute to the overall characteristics of the data. Reference [16] proposed a correlation-based filter solution using a genetic algorithm for feature selection, which was able to identify relevant features quickly and accurately in high-dimensional datasets. The last case is found in the field of computer vision. Authors from work [1] enhance the accuracy of identifying apple leaf disease and reduce the dimensionality of the feature space. They select the most valuable features through a combination of genetic algorithm and CFS.

While there is a vast amount of technical literature available, there is no evidence of research that addresses user-generated data from non-transactional webpages. Online activity data provides non-intrusive means of gaining insight into consumers' purchasing behavior, eliminating the need for interviews or surveys that may force consumers to rationalize irrational thought processes. This proposed methodology aims to find the criteria that can effectively identify potential consumers and assist in targeted marketing efforts.

3   Dataset Description

The Car Configurator (CC) webpage guides users through a series of screens where they select different attributes of the car. The information entered by each user is saved and anonymous, as there is no login option. The plain clickstream data spans from April 2017 to January 2020 for the Spanish national market. The information is contained in 3,689,492 rows for 1,890,641 users. It's important to note that each row now represents a specific car variant and date.

Car variant has been defined as the combination of user's geographical location (*GeoSeg*), *TRIM*, *Engine* and Exterior Color (*ExtColor*). Clickstream data collects the information of four car models. We name them from *Model A* to *Model D*, as a request of the source OEM to save privacy. Two of them belongs to car segment B, and the rest fits in car segment C. The range of equipment levels spans from 4 to 6 options per car model. The number of eligible engines and exterior colors per TRIM lays in the range from 3 to 16, and from 10 to 46, respectively. Finally, geographical location refers to Spanish provinces, i.e., 50 in total, as OEM aggregates four of them in two couples. Additionally, the last attribute to consider is the date, in the form of day of the week. Table 1 summarizes the main statistics of the raw clickstream data.

Table 1. Main statistics values of the elements contained in clickstream data.

	Dayname	GeoSeg	TRIM	Engine	ExtColor
No. elems	7.0	50.0	19.0	48.0	51.0
Avg %	14.29	2.00	5.26	2.08	1.96
Std %	13.31	0.03	1.66	0.02	0.00
Max %	15.05	28.73	14.78	16.73	14.47
Min %	13.31	0.03	1.66	0.02	0.00

On the other side, the OEM source has also provided sales record for the same historical period, car models and regions. During this age, 107,804 cars were sold within the national market. Hence, considering the behavior for 149 weeks within the time-span, average weekly sales are 723.52 ± 308.49 cars. During first week of December 2018 occurred the sales peak, with 1701 cars sold. On the other side, the minimum amount are 149 cars sold at April 2017 first week.

4   Methodology

This segment describes the procedure followed to answer the research question. Firstly, it is presented the strategy to obtain the correlation. Afterwards, genetic algorithm's structure is detailed. Finally, the assessment procedure is exposed.

4.1   Weekly Lagged Correlation

Paper [6] is an example about managing clickstream data from a non-transactional webpage of a door-selling company. Nevertheless, within our framework, it is not possible to replicate their linking method. So, we use correlation, that has been proved to be a valid metric in work [2]. To conduct this analysis, we utilize the R2 Score, which involves transforming both data sources into time series. This score is calculated as the square of the ratio between the covariance of the two variables and the product of their standard deviations.

Customers typically research about cars online before purchasing them from a dealer. To account for this delay, we set it to 8 weeks. This number was chosen based on the cars' manufacturing process, which includes a preparation phase that can take up to 6 weeks. Within this time, it is defined cars' wire-harness system [14], and established the sequence in the production line [4]. This is the minimum time required to follow the mass customization philosophy of automotive OEMs [3]. Just in case, we expand the range by one week to ensure we capture all relevant data. Given the delay period, our computation strategy is as follows. Instead of lagging the entire sales record over the entire clickstream (CC) time series and performing the computation, we have processed the data monthly. For each month of CC data within the given time range, we select the sales record from 8 weeks in advance of the first week to compute the R2 score. The sales range extends for the duration of the month, based on the number of weeks. Finally, the outcomes are averaged.

4.2   Genetic Algorithm's Structure

The chromosomes of the population contain the attributes that define a car variant (*GeoSeg, TRIM, Engine* and *ExtColor*), and the day of the week the user visited the webpage (*Dayname*). The size of the chromosome is the same for all the population and determined by the number of rules to be found. However, if the chromosome contains duplicated rules, only one remains and the others are deleted, reducing the size of the chromosome, consequently. Thus, raw clickstream data is filtered according to the rules defined in the chromosome and the weekly time series of users visiting the CC webpage is built. Therefore, the procedure described in Sect. 4.1 takes part. In case there are not users that fulfill the filtering criteria, the fitness is penalized according to the maximization problem requirements.

The mechanisms used to create new solutions are crossover and mutation of chromosomes. To perform crossover, the algorithm randomly chooses a single intersection point on the parent. Regarding mutation, the element's rule is permuted by means of an uniform distribution by other permitted value of the same attribute. The feasibility is relevant for *Engine* and *ExtColor*, such as they are conditioned by the *TRIM*.

Finally, elitism is employed to prevent fitness from decreasing in successive generations. In our approach, we only transfer the best solution. In addition, if fitness does not vary beyond a certain tolerance for a specified number of consecutive generations, an anti-stagnation mechanism is triggered. This mechanism involves increasing the mutation probability for the next generations until the mutation probability returns to its original value after a certain period. If the mechanism is activated a certain number of times, the algorithm terminates. In this framework, the permitted tolerance is 0.001, the number of consecutive generations to activate or deactivate the anti-stagnation mechanism is 5% of the population size, and the activation limit is set to five.

4.3   Assessment Procedure

In order to ensure the reliability of our findings, we carried out a total of five independent trials under identical initial conditions. Outcomes are averaged and compared with respect to the benchmark value from plain clickstream data. It follows to select the best solution candidate and evaluate it individually. The frequency of the elements chosen by each rule is analysed and related with the position they place in the clickstream data. Additionally, the fitness of each single rule that compose the best candidate is computed. Therefore, we understand the weight each individual rule has and we are capable of finding which are the Pareto optimum and associate them with sales frequency rate.

5   Results

The conditions of the experiments are: (a) population size: 250; (b) number of rules within chromosome: 100; (c) number of generations: 100; (d) tournament probability: 0.3 of *population size*; (e) crossover probability: 0.9; (f) mutation probability: 1/*population size*; (g) theoretical limit fitness value: 100.

Table 2 shows which is the maximum correlation achieved by each trial, the average measure and the benchmark value. We observe that Trial 3 provides the largest fitness value. Thus, we present the insights of the best candidate. Firstly,

Table 2. Maximum correlation achieved by each trial together with the average. Benchmark value. Bold text refers to best solution

Benchmark	Average	Trial 1	Trial 2	Trial 3	Trial 4	Trial 5
29.42	91.21 ± 3.8	85.34	90.27	**95.45**	91.72	93.28

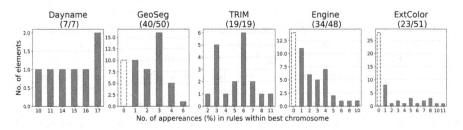

Fig. 1. The graph displays the frequency of each element in the best chromosome's rules for each attribute. The x-axis shows the percentage of appearances, and the y-axis represents the number of elements. The title lists the number of unique elements found in the chromosome and the quantity of unique elements available in the attribute. Colorless bars represent available elements not chosen by the chromosome

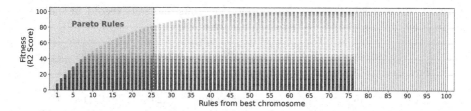

Fig. 2. Stacked bars depict the accumulated fitness value of each rule in the best chromosome, with each block representing a single rule. White bars indicate zero individual fitness, while the blue region represents rules contributing to 80% of the total accumulated fitness value. (Color figure online)

it has been studied the percentage each element from each attribute appears in the filtering candidate. These outputs are found in Fig. 1. Finally, the fitness of each single rule derived from the best candidate is computed. Figure 2 presents the accumulated fitness outcomes sorted from highest to lowest rules.

6 Discussion

Firstly, outcomes placed in Table 2 reveals a massive improvement with respect to benchmark line. Looking up each one of them, Trial 1 delivered the poorest results. Trial 2 and Trial 4 are the ones closer to the average best fitness. It follows Trial 5, with the second largest mark. Finally, Trial 3 delivered the candidate more alike to the theoretical limit value. That's why we proceed to analysis more in detail this candidate. The frequency of the elements that appears in the chromosome's attributes is shown in Fig. 1. From all the attributes, only all available elements in *Dayname* and *TRIM* are included in the filtering rules. The days of the week with the largest percentage of appearances are Sunday and Friday, both with 17%. In terms of car's equipment, the most common TRIM is unique with 11% appearance rate. It belongs to the most dressed version from *Model A* car. With respect the geographical location, only one province is the most repeated, with 6% of appearance rate. Regarding engines, only one of them is the most repeated with 10%, and it is an engine that can be assembled in any TRIM from cars of segment B, i.e., *Model A* or *Model B*. Finally, the most repeated color has 11% of appearance rate. All the cars under study includes this color in their portfolio. The ranking position these elements occupy in the clickstream data is shown in Table 3.

Finally, the study of the weight of each rule is performed and plotted in Fig. 2. The first rule delivers individually a correlation with respect to sales records of

Table 3. Relationship between elements with more appearances within best candidate rules and position placed in the clickstream data.

	Dayname	GeoSeg	TRIM	Engine	ExtColor
Top Rules Appearances	2 (17%)	1 (6%)	1 (11%)	1 (10%)	1 (11%)
Clickstream Ranking	4th (14.33%) 7th (13.31%)	37th (0.41%)	2nd (12.42%)	7th (3.42%)	5th (9.51%)

Table 4. Relationship between Pareto rules' elements and sales record. It indicates the position ranking and the sales percentage, in brackets.

	Dayname	GeoSeg	TRIM	Engine	ExtColor
Rule 1	5th (18.41%)	2nd (15.42%)	18th (0.63%)	16th (1.86%)	1st (24.39%)
Rule 2	6th (4.75%)	1st (15.87%)	1st (11.94%)	1st (20.86%)	5th (6.54%)
Rule 3	3rd (19.17%)	16th (1.89%)	12th (2.81%)	1st (20.86%)	12th (1.84%)
Rule 4	4th (18.65%)	3rd (5.49%)	4th (10.92%)	16th (1.86%)	1st (24.39%)
Rule 5	6th (4.75%)	9th (2.56%)	15th (0.96%)	22th (0.76%)	8th (4.86%)
Rule 6	1st (19.59%)	23th (1.31%)	15th (0.96%)	37th (0.17%)	4th (8.84%)
Rule 7	7th (0.02%)	26th (1.13%)	7th (6.58%)	15th (1.99%)	4th (8.84%)
Rule 8	2nd (19.41%)	18th (1.74%)	7th (6.58%)	15th (1.99%)	4th (8.84%)
Rule 9	5th (18.41%)	12th (2.15%)	14th (1.89%)	20th (0.97%)	5th (6.54%)
Rule 10	7th (0.02%)	19th (1.7%)	7th (6.58%)	2nd (14.69%)	4th (8.84%)
Rule 11	5th (18.41%)	19th (1.7%)	15th (0.96%)	34th (0.26%)	3rd (10.65%)
Rule 12	2nd (19.41%)	23th (1.31%)	13th (2.5%)	16th (1.86%)	1st (24.39%)
Rule 13	5th (18.41%)	9th (2.56%)	10th (4.18%)	4th (4.84%)	5th (6.54%)
Rule 14	6th (4.75%)	1st (15.87%)	13th (2.5%)	4th (4.84%)	4th (8.84%)
Rule 15	1st (19.59%)	1st (15.87%)	18th (0.63%)	17th (1.64%)	4th (8.84%)
Rule 16	6th (4.75%)	50th (0.02%)	15th (0.96%)	37th (0.17%)	8th (4.86%)
Rule 17	7th (0.02%)	15th (2.08%)	12th (2.81%)	9th (3.93%)	12th (1.84%)
Rule 18	7th (0.02%)	16th (1.89%)	8th (5.71%)	5th (4.82%)	5th (6.54%)
Rule 19	4th (18.65%)	36th (0.7%)	4th (10.92%)	7th (4.2%)	7th (4.88%)
Rule 20	5th (18.41%)	7th (3.5%)	15th (0.96%)	34th (0.26%)	10th (3.54%)
Rule 21	7th (0.02%)	21th (1.43%)	7th (6.58%)	3rd (7.13%)	3rd (10.65%)
Rule 22	5th (18.41%)	23th (1.31%)	18th (0.63%)	7th (4.2%)	6th (4.89%)
Rule 23	1st (19.59%)	35th (0.71%)	4th (10.92%)	16th (1.86%)	3rd (10.65%)
Rule 24	3rd (19.17%)	31th (0.75%)	11th (3.38%)	1st (20.86%)	12th (1.84%)

19.13 R2 Score, representing 7.83% of the aggregated value. It contains *Monday* as the day of the week; geographical location is one of the most populated provinces in Spain; TRIM is the entrance level of *Model D*; car engine is only assembled in cars from segment C; exterior color is valid for all car models of the study. On one side, it is appreciated that there are rules with null individual correlation. They are from the 77th rule onwards. On the other hand, the first 24 rules deliver the 80% of the aggregated individual fitness outcomes. They are called Pareto Rules. The relation between each Pareto rule's element and the sales record is found in Table 4.

Among the Pareto rules, the first tier of dayname sales was selected by 12.5%, while the most frequent dayname (25%) is in the fifth position in the sales record. For the GeoSeg chromosome attribute, there is a tie between the first and thirteenth best-selling locations, both appearing in 12.5% of the Pareto rules. Regarding TRIM, the best-selling car equipment is selected by 4.16% of the Pareto rules, and it is the fifteenth most popular TRIM (20.8%) among the Pareto rules. As for car engines, the most frequent one in the Pareto rules is the sixteenth (16.7%), but the best-selling engine is the second most popular (12.5%). Lastly, for exterior color, the top tier sales color occupies the third place in popularity (12.5%) among the Pareto rules, while the fourth most sold color is the top in appearances (25%) within the Pareto rules.

7   Conclusions

In conclusion, our results demonstrate the benefits of applying data mining techniques in the form of genetic algorithms. We have identified and evaluated the best filtering rules for car configurator webpage data from a specific automotive OEM, which allows us to differentiate users with purchasing interest from the noisy and vast data generated by the online tool. Therefore, we suggest that car manufacturers include this data source in their planning operations to improve their ability to identify potential consumers and better target their marketing efforts.

The correlation between sales records and clickstream data has surpassed the established reference value by a significant margin. We improved from a 29.42 R2 score to an average of 91.21 ± 3.8. We used a genetic algorithm to identify rules that maximize the correlation with sales records. We conducted five independent trials under identical conditions to obtain robust results. Subsequently, we decomposed and assessed the best candidate, evaluating the frequency of appearance of filtering rules and the weight of each individual rule on the overall outcome achieved by the best chromosome. We compared these counts with the frequency ranking of sales and clickstream data. Our findings suggest that the most popular elements from these sources are not necessarily the best indicators of potential consumers among online tool users.

Although the best trial achieved a fitness value close to the theoretical maximum, we were unable to explore the majority of the search space. With slightly over 125k potential candidates, this figure represents less than 1% of all possible combinations. A larger sample would enable us to perform an analysis of rule convergence and verify the existence of a global maximum in the fitness function. For this reason, we will focus our efforts on optimizing the computational cost to facilitate exploration of a larger portion of the search space.

In conclusion, we believe that data mining in the form of a genetic algorithm is a versatile tool, as its ease of use allows for adaptation to various contexts. Therefore, we propose adapting the methodology developed in this study to the problem of demand prediction. This would involve not only verifying the correlation between clickstream data and sales records, but also assessing whether the car configurator webpage can be used to make more accurate forecasts.

References

1. Chuanlei, Z., Shanwen, Z., Jucheng, Y., Yancui, S., Jia, C.: Apple leaf disease identification using genetic algorithm and correlation based feature selection method. Int. J. Agric. Biol. Eng. **10**, 74–83 (2017). https://doi.org/10.3965/j.ijabe.20171002.2166

2. García Sánchez, J.M., Vilasís Cardona, X., Lerma Martín, A.: Influence of car configurator webpage data from automotive manufacturers on car sales by means of correlation and forecasting. Forecasting **4**(3), 634–653 (2022). https://doi.org/10.3390/forecast4030034. https://www.mdpi.com/2571-9394/4/3/34

3. Heradio, R., Perez-Morago, H., Salinas, E.A., Fernandez-Amoros, D., Alférez, G.: Augmenting measure sensitivity to detect essential, dispensable and highly incompatible features in mass customization. Eur. J. Oper. Res. **248**, 1066–1077 (2016). https://doi.org/10.1016/j.ejor.2015.08.005

4. Hottenrott, A., Waidner, L., Grunow, M.: Robust car sequencing for automotive assembly. Eur. J. Oper. Res. **291**, 983–994 (2020). https://doi.org/10.1016/j.ejor.2020.10.004

5. Huang, C.L., Wang, C.J.: A GA-based feature selection and parameters optimizationfor support vector machines. Expert Syst. Appl. **31**(2), 231–240 (2006). https://doi.org/10.1016/j.eswa.2005.09.024. https://www.sciencedirect.com/science/article/pii/S0957417405002083

6. Huang, T., Van Mieghem, J.: Clickstream data and inventory management: model and empirical analysis. Prod. Oper. Manag. **23**, 333–347 (2014). https://doi.org/10.2139/ssrn.1851046

7. Kira, K., Rendell, L.A., et al.: The feature selection problem: traditional methods and a new algorithm. In: AAAI, vol. 2, pp. 129–134 (1992)

8. Manowicz, A.A., Bacher, N.: Digital auto customer journey - an analysis of the impact of digitalization on the new car sales process and structure. Int. J. Sales Retail. Mark. **20**, 16 (2020)

9. Rijnsoever, F.V., Farla, J., Dijst, M.: Consumer car preferences and information search channels. Transp. Res. Part D Transp. Environ. **14**, 334–342 (2009). https://doi.org/10.1016/j.trd.2009.03.006

10. Scholz, M., Dorner, V., Schryen, G., Benlian, A.: A configuration-based recommender system for supporting e-commerce decisions. Eur. J. Oper. Res. **259**, 205–215 (2017). https://doi.org/10.1016/j.ejor.2016.09.057

11. Shah, S., Kusiak, A.: Cancer gene search with data-mining and genetic algorithms. Comput. Biol. Med. **37**(2), 251–261 (2007). https://doi.org/10.1016/j.compbiomed.2006.01.007. https://www.sciencedirect.com/science/article/pii/S0010482506000217

12. Shroff, K.P., Maheta, H.H.: A comparative study of various feature selection techniques in high-dimensional data set to improve classification accuracy. In: 2015 International Conference on Computer Communication and Informatics (ICCCI), pp. 1–6 (2015). https://doi.org/10.1109/ICCCI.2015.7218098

13. Tiwari, R., Singh, M.: Correlation-based attribute selection using genetic algorithm. Int. J. Comput. Appl. **4**, 28–34 (2010). https://doi.org/10.5120/847-1182

14. Vié, M.S., Zufferey, N., Cordeau, J.F.: Solving the wire-harness design problem at a European car manufacturer. Eur. J. Oper. Res. **272**, 712–724 (2018). https://doi.org/10.1016/j.ejor.2018.06.047

15. Witten, I.H., Frank, E., Hall, M.A., Pal, C.J.: Data Mining, Fourth Edition: Practical Machine Learning Tools and Techniques, 4th edn. Morgan Kaufmann Publishers Inc., San Francisco (2016)

16. Yu, L., Liu, H.: Feature selection for high-dimensional data: a fast correlation-based filter solution. In: Proceedings of the 20th International Conference on Machine Learning (ICML 2003), pp. 856–863 (2003)

Multi-population Algorithm Using Surrogate Models and Different Training Plans

Daniel Kucharski[ID] and Krzysztof Cpałka[(✉)][ID]

Department of Computational Intelligence, Czestochowa University of Technology,
Czestochowa, Poland
xdaniel@onet.eu, krzysztof.cpalka@pcz.pl

Abstract. Population-based algorithms (PBAs) are effective meta-heuristic methods. Their important feature is their ability to define a complex objective function depending on a given problem need not be differentiable. This allows PBAs to be used to solve continuous and discrete problems for which it is difficult to use gradient algorithms. Another advantage of PBAs is the ability to search the problem domain using a population of individuals. Therefore, an important issue regarding PBAs is to reduce their complexity and increase their efficiency. In this article, we propose a new PBA that uses both surrogate and temporary subpopulation models to (a) reduce the number of evaluation function calls and (b) increase the efficiency of finding a solution. The underlying algorithm for the application of these mechanisms is the Particle Swarm Optimization (PSO) algorithm. For the initial testing of the proposed method, we used well known test functions. We consider the obtained results to be good.

Keywords: metaheuristic algorithm · population-based algorithm · Particle Swarm Optimization algorithm · multi-population algorithm · surrogate models

1 Introduction

Population-based algorithms (PBAs) are effective metaheuristic methods [20,30,33]. Their important feature is the ability to define a complex objective function, depending on the problem [2,7,38]. It need not be differentiable. This allows PBAs to be used to solve continuous and discrete problems for which it is difficult to use gradient algorithms (see e.g. [10,26,31,36,41,43,44]). Another advantage of PBAs is the ability to search the problem domain using a population of individuals. An important issue regarding PBAs is to reduce their complexity and increase their efficiency. Examples of approaches include: increasing the efficiency of the search mechanisms, reducing the number of evaluation function calls, changing the precision of determining the evaluation function during the operation of the algorithm, using surrogate models, controlling the size of the

L. Rutkowski et al. (Eds.): ICAISC 2023, LNAI 14125, pp. 385–398, 2023.
https://doi.org/10.1007/978-3-031-42505-9_33

population, using multiple subpopulations, choosing the topology for exchanging individuals between subpopulations, controlling the parameters of the algorithm, changing the algorithm operation mode (exploration and exploitation) during its operation, the use of training plans, and the creation of hybrid methods.

Among the mentioned approaches, the use of surrogate models is interesting. This is an important technique to improve various aspects of PBAs operation. One such aspect is estimating the value of a computationally complex evaluation function. It is done using an approximate but computationally simpler substitute model. This approach is not always beneficial to use, which results from the specificity of the problem and the complexity of the evaluation function estimation procedure. However, its use often allows to significantly reduce the computational effort of PBA operation. There are many references in the literature regarding the use of surrogate models. In [49], the authors reviewed PBAs using surrogate models, presented approaches to creating and updating models, and indicated how to use them. In [25], the authors considered the possibility of using surrogate models in multi-criteria optimization, presented examples of applications and indicated trends in the considered area of research. In [11], the authors considered the issue of using deep learning models as surrogate models in PBAs. They described the methods of building and updating substitute models, presented examples of their applications, indicated trends in the research area under consideration. In [4], the authors reviewed PBAs using surrogate models. Focused on engineering applications, they considered other search methods (besides PBAs) including genetic, simulated annealing, and memetic algorithms. In [5], the authors proposed a PSO-based approach to feature selection in classification problems. Their approach uses surrogate models to determine the evaluation function and the concept of a temporary population of individuals (as in evolutionary strategies), the best of which are selected for the main population.

Another interesting approach to building PBAs is the use of multiple populations. It aims to increase the efficiency of the search by reducing the impact of local minima on the results of the operation. In [22,48], the authors reviewed multi-population PBAs, described approaches to their construction, presented examples of applications, pointed out the advantages and disadvantages of the considered algorithms and trends in their development. In [19], the authors characterized various approaches to building and updating multi-population PBAs, presented interesting applications of the considered algorithms, and referred to their connection with surrogate models. We also presented interesting solutions in this area in our earlier works [6,8,21,37].

In this article, we propose a new PBA that uses both surrogate and subpopulation models to (a) reduce the number of evaluation function calls and (b) increase the efficiency of finding a solution. The underlying algorithm for the application of these mechanisms is the Particle Swarm Optimization (PSO) algorithm. For the initial testing of the proposed method, we used well known test functions.

1.1   Motivation

The article aims to develop an algorithm that uses surrogate models and multiple populations simultaneously. It seems to us that this approach has great potential in terms of creating effective PBAs and reducing their computational complexity. At the same time, this approach has not been considered in the literature so far.

1.2   Contribution of the Paper

The contribution of the paper can be summarized as follows:

- We developed an original algorithm that uses multiple populations and surrogate models. It uses the surrogate model approach described in [5] and is based on the Particle Swarm Optimization (PSO, [13,14]) formula. Any other PBA may be used in place of a PSO. Similarly, the use of surrogate models can also be changed. In this work, it is interesting to combine both approaches (multiple populations and surrogate models), therefore the proposed algorithm can be treated as a basic method that can be rebuilt as needed.
- We tested the proposed algorithm using the CEC2017 functions. In the tests, we took into account the accuracy of the indirect modeling of the evaluation function, also in the context of the individual steps of the algorithm.

1.3   Structure of the Paper

In Sect. 3 we have characterized the algorithm proposed in this article. In Sect. 2 we have described the symbols and notations used throughout the article. In Sect. 4 we have included sample simulation results. In Sect. 5 we have summarized the most important conclusions and plans for future research.

2   Symbols and Markings

The Table 1 contains the parameters of the algorithm. The information contained in this table is supplemented by the following symbols and markings:

- $\mathbf{X}_{ch} = \{\mathbf{X}_{ch}^{par}, \mathbf{X}_{ch}^{vel}, \mathbf{X}_{ch}^{bst}\}$ is an individual of the population with an index ch.
- ch is the index of individual $\mathbf{X}_{ch}$ in the population
- $\mathbf{X}_{ch}^{par} = \{X_{ch,1}^{par}, X_{ch,2}^{par}, ..., X_{ch,Npar}^{par}\}$ is a component with solution parameters encoded in individual $\mathbf{X}_{ch}$. Each position component $\mathbf{X}_{ch}^{par}$ encodes a complete solution to the problem under consideration.
- $Npar$ is the number of dimensions of the considered problem.
- $\mathbf{X}_{ch}^{bst} = \{X_{ch,1}^{bst}, X_{ch,2}^{bst}, ..., X_{ch,Npar}^{bst}\}$ is a component with the parameters of the best (found so far) solution encoded in individual $\mathbf{X}_{ch}$ (best for a given individual). This is a component typical of the PSO algorithm.
- $\mathbf{X}_{ch}^{vel} = \{X_{ch,1}^{vel}, X_{ch,2}^{vel}, ..., X_{ch,Npar}^{vel}\}$ is a component with velocity values coded for individual $\mathbf{X}_{ch}$. This is a component typical of the PSO algorithm.

- $\mathbf{X}^{\mathrm{glb}} = \{X_1^{\mathrm{glb}}, X_2^{\mathrm{glb}}, ..., X_{Npar}^{\mathrm{glb}}\}$ is the component with the parameters of the best (found so far) solution by the algorithm. This is a component typical for the PSO algorithm.
- $\mathbf{P} = \{\mathbf{X}_{ch=1}, \mathbf{X}_{ch=2}, ..., \mathbf{X}_{ch=Nind}\}$ is the base population of the algorithm.
- $\mathbf{P}' = \{\mathbf{X}'_{ch=1}, \mathbf{X}'_{ch=2}, ..., \mathbf{X}'_{ch=Nind\cdot(Nc+1)}\}$ is the auxiliary population of the algorithm.
- $\mathbf{ff} = \{ff_{ch=1}, ff_{ch=2}, ..., ff_{ch=Nind}\}$ is a collection of values of population evaluation function $\mathbf{P}$.
- $\mathbf{ff}' = \{ff'_{ch=1}, ff'_{ch=2}, ..., ff'_{ch=Nind}\}$ is a collection of values of population evaluation function $\mathbf{P}'$.
- $\mathbf{Xl}^{\mathrm{par}} = \{Xl_1^{\mathrm{par}}, Xl_2^{\mathrm{par}}, ..., Xl_{Npar}^{\mathrm{par}}\}$ is a set of minimum (acceptable) values for each parameter of the considered problem. At the same time $\mathbf{Xh}^{\mathrm{par}} = \{Xh_1^{\mathrm{par}}, Xh_2^{\mathrm{par}}, ..., Xh_{Npar}^{\mathrm{par}}\}$ is a set of maximum (acceptable) values for each parameter of the considered problem. Therefore, any g-th parameter encoded in an individual of the population satisfies assumption $X_{ch,g}^{\mathrm{par}} \in [Xl_g^{\mathrm{par}}, Xh_g^{\mathrm{par}}]$.
- $U(a, b)$ is a function returning a random number from range $[a, b]$.
- Uint (a, b) is a function returning a random integer from range $[a, b]$.
- $N(\bar{x}, \sigma)$ is a normal distribution with expectation $\bar{x}$ and variance σ^2.

3   Multi-population Algorithm Using Surrogate Models and Different Training Plans

The algorithm proposed in this paper uses the concept of using surrogate models described in [5] and the capabilities of the following algorithms, i.e. PSO and kNN (k Nearest Neighbours, [47]). Its block diagram is shown in Listing 1.

The operation method of the algorithm proposed in this article is shown in Listing 1. Its steps are described later in this section.

At the beginning of the algorithm (Step 1), the values of its parameters are set. They are listed and described in Table 1. Then, follows (Step 2), in which the components of position $\mathbf{X}_{ch}^{\mathrm{par}}$ and velocity $\mathbf{X}_{ch}^{\mathrm{vel}}$ for $Nind$ individuals of population $\mathbf{P}$ are drawn. When drawing $\mathbf{X}_{ch}^{\mathrm{par}}$, the search range for a solution defined by $\{\mathbf{Xl}^{\mathrm{par}}, \mathbf{Xh}^{\mathrm{par}}\}$ is accounted for. Once drawn, the individuals of the $\mathbf{P}$ population are evaluated using the assumed evaluation function (Step 3). It is defined depending on the problem under consideration. The determined individual rating values are stored in $\mathbf{ff}$. In Step 4, the best individual of the $\mathbf{P}$ population is found (i.e. $\mathbf{X}^{\mathrm{glb}}$) and the components are set $\mathbf{X}_{ch}^{\mathrm{bst}}$, $ch = 1, 2, ..., Nind$ (see Sect. 2). In the next step of the algorithm (Step 5), a copy of the $\mathbf{P}$ population is created and marked as $\mathbf{P}'$. It is used to store individuals for which the assessment function is determined using the surrogate approach. This approach tries to avoid calls to the evaluation function, which may be computationally expensive to determine. Indirectly determined evaluation function values are stored in $\mathbf{ff}'$. The individuals with the best (estimated) evaluation function value from $\mathbf{ff}'$ are then selected and transferred to $\mathbf{P}$ (Step 9). Such individuals are scored in the usual way - using the rating function (Step 10).

Algorithm 1. Block diagram of the multi-population algorithm proposed in this work using surrogate models and training plans

1: Setting the values of the algorithm parameters: $Nsteps$, $Nind$, Nc, $Nnei$, $\{c_1^{\text{up}}, c_2^{\text{up}}, w^{\text{up}}\}$, $\{c_1^{\text{mi}}, c_2^{\text{mi}}, w^{\text{mi}}\}$, $\{c_1^{\text{lo}}, c_2^{\text{lo}}, w^{\text{lo}}\}$, and $\{\sigma_b, \sigma_e\}$ (see Table 1).
2: Randomizing position $\mathbf{X}_{ch}^{\text{par}}$ and velocity $\mathbf{X}_{ch}^{\text{vel}}$ for $Nind$ of individuals of population $\mathbf{P}$ including ranges $\{\mathbf{Xl}^{\text{par}}, \mathbf{Xh}^{\text{par}}\}$.
3: Evaluating the individuals of the $\mathbf{P}$ population using the adopted evaluation function (update $\mathbf{ff}$).
4: Searching for individual $\mathbf{X}^{\text{glb}}$ and setting components $\mathbf{X}_{ch}^{\text{bst}}$, $ch = 1, 2, ..., Nind$.
5: Creating a copy of the $\mathbf{P}$ population named/designated as/marked as $\mathbf{P}'$.
6: Updating components $\mathbf{X'}_{ch}^{\text{par}}$ of the individuals in $\mathbf{P}'$ according to the PSO formula.
7: Randomizing Nc of new individuals for each individual of the $\mathbf{P}'$ population (in its vicinity, according to the adopted distribution) and including them in $\mathbf{P}'$.
8: Determining for each individual $\mathbf{P}'$ the value of the evaluation function indirectly based on components $\mathbf{X'}_{ch}^{\text{par}}$ and $\mathbf{X}_{ch}^{\text{par}}$, and $\mathbf{ff}$ values (updating $\mathbf{ff}'$).
9: Selecting individuals from population $\mathbf{P}'$ for population $\mathbf{P}$ (Algorithm 2)
10: Evaluating individuals in/from population $\mathbf{P}$ using the adopted evaluation function (updating $\mathbf{ff}$).
11: Updating individual $\mathbf{X}^{\text{glb}}$ and updating component $\mathbf{X}_{ch}^{\text{bst}}$, $ch = 1, 2, ..., Nind$.
12: Dividing population $\mathbf{P}$ individuals into three subpopulations based on their rating function values, i.e. the best, the average, and the worst.
13: Updating velocity vector $\mathbf{X}_{ch}^{\text{vel}}$ of each individual $\mathbf{P}$ depending on its subpopulation assignment (see Eq. (4)).
14: Checking the algorithm's stop condition: if it is met, it moves to the next step. Otherwise, return to step 5.
15: Presenting $\mathbf{X}^{\text{glb}}$ as the best solution found by the algorithm.

Algorithm 2. Block diagram of the procedure for selecting individuals from the $\mathbf{P}'$ population to the $\mathbf{P}$ population of the multi-population algorithm proposed in this work using surrogate models and training plans (Algorytm 1, step 9).

1: Removing individuals from population $\mathbf{P}$.
2: Sort $\mathbf{P}'$ by $\mathbf{ff}'$ in ascending order (for the problem of finding the minimum of the evaluation function).
3: **for** $ch := 1$ **to** $Nind$ **do**
   Finding in $\mathbf{P}'$ the individual closest to $\mathbf{X}'_1$
4:     in terms of the Euclidean distance (based on the components of $\mathbf{X'}_{ch}^{\text{par}}$) and removing it from $\mathbf{P}'$.
5:     Including $\mathbf{X}'_1$ in $\mathbf{P}$ and removing it from $\mathbf{P}'$.
6: **end for** ch

Returning to Step 6, the components of the $\mathbf{X'}_{ch}^{\text{par}}$ items in $\mathbf{P}'$ are updated according to the simple PSO formula:

$$X'^{\text{par}}_{ch,g} := X'^{\text{par}}_{ch,g} + X'^{\text{vel}}_{ch,g}, \tag{1}$$

where g ($g = 1, 2, ..., Npar$) is the index of the solution parameter. Each of the individuals modified by using formula (1) is used in the next step to generate

Table 1. List of algorithm parameters.

No.	Parameter marking	Parameter description
1	$Nsteps$	number of steps of the algorithm (stop criterion)
2	$Nind$	number of individuals of the **P** population for which the value of the evaluation function is determined
3	Nc	the number of surrogates - helper individuals generated from each individual individual in the population **P**
4	$Nnei$	the number of nearest neighbors used in estimating the value of the evaluation function
5	$\left\{c_1^{\mathrm{up}}, c_2^{\mathrm{up}}, w^{\mathrm{up}}\right\}$	PSO parameters to updatesubpopulation of the best individuals
6	$\left\{c_1^{\mathrm{mi}}, c_2^{\mathrm{mi}}, w^{\mathrm{mi}}\right\}$	PSO parameters to update subpopulation of average individuals
7	$\left\{c_1^{\mathrm{lo}}, c_2^{\mathrm{lo}}, w^{\mathrm{lo}}\right\}$	PSO parameters to update worst subpopulations
8	$[\sigma_b, \sigma_e]$	range of changes in the σ parameter of the distribution used to generate individuals of the population **P**$'$ during the operation of the algorithm
9	$Nlocalnei \in \{2, 4, 6, ...\}$	parameter used in updating the $\mathbf{X}_{ch}^{\mathrm{vel}}$ component of the worst subpopulation included in the population **P** in the final part of the algorithm; it means the number of individuals neighboring with the individual $\mathbf{X}_{ch}$, which provide this individual with information about their location

solutions according to the surrogate approach. Thus, in Step 7, Nc new individuals are drawn for each individual in the **P**$'$ population. Each of the created individuals is included in **P**$'$. Of course, individuals added to **P**$'$ no longer create their individuals according to Step 7. In this article, we have adopted the following rule for creating a new individual with index $ch2$:

$$\begin{cases} X'^{\mathrm{par}}_{ch2,g} = N\left(X'^{\mathrm{par}}_{ch,g}, \frac{(\sigma_e - \sigma_b) \cdot step - \sigma_e \cdot 1 + \sigma_b \cdot Nsteps}{Nsteps - 1}\right) \\ X'^{\mathrm{vel}}_{ch2,g} = X^{\mathrm{vel}}_{ch,g} \\ X'^{\mathrm{bst}}_{ch2,g} = X^{\mathrm{bst}}_{ch,g}, \end{cases} \tag{2}$$

where $step = 1, 2, ..., Nsteps$ is the current step of the algorithm. Note that for $step = 1$ in formula (2) the distribution is $N\left(X'^{\mathrm{par}}_{ch,g}, \sigma_b\right)$, while for $step = Nsteps$ it is the distribution $N\left(X'^{\mathrm{par}}_{ch,g}, \sigma_e\right)$ (with less variance). That is why $\sigma_b \gg \sigma_e$ as to ensure a smooth transition from exploration to exploitation in the operation of the algorithm. So after Step 7, the **P**$'$ count increases to $Nind \cdot (Nc + 1)$. Therefore, it is possible to evaluate the individuals (Step 8) and select the best individuals for the new **P** population (Step 9; Algorithm 2). The individuals of the **P** population were evaluated using the real fitness function. On that basis, in Step 8, each individual of the $\mathbf{P}'$ population is evaluated indirectly. We will describe how this is done for a single individual. Suppose that for individual ch from the population $\mathbf{P}'$, the kNN algorithm found collection $Nnei$ of its nearest neighbors from population $\mathbf{P}$. The similarity of the $\mathbf{X}'^{\mathrm{par}}_{ch}$ component from the $\mathbf{P}'$ population to $\mathbf{X}^{\mathrm{par}}_{ch2}$ ($ch2 = 1, 2, ..., Nind$) from population $\mathbf{P}$. Denoting the evaluation functions of the found individuals $Nnei$ as $\overline{ff}_{ch2}$ ($ch2 = 1, 2, ..., Nnei$) we can indirectly determine the component of the evaluation function of the considered individual with index ch from population $\mathbf{P}'$:

$$ff'_{ch} = \frac{1}{Nnei} \cdot \sum_{ch2}^{Nnei} \overline{ff}_{ch2}. \tag{3}$$

This procedure is an attempt to eliminate the need to directly determine the value of the evaluation function for individuals $\mathbf{P}'$. After evaluating individuals from $\mathbf{P}'$, $\mathbf{P}$ is cleared, $Nind$ best individuals from $\mathbf{P}'$ are transferred to population $\mathbf{P}$, and then population $\mathbf{P}'$ is cleared (Step 9). This step is implemented with the suggestions provided in [5], which ensures the appropriate variety and quality of individuals transferred from $\mathbf{P}'$ to $\mathbf{P}$. When population $\mathbf{P}$ is rebuilt, then its individuals are evaluated using the adopted evaluation function - update $\mathbf{ff}$ (Step 10). The $\mathbf{P}$ population generated and evaluated in this way is subject to further modification. In particular, (Step 11) individual $\mathbf{X}^{\mathrm{glb}}$ and its components $\mathbf{X}^{\mathrm{bst}}_{ch}$, $ch = 1, 2, ..., Nind$ are updated. Then, the $\mathbf{P}$ individuals are divided into three subpopulations depending on the value of the evaluation function, i.e. the best, the average and the worst (Step 12). It has been assumed that the number of individuals in these subpopulations is the same. This division makes it possible to update the velocity vectors $\mathbf{X}^{\mathrm{vel}}_{ch}$ of each $\mathbf{P}$ individual depending on its assignment to a given subpopulation (Step 13). The assumption in this approach is that the subpopulations associated with the best and average individuals are much less numerous and less intensively modified than the subpopulation of the worst individuals. The formula for updating the g component of the ch individual (in accordance with the PSO) takes the following form:

$$X^{\mathrm{vel}}_{ch,g} := \begin{cases} w^{\mathrm{up}} \cdot X^{\mathrm{vel}}_{ch,g} + c^{\mathrm{up}}_1 \cdot \mathrm{U}(0,1) \cdot \left(X^{\mathrm{bst}}_{ch,g} - X^{\mathrm{par}}_{ch,g}\right) + \\ +c^{\mathrm{up}}_2 \cdot \mathrm{U}(0,1) \cdot \left(X^{\mathrm{glb}}_g - X^{\mathrm{par}}_{ch,g}\right) \\ \text{for best population} \\ w^{\mathrm{mi}} \cdot X^{\mathrm{vel}}_{ch,g} + c^{\mathrm{mi}}_1 \cdot \mathrm{U}(0,1) \cdot \left(X^{\mathrm{bst}}_{ch,g} - X^{\mathrm{par}}_{ch,g}\right) + \\ +c^{\mathrm{mi}}_2 \cdot \mathrm{U}(0,1) \cdot \left(X^{\mathrm{glb}}_g - X^{\mathrm{par}}_{ch,g}\right) \\ \text{for middle population} \\ w^{\mathrm{lo}} \cdot X^{\mathrm{vel}}_{ch,g} + c^{\mathrm{lo}}_1 \cdot \mathrm{U}(0,1) \cdot \left(X^{\mathrm{bst}}_{ch,g} - X^{\mathrm{par}}_{ch,g}\right) + \\ +c^{\mathrm{lo}}_2 \cdot \mathrm{U}(0,1) \cdot \left(X^{\mathrm{par}}_{\mathrm{Uint}\left(\frac{2}{3} \cdot Nind+1, Nind\right)/\{ch\},g} - X^{\mathrm{par}}_{ch,g}\right) \\ \text{for lower population.} \end{cases} \tag{4}$$

The interpretation of the designations used is given in Sect. 2. Please note that in formula (4) the update of $X_{ch,g}^{vel}$ takes place depending on the subpopulation it belongs to, i.e. for the best subpopulation (implementing the exploitation of the search space) and the average one, the best individual X_g^{glb} is taken into account. However, for the worst subpopulation (exploring the search space), another individual from this subpopulation is taken into account. Its index is randomized from Uint $\left(\frac{2}{3} \cdot Nind + 1, Nind\right) / \{ch\}$. The individual update procedures in formula (4) also differ in the values of the constants.

After updating the $\mathbf{X}_{ch}^{vel}$ components of all individuals of the $\mathbf{P}$ population, the stopping condition of the algorithm is checked (Step 14). If this condition is met, the transition to the next step takes place. Otherwise, it returns to Step 5. In the simulations, we assumed that the stopping condition is based on the allowable number of steps. The last step of the method is to present the individual $\mathbf{X}^{glb}$ as the best solution found.

Notes on the proposed algorithm are as follows:

- The disadvantage of the indirect method of evaluating the evaluation function is the need to use the nearest neighbor algorithm. An additional disadvantage of this mechanism may affect the accuracy of the evaluation of the evaluation function for some types of problems. This is the case, for example, when the problem has a lot of adjacent local extremes and the population size is too small. Therefore, the algorithm could, in the future, include additional methods such as performance verification that could compare estimated values of $\mathbf{ff}'$ with exact values of $\mathbf{ff}$.
- After eliminating in Step 8 the indirect determination of the evaluation function (using the evaluation function directly), the algorithm could function as a typical PBA without surrogate models. Then, Step 7 would operate as a typical local search focused on exploring the search space. This variant of the algorithm was additionally tested in the simulations.

4 Simulations

The simulation considerations are as follows:

- The main goal of the simulation was to test the proposed algorithm and compare it with other PBAs. 19 popular test functions from CEC2017 [18] were used in the simulations. For each of the functions, the PBA tried to find a minimum in the defined solution space. The algorithm was tested for a different number of dimensions: $Npar \in \{10, 30\}$.
- The parameters of our algorithm were as follows: $Nsteps = 1000$, $Nind = 40$, $Nc = 2$, $Nnei = 3$, $c_1^{up} = 1.0$, $c_2^{up} = 1.5$, $w^{up} = 0.2$, $c_1^{mi} = 2.0$ $c_2^{mi} = 1.0$, $w^{mi} = 0.4$, $c_1^{lo} = 1.2$ $c_2^{lo} = 1.8$, $w^{lo} = 0.6$, $\sigma_b = 0.5$, $\sigma_e = 0.1$.
- The parameter values of the remaining algorithms were adopted in accordance with the suggestions given in the literature.

- The algorithm was compared with three other PBAs: PSO, PSO+ring topology and PSO+dynamic topology [8]. The calculations were conducted in a proprietary test environment written in Python. This allowed us to test all variations of the algorithms in a consistent way. Each simulation was repeated 50 times and the presented results were averaged. They are shown in Tables 2 and 3.

The conclusions of the simulations can be summarized as follows:

- The aim of our simulations was to demonstrate the effectiveness of linking surrogate models and subpopulations. This goal was achieved, and the effectiveness of the algorithm was confirmed by the obtained results. They are especially favorable for the variant $Npar = 10$ (see Table 2).
- The mechanism of combining surrogate models and training plans meant that the proposed algorithm coped very well with searching the space and did not stop at local minima. It obtained results comparable to those for other PBAs under consideration. For 57% of the functions for $Npar = 10$ and for 42% of the functions for $Npar = 30$, it achieved either the first or second place out of the four methods tested. The analysis of the results confirmed that the space exploitation mechanism based on surrogate models reduces the precision of exploration of the found optimum. This will be the subject of further research.

The algorithm proposed in this paper can be used in typical application areas of PBAs. Moreover, it can support other computational intelligence methods, such as: designing recommendation systems and their applications [24,40], designing fuzzy systems [27–29] and their applications [16], parallelizing algorithms and systems [3], generating 3D objects using various methods [39], designing electronic circuits [32,34,35], extracting semantic content from data [1], detecting anomalies in data [9,23], data hashing [12], data classification [15,17], and signature verification [42,45,46].

Table 2. Summary of the averaged results for CEC2017 test functions for $Npar = 10$. The best results have been highlighted.

Name of the function	our method	PSO	PSO+ring topology	PSO+dynamic topology
bent cigar	1.24E-11	**8.35E-50**	**7.16E-62**	1.95E-20
sum diff pow	3.06E-06	**1.62E-46**	**9.28E-65**	3.88E-31
zakharov	1.60E-07	**1.14E-22**	**1.21E-18**	1.22E-06
rosenbrock	**1.92E-01**	**1.24E+00**	1.54E+00	3.09E+00
rastrigin	**5.47E-06**	8.76E+00	7.21E+00	**3.67E+00**
expanded schaffers f6	**1.26E-01**	1.65E+00	**1.32E+00**	1.75E+00
lunacek bi rastrigin	**2.56E+00**	1.64E+01	1.79E+01	**1.52E+01**
non cont rastrigin	**3.32E-07**	1.03E+01	7.97E+00	**3.93E+00**
levy	**1.59E-08**	4.43E+00	1.51E-02	**8.15E-26**
modified schwefel	4.86E+01	4.31E+02	2.71E+02	**2.63E+02**
high conditioned elliptic	1.70E-11	**3.48E-53**	**6.73E-65**	1.71E-24
discus	2.32E-06	**6.67E-56**	**2.75E-66**	8.69E-27
ackley	**1.32E+00**	2.00E+01	**1.94E+01**	2.00E+01
weierstrass	**1.12E-03**	6.25E-01	**0.00E+00**	**0.00E+00**
griewank	9.27E-02	4.56E-02	**1.20E-02**	**2.84E-02**
happy cat	**7.46E-02**	1.89E-01	**1.18E-01**	1.88E-01
h g bat	**1.77E-01**	2.75E-01	2.53E-01	**1.81E-01**
expanded griewanks plus rosenbrock	**5.39E-01**	**1.04E+00**	1.17E+00	1.72E+00
schaffers f7	9.57E-04	1.18E+00	**2.03E-05**	**8.74E-07**
number of functions for which the algorithm took 1st or 2nd place:	**11/19(57.89%)**	7/19(36.84%)	**11/19 (57.89%)**	9/19 (47.37%)

Table 3. Summary of the averaged results for CEC2017 test functions for $Npar = 30$. The best results have been highlighted.

Name of the function	our method	PSO	PSO+ring topology	PSO+dynamic topology
bent cigar	3.22E-22	**4.63E-87**	5.63E-38	**7.88E-91**
sum diff pow	8.35E-04	**5.18E-113**	3.36E-63	**3.62E-118**
zakharov	2.54E-02	**8.35E-04**	3.11E-03	**2.69E-07**
rosenbrock	2.09E-02	**4.79E-03**	1.05E-02	**3.79E-03**
rastrigin	**1.49E+01**	**1.23E+01**	1.59E+01	1.53E+01
expanded schaffers f6	7.02E+00	**5.31E+00**	6.60E+00	**5.32E+00**
lunacek bi rastrigin	4.46E+01	**3.94E+01**	1.05E+02	**3.72E+01**
non cont rastrigin	1.47E+01	**1.30E+01**	1.34E+01	**1.04E+01**
levy	**1.40E-25**	1.55E+01	**9.09E-02**	1.69E+01
modified schwefel	**2.94E+02**	8.30E+02	**6.55E+02**	7.66E+02
high conditioned elliptic	3.16E-26	**1.39E-91**	1.60E-40	**1.61E-95**
discus	5.49E-29	**1.57E-96**	1.60E-43	**2.52E-99**
ackley	**2.45E-05**	4.99E-01	**2.25E-05**	1.86E-01
weierstrass	**1.50E-11**	7.59E-01	**3.15E-01**	1.06E+00
griewank	**5.24E-03**	7.69E-02	**4.93E-03**	2.11E-02
happy cat	**1.11E-01**	**1.36E-01**	1.61E-01	1.48E-01
h g bat	1.42E-01	**1.17E-01**	**1.26E-01**	1.29E-01
expanded griewanks plus rosenbrock	9.35E+00	**4.48E+00**	7.09E+00	**3.82E+00**
schaffers f7	**2.36E-04**	5.51E-01	**8.18E-09**	5.61E-01
number of functions for which the algorithm took 1st or 2nd place:	8/19 (42.11%)	**13/19 (68.42%)**	7/19 (36.84%)	**10/19 (52.63%)**

5 Conclusions

In this work, we have considered a multi-population algorithm using surrogate models and training plans. It worked as expected, i.e. it was resistant to local minima and in the vast majority of cases it found the global optimum in the given search interval. The algorithm can be easily adapted to solve various practical problems, but it is mainly dedicated to solving problems in which the direct determination of the evaluation function of individuals is difficult, i.e. it is computationally complex or requires taking into account expensive physical resources. Then, the use of surrogate models makes it possible to reduce the number of calls to the evaluation function. It is worth noting that the concept of the algorithm and the search formulas used are basic - they will be developed in the future, which could, for example, improve the efficiency of the exploitation mechanism or reduce the complexity resulting from the use of the k nearest neighbors method.

Our plans for further research include using surrogate models with a different structure, selecting training plans, and performing simulations for other test problems.

Acknowledgment. The project financed under the program of the Polish Minister of Science and Higher Education under the name "Regional Initiative of Excellence" in the years 2019-2023, project number 020/RID/2018/19, the amount of financing PLN 12,000,000.

References

1. Aghdam, M.: Automatic extractive and generic document summarization based on NMF. J. Artif. Intell. Soft Comput. Res. **13**(1), 37–49 (2023)
2. Bartczuk, Ł, Przybył, A., Cpałka, K.: A new approach to nonlinear modelling of dynamic systems based on fuzzy rules. Int. J. Appl. Math. Comput. Sci. (AMCS) **26**(3), 603–621 (2016)
3. Bilski, J., Smoląg, J., Kowalczyk, B., Grzanek, K., Izonin, I.: Fast computational approach to the Levenberg-Marquardt algorithm for training feedforward neural networks. J. Artif. Intell. Soft Comput. Res. **13**(2), 45–61 (2023)
4. de Castro, L.N., Von Zuben, F.J.: A review on surrogate-assisted evolutionary algorithms for engineering optimization. Eng. Comput. **36**(4), 563–582 (2020)
5. Chen, K., Xue, B., Zhang, M., Zhou, F.: Correlation-guided updating strategy for feature selection in classification with surrogate-assisted particle swarm optimization. IEEE Trans. Evol. Comput. **26**(5), 1015–1029 (2021)
6. Łapa, K., Cpałka, K., Kisiel-Dorohinicki, M., Paszkowski, J., Dębski, M., Le, V.-H.: Multi-population-based algorithm with an exchange of training plans based on population evaluation. J. Artif. Intell. Soft Comput. Res. **12**(4), 239–253 (2022)
7. Cpałka, K., Łapa, K., Przybył, A.: Genetic programming algorithm for designing of control systems. Inf. Technol. Control **47**(4), 668–683 (2018)
8. Cpałka, K., Łapa, K., Rutkowski, L.: A multi-population-based algorithm with different ways of subpopulations cooperation. In: Rutkowski, L., Scherer, R., Korytkowski, M., Pedrycz, W., Tadeusiewicz, R., Zurada, J.M. (eds.) ICAISC 2022. LNCS, vol. 13588, pp. 205–218. Springer, Cham (2022). https://doi.org/10.1007/978-3-031-23492-7_18

9. Gabryel, M., Lada, D., Filutowicz, Z., Patora-Wysocka, Z., Kisiel-Dorohinicki, M., Chen, G.: Detecting anomalies in advertising web traffic with the use of the variational autoencoder. J. Artif. Intell. Soft Comput. Res. **12**(4), 255–256 (2022)

10. Gabryel, M., Cpałka, K., Rutkowski, L.: Evolutionary strategies for learning of neuro-fuzzy systems. In: Proceedings of the I Workshop on Genetic Fuzzy Systems, pp. 119–123 (2005)

11. García-Nieto, D., Bäck, T., Bosman, P.A., De Jong, K.: Deep learning surrogates for evolutionary optimization. Evol. Comput. **28**(1), 1–28 (2020)

12. Grycuk, R., Scherer, R., Marchlewska, A., Napoli, C.: Semantic hashing for fast solar magnetogram retrieval. J. Artif. Intell. Soft Comput. Res. **12**(4), 299–306 (2022)

13. Kennedy, J.: Small worlds and mega-minds: effects of neighborhood topology on particle swarm performance. In: Proceedings of the 1999 Congress on Evolutionary Computation-CEC99 (Cat. No. 99TH8406), vol. 3, pp. 1931–1938. IEEE (1999)

14. Kennedy, J., Eberhart, R.: Particle swarm optimization. In: Proceedings of the IEEE International Conference on Neural Networks, vol. 4, pp. 1942–1948 (1995)

15. Kumar, D., Sharma, D.: Feature map augmentation to improve scale invariance in convolutional neural networks. J. Artif. Intell. Soft Comput. Res. **13**(1), 51–74 (2023)

16. Laktionov, I., Vovna, O., Kabanets, M.: Information technology for comprehensive monitoring and control of the microclimate in industrial greenhouses based on fuzzy logic. J. Artif. Intell. Soft Comput. Res. **13**(1), 19–35 (2023)

17. Lewy, D., Mańdziuk, J.: Training CNN classifiers solely on webly data. J. Artif. Intell. Soft Comput. Res. **13**(1), 75–92 (2023)

18. Liang, J.J., Qu, B.Y., Suganthan, P.N.: Problem definitions and evaluation criteria for the CEC 2017 special session and competition on single objective real-parameter numerical optimization. Technical report, Computational Intelligence Laboratory, Zhengzhou University, Zhengzhou China and Nanyang Technological University, Singapore (2017)

19. Li, J., De Jong, K.: Multi-population evolutionary algorithms: a review and some new developments. IEEE Trans. Evol. Comput. **26**(1), 1–21 (2022)

20. Lapa, K.: Meta-optimization of multi-objective population-based algorithms using multi-objective performance metrics. Inf. Sci. **489**, 193–204 (2019)

21. Lapa, K., Cpałka, K., Paszkowski, J.: Hybrid multi-population based approach for controllers structure and parameters selection. In: Rutkowski, L., Scherer, R., Korytkowski, M., Pedrycz, W., Tadeusiewicz, R., Zurada, J.M. (eds.) ICAISC 2019. LNCS (LNAI), vol. 11508, pp. 456–468. Springer, Cham (2019). https://doi.org/10.1007/978-3-030-20912-4_42

22. Ma, W., Gao, S., Li, X.: A survey on multi-population evolutionary algorithms. Inf. Sci. **508**, 90–107 (2023)

23. Park, C.: A comparative study for outlier detection methods in high dimensional text data. J. Artif. Intell. Soft Comput. Res. **13**(1), 5–17 (2023)

24. Pawłowska, J., Rydzewska, K., Wierzbicki, A.: Using cognitive models to understand and counteract the effect of self-induced bias on recommendation algorithms. J. Artif. Intell. Soft Comput. Res. **13**(2), 73–94 (2023)

25. Reyes-Pérez, M., Martí, R.: Surrogate modeling in multiobjective optimization: a review. Mathematics **9**(5), 653 (2021)

26. Rutkowski, L., Cpałka, K.: Flexible structures of neuro-fuzzy systems. In: Quo Vadis Computational Intelligence. Studies in Fuzziness and Soft Computing, vol. 54, pp. 479–484 (2000)

27. Scherer, R.: Neuro-fuzzy systems with relation matrix. In: Rutkowski, L., Scherer, R., Tadeusiewicz, R., Zadeh, L.A., Zurada, J.M. (eds.) ICAISC 2010. LNCS (LNAI), vol. 6113, pp. 210–215. Springer, Heidelberg (2010). https://doi.org/10.1007/978-3-642-13208-7_27

28. Scherer, R., Rutkowski, L.: Neuro-fuzzy relational classifiers. In: Rutkowski, L., Siekmann, J.H., Tadeusiewicz, R., Zadeh, L.A. (eds.) ICAISC 2004. LNCS (LNAI), vol. 3070, pp. 376–380. Springer, Heidelberg (2004). https://doi.org/10.1007/978-3-540-24844-6_54

29. Scherer, R., Rutkowski, L.: Neuro-fuzzy relational systems. In: FSKD, pp. 44–48 (2002)

30. Słowik, A.: Steering of balance between exploration and exploitation properties of evolutionary algorithms - mix selection. In: Rutkowski, L., Scherer, R., Tadeusiewicz, R., Zadeh, L.A., Zurada, J.M. (eds.) ICAISC 2010. LNCS (LNAI), vol. 6114, pp. 213–220. Springer, Heidelberg (2010). https://doi.org/10.1007/978-3-642-13232-2_26

31. Słowik, A.: Application of evolutionary algorithm to design minimal phase digital filters with non-standard amplitude characteristics and finite bit word length. Bull. Polish Acad. Sci.-Tech. Sci. **59**(2), 125–135 (2011)

32. Słowik, A., Białko, M.: Design and optimization of combinational digital circuits using modified evolutionary algorithm. In: Rutkowski, L., Siekmann, J.H., Tadeusiewicz, R., Zadeh, L.A. (eds.) ICAISC 2004. LNCS (LNAI), vol. 3070, pp. 468–473. Springer, Heidelberg (2004). https://doi.org/10.1007/978-3-540-24844-6_69

33. Słowik, A., Białko, M.: Modified version of roulette selection for evolution algorithms – the fan selection. In: Rutkowski, L., Siekmann, J.H., Tadeusiewicz, R., Zadeh, L.A. (eds.) ICAISC 2004. LNCS (LNAI), vol. 3070, pp. 474–479. Springer, Heidelberg (2004). https://doi.org/10.1007/978-3-540-24844-6_70

34. Słowik, A., Białko, M.: Partitioning of VLSI circuits on subcircuits with minimal number of connections using evolutionary algorithm. In: Rutkowski, L., Tadeusiewicz, R., Zadeh, L.A., Żurada, J.M. (eds.) ICAISC 2006. LNCS (LNAI), vol. 4029, pp. 470–478. Springer, Heidelberg (2006). https://doi.org/10.1007/11785231_50

35. Słowik, A., Bialko, M.: Design of IIR digital filters with non-standard characteristics using differential evolution algorithm. Bull. Polish Acad. Sci.-Tech. Sci. **55**(4), 359–363 (2007)

36. Slowik, A., Bialko, M.: Design and optimization of IIR digital filters with non-standard characteristics using continuous ant colony optimization algorithm. In: Darzentas, J., Vouros, G.A., Vosinakis, S., Arnellos, A. (eds.) SETN 2008. LNCS (LNAI), vol. 5138, pp. 395–400. Springer, Heidelberg (2008). https://doi.org/10.1007/978-3-540-87881-0_39

37. Słowik, A., Cpałka, K., Łapa, K.: Multi-population nature-inspired algorithm (MNIA) for the designing of interpretable fuzzy systems. IEEE Trans. Fuzzy Syst. **28**(6), 1125–1139 (2020)

38. Szczypta, J., Przybył, A., Cpałka, K.: Some aspects of evolutionary designing optimal controllers. In: Rutkowski, L., Korytkowski, M., Scherer, R., Tadeusiewicz, R., Zadeh, L.A., Zurada, J.M. (eds.) ICAISC 2013. LNCS (LNAI), vol. 7895, pp. 91–100. Springer, Heidelberg (2013). https://doi.org/10.1007/978-3-642-38610-7_9

39. Szmuc, T., Mrówka, R., Brańka, M., Ficoń, J., Pięta, P.: Nowatorska metoda szybkiego generowania obiektów 3D z wielu czujników głębokości. J. Artif. Intell. Soft Comput. Res. **13**(2), 95–105 (2023)

40. Woldan, P., Duda, P., Cader, A., Laktionov, I.: A new approach to image-based recommender systems with the application of heatmaps maps. J. Artif. Intell. Soft Comput. Res. **13**(2), 63–72 (2023)

41. Zalasiński, M.: New algorithm for on-line signature verification using characteristic global features. Adv. Intell. Syst. Comput. **432**, 137–146 (2016)

42. Zalasiński, M., Cpałka, K., Er, M.J.: A new method for the dynamic signature verification based on the stable partitions of the signature. In: Rutkowski, L., Korytkowski, M., Scherer, R., Tadeusiewicz, R., Zadeh, L.A., Zurada, J.M. (eds.) ICAISC 2015. LNCS (LNAI), vol. 9120, pp. 161–174. Springer, Cham (2015). https://doi.org/10.1007/978-3-319-19369-4_16

43. Zalasiński, M., Cpałka, K., Hayashi, Y.: A new approach to the dynamic signature verification aimed at minimizing the number of global features. In: Rutkowski, L., Korytkowski, M., Scherer, R., Tadeusiewicz, R., Zadeh, L.A., Zurada, J.M. (eds.) ICAISC 2016. LNCS (LNAI), vol. 9693, pp. 218–231. Springer, Cham (2016). https://doi.org/10.1007/978-3-319-39384-1_20

44. Zalasiński, M., Cpałka, K., Hayashi, Y.: New fast algorithm for the dynamic signature verification using global features values. In: Rutkowski, L., Korytkowski, M., Scherer, R., Tadeusiewicz, R., Zadeh, L.A., Zurada, J.M. (eds.) ICAISC 2015. LNCS (LNAI), vol. 9120, pp. 175–188. Springer, Cham (2015). https://doi.org/10.1007/978-3-319-19369-4_17

45. Zalasiński, M., Łapa, K., Cpałka, K.: Feature selection for on-line signature verification using genetic programming. Expert Syst. Appl. **104**, 86–96 (2018)

46. Zalasiński, M., Łapa, K., Cpałka, K., Przybyszewski, K., Yen, G.G.: On-line signature partitioning using a population based algorithm. J. Artif. Intell. Soft Comput. Res. **10**(1), 5–13 (2020)

47. Zhang, T.: Solving large scale linear prediction problems using stochastic gradient descent algorithms. In: Proceedings of the Twenty-first International Conference on Machine Learning, vol. 116, pp. 1–8 (2004)

48. Zhang, W., Chen, Y., Li, J.: Multi-population evolutionary algorithms: a survey. IEEE Access **10**, 89934–89953 (2022)

49. Zhang, W., Chen, Y., Liu, M., Li, J.: Surrogate-assisted evolutionary algorithms: a survey. IEEE Access **9**, 113659–113678 (2021)

Multi-population-based Algorithms with Different Migration Topologies and Their Improvement by Population Re-initialization

Krystian Łapa[✉][iD]

Częstochowa University of Technology, 42-201 Częstochowa, Poland
krystian.lapa@pcz.pl

Abstract. In this paper, the possibilities of improving the performance of multi-population-based algorithms were tested. In the proposed approach, it was decided to test various methods and parameters of the population re-initialization mechanism, aimed at improving the diversity of individuals and preventing premature convergence, which is associated with a possible improvement in obtained results. In addition to the standard approach with random re-initialization of a new population, it was decided to test an approach in which selected populations are initialized with the use of modified individuals from better-performing populations. This approach has not been thoroughly tested so far, in particular for many different migration topologies and different population-based algorithms. The presented approach was specifically tested for the MNIA algorithm, eliminating the need to select one specific algorithm for the optimization. The simulations were performed for typical benchmark functions. The results of the simulations allow us to conclude that the proposed approach, depending on the parameters, improved the optimization process.

Keywords: Multi-Population-Based algorithms · Migration topologies · Population re-initialization

1 Introduction

Population-based algorithms (PBAs) are great methods for optimizing the parameters of arbitrary problems as they do not need a derivative of the evaluation function and can take into account multiple evaluation criteria for a given problem at the same time (see e.g. [6,10,56]). The advantages of population-based algorithms make them more and more applicable to various problems (e.g. [58–61]). Compared to optimization using, for example, back-propagation methods (see e.g. [51,54]), PBAs disadvantage is their computational complexity. However, with technological progress, this factor is less and less important in relation to achievable results. And although population-based algorithms with

© The Author(s), under exclusive license to Springer Nature Switzerland AG 2023
L. Rutkowski et al. (Eds.): ICAISC 2023, LNAI 14125, pp. 399–414, 2023.
https://doi.org/10.1007/978-3-031-42505-9_34

lower computational complexity are currently being developed (e.g. using surrogate models or a dynamic number of individuals-see e.g. [2,48]), at the same time it is possible to observe the development process of more and more multi-population-based algorithms (MPBAs) that usually require more individuals and have greater computational complexity (see e.g. [19,41,44]). This is due to many reasons, the most important of which are reducing the chance of getting stuck in the local optimum and improving the convergence of the algorithm. Thus, the complexity issues are not an aspect of this study. The universality of population algorithms means that they are not only applicable to many fields but also create interesting solutions that use versatile mechanisms or allow to support other methods (see e.g. [28,47]). The algorithm proposed in this paper can be used in typical application areas of PBAs. Moreover, it can support other computational intelligence methods, such as: designing recommendation systems and their applications [40], designing fuzzy systems and their applications [22], parallelizing algorithms and systems [4], detecting anomalies in data [13], data classification [20], etc.

1.1 Motivation

MPBAs are effective, but their effectiveness depends on many factors. One of them is the topology of connections between populations, which determines the manner, direction, and number of individuals being exchanged [26]. Other parameters of these algorithms related to the topology are the mechanisms for selecting individuals for exchange and determining the frequency of such an exchange. In the literature, there are also approaches in which the topology can be dynamically changed, and the number of populations itself can be dynamic (see e.g. [1,12,32]). However, not only the topology issues are crucial, but the choice of the underlying population-based algorithm or algorithms is also important, not to mention the problem of selecting the parameters of these algorithms. Most often, however, one underlying algorithm is chosen. In the case of using dynamic populations or population re-initialization, the new populations are created by random initialization, or by initialization with the use of individuals stored in the archive-the group of the most promising individuals (see e.g. [49]). The development of effective methods aimed at improving the performance of multi-population-based algorithms is therefore a difficult task that has been undertaken and moved a step forward in this paper.

1.2 Contribution

As a goal of this paper, we want to investigate the possibilities of further improving the performance of multi-population algorithms. The paper, among others, extends the approach presented in [7], which presents an investigation of MPBAs including Multi Nature Inspired Algorithm (MNIA)-algorithm where populations can be based on different PBAs with the use of different topologies and migration parameters. As a novel element, it was decided to test various methods and parameters of population re-initialization, aimed at improving the diversity of individuals and preventing premature convergence, which is also associated with a possible improvement in results. In addition to the standard approach with random re-initialization of a new population, it was decided to test an approach in which selected populations are initialized with the use of modified individuals from better-performing populations. This approach has not been thoroughly tested so far, in particular for many different migration topologies and different multi-population-based algorithms.

1.3   Structure of the Paper

The structure of this paper is as follows: Sect. 2 reviews the methods related to the issues considered in this paper; Sect. 3 describes the proposed approach and how to perform comparative experiments; and a summary is provided in Sect. 4.

2   Background

Basic population-based algorithms use one population where each individual encodes the parameters of one solution. This approach, depending on the exploration and exploitation mechanisms and the problem under consideration, can often lead to getting stuck in a local optimum (see e.g. [9,37]). One of the approaches to improve the performance of population-based algorithms is to diversify the behavior of individuals in the population, most often the population is divided into several parts, e.g. a part including individuals that are focused on exploration and part on exploitation. Such a mechanism can be observed, for example, in the Bison Algorithm [18]. Other approaches include differentiating the optimization parameters of individuals, changing the mechanisms depending on the ranking of the individual in the population, or depending on the iteration of the algorithm (e.g. Grey Wolf Optimizer [34]). In the literature, also hybrid approaches in which individuals of a population use mechanisms derived from different population algorithms can be found (see e.g. [45]). In all the mentioned cases, still, a single population is used. In multi-population-based algorithms, the distinction between populations (also called islands) must be clear, and the migration of an individual from population to population (which does not have to take place at all) can only take place under certain rules. In this section, various approaches to multi-population-based algorithms and the related problems will be described.

2.1   Multi-population-Based Algorithms

MPBAs can be divided according to whether each population optimizes the same parameters of the problem, or different parameters or different parts of the problem. In the latter case, we are dealing with cooperation, which can also occur in the case of a single population. Cases of cooperation will not be considered in this paper due to the characteristics of optimization problems, but an interesting overview of them can be found in [29], and the development of methods related to this approach is not excluded in the future. Other ways of dividing MPBAs can be made regarding the number of sub-populations (fixed or dynamic), sub-population communication (distinguishing rate, policy, interval, and topology), search area (distinguishing size and overlap), and search strategy (same strategy or different strategy in different populations). This division of MPBAs issues was made and described in detail in [30].

Distinguishing between the choice of different strategies for optimizing different populations is very important. This is because in the case of population-based algorithms, different results can be achieved depending on the problem and the algorithm, i.e. there is no algorithm that will be the best for solving all problems [7]. To deal with that different solutions can be found in the literature, starting with those in which there are only two populations optimized according to strategies from different population-based algorithms (see e.g. [50]), through solutions in which there are several populations optimized on the basis of one population-based algorithm, but with different parameters for each sub-population (see e.g. [39]), ending with solutions with multiple populations where each can be optimized based on a dynamic optimization plan that changes during the optimization process (see e.g. [46]). The use of different algorithms instead of one eliminates the need to look for a good algorithm for a given simulation problem and such an approach will be considered in this paper.

2.2   Migration Topologies and Strategies

Migration topologies are one of the key factors determining the effectiveness of multi-population-based algorithms. In the literature, a number of papers in which various topologies are considered can be found. The most commonly used migration topologies include star and ring topologies [17], which additionally can occur in many variations (see e.g. star1d, star2d, ring1d, ring2d, ringp1 in Fig. 1). Other common topologies according to [17] are torus and lattice (also called mesh)-see mesh4 and torus in Fig. 1. To the successful topologies summarized as topologies from [31] with structures such as fully connected, toroidal, or tree we can also add-see full, tor04, and tree on Fig. 1. Many topologies are also combinations of some topologies, e.g. star and ring called cartwheel [38,43]-see strnc on Fig. 1. Another topology approach is to add random connections between the populations or use only random connections-see swrl02, swrl03, rtree, rand2, rand3, and rand4 respectively presented in Fig. 1. In addition, in some solutions, the topologies are changed dynamically during the operation of the algorithm (some or all connections are re-established in accordance with the algorithm's guidelines). An example is proposed in [7] where the worst or best population is placed as a specific element of the topology-see e.g. starb, starw, pathb, and pathw in Fig. 1. An interesting summary of the topology was made in the paper [7], and the topologies presented there are shown in Fig. 1. Choosing the best topology is therefore another challenge when designing an algorithm. Unfortunately in most approaches from the literature, only a few topologies which additionally use only one specified population-based algorithm are tested simultaneously. In this paper, it was undertaken to test a number of different topologies for several population algorithms. In addition, it was decided to test the behavior of these topologies in the case of population re-initialization during the operation of the algorithm. Such a complete approach has not been presented in the literature so far.

2.3 Convergence

Convergence in population-based algorithms plays a major role in their operation (see e.g. [33,42,52]). Too fast and premature convergence makes it possible to get stuck in the local optimum and stops results from improving. Various techniques are used to avoid the convergence of individuals to one point in space (or several points). One of the basic techniques is to provide a continuous global search (exploration), an example of which is the use of the mutation operator in the genetic algorithm [23]. Another example is to ensure changes in parameters, e.g. the use of a condition in the Differential Evolution algorithm, thanks to which at least one parameter in a new individual will be modified [11]. At some point, however, an improvement of the solutions found occurs only with intensive local search (exploitation). Thus, finding a good balance between exploration and exploitation is of very great significance. A very good example is the previously mentioned Gray Wolf Optimizer [34], in which the algorithm parameter smoothly changes the search range along with the iterations of the algorithm. However, the said change is linear and depends on the number of adopted steps of the algorithm. It is also not dynamic, and thus new variants of this and other PBA algorithms are constantly being developed to improve their performance.

The issue of population-based algorithm convergence is broad. Interesting summaries can be found, among others, in [5,15,36,52,62]. An important mechanism that can be introduced to any population-based algorithm is to ensure the appropriate differentiation of individuals. The differentiation of the individuals can be tested by various criteria, and the increase in the differentiation can be introduced, inter alia, by re-initializing the individuals. Such re-initialization may concern both single individuals (usually in single-population-based algorithms-see e.g. [14,21]) and the entire population (which may work better in multi-population algorithms-see e.g. [53,55]). Most often, new populations are created by random initialization of individuals, or by initialization with the use of individuals stored in the archive/memory-the group of the most promising individuals (see e.g. [49,53]). The latter, however, may have a different impact on further convergence. In the literature, approaches in which the worst populations are removed, or individuals are removed from them can be also found-such an example is the ICA [3] algorithm. The re-initialization process itself also requires specifying when it is to occur, it can be e.g. a certain number of iterations, or reaching some replacement criterion (see e.g. [8]). Re-initialization can also help when populations are overlapping [24]. In the case of a re-initialization of entire populations, there are no relevant reviews of approaches in the literature where the impact of population restart is tested for many population algorithms and many different migration topologies. The author decided to address this aspect in this paper, especially for MNIA and dynamic changes in topologies proposed in [7].

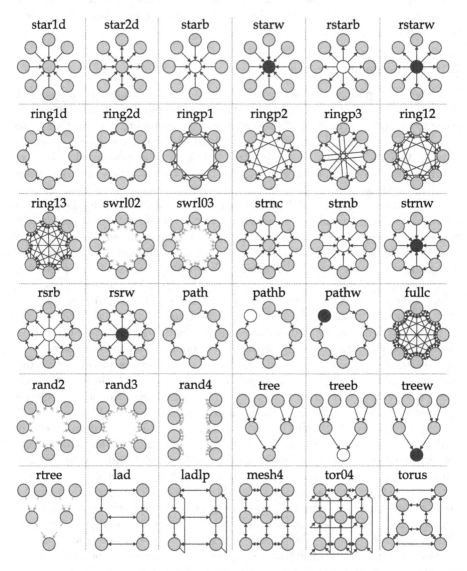

Fig. 1. Migration topologies by [7]. The arrowhead indicates the sub-population that has been modified. A dark circle means an additional population replacement after the adopted interval for the population that is the worst of all others in terms of the mean fitness function value. A light-colored circle means an additional replacement of the population with the best sub-population. Light lines indicate connections from sub-populations selected at random

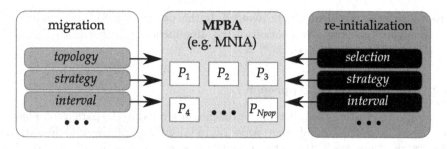

Fig. 2. Approaches that determine the performance of MPBAs. Elements with the greatest emphasis in this paper have been marked with black rectangles. P denotes a population algorithm, in the case of the MNIA algorithm, each algorithm P may follow rules from different population algorithms.

3   Comparative Experiments

In the paper [7], the impact of the choice of migration parameters on the results of the optimization was examined. In particular, the migration topologies presented in Fig. 1 were tested. In addition, parameters related to the migration interval, migration model (how to select individuals for migration), and various numbers of islands were considered. The best results, regardless of the given topology, were obtained for a migration interval of 10 ($Nivl$), the selection of an individual for migration using a roulette wheel, and 8 islands ($Npop$ sub-populations) consisting of 32 individuals each ($Nind$). The above parameters were adopted in the simulations in this paper.

3.1   Proposed Approach and Experiments

This paper proposes investigating the effect of population re-initialization in multi-population-based algorithms with different migration topologies. First, all migration topologies presented in Fig. 1 were considered. This applies to both the standard topologies often used in the literature, as well as to the author's proposed topologies, in which the population is castling according to the adopted mechanisms (for the details see [7]). Secondly, a different population re-initialization interval ($Rinv$) was considered: every 10 (M10), 25 (M25), and 40 (M40) iterations. Thirdly, different ways of selecting the population for re-initialization were tested: selecting the worst population in terms of the best individual rating function (SBI) and selecting the worst population in terms of the average rating function of all individuals (SAV). As part of the optimization, it was decided to take into account both well-known population algorithms (Cuckoo Search-CS [57], Grey Wolf Optimizer-GWO [34], and Whale Optimization Algorithm-WOA [35]) and the MNIA algorithm, in which populations based on different population-based algorithms are used. Thanks to MNIA, in which the problem of choosing a single algorithm, which is not always optimal for a given simulation problem, can be avoided. In this paper for MNIA as population-based algorithms, the combination of the aforementioned algorithms (i.e. CS, GWO, and WOA) was used.

3.2 Re-initialization Approach

In addition to testing the different approaches described in the paragraph above, it was decided to test different ways of re-initializing of the individuals. In the standard approach, the entire population is replaced with individuals with random parameters (RAND). In the first supplementary approach, individuals replacing the worst populations are created based on the crossover and mutation of individuals from the remaining populations, in accordance with the crossover and mutation operators from the genetic algorithm (CMGA). In the second supplementary approach, individuals are created based on an operator from Differential Evolution (CRDE). In both CMGA and CRDE, the individuals used to create new individuals are selected using a roulette wheel. It should be added that the proposed re-initialization approaches have not been tested for the mentioned topologies, parameters, and their combinations with the mentioned algorithms, in particular with MNIA, and have a great potential to improve the optimization process. All proposed variants will be tested according to the following idea. In the first step $Npop$ of the population is initialized with $Nind$ individuals each. In the case of MNIA, each population can be based on a different algorithm. In the second step, the populations are combined according to the migration topologies in Fig. 1. Then, all populations are processed through $Niter$ iterations. Every $Nivl$ of iterations, individuals are replaced in accordance with the adopted strategy, and in the case of selected topologies, they are dynamically updated. However, for every $Rivl$ of iterations, the population selected in accordance with the considered strategy is reinitialized. In the last step of the algorithm, after completing the processing of individuals, the best solution found from all populations is presented. The idea of topology selection and reinitialization is shown in Fig. 2.

3.3 Simulation Parameters

Simulations were performed on the CEC 2013 benchmark functions [25], assuming 50 as the number of problem dimensions. The number of simulation repetitions for each variant was set at 50, and the number of $Niter$ iterations at 1000. In the CS, GWO, and WOA population algorithms, standard parameters suggested in the literature were adopted. The crossover probability of 0.9, the mutation probability of 0.5, and the mutation range of 0.1 were assumed for CMGA re-initialization, while the value of the F parameter equal to 0.9 and the CR parameter equal to 0.9 were assumed for the CRDE re-initialization. MNIA settings were adopted as described in the previous section.

3.4   Simulation Results

The possibility of improving the results using re-initialization of the population for each of the topologies presented in Fig. 1 is shown in Table 1, while the possi-

Table 1. Improvement over the **given** topology and case without re-initialization averaged for all simulation problems and all population-based algorithms. A value of x in the table means an improvement by $(1+x)$ times. Re-init stands for method, interv. for interval, and select. for selecting the method of the worst population for re-initialization.

re-init	RAND						CMGA						CRDE					
interv.	M10		M25		M40		M10		M25		M40		M10		M25		M40	
select.	SBI	SAV	SBI	SAV	SBI	SAV	SBI	SAV	SBI	SAV	SBI	SAV	SBI	SAV	SBI	SAV	SBI	SAV
starld	0.7	0.7	0.4	0.4	0.4	0.3	1.7	1.7	1.1	1.0	0.8	0.8	3.0	2.9	1.2	1.4	1.0	1.0
star2d	0.6	0.8	0.3	0.4	0.3	0.3	1.1	1.0	0.6	0.6	0.4	0.4	1.0	1.1	0.5	0.5	0.3	0.4
starb	0.6	0.6	0.3	0.3	0.2	0.3	1.5	1.6	1.0	0.9	0.7	0.7	2.9	2.7	1.1	1.1	0.9	0.7
starw	0.5	0.4	0.3	0.3	0.2	0.3	0.9	0.9	0.4	0.4	0.3	0.3	1.0	1.1	0.4	0.5	0.3	0.3
rstarb	0.5	0.8	0.3	0.5	0.2	0.3	0.9	1.0	0.4	0.5	0.3	0.3	1.0	1.2	0.4	0.5	0.3	0.3
rstarw	2.4	2.2	1.2	1.0	0.7	0.7	4.8	5.0	3.1	3.2	2.7	2.8	**6.6**	**6.6**	3.2	3.1	2.3	2.4
ringld	0.4	0.5	0.3	0.3	0.2	0.2	1.0	0.9	0.5	0.4	0.4	0.4	1.2	1.2	0.5	0.6	0.4	0.4
ring2d	0.4	0.5	0.2	0.3	0.1	0.2	0.7	0.8	0.3	0.4	0.3	0.3	1.0	0.9	0.4	0.4	0.3	0.3
ringp1	0.5	0.7	0.4	0.4	0.3	0.3	0.9	0.9	0.5	0.5	0.4	0.3	1.0	1.0	0.5	0.5	0.3	0.4
ringp2	0.5	0.6	0.3	0.4	0.2	0.2	0.7	0.9	0.5	0.5	0.4	0.4	1.1	1.0	0.4	0.5	0.4	0.3
ringp3	0.4	0.5	0.3	0.3	0.2	0.2	0.8	0.9	0.4	0.4	0.3	0.3	0.9	1.0	0.4	0.5	0.3	0.3
ring12	0.5	0.7	0.3	0.4	0.2	0.3	0.8	0.9	0.4	0.4	0.3	0.3	0.9	1.0	0.4	0.5	0.3	0.3
ring13	0.4	0.6	0.2	0.3	0.2	0.2	0.6	0.8	0.3	0.4	0.2	0.3	0.8	0.8	0.4	0.4	0.2	0.3
swrl02	0.5	0.6	0.3	0.3	0.3	0.2	0.7	0.8	0.4	0.4	0.3	0.3	0.9	0.9	0.4	0.4	0.3	0.3
swrl03	0.4	0.5	0.3	0.3	0.2	0.2	0.7	0.7	0.3	0.4	0.2	0.3	0.7	0.8	0.3	0.3	0.2	0.2
strnc	0.3	0.4	0.1	0.2	0.1	0.1	0.8	0.9	0.4	0.4	0.3	0.3	1.0	1.0	0.4	0.5	0.3	0.3
strnb	0.6	0.6	0.3	0.4	0.2	0.3	1.2	1.1	0.7	0.7	0.5	0.5	1.4	1.5	0.7	0.7	0.6	0.6
strnw	0.5	0.7	0.3	0.4	0.3	0.3	0.9	1.0	0.4	0.5	0.4	0.3	0.9	1.0	0.5	0.5	0.4	0.4
rsrb	0.5	0.9	0.3	0.5	0.3	0.3	0.8	1.0	0.4	0.5	0.4	0.4	0.8	1.1	0.4	0.5	0.3	0.3
rsrw	0.5	0.5	0.2	0.3	0.2	0.2	0.9	0.9	0.5	0.5	0.4	0.4	1.2	1.1	0.5	0.5	0.4	0.4
mesh4	0.9	1.1	0.5	0.6	0.4	0.5	1.9	2.0	1.1	1.2	0.9	1.0	2.1	2.2	1.1	1.2	0.9	0.9
toro4	0.4	0.6	0.3	0.3	0.2	0.2	0.9	0.9	0.5	0.5	0.4	0.3	1.1	1.1	0.6	0.5	0.4	0.4
torus	0.6	0.8	0.4	0.4	0.4	0.3	0.9	0.9	0.5	0.6	0.3	0.4	1.0	1.0	0.5	0.5	0.3	0.4
fullc	0.4	0.5	0.3	0.3	0.2	0.3	0.6	0.7	0.4	0.4	0.3	0.3	0.7	0.8	0.4	0.4	0.2	0.3
path	0.7	0.8	0.4	0.5	0.3	0.3	1.6	1.7	0.9	0.9	0.7	0.7	1.9	2.2	0.9	0.9	0.7	0.7
pathb	0.7	0.9	0.4	0.5	0.3	0.3	1.7	1.5	1.1	1.0	0.7	0.8	1.9	1.9	0.9	1.0	0.7	0.7
pathw	0.5	0.6	0.3	0.4	0.2	0.3	1.0	1.1	0.6	0.6	0.4	0.4	1.2	1.2	0.6	0.6	0.4	0.4
tree	0.7	0.7	0.3	0.4	0.2	0.2	1.7	1.8	1.0	1.0	0.8	0.7	2.5	2.3	1.1	1.2	0.8	0.8
treeb	0.5	0.6	0.3	0.3	0.2	0.3	1.3	1.5	0.9	0.8	0.6	0.6	2.2	2.0	0.9	0.9	0.7	0.6
treew	0.7	0.7	0.4	0.4	0.2	0.3	1.7	1.6	1.0	1.0	0.8	0.7	2.3	2.4	1.3	1.2	0.8	0.9
rtree	0.7	0.7	0.5	0.5	0.3	0.4	1.3	1.2	0.8	0.7	0.5	0.5	1.6	1.4	0.7	0.8	0.5	0.5
lad	0.6	0.7	0.3	0.4	0.2	0.3	1.2	1.2	0.6	0.7	0.5	0.5	1.4	1.5	0.7	0.7	0.5	0.6
ladlp	0.5	0.7	0.4	0.4	0.2	0.3	0.9	0.9	0.5	0.5	0.4	0.4	1.0	1.1	0.5	0.5	0.4	0.4
rand2	0.5	0.6	0.2	0.3	0.2	0.2	0.9	0.9	0.5	0.5	0.4	0.4	1.0	1.0	0.5	0.5	0.3	0.4
rand3	0.5	0.6	0.2	0.3	0.2	0.3	0.8	0.8	0.5	0.4	0.4	0.3	0.9	0.9	0.4	0.5	0.3	0.3
rand4	0.6	0.7	0.5	0.4	0.3	0.3	0.9	0.9	0.5	0.5	0.3	0.4	0.9	1.1	0.5	0.5	0.3	0.4
AVG	0.6	0.7	0.3	0.4	0.3	0.3	1.2	1.2	0.7	0.7	0.5	0.5	**1.5**	**1.5**	0.7	0.7	0.5	0.5

bility of improving the results against the best topology without re-initialization is shown in Table 2 and in detail in Table 3. A comparison of the tested algorithms in terms of each simulation problem is presented in Table 4.

3.5   Simulation Conclusions

The best improvement in relation to a given topology was achieved for rstarw and the cases of CRDE, M10, SBI, and SAV (see Table 1). In addition, in the

Table 2. Improvement over the **best** topology and case without re-initialization averaged for all simulation problems and all population-based algorithms. A value of x in the table means an improvement by $(1+x)$ times. Re-init stands for method, interv. for interval, and select. for selecting the method of the worst population for re-initialization

re-init	RAND						CMGA						CRDE					
interv.	M10		M25		M40		M10		M25		M40		M10		M25		M40	
select.	SBI	SAV	SBI	SAV	SBI	SAV	SBI	SAV	SBI	SAV	SBI	SAV	SBI	SAV	SBI	SAV	SBI	SAV
star1d	−0.6	−0.7	−0.8	−0.7	−0.8	−0.8	0.2	0.2	−0.1	−0.1	−0.3	−0.3	0.4	0.3	−0.1	−0.1	−0.2	−0.2
star2d	−0.1	0.1	−0.3	−0.1	−0.3	−0.3	0.3	0.3	0.0	0.0	−0.1	−0.1	0.3	0.3	0.0	0.0	−0.2	−0.1
starb	−0.6	−0.6	−0.8	−0.8	−0.9	−0.9	0.2	0.2	−0.1	−0.1	−0.3	−0.2	0.4	0.3	−0.1	−0.1	−0.2	−0.3
starw	−0.1	−0.5	−0.2	−0.2	−0.3	−0.2	0.3	0.2	0.0	−0.1	−0.1	−0.1	0.3	0.4	−0.1	−0.1	−0.2	−0.1
rstarb	0.0	0.2	−0.1	0.0	−0.2	−0.1	0.3	0.4	0.0	0.1	−0.1	−0.1	0.4	0.5	0.0	0.1	0.0	−0.1
rstarw	−0.9	−0.9	−1.3	−1.5	−1.6	−1.5	0.2	0.2	−0.2	−0.2	−0.3	−0.4	0.3	0.3	−0.2	−0.3	−0.4	−0.4
ring1d	−0.2	−0.2	−0.3	−0.3	−0.4	−0.3	0.3	0.2	−0.1	−0.1	−0.1	−0.1	0.4	0.4	−0.1	0.0	−0.1	−0.1
ring2d	0.0	0.1	−0.1	−0.1	−0.2	−0.1	0.3	0.3	0.0	0.0	0.0	0.0	0.5	0.4	0.1	0.1	0.0	0.0
ringp1	0.0	0.1	−0.1	−0.1	−0.2	−0.1	0.3	0.3	0.0	0.0	0.0	−0.1	0.4	0.4	0.1	0.1	−0.1	0.0
ringp2	0.0	0.0	−0.1	0.0	−0.2	−0.2	0.2	0.3	0.0	0.1	0.0	0.0	0.5	0.4	0.0	0.1	0.0	−0.1
ringp3	−0.1	0.0	−0.1	−0.1	−0.2	−0.2	0.3	0.3	0.0	0.0	−0.1	−0.1	0.4	0.4	0.0	0.1	−0.1	−0.1
ring12	0.1	0.2	−0.1	0.0	−0.1	−0.1	0.3	0.4	0.0	0.1	0.0	0.0	0.4	0.5	0.1	0.1	0.0	0.0
ring13	0.1	0.2	0.0	0.0	0.0	0.0	0.3	0.4	0.1	0.1	0.0	0.0	0.4	0.4	0.1	0.1	0.0	0.0
swrl02	0.1	0.2	0.0	0.0	0.0	0.0	0.4	0.4	0.1	0.1	0.0	0.0	0.5	0.5	0.1	0.1	0.0	0.0
swrl03	0.1	0.3	0.1	0.1	0.0	0.0	0.4	0.4	0.1	0.1	0.1	0.1	0.5	0.5	0.1	0.1	0.0	0.0
strnc	−0.2	−0.2	−0.3	−0.2	−0.3	−0.3	0.3	0.4	0.0	0.0	−0.1	−0.1	0.4	0.4	0.0	0.0	−0.1	−0.1
strnb	−0.2	−0.2	−0.3	−0.2	−0.4	−0.3	0.3	0.3	0.0	0.0	−0.1	−0.1	0.4	0.5	0.0	0.0	−0.1	−0.1
strnw	0.0	0.1	−0.1	0.0	−0.1	−0.1	0.3	0.4	0.0	0.1	0.0	−0.1	0.4	0.4	0.1	0.1	0.0	0.0
rsrb	0.1	0.4	0.0	0.1	0.0	−0.1	0.3	0.4	0.1	0.1	0.0	0.0	0.4	0.5	0.1	0.1	0.0	0.0
rsrw	−0.1	0.0	−0.3	−0.2	−0.3	−0.3	0.3	0.3	0.0	0.0	−0.1	−0.1	0.5	0.3	0.0	0.0	−0.1	−0.1
mesh4	−0.3	−0.2	−0.5	−0.4	−0.5	−0.4	0.3	0.3	0.0	0.0	−0.1	−0.1	0.4	0.4	0.0	0.0	−0.1	−0.1
toro4	0.0	0.1	−0.1	−0.1	−0.1	−0.2	0.3	0.3	0.0	0.1	0.0	0.0	0.5	0.5	0.1	0.1	0.0	0.0
torus	0.2	0.3	0.0	0.0	0.0	0.0	0.4	0.4	0.1	0.2	0.0	0.0	0.5	0.5	0.1	0.1	0.0	0.0
fullc	0.3	0.4	0.2	0.2	0.1	0.2	0.5	**0.6**	0.2	0.2	0.2	0.1	0.5	**0.6**	0.3	0.2	0.1	0.2
path	−0.4	−0.3	−0.5	−0.5	−0.6	−0.6	0.3	0.3	−0.1	−0.1	−0.2	−0.2	0.4	0.4	−0.1	−0.1	−0.2	−0.2
pathb	−0.4	−0.3	−0.6	−0.5	−0.6	−0.6	0.3	0.2	0.0	−0.1	−0.2	−0.2	0.3	0.4	−0.1	−0.1	−0.2	−0.3
pathw	−0.2	−0.2	−0.3	−0.2	−0.4	−0.3	0.3	0.3	−0.1	0.0	−0.1	−0.2	0.3	0.4	0.0	0.0	−0.1	−0.1
tree	−0.5	−0.5	−0.8	−0.7	−0.9	−0.8	0.3	0.3	−0.1	−0.1	−0.2	−0.3	0.4	0.4	−0.1	−0.1	−0.3	−0.2
treeb	−0.5	−0.5	−0.6	−0.7	−0.8	−0.7	0.2	0.3	0.0	−0.1	−0.2	−0.2	0.4	0.3	−0.1	−0.1	−0.2	−0.3
treew	−0.5	−0.5	−0.7	−0.6	−0.9	−0.8	0.2	0.2	−0.1	−0.2	−0.2	−0.3	0.3	0.3	0.0	0.0	−0.2	−0.2
rtree	−0.2	−0.4	−0.3	−0.3	−0.3	−0.3	0.2	0.3	0.0	0.0	−0.2	−0.2	0.5	0.4	0.0	0.0	−0.2	−0.2
lad	−0.2	−0.1	−0.4	−0.3	−0.5	−0.4	0.3	0.3	−0.1	0.0	−0.1	−0.1	0.4	0.4	0.0	0.0	−0.1	−0.1
ladlp	0.0	0.1	−0.1	−0.1	−0.2	−0.1	0.3	0.3	0.0	0.0	−0.1	0.0	0.4	0.5	0.0	0.1	0.0	0.0
rand2	0.0	0.1	−0.2	−0.1	−0.2	−0.2	0.3	0.3	0.0	0.1	0.0	0.0	0.4	0.4	0.0	0.0	−0.1	−0.1
rand3	0.1	0.2	−0.1	0.0	−0.1	−0.1	0.4	0.4	0.1	0.1	0.0	0.0	0.4	0.5	0.1	0.1	0.0	0.0
rand4	0.2	0.3	0.1	0.1	0.0	0.0	0.4	0.4	0.1	0.1	0.0	0.0	0.5	**0.6**	0.1	0.1	0.0	0.0
AVG	−0.1	−0.1	−0.3	−0.2	−0.3	−0.3	0.3	0.3	0.0	0.0	−0.1	−0.1	**0.4**	**0.4**	0.0	0.0	−0.1	−0.1

Table 3. Improvement over the **best** topology and case without re-initialization averaged for all simulation problems, all population-based algorithms, and all topologies. A value of x in the table means an improvement by $(1+x)$ times. Interv. stands for interval, and select. for selecting the method of the worst population for re-initialization.

interv	M10		M25		M40	
select.	SBI	SAV	SBI	SAV	SBI	SAV
RAND	−0.138	−0.085	−0.281	−0.244	−0.345	−0.311
CMGA	0.306	0.319	0.006	0.007	−0.092	−0.099
CRDE	0.402	**0.417**	0.013	0.030	−0.104	−0.094

Table 4. A comparison of the tested algorithms in terms of each simulation problem. The best results are marked in bold.

	improvement for best strategy related to base topology				improvement for best strategy related to the best topology				normalized error			
	CS	GWO	WOA	MNIA	CS	GWO	WOA	MNIA	CS	GWO	WOA	MNIA
C01	11.1	4.4	3.7	0.4	2.4	3.4	0.9	−0.6	**0.000**	1.000	0.305	0.002
C02	0.1	1.1	0.4	0.3	−0.1	0.6	0.0	0.0	0.210	1.000	0.519	**0.000**
C03	0.5	4.7	1.5	0.3	−0.3	0.6	0.1	−0.4	**0.000**	1.000	0.794	0.098
C04	−0.1	0.2	0.1	0.3	−0.7	0.1	−0.1	0.0	1.000	0.385	0.148	**0.000**
C05	1.0	3.3	1.8	0.4	0.5	2.4	0.4	0.0	**0.000**	1.000	0.386	0.025
C06	0.3	2.9	1.1	0.2	−0.1	1.8	0.3	−0.1	**0.000**	1.000	0.499	0.040
C07	0.1	1.1	1.0	0.2	−0.1	0.3	0.0	0.1	1.000	0.953	0.995	**0.000**
C08	0.0	0.0	0.0	0.2	0.0	0.0	0.0	−0.1	0.181	0.052	**0.000**	1.000
C09	5.4	2.4	2.1	0.7	0.8	1.7	0.5	−0.1	**0.000**	1.000	0.518	0.009
C10	0.5	2.4	1.1	0.5	0.1	1.5	0.3	0.2	0.556	1.000	**0.000**	0.307
C11	0.2	3.7	1.3	0.9	−0.2	1.3	0.3	−0.2	**0.000**	1.000	0.983	0.406
C12	0.3	0.7	0.8	0.3	−0.5	0.3	−0.1	0.3	1.000	**0.000**	0.614	0.519
C13	0.9	1.9	1.0	0.4	0.2	1.2	0.2	0.0	0.337	1.000	**0.000**	0.198
C14	3.0	2.8	1.5	0.7	0.4	1.8	0.5	0.0	**0.000**	1.000	0.918	0.193
C15	0.5	1.8	1.2	1.0	0.0	1.0	0.1	0.4	1.000	**0.000**	0.660	0.848
C16	0.4	2.0	0.9	1.1	−0.1	0.6	0.2	0.0	1.000	**0.000**	**0.000**	0.536
C17	3.2	1.4	1.7	0.7	0.2	1.0	0.2	0.2	**0.000**	1.000	0.928	0.386
C18	0.8	2.2	0.9	0.7	0.3	1.4	0.2	0.3	0.300	1.000	**0.000**	0.290
C19	2.0	3.5	1.6	1.0	0.2	1.7	0.5	0.1	**0.000**	0.026	1.000	0.087
C20	0.4	1.3	1.1	0.8	−0.3	0.7	0.1	0.4	**0.000**	1.000	0.862	0.112
C21	1.0	2.0	0.8	1.4	0.0	0.9	0.2	0.1	0.524	**0.000**	**0.000**	1.000
C22	3.3	2.1	1.6	1.1	0.3	1.4	0.3	0.1	**0.000**	0.505	1.000	0.211
C23	0.8	2.1	1.2	1.2	0.1	1.3	0.2	0.5	0.083	1.000	0.922	**0.000**
C24	1.5	2.8	1.3	1.7	0.2	1.2	0.4	0.2	1.000	**0.000**	**0.000**	**0.000**
C25	2.1	1.4	1.4	1.3	0.0	1.0	0.1	0.5	**0.000**	0.427	0.979	1.000
C26	1.0	2.1	0.9	1.4	0.2	1.3	0.2	0.3	0.171	0.485	1.000	**0.000**
AVG	1.5	**2.2**	1.2	0.7	0.1	**1.2**	0.2	0.1	0.322	0.647	0.540	**0.280**

case of CRDE, M10 allowed for the best improvement on average for each of the topologies (see AVG in Table 1). This shows that the re-initialization strategy can improve the performance of any topology (in Table 1 there are no negative values-performance degradation). The rstarw topology was improved the most, but that was because it gave the worst results relative to the best topology (see rstarw in Table 2). The best-performing combination against the best topology without re-initialization was fullc for CMGA and CMDE, M10 and SAV, and rand4 for CMDE and M10 (see Table 2). The use of CMDE, M10, and SAV re-initialization turned out to be the best solution in averaging and allowed to improve the results by 1.4 times (see AVG in Table 3). The best improvement in relation to a specific algorithm was achieved for GWO, which may be due to the fact that it gave the weakest results in terms of the fitness function on average (see Table 4). The better the algorithm performed, the less improvement using re-initialization was achieved, but the improvement was still visible (see AVG in Table 4). Looking at the algorithms in terms of the accuracy of the results, there is no one best algorithm for all problems, however, the MNIA algorithm worked best on average (see error in Table 4).

4 Conclusions

In this paper, different approaches to population re-initialization in multi-population-based algorithms were tested and it was shown that such an approach with an appropriate configuration and mechanism for creating new individuals allows to improve the results of any topology. The configuration of CRDE, M10 and BAV re-initialization yielded better results than the best topology for the given problem and algorithm. In addition, looking at the MNIA algorithm that eliminates the need to choose a specific algorithm for a given problem, improved results were also achieved. Further research requires testing the developed method for a larger number of population-based algorithms, using other approaches to re-initialization and checking the effectiveness of this approach for other simulation problems.

Acknowledgement. The project financed under the program of the Polish Minister of Science and Higher Education under the name "Regional Initiative of Excellence" in the years 2019-2023 project number 020/RID/2018/19 the amount of financing PLN 12,000,000.

References

1. Akhmedova, S., Stanovov, V., Semenkin, E.: Soft island model for population-based optimization algorithms. In: Tan, Y., Shi, Y., Tang, Q. (eds.) ICSI 2018. LNCS, vol. 10941, pp. 68–77. Springer, Cham (2018). https://doi.org/10.1007/978-3-319-93815-8_8
2. Akhtar, T., Shoemaker, C.A.: Efficient multi-objective optimization through population-based parallel surrogate search. arXiv preprint arXiv:1903.02167 (2019)

3. Atashpaz-Gargari, E., Lucas, C.: Imperialist competitive algorithm: an algorithm for optimization inspired by imperialistic competition. In: 2007 IEEE Congress on Evolutionary Computation, pp. 4661–4667 (2007)
4. Bilski, J., Smolag, J., Kowalczyk, B., Grzanek, K., Izonin, I.: Fast computational approach to the Levenberg-Marquardt algorithm for training feedforward neural networks. J. Artif. Intell. Soft Comput. Res. **13**(2), 45–61 (2023)
5. Birbil, Şİ, Fang, S.C., Sheu, R.L.: On the convergence of a population-based global optimization algorithm. J. Global Optim. **30**, 301–318 (2004)
6. Chen, M.R., Zeng, G.Q., Lu, K.D.: Constrained multi-objective population extremal optimization based economic-emission dispatch incorporating renewable energy resources. Renewable Energy **143**, 277–294 (2019)
7. Cpałka, K., Łapa, K., Rutkowski, L.: A multi-population-based algorithm with different ways of subpopulations cooperation. In: Rutkowski, L., Scherer, R., Korytkowski, M., Pedrycz, W., Tadeusiewicz, R., Zurada, J.M. (eds.) ICAISC 2022. LNCS, vol. 13588, pp. 205–218. Springer, Cham (2023). https://doi.org/10.1007/978-3-031-23492-7_18
8. Cui, H., Li, X., Gao, L.: An improved multi-population genetic algorithm with a greedy job insertion inter-factory neighborhood structure for distributed heterogeneous hybrid flow shop scheduling problem. Expert Syst. Appl. **222**, 119805 (2023)
9. Dang, D.C., Eremeev, A., Lehre, P.K.: Escaping local optima with non-elitist evolutionary algorithms. In: Proceedings of the AAAI Conference on Artificial Intelligence, vol. 35, no. 14, pp. 12275–12283 (2021)
10. Dziwiński, P., Przybył, A., Trippner, P., Paszkowski, J., Hayashi, Y.: hardware implementation of a Takagi-Sugeno neuro-fuzzy system optimized by a population algorithm. J. Artif. Intell. Soft Comput. Res. **11**(3), 243–266 (2021)
11. Feoktistov, V.: Differential Evolution, pp. 1–24. Springer, New York (2006). https://doi.org/10.1007/978-0-387-36896-2
12. Fernandes, C.M., Rosa, A.C., Laredo, J.L., Merelo, J.J., Cotta, C.: Dynamic models of partially connected topologies for population-based metaheuristics. In: 2018 IEEE Congress on Evolutionary Computation (CEC), pp. 1–8. IEEE (2018)
13. Gabryel, M., Lada, D., Filutowicz, Z., Patora-Wysocka, Z., Kisiel-Dorohinicki, M., Chen, G.: Detecting anomalies in advertising web traffic with the use of the variational autoencoder. J. Artif. Intell. Soft Comput. Res. **12**(4), 255–256 (2022)
14. Gupta, A., Lanctot, M., Lazaridou, A.: Dynamic population-based meta-learning for multi-agent communication with natural language. Adv. Neural. Inf. Process. Syst. **34**, 16899–16912 (2021)
15. Harrison, K.R., Engelbrecht, A.P., Ombuki-Berman, B.M.: Self-adaptive particle swarm optimization: a review and analysis of convergence. Swarm Intell. **12**, 187–226 (2018)
16. Holly, S., Nieße, A.: Dynamic communication topologies for distributed heuristics in energy system optimization algorithms, pp. 191–200 (2021)
17. Karaboga, D., Aslan, S.: A new emigrant creation strategy for parallel artificial bee colony algorithm. In: 9th International Conference on Electrical and Electronics Engineering (ELECO), pp. 689–694 (2015). https://doi.org/10.1109/eleco.2015.7394477
18. Kazikova, A., Pluhacek, M., Senkerik, R., Viktorin, A.: Proposal of a new swarm optimization method inspired in bison behavior. In: Matoušek, R. (ed.) MENDEL 2017. AISC, vol. 837, pp. 146–156. Springer, Cham (2019). https://doi.org/10.1007/978-3-319-97888-8_13

19. Kavoosi, M., Dulebenets, M. A., Mikijeljević, M.: A universal island-based meta-heuristic for effective berth scheduling. In: XXIII International Conference on Material Handling, Constructions and Logistics (MHCL 2019) (2019)

20. Kumar, D., Sharma, D.: Feature map augmentation to improve scale invariance in convolutional neural networks. J. Artif. Intell. Soft Comput. Res. **13**(1), 51–74 (2023)

21. Kupfer, E., Le, H.T., Zitt, J., Lin, Y.C., Middendorf, M.: A hierarchical simple probabilistic population-based algorithm applied to the dynamic TSP. In: 2021 IEEE Symposium Series on Computational Intelligence (SSCI), pp. 1–8. IEEE (2021)

22. Laktionov, I., Vovna, O., Kabanets, M.: Information technology for comprehensive monitoring and control of the microclimate in industrial greenhouses based on fuzzy logic. J. Artif. Intell. Soft Comput. Res. **13**(1), 19–35 (2023)

23. Lambora, A., Gupta, K., Chopra, K.: Genetic algorithm-a literature review. In: 2019 International Conference on Machine Learning, Big Data, Cloud and Parallel Computing (COMITCon), pp. 380–384. IEEE (2019)

24. Li, C., Nguyen, T.T., Yang, M., Yang, S., Zeng, S.: Multi-population methods in unconstrained continuous dynamic environments: the challenges. Inf. Sci. **296**, 95–118 (2015)

25. Liang, J.J., Qu, B.Y., Suganthan, P.N., Hernández-Díaz, A.G.: Problem definitions and evaluation criteria for the CEC 2013 special session on real-parameter optimization. Computational Intelligence Laboratory, Zhengzhou University, Zhengzhou, China and Nanyang Technological University, Singapore, Technical report 201212(34), pp. 281–295 (2013)

26. Lynn, N., Ali, M.Z., Suganthan, P.N.: Population topologies for particle swarm optimization and differential evolution. Swarm Evol. Comput. **39**, 24–35 (2018)

27. Łapa, K., Cpałka, K., Kisiel-Dorohinicki, M., Paszkowski, J., Debski, M., Le, V.H.: Multi-population-based algorithm with an exchange of training plans based on population evaluation. J. Artif. Intell. Soft Comput. Res. **12**(4), 239–253 (2022)

28. Łapa, K., Cpałka, K., Laskowski, Ł, Cader, A., Zeng, Z.: Evolutionary algorithm with a configurable search mechanism. J. Artif. Intell. Soft Comput. Res. **10**(3), 151–171 (2020)

29. Ma, X., et al.: A survey on cooperative co-evolutionary algorithms. IEEE Trans. Evol. Comput. **23**(3), 421–441 (2018)

30. Ma, H., Shen, S., Yu, M., Yang, Z., Fei, M., Zhou, H.: Multi-population techniques in nature inspired optimization algorithms: a comprehensive survey. Swarm Evol. Comput. **44**, 365–387 (2019)

31. Medina, A., Tosca P.G., Ramírez-Torres, J.: A Comparative Study of Neighborhood Topologies for Particle Swarm Optimizers, pp. 152–159 (2009)

32. Meng, Q., Wu, J., Ellis, J., Kennedy, P.J.: Dynamic island model based on spectral clustering in genetic algorithm. In: 2017 International Joint Conference on Neural Networks (IJCNN), pp. 1724–1731. IEEE (2017)

33. Ming, M., Trivedi, A., Wang, R., Srinivasan, D., Zhang, T.: A dual-population-based evolutionary algorithm for constrained multiobjective optimization. IEEE Trans. Evol. Comput. **25**(4), 739–753 (2021)

34. Mirjalili, S., Mirjalili, S.M., Lewis, A.: Grey wolf optimizer. Adv. Eng. Softw. **69**, 46–61 (2014)

35. Mirjalili, S., Lewis, A.: The whale optimization algorithm. Adv. Eng. Softw. **95**, 51–67 (2016)

36. Mishra, D.K., Shinde, V., Bharadwaj, S.K.: A convergence study of firefly algorithm. Int. J. Res. Sci. Eng. (IJRISE) **2**(03), 17–25 (2022). ISSN 2394-8299

37. Mousavirad, S.J., Schaefer, G., Jalali, S.M.J., Korovin, I.: A benchmark of recent population-based metaheuristic algorithms for multi-layer neural network training. In: Proceedings of the 2020 Genetic and Evolutionary Computation Conference Companion, pp. 1402–1408 (2020)
38. Najmeh, S.J., Salwani, A., Abdul, R.H.: Multi-population cooperative bat algorithm-based optimization of artificial neural network model. Inf. Sci. **294**, 628–644 (2015)
39. Osaba, E., Diaz, F., Onieva, E.: Golden ball: a novel meta-heuristic to solve combinatorial optimization problems based on soccer concepts. Appl. Intell. **41**, 145–166 (2014)
40. Pawłowska, J., Rydzewska, K., Wierzbicki, A.: Using cognitive models to understand and counteract the effect of self-induced bias on recommendation algorithms. J. Artif. Intell. Soft Comput. Res. **13**(2), 73–94 (2023)
41. Price, D., Radaideh, M.I.: Animorphic ensemble optimization: a large-scale island model. Neural Comput. Appl. **35**(4), 3221–3243 (2023)
42. Sahu, A., Panigrahi, S.K., Pattnaik, S.: Fast convergence particle swarm optimization for functions optimization. Procedia Technol. **4**, 319–324 (2012)
43. Sanu, M., Jeyakumar, G.: Empirical performance analysis of distributed differential evolution for varying migration topologies. Int. J. Appl. Eng. Res. **10**, 11919–11932 (2015)
44. Skakovski, A., Jędrzejowicz, P.: A multisize no migration island-based differential evolution algorithm with removal of ineffective islands. IEEE Access **10**, 34539–34549 (2022)
45. Słowik, A., Cpałka, K.: Guest editorial: hybrid approaches to nature-inspired population-based intelligent optimization for industrial applications. IEEE Trans. Industr. Inf. **18**(1), 542–545 (2021)
46. Słowik, A., Cpałka, K., Łapa, K.: Multipopulation nature-inspired algorithm (MNIA) for the designing of interpretable fuzzy systems. IEEE Trans. Fuzzy Syst. **28**(6), 1125–1139 (2019)
47. Szczypta, J., Przybył, A., Cpałka, K.: Some aspects of evolutionary designing optimal controllers. In: Rutkowski, L., Korytkowski, M., Scherer, R., Tadeusiewicz, R., Zadeh, L.A., Zurada, J.M. (eds.) ICAISC 2013. LNCS (LNAI), vol. 7895, pp. 91–100. Springer, Heidelberg (2013). https://doi.org/10.1007/978-3-642-38610-7_9
48. Thiruvady, D., Nguyen, S., Shiri, F., Zaidi, N., Li, X.: Surrogate-assisted population based ACO for resource constrained job scheduling with uncertainty. Swarm Evol. Comput. **69**, 101029 (2022)
49. Turky, A.M., Abdullah, S.: A multi-population harmony search algorithm with external archive for dynamic optimization problems. Inf. Sci. **272**, 84–95 (2014)
50. Wang, H., Zuo, L.L., Liu, J., Yi, W.J., Niu, B.: Ensemble particle swarm optimization and differential evolution with alternative mutation method. Nat. Comput. **19**, 699–712 (2020)
51. Wright, L.G., et al.: Deep physical neural networks trained with backpropagation. Nature **601**(7894), 549–555 (2022)
52. Wu, G., Mallipeddi, R., Suganthan, P.N.: Ensemble strategies for population-based optimization algorithms-a survey. Swarm Evol. Comput. **44**, 695–711 (2019)
53. Vafashoar, R., Meybodi, M.R.: A multi-population differential evolution algorithm based on cellular learning automata and evolutionary context information for optimization in dynamic environments. Appl. Soft Comput. **88**, 106009 (2020)
54. Vlachas, P.R., et al.: Backpropagation algorithms and reservoir computing in recurrent neural networks for the forecasting of complex spatiotemporal dynamics. Neural Netw. **126**, 191–217 (2020)

55. Xiao, L., Zuo, X.: Multi-DEPSO: a DE and PSO based hybrid algorithm in dynamic environments. In: 2012 IEEE Congress on Evolutionary Computation, pp. 1–7. IEEE (2012)

56. Xu, Y., et al.: A multi-population multi-objective evolutionary algorithm based on the contribution of decision variables to objectives for large-scale multi/many-objective optimization. IEEE Trans. Cybern. (2022)

57. Yang, X.S., Deb, S.: Cuckoo search via Lévy flights. In: 2009 World Congress on Nature & Biologically Inspired Computing (NaBIC), pp. 210–214. IEEE (2009)

58. Zalasiński, M., Cpałka, K., Hayashi, Y.: New fast algorithm for the dynamic signature verification using global features values. In: Rutkowski, L., Korytkowski, M., Scherer, R., Tadeusiewicz, R., Zadeh, L.A., Zurada, J.M. (eds.) ICAISC 2015. LNCS (LNAI), vol. 9120, pp. 175–188. Springer, Cham (2015). https://doi.org/10.1007/978-3-319-19369-4_17

59. Zalasiński, M., Cpałka, K., Przybyszewski, K., Yen, G.G.: On-line signature partitioning using a population based algorithm. J. Artif. Intell. Soft Comput. Res. **10**(1), 5–13 (2020)

60. Zalasinski, M., Cpalka, K., Laskowski, L., Wunsch, D.C., Przybyszewski, K.: An algorithm for the evolutionary-fuzzy generation of on-line signature hybrid descriptors (2020)

61. Zalasiński, M., et al.: Evolutionary algorithm for selecting dynamic signatures partitioning approach. J. Artif. Intell. Soft Comput. Res. **12**(4), 267–279 (2022)

62. Zhou, Y., Li, S., Pedrycz, W., Feng, G.: ACDB-EA: adaptive convergence-diversity balanced evolutionary algorithm for many-objective optimization. Swarm Evol. Comput. **75**, 101145 (2022)

Machine Learning Assisted Interactive Multi-objectives Optimization Framework: A Proposed Formulation and Method for Overtime Planning in Software Development Projects

Hammed A. Mojeed$^{(\boxtimes)}$ ⓘ and Rafal Szlapczynski ⓘ

Department of Applied Computer Science, Institute of Ocean Engineering and Ship Technology, Gdansk University of Technology, Gdansk, Poland
{Hammed.mojeed,rafal.szlapczynski}@pg.edu.pl

Abstract. Software development project requires proper planning to mitigate risk and uncertainty. Overtime planning within software project management has been receiving attention recently from search-based software engineering researchers. Multi-objective evolutionary algorithms are used to build automated tools that could effectively help Project Managers (PM) plan overtime on project schedules. Existing models however lack applicability by the PMs due to their disregard for expert knowledge in planning overtime. This study proposes a new interactive problem formulation for software overtime planning and presents a framework for building a machine learning-based interactive multi-objective optimization algorithm for overtime planning in software development projects. The framework is designed to train a priori a machine learning model to mimic the PM's subjective judgment of overtime plans within the project schedule. The machine learning model is integrated with a memetic multi-objective optimization algorithm via an interactive module. Also, the memetic algorithm incorporates a preference-based w-dominance method for selecting non-dominated solutions. The proposed framework will be developed to assist software project managers to better plan overtime in order to prevent the expected risk of software development overrun.

Keywords: Interactive Multi-Objective Optimization · Machine Learning · Software project management · Overtime Planning

1 Introduction

Software engineering applies systematic approaches to the development of software. The goal is to produce software that is built fast, produced cheaper, qualitatively reliable, absolutely testable, largely scalable, and simply maintainable [1]. Therefore, Software development projects require proper management and planning to guarantee quick completion, minimum development cost, and quality product. Software project planning is a kind of optimization process that seeks

© The Author(s), under exclusive license to Springer Nature Switzerland AG 2023
L. Rutkowski et al. (Eds.): ICAISC 2023, LNAI 14125, pp. 415–426, 2023.
https://doi.org/10.1007/978-3-031-42505-9_35

to find an optimal schedule for software development so that the final cost and duration are minimized satisfying the precedence and resource constraints. The high complexity of software projects underscores the need for computer-aided tools to properly plan the project development as studies have revealed that 60–80% of software development projects are delivered late [2,3]. As an optimization problem, software project planning has attracted the attention of the Search-Based Software Engineering (SBSE) community for the past decades with the application of search-based optimization algorithms to develop automated tools for software project managers [4–8].

Nonetheless, when these tools are inadequate or the project encounters unexpected 'mission creep' due to time pressure and/or late change in requirements, the only remaining option for Project Managers (PM) is to rely on the allocation of overtime [1]. However, unplanned overtime has constantly been reported to cause increased stress on developers and low-quality software products [2,9–14]. Therefore, new approaches in software project planning consider planning overtime allocation along with the project schedule to cater for any uncertainty or failure risks that may occur as the development progresses. Although managing overtime depends on the project management/planning approach employed in the development of software, agile developmental approaches have now been widely used as a de-facto approach in software development [15–17], scaling Agile methods for large-scale software development teams is still an issue due to some de-motivators identified by studies documented in [18,19]. This has affected the adoption of agile approaches in planning large-scale software development projects in recent times. Consequent to the above findings, this work focuses on planning overtime within the classical developmental approach.

State-of-the-art approaches in software project planning integrate overtime allocation with the project schedule by balancing between optimal overtime, project cost, project duration and risks of overrun using multi-objective search-based optimization approaches such as NSGA II [9,20], Adaptive NSGA II [21], memetic MOSFLA [22]. These algorithms suggest appropriate solutions for software engineers to guide their decision in planning overtime appropriately without considering subjective feedback from the PM except the work of [21] that constructs solutions from the initial plans of the PM. Studies have revealed that relying only on explicit solutions of automated tools for software engineering problems has not been realistic [1,21,23]. PMs usually prefer their own judgments for the applicable solutions due to the fact that software project management requires implicit and subjective human-centric decisions which an automated tool cannot sufficiently handle. There are shreds of evidence on the development of interactive techniques that integrates the subjective evaluation of the PM within the evolution steps of optimization algorithms in some other software engineering processes such as requirement engineering, software design, testing, and maintenance [23–28].

Previous studies on interactive approaches in software engineering modeled interactions between the search algorithms and software engineers as direct or semi-indirect interactions. These kinds of interactions between the algorithms and PMs could lead to serious and overwhelming fatigue as it requires a high amount of physical involvement to guide the search towards an optimal solution. The fatigue could in turn leads to inconsistent judgment by the PM. Thus, there is a need for an interactive framework capable of mimicking the PM's subjective judgments to guarantee indirect interaction without any physical involvement of the PM in the SBSE optimization process. Machine learning has been identified as a suitable method to synergically supercharge SBSE in its various applications [29–31]. Moreover, to the best of our knowledge, no work has been carried out on developing interactive search-based optimization methods in software project planning, especially for overtime planning. This study, therefore, proposes an interactive overtime planning framework based on the integration of a memetic search-based optimization algorithm and machine learning predictive model to produce optimal solutions that simultaneously satisfy the objective constraints and the PM interests.

2   Literature Review

Considering SBSE-based approaches in planning overtime alongside the project schedule, Ferrucci et al. [9] introduced the multi-objective SBSE approach to software overtime planning. They investigated the effects of choices of overtime allocations on the project schedule to minimize the risk of overrun, the total amount of overtime, and project duration with the application of NSGA-IIv specifically designed for overtime planning. An empirical study on six real-life software projects showed that the approach significantly outperformed standard overtime planning strategies in 100% of the experiments. Sarro et al. [21] introduced an adaptive method for operator selection in NSGA-II to extend the work of Ferrucci et al. [9]. The proposed adaptive NSGA-II outperformed Standard NSGA-II with a 93% win.

Barros and Araujo [20] advanced the formulation by considering the reported effect of overtime work on the quality of software. The authors integrated simulation within the optimization process of NSGA-II to study the overtime dynamics on increased number of defects as it affects the project's duration and cost. The problem was formulated to minimize the overall project make-span, cost, and project duration. Empirical results with their formulation showed the superiority of NSGA-II in planning overtime to existing overtime strategies in the industry. Using the same formulation and software project dataset as in [20], Mojeed et al. [22] applied and investigated the performance of a memetic algorithm: Multi-Objective Shuffled Frog-Leaping Algorithm (MOSFLA) in software overtime planning. Results from experiments revealed that it outperformed the widely applied NSGA-II. Existing studies in overtime management lack interactive feature and this undermine their applicability in the software industry.

Various interactive search-based optimization algorithms have been proposed and applied in different subfields of software engineering. Considering requirements engineering, Saraiva [23] proposed an architecture for incorporating human experience and preferences in the search process of the Interactive

Genetic Algorithm (IGA). The architecture employs a learning model to replace PM's interactions with the search process at a point when it becomes overwhelming. Dantas et al. [28] proposed an interactive approach to software release planning using a Preferences Base sup-plied by the PM during interaction with the search process of an IGA. The approach integrates the PM preferences as a penalty for a candidate solution based on the importance level of each preference that was not satisfied.

With respect to software design optimization, Simons et al. [24] focused on interactive Ant Colony Optimization (iACO) for software design lifecycle in which the search process is guided by objective and subjective factors. The user interacts with the search process of the algorithm by giving a numeric evaluation (from 1 to 100) of a feasible candidate solution represented as a UML diagram. Bavota et al. [27] proposed the inclusion of the developer in tasks of software re-modularization using IGA. The proposed algorithm uses a fitness composed of modularization quality achieved by the solution and a human-evaluated factor that determines if two components must be in the same module or not, as a constraint to penalize the solution. Results indicated the effectiveness of the approach with respect to cohesion.

With respect to software testing, Marculecu et al. [32] proposed a Differential Evolution algorithm for the development of a system for testing embedded software by applying a technique that largely automates the generation of test data while still enabling domain specialists to contribute with their knowledge and experience. To guide the search, the domain specialist decides the relative importance of the quality objectives. Regarding software maintenance, Ghannem, and Kessentini [33] proposed an IGA approach to finding appropriate refactoring suggestions using a set of examples. The fitness function combines the objective value of refactoring solutions proposed during the execution of the IGA with the developer's ratings. Results showed that this approach is stable regarding its accuracy. Analysis of the limitation of the existing studies in comparison with the proposed study is presented in Table 1.

Table 1. Gab Analysis of the proposed and existing studies.

Studies	Overtime planning	Multi-objective	Interactive approach	Interaction	Machine Learning
[9]	✓	✓		None	
[24]		✓	✓	Direct	
[28]			✓	Direct	
[20]	✓	✓		None	
[32]		✓	✓	Direct	
[21]	✓	✓	✓	Partial	
[23]			✓	Semi-indirect	✓
[22]	✓	✓		None	
Proposed	✓	✓	✓	Indirect	✓

3   Methodology

3.1   Interactive Overtime Planning Problem Formulation

A software project schedule is usually represented with a Direct Acyclic Graph (DAG) composed of a set of nodes $WP = \{wp_1, wp_2, ...wp_n\}$ representing a set of work packages, and set of edges $DP = (wp_i, wp_j) : i, j \leq n$ representing dependencies. Each wp is described by the amount of effort (represented as function points) required to finish it, its estimated duration, and the cost of completing it (for example in dollars). Building a good software project schedule has been studied extensively by researchers. The focus of this study is not on building such a schedule, but rather, on analyzing the effect of overtime assignments on an already-made schedule. For the purpose of this study, Critical Path Method (CPM), which has been used widely for decades, is adopted to plan the schedule. An overtime plan on the schedule can be represented by a linear and finite set of N (N is the number of work packages in the project) integer values in the interval $[0, 8]$ denoting the number of daily overtime spent on each wp. Each value corresponds to a multiple of 30 min. An example of the overtime plan on a project consisting of ten packages is given in the following:

0	4	3	8	0	2	5	4	6	3

From the example, the second work package is assigned 4×30 min which equals 2 h daily. The problem is to produce an optimal overtime plan for the schedule based on certain objectives. The interactive overtime planning problem considered in this study is formulated as a multi-objective optimization problem consisting of four separate objectives. Due to the interactive nature of the formulation, the first three objectives (total overtime, cost, and quality of code) are measured based on explicit characteristics of the project schedules, and the remaining one; PM's satisfaction will be predicted by a pre-trained machine learning model. This is the first time quality of code will be considered as objective in the formulation and machine learning included in the formulation.

Objectives: The four objectives considered in our formulation are as follows:
1. Total overtime: This represents the sum of overtime hours spent on all work packages to complete the project as produced by the optimization algorithm. A good solution should minimize the total amount of overtime hours spent on the project. Equation 1 denotes its computation.

Minimize:

$$OH = \sum_{i=1}^{n} O_{wp_i} \cdot D_{duration(wp_i)} \tag{1}$$

Where O_{wp_i} denotes the amount of daily overtime spent on ith work package and $D_{duration(wp_i)}$ is its duration in days.

2. Cost: The project cost estimates the total amount of money spent to complete the project. The cost of each work package is determined by the product of the cost of regular developer working hours and the duration of the work package. The effect of overtime allocation on the project cost is modeled based on the Brazilian Cost law which suggests that if a regular working hour costs X, the first two overtime hours cost 120% of X, and the next two hours cost 150% of X. The cost is also expected to be minimized by a candidate solution. It is calculated as given in Eq. 2.

Minimize:

$$Cost = \sum_{i=1}^{n} \begin{cases} X_{wp_i} + \frac{5X_{wp_i}}{6}, & if \ O_{wp_i} \leq 4, \\ X_{wp_i} + \frac{3X_{wp_i}}{2}, & if \ O_{wp_i} > 4, \end{cases} \tag{2}$$

Where X_{wp_i} denotes the regular cost of the work packages.

3. Quality of code: it has been revealed that a developer working overtime may produce software below quality standards. The quality of the software code is computed as the rate of error generated due to overtime as modeled in [20]. The model estimates an introduction of 20% more errors by a developer working 2 h overtime daily and 50% more errors by developers working 4 h/day. The lesser the error rate, the better the quality of code. The error rate should therefore be minimal in the expected optimal solution.

Minimize:

$$E_{overtime} = \sum_{i=1}^{n} \begin{cases} \frac{E_{wp_i}}{5}, & if \ O_{wp_i} \leq 4, \\ \frac{E_{wp_i}}{2}, & if \ O_{wp_i} > 4, \end{cases} \tag{3}$$

4. Maximized PM's satisfaction: the PM's subjective evaluation of a solution is modeled as a separate objective that needs to be maximized. PM satisfaction on a scale of (0–100) is estimated and predicted by a trained machine learning model based on annotated solutions by the PM.

Constraint: The above-listed objectives are subject to the following constraint:

$$0 \leq O_{wp_i} \leq maxovertime$$

where $maxovertime$ is the maximum daily overtime allowed.

3.2   Handling Multiple Objectives

To handle multiple objectives simultaneously Pareto optimality has been widely used based on dominance relation of the objective values. Due to the interactive nature of the proposed multi-objective optimization model and our goal of producing solutions that are usable by the PMs, a preference-oriented dominance relation based on tradeoffs (w-dominance) as proposed by Szlapczynski and Szlapczynska [34] is adopted. The method allows the Decision Maker (DM) to specify weights of objectives as intervals (i.e. in the range [0, 1]) instead of a singular value as often represented in the weighted average method. The mean value of each interval represents DM's estimate of the objective's importance and the width of intervals denotes his uncertainty of the estimate. Also, a wide interval denotes a deeper search by the optimization algorithm into non-convex parts of the solution space. The w-dominance method is adopted to reduce the computational complexity of the proposed multi-objective optimization method and cater for the PM's preference during optimization. If follows that for minimization problems, a solution x w-dominates another solution y given the weight intervals $(w_i^{\min}, w_i^{\max})$ for each objective i, if and only if the following condition is satisfied:

$$\sum_{i=1}^{n} \min \left(w_i^{\min} \cdot d_i \left(x, y \right), \ w_i^{\max} \cdot d_i \left(x, y \right) \right) > 0 \qquad (4)$$

Where:

$$d_i \left(x, y \right) = f_i \left(y \right) - f_i \left(x \right) \qquad (5)$$

$f_i(x)$ denotes the normalized i^{th} objective function and n is the number of objectives. Extensive details on the w-dominance method and its derivation can be found in [34,35].

3.3   Machine Learning-Based Memetic Optimization Framework

The machine learning-based interactive memetic framework proposed in this study as presented in Fig. 1 is composed of three major steps: problem modeling/formulation as discussed in the previous section, framework development, and Evaluation.

The framework is built on three separate but integrated components- the machine learning model, the memetic multi-objective search-based optimization algorithm, and the interaction module.

Machine Learning (ML) Model: In this study, the ML model is built a priori separately before the optimization process begins. To build an effective and accurate predictive model, training data is required which is very scarce in software project management. A suitable machine learning model that can work on a small dataset would be applied. First, a usable number of random solutions (i.e. overtime plans) based on the problem modeling and from empirical data will be generated. Then experts in software project management will be approached to subjectively evaluate the solution based on their understanding of the problem at hand by giving a numeric evaluation score (as a measure of the applicability of the overtime plan) between 1 and 100 as adapted from [24] representing their satisfaction. The annotated data is then used to build a predictive model to evaluate the actual solutions from the optimization algorithm.

Due to the enormous efforts needed from the project management expert, which might lead to the small annotated dataset and expected high dimensionality, an optimized Tree-based learning model is proposed based on their recorded

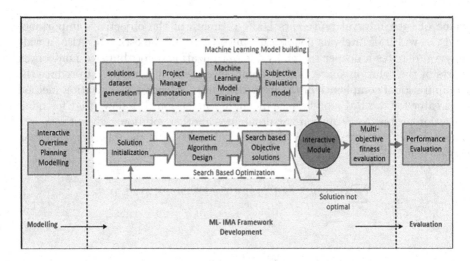

Fig. 1. ML-IMA Framework for Interactive Overtime Planning.

performance in preventing bias and over-fitting. Also, the numeric nature of the attributes and the continuous nature of the predicted value with small number of instances directs the decision that a regression-based approach is more suitable for the ML model. Consequently, this study will employ an optimized Random Forest Regression model - a meta-estimator that fits a number of regression-based decision trees such as CART on various sub-samples of the dataset and uses averaging to improve the predictive accuracy and control over-fitting - in estimating PM satisfaction from overtime allocations.

Memetic Multi-objective Optimization Algorithm: Due to the multi-objective nature of the overtime planning problem and its complexity, a memetic approach that combines a population-based global technique and a local search made by each individual in the population to guide the search to a global optimum is proposed. Memetic algorithms are known for effective exploration of the solution space and robust exploitation of promising regions within the solution space. The MOSFLA specifically designed for overtime planning by [22] is adopted in this study. The algorithm is integrated with a machine learning model to capture the subjective PM evaluation of solutions and an interactive multi-objective fitness function module evaluates the fitness of each solution based on the w-dominance relation. Figure 2 depicts the flowchart for the proposed machine learning-based interactive MOSFLA.

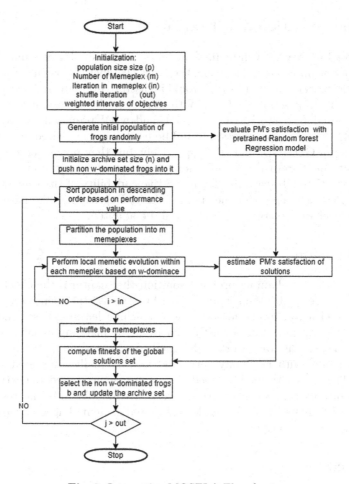

Fig. 2. Interactive MOSFLA Flowchart.

Interaction Module: The interaction module provides a medium for a hand-shake between the machine learning model and the memetic algorithm. This study extends the interaction model employed in [23] for the Next Release Problem (NRP) by removing the direct involvement of the PM during the optimization process and replacing him completely with a trained predictive machine learning model. Specifically, the interaction module takes the individual solution from the memetic algorithm and passes it to the machine learning model for implicit evaluation. The subjective evaluation score is incorporated into the individual solution for fitness evaluation. Consequently, the interaction module communicates with the IMA, the predictive model, and the fitness function. The fitness function employs preference-based dominance as the Pareto optimality relation to measure the superiority of a candidate interactive solution.

4   Implementation and Evaluation

The proposed framework will be implemented using Java. The machine learning model would be implemented by using the Weka classifier library in Java. Dataset on software project collected by [20] would be used to evaluate and test the effectiveness of the proposed framework. With respect to the performance evaluation of the proposed framework, wGD, wIGD, and wHV proposed for preference-based multi-objective optimization would be used. They are based on commonly used metrics of GD, IGD, and HV respectively, but they pre-screen the original solution set and Pareto Front: only non-w-dominated solutions are considered in computing them. To capture the interactive capability of the framework, the standard interactive algorithm metrics: Similarity Degree (SD), Similarity Factor (SF), and Price of Preference (PP) [23] will be adapted.

5   Conclusion

Producing overtime planning problem solution that captures the effect of overtime on software quality and is applicable by PMs is still open research. This work proposed a framework for building a machine learning-based interactive multi-objective optimization algorithm for overtime planning in software development projects. The framework is designed to train a priori a Random Forest regression model with randomly generated and manually annotated solutions by PMs. The model trained is fused with a preference-based memetic multi-objective optimization algorithm via an interactive module. In the nearest future, the proposed framework will be implemented and evaluated against the existing state-of-the-art approaches.

References

1. Ferrucci, F., Harman, M., Sarro, F.: Search-based software project management. In: Ruhe, G., Wohlin, C. (eds.) Software Project Management in a Changing World, pp. 373–399. Springer, Heidelberg (2014). https://doi.org/10.1007/978-3-642-55035-5_15
2. Kuutila, M., Mäntylä, M., Farooq, U., Claes, M.: Time pressure in software engineering: a systematic review (2020). https://doi.org/10.1016/j.infsof.2020.106257
3. Moløkken, K., Jørgensen, M.: A review of surveys on software effort estimation. In: International Symposium on Empirical Software Engineering, ISESE 2003, pp. 223–230. IEEE (2003)
4. Alba, E., Francisco Chicano, J.: Software project management with GAs. Inf. Sci. (NY) **177**, 2380–2401 (2007). https://doi.org/10.1016/j.ins.2006.12.020
5. Crawford, B., Soto, R., Johnson, F., Monfroy, E., Paredes, F.: A max-min ant system algorithm to solve the software project scheduling problem. Expert Syst. Appl. **41**, 6634–6645 (2014). https://doi.org/10.1016/j.eswa.2014.05.003
6. Luna, F., González-Álvarez, D.L., Chicano, F., Vega-Rodríguez, M.A.: The software project scheduling problem: a scalability analysis of multi-objective metaheuristics. Appl. Soft Comput. J. **15**, 136–148 (2014). https://doi.org/10.1016/j.asoc.2013.10.015

7. Oladele, R.O., Mojeed, H.A.: A shuffled frog-leaping algorithm for optimal software project planning. Afr. J. Comput. ICT. **7**, 147–152 (2014)
8. Rachman, V., Ma'sum, A.M.: Comparative analysis of ant colony extended and mix min ant system in SW project scheduling problem. In: Proceedings - WBIS 2017 2017 International Workshop on Big Data and Information Security, vol. 8, pp. 85–91 (2017)
9. Ferrucci, F., Harman, M., Ren, J., Sarro, F.: Not going to take this anymore: multi-objective overtime planning for software engineering projects. In: Proceedings - International Conference on Software Engineering, pp. 462–471 (2013). https://doi.org/10.1109/ICSE.2013.6606592
10. Akula, B., Cusick, J.: Impact of overtime and stress on software quality. In: WMSCI 2008 - The 12th World Multi-Conference on Systemics, Cybernetics, and Informatics, Jointly with the 14th International Conference on Information Systems Analysis and Synthesis, ISAS 2008 - Proceedings, p. 214 (2008). https://doi.org/10.13140/RG.2.2.12815.59041
11. Kleppa, E., Sanne, B., Tell, G.S.: Working overtime is associated with anxiety and depression: the Hordaland health study. J. Occup. Environ. Med. **50**, 658–666 (2008). https://doi.org/10.1097/JOM.0b013e3181734330
12. Claes, M., Mäntylä, M., Kuutila, M., Adams, B.: Abnormal working hours: effect of rapid releases and implications to work content. In: 2017 IEEE/ACM 14th International Conference on Mining Software Repositories (MSR), pp. 243–247 (2017). https://doi.org/10.1109/MSR.2017.3
13. Kuutila, M., Mäntylä, M.V., Claes, M., Elovainio, M.: Daily questionnaire to assess self-reported well-being during a software development project. In: 2018 IEEE/ACM 3rd International Workshop on Emotion Awareness in Software Engineering (SEmotion), pp. 39–43 (2018)
14. Van Der Hulst, M., Geurts, S.: Associations between overtime and psychological health in high and low reward jobs. Work Stress. **15**, 227–240 (2001). https://doi.org/10.1080/026783701110.1080/02678370110066580
15. Hajjdiab, H., Taleb, A.S.: Adopting agile software development: issues and challenges. Int. J. Manag. Value Supply Chain. **2**, 1–10 (2011). https://doi.org/10.5121/ijmvsc.2011.2301
16. Capodieci, A., Mainetti, L., Manco, L.: A case study to enable and monitor real IT companies migrating from waterfall to agile. In: Murgante, B., et al. (eds.) ICCSA 2014. LNCS, vol. 8583, pp. 119–134. Springer, Cham (2014). https://doi.org/10.1007/978-3-319-09156-3_9
17. Alashqur, A.: Towards a broader adoption of agile software development methods. Int. J. Adv. Comput. Sci. Appl. **7**, 94–98 (2016). https://doi.org/10.14569/ijacsa.2016.071212
18. Faisal Abrar, M., et al.: De-motivators for the adoption of agile methodologies for large-scale software development teams: an SLR from management perspective (2020). https://doi.org/10.1002/smr.2268
19. Ali, S., Hongqi, L., Abrar, M.F.: Systematic literature review of critical barriers to software outsourcing partnership. In: 2018 5th International Multi-Topic ICT Conference (IMTIC), pp. 1–8 (2018). https://doi.org/10.1109/IMTIC.2018.8467254
20. DeO Barros, M., De Araujo, L.A.O.: Learning overtime dynamics through multi-objective optimization. In: GECCO 2016 - Proceedings 2016 Genetic and Evolutionary Computation Conference, pp. 1061–1068 (2016). https://doi.org/10.1145/2908812.2908824

21. Sarro, F., Ferrucci, F., Harman, M., Manna, A., Ren, J.: Adaptive multi-objective evolutionary algorithms for overtime planning in software projects. IEEE Trans. Softw. Eng. **43**, 898–917 (2017). https://doi.org/10.1109/TSE.2017.2650914

22. Mojeed, H.A., Bajeh, A.O., Balogun, A.O., Adeleke, H.O.: Memetic approach for multi-objective overtime planning in software engineering projects. J. Eng. Sci. Technol. **14**, 3213–3233 (2019)

23. Saraiva, R., Araújo, A.A., Dantas, A., Yeltsin, I., Souza, J.: Incorporating decision maker's preferences in a multi-objective approach for the software release planning. J. Braz. Comput. Soc. **23** (2017). https://doi.org/10.1186/s13173-017-0060-0

24. Simons, C.L., Smith, J., White, P.: Interactive ant colony optimization (iACO) for early lifecycle software design. Swarm Intell. **8**, 139–157 (2014). https://doi.org/10.1007/s11721-014-0094-2

25. Tonella, P., Susi, A., Palma, F.: Interactive requirements prioritization using a genetic algorithm. Inf. Softw. Technol., 173–187 (2013). https://doi.org/10.1016/j.infsof.2012.07.003

26. Wang, T., Zhou, M.: A method for product form design of integrating interactive genetic algorithm with the interval hesitation time and user satisfaction. Int. J. Ind. Ergon. **76**, 102901 (2020). https://doi.org/10.1016/j.ergon.2019.102901

27. Bavota, G., Carnevale, F., De Lucia, A., Di Penta, M., Oliveto, R.: Putting the developer in-the-loop: an interactive GA for software re-modularization. In: Fraser, G., Teixeira de Souza, J. (eds.) SSBSE 2012. LNCS, vol. 7515, pp. 75–89. Springer, Heidelberg (2012). https://doi.org/10.1007/978-3-642-33119-0_7

28. Dantas, A., Yeltsin, I., Araújo, A.A., Souza, J.: Interactive software release planning with preferences base. In: Barros, M., Labiche, Y. (eds.) SSBSE 2015. LNCS, vol. 9275, pp. 341–346. Springer, Cham (2015). https://doi.org/10.1007/978-3-319-22183-0_32

29. Nair, V., et al.: Data-driven search-based software engineering. In: Proceedings - International Conference on Software Engineering, pp. 341–352 (2018). https://doi.org/10.1145/3196398.3196442

30. Shafiq, S., Mashkoor, A., Mayr-Dorn, C., Egyed, A.: Machine learning for software engineering: a systematic mapping. arXiv Prepr. arXiv:2005.13299 (2020)

31. Shafiq, S., Mashkoor, A., Mayr-Dorn, C., Egyed, A.: A literature review of using machine learning in software development life cycle stages. IEEE Access **9**, 140896–140920 (2021). https://doi.org/10.1109/ACCESS.2021.3119746

32. Marculescu, B., Poulding, S., Feldt, R., Petersen, K., Torkar, R.: Tester interactivity makes a difference in search-based software testing: a controlled experiment. Inf. Softw. Technol. **78**, 66–82 (2016). https://doi.org/10.1016/j.infsof.2016.05.009

33. Ghannem, A., El Boussaidi, G., Kessentini, M.: Model refactoring using interactive genetic algorithm. In: Ruhe, G., Zhang, Y. (eds.) SSBSE 2013. LNCS, vol. 8084, pp. 96–110. Springer, Heidelberg (2013). https://doi.org/10.1007/978-3-642-39742-4_9

34. Szlapczynski, R., Szlapczynska, J.: W-dominance: tradeoff-inspired dominance relation for preference-based evolutionary multi-objective optimization. Swarm Evol. Comput. **63**, 100866 (2021). https://doi.org/10.1016/j.swevo.2021.100866

35. Szlapczynska, J., Szlapczynski, R.: Preference-based evolutionary multi-objective optimization in ship weather routing. Appl. Soft Comput. J. **84**, 105742 (2019). https://doi.org/10.1016/j.asoc.2019.105742

Improved Barnacles Movement Optimizer (IBMO) Algorithm for Engineering Design Problems

Syed Kumayl Raza Moosavi[1] [ID], Muhammad Hamza Zafar[2] [ID],
Seyedali Mirjalili[3] [ID], and Filippo Sanfilippo[2,4(✉)] [ID]

[1] National University of Sciences and Technology, Islamabad 44000, Pakistan
[2] Department of Engineering Sciences, University of Agder, 4879 Grimstad, Norway
`filippo.sanfilippo@uia.no`
[3] Centre for Artificial Intelligence Research and Optimization, Torrens University
Australia, Fortitude Valley, Brisbane, QLD 4006, Australia
[4] Department of Software Engineering, Kaunas University of Technology,
44029 Kaunas, Lithuania

Abstract. A better understanding of natural behavior modeling in mathematical systems has enabled a new class of stochastic optimization algorithms that can estimate optimal solutions using reasonable computational resources for problems where exact algorithms show poor performance. The position up-dating mechanism in various optimization algorithms utilizes similar chaotic random behavior which impedes the performance of the search for a globally optimum solution in monotonic nonlinear search space. In this work, an approach is proposed that tackles these issues on an already established algorithm; Improved Barnacle Mating Optimization (IBMO) Algorithm, inspired by the movement and mating of Gooseneck Barnacles. The algorithm introduces the mimicry of the movement and mating behavior in nature to model an optimization process. Several benchmark functions are employed to gauge the performance of the proposed optimization technique. Results are compared with several meta-heuristics and conventional optimization algorithms. It is observed that the IBMO algorithm performs generally better and provides a huge potential for solving real-world problems.

Keywords: Metaheuristic Algorithms · Artificial Intelligence · Improved Barnacles Mating Optimization · Engineering Design Problems

1 Introduction

The process of evolution in nature has made many micro and major processes integrate mutually for a common goal. In recent decades, the complexity of real-world problems has resulted in the need for highly intelligent and reliable optimization techniques [4]. During the past century computing resources have

L. Rutkowski et al. (Eds.): ICAISC 2023, LNAI 14125, pp. 427–438, 2023.
https://doi.org/10.1007/978-3-031-42505-9_36

exploded and brought forth a new class of optimization and control known as meta-heuristics into both science and industry. Such optimization techniques belong to the field of Computational Intelligence with three main branches of fuzzy logic, neural network and evolutionary computation. Swarm intelligence techniques belong to the family of evolutionary computation, which is unique in the sense as it mimics the simplest tasks performed by the swarm of a less intelligent species that require collective behavior for survival. The shared distributive tasks and ability to share information among the swarm particle/agents/members enable the solution for complex problems.

These solutions of a swarm-based movement/mating technique supersede conventional algorithms due to it being free of the gradient based technique which inherently gets trapped in local optima [15,19]. The main obstacle comes from the chaotic behavior of individual particles with nonlinear activity models. Despite the connotation of 'chaos' which suggests unpredictable and irregular systems, chaos theory suggests that seemingly random events can lead to a pattern over time [12]. This also holds authentic for modern swarm intelligence-based systems which randomly initiate problem formulation and improvise the random solutions over some time. The main role in swarm intelligence is played by random exploratory and exploitative phases. In the exploration phase, the expectation is to get a high enough variance between agents to cover a massive area of the search space while the exploitation phase focuses on a small subset of the search space that already contains the best solution at any given time. The exploration task facilitates the avoidance of local minima entrapment while the exploitation task explores nearby promising solutions [1]. Most techniques utilize pre-defined criteria for the balancing of exploration and exploitation behavior such as in [8].

The most popular swarm-based algorithm, encouraged by the motion of a swarm of birds, started this field of study is the Particle Swarm Optimization (PSO) algorithm [7]. Other similar swarm-based algorithms proposed in the literature include Grey Wolf Optimization (GWO) Algorithm [10], where the alpha wolf carries the best solution and the consequent wolf classes, Ant Colony Optimization (ACO) algorithm [5], Grasshopper Optimization Algorithm (GOA) [11], Fruit fly Optimization Algorithm (FOA) [16] and many more.

From all the optimization algorithms described in the literature, two things can be surmised; (1) one single algorithm cannot be termed as the best suited for all optimization related problems and (2) determination of the exploration and exploitation phase requirements vary with each proposed optimization problem. The former has been logically proven by the No-Free Lunch (NFL) Theorem [6]. If one algorithm works for one type of dataset problem, it cannot be guaranteed that it will be best suited for another. This continuously encourages the research field to bring forth new techniques. In case of the latter, each algorithm has a specific set of instructions for determining the exploration and exploitation phases. Both vary using tuning parameters within the algorithms. Hence, finding a proper balance of the two, especially keeping in mind the stochastic nature of meta-heuristic algorithms, is a difficult task.

Barnacles movement Optimizer (BMO) [14], a newly proposed bio-inspired algorithm, has the features of fewer parameters and mathematical manipulation to search for promising search space solutions. It can be conferred that with a smaller mathematical model, the computation time is low but the tradeoff be-tween accuracy is too high and warrants improvement in the areas of performance and parameter tuning. In addition, the random behavior impedes the performance for the search of a globally optimum solution in monotonic nonlinear search space. This paper proposes an improved version of the bio-inspired meta-heuristic algorithm in which the mimicry of the movement and mating behavior of gooseneck barnacles is modelled. The effectiveness of the Improved Barnacles Mating Algorithm (IBMO) is evaluated using 23 benchmark test functions. These functions contain unimodal, multi-modal and fixed dimension multi-model functions. Secondly it has been put into comparison with other meta-heuristic algorithms that are; PSO, GWO, BMO, Arithmetic Optimization Algorithm (AOA) [2], Flower Pollination Algorithm (FPA) [17] and Dragonfly Algorithm (DFA) [9].

2   Improved Barnacles Mating Algorithm

This section first presents the inspiration for the algorithm studied from Goose-neck Barnacles' movement and mating technique. Successively, the initialization and selection process for mating of the barnacles is discussed. Next the barna-cles' reproduction probabilistic model and the resulting exploration/exploitation phases are studied. Finally, the improvement from the BMO technique is introduced i.e., the movement of the barnacles, prior to the mating process, is articulated.

2.1   Inspiration

Found in the rocky shores of the Eastern Atlantic, gooseneck barnacles (GB), a species of filter-feeding crustaceans, begin their life cycle as free moving larvae in the ocean [3]. Unlike their counterpart crustaceans such as crabs, lobsters and shrimp that have free ranging lives, these barnacles grow to eventually be attached to a hard surface. Once their growth is completed from free moving nauplius larvae to cyprid larvae to adults, they attach on a rocky surface using their heads with a cement like strong substance. The complete life cycle of GB is shown in Fig. 1.

Once a GB finds its suitable location on the marine shores, other GBs also fol-low the initial GB's location and attach themselves close by for feeding and mating purposes primarily because they do not physically move from their position of attachment. Barnacles are hermaphroditic, meaning they have both male and female reproductive organs. The life cycle of these barnacles is illustrated in Fig. 1. Prior to the mating ritual, the movement and search of these barnacles during the Nauplius to Cyprid Larvae to adulthood stage is used as the inspiration for the improvement of the algorithm explained in the coming sections.

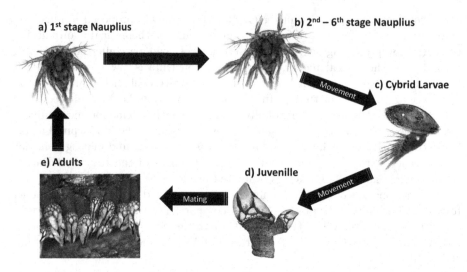

Fig. 1. Life Cycle of Gooseneck barnacles: a) Eggs develop and hatch inside the adults and are released into the water. b) Different stages of the nauplius larvae are developed drifting overall several weeks developing complex structure. c) Cyprid larvae begin searching for a suitable place to attach. d) Attached at the trunk (peduncle) of an adult initially and later moves to the surface for permanent attachment. e) Adults attached on rocks or hard surfaces mating either by the penis elongation or by the sperm cast process

2.2   Initialization

In IBMO, the candidate solutions are termed here as GB. The initial population is initialized as:

$$GB = \begin{pmatrix} g_1^1 \cdots g_1^N \\ \vdots \ddots \vdots \\ g_t^1 \cdots g_t^N \end{pmatrix} \tag{1}$$

where g is the generic candidate and t is the complete population of the GB's size and N here represents the size of the control variables within each GB in the population. The boundary conditions on the movement of the GB population are applied using Eqs. (2);

$$ub = \begin{bmatrix} ub, \ldots, ub_i \end{bmatrix}$$
$$lb = \begin{bmatrix} lb, \ldots, lb_i \end{bmatrix} \tag{2}$$

where lb and ub is the bound for lower and upper respectively.

2.3   Mating Selection Method

The mating of every two barnacles in the selection process is dependent on the length of the penis size (ps) of the male barnacle. The mating ritual is dependent on the following principle:

– Random selection of the barnacles and restriction based upon the length of the penis i.e., penis size. Since barnacles are hermaphrodites, each barnacle can provide and receiving sperm from other barnacles. If the position of the two barnacles in the mating process is larger than the penis size, sperm casting is applied. Sperm cast happens when adjacent male penis is out of range of the GB, so the male-acting barnacle ejects sperm in the ocean towards the direction of the female-acting barnacle for reproduction.

In the above-mentioned principal assumptions, the exploitation phase and exploration phase are prescribed in the IBMO. The choosing strategy male-female barnacles is expressed as:

$$GB_{male} = rand(n)$$
$$GB_{female} = rand(n)$$

$$(3)$$

where n is the total number of barnacles.

2.4   Reproduction

The Hardy-Weinberg principle [13] states that in a random population of alleles i.e., variant form of genes, with no external factors such as selection, crossover or mutation, the offspring generation can be surmised as a simple relationship be-tween allele frequency and genotype frequency. The expected genotype process can be expressed as such that the frequency of Male plus Male self-mating process generate offspring with the probability of p^2. Similarly, the Female plus Female process has a probability of q^2 and Male plus Female generates with the probability of $2pq$. The sum of these probability entries is seen in Eq. (4):

$$p^2 + 2pq + q^2 = 1 \qquad (4)$$

Thus, in supposition, we can deduce that the offspring selection is dependent on these two probabilities.

2.5   Exploration/Exploitation Phase

In order to produce the new variables, Eqs. (5), (6) and (7) are used for the reproduction phase:

$$GB_i^{new} = A \cdot GB_{male}^N + B \cdot GB_{female}^N \qquad (5)$$

where A is the random number between $[0, 1]$ and $B = (1 - A)$. GB_{male}^N and GB_{female}^N are the male and female variables that are selected from Eq. (3). A and B dictate the weightage of the Male and Female's positional characteristics which are going to be passed down onto the new offspring. ps is responsible for the determination of the exploration, exploitation phases. If the barnacle's selection is within the range of penile length of the chosen male, the former exploitation phase occurs.

During the first half of the iteration process, the exploration phase needs to be widened to find better optimum solutions in the search space. Therefore, a parameter k is multiplied into the values of A and B as shown by the Eq. (6). Using this parameter enhances the exploration phase from the traditional Barnacles Mating Optimizer Algorithm.

$$A = k \cdot A$$
$$B = k \cdot B \tag{6}$$

In IBMO, the process of sperm casting is considered the exploration phase and it happens when the selection of barnacles that are to be mated in the current iteration becomes greater than the penis size ps. The process can be expressed as:

$$GB_i^{new} = rand() \cdot GB_{barnacle\_male}^{N} \tag{7}$$

2.6   Movement

GB larvae move across the ocean and attach on a rocky surface once fully grown. For the purposes of mating, the GB attaches itself onto a surface with either a GB already present or follows another GB that is going to attach itself onto the rocky surface. This movement of following and attaching of the GB is represented as following the entire population of GB's best solution i.e., the global minima GB for each iteration of the exploitation and exploration phase. This consideration of the global minima is added in Eq. (5) and subtracted in Eq. (7) as shown below:

$$GB_i^{new} = A \cdot GB_{male}^{N} + B \cdot GB_{female}^{N} + r \cdot GB_{best}$$
$$GB_i^{new} = rand() \cdot GB_{barnacle\_male}^{N} - r \cdot GB_{best} \tag{8}$$

where r is a random number within the range $[0, 1]$ and GB_{best} is the position of the gooseneck barnacle with the global best solution from all previous iterations. The pseudo code for the IBMO technique is shown in Algorithm 1. The detailed process flow diagram of IBMO is illustrated in Fig. 2.

The main contribution of this work is the inclusion of the parameter k. The inclusion of the k parameter and the movement algorithm enhancement from the traditional barnacles mating optimizer helps expand the search range of the algorithm and helps traverse towards the global minima solution much quickly. This makes it easier also to move away from the local minima cost solutions and increases the diversity of the search space solution for the barnacle population.

3   Experimental Results

In this section, numerous simulations are conducted to illustrate the efficacy of the IBMO algorithm. First and foremost, 23 point of reference test functions are utilized to observe the features of the IBMO. The benchmark test functions are categorized into; unimodal, multimodal, and composite functions. As the name suggests the unimodal functions have single global minima point. Therefore, the basic criteria of finding the minima solution with IBMO is tested. Next, the multimodal and composite functions are tested which have multiple local minima solutions so while the unimodal functions test the exploitation phase of the algorithm, these two categories of functions test the exploration phase and the avoidance of getting trapped in local minima solutions.

Algorithm 1: Pseudo Code of Proposed Algorithm

Initialize population $GB_i, i = 1, 2, \ldots, N$
Evaluate the fitness of each barnacle
Sort the solutions and find the best solution
while $iter < iter\_max$ **do**
    set the value of ps
    select male and female GB using eq. (3)
    if *Distance of male and female* $\leq ps$ **then**
        for *Each variable* **do**
            Generate offspring using eq. (8)-A

    Else if *Distance of male and female* $> ps$ **then**
        for *Each variable* **do**
            Generate offspring using eq. (8)-B

    Apply boundary conditions on updated solution Calculate Fitness and sort
    population to update the best solution iter = iter + 1
return *Best Solution*;

For a fair quantitative comparison of the test functions, the base parameters of the multi-agent algorithm needed to be kept the same. While the upper and lower boundaries for each test function is different, the number of barnacles chosen for the test is 30 and a maximum of 50 iterations were employed for the barnacles to search the global minima solution. Each test for performed a total of 30 times to generate statistical results. Different performance indicators were used to test out the features of the algorithm which is the average of the 30 generated tests and the standard deviation of the best solutions.

For comparison, six recent and traditional algorithms were used under the same light of parameters namely, BMO, AOA, GWO, PSO, FPA, DFA. These algorithms were chosen to distinguish the different capabilities IBMO has over the characteristics of such nature of algorithms. The tuning parameters are chosen for each algorithm, as suggested by the respective original papers. A computational complexity analysis is also presented using the CEC-2020 test functions. The first set of simulation results is performed on all 23 test functions with IBMO with tuning parameters at $ps = 0.4$ and $k = 2.0$, 30 barnacles, and 50 iterations run 30 times. All values recorded as 0 represent values below 1.0e-300. The convergence curve comparison for the algorithms can be seen in Fig. 3.

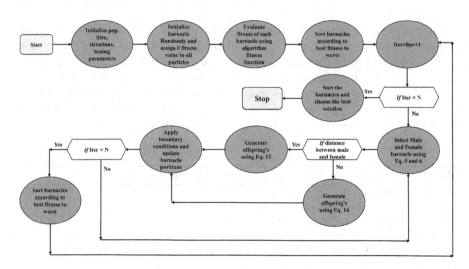

Fig. 2. Flow chart of Proposed Algorithm

Table 1. Comparison of meta heuristic algorithms with IBMO for unimodal and multimodal functions.

Func	Dim	IBMO	BMO	AOA	PSO	GWO	FPA	DFA
F1	2	**0**	3.34E-184	**0**	1.59E-04	**0**	1.94E-39	1.17E-123
	10	**0**	3.12E-131	**0**	4.11E-01	1.94E-64	3.82E-10	4.21E-03
	30	**5.34E-272**	1.38E-123	2.39E-28	4.64E+01	4.47E-06	2.98E+00	1.22E+03
F2	2	**0**	3.41E-90	**0**	8.14E-04	**0**	9.42E-21	2.35E-62
	10	**1.25E-160**	1.36E-69	0	1.88E-01	6.64E-18	1.72E-05	2.87E-01
	30	**1.23E-143**	8.33E-66	0	3.25E+00	5.13E+00	2.47E+00	1.23E+01
F3	2	**0**	4.57E-176	**0**	3.53E-07	**0**	3.91E-33	8.96E-124
	10	**0**	1.09E-107	**0**	3.04E+00	9.07E-02	1.40E+00	1.57E+00
	30	**2.54E-212**	7.37E-91	3.68E-03	8.08E+02	6.06E+03	1.68E+04	1.17E+04
F4	2	**0**	3.06E-87	**0**	4.84E-03	1.07E-304	8.86E-17	5.89E-62
	10	1.88E-144	2.07E-58	**0**	4.03E-01	3.65E-22	9.62E-03	9.19E-01
	30	**2.55E-137**	1.55E-56	4.86E-33	6.58E+00	1.11E+01	1.36E+01	1.75E+01
F5	2	6.54E-07	1.00E+00	4.55E-02	1.16E-04	2.14E-03	6.54E-07	**6.54E-07**
	10	**2.26E+00**	8.82E+00	5.69E+00	1.14E+01	3.54E+00	6.56E+00	2.27E+00
	30	**2.70E+01**	2.90E+01	2.88E+01	2.15E+03	2.89E+01	2.46E+02	2.24E+04
F6	2	**1.03E-04**	6.45E-06	1.51E-05	2.04E-04	2.52E-04	2.42E-04	1.01E-05
	10	6.04E-01	2.50E+00	3.18E-02	8.62E-02	6.02E-02	7.01E-10	3.18E-02
	30	**1.56E+01**	2.39E+01	1.69E+01	1.63E+03	1.01E+04	4.19E+03	1.92E+04
F7	2	1.92E-04	7.84E-05	**3.75E-05**	3.22E-04	4.88E-03	1.17E-04	7.97E-05
	10	**4.60E-05**	3.63E-04	4.69E-05	3.61E-03	1.12E-02	7.32E-03	8.91E-03
	30	**1.79E-04**	3.86E-04	8.34E-03	7.45E-02	4.90E-01	7.08E-02	3.03E-01
F8	2	−8.38E+02	−6.21E+02	−7.19E+02	−7.20E+02	−8.38E+02	−8.36E+02	−8.35E+02
	10	**−3.24E+03**	−1.77E+03	−3.23E+03	−2.11E+03	−2.65E+03	−3.24E+03	−2.83E+03
	30	−4.41E+03	−3.97E+03	−4.79E+03	−5.20E+03	**−5.53E+03**	−5.37E+03	−3.42E+03
F9	2	**0**	**0**	**0**	3.31E-05	9.95E-01	**0**	**0**
	10	**0**	**0**	**0**	5.46E+00	2.31E+01	2.44E+01	1.39E+01
	30	**0**	**0**	4.16E+00	5.35E+01	1.42E+02	2.30E+02	1.77E+02
F10	2	8.88E-16	8.88E-16	**8.88E-16**	6.73E-03	**8.88E-16**	8.88E-16	**8.88E-16**
	10	**8.88E-16**	**8.88E-16**	1.31E-03	1.41E+00	8.41E+00	8.24E-03	6.60E+00
	30	**8.88E-16**	**8.88E-16**	1.79E+01	3.75E+00	1.10E+01	6.74E+00	2.00E+01
F11	2	**0**	**0**	**0**	1.36E-02	7.40E-03	7.12E-10	7.40E-03
	10	**0**	**0**	3.49E+00	4.60E-01	5.16E+00	2.09E-01	2.75E-01
	30	**0**	**0**	4.64E+02	1.44E+00	5.44E+01	7.97E-01	7.64E+00
F12	2	**2.36E-31**	5.82E-04	5.54E-03	2.53E-06	1.38E-04	1.38E-04	2.12E-25
	10	**1.92E-04**	1.47E-01	9.78E-02	5.59E-04	5.82E-01	4.77E-10	8.48E-02
	30	**7.37E-03**	1.29E+00	6.79E+00	2.25E-01	1.45E+00	1.58E-02	7.40E-01
F13	2	1.35E-32	2.23E-03	1.17E-02	8.31E-08	**1.35E-32**	1.49E-04	**1.35E-32**
	10	**9.96E-12**	7.30E-01	8.43E-02	1.06E-03	4.66E-01	9.66E-02	9.18E-03
	30	**4.31E-03**	2.85E+00	1.03E+00	3.03E-02	4.36E+00	1.98E+00	1.32E+00

Detailed analysis of each function against different dimensions is prepared. Referring to Table 1 and Table 2, IBMO has gained the far most performance by finding the global minima solution mostly better than other compared optimizers. The best results are written in bold for better visualization of each test function.

Tabular results indicates that IBMO is far better at balancing between exploitation and exploration phases compared to other meta-heuristic algorithms.

Table 2. Comparison of meta heuristic algorithms with IBMO for fixed dimension multimodal functions.

Func	IBMO	BMO	AOA	PSO	GWO	FPA	DFA
F14	**9.98E-01**	3.80E+00	1.13E+01	9.98E-01	3.97E+00	**9.98E-01**	2.98E+00
F15	**5.98E-04**	5.64E-03	9.83E-04	1.63E-03	1.04E-03	6.86E-04	2.24E-03
F16	**−1.03E+00**	**−1.03E+00**	**−1.03E+00**	**−1.03E+00**	**−1.03E+00**	**−1.03E+00**	**−1.03E+00**
F17	**3.98E-01**	4.45E-01	3.98E-01	4.00E-01	**3.98E-01**	4.00E-01	**3.98E-01**
F18	**3.00E+00**	1.99E+01	**3.00E+00**	3.01E+00	3.01E+00	3.01E+00	3.01E+00
F19	**−3.86E+00**	−3.81E+00	−3.84E+00	−3.86E+00	**−3.86E+00**	−3.84E+00	−3.84E+00
F20	−3.20E+00	−1.55E+00	−2.94E+00	−3.20E+00	−2.59E+00	**−3.32E+00**	−2.84E+00
F21	**−6.03E+00**	−4.40E+00	−4.81E+00	−5.05E+00	−5.06E+00	−1.02E+01	−1.02E+01
F22	**−8.36E+00**	−3.67E+00	−3.72E+00	−1.04E+01	−1.04E+01	−1.04E+01	−3.72E+00
F23	**−7.02E+00**	−1.65E+00	−4.97E+00	−1.05E+01	−5.13E+00	−1.05E+01	−3.83E+00

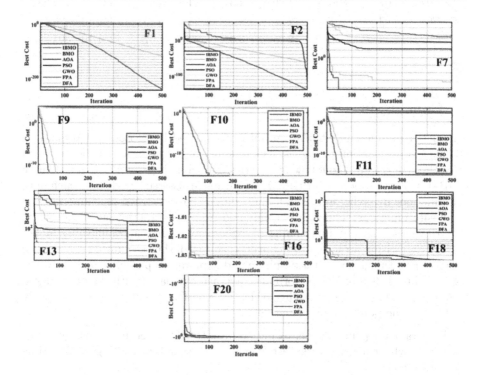

Fig. 3. Convergence Curves

3.1   Computational Cost Analysis

A time-based computational cost investigation has been conducted in this section with the IBMO algorithm. It can be determined by testing the algorithm on the benchmark test functions for CEC-2020 protocol [18]. The proposed algorithm of IBMO tested on the computational times and is compared with other similar metaheuristic algorithms on each CEC benchmark test function with a population size of 10. The results of the experiment is shown in Table 3. Rest of the parameters are same as used in the previous section. The machine used for the complete analysis is a Core i7 9750h with 16 GB RAM.

Table 3. Comparison of meta heuristic algorithms with IBMO for $\overrightarrow{T}$ (sec) time complexity analysis

Func.	$\overrightarrow{T}$IBMO	$\overrightarrow{T}$FDO	$\overrightarrow{T}$BMO	$\overrightarrow{T}$AOA	$\overrightarrow{T}$PSO	$\overrightarrow{T}$GWO	$\overrightarrow{T}$FPA	$\overrightarrow{T}$DFA
CEC01	335.14	10213.71	329.9	316.47	317.4	317	464.89	594.96
CEC02	14.54	197.15	13.41	5.82	4.92	5.27	242.62	542.33
CEC03	18.96	254.5	18.83	10.6	10.33	10.58	274.56	2075.9
CEC04	14.31	342.83	12.12	3.88	3.72	3.89	153.3	303.76
CEC05	14.77	615.55	13.74	4.4	4.36	4.97	153.31	302.95
CEC06	125.59	3312.43	115.17	110.05	110.4	111.38	259.73	410.83
CEC07	15.07	646.37	11.99	4.37	4.24	4.4	149.01	294.98
CEC08	13.52	191.17	12.08	4.51	4.25	4.39	149.83	302.48
CEC09	13.78	232.48	12.05	3.9	4.29	4.07	151.19	301.13

4   Conclusion

This paper presents an efficient optimizer motivated by gooseneck barnacles to tackle the optimization problems. The qualitative investigation of the proposed algorithm consists of the following metrics, namely; speed of convergence curve of IBMO. Furthermore, the IBMO algorithm is assessed with 23 benchmark test functions involving uni-modal, multi-modal, fix-dimension multi-modal, and composite functions. The results conducted from the experiments demonstrate that IBMO assures the functioning of explorations while accomplishing higher exploitation within an acceptable convergence speed, thus keeping an exceptional balance between the exploitation phase and exploration phase. Statistically, the algorithm returns a higher performance average compared with the other metaheuristic algorithms the suitability of IBMO's performance can be theoretically credited to the points as discussed below:

- The parameter penis size i.e. *ps* permits the IBMO to retain a constant disorder rate whilst also assuring fast convergence, therefore evading local optima solution traps.

– k guarantees the effectiveness of the early exploration and later exploitation.
– Based on historical data, suitable use of the discrete fitness values allows IBMO to find better positional variables that evidently allow better adaptability of the IBMO in different search phases.

Acknowledgment. This work was supported by Top Research Centre Mechatronics (TRCM), University of Agder (UiA), Norway.

References

1. Abualigah, L.: Group search optimizer: a nature-inspired meta-heuristic optimization algorithm with its results, variants, and applications. Neural Comput. Appl. **33**(7), 2949–2972 (2021)
2. Abualigah, L., Diabat, A., Mirjalili, S., Abd Elaziz, M., Gandomi, A.H.: The arithmetic optimization algorithm. Comput. Methods Appl. Mech. Eng. **376**, 113609 (2021)
3. Chan, B.K., et al.: The evolutionary diversity of barnacles, with an updated classification of fossil and living forms. Zool. J. Linn. Soc. **193**(3), 789–846 (2021)
4. Dong, Y., Hou, J., Zhang, N., Zhang, M.: Research on how human intelligence, consciousness, and cognitive computing affect the development of artificial intelligence. Complexity **2020**, 1–10 (2020)
5. Dorigo, M., Stützle, T.: Ant colony optimization: overview and recent advances. In: Gendreau, M., Potvin, J.Y. (eds.) Handbook of Metaheuristics. International Series in Operations Research & Management Science, vol. 146, pp. 227–263. Springer, Boston (2019). https://doi.org/10.1007/978-1-4419-1665-5_8
6. Igel, C.: No free lunch theorems: limitations and perspectives of metaheuristics. In: Borenstein, Y., Moraglio, A. (eds.) Theory and Principled Methods for the Design of Metaheuristics. NCS, pp. 1–23. Springer, Heidelberg (2014). https://doi.org/10.1007/978-3-642-33206-7_1
7. Kennedy, J., Eberhart, R.: Particle swarm optimization. In: Proceedings of ICNN 1995-International Conference on Neural Networks, vol. 4, pp. 1942–1948. IEEE (1995)
8. Mafarja, M., Mirjalili, S.: Whale optimization approaches for wrapper feature selection. Appl. Soft Comput. **62**, 441–453 (2018)
9. Mirjalili, S.: Dragonfly algorithm: a new meta-heuristic optimization technique for solving single-objective, discrete, and multi-objective problems. Neural Comput. Appl. **27**, 1053–1073 (2016)
10. Mirjalili, S., Mirjalili, S.M., Lewis, A.: Grey wolf optimizer. Adv. Eng. Softw. **69**, 46–61 (2014)
11. Mirjalili, S.Z., Mirjalili, S., Saremi, S., Faris, H., Aljarah, I.: Grasshopper optimization algorithm for multi-objective optimization problems. Appl. Intell. **48**, 805–820 (2018)
12. Oestreicher, C.: A History of Chaos Theory. Dialogues in Clinical Neuroscience (2022)
13. Stark, A.E.: The Hardy-Weinberg principle. Genet. Mol. Biol. **28**, 485–485 (2005)
14. Sulaiman, M.H., Mustaffa, Z., Saari, M.M., Daniyal, H.: Barnacles mating optimizer: a new bio-inspired algorithm for solving engineering optimization problems. Eng. Appl. Artif. Intell. **87**, 103330 (2020)

15. Wang, C., Koh, J.M., Yu, T., Xie, N.G., Cheong, K.H.: Material and shape optimization of bi-directional functionally graded plates by giga and an improved multiobjective particle swarm optimization algorithm. Comput. Methods Appl. Mech. Eng. **366**, 113017 (2020)

16. Xing, B., Gao, W.-J.: Fruit fly optimization algorithm. In: Innovative Computational Intelligence: A Rough Guide to 134 Clever Algorithms. ISRL, vol. 62, pp. 167–170. Springer, Cham (2014). https://doi.org/10.1007/978-3-319-03404-1_11

17. Yang, X.S., Karamanoglu, M., He, X.: Flower pollination algorithm: a novel approach for multiobjective optimization. Eng. Optim. **46**(9), 1222–1237 (2014)

18. Yue, C., et al.: Problem definitions and evaluation criteria for the CEC 2020 special session and competition on single objective bound constrained numerical optimization. Computational Intelligence Laboratory, Zhengzhou University, Zhengzhou, China, Technical report 201911 (2019)

19. Zhang, J., Xiao, M., Gao, L., Pan, Q.: Queuing search algorithm: a novel metaheuristic algorithm for solving engineering optimization problems. Appl. Math. Model. **63**, 464–490 (2018)

Evolutionary-Based Generative Design for Electric Transmission Towers

Hugo Moreno[1], Pablo S. Naharro[2]([✉]), Antonio LaTorre[3], and José-María Peña[4]

[1] Environmental and Geomatic Engineering Department,
University College London, London, UK
`hugo.manresa.21@ucl.ac.uk`
[2] Lurtis Rules, Madrid, Spain
`p.sanchez@lurtis.com`
[3] Center for Computational Simulation,
Technical University of Madrid, Madrid, Spain
`a.latorre@upm.es`
[4] Lurtis Ltd., Oxford, UK
`jm.penya@lurtis.com`

Abstract. Evolutionary Algorithms have shown during the last decades that they can solve a wide range of real-world problems in different fields, such as science or engineering. In this paper, we explore the application of Hybrid Evolutionary Algorithms (a Differential Evolution algorithm plus a tailor-made local search called MLS) to the generative design of electric transmission towers. This problem is modelled as a mesh of beams with a given thickness than can be either present or not depending on the value of an additional threshold parameter. For each beam, the algorithm optimises both parameters (thickness and threshold) with the objective of minimising the overall weight of the structure subject to the constraint of a maximum allowed displacement of 7 mm. The experimental results show that this is a promising application of Evolutionary Algorithms as they were able to improve the design of a human expert in the most complex of the considered scenarios, when the structure must deal with external forces due to wind.

Keywords: Generative Design · Evolutionary Algorithms · MOS · MLS · Electric Transmission Towers

1 Introduction

Most optimisation techniques work in a similar way: they start from one or multiple candidate solutions initialised following a given strategy and iteratively refine them by applying some kind of perturbation to existing solutions. This is far more efficient than brute force approaches, as the information created during the search, in the form of candidate solutions, is exploited to create new, hopefully better, solutions. This is the case of Evolutionary Algorithms (EAs). These techniques start with an initial population of solutions that are evolved by means

L. Rutkowski et al. (Eds.): ICAISC 2023, LNAI 14125, pp. 439–450, 2023.
https://doi.org/10.1007/978-3-031-42505-9_37

of the application of some recombination operators that create new solutions. A certain replacement strategy is then applied to decide which solutions take over to the next generation. This process is repeated until a predefined convergence criterion is met. This behaviour makes EAs a suitable approach to deal with generative design problems.

The aim of this study is to propose a generative design method for structures based on a hybrid evolutionary algorithm. To evaluate the convenience of this method, it will be applied to the generative design of electric transmission towers. The motivation of this study is as follows. At the beginning of 2022 the UK erected the first T-pylons in the world. These new T-pylons were the first redesign of the standard pylon in 100 years. Their design reduces the visual impact of the pylons, while also using lightweight and recyclable materials to reduce their impact on the environment. The new pylons also require less land, which helps to reduce their overall costs. This design was the result of a competition run by the UK's National Grid in which teams from around the world competed to develop an efficient and aesthetically pleasing design. The T-Pylon was the chosen one, and it is expected to be rolled out across the UK in the near future. Our objective is to evaluate if evolutionary-based generative design can be a useful tool for designers of this kind of structures.

The remainder of this paper is structured as follows. Section 2 provides an introduction to optimisation and surrogate models. Section 3 describes the optimisation proposal of this paper for addressing the generative design, which uses DE and a tailored-made local search algorithm, MLS, in combination with a Decision Tree that acts as a surrogate model. Section 4 proposes a method to encode the generative design problem. To follow, Sect. 5 defines the experimental scenario to evaluate the performance of the new proposal. Later, Sect. 6 analyses the results of the aforementioned experiments. Finally, Sect. 7 concludes the study by summarising the most important outcomes.

2   Optimisation in Engineering

Optimisation has been shown to be effective in many application fields, such as engineering or science. The aim of optimisation algorithms is to conduct the process as efficiently as possible, aiming to reduce the number of evaluations needed to reach the optimum. However, even if the most efficient optimisation algorithm were used, it would still require performing an iterative trial-and-error process, which might take a long time to converge. Besides, in these fields, the fitness function normally implies the execution of costly simulations. Given this, time is still a limiting factor, as the evaluation of current solutions need to be completed before continuing with the optimisation process. In this context, surrogate models arise, aiming to reduce this limitation by preventing some samples from being fully executed by approximating them.

There are two main types of surrogate models. On the one hand, offline surrogate models replace the whole fitness function with an approximation. This is achieved by using all the fitness function evaluations but one to create the training dataset that contains the information about the real fitness function. The samples used to build the dataset are selected using a sampling technique such as Latin Hypercube [8]. Later, a model that replaces the fitness is trained, and the optimisation is launched using the newly trained model, which is quasi-instantaneous, waiving the restriction of the amount of fitness function evaluations from hundreds/thousands to millions. After finishing the process, the minimum found with this strategy is evaluated with the real function using the remaining fitness function evaluation. The main advantage of this approach is the fact that all the fitness function evaluations are decoupled, and therefore, all can be run in parallel. Nonetheless, the optimisation is highly dependent on the limitations of the sampling technique and the errors made by the surrogate model.

On the other hand, in online surrogate models, the real fitness function is still present throughout the optimisation process. Models act as a filter that prevents non-worthy attempts from being executed, instead of replacing the full fitness function. Unlike offline surrogate models, the training dataset is built during the optimisation process with the samples calculated using the actual fitness function, which makes it necessary to retrain the model when new data is added to the dataset. This approach has a significant drawback: samples and training cannot be fully parallelised, as there is a sequential dependency. This situation can still lead to a limitation if the fitness function is extremely costly. However, online surrogate models reduce the dependency on the model error because the model is updated multiple times with incremental real data, and on the sampling method, because data is sampled around the region on which the optimiser is focusing.

The most straightforward approach for surrogate models is to use regressors that approximate the fitness function value (assuming continuous optimisation). Nonetheless, recent studies have proposed alternative approaches that reformulate the problem as a classifier instead of a regressor. This new approach has synergies with some optimisation methods that perform a comparison between samples to accept them into the population. For instance, CADE [4] uses a classifier to predict improvement based on neighbourhood data. Furthermore, CRADE [3], an extension of CADE, combines classification with regression. In [10], Particle Swarm Optimization (PSO) is combined with a level-based classifier that splits the population into four groups depending on its estimated quality value. Also, [5] proposes the use of pairwise surrogate models, which presents some benefits compared to the use of regressors.

Another point to address is the selection of the optimisation algorithm. Since the No Free Lunch Theorem [11] states that "any two algorithms are equivalent when their performance is averaged across all possible problems," it cannot be assumed that there is a best overall algorithm for every potential problem. However, research on different optimisation methods has revealed that some methods tend to perform better or worse depending on certain features of the problem to be optimised. Based on this, multiple approaches that combine different optimisation methods have emerged. The key factor lies in the capability of hybrid algorithms to exploit the different features of the algorithms of which they are composed. Among them, Multiple Offspring Sampling (MOS) [1,2] is a method that periodically evaluates the performance of internal algorithms and reassigns available resources accordingly. MOS divides the optimisation process into several splits in which every individual algorithm is assigned a budget of fitness function evaluations. Each algorithm is run until it runs out of fitness evaluations and then hands over to the next algorithm on the list. Once all algorithms have exhausted their budget, their performance is analysed, and new budgets are calculated for the new split. MOS has been used successfully on several problems, including real-world problems such as optimising finite elements models [6], in which MOS was used as a tool for hybridising DE [7] with MTS [9].

3   Evolutionary-Based Generative Design

This paper proposes a hybrid optimisation algorithm combined with surrogate models. Specifically, it combines a population-based algorithm, Differential Evolution (DE), with a customised local search algorithm called Mirror Local Search (MLS). Ideally, the hybrid algorithm should be able to balance the exploration ability of the population-based method (DE) with the exploitation capabilities of the local search (MLS). Once a promising region has been found by DE, MLS should gradually refine the structure by enabling and disabling one or more beams.

Additionally, as the proposed fitness function implies running heavy simulations that limit the number of available fitness evaluations, surrogate models are introduced aiming to increase the performance of the algorithm. A Decision Tree classifier (DT/C) is used following the *pairwise surrogate model* approach proposed in [5]. The success of this approach is based on focusing the efforts of the model on distinguishing whether a sample is better than another one or not, instead of being able to predict its exact fitness value. This is the case of both DE and MLS, which perform a comparison between two samples in their elitism phase to decide which one will be kept. As an additional feature, this approach provides a mechanism to augment the dataset when only few fitness function evaluations can be carried out (as in this problem). Finally, *pairwise surrogate models* have shown to be very effective and outperformed several other common surrogate approaches in the analysis performed in [5].

3.1   Mirror Local Search (MLS)

MLS is a heuristic search algorithm that assumes that the problem to be optimised involves selecting the weight of beams in a given structure, usually the full mesh. The algorithm also assumes that for each beam two parameters need to be optimised: its thickness and an additional parameter that defines a threshold below which the beam disappears from the structure.

MLS performs an iterative process that generates new candidate solutions based on the previous ones, as shown in Algorithm 1. Its mutation iterates over all variables except the threshold, pivoting the value of the selected variable over the threshold value. This behaviour is essentially a switch that enables or disables a beam. An example of this is shown in Fig. 1, for which the strategy for mirroring the values is given in Definition 1.

It is also essential to consider that beams whose value is close to the threshold (compared to others) may hold more uncertainty in being enabled or disabled by other optimisation techniques used within the MOS framework. To maintain the neighbourhood between uncertainty regions, the relative distance from the value to the threshold is kept before and after the mutation. This allows the algorithm to keep the variables currently close to the threshold at a similar position while maintaining the on/off switching behaviour.

Algorithm 1: Mirror Local Search (MLS). One generation carried out.

Data: A solution x
Result: A new solution $newX$
// Create new candidates using Mutation as in Figure 1
newCandidates = CreateNewCandidates(x)
// Select the best candidate using Elitism as in Algorithm 2
$newX$ = GetBestCandidate(x, $newCadidates$)
return $newX$

Algorithm 2: Elitism function.

Data: A solution x and a challenger solutions list x'
Result: The best one among x and x'
$best \leftarrow x$
for *candidate in x'* **do**
  if $\hat{w}(x, candidate)$ **then**
      // The challenger seems to improve the current solution
      // Therefore, the actual quality function is computed
      if $q(candidate) \prec q(best)$ **then**
          // The actual quality value of *candidate* is better than that of *best*
          $best \leftarrow candidate$
      end
  end
end
return *best*

Definition 1. *Let X be the original value, X_N the new value, T the threshold, L the lower problem bound and U the upper bound of the problem. Equation 1 defines the mirroring process of the MLS mutation phase.*

$$X_N = \begin{cases} X >= T, & T - ((X - T) * \frac{T-L}{U-T}) \\ X < T, & T + ((T - X) * \frac{U-T}{T-L}) \end{cases} \tag{1}$$

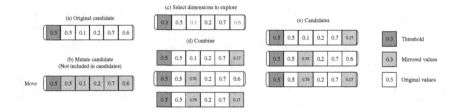

Fig. 1. MLS Mutation example

Once the new candidates has been proposed, an elitism function (Algorithm 2) chooses which individuals are accepted and get into the population. This function also includes the use of a surrogate model in the elitism phase, aiming to boost the performance of the algorithm.

4   Design of Transmission Towers

In this section, we characterise the problem by defining both the objective function and the encoding used in our experiments. Our goal is to create a structure for our experiments in which the optimiser would delete beams or change their cross-section, aiming to shape it and reach the lowest weight possible without exceeding a certain maximum displacement.

Moreover, MLS, one of the optimisation techniques described in Sect. 3.1, requires a specific coding scheme where each dimension acts as a unique identifier of the beam configuration, which, in this case, is the unit weight of the beam (kg/m). The only exception is the first dimension, which defines the threshold of the unit weight under which the beam is disabled.

Definition 2. *The objective function f calculates the total weight y of the structure based on the input values x and th, as shown in Eq. 2. The array x consists of values that represent the unit weight of each beam, and their mapping with the specific beam in the structure remains constant throughout the optimisation process. The parameter th corresponds to the threshold of x, below which the beam is considered to be disabled.*

$$y = f(th, x) \tag{2}$$

Furthermore, this function calculates the maximum displacement of the nodes and marks the solution as invalid if it exceeds 7 mm. This is to ensure that the final design meets its intended purpose.

Figure 2 displays the complete mesh that serves as a template for modifications. All beams in the figure are tubular structures, and their general cross-section is also shown in Fig. 2. However, each beam in this structure must be assigned a value for its diameter D and thickness t, or it must be disabled.

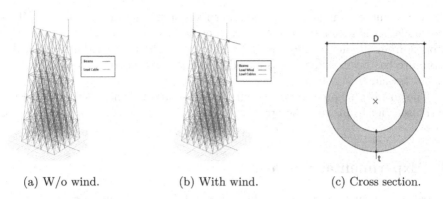

(a) W/o wind.   (b) With wind.   (c) Cross section.

Fig. 2. Structure that gets modified and cross-section of the beam of the structure.

In order to assign a cross-section, a procedure needs to be defined. Firstly, the unit weight (uw_i) of the section i is obtained from its x_i value using Eq. 3. Secondly, the nearest neighbour configuration is selected based on the distance between the unit weights. Finally, the D and t that characterise the selected configuration are obtained and assigned to the beam.

Definition 3. *Let uw_i denote the expected unit weight of beam i, and uw_{max} the maximum unit weight in the configuration space. Equation 3 calculates the expected unit weight uw_i of beam i based on the value assigned by the optimiser x_i.*

$$uw_i = (x_i - th)/(1 - th) * uw_{max} \qquad (3)$$

Finally, to preserve the nature of the problem, we applied two loads of 10KN to the top corners of the structure to simulate the weight of two electricity cables. We considered two scenarios, one with wind forces and one without. To simulate the wind, we applied a horizontal load of 10kN to the upper points of the structure.

4.1 Initialisation

The search space is quite large compared to the number of feasible solutions that can be simulated. Many designs do not fully connect the loads to the floor, which would cause the simulator to fail. Others represent structures whose equations do not converge. This means that a randomly initialised population is likely to contain many infeasible configurations.

However, the optimisation algorithms that we use require valid solutions to be initialised. Therefore, we have implemented the following procedure. First, we select a node at the top of the structure. From that node, there is a 60% chance of going down to the lower level and a 40% chance of staying at the current level. Then, we randomly choose a node among the neighbour nodes that meets this constraint of going down to the lower level or staying in the same one. This new node is then connected to the previous node with a beam. We repeat this process from the newly selected node until we reach the floor. Once a feasible structure has been defined, it is encoded as the corresponding array of values, x, and a valid th.

The goal of this process is not to find good solutions, which is the task of the optimiser, but to provide the optimiser with some solutions to start the process with.

5   Experimental Scenario

In order to evaluate and analyse the structural designs of the electricity pylons, the software used was Oasys GSA. GSA allows for real-life structural designs to be modelled and gives a detailed analysis of the forces and movements of a structure due to its own weight or any external loads. The problem has been configured using the mesh of Fig. 2 and according to the parameters in Table 1.

Table 1. Parameters of the problem.

Parameter	Value	Units
D	{20, 21, ..., 149, 150}	mm
t	{5, 10}	mm
Loads (cables)	10	kN
Loads (wind)	10	kN
Max. displacement	7	mm

To simplify the problem, the structure was divided into four quadrants, as viewed from above. For this study, the optimiser only had access to the first quadrant, and the results were later mirrored to the other quadrants to ensure symmetry. This also reduced the complexity of the problem by a factor of four, resulting in a total of 194 dimensions (193 beams plus threshold). The authors acknowledge that this approach may limit the structure's capabilities by prohibiting asymmetric designs, which would have been especially problematic if the boundary conditions were asymmetric as well.

5.1   Optimiser Configuration

We have used MOS as the hybridisation technique for combining a DE and a MLS. MOS allocates fitness evaluations based on the performance of the algorithms. To accomplish this, it defines steps in which the algorithms' performance is measured, and fitness evaluations are reassigned accordingly.

The surrogate model used is a Decision Tree classifier (DT/C) that is trained at the end of each algorithm phase. Since the surrogate might not be reliable throughout the optimisation, a warm-up phase in which the surrogate is not used has been included. Additionally, a probability of recovering a solution has been set up to prevent the surrogate from discarding every solution. For MLS, a probability of recovering a solution has been added based on the "Qual." strategy proposed in [5].

One of the strengths of pairwise surrogate models is the ability to augment training data to (N^2). However, this approach is not feasible with the amount of fitness function evaluations used. As a result, growth has been limited with the "trail size" parameter, which restricts comparisons to the last 5 calculated samples, i.e., $(5N)$ (Table 2).

Table 2. Parameters values for the considered algorithms.

Parameter Values of DE		Parameter Values of MLS	
strategy	rand/1/exp	dimensions to explore	5
F	0.5	recover probability	0.05
CR	0.5	Qual. probability	0.4
recover probability	0.05	initial resource proportion	0.5
initial resource proportion	0.5		
Parameter Values of MOS			
number of steps	20		
trail size	5		
warm up	100 ffe.		

5.2 Reference Structures

To analyse the performance of the optimiser, we used some reference solutions created by a human who attempted to find the minimum weight while keeping the solution within the boundary conditions and complying with the displacement restriction of 7 mm.

Figure 3 shows, on the left, the structure for the case with no wind, with D set to 80 and t set to 5. Alternatively, on the right, we show the case with wind, with parameters D and t set to 60 and 10 respectively.

6 Results Analysis

Table 3 displays the minimum, average, and maximum weight attained by the optimiser. When compared to the reference case, we can observe that the optimiser achieves a less favourable solution when no external loads (wind) are applied. However, in cases where there are more loads than just holding the electricity cables, the optimiser achieves a satisfactory outcome (an improvement of over 8.03%).

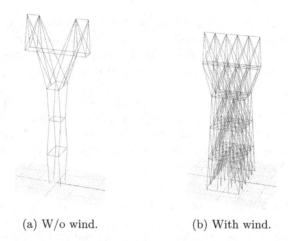

(a) W/o wind.   (b) With wind.

Fig. 3. Reference structures.

Table 3. Summary of the results.

	No wind		Wind	
	Optimiser	Human	Optimiser	Human
Min	6,16E+03	4,37E+03	2,27E+04	3.18E+04
Mean	8,75E+03		2,92E+04	
Max	1,43E+04		3,63E+04	
Max displacement	2,79E-03	3,76E-03	6,99E-03	3,76E-03
Improvement	−100,10%		8.03%	

Figure 4 displays the best solutions for both cases, with and without wind. The best solutions in the scenario with no wind have fewer beams due to having less load applied to them. Since the load is vertical in this scenario, the structures have two pillars that support the loads and transfer them to the ground. The structures generated in the scenario with wind show cross bracing, which supports the lateral load. They also have more connections to transfer the load more efficiently.

However, this method is limited to the subset of possibilities that the initial mesh is able to define. The authors believe that it is possible to improve the solution by increasing the flexibility of the mesh.

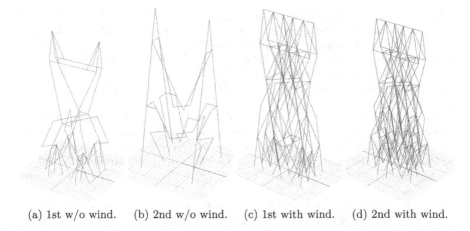

(a) 1st w/o wind.   (b) 2nd w/o wind.   (c) 1st with wind.   (d) 2nd with wind.

Fig. 4. Best solutions obtained with the optimiser.

7   Conclusion

In this paper we have conducted an experimentation with a Hybrid Evolutionary Algorithm combining Differential Evolution and a tailor-made local search called MLS to the generative design of electric transmission towers. The objective was to minimize the overall weight of the structure while satisfying a constraint of maximum displacement. Two different scenarios were considered, with and without wind, and the experimental results show that the proposed method yields promising improvements in the first one. However, results were not as good in the second scenario, probably due to the fact that simpler designs are easy to obtain by a human expert in that particular case. Nonetheless, we believe that this approach could still be useful in those scenarios by using the Hybrid EA to refine human designs. This opens new research lines in the definition of specific initialisation procedures that take into account human designs and recommendations.

Acknowledgment. PSN, JMP and ALT would like to thank the Industrial PhD Programme of *Comunidad de Madrid* (grant IND2019/TIC-17140). ALT and JMP thank the Spanish Ministry of Science (grant PID2020-113013RB-C22). This publication is part of the project PLEC2021-007962, funded by MCIN/AEI/10.13039/501100011033 and the European Union "NextGenerationEU"/PRTR.

References

1. LaTorre, A., Muelas, S., Peña, J.M.: A MOS-based dynamic memetic differential evolution algorithm for continuous optimization: a scalability test. Soft. Comput. **15**(11), 2187–2199 (2011)
2. LaTorre, A., Sánchez, J.M.P.: A framework for hybrid dynamic evolutionary algorithms: multiple offspring sampling (MOS). Ph.D. thesis, Ph.D. dissertation, Computer Science Faculty, University Polytechnic of Madrid (2009)

3. Lu, X.F., Tang, K.: Classification- and regression-assisted differential evolution for computationally expensive problems. J. Comput. Sci. Technol. **27**(5), 1024–1034 (2012). https://doi.org/10.1007/s11390-012-1282-4

4. Lu, X., Tang, K., Yao, X.: Classification-assisted differential evolution for computationally expensive problems. In: 2011 IEEE Congress of Evolutionary Computation, CEC 2011, pp. 1986–1993 (2011). https://doi.org/10.1109/CEC.2011.5949859

5. Naharro, P.S., Toharia, P., LaTorre, A., Peña, J.M.: Comparative study of regression vs pairwise models for surrogate-based heuristic optimisation. Swarm Evol. Comput. **75**, 101176 (2022). https://doi.org/10.1016/j.swevo.2022.101176

6. Peña, J.M., LaTorre, A., Jérusalem, A.: SoftFEM: the soft finite element method. Int. J. Numer. Meth. Eng. **118**(10), 606–630 (2019). https://doi.org/10.1002/nme.6029

7. Price, K., Storn, R.M., Lampinen, J.A.: Differential Evolution: A Practical Approach to Global Optimization. Springer, Heidelberg (2006). https://doi.org/10.1007/3-540-31306-0

8. Stein, M.: Large sample properties of simulations using Latin hypercube sampling. Technometrics **29**(2), 143–151 (1987)

9. Tseng, L.Y., Chen, C.: Multiple trajectory search for large scale global optimization. In: 2008 IEEE Congress on Evolutionary Computation, CEC 2008, pp. 3052–3058 (2008). https://doi.org/10.1109/CEC.2008.4631210

10. Wei, F.F., et al.: A classifier-assisted level-based learning swarm optimizer for expensive optimization. IEEE Trans. Evol. Comput. **25**(2), 219–233 (2021). https://doi.org/10.1109/TEVC.2020.3017865

11. Wolpert, D., Macready, W.: No free lunch theorems for optimization. IEEE Trans. Evol. Comput. **1**(1), 67–82 (1997). https://doi.org/10.1109/4235.585893. Conference Name: IEEE Transactions on Evolutionary Computation

Ehnanced Grey Wolf Optimizer

Radka Poláková$^{(\boxtimes)}$ and Daniel Valenta

Silesian University in Opava, Bezručovo náměstí 1150/13, 746 01 Opava,
Czech Republic
{radka.polakova,daniel.valenta}@fpf.slu.cz

Abstract. In this paper, we propose EGWO, a new version of Grey Wolf Optimizer. The EGWO algorithm works in almost the same way as the original algorithm, only a simple tool was added into this algorithm. Both algorithms, original and also its new version, are tested on benchmark set of CEC2014 at three levels of dimension, 10, 30, and 50. Our results show that the implementation of our tool makes the Grey Wolf Optimizer significantly more effective in more than 64% of tested problems.

Keywords: Nature-inspired algorithms · Function optimization · GWO · Experimental comparison

1 Introduction

There are many fields in human life in which a solved problem should be formalized as an optimization problem defined as follows.

Let's have a real function $f : S \rightarrow R$, $S \subset R^D$, f is an objective function and to solve the optimization problem for the function f in search space S, it means to find a point $\boldsymbol{X}^*$ (optimum) such that for all $\boldsymbol{X} \in S$ in case of minimization formula $f(\boldsymbol{X}^*) \leq f(\boldsymbol{X})$ or in case of maximization formula $f(\boldsymbol{X}^*) \geq f(\boldsymbol{X})$ holds. It is easy to understand that if you maximize the function f in search space S, it is the same process as to minimize the function $-f$ in search space S. That is why we can focus only on the minimization.

Many researchers, and also specialists from the industry, work with such issues. Almost all of them are solving optimization problems by a nature-inspired or an evolutionary algorithm because they are often easy to implement and they can usually find sufficient solution of the problem during a relatively short time. Using the two types of algorithms is often an effective way to solve an optimization problem. We study the GWO algorithm [1]. It is fast and relatively effective tool for optimization. In this paper, we implement an easy tool into this nature-inspired algorithm. New algorithm Enhanced Grey Wolf Optimizer (EGWO) is introduced and tested on CEC2014 benchmark set [2] which includes 30 different functions of different hardness.

The rest of this paper is organized as follows. The following section describes the original GWO algorithm. In Sect. 3, we introduce the proposed tool and describe our new EGWO algorithm. Then we briefly explain our experiments and discuss the results. In the last section, we conclude our findings.

L. Rutkowski et al. (Eds.): ICAISC 2023, LNAI 14125, pp. 451–460, 2023.
https://doi.org/10.1007/978-3-031-42505-9_38

2   Original GWO Algorithm

The Grey Wolf Optimizer is an efficient algorithm for global optimization. It simulates a real life hunting of a grey wolf pack. In the nature, there are several wolves in such pack and each grey wolf has a clearly defined role here. There is a hierarchy in the wolf pack where we can observe four types of wolves. Wolves of the first type are so-called alpha wolves. Precisely, there are two alphas, male and female, and they form the alpha pair. Each wolf from the pack should follow instructions of the alpha pair.

Further, there is usually another pair in the wolf pack. Beta male and beta female. This pair can substitute the alpha pair when necessary. These wolves behave in keeping up with the instructions of the alpha pair similarly to the rest of the wolf pack. Beta wolves help and support the alpha pair. The rest of the wolves (except the alpha pair) also follows instructions of the beta pair.

In such wolf pack, there are also wolves which are on the lowest position of the hierarchy. They are called omega wolves. They are the last, but they are very important. All of other wolves can take out their frustration on these omega wolves. It keeps the wolf pack stable. They play the role of a punching bag in the pack. Losing these wolves can disturb both the hierarchy and their discipline, and it can lead to destruction of the pack. Other wolves in the pack are called delta ones. They are between the leaders (alpha and beta wolves) and omega wolves in the hierarchy. The wolves in the pack are searching for and then following the prey, they encircle it, and then they attack it. They hunt and cooperate in order to catch the prey. In optimization, the prey is the optimum.

The GWO algorithm [1] was introduced in 2014 and it was inspired by behavior inside the wolf pack where the wolves are searching and hunting the prey together. They do it by cooperating with each other. In the GWO algorithm, there is only one alpha wolf, one beta wolf, and one delta wolf. The importance of their position in the hierarchy is the same in the algorithm. Other ones are omega wolves. Wolves are points and they are moving in the search space S to find a better position closer to the optimum and behave like the wolves in the pack. The algorithm is an iterative one. In each iteration, every wolf in the pack moves to a new position which is influenced by the current positions of the three best points, i.e. alpha, beta, and delta wolves. They have the three best values of all the values of the optimized function at all n wolves-points. The best values mean the smallest ones (in the case of minimization). The parameter n represents the size of the wolf pack.

So, there are n wolves - points in the algorithm and they are moving inside the search space. At the beginning of the search, they are placed randomly into the search space S. Then the iterative process starts. The hierarchy is recognized, i.e. alpha, beta, and delta wolves are found in the iteration. So, it is necessary to know a value of the optimized function in each point - wolf of the pack. The optimum (prey) is expected somewhere close to these three best points, but it could not be the right idea because the area may be the area of a local optimum. Therefore, every point-wolf move either close to this place (where the three best points are located) or far from this place. It depends on which strategy the wolf currently prefers, hunting or scouting. It is chosen randomly, but in the first iterations, the probability that the wolf will search is higher, and as iterations increase, the probability that the wolf will hunt increases. Note, that the simulation goes separately in each of all the dimensions.

In nature, wolves sometimes could pass by some obstacles, such as trees, bushes, and water areas. It means that they often do not move straight to the prey. Also this aspect of the wolves' behavior is simulated in the algorithm.

In each iteration, after finding the three best points - wolves in the pack, $X_\alpha(it)$, $X_\beta(it)$, and $X_\delta(it)$, new position $X_j(it+1)$ is calculated for j-th member of the pack, $1 \leq j \leq n$, where n is the number of the wolves in the pack. The current position $X_j(it)$, positions of current alpha, beta, and delta wolves, and two triples of vectors (A_1, A_2, A_3, C_1, C_2, and C_3, these are generated separately for each wolf from the pack) are used for computation of the new position of a wolf.

In each iteration it, new three positions are computed for j-th wolf, X_1, X_2, and X_3. It is done according to the following description.

$$X_1 = X_\alpha(it) - A_1 \times D_\alpha,$$
$$X_2 = X_\beta(it) - A_2 \times D_\beta,$$
$$X_3 = X_\delta(it) - A_3 \times D_\delta,$$

where the operation $\times$ is a multiplication of components, which means that $A \times D$ for $A = (a_1, a_2, \ldots, a_m)$ and $D = (d_1, d_2, \ldots, d_m)$ is $A \times D = (a_1 d_1, a_2 d_2, \ldots, a_m d_m)$. $X_\alpha(it)$, $X_\beta(it)$, and $X_\delta(it)$ is current position of alpha, beta, and delta wolf, respectively. Vectors A_1, A_2, and A_3 are three different instances of vector A. Vector A has components equal to $rand(-1, 1) \times a$, where $rand(-1, 1)$ means a random number between -1 and 1 and a equals to $2 - (2it/it_{max})$, where it is the algorithm current iteration, it_{max} is the maximum number of iterations. Each component of vector A influences movement of the point-wolf towards or away from the position of the elite wolf (alpha, beta, and delta) in a specific dimension of the search space S. Each component of vector A is generated separately. Parameter a decreases during the whole run from 2 to 0. It implies that interval in which components of vector A lie is narrowing, we can say, linearly from $[-2, 2]$ to $[0, 0]$ as number of iterations increases. The closer the value of the component of A to 0, the higher probability that the wolf chooses the hunting phase instead of the scouting one in relevant dimension.

Vectors D_α, D_β, D_δ represent the distance of the wolf X_j in iteration it from prey. They are computed in the following way.

$$D_\alpha = |C_1 \times X_\alpha(it) - X_j(it)|,$$
$$D_\beta = |C_2 \times X_\beta(it) - X_j(it)|,$$
$$D_\delta = |C_3 \times X_\delta(it) - X_j(it)|,$$

where the operation × is again the multiplication of components, similarly as in equations for computation of X_1, X_2, and X_3. $|X|$ is the vector whose components are the absolute values of relevant components of X.

Vectors C_1, C_2, and C_3 are three different instancies of vector C. Vector C has components set to $rand(0, 2)$ (a random number between 0 and 2, each component can be different, each component is generated separately). The closer value to 0, the higher probability that the wolf chooses the hunting phase in a relevant dimension. This vector helps to simulate a situation in which there are various obstacles in the environment, like bushes, stones or trees in the nature. So, the wolves may not move directly to the prey in current iterations. The higher the value of the component of C, the higher deviation from straight direction to the prey.

The three points with positions X_1, X_2, and X_3 are used for finding new current position $X_j(it + 1)$ of X_j member of our wolf pack. The position of X_j is updated according to the following formula.

$$X_j(it + 1) = \frac{X_1 + X_2 + X_3}{3}.$$

GWO has only two parameters, the size of the wolf pack n and the length of the time it can search the optimum. In the original proposal, GWO works with maximum count of iterations it can make. Here, we use the maximum number of function evaluations in order to fullfil conditions of CEC2014 benchmark set.

We can summarize the process. Wolves of the pack are randomly placed into the search space at the beginning of the search process. Next, in each iteration, the algorithm makes the following five steps.

1. It calculates the value of objective function f in the position of each wolf,
2. it determines the social hierarky of the pack, picks the alpha, beta, and delta wolves,
3. it generates vectors A_1, A_2, A_3, C_1, C_2, and C_3 separately for each wolf of the pack,
4. then it calculates the new position of each wolf X_j according to the description written above,
5. it checks if it reaches maximum number of iterations (here maximum number of objective function evaluations) and if so, it stops, otherwise, it performs the next iteration.

3   New Version of GWO

We study results of the original GWO algorithm on optimization problems of CEC2014 benchmark set. The behavior on large part of these optimization problems was very similar to each other. GWO found a result which was given as the optimization problem result for a relatively long time during the search process. Sometimes it was improved in the following part of the run of the algorithm, but sometimes it was also given as the final result of the problem (the algorithm was not able to improve it). The algorithm sticks its result on a local optimum and it already cannot escape from this place, or it was stuck there for a long time. It inspired us to propose a modification of the algorithm in order to improve this fact. It is possible to stop the algorithm after several iterations when it cannot move from a local optimum, and after this to run the algorithm again and again (the result of the first run is stored, then re-written if the next one is better). However, this is the most naive variant of enhancing not only the GWO algorithm (see also [3]). We wanted to propose such improvement for which we can find a similarity in real life of the grey wolf pack.

It is maybe not fully feasible, but it is at least imaginable. Envision a hunting pack. There are n members of the pack and wolves know that the prey they are hunting is smaller than would be optimal. It is clear that there would not be enough food for all members of the pack. So, wolves that are the nearest to the prey continue hunting and another part of the pack, only few wolves, starts searching for a new prey. In our just proposed algorithm, it happens only if searched optimum seems not to be improved, i.e. it is the same for several iterations. Some wolves from the pack change their positions to new random ones in the search space S in that time. And then everything goes as before these positions change.

So, in our modification of the GWO algorithm, the Enhanced Grey Wolf Optimizer (EGWO), there are two more parameters in comparison with the original version of the algorithm. The first one is the count of iterations after which the algorithm will move several wolves (not equal to alpha, beta, and delta) to the new random positions if the result of optimization problem does not change during them. We named this parameter nit. Thus, if the result is not changed for nit iterations, the ne randomly chosen wolves which are not the elite wolves (alpha, beta, and delta) change their positions to new random positions in the search space S. The ne parameter determines the count of these we can say explorers. These are wolves which start to search the new prey when the rest of the pack is still hunting the old one. We set ne equal to 2 and nit parameter equal to 10 in this paper.

4 Experiments

In order to find if the new EGWO algorithm is more effective than the original one we tested both algorithms on CEC2014 benchmark set at three levels of dimension, 10, 30, and 50. It means that we solved 30 optimization problems by GWO and then by EGWO at each of the three mentioned dimensions. Because of the fact that GWO and EGWO are stochastic, we have to run each of them several times for each problem. We did it fifteen times for each problem, which means that we made $30 \times 3 \times 15 \times 2$ (functions $\times$ dimensions $\times$ runs for a setting (runs for a problem) $\times$ algorithms) runs.

Benchmark set named CEC2014 was developed for a single objective optimization competition organized at the CEC2014 world congress which was held in Peking that year. It includes 30 different functions for each dimension. When

Table 1. Results of both tested algorithms (minimum, median, mean, standard deviation) and results of Wilcoxon rank sum tests, $D = 10$

f	GWO				EGWO				W
	min	median	mean	std	min	median	mean	std	
1	$1.68E+07$	$5.16E+07$	$1.31E+08$	$1.81E+08$	$1.43E+07$	$3.03E+07$	$2.96E+07$	$1.07E+07$	$+$
2	$1.56E+08$	$2.71E+09$	$2.57E+09$	$1.51E+09$	$1.28E+07$	$2.34E+08$	$3.51E+08$	$3.51E+08$	$+$
3	$1.06E+04$	$1.79E+04$	$1.89E+04$	$5.78E+03$	$9.15E+03$	$1.66E+04$	$1.71E+04$	$4.61E+03$	$\approx$
4	$1.12E+02$	$4.80E+02$	$9.72E+02$	$1.08E+03$	$4.75E+01$	$8.37E+01$	$9.18E+01$	$3.79E+01$	$+$
5	$2.02E+01$	$2.06E+01$	$2.06E+01$	$2.20E-01$	$2.05E+01$	$2.07E+01$	$2.07E+01$	$1.12E-01$	$\approx$
6	$6.13E+00$	$8.30E+00$	$8.26E+00$	$1.50E+00$	$2.55E+00$	$6.03E+00$	$6.04E+00$	$1.53E+00$	$+$
7	$1.04E+01$	$7.59E+01$	$8.16E+01$	$3.53E+01$	$1.97E+00$	$5.05E+00$	$9.04E+00$	$1.03E+01$	$+$
8	$3.81E+01$	$6.37E+01$	$6.52E+01$	$1.47E+01$	$3.25E+01$	$4.39E+01$	$4.30E+01$	$6.57E+00$	$+$
9	$3.90E+01$	$5.86E+01$	$5.84E+01$	$9.65E+00$	$2.15E+01$	$4.17E+01$	$3.87E+01$	$1.18E+01$	$+$
10	$8.89E+02$	$1.24E+03$	$1.30E+03$	$2.12E+02$	$8.71E+02$	$1.31E+03$	$1.37E+03$	$2.64E+02$	$\approx$
11	$7.62E+02$	$1.73E+03$	$1.53E+03$	$3.93E+02$	$7.63E+02$	$1.48E+03$	$1.50E+03$	$4.61E+02$	$\approx$
12	$4.16E-01$	$1.48E+00$	$1.43E+00$	$5.69E-01$	$1.33E+00$	$2.43E+00$	$2.30E+00$	$5.63E-01$	$-$
13	$3.00E-01$	$8.79E-01$	$1.44E+00$	$1.15E+00$	$2.88E-01$	$4.85E-01$	$5.12E-01$	$1.29E-01$	$\approx$
14	$6.73E-01$	$5.73E+00$	$8.16E+00$	$8.38E+00$	$3.22E-01$	$4.35E-01$	$1.08E+00$	$1.45E+00$	$+$
15	$5.82E+00$	$1.25E+01$	$7.19E+02$	$2.27E+03$	$3.27E+00$	$5.76E+00$	$6.12E+00$	$2.15E+00$	$+$
16	$3.90E+00$	$4.28E+00$	$4.28E+00$	$2.38E-01$	$3.35E+00$	$3.89E+00$	$3.84E+00$	$2.05E-01$	$+$
17	$3.50E+05$	$9.55E+05$	$9.75E+05$	$3.41E+05$	$7.36E+04$	$5.14E+05$	$4.77E+05$	$2.63E+05$	$+$
18	$5.05E+03$	$1.40E+04$	$2.17E+05$	$6.02E+05$	$5.48E+03$	$1.17E+04$	$3.19E+04$	$5.49E+04$	$\approx$
19	$6.98E+00$	$1.40E+01$	$2.08E+01$	$1.77E+01$	$4.36E+00$	$7.10E+00$	$6.78E+00$	$1.78E+00$	$+$
20	$5.62E+03$	$1.17E+04$	$1.44E+04$	$7.97E+03$	$2.72E+02$	$7.55E+03$	$9.24E+03$	$6.72E+03$	$\approx$
21	$1.20E+04$	$3.56E+05$	$1.40E+06$	$3.20E+06$	$6.27E+03$	$7.57E+04$	$1.76E+05$	$1.95E+05$	$+$
22	$2.00E+02$	$2.62E+02$	$2.76E+02$	$6.70E+01$	$6.70E+01$	$1.90E+02$	$1.95E+02$	$6.55E+01$	$+$
23	$2.01E+02$	$3.52E+02$	$3.37E+02$	$5.45E+01$	$2.00E+02$	$3.45E+02$	$3.37E+02$	$3.81E+01$	$+$
24	$1.67E+02$	$2.01E+02$	$1.99E+02$	$8.84E+00$	$1.37E+02$	$2.00E+02$	$1.89E+02$	$2.21E+01$	$\approx$
25	$1.97E+02$	$2.00E+02$	$2.00E+02$	$8.55E-01$	$2.00E+02$	$2.00E+02$	$2.00E+02$	$3.37E-01$	$\approx$
26	$1.02E+02$	$1.87E+02$	$1.57E+02$	$4.71E+01$	$1.00E+02$	$1.00E+02$	$1.01E+02$	$1.35E+00$	$+$
27	$4.13E+02$	$6.16E+02$	$5.75E+02$	$8.94E+01$	$3.66E+02$	$4.26E+02$	$4.27E+02$	$3.97E+01$	$+$
28	$8.53E+02$	$1.22E+03$	$1.34E+03$	$3.54E+02$	$6.13E+02$	$9.63E+02$	$9.91E+02$	$3.12E+02$	$+$
29	$7.23E+02$	$4.55E+07$	$4.71E+07$	$4.44E+07$	$5.01E+02$	$1.97E+03$	$3.10E+05$	$1.18E+06$	$+$
30	$1.97E+03$	$3.46E+04$	$5.80E+04$	$6.02E+04$	$2.40E+03$	$5.86E+03$	$9.36E+03$	$7.56E+03$	$+$

$\# +/\approx/-$

$20/9/1$

you use all four dimensions for which functions are prepared for testing, you obtain 120 different optimization problems. We use only 90 of them here, we tested at three levels of dimension as written above. The set of 30 functions includes four types of it, unimodal functions ($f1$–$f3$), simple multimodal functions ($f4$–$f16$), hybrid functions ($f17$–$f22$), and composition functions ($f23$–$f30$).

Taking into account the conditions of CEC2014 benchmark set, the GWO algorithm has only one parameter, it is size n of the wolf pack. It is set to $n = 6$, in this paper. The setting is recommend by the algorithm authors in [1]. The EGWO has two more parameters, as it was already mentioned above, ne is set to the value 2 here, and nit is set to $nit = 10$. The original parameter, inherited from GWO, the size of wolf pack n, is set to $n = 6$ also in EGWO.

Tested algorithms were implemented in GNU Octave, version 7.1.0 and all computations were carried out on a standard PC with Windows 10 Home, Intel(R) Core(TM) i7-7500U CPU 2.70 GHz 2.90 GHz, 8 GB RAM.

5 Results

The results of our experiments are displayed in Tables 1, 2, and 3. In each table, there are results for a tested dimension of $D = 10$, $D = 30$, and $D = 50$. In Table 1, there are minimum (min), median, mean, and standard deviation of relevant fifteen reached results for each of 30 test problems for both tested algorithms at dimension $D = 10$. There are also results of 30 Wilcoxon rank sum tests, comparisons of two relevant sets of results (the last column). The mark + in this column means that reached results of EGWO are statistically better than the ones of the GWO algorithm for the problem (function) at dimension $D = 10$. The mark $-$ means that reached results of EGWO are statistically worse than the ones of the GWO algorithm for the relevant problem (function) at dimension $D = 10$. And the mark $\approx$ means that reached results of EGWO and the ones of GWO are statistically the same for the relevant problem (function) at dimension $D = 10$. All Wilcoxon rank sum tests done in this paper were computed with statistical significance level set to $\alpha = 0.05$. Results for dimensions $D = 30$ and $D = 50$ are in the same form displayed in Tables 2 and 3, respectively.

When we look into Table 1, we can see that the results of our new EGWO algorithm are statistically better in 20 of 30 cases. There is also a function (problem) - f12 at dimension $D = 10$, where the original GWO is more efficient in comparison with new EGWO and also 9 functions, where the results of GWO does not change significantly by the implementation of the proposed tool.

From Table 2, we see that the results of our new EGWO algorithm are statistically better in 21 of 30 optimization problems. For other 6 cases, the more efficient algorithm is the original one, the GWO. The implementation of proposed improvement does not cause any significant changes in efficiency of the GWO algorithm in 3 rest cases.

In the case of dimension $D = 50$ (see Table 3), there are 17 of 30 functions, where our tool improves the results of the GWO algorithm significantly. The efficiency of algorithm stays statistically the same in 5 problems here. The original GWO algorithm has statistically better results than EGWO has in 8 problems for dimension $D = 50$.

Table 2. Results of both tested algorithms (minimum, median, mean, standard deviation) and results of Wilcoxon rank sum tests, $D = 30$

f	GWO min	median	mean	std	EGWO min	median	mean	std	W
1	$4.26E+08$	$7.51E+08$	$8.10E+08$	$2.54E+08$	$1.57E+08$	$2.48E+08$	$2.49E+08$	$6.88E+07$	+
2	$3.03E+10$	$4.64E+10$	$4.63E+10$	$6.34E+09$	$1.27E+09$	$5.83E+09$	$5.68E+09$	$1.79E+09$	+
3	$7.20E+04$	$8.42E+04$	$8.35E+04$	$4.46E+03$	$7.09E+04$	$8.67E+04$	$8.80E+04$	$1.08E+04$	≈
4	$4.14E+03$	$5.31E+03$	$5.75E+03$	$1.31E+03$	$4.39E+02$	$7.68E+02$	$8.35E+02$	$2.60E+02$	+
5	$2.06E+01$	$2.11E+01$	$2.10E+01$	$1.65E-01$	$2.10E+01$	$2.12E+01$	$2.12E+01$	$6.00E-02$	−
6	$3.41E+01$	$3.57E+01$	$3.65E+01$	$2.12E+00$	$2.01E+01$	$2.61E+01$	$2.59E+01$	$3.33E+00$	+
7	$3.07E+02$	$4.30E+02$	$4.43E+02$	$7.89E+01$	$1.79E+01$	$8.38E+01$	$8.02E+01$	$4.95E+01$	+
8	$2.90E+02$	$3.22E+02$	$3.19E+02$	$2.38E+01$	$1.41E+02$	$2.05E+02$	$1.97E+02$	$3.96E+01$	+
9	$2.63E+02$	$3.16E+02$	$3.13E+02$	$2.15E+01$	$1.27E+02$	$1.97E+02$	$1.94E+02$	$3.62E+01$	+
10	$5.73E+03$	$6.83E+03$	$6.85E+03$	$5.58E+02$	$3.76E+03$	$4.99E+03$	$4.94E+03$	$6.83E+02$	+
11	$6.18E+03$	$7.23E+03$	$7.43E+03$	$7.87E+02$	$4.63E+03$	$6.16E+03$	$6.11E+03$	$8.39E+02$	+
12	$7.71E-01$	$2.52E+00$	$2.30E+00$	$7.42E-01$	$1.72E+00$	$3.70E+00$	$3.63E+00$	$9.17E-01$	−
13	$4.62E+00$	$6.29E+00$	$6.10E+00$	$5.34E-01$	$5.90E-01$	$2.00E+00$	$1.63E+00$	$9.05E-01$	+
14	$1.34E+02$	$1.75E+02$	$1.73E+02$	$2.29E+01$	$9.27E+00$	$2.43E+01$	$2.48E+01$	$1.01E+01$	+
15	$3.37E+04$	$5.47E+04$	$8.04E+04$	$5.28E+04$	$1.13E+02$	$6.00E+02$	$1.26E+03$	$1.37E+03$	+
16	$1.35E+01$	$1.39E+01$	$1.38E+01$	$1.31E-01$	$1.30E+01$	$1.35E+01$	$1.35E+01$	$2.43E-01$	+
17	$2.86E+07$	$7.14E+07$	$7.86E+07$	$4.06E+07$	$4.84E+06$	$1.77E+07$	$1.67E+07$	$9.09E+06$	+
18	$1.09E+08$	$2.47E+08$	$1.42E+09$	$1.99E+09$	$2.66E+06$	$6.24E+06$	$1.93E+07$	$2.38E+07$	+
19	$2.08E+02$	$2.96E+02$	$2.89E+02$	$4.01E+01$	$6.53E+01$	$1.09E+02$	$1.13E+02$	$3.13E+01$	+
20	$5.77E+04$	$2.55E+05$	$2.37E+05$	$9.55E+04$	$3.94E+04$	$9.30E+04$	$1.10E+05$	$5.80E+04$	+
21	$1.50E+07$	$2.63E+07$	$3.37E+07$	$2.10E+07$	$3.83E+06$	$7.04E+06$	$7.36E+06$	$2.81E+06$	+
22	$1.20E+03$	$2.99E+03$	$3.16E+03$	$1.37E+03$	$3.62E+02$	$8.56E+02$	$8.49E+02$	$2.73E+02$	+
23	$2.00E+02$	$4.61E+02$	$4.32E+02$	$1.82E+02$	$2.00E+02$	$3.97E+02$	$3.87E+02$	$5.52E+01$	≈
24	$2.00E+02$	$2.00E+02$	$2.00E+02$	$5.03E-02$	$2.00E+02$	$2.01E+02$	$2.01E+02$	$1.19E+00$	−
25	$2.00E+02$	$2.00E+02$	$2.00E+02$	$0.00E+00$	$2.00E+02$	$2.00E+02$	$2.01E+02$	$3.91E+00$	−
26	$2.00E+02$	$2.00E+02$	$2.00E+02$	$2.15E-04$	$1.07E+02$	$1.61E+02$	$1.63E+02$	$3.79E+01$	+
27	$2.00E+02$	$2.00E+02$	$7.28E+02$	$7.31E+02$	$9.40E+02$	$1.07E+03$	$1.06E+03$	$8.97E+01$	≈
28	$2.00E+02$	$2.00E+02$	$7.50E+02$	$7.29E+02$	$2.69E+03$	$7.19E+03$	$6.66E+03$	$1.27E+03$	−
29	$4.93E+02$	$4.69E+04$	$8.84E+07$	$1.61E+08$	$1.34E+05$	$2.13E+06$	$8.21E+06$	$1.78E+07$	−
30	$4.08E+02$	$3.84E+06$	$3.30E+06$	$2.01E+06$	$2.32E+05$	$8.56E+05$	$8.63E+05$	$3.48E+05$	+

+/≈/−
21/3/6

Table 3. Results of both tested algorithms (minimum, median, mean, standard deviation) and results of Wilcoxon rank sum tests, $D = 50$

| | GWO | | | | EGWO | | | | |
f	min	median	mean	std	min	median	mean	std	W
1	$2.14E+09$	$2.93E+09$	$2.98E+09$	$6.62E+08$	$1.95E+08$	$3.73E+08$	$3.75E+08$	$1.37E+08$	+
2	$1.01E+11$	$1.09E+11$	$1.11E+11$	$6.76E+09$	$1.27E+10$	$1.84E+10$	$2.01E+10$	$6.12E+09$	+
3	$1.38E+05$	$1.50E+05$	$1.50E+05$	$7.42E+03$	$1.41E+05$	$1.67E+05$	$1.66E+05$	$1.31E+04$	−
4	$1.99E+04$	$2.81E+04$	$2.63E+04$	$4.69E+03$	$2.06E+03$	$3.09E+03$	$3.19E+03$	$1.03E+03$	+
5	$2.12E+01$	$2.12E+01$	$2.12E+01$	$6.23E-02$	$2.12E+01$	$2.13E+01$	$2.13E+01$	$3.58E-02$	≈
6	$6.70E+01$	$6.99E+01$	$6.98E+01$	$1.77E+00$	$4.28E+01$	$4.79E+01$	$4.73E+01$	$2.42E+00$	+
7	$8.68E+02$	$1.01E+03$	$1.04E+03$	$1.24E+02$	$9.90E+01$	$1.78E+02$	$1.80E+02$	$5.10E+01$	+
8	$5.89E+02$	$6.53E+02$	$6.44E+02$	$2.85E+01$	$2.61E+02$	$3.46E+02$	$3.65E+02$	$6.39E+01$	+
9	$5.73E+02$	$6.55E+02$	$6.45E+02$	$3.51E+01$	$3.08E+02$	$3.89E+02$	$3.84E+02$	$5.36E+01$	+
10	$1.15E+04$	$1.35E+04$	$1.34E+04$	$7.15E+02$	$8.46E+03$	$9.76E+03$	$1.00E+04$	$1.31E+03$	+
11	$1.29E+04$	$1.46E+04$	$1.45E+04$	$7.55E+02$	$8.16E+03$	$1.05E+04$	$1.03E+04$	$1.16E+03$	+
12	$2.82E+00$	$3.71E+00$	$3.84E+00$	$7.91E-01$	$1.94E+00$	$4.08E+00$	$3.94E+00$	$1.18E+00$	≈
13	$6.61E+00$	$6.88E+00$	$6.90E+00$	$2.27E-01$	$7.64E-01$	$2.78E+00$	$2.50E+00$	$9.77E-01$	+
14	$2.19E+02$	$2.66E+02$	$2.69E+02$	$2.81E+01$	$2.10E+01$	$4.34E+01$	$4.85E+01$	$2.09E+01$	+
15	$5.69E+05$	$1.20E+06$	$1.32E+06$	$5.09E+05$	$3.41E+03$	$2.44E+04$	$2.66E+04$	$2.17E+04$	+
16	$2.28E+01$	$2.31E+01$	$2.31E+01$	$1.78E-01$	$2.25E+01$	$2.31E+01$	$2.30E+01$	$3.13E-01$	≈
17	$1.34E+08$	$3.31E+08$	$4.24E+08$	$1.69E+08$	$8.40E+06$	$3.19E+07$	$3.40E+07$	$1.63E+07$	+
18	$6.28E+09$	$1.14E+10$	$1.06E+10$	$3.43E+09$	$8.87E+06$	$4.20E+07$	$9.04E+07$	$1.08E+08$	+
19	$6.70E+02$	$1.24E+03$	$1.24E+03$	$3.84E+02$	$1.48E+02$	$2.40E+02$	$2.31E+02$	$5.08E+01$	+
20	$6.84E+04$	$1.55E+05$	$1.43E+05$	$4.25E+04$	$4.96E+04$	$1.01E+05$	$1.11E+05$	$5.08E+04$	≈
21	$2.37E+07$	$4.64E+07$	$5.31E+07$	$2.53E+07$	$4.29E+06$	$8.09E+06$	$7.96E+06$	$2.83E+06$	+
22	$6.37E+03$	$1.91E+04$	$4.26E+04$	$3.79E+04$	$7.54E+02$	$1.83E+03$	$1.80E+03$	$4.87E+02$	+
23	$2.00E+02$	$2.00E+02$	$2.00E+02$	$0.00E+00$	$4.76E+02$	$5.73E+02$	$5.73E+02$	$6.66E+01$	−
24	$2.00E+02$	$2.00E+02$	$2.00E+02$	$9.09E-03$	$2.00E+02$	$2.01E+02$	$2.04E+02$	$1.13E+01$	−
25	$2.00E+02$	$2.00E+02$	$2.00E+02$	$0.00E+00$	$2.00E+02$	$2.00E+02$	$2.00E+02$	$2.48E-01$	≈
26	$2.00E+02$	$2.00E+02$	$2.00E+02$	$0.00E+00$	$2.00E+02$	$2.00E+02$	$2.00E+02$	$1.10E-01$	−
27	$2.00E+02$	$2.00E+02$	$2.41E+02$	$1.59E+02$	$1.32E+03$	$1.66E+03$	$1.61E+03$	$1.38E+02$	−
28	$2.00E+02$	$2.00E+02$	$2.00E+02$	$5.16E-05$	$9.50E+03$	$1.33E+04$	$1.29E+04$	$1.73E+03$	−
29	$2.01E+02$	$2.04E+02$	$2.06E+02$	$5.26E+00$	$2.01E+02$	$1.01E+07$	$1.42E+07$	$1.66E+07$	−
30	$2.00E+02$	$2.01E+02$	$2.95E+02$	$2.77E+02$	$5.16E+05$	$1.38E+06$	$1.57E+06$	$7.59E+05$	−

$\# +/\approx/-$
$17/5/8$

On 17% of tested problems, the new algorithm has significantly worse results than the original one. It means that our new version of algorithm is either significantly more effective than the original algorithm or the results are statistically the same on more then 80% of tested problems. EGWO has statistically better results than the GWO in almost two thirds of tested problems.

We can say that the implementation of the proposed simple tool into the GWO algorithm improves significantly the solution of this algorithm.

6   Conclusion

In this paper, we propose a modification of the well-known nature-inspired GWO algorithm. It is named the Enhanced Grey Wolf Optimizer.

Only a simple tool was included into the Grey Wolf Optimizer. In order to enhance the effectivity of the algorithm, we implemented wolves, which are explorers and they change their positions to random positions in the search space when the algorithm tends to stick on a local optimum.

The experimental comparison of the new algorithm and the original one shows that such simple tool improves the solution of the GWO significantly in 64% of tested problems.

For future work, we plan on exploring more the way of GWO enhancing we proposed in this paper. Perhaps by implementing other types of generating new positions of explorers.

References

1. Mirjalili, S., Mirjalili, S.M., Lewis, A.: Grey Wolf optimizer. Adv. Eng. Softw. **69**, 46–61 (2014)
2. Liang, J.J., Qu, B.Y., Suganthan, P.N.: Problem definitions and evaluation criteria for the CEC 2014 special session and competition on single objective real-parameter numerical optimization. Technical report for single objective optimization competition on CEC 2014 (2013)
3. Poláková, R., Tvrdík, J., Bujok, P.: Controlled restart in differential evolution applied to CEC2014 benchmark functions. In: IEEE Congress on Evolutionary Computation 2014, pp. 2230–2236. IEEE, Peking (2014)

Artificial Intelligence in Modeling and Simulation

Security Intelligence for Real-Time Security Monitoring Software

Aneta Poniszewska-Marańda[1]($\boxtimes$) [iD], Radoslaw Grela[1],
and Natalia Kryvinska[2] [iD]

[1] Institute of Information Technology, Lodz University of Technology, Lodz, Poland
aneta.poniszewska-maranda@p.lodz.pl
[2] Information Systems Department, Comenius University in Bratislava,
Bratislava, Slovakia
natalia.kryvinska@uniba.sk

Abstract. Security Intelligence (SI) describes the practice of collecting, standardizing and analysing data generated by networks, applications and other IT infrastructure in real time and using this information to assess and improve the security status of an organization. Security Intelligence involves deploying software and personnel resources to discover practical and useful insights that impact risk mitigation and risk reduction for the organization. Security Intelligence may also be referred to as intelligent security analysis. The paper presents the analysis of current state-of-the-art in the use of Security Intelligence and its impact on the development of current software engineering methods and approaches together with the built solution monitoring the software security with the use of SI and ML.

Keywords: Security Intelligence · Artificial Intelligence · Machine Learning (ML) · security monitoring · data security · event management

1 Introduction

Security Intelligence (SecInt) describes the practice of collecting, standardizing and analysing data generated by networks, applications and other IT infrastructure in real time and using this information to assess and improve the security status of an organization. Security Intelligence involves deploying software and personnel resources to discover practical and useful insights that impact risk mitigation and risk reduction for the organization. Security Intelligence may also be referred to as intelligent security analysis [1–3].

Gathering safety information is not a single activity undertaken by organizations. Rather, it is a series of related activities, technologies, and tools that work together to achieve the intended result. Security intelligence brings significant benefits to IT organizations that face stringent regulatory compliance requirements for sensitive data collected via web applications. The security information gathering process influences other downstream SecInt and SecOps processes that help protect our IT infrastructure from cyber attacks.

L. Rutkowski et al. (Eds.): ICAISC 2023, LNAI 14125, pp. 463–474, 2023.
https://doi.org/10.1007/978-3-031-42505-9_39

Security analysts use industry-leading technologies such as machine learning and big data analytics to automate the detection and analysis of security incidents and extract security information from network-wide event logs. The SecOps approach, named as Security and Operations, is to facilitate collaboration between IT security and operations teams, and to integrate the technologies and processes they use to keep systems and data secure, to reduce risk and improve business agility [1,4].

This paper presents the analysis of current state-of-the-art in the aspect of use of security intelligence for current software engineering processes and approaches. It presents the basic key elements and concepts of security intelligence, outlining its advantages when used for software engineering together with the prototype design for monitoring the security of a given software. The paper is structured as follows: Sect. 2 presents the key elements of security intelligence – the main concepts, terms and benefits. Section 3 outlines the related works in SecInt domain while Sect. 4 deals with the practical implementation of SecInt approach for current software engineering.

2   Key Elements of Security Intelligence

The concept of Security Intelligence can be further explained by understanding its key elements [3,5]. Organizations collect many types of information as part of their IT security and operational tasks. And here are the questions: How do you know if a given piece of information is considered a "security intelligence"? What are the features of intelligent security processes in IT organizations in various industries?

(1) Intelligent security is realized as real-time Real-time monitoring is a key aspect of security information gathering in today's high-tech IT organizations. In the past, manual browsing through historical log data was a tedious job of security analysts who used their knowledge to correlate event logs from across the network to better understand potential security threats. Today, IT organizations use technology tools such as Security Information and Event Management (SIEM) software to collect real-time security information.

Security Information and Event Management (SIEM) is software that aggregates and analyses activities from many different resources across the entire IT infrastructure. Collects security data from network devices, servers, domain controllers. This data then stores, normalizes, aggregates, and applies analytics to that data to detect trends, detect threats, and allow organizations to investigate any alerts. SIEM provides two basic functions:

- reporting and "investigating" security incidents,
- analysis-based alerts that match a specific set of rules that indicate a security issue.

The main features of SIEM systems are: threat detection, investigation, time to respond. Moreover, it is possible to distinguish also their additional features such as: basic security monitoring, advanced thread detection, forensics and incident response, log collection, normalization, notifications and alerts about the security threads and attacks, security incident detection, threat response workflow.

(2) Security Intelligence requires the collection, standardization and analysis of data Merely aggregating data from the IT infrastructure in the form of network, event and application logs is not enough to develop intelligent security. IT organizations use complex machine learning, pattern recognition, and big data analytics to sift through millions of logs from a variety of applications, translate aggregated data into a standardized human-readable format, and analyse data to spot attacks or vulnerabilities that a human can easily miss.

(3) Security Intelligence must be executable True security intelligence must be operational for the organization. The purpose of security analysis is not simply to collect and store additional data and information, but also to generate actionable data that drives the informed and targeted implementation of security controls and countermeasures.

(4) Security Intelligence must be useful Here we can ask a question: Can intelligence be useful in action, but not useful? When responding to them, we must remember that IT organizations are able to collect security information that does not correspond to a known vulnerability. Therefore, in order for a part of the safety-related information to be useful, it should significantly correspond to the vulnerability that can be secured by introducing new security rules or control mechanisms [6,7].

2.1 Concepts and Terms of Security Intelligence

The intelligent security discipline is full of jargon, acronyms that can be confusing - developers can find the acronyms such as CIA, CIO, APT, IoC, TTP, ... Of course, they have their own meaning as follows:

CIA (Confidentiality, Integrity, Availability) is a model used to guide the development of information security rules in an IT organization. In this context, the CIA stands for confidentiality, integrity and availability. IT organizations must maintain an IT security system that ensures data privacy, prevents unauthorized changes to data, and allows only authorized users to access protected or sensitive information.

CIO (Intent, Capability, Opportunity) represents three requirements for the existence of a security risk: intention, capability, and opportunity. A cyber threat occurs when a malicious actor wants to harm an organization (intention) that has access to the necessary tools (opportunity), and when there is a potential vulnerability that can be exploited (opportunity).

IoC (Indicators of Compromise) are indicators of compromise. They represent forensic data whose characteristics indicate or identify malicious activity or an attack on a network. SIEM tools can be configured to send alerts to security analysts upon an IoC detection, ensuring rapid response to cyber threats.

APT (Advanced Persistent Threat) is a cyberattack initiated by an organization aimed at securing long-term access to internal networks and data of an

IT organization. APT attacks are strongly targeted at a specific organization and are usually aimed at compromising a target and keeping it accessible for a longer period of time. An attack can infect an entire network, covering its traces, eventually stealing well-protected and valuable data.

TTP (Techniques, Tactics, Procedures) stands for "techniques, tactics and procedures". IoC refers to the cyberattack data signature. TTP is a direct reference to the methodology used by cyber attacks to launch an attack on a network. This should be understood as techniques, tactics, and procedures used by hackers to implement appropriate security controls to prevent data breaches.

2.2   Benefits of Security Intelligence

IT organizations use security information and event management (SIEM) tools to bolster their security intelligence collection efforts. There are three main ways IT organizations can benefit from faster and more efficient gathering of security information:

- improved compliance with regulations and standards,
- improved threat detection and removal,
- simplified security operations.
- reduction of internal fraud, theft and data leakage.

Compliance is a key force in IT security initiatives for organizations covered by HIPAA (Health Insurance Portability and Accountability Act of 1996), PCI DDS (Payment Card Industry Data Security Standard) or seeking ISO 27001 (international information security management standard) compliance. Tools that collect, standardize, and analyse log data can help IT organizations demonstrate compliance with a specific security standard. Detecting security threats and their removal are the core feature of SIEM tools. Today's best tools use machine learning and Big Data to correlate hidden events in millions of log files from across the web. This translates into faster threat detection and better response times in the event of an IoC detection.

IT organizations can automate many different types of security information gathering tasks using state-of-the-art SIEM tools. IT organizations can achieve this by simplifying their operations, reducing the cost of collecting useful and actionable cybersecurity data. Much more often we can hear about threats that have been made from the outside, but internal threats can be even more harmful. In the case of government software, even this could threaten national security. Thanks to Security Intelligence, organizations can identify and mitigate internal threats by detecting the threats such as: unauthorized access or use of the application, loss of data by sending to unauthorized destinations, application configuration problems, such as access exceptions privileged accounts (e.g. administrator), application performance problems (excessive use).

3   Related Works on Security Intelligence

To create the solution for software monitoring systems, it is necessary to analyse how current approaches behave. It is important to analyse the works on Security Intelligence and software monitoring systems.

The main purpose of work [13] is to discuss the use of artificial intelligence in application security. This technology is evolving more and more, and it's happening so fast that it's hard to tell if its impact is revolutionary or the next evolution. Some of the AI experts argue whether this new technology will be able to be used in IT security. However, it undoubtedly has potential in every industry sector. The fourth industrial revolution (Industry 4.0), in which we are now, is driven by artificial intelligence. Organizations produce endless amounts of data, both internally through business processes and externally through customer, supplier or user data. No human can analyse all this data to find a security breach. This is mainly because information systems are becoming more and more complex and data-driven. However, when they are combined with the right Big Data tools, artificial intelligence becomes much more effective in processing huge amounts of data, and then in detecting patterns and anomalies. What is worth noting, the more data is used to train the model, the smarter the neural networks become.

The author of paper [8] describes the key tools to combat threats such as theft of data from credit cards or other legally protected information. These are Security Intelligence, SIEM and Big Data for Security solutions. They can detect application usage and access patterns that are not visible to the naked eye, qualify threats to reduce false positives, or alert the organization when needed. The author points out that by combining a SIEM solution with security solutions requiring access to data, we obtain an almost perfect tool for data protection. After collecting logs about processes, users, infrastructure, they are further analysed by SIEM to identify certain patterns that may represent a threat. This type of situation shows that the use of Big Data gives a big advantage compared to generally available SIEM solutions. Massive amounts of data can be correlated with each other and analysed in much greater detail.

The main purpose of work [10] was to show how to better secure the computer systems. From the very beginning, the author describes how important data is stored in today's software. Once it was enough to observe the operation of the system and be aware of the use of its modern security features. Currently, internal security policies are being developed and SIEM tools are being implemented. Instead of taking a centralized approach to collecting and analysing logs from critical sources, software administrators must think like hackers to anticipate or respond to a system breach. Moreover, special attention should be paid to the fact that depending on the protected data, attacks may be carried out differently. Additionally, the administrator should be familiar with the most common attacks in order to be aware of what to expect when a system is compromised.

The authors of [9] present own solution, using existing SIEM Splunk software [12]. The concepts of software security, general assumptions of threat intelligence were described, and it was similarly stated that it is impossible to predict and prevent all hacker attacks. The Splunk and Splunk forwarder tools and the entire security analysis process were described using these tools, which is as follows: (1) Suspicious activities are associated with a given time window. (2) Detecting threats and preventing their use as a hacking attack. (3) Validation of threats through their visualization. (4) Ensuring that once a bug is fixed, no more room is left for future attacks.

4   Security Monitoring Software with Security Intelligence

Real-time security monitoring solution with the use of Security Intelligence should detect potential threats to the security of IT systems based on data collected from various heterogeneous sources, subjected to comprehensive analysis and processing thanks to big data, machine learning and security intelligence methods.

The analysis of such solutions showed the need to provide the following services: (1) Collecting application logs is one of the most basic functions of security systems. Without this, the analyst cannot check what happened in the monitored software. (2) SIEM tool must have a system of notifications and alerts that inform about any incidents of the administrator or analyst of the monitored application. In addition, notifications must also be able to be automatically prioritized, minor bugs can be overlooked, but system intrusions cannot be ignored. (3) The monitoring system should have an appropriate layer of view – data preview, because charts with data or maps of incident locations cannot be easily transferred on the console or set up an endpoint under which such data would be returned. 4 The efficiency of the system is primarily the speed of reaction to given threats – this is a very important feature of the proposed solution, because if the system does not react quickly enough, the longer it will be exposed to danger from the attacker. (5) The last important service is the artificial intelligence module, containing a set of appropriate algorithms, including a classification algorithm based on the collected logs, an anomaly detection algorithm and an intrusion detection algorithm Based on the logs of individual users, the system is able to learn them will keep. Thanks to this, when suspicious behaviour is detected, the account of such a user can be blocked, and appropriate alerts will be sent to data administrators.

The prototype of proposed solution of the SIEM type system consists of five components (Fig. 1):

- Database – PostgreSQL database – storing all data required for system operation. It contains, among others, user data, notifications, logs from the monitored application, configuration of the module sending notifications.
- View – application view, which is designed to display notifications, events from the monitored application and the configuration of entire monitoring system.
- MailSender – component responsible for sending messages with security notifications.

- Security Intelligence (Machine Learning) – component responsible for processing logs from the monitored application. It contains appropriate proposed artificial intelligence algorithms to support software security.
- Core – the main part of the system, responsible for the initial processing of logs, controlling the entire software, transferring information between individual components.

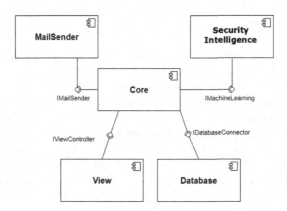

Fig. 1. Architecture of proposed solution of SIEM type system.

In the component responsible for intelligent processing of logs from the system, i.e. Security Intelligence, three algorithms have been implemented, which are designed to prevent intrusions, detect anomalies and an incorrectly functioning monitored application.

Abnormality Detection
The first algorithm responsible for detecting a malfunctioning application works on the principle of classification. After collecting logs for a period of one minute, the logs are filtered according to the logging level, the lowest levels will not be important from the point of view of the application's operation – logged errors and warnings from the monitored application are marked as WARN, ERROR, FATAL, and other logging levels (INFO, DEBUG, TRACE) are primarily to signal how the application is working at a given moment [11].

After the filtering of useless logs, classification and recognition of which module or part of the monitored application stopped working properly takes place. The monitoring system is able to notice that something is going wrong and notify the people responsible for fixing the errors. To a large extent, these are errors of the application developers, but sometimes a microservice ends up with an error and causes the application to malfunction. In both situations, outside intervention is required. If the vast majority of the captured logs concern one library/module, it will be reported as inoperative, and a notification will be sent to the administrator and the dashboard.

Anomaly Detection

The next algorithm is anomaly detection. Based on several weeks of system operation, it can determine certain trends and behaviours of individual users. Thanks to this, it is able to notice undesirable activity, such as, for example, working outside the specified hours of a given user or performing activities without first logging into the system. Then, his account can be blocked until the situation is clarified with the administrator. The algorithm works as follows:

1. The system learns the daily behaviour of each new employee who uses the application. It saves his login, work and logout data in the database for the first month.
2. After collecting the appropriate amount of data, the system generates a model that is saved in the database. Later, on its basis, the correctness of its work and whether there are any anomalies will be checked.
3. The software can now detect suspicious activity, such as logging in outside of normal business hours or doing much more at work. At the same time, it further corrects any changes in the employee's habits.
4. If suspicious behaviour is detected, appropriate alerts are sent to the administrator (mail, dashboard), and the system additionally sends information to the appropriate topic of the message broker that the monitored application can handle and block this user for time to explain the situation.

The following listing shows the operation of the entire anomaly detection algorithm (it should be assumed that the logs have already been downloaded and pre-processed):

```
Filter logs containing user data or login/logout attempts
For every user
Filter this user's logs
Sort by date
If the database contains a trained model:
If the data matches the model
Update the model
Go further
If the data does not match the model
Send notification
Block the user
Go to the next user
If the database does not contain a model:
If user logs are shorter than 20 entries
Add a new temporary model
If user logs are not shorter than 20 entries
Add a new model
Go to the next user
```

Intrusion Detection

The last part of the Security Intelligence module is the intrusion detection algorithm. The monitored application must properly send data regarding the connection with it. The components of entire intrusion detection process are based on several important parts.

The first is to check for repetitive actions. Typically, when an attacker fails to access a desired resource the first time, more attempts follow. Thanks to such action, the system is able to notice that there is an attempt to access data several times and it is necessary to react. The problem will only occur if the intruder manages to access the protected resource the first time. Then such action cannot be detected in this way.

Similar to the verification of recurring actions, the relevant rules for repeating events can be checked. In this case, it is most often used when trying to log into the system and to determine the number of such authentication attempts. However, it must be remembered that if the repetition rules are not properly defined, no notifications may be sent or false ones may be sent, indicating a potential attack.

For example, the attacker knows the user's login, but does not know his password. Based on another hack he managed to make on another website, he predicts that the same user may have a similar password here as well. After making several attempts to log in, he fails to crack the password and enter the system, because the configured SIEM blocks access after five failed attempts. If the number of allowed attempts were increased to 20, the attacker would most likely get into the application, and the data from it could be used by the hacker in his own way. Otherwise, the system could be configured so that even one failed login attempt would lock the user's account. Then, the employee, making a typo, would have his account blocked every time, which would make his work more difficult.

The last component of intrusion detection is checking for invalid commands. All exceptions that appeared in the logs and are related to errors regarding incorrectly sent query or response to requests are verified separately. For example, a hacker tries to access protected resources in a web application. Using a browser, he notices that the application sends queries to a given endpoint. Changes its parameters to force the download of data that is not allowed, for example, for an unregistered user. By changing the query, the server part of the application throws an exception, which is logged by the SIEM system. A notification is sent to the administrator to check whether the monitored application is working as it should and whether there may have been a data leak (Fig. 2).

The entire system was built to be universal and available for any type of application and possibly any technology. To check whether the built system works, several different test scenarios were developed. Then, on their basis, various types of logs were generated, which verify the correct operation of each of the Security Intelligence algorithms.

The first scenario checked abnormality detection. By incorrectly setting the server address, exceptions were generated in the code, which signalled a problem connecting to the PostgreSQL database. Then, after a minute, the SIEM system noticed that there are a lot of messages and exceptions in the logs regarding this database. The algorithm collected the most frequently occurring words, filtered the corresponding exceptions and sent a message about the incorrect operation of the monitored application. In another similar scenario, several different excep-

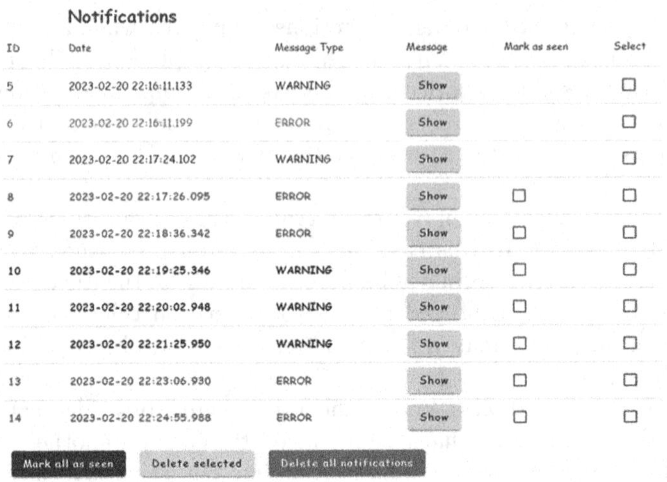

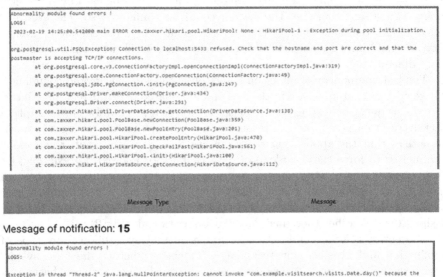

Fig. 2. View of proposed SIEM type system – notifications.

Fig. 3. Malfunction application monitored by SIEM system – notification.

tions were thrown, which indicate a wrong setting of some field when invoking the search for visits based on a date. This caused a NullPointerException to be thrown (Fig. 3).

In order to test the detection of anomalies, logs of an exemplary medical application were generated, the assumption of which is to book appointments

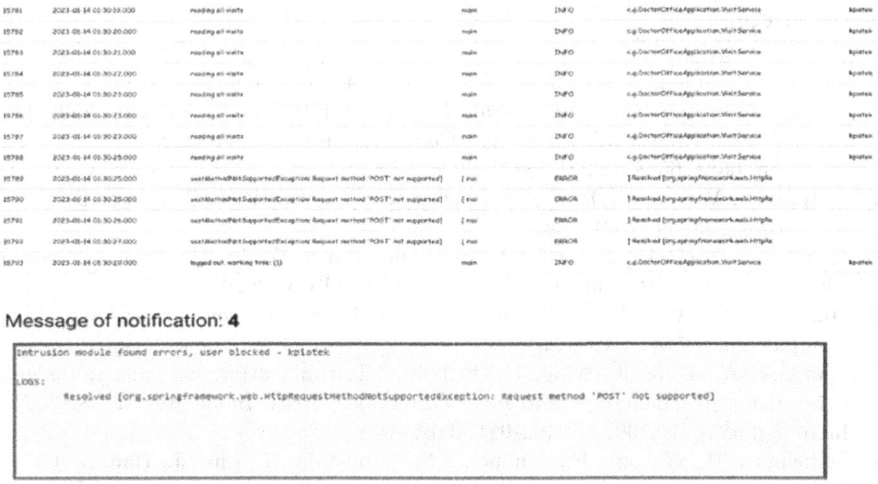

Fig. 4. Correct anomaly detection by SIEM system – notification.

and search for them by various employees. Users of this application work at different hours and for different working hours, for example, one works 8–16 and another 6–12. After a month of standard work, when all users had their habits recorded in the database, an unusual activity was generated, consisting in starting work at 3 am by an employee who should start his work at 8 am. The SIEM system correctly detected an unusual activity and blocked the user until the situation was clarified with the administrator.

Intrusion detection was tested with previously generated data, but this time, after a user logged into the system after several failed login attempts, a lot of queries were performed and exceptions of the type HttpRequestMethodNotSupportedException occurred at the same time. The SIEM system detected a hacking attempt, blocked the user and sent an urgent notification to the application administrator (Fig. 4).

5   Conclusions

The created SIEM system prototype is able to catch errors in the monitored application, detect anomalies of users who use it and possible intrusions into the system. Each time security is breached, alerts are sent to data administrators. In addition, we can view logs and notifications from the application, and in the event of suspicious behaviour of the user, block access to his account. The entire system can be further expanded with further components and artificial intelligence algorithms can be added to improve the security of the monitored application. In addition to the proposed three algorithms for detecting irregularities, intrusions and anomalies, it is possible to add other algorithms that will increase the system's sensitivity to external threats, for example detecting suspicious network traffic.

References

1. Jatain, D., Singh, V., Dahiya, N.: A contemplative perspective on federated machine learning: taxonomy, threats & vulnerability assessment and challenges. In: Journal of King Saud University - Computer and Information Sciences, vol. 34, no. 9, pp. 6681–6698 (2022). ISSN 1319–1578
2. Puthal, D., Mohanty, S.P.: Cybersecurity Issues in AI. IEEE Consumer Electron. Mag. **10**(4), 33–35 (2021)
3. Bertino, E.: Attacks on artificial intelligence [Last Word]. IEEE Secur. Privacy **19**(1), 103–104 (2021). https://doi.org/10.1109/MSEC.2020.3037619
4. Hu, Y., et al.: Artificial intelligence security: threats and countermeasures. ACM Comput. Surv. **55**(1), 1 (2023)
5. Qammar, A., Ding, J., Ning, H.: Federated learning attack surface: taxonomy, cyber defences, challenges, and future directions. Artif. Intell. Rev. 1–38 (2021). https://doi.org/10.1007/s10462-021-10098-w
6. Sedjelmaci, H., Guenab, F., Senouci, S.M., Moustafa, H., Liu., J., Han, S.: Cyber security based on artificial intelligence for cyber-physical systems. IEEE Netw. **34**(3), 6–7 (2020)
7. Sree, S., et al.: Ontology driven AI and access control systems for smart fisheries. In: Proceedings of 2021 ACM Workshop on Secure and Trustworthy Cyber-Physical Systems (SAT-CPS 2021), pp. 59–68 (2021)
8. Cates, S.: The evolution of security intelligence. Netw. Secur. **2015**(3), 8–10 (2015)
9. Eswaran, S., Srinivasan, A., Honnavalli, P.: A thresholdbased, real-time analysis in early detection of endpoint anomalies using SIEM expertise. Netw. Secur. **2021**(4), 7–16 (2021)
10. Howell, D.: Building better data protection with SIEM. Comput. Fraud Secur. **2015**(8), 19–20 (2015)
11. Logging levels explained. https://www.crowdstrike.com/cybersecurity-101/observ ability/logging-levels/ (2020). Accessed Jan 2023
12. Splunk Enterprise Security. https://www.splunk.com/en_us/products/enterprise-security.html (2020). Accessed Jan 2023
13. Talwar, R., Koury, A.: Artificial intelligence - the next frontier in IT security? Netw. Secur. **2017**(4), 14–17 (2017)

Examining Effects of Class Imbalance on Conditional GAN Training

Yang Chen$^{(\boxtimes)}$, Dustin J. Kempton, and Rafal A. Angryk

Georgia State University, Atlanta, GA 30302, USA
ychen113@student.gsu.edu, {dkempton1,angryk}@cs.gsu.edu

Abstract. In this work, we investigate the impact of class imbalance on the accuracy and diversity of synthetic samples generated by conditional generative adversarial networks (CGAN) models. Though many studies utilizing GANs have seen extraordinary success in producing realistic image samples, these studies generally assume the use of well-processed and balanced benchmark image datasets, including MNIST and CIFAR-10. However, well-balanced data is uncommon in real world applications such as detecting fraud, diagnosing diabetes, and predicting solar flares. It is well known that when class labels are not distributed uniformly, the predictive ability of classification algorithms suffers significantly, a phenomenon known as the "class-imbalance problem." We show that the imbalance in the training set can also impact sample generation of CGAN models. We utilize the well known MNIST datasets, controlling the imbalance ratio of certain classes within the data through sampling. We are able to show that both the quality and diversity of generated samples suffer in the presence of class imbalances and propose a novel framework named Two-stage CGAN to produce high-quality synthetic samples in such cases. Our results indicate that the proposed framework provides a significant improvement over typical oversampling and undersampling techniques utilized for class imbalance remediation.

Keywords: class-imbalance issue · generative adversarial networks · synthetic data

1 Introduction

Most classification algorithms assume that training data classes are distributed uniformly. When this assumption is questioned, regular algorithms suffer from the class-imbalance problem, i.e., their ability to predict minority classes decreases significantly. This well-known issue can also have a profound effect on training generative adversarial networks (GAN). So much so, that the authors of [1] state that traditional GANs cannot be employed to generate minority-class images from an imbalanced dataset. There have been few studies conducted to address this imbalance issue, one of which being BAGAN [2]. In the BAGAN work, an augmentation tool for generating high-quality images of minority classes

© The Author(s), under exclusive license to Springer Nature Switzerland AG 2023
L. Rutkowski et al. (Eds.): ICAISC 2023, LNAI 14125, pp. 475–486, 2023.
https://doi.org/10.1007/978-3-031-42505-9_40

was developed by achieving the following: (1) Using an autoencoder to initiate the GAN training, allowing the model to learn accurate class-conditioning information in the latent space. (2) Combining the real/fake loss and classification loss at the discriminator into a single output. Based on BAGAN, authors of [1] utilize the supervised Autoencoder and gradient penalty to solve the instability problem when images from different classes appear similar. Nevertheless, the aforementioned works attempt to address the imbalance issue at the algorithm level, either by employing Autoencoder to learn latent features or by modifying objective functions during the training procedure. In this work, we investigate the issue of class imbalance inherent to GAN training at the data-level, and develop a solution through the following contributions:

- Show how the imbalance in the training set has a negative effect on the performance of GANs.
- Show the ineffectiveness of common remedies for training GANs on imbalanced datasets, such as oversampling and undersampling.
- Propose a novel solution, Two-stage CGAN, to enhance the quality of samples from minority classes when training GAN models on imbalanced datasets.
- Show that the proposed framework can generate synthetic samples of higher quality than scenarios that use the original imbalanced set or sets that are rebalanced by oversampling or undersampling.

2   Related Work

In this section, we begin with an overview of the issue of class imbalance and the traditional methods used to overcome it. Next, we introduce the concept of a generative adversarial network (GAN) and its many variants, including the conditional GAN (CGAN) employed in this study. Additionally, we present Fréchet Inception Distance, or FID, as the standard measure for assessing the quality of generative models.

2.1   Imbalance Issue

Class imbalance typically occurs when there are more instances of some classes than others. It is common to use special remedies to address the class imbalance if it is present, since standard classifiers can be overwhelmed by the majority classes and neglect the minority ones. In typical class-imbalance situations, the minority class is the class of interest and therefore cannot be ignored. As a result, two approaches to overcoming the imbalance issue are established: either reduce the class skew at the data level or alternate the learning procedure at the algorithm level. As the representative method of data level, resampling is a classifier-independent technique for addressing imbalanced data, and it is accomplished in one of three ways: (1) Oversampling: selecting and duplicating samples of the minority class; (2) Undersampling: removing samples of the majority class; or (3) Hybrid: coupling the oversampling and undersampling methods when multi-class data are present [3]. The authors of [4] show that the classification performance improves when the above class-imbalance remedies are applied to a solar flare benchmark dataset, namely SWAN-SF [5]. However, random undersampling can jeopardize the preservation of important concepts because it removes the most samples from the majority classes [6]. Random oversampling is susceptible to the risk of overfitting because it neither introduces nor utilizes new data. To reduce such risks in the image domain, we can perform transformation-based data augmentation, a heuristic oversampling strategy for dealing with the lack of data. To achieve this, the current examples are subjected to one or more data transformations, such as random rotation, translation, reflection, cropping, blurring, sharpening, and hue adjustment. These transformations are not applicable in all circumstances. A reflection or affine transformation, for instance, would alter the chirality of a picture of a solar filament. In addition, it is challenging to apply transformation-based data augmentation to feature-based data points or sequential data such as time series and text data [7]. To deal with such a situation, SMOTE [8], a heuristic oversampling method, is introduced by constructing new synthetic samples between minority instances and their nearest neighbors of the same class, but it may suffer when the separation between majority and minority clusters is not always obvious, resulting in noisy samples [6]. In addition, the method is based on information from the local area, not the overall distribution of minority classes [9]. Generative Adversarial Networks provide an alternative method for addressing the lack of data by learning the underlying distribution of real samples and then generating new realistic samples [10,11].

In contrast to the solutions discussed at the data level, algorithm-level approaches are promptly implemented within the training procedures of the classifiers under consideration in three ways: (1) Classifier adaptation: adapting existing machine learning algorithms to a particular imbalanced dataset [12]; (2) Ensemble learning: combining several base models to construct an optimal predictive model. One example is dividing the sample set of majority classes into multiple small portions that are balanced with minority classes, and then, training multiple individual classifiers to classify the data, yielding the final decision through a voting mechanism [13]; (3) Cost-sensitive learning: designating a high misclassification cost to minority classes with the objective of minimizing the total cost [14]. There are a variety of approaches to the class-imbalance problem, but resampling methods that manipulate existing data or generate synthetic data to accomplish a balanced class distribution are more versatile than algorithm modifications. In this work, we therefore place greater emphasis on data-level solutions.

2.2 Generative Adversarial Network

Generative Adversarial Network is an emerging method for modeling implicitly the high-dimensional distributions of actual samples [15]. Originally proposed in [10], the GAN learns to generate plausible data by training two adversarial components, the generator and the discriminator. First, the generator is used to capture the data distribution by sampling random vectors from a latent space as inputs and producing samples that resemble the actual data. Next, the discriminator receives both generated and actual samples as inputs and estimates the probability that the input originated from the real data space. By simultaneously training the generator and the discriminator, a generator can generate progressively more realistic samples under the supervision of actual samples. This procedure is repeated until the discriminator is unable to distinguish between generated and actual samples. Depending on the actual data source, either the generator or the discriminator can typically be implemented by arbitrary multilayer neural networks consisting of fully connected networks, convolutional neural networks, and recurrent neural networks.

The vanilla GAN has limitations regarding the stability of model training and the diversity of the samples it generates [16]. Consequently, a number of studies have investigated the design of novel architectures to mitigate training issues and enhance the quality of generated samples. Deep Convolutional GAN (DCGAN) replaces pooling layers with strided convolutions (discriminator) and fractional-strided convolutions (generator) to enhance training stability [17]. The Wasserstein GAN implements the Earth-Mover distance to enhance learning stability and provide a meaningful learning curve for hyperparameter tuning [16]. Conditional information is incorporated into the Conditional GAN (CGAN) to enhance the quality of the generated samples and control the classes of synthetic samples [18]. Class labels are the most common type of conditional information.

2.3   Fréchet Inception Distance

Introduced in 2017, the Fréchet Inception Distance (FID) score is the current standard metric for evaluating the quality of generative models. Using the feature vectors derived from the Inception v3 model [19], FID calculates the distance between real and generated images. Specifically, the final pooling layer preceding the classification of output images is used to capture computer-vision-specific features of an input image. In practice, each input image is represented as a vector of 2048 units. Suppose that if we select 1,000 real samples and 1,000 synthetic samples, X and Y are feature vectors of the real and synthetic samples with the same shape $[1000, 2048]$. Then, multivariate FID can be computed based on the formulation in Eq. 1. μ_X and μ_Y are the vector magnitudes X and Y, respectively. $Tr(.)$ is the trace of the matrix, while Σ_X and Σ_Y are the covariance matrices of X and Y. Lower FID values indicate higher quality and diversity in synthetic samples.

$$FID = ||\mu_X - \mu_Y||^2 + Tr(\Sigma_X + \Sigma_Y - 2\sqrt{\Sigma_X \Sigma_Y})$$
(1)

3   Methodology

3.1   Recap: CGAN

In this project, we use the Conditional Generative Adversarial Network (CGAN), and there are two main justifications for doing so: To begin, CGAN allows us to control the category of generated samples, enabling us to generate samples of minority classes to alleviate the class imbalance problem. Second, when compared to the vanilla GAN [20], it can provide more stable and quicker training. Figure 1 depicts the design of CGAN. The generator's (G) ultimate goal is to produce output that is similar to the real data. The method begins by taking a random input vector (Z) and a conditional vector (C). The generator's outputs, known as generated or synthetic samples, are computed by feeding them through the LSTM and Dense layers pipelines.

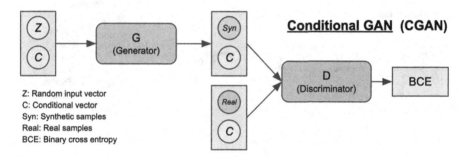

Fig. 1. This is the framework of the CGAN model, including components of the generator (G) and the discriminator (D). The inputs of the generator are random input vectors concatenated with conditional vectors. The inputs of the discriminator are either synthetic or real samples with conditional vectors. The binary cross-entropy is the criterion for optimizing the model.

A discriminator (D) is responsible for classifying inputs as either real or generated samples produced by the generator. The discriminator accepts as inputs both the real and generated samples. By inputting C into D, the discriminator determines whether the sample is generated or real and assesses whether the generated sample's category corresponds to its conditional information. Backpropagation is then used to adjust the weighting parameters of the generator and discriminator based on the binary cross-entropy loss calculated between the predicted and actual values.

3.2   Two-stage CGAN

After describing how CGAN is constructed, we present a new framework named Two-stage CGAN for addressing the class imbalance problem in CGAN model training. The proposed pipeline consists of three steps. To begin with, if the original set is unbalanced, we use random undersampling to reduce it to a smaller, more balanced set (i.e., Training-set-1 in Fig. 2) and then train the first CGAN model ($CGAN_1$) on it. After completing $CGAN_1$ training, we can generate synthetic minority class samples, resulting in Synthetic-set-1. The reason for performing undersampling and generating the Synthetic-set-1 dataset based on it is that we discovered that the $CGAN_1$ can generate synthetic samples of minority classes with acceptable diversity. In the intermediary step, the original set and Synthetic-set-1 are merged to create Training-set-2 in Fig. 2, a balanced and much larger set. This dataset is then used to train the second CGAN model ($CGAN_2$). Again, we generate synthetic minority class samples to construct the Synthetic-set-2. In the final step, the Original-set and Synthetic-set-2 will be combined to form the final training set (i.e., Final-set in Fig. 2) for subsequent applications.

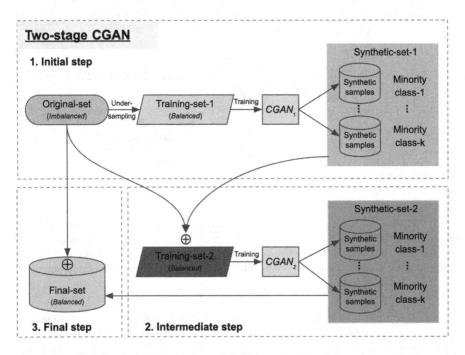

Fig. 2. The Two-stage CGAN framework consists of three steps: (1) undersampling Original-set and training the $CGAN_1$ model on it to form Synthetic-set-1 for minority classes; (2) merging Original-set and Synthetic-set-1 to training the $CGAN_2$ model to produce Synthetic-set-2 for minority classes; and (3) combining Original-set and Synthetic-set-2 to obtain Final-set for subsequent applications.

4   Experiments and Results

4.1   Dataset

MNIST is a benchmark database of handwritten digits that is frequently used to train and evaluate machine learning algorithms [21]. The original dataset consists of 10 classes, which are distributed evenly across 60,000 training images

Table 1. The table lists five datasets intended to assess the performance of CGAN training. A is directly taken from the original MNIST. B is produced by reducing the minority classes of $'3'$ and $'4'$ to 500 and 100 samples, respectively, based on A. C and D are obtained by employing oversampling and undersampling strategies to B. E is the dataset that has been augmented on B using Two-stage CGAN.

Dataset	Type	Digit Class					Total
		0	1	2	3	4	
A	Balanced	5923	6742	5958	6131	5842	30596
B	Imbalanced	5923	6742	5958	500	100	19223
C	Oversampling (OS)	5923	6742	5958	6000	6000	30623
D	Undersampling (US)	100	100	100	100	100	500
E	Two-stage CGAN	5923	6742	5958	6000	6000	30623

and 10,000 testing images. For the sake of brevity, we use only a subset of the original MNIST and perform the necessary resampling operations to meet the experimental requirements. More specifically, we select five digit classes out of ten, and we consider $\{'0','1','2'\}$ to be the majority classes and $\{'3','4'\}$ to be the minority classes, as shown in Table 1. In addition, we manually generate five different datasets to evaluate the efficacy of CGAN models trained on them. The dataset-A is derived directly from the original MNIST, which has approximately 6,000 samples per class and is balanced. The dataset-B is created based on A by reducing the minority classes of $'3'$ and $'4'$ to 500 and 100 samples, respectively. We chose 500 and 100 because we wish to examine two distinct imbalance ratios, which are approximately 1:12 and 1:60. If the assumption that the class imbalance issue affects the performance of CGAN models holds true, we consider two common resampling strategies in practice: oversampling and undersampling. The dataset C is created by duplicating and rebalancing existing samples of classes $'3'$ and $'4'$ with majority classes. We can also determine if the overfitting issue resulting from oversampling the underrepresented classes is affecting the sample quality. The dataset D is generated by removing the existing samples of majority classes to align their size with the size of minority classes. The dataset E differs from the dataset C in that it was oversampled using Two-stage CGAN, a newly devised framework. Instead of duplicating existing samples, we rebalance the dataset by adding 5,500 and 5,900 synthetic samples, respectively, to the minority classes of $'3'$ and $'4'$.

4.2 Experimental Settings

We evaluate the performance of CGAN model with the same hyper-parameter configuration across different experiments, setting the latent space dimension to 3, the learning rates to 0.1, the batch size to 32, and the LSTM hidden size of 100. The models were trained with 500 epochs. Empirically, we use the Adam Optimizer for the generator and the Gradient Descent Optimizer for the discriminator. The CGAN model is implemented based on the TensorFlow 2.1 library [22].

For the sake of simplicity, we only display the FID score distribution of the CGAN trained on dataset-A in Fig. 3 when performing model selection based on FID scores. We review the checkpoints every 25 epochs, between the 200th and 500th epochs. We conclude that the 300th epoch is a reasonable option given the trade-off between performance and computational cost. We use the 300th checkpoint in evaluation with experiments A, B, C, and E because the dataset size variation is insignificant. Since the experiment D dataset is much smaller than other datasets, we repeat the FID-based model selection process for it, and we choose to use the 900th checkpoint in the evaluation that follows.

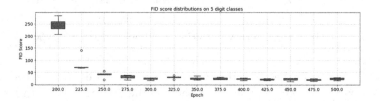

Fig. 3. The box plots depict the distributions of FID scores for five digit classes (i.e., $'0'$, $'1'$, $'2'$, $'3'$, and $'4'$) as calculated by the CGAN model trained on dataset-A. The x-axis represents the models per 25 epochs between the 200th and 500th epochs, and the y-axis represents the corresponding FID scores for each class. This metric is considered the selection criterion for models.

4.3   Results and Analysis

Using the setup shown in Table 1, we trained CGAN models on each of the five datasets separately. Figure 4 shows examples of the output from these models. By looking at the outputs in subplot (A), it is evident that a CGAN trained on a balanced training set is capable of producing acceptable synthetic samples for all classes. However, in the subplot (B), we discovered that the generated samples of class $'4'$ are of lesser quality, whereas we can generate samples of comparable quality for other classes using A. This confirms the assumption that the imbalance ratio in the training set can affect the performance of a GAN, i.e. that GANs give more attention to the majority classes in practice. In scenario (C), we observe that both $'3'$ and $'4'$ synthetic samples have low diversity and low quality. This may be because the random oversampling strategy typically involves duplicating samples exactly to expand the data space, which may lead to the overfitting issue. Therefore, balancing the training set by randomly over-sampling minority class samples cannot enhance the performance of the CGAN and generate high-quality synthetic samples. In (D), we can observe that the diversity of minority classes is greater than in (C), despite the fact that this strategy puts at risk the loss of important concepts. Insufficient training data is responsible for the lower-quality results. The subplot (E) depicts the synthetic samples generated by Two-stage CGAN, which enhance both quality and diversity simultaneously.

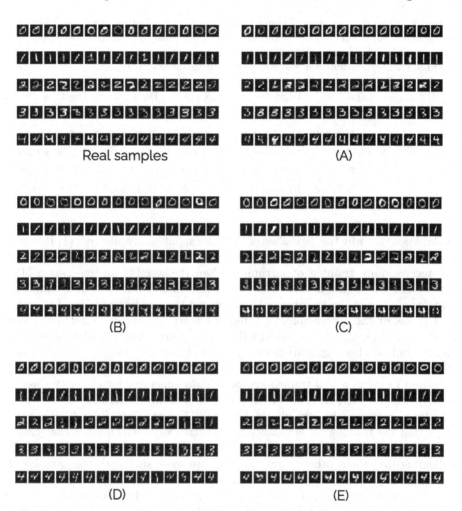

Real samples

(A)

(B)

(C)

(D)

(E)

Fig. 4. The diagram shows real samples and synthetic samples generated by CGAN models trained on five datasets listed in Sect. 4.1.

The FID score is then utilized to quantitatively assess the similarity between the real and synthetic samples. Specifically, 1,000 real samples per class are selected at random, and 1,000 synthetic samples per class are generated using CGAN models trained on five training sets. The results of the FID are shown in Table 2. Row-A displays the FID scores of five classes for a balanced training set, which can be interpreted as the baseline similarity between real and synthetic samples. Row B is the result of an imbalanced training set. We discovered that the FID scores for the majority classes (i.e., '3' and '4') are lower than A while the scores for the minority classes (i.e., '3' and '4') are higher than A, with means of 32.89 and 86.79, respectively. The '4' digit class, which has the greatest imbalance in our design (approximately 1:60), is especially affected. There are two possible

Table 2. The table provides a summary of the FID evaluation outcomes from five experiments. Each FID score is determined by comparing 1,000 actual and 1,000 synthetic samples of the same class. Five separate simulations are performed to calculate the final results, guaranteeing the correctness of the assessment.

FID$_{(mean \pm std)}$	Digit - 0	Digit - 1	Digit - 2	Digit - 3	Digit - 4
A	21.44 ± 0.32	15.81 ± 0.20	27.47 ± 0.36	26.62 ± 0.45	24.99 ± 0.55
B	15.28 ± 0.38	11.07 ± 0.26	15.11 ± 0.15	32.89 ± 0.23	86.79 ± 0.50
C	15.12 ± 0.19	14.16 ± 0.36	25.46 ± 0.44	51.75 ± 0.81	142.59 ± 0.59
D	55.36 ± 0.48	30.31 ± 0.28	59.81 ± 0.39	53.73 ± 0.57	45.32 ± 0.46
E	12.44 ± 0.28	10.03 ± 0.39	17.11 ± 0.52	10.31 ± 0.23	9.81 ± 0.19

explanations for why the digit class of '3' is not significantly affected: (1) Because the class of '3' is not the rarest, the weights in the generator for generating '3's receive more training opportunities than the weights for generating '4's; (2) because the digits '2' and '3' are naturally more similar, feeding sufficient samples of '2' into the training process can aid the training process of '3'. The FID scores of the oversampling strategy as a remedy for class imbalance are displayed in Row C. The increased FID scores of both minority classes (i.e., '3' and '4') indicate less similarity between real and synthetic samples. This is more evident for '4', indicating that oversampling cannot mitigate the data deficiency issue and result in a well-trained synthetic data generator for minority classes. Row D displays the FID score of using the undersampling strategy as the class imbalance remedy, which results in higher FID scores than Row A. However, given that the training set is balanced, the variances in FID are not that great. In D, the FID score of the digit '4' is 45.81, which is lower than in B and C, indicating that the synthetic samples of '4' are more similar to real samples of '4'. Therefore, we are considering utilizing this advantage to generate synthetic samples of minority classes to supplement the imbalance dataset (i.e., dataset B), and then training a final CGAN model on a larger and more balanced training set, yielding the result of Row E. Observing the FID results for Row E, we can see that it achieves the lowest FID scores of all classes, indicating the proposed framework provides a significant improvement over typical oversampling and undersampling techniques utilized for class imbalance remediation.

5 Conclusion

In this study, we show how the imbalance in the training set has a negative effect on the performance of GANs. In addition, we show the ineffectiveness of common remedies for training GANs on imbalanced datasets, such as oversampling and undersampling. We propose a novel solution named Two-stage CGAN, to improve the quality of samples from minority classes in two stages. Our experimental results show that the proposed framework can generate synthetic samples of higher quality than scenarios that use the original imbalanced set or sets that are rebalanced by oversampling or undersampling. In our future work, we plan to improve the algorithm in multiple ways. The first is to investigate heuristic-based undersampling techniques to preserve as much diversity as possible for the majority classes in the original set. The second is to extend the usage of Two-stage CGAN to time series data, including univariate and multivariate time series. A FID-like score is expected to be implemented using representation learning methods such as Autoencoder and dictionary learning to evaluate the quality of generated time series. Furthermore, we would like to investigate if adding more stages to the current framework would increase the quality and diversity of synthetic samples for minority classes.

Acknowledgment. This project has been supported in part by funding from the Division of Advanced Cyberinfrastructure within the Directorate for Computer and Information Science and Engineering, the Division of Atmospheric & Geospace Sciences within the Directorate for Geosciences, under NSF awards #1931555 and # 1936361. It has also been supported by NASA's Space Weather Science Application Research-to-Operations-to-Research program grant #80NSSC22K0272.

References

1. Huang, G., Jafari, A.H.: Enhanced balancing GAN: minority-class image generation. Neural Comput. Appl. 1–10 (2021). https://doi.org/10.1007/s00521-021-06163-8
2. Mariani, G., Scheidegger, F., Istrate, R., Bekas, C., Malossi, C.: Bagan: data augmentation with balancing GAN, arXiv preprintar Xiv:1803.09655 (2018)
3. Ahmadzadeh, A., et al.: Challenges with extreme class-imbalance and temporal coherence: a study on solar flare data. In: 2019 IEEE International Conference on Big Data (Big Data), pp. 1423–1431 (2019). https://doi.org/10.1109/BigData47090.2019.9006505
4. Ahmadzadeh, A., et al.: How to train your flare prediction model: revisiting robust sampling of rare events. Astrophys. J. Supplement Ser. **254**(2), 23 (2021). https://doi.org/10.3847/1538-4365/abec88
5. Angryk, R.A., et al.: Multivariate time series dataset for space weather data analytics. Sci. Data **7**(1) (2020). https://doi.org/10.1038/s41597-020-0548-x
6. Douzas, G., Bacao, F., Last, F.: Improving imbalanced learning through a heuristic oversampling method based on k-means and smote. Inf. Sci. **465**, 1–20 (2018)
7. Wen, Q., et al.: Time series data augmentation for deep learning: a survey, arXiv preprintar Xiv:2002.12478 (2020)
8. Chawla, N., Bowyer, K., Hall, L., Kegelmeyer, W.P.: Smote: synthetic minority over-sampling technique. J. Artif. Intell. Res. **16**, 321–357 (2002). https://doi.org/10.1613/jair.953
9. Douzas, G., Bacao, F.: Effective data generation for imbalanced learning using conditional generative adversarial networks. Exp. Syst. Appl. **91**, 464–471 (2018). https://www.sciencedirect.com/science/article/pii/S0957417417306346
10. Goodfellow, et al.: Generative adversarial nets. In: Proceedings of the 27th International Conference on Neural Information Processing Systems - Volume 2, ser. NIPS 2014. Cambridge, MA, USA, MIT Press, pp. 2672–2680 (2014). https://dl.acm.org/doi/10.5555/2969033.2969125

11. Chen, Y., Kempton, D.J., Ahmadzadeh, A., Angryk, R.A.: Towards synthetic multivariate time series generation for flare forecasting. In: Rutkowski, L., Scherer, R., Korytkowski, M., Pedrycz, W., Tadeusiewicz, R., Zurada, J.M. (eds.) ICAISC 2021. LNCS (LNAI), vol. 12854, pp. 296–307. Springer, Cham (2021). https://doi.org/10.1007/978-3-030-87986-0_26

12. Chen, K., Lu, B.-L., Kwok, J.T.: Efficient classification of multi-label and imbalanced data using min-max modular classifiers. In: The 2006 IEEE International Joint Conference on Neural Network Proceedings, pp. 1770–1775. IEEE (2006)

13. Tahir, M.A., Kittler, J., Yan, F.: Inverse random under sampling for class imbalance problem and its application to multi-label classification. Pattern Recogn. **45**(10), 3738–3750 (2012). https://www.sciencedirect.com/science/article/pii/S0031320312001471

14. Sun, Y., Kamel, M.S., Wong, A.K., Wang, Y.: Cost-sensitive boosting for classification of imbalanced data. Pattern Recogn. **40**(12), 3358–3378 (2007)

15. Creswell, A., White, T., Dumoulin, V., Arulkumaran, K., Sengupta, B., Bharath, A.A.: Generative adversarial networks: An overview. IEEE Sig. Process. Mag. **35**(1), 53–65 (2018). https://doi.org/10.1109/MSP.2017.2765202

16. Arjovsky, M., Chintala, S., Bottou, L.: Wasserstein generative adversarial networks. In: Proceedings of the 34th International Conference on Machine Learning - Volume 70. JMLR.org, pp. 214–223 (2017). https://dl.acm.org/doi/10.5555/3305381.3305404

17. Radford, A., et al.: Unsupervised representation learning with deep convolutional generative adversarial networks, CoRR, vol. abs/1511.06434 (2016)

18. Mirza, M., Osindero, S.: Conditional generative adversarial nets (2014). http://arxiv.org/abs/1411.1784

19. Szegedy, C., Vanhoucke, V., Ioffe, S., Shlens, J., Wojna, Z.: Rethinking the inception architecture for computer vision. In: IEEE Conference on Computer Vision and Pattern Recognition (CVPR), vol. 2016, pp. 2818–2826 (2016)

20. Brownlee, J.: Generative adversarial networks with python: deep learning generative models for image synthesis and image translation. Machine Learning Mastery (2019). https://books.google.com/books?id=YBimDwAAQBAJ

21. Lecun, Y., Bottou, L., Bengio, Y., Haffner, P.: Gradient-based learning applied to document recognition. Proc. IEEE **86**(11), 2278–2324 (1998)

22. Abadi, M., et al.: TensorFlow: large-scale machine learning on heterogeneous systems (2015). software available from tensorflow.org

Stochastic Model for Wildfire Simulation Based on the Characteristics of the Brazilian Cerrado

Heitor F. Ferreira[ID], Claudiney R. Tinoco[(✉)][ID], Luiz G. A. Martins[ID],
and Gina M. B. Oliveira[ID]

Federal University of Uberlândia (UFU), Uberlândia, MG, Brazil
{heitor.ff,claudineyrt,lgamartins,gina}@ufu.br

Abstract. As a result of an upsurge in the number of wildfires, several studies are underway to discover methods to mitigate the side effects of the flames on the ecosystem and in marginalised settlements. This work proposes an improvement to a stochastic model based on cellular automata that simulates wildfires. The main objective is to increment the model's representation based on the characteristics of the Brazilian Cerrado, enabling a better understanding of the dynamics of these wildfires, aiming to increase the speed and assertiveness in the decision-making of firefighting forces. We propose some improvements to the model, including the incorporation of additional states to represent the different phytophysiognomies of the mentioned biome, a novel approach to representing wind currents that redirect the flames, and a function that considers the air humidity of the region being analysed to influence the fire spread probability. Based on the experimental results, it was possible to conclude that the model achieves the expected objectives, effectively simulating the phenomenon under analysis.

Keywords: Cellular automata · Stochastic rules · Wildfire simulation · Cerrado Biome · Complex phenomena · Firefighting efficiency

1 Introduction

In recent decades, the occurrence of wildfires has exponentially increased, mainly due to the indiscriminate exploitation and extraction of natural resources, which results in the intensification of the greenhouse effect and climate changes. In some biomes, such as the Brazilian Cerrado, wildfires are a natural part of their life cycle [12]. However, these biomes are not able to withstand this unnatural growth of wildfires, and, in most cases, end up collapsing. Other aspects to consider are the immeasurable loss of fauna and flora, and the potential for these wildfires to advance into areas of human occupation [9], especially those of marginalised populations (e.g., indigenous tribes, *quilombolas*, *favelas* and riverside dwellers), which lack ideal physical infrastructures.

Authors are grateful to FAPEMIG, CNPq and CAPES support and scholarships.

L. Rutkowski et al. (Eds.): ICAISC 2023, LNAI 14125, pp. 487–496, 2023.
https://doi.org/10.1007/978-3-031-42505-9_41

Research studies are being carried out in order to identify effective solutions to address the problem at hand. In the work by Jazebi et al. [8], a review of wildfire management techniques is presented considering monitoring, surveillance, detection, suppression, and prevention. Simulation is another important technique as a mean to understanding the behaviour and effects of wildfires. By comprehending the evolution of the flames, proactive countermeasures can be implemented, thereby enhancing the ability to prevent and suppress fires and safeguarding human lives, natural habitats, and property.

Due to its simplicity and capability to predict a wide range of complex phenomena, including wildfires, the Cellular Automata (CA) [4] stands out as a simulation technique: pedestrian dynamics [2], coordination of swarm of robots [15], epidemiological analysis [11], among others. Define as a machine of transitions, discrete in both time and space, composed of lattices of identical regular cells, at each time-step, each cell evolves considering its local neighbourhood and according to a finite set of states and transition rules.

Accordingly, this work proposes an improvement to the wildfire simulation model proposed by Tinoco et al. [14], aiming to reproduce the characteristics of the Cerrado biome. Given the importance of this biome to the Brazilian biodiversity and the fact that it has been frequently affected by the increase in wildfires, a specific study considering its main characteristics becomes of great importance. Implementing the native flora of the Cerrado, the model maintains as its basis a CA with stochastic rules for fire propagation. Moreover, it takes into account not only the burning time, but other crucial characteristics during a wildfire, such as fire intensity, air humidity, the state of the vegetation before the fire, the presence of wind currents, and obstacles. Furthermore, this work contributes from an experimental standpoint by conducting a comprehensive set of experiments to analyse different parameters on the evolution of wildfires.

2   Related Literature

A brief literature review that includes some important works related to the application of CA in wildfires simulation is presented. Table 1 compares key characteristics of these models with our proposed model.

One of the seminal studies proposing a CA model to simulate fire spreading is the work of Chopard [5]. The model employs three states and stochastic transition rules to recover burnt cells and provide spontaneous combustion.

In the work of Yongzhong et al. [18] it was proposed the application of hexagonal tessellation spaces in the CA. Experiments allowed to conclude that the model can be useful in managing wildfires with heterogeneous characteristics.

Exploring solutions for Geographic Information Systems (GIS), in the work of Yassemi et al. [17], the authors proposed the integration of CA and GIS for the simulation of forest fires. The system presents different options for terrain, vegetation and weather. According to the authors, the model can be adapted to other CA-based spatio-temporal modelling applications.

Table 1. Detailed comparison between CA-based wildfire simulation models

Authors	Year	CA States				Prblty.	Wind	Topog.	Veg. recover
		Veg.	Fire	Obst.	Total				
Chopard et al. [5]	1998	1	2	0	3	Yes	No	2D	Linear
Yongzhong et al. [18]	2004	1	2	0	3	No	Yes	3D	No
Yassemi et al. [17]	2008	1	[0.0...1.0]	0	~	Yes	Yes	3D	No
Alexandridis et al. [1]	2008	1	2	1	4	Yes	Yes	3D	No
Ghisu et al. [7]	2015	1	2	0	3	No	Yes	3D	No
Xuehuaet al. [16]	2016	1	2	1	4	No	Yes	3D	No
Sun et al. [13]	2021	1	4	0	5	No	Yes	3D	No
Previous Model [14]	**2022**	**1**	**4**	**1**	**6**	**Yes**	**Yes**	**2D**	**Non-linear**
Proposed Model	**2023**	**3**	**4**	**1**	**8**	**Yes**	**Yes**	**2D**	**Non-linear**

Bringing the models closer to reality, a case study related to a forest fire (Spetses Island, 1990) was carried out in the work of Alexandridis et al. [1]. The authors proposed a simulation model using a non-linear optimisation approach to approximate its behaviour to that of the analysed event. The simulation results were promising in terms of the predictive capacity of the model.

More current works still present CA as an important tool for fire simulation models. In the work of Ghisu et al. [7], the authors proposed a model for the simulation of forest fires based on CA that applies a numerical optimisation approach to find values that correlate the model parameters. Simulations showed promising results, bringing the proposal closer to classical methods.

In the work by Xuehua et al. [16], the authors evaluated a set of factors that influence the spread of flames in forest fires. Among the analysed factors, the authors highlight combustible materials, wind, temperature, and terrain. Implemented through CA rules, the model demonstrates to be able to satisfactorily simulate the flame spread trends under different conditions.

Finally, in the work of Sun et al. [13], a model based on CA was proposed for simulating wildfires. The main objective was to improve the accuracy in relation to the spread speed of the flames. According to the results, the model demonstrated a good accuracy to simulate and predict fire spread.

3   The Cerrado Biome

The Cerrado biome is located on the central plateau of Brazil and it is the second largest biome in the country. In terms of size, it covers an area of ≈ 2 million km^2 (≈ 204 million hectares), which represents almost a quarter of the entire territorial extension [10]. Moreover, it is considered a "global hotspot of biodiversity" due to its flora, which contains around 12,385 different types of plants, and its fauna, with 320,000 animal species catalogued to date.

Concerning the phytophysiognomy of the Cerrado, i.e., the characteristics of its vegetation (as illustrated in Fig. 1), it can be divided into three major formations [10]: forest, meadow and savannah. Forest formations are characterised

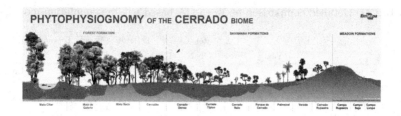

Fig. 1. Phytophysiognomies of the Brazilian Cerrado, with three main formations: meadow, savannah and forest [Adapted from [10]].

by a continuous vegetative canopy, having a predominance of trees, with a small amount of shrubs and undergrowth. It occurs near bodies of water or in places with a high density of nutrients. Due to its dense vegetation and water bodies, there is a greater presence of moisture compared to the other two formations. In contrast, savannah formations are characterised by a random distribution of trees, without the formation of a continuous vegetative canopy. It still contains shrubs, but with a larger volume of vegetation than the meadow formation. Finally, meadow formations have the least amount of vegetation in volume. It is characterised by the predominance of bushes and a rocky substrate.

4   Model Description

This work proposes an improvement to the wildfire simulation model proposed by Tinoco et al. [14]. The fundamental aspects of the previous model, including stochastic evolution, a non-linear recovery function based on an exponential probability, and the composition of a combustion matrix with wind currents, are preserved. In addition, this improved model incorporates heterogeneous vegetation states based on the phytophysiognomy of the Brazilian Cerrado biome and the influence of relative humidity on the fire dynamics.

Figure 2 shows the possible states for each CA cell. The states "initial-fire", "stable-fire" and "ember" (orange, red and dark-red, respectively) representing the fire states, the state "ash" (grey) and the state "water" (blue) have been defined in our previous model [14]. The states "meadow", "savannah" and "forest" (in green), represent cells with different types of vegetation of the Cerrado biome. These vegetation states do not influence each other, but can be influenced by the fire states, i.e., they are susceptible to combustion. Besides, each type of vegetation has a different amount of combustible material, with meadow having the lowest, forest intermediate, and savannah the highest amount.

To determine the probability of fire spread, it is important to consider not only the type of vegetation but also the air humidity. It has an inversely proportional influence on the probability of burning, i.e., the higher the humidity, the lower the probability that a cell to ignite. The effect of air humidity is captured by a factor ω determined by predefined thresholds, and it is incorporated into the ignition probability calculation, where: $\omega = 1.5 \ \ if \ \big((\gamma > 0\%) \ and \ (\gamma \le 25\%)\big)$;

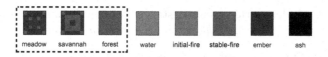

Fig. 2. States for the CA cells described by different colours. (Color figure online)

$\omega = 1.0$ if $((\gamma > 25\%)$ and $(\gamma \leq 50\%))$; $\omega = 0.8$ if $((\gamma > 50\%)$ and $(\gamma \leq 75\%))$; and, $\omega = 0.6$ if $((\gamma > 75\%)$ and $(\gamma \leq 100\%))$.

Air humidity also affects the duration of fire states. Specifically, in conditions where the air humidity is less than 30% ($\gamma \leq 0.3$), the transition time from state "stable-fire" to state "ember" increases by a factor of 5, whereas the transition time from state "ember" to state "ash" decreases by a factor of 3. This effect is due to the increase in flame intensity, which leads to faster consumption of flammable materials. On the other hand, if air humidity is greater than 30% ($\gamma > 0.3$), cells at state "initial-fire" change to state "stable-fire" after two time-steps. Cell stays at state "stable-fire" for four time-steps and change to state "ember", in which it stays for 10 time-steps before transitioning to state "ash", representing the absence of flammable material.

Each cell in the neighbourhood of the central cell has a probability of propagating the fire based on the formula of Eq. 1.

$$\phi_{i,j} = \beta - (\delta * r) \tag{1}$$

where: (i) $\phi_{i,j}$ is the probability P of the fire on the (i, j) position spread to the central cell; (ii) β is the base intensity of the flames; (iii) δ is the decay of the base intensity, the greater the decay, the more directional is the wind, if $\delta = 0$ there is no wind, creating a circular pattern; and (iv) r is the direction factor, representing the orientation ($\{cardinal\} \cup \{collateral\}$) of the wind current.

Cells change state according to transition rules, here defined as fire propagation rules. These rules employ a combustion probability matrix [14], which quantifies the probability of a given cell igniting through the propagation of fire from its closest cells (considering the Moore's Neighbourhood).

In addition to the transitions between fire states, the previous model implemented a transition from the "ash" state to a vegetation state, representing the capability of burnt cells to recover. Vegetation recovery is an essential process to consider, especially in biomes like the Cerrado, which are highly resilient to wildfires. Equation 2 [14] describes the recovery probability P_r of a cell x_{ij} on the 2D lattice. If a period of idleness is defined, then the probability is zero. Otherwise, the probability is equal to the square of the time steps counted since the cell x_{ij} turned to ash (ts_r) over 10 to the ath power. This exponential represents the longitudinal extent of a probability distribution.

$$P_r(x_{ij}) = \begin{cases} 0.0, & \text{if } idle \\ (ts_r)^2/10^a, & \text{otherwise, such that } ts_r \geq 1 \text{ and } a \geq 1 \end{cases} \tag{2}$$

CA Rules: Considering the characteristics presented, the fire propagation rules can be described as follows. *If the central cell is in the state:*

- *"vegetation"* and there are no cells in a fire state in its neighbourhood → maintain the same state;
- *"vegetation"* and a cell *'cl'* in its neighbourhood is in a fire state → there is a probability to change to the state *"initial_fire"*;

$$\{P(\textit{"initial\_fire"}) = \textit{combustion-matrix(cl)} \times \textit{local-fire-intensity} \times (\lambda)\}$$

- *"initial_fire"* (it is not influenced by other cells) → maintains this state for 3 time-steps and switches to the state *''stable_fire"*;
- *"stable_fire"* (it is not influenced by other cells) → maintains this state for 3 time-steps and switches to the state *"ember"*;
- *"ember"* (it is not influenced by other cells) → maintains this state for 10 time-steps and switches to the state *"ash"*;
- *"ash"* (it is not influenced by other cells) → it can change to the state *"vegetation"* according to the recovery function (Eq. 2);
- *"water"* → there is no interaction with others states.

Model Parameters (Values Obtained by Preliminary Experiments): fire spread probability ($\phi = P(c_{ij} \rightarrow c_{central})$, given Eq. 1); local fire intensity (*"initial_fire"* = 0.6; *"stable_fire"* = 1.0; *"ember"* = 0.2); dwell time of states with active fire (*"initial_fire"* = $2ts$; *"stable_fire"* = $4ts$; *"ember"* = $10ts$); recovery time-step ($ts_r = \{1..\} \parallel ts_r \in \mathbb{N}^*$); and, the exponent ($a = 6$).

5   Simulations and Analyses

The proposed model was implemented in the GameMaker Studio [6] and in the C programming language, in which the former was used for visualisation and the latter for mass processing. All simulations have run for 300 time-steps, while the mass experiments consist of 100 executions to ensure statistical significance, and different seeds to avoid outliers. Screenshots are composed of a CA lattice (128×128) in the same time-step intervals $ts = \{20, 50, 100, 200, 300\}$.

As the first simulation, a visual assessment of fire behaviour was carried out in the three types of implemented vegetation: forest, savannah and meadow. The objective of this assessment is to observe the differences in the proportion and speed of the fire spreading when the type of combustible material is changed. For this, the same variables were used in these three scenarios, and a spark was placed in the same spot (centre of the lattice) to start the fire. It is noteworthy that, the intensity of the fire in each vegetation type was defined based on an approximation of the natural characteristics of the Cerrado biome.

Figure 3 depicts the simulation of wildfires in different vegetation formations, where Fig. 3a represents forest, Fig. 3b savannah, and Fig. 3c meadow formations. The scarcity of combustible material in meadow formations leads to a slower rate of fire propagation compared to savannah and forest formations (see Sect. 3).

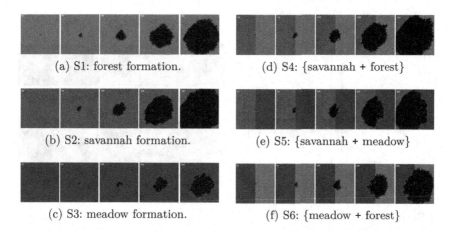

(a) S1: forest formation.

(b) S2: savannah formation.

(c) S3: meadow formation.

(d) S4: {savannah + forest}

(e) S5: {savannah + meadow}

(f) S6: {meadow + forest}

Fig. 3. Wildfire simulations with the three major groups of the Cerrado phytophysiognomy (forest, savannah and meadow) - disjoined (a–c) and merged (d–f).

As a result, upon reaching 300 time-steps, the extent of the burned area in the meadow formation (Fig. 3c) approaches the burning areas in the savannah and forest formations with 100 and 200 time-steps, respectively. In turn, given the higher concentration of moisture in forest formations, it is expected that the burning rate would be lower. This behaviour can be observed where, after 300 time-steps, the burned area of the forest formation (Fig. 3a) has not yet encompassed the entire analysed area, unlike the simulation in the savannah formation (Fig. 3b), approaching the real characteristics of the biome.

It is important to analyse scenarios that include more than one type of vegetation. Figure 3 illustrates wildfire simulations in areas that have two different vegetation formations: Fig. 3d combines savannah and forest formations, Fig. 3e savannah and meadow, and Fig. 3f meadow and forest. According to the simulations, one can observe that the behaviour of flames in savannah and forest formations (Fig. 3d) are more similar. This similarity is a result of a large amount of combustible material present in both formations. However, forest formations have a higher humidity rate, which contributes to a slower spread of fire. On the other hand, when meadow formations are present (Fig. 3e and Fig. 3f), there is a distinct difference in the propagation of flames. This can be attributed to the undergrowth nature of meadow formations and their low amount of combustible material. For instance, with 300 time-steps (Fig. 3e), almost the entire savanna region was consumed by the flames, while in the meadow formation, only around 50% of the region was consumed.

Humidity varies among different types of vegetation. Forest formations, for example, exhibit higher levels of humidity and moisture compared to savannah and meadow formations. Thus, it is important to assess wildfires under such conditions. Figure 4 illustrates experiments conducted to examine the impact of the humidity level on wildfires: a quantitative analysis (percentage of burned area (Fig. 4a)) and simulations in forest formations (scenario S1 with 20% humidity

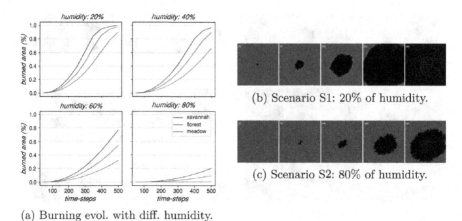

(a) Burning evol. with diff. humidity.

(b) Scenario S1: 20% of humidity.

(c) Scenario S2: 80% of humidity.

Fig. 4. Wildfire simulations varying the humidity coefficient.

(Fig. 4b) and S2 with 80% (Fig. 4c)). According to the charts, one can observe the influence of humidity on the proportion of burned area and the burning behaviour in different types of vegetation. Furthermore, simulations in scenario S1 (Fig. 4b), where the humidity is lower, nearly the entire environment was burned after 200 time-steps, in scenario S2 (Fig. 4c), where the humidity is higher, only about 50% of the cells were burned.

Another important analysis is the evaluation of burning edges (cells in fire states) and the proportion of unburnt cells. It is expected that the model can accurately mimic fire propagation resistance under high humidity conditions. This characteristic can be observed by comparing the burning edges of each simulation. In scenario S1 (Fig. 4b), in which humidity is low, the burning edges demonstrate a higher homogeneity. In turn, with a high humidity rate in scenario S2 (Fig. 4c), the burning edge becomes entirely irregular, and it is possible to observe areas where the flames have even been extinguished. Moreover, with high humidity rates, some cells within the burnt area did not ignite (in scenario S2 with 100 time-steps, several cells within the burnt area remained in a vegetation state), which is a striking feature of humid environments.

One of the main objectives of this work is to comprehend the behaviour of wildfires in the Cerrado biome, aiming to prevent and minimise the adverse impacts of wildfires. Hence, it is important to analyse real-world data. Figure 5 presents a simulation of a wildfire in the Pau-Furado State Park, a conservation unit located in the state of Minas Gerais, Brazil. Figure 5a shows an area of interest within the park where simulations were conducted. Figure 5b illustrates the time sequence of the wildfire simulation in this region. Simulations show the fire starting in the centre of the area and spreading radially, with the speed and intensity of scattering varying according to the vegetation formations. As forest formations are predominant in this region, the humidity rate strongly affects the intensity of the flames. An important characteristic to be highlighted is the capability of watercourses to function as fire barriers in this scenario.

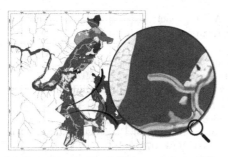
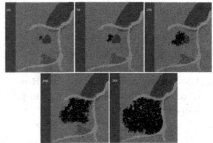

(a) Pau-Furado Park [Adapted from [3]].   (b) Simulation in the highlighted area.

Fig. 5. Wildfire simulation of an approximate reproduction of the highlighted area of the Pau-Furado State Park (Protected Cerrado area in Brazil).

6   Conclusion and Future Work

This study proposed an enhanced wildfire simulation model based on Cellular Automata to more accurately represent the unique features of the Brazilian Cerrado biome. The improvements include the following: (i) incorporating different vegetation states based on the phytophysiognomy of the Cerrado, allowing for the simulation of various fire spread scenarios; (ii) application of different humidity coefficients for the assessment of the intensity of the flames; and (iii) reproduction of a real Cerrado-dominated environment for simulating forest fires.

Based on preliminary analyses, it can be concluded that the proposed improvement to the wildfire simulation model produced the expected outcomes. The model satisfactorily simulated fire behaviour under different vegetation states and humidity coefficients. The representation of environments with various types of vegetation and their respective particularities, represents a significant improvement over the previous model, which only accounted for a single type of vegetation. Furthermore, the results showed the expected correlation between the spread of flames and low air humidity, whereas an inverse correlation was observed with increasing air humidity.

In terms of future work, we intend (i) to update the recovery function to take into account different characteristics of each area; (ii) to incorporate the influence of terrain relief, accounting for how the topography can impact the spread of wildfires; and (iii) to apply evolutionary computation in the optimisation of the model's parameters, taking into account real wildfire data.

References

1. Alexandridis, A., Vakalis, D., Siettos, C., Bafas, G.: A cellular automata model for forest fire spread prediction: the case of the wildfire that swept through Spetses Island in 1990. Appl. Math. Comput. **204**(1), 191–201 (2008). https://doi.org/10. 1016/j.amc.2008.06.046

2. Bandini, S., Crociani, L., Vizzari, G.: An approach for managing heterogeneous speed profiles in cellular automata pedestrian models. J. Cell. Autom. **12**(5) (2017). https://doi.org/10.17815/CD.2020.85

3. Bevilaqua, A.C.: Plano de manejo parque estadual do pau furado (2011). http://biblioteca.meioambiente.mg.gov.br/index.asp?codigo_sophia=13597

4. Bhattacharjee, K., Naskar, N., Roy, S., et al.: A survey of cellular automata: types, dynamics, non-uniformity and applications. Nat. Comput. **19**(2), 433–461 (2020). https://doi.org/10.1007/s11047-018-9696-8

5. Chopard, B., Droz, M.: Cellular Automata Modeling of Physical Systems. Cambridge Univ. Press (1998). https://doi.org/10.1007/978-0-387-30440-3_57

6. Games, Y.: Gamemaker: Studio (2014). https://www.yoyogames.com/gamemaker

7. Ghisu, T., Arca, B., Pellizzaro, G., Duce, P.: An improved cellular automata for wildfire spread. Procedia Comput. Sci. **51**, 2287–2296 (2015). https://doi.org/10.1016/j.procs.2015.05.388

8. Jazebi, S., De Leon, F., Nelson, A.: Review of wildfire management techniques-part I: causes, prevention, detection, suppression, and data analytics. IEEE Trans. Power Deliv. **35**(1), 430–439 (2019). https://doi.org/10.1109/TPWRD.2019.2930055

9. Lozano, O.M., Salis, M., Ager, A.A., et al.: Assessing climate change impacts on wildfire exposure in mediterranean areas. Risk Anal. **37**(10), 1898–1916 (2017). https://doi.org/10.1111/risa.12739

10. Ribeiro, J.F., Walter, B.M.T.: As principais fitofisionomias do bioma cerrado. Cerrado ecologia e flora **1**, 151–212 (2008)

11. Schimit, P.H.T.: A model based on cellular automata to estimate the social isolation impact on COVID-19 spreading in Brazil. Comput. Meth. Prog. Biomed. **200**, 105832 (2021). https://doi.org/10.1016/j.cmpb.2020.105832

12. Schmidt, I.B., Eloy, L.: Fire regime in the Brazilian Savanna: recent changes, policy and management. Flora **268**, 1–5 (2020). https://doi.org/10.1016/j.flora.2020.151613

13. Sun, L., Xu, C., et al.: Adaptive forest fire spread simulation algorithm based on cellular automata. Forests **12**, 1431 (2021). https://doi.org/10.3390/f12111431

14. Tinoco, C.R., Ferreira, H.F., Martins, L.G.A., Oliveira, G.M.B.: Wildfire simulation model based on cellular automata and stochastic rules. In: Chopard, B., Bandini, S., Dennunzio, A., Arabi Haddad, M. (eds.) Cellular Automata ACRI 2022. LNCS, vol. 13402, pp. 246–256. Springer, Cham (2022). https://doi.org/10.1007/978-3-031-14926-9_22

15. Tinoco, C.R., Oliveira, G.M.B.: Heterogeneous teams of robots using a coordinating model for surveillance task based on cellular automata and repulsive pheromone. In: IEEE Congress on Evolutionary Computation (CEC), pp. 747–754. IEEE (2019). https://doi.org/10.1109/CEC.2019.8790266

16. Xuehua, W., Chang, L., Jiaqi, L., et al.: A cellular automata model for forest fire spreading simulation. In: IEEE Symposium Series on Computational Intelligence, pp. 1–6 (2016). https://doi.org/10.1109/SSCI.2016.7849971

17. Yassemi, S., Dragićević, S., Schmidt, M.: Design and implementation of an integrated GIS-based cellular automata model to characterize forest fire behaviour. Ecol. Model. **210**(1–2), 71–84 (2008). https://doi.org/10.1016/j.ecolmodel.2007.07.020

18. Yongzhong, Z., Feng, Z.D., Tao, H., et al.: Simulating wildfire spreading processes in a spatially heterogeneous landscapes using an improved cellular automaton model. In: IEEE International Geoscience and Remote Sensing Symposium, vol. 5, pp. 3371–3374 (2004). https://doi.org/10.1109/IGARSS.2004.1370427

Test Case Generator for Problems of Complete Coverage and Path Planning for Emergency Response by UAVs

Jakub Grzeszczak$^{(\boxtimes)}$ (ID), Krzysztof Trojanowski (ID), and Artur Mikitiuk (ID)

Cardinal Stefan Wyszyński University in Warsaw, Warsaw, Poland
{jakub.grzeszczak,k.trojanowski,a.mikitiuk}@uksw.edu.pl

Abstract. Unmanned Aerial Vehicles (UAVs) can aid rescue workers during operational emergency response procedures in tasks such as communication delivery or aerial reconnaissance of the area. Before a UAV team starts operating in the natural environment, multiple simulations aimed at experimental verification of their paths' effectiveness are necessary. Simulations require demanding test cases that exhibit different types of problem complexity and are easily controlled by a simple set of parameters. We develop a model of the problem adjusted to the specific requirements of the optimization algorithm. Then, we generate a set of problem-specific benchmarks using the model and available statistical information about population density levels for the entire area of Poland. The proposed generator divides the selected area into convex regions with a given population density level. Depending on the parameter settings, it generates more than one map of convex regions from a single raw data. The simulation results show the diversity of the obtained test cases and their main features.

Keywords: Coverage Path Planning · Unmanned Aerial Vehicles · Terrain Coverage · Heuristic Optimization

1 Introduction

Reconnaissance and delivering services by swarms of UAVs for ground users in the case of disaster areas management, military operations, or any other scenarios when ad-hoc support is needed becomes a subject of increasing interest. In such a remote or dangerous field, UAVs' operational problems belong to several distant classes like connectivity problems, coverage or transmission parameters optimization, or path planning and navigation. Each requires a different environment model for developing respective methods and algorithms and finding solutions useful in real-world applications.

In this research, we assume that a swarm of UAVs works in a disaster area when the locations of the victims are unknown; however, the number of victims can be estimated from external sources of information. We have no contact with them because they are out of the base transceiver stations (BTSs) range.

© The Author(s), under exclusive license to Springer Nature Switzerland AG 2023
L. Rutkowski et al. (Eds.): ICAISC 2023, LNAI 14125, pp. 497–509, 2023.
https://doi.org/10.1007/978-3-031-42505-9_42

To help victims effectively, we need a path-planning algorithm that solves the complete coverage problem. Such an algorithm searches for UAVs' paths to find and contact all ground users while maximizing the number of them in the area over the running time, namely, a Prediction Based Path Planning Algorithm for Victim Detection Optimization (PBPPA). However, the first step of such an algorithm development is building a testbed where the algorithm's effectiveness can be tested and verified. Hence, we need to develop a model of the environment for the problem of UAVs paths optimization first. The model must consider all the goals, assumptions, and constraints imposed on the creators of PBPPA. In our case, the model concerns just the terrain with its natural features and the location of victims. Any other issues, such as UAV effective power management and communication constraints, are omitted.

When the model is ready, the next step is to generate test cases representing reliable and demanding benchmarks for PBPPA. We are interested in the test cases as close to natural environments as possible. Therefore, we use data on residents in a 1 km grid from the "2021 Population and Housing Census in Poland" published by "Statistics Poland". Raw data are an input for the test case generator developed in the presented research.

Since the test cases must fit the model assumptions and constraints, the proposed Test Case Generator for Problems of Complete Coverage and Path Planning (TCG-CCPP) requires non-trivial raw data analysis and transformation methods. In this case, we assume that PBPPA can easily find a path in a simple rectangle region using already known methods generating single spiral, zig-zag, or back-and-forth (boustrophedon) patterns [2,3,5]. Therefore, the optimization goal of PBPPA is finding just sequences of regions to visit in the area by UAVs of the swarm that maximize the number of already-found victims over time based on the prediction of population density in these regions. In most approaches to the problem of complete coverage and path planning, authors also started building the problem model with a decomposition of the area into simple, non-overlapping convex regions containing no obstacles [1,4,6–9].

A good benchmark for PBPPA evaluation represents a division of the disaster area into convex regions with a given population density level. The complexity of such a test case follows from the structure of the area decomposition into regions and their population density levels. Hence, the division into regions should not be random but reflect the distribution of population density in authentic villages and cities. The division is not a deterministic process. For two reasons, we can get more than one map of convex regions from a single raw population density map. First, the shape of both convex and concave raw regions obtained in the area depends on the applied number of density thresholds and the values of these thresholds. Second, the concave raw regions are unacceptable and have to be divided into several convex regions, which can be done in multiple ways. In this research, the novelty concerns a new model of the disaster area and the method of test case generation. In the experimental part, we implement a novel Test Case Generator, which produces a set of test cases based on the population density data for selected regions of Poland.

Section 2 presents the goals, assumptions, and constraints of PBPPA, which impact the model of the problem instances created by the Test Case Generator. Section 3 describes the source data and the main idea of their translation into representation in the model space. Section 4 contains pseudocodes and the description of the Test Case Generator. The experimental part of the research is described in Sect. 5. Finally, Sect. 6 summarizes the paper.

2   The Problem Model

The problem of achieving complete coverage of a convex region can be addressed through various known algorithms. PBPPA includes at least one of these algorithms; hence one can simplify the given path-planning problem to a combinatorial one optimizing just the order of visiting convex regions to minimize the length of paths for respective UAVs. Each path considers both the overall time of region coverage and the time necessary to traverse between them.

We aim to provide an area partition scheme that translates the entire input area into a series of smaller regions for PBPPA to work with. The resulting regions can differ in size or shape as long as they are convex.

PBPPA uses the surface area of each region to calculate the time required for a complete coverage traversal, assuming that in the given convex region, we can find a similar in-length solution for any pair of entry and exit points. Hence, the path trajectory within a convex region should not influence the estimated number of found victims over time. This requirement can be fulfilled when the considered region's population density is at least uniform to a reasonable degree. Finding appropriate density thresholds for regions' selection and classification is not a context-free task. Still, it depends on the population densities in the particular disaster area's farmlands, villages, and cities. In the following sections, we explore the impact of different accepted density thresholds on the generated list of regions.

With the following in mind, we model the UAVs' workspace as a set of rectangular regions of different sizes whose union exactly occupies the target area. Since the regions satisfy the convexity constraint, UAVs can explore them by simple motions, like spiral, zig-zag, or back-and-forth. In this way, the motion planning problem in our model is reduced to motion planning from one region to another. Moreover, the path has no strict adjacency requirements for the neighboring regions. A UAV can traverse between two regions directly through any point on a common boundary or by following a straight line between the two closest points of the region boundaries. The cost of such traversal is also considered during the PBPPA's path-finding process.

The regions get labels based on population density ranges defined by the above-mentioned density thresholds. The label assignment means that population density in the entire region strictly fits the range of respective density thresholds. Suppose the region's population density locally exceeds the associated threshold values. In that case, the region must be split into smaller rectangular parts, creating new regions with reassigned labels. The labels introduce yet another dimension to the representation of our model.

Finally, the rectangular shape of the regions is advantageous because a map of the population density of an area can be obtained directly from datasets containing numbers of residents in squares of a regular grid. It is crucial because the grid is a common statistical data format about residents. Moreover, resizing the grid square size in the input dataset, e.g., from 1-kilometer to 0.1-kilometer, does not invalidate the convexity of each region. Hence, we have complete control over the resolution of the problem instance, regardless of the actual area dimensions and resolution of the population density data represented by the grid square size.

3   Case Study of the Emergency Areas

The proposed model implementation converts the source statistical data into its discrete representation. To create our benchmark, we used the Population and Housing Census Dataset published in 2021[1] where Poland is divided into a 1-km grid of cells. To further study the layout of Polish cities, we extracted four areas with differently spread population densities. The selected areas varied in the number of densely populated cells and the overall shape of the population gradients.

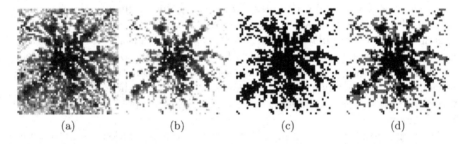

(a)   (b)   (c)   (d)

Fig. 1. (a) Input data area representation; (b) Step 1—denoised area representation; (c) Step 2—cells labels' binarization; (d) Step 3—assignment of new labels based on grid density levels.

To correctly translate the data into the problem's model representation, we wanted to ensure a relatively even spread of all available labels between the grid cells. Unfortunately, the extracted areas mainly consist of cells with different but relatively small or even close to zero population densities, which prompted us to pre-process input data. We transform raw data in three major steps (Fig. 1). In Step 1, we introduce a hard cut-off for values treated as empty cells, marking every cell with a density level below 200 people per cell with a label 0. Examples of such change are presented in Figs. 1a and 1b.

As seen in Fig. 1b, execution of Step 1 clears out a large part of the example area. In Step 2, we binarize the area based on the selected label 0 threshold

---

[1] Geostatistics Portal, https://geo.stat.gov.pl, the date of access: Dec 28, 2022.

(Fig. 1c). In Step 3, for all cells with non-zero labels, we create a histogram of their density levels. Then, we extract the necessary thresholds to evenly partition and label non-empty cells according to their population density. The numbers of cells in each group defined by the obtained thresholds are not strictly equal, but the difference is usually negligible. The example result of Step 3 is shown in Fig. 1d, where we defined only three labels.

The results of the execution of the three steps provide us with helpful information about the structure of the area. In this example, unsurprisingly, we can also see that the center of the populated area is denser than its borders. Splitting the data into more groups would reveal even more details. Nevertheless, the number of cells in each group has no value to us, as it is expected from how the previous step was performed. Instead, we compare the numbers of raw regions generated for each rank.

The observations varied depending on the number of defined labels or the method behind threshold extraction. With our approach, we wanted to examine which cells will change when the number of labels increases and how the number of raw regions in each group changes.

4   Test Case Generator for Problems of Complete Coverage and Path Planning

If the discrete model of the disaster area does not exist, it can be obtained using the procedure described in the previous section. An example emergency response procedure generating paths for the UAVs would be then defined by the following Algorithm 1. The steps introduced in lines 2–5 directly correspond to the procedure described in the previous section. Before PBPPA is called with the generated raw regions' list (line 7), we must satisfy the convexity constraint of each raw region. Hence, we introduce a separate step into this pipeline (line 6) called Concave Region Sub-Division Procedure (CRSD). The point of CRSD is to intercept the generated list of raw regions and substitute every detected concave region with a list of smaller, convex sub-regions. Technically, CRSD could be implemented as a part of PBPPA being an input data preprocessing step aimed at the problem representation adjustment to PBPPA requirements.

We approached the raw region sub-division with one goal: to maintain a relatively short length of PBPPA's input vector V and introduce minimal changes

---

Algorithm 1. Emergency Response Solution Generator

1: **procedure** EMERGENCY RESPONSE($location, n\_labels$)
2:     $PDM \leftarrow$ PopulationDensityMap($location$)
3:     $T \leftarrow$ CalculateLabelThresholds(PDM, n_labels)
4:     $PDM \leftarrow$ AssignLabels(PDM, T)
5:     $V \leftarrow$ MergeByLabel(PDM)
6:     $V \leftarrow$ CRSD(V)
7:     **return** PBPPA(V)

---

to the raw region's structure. It is important to note that any given concave raw region containing more than two cells can be divided in multiple valid ways that may lead to the same number of convex sub-regions. The shape and placement of the generated sub-regions can impact the solution quality of PBPPA, so we decided to construct an algorithm that exploits this fact. The solution generation scheme should not be biased towards any given grid cell, letting the raw region's features have the only measurable impact on the quality of the generated vector V. The main steps of CRSD (line 6 in Algorithm 1) are described in Algorithm 2.

Algorithm 2. Concave Region Sub-Division Procedure

1: **procedure** CRSD($raw\_regions$)
2:     $output \leftarrow$ **empty()**
3:     **for** raw_region **in** $raw\_regions$ **do**
4:         **if** isConvex(raw_region) **then**
5:             send raw_region to $output$
6:         **else**
7:             **while** raw_region is not empty **do**
8:                 $cell \leftarrow$ random(raw_region)
9:                 $bounds \leftarrow$ rect($cell$)
10:                **while** canExpand($bounds, raw\_region$) **do**
11:                    expand($bounds, raw\_region$)
12:                $subset \leftarrow$ withinBounds($raw\_region, bounds$)
13:                **send** $subset$ **to** $output$
14:                remove $subset$ from raw_region

Algorithm 2 handles the raw input regions one by one. Each raw region is evaluated (line 4), and if its cells form a convex polygon, it is left unchanged and pushed onto the output queue. Otherwise, we perform necessary actions that lead to the generation of smaller, convex sub-regions (lines 7+).

To divide a raw concave region into multiple convex ones, we randomly select a cell and define a bounding rectangle around it (lines 8–9). Then, we check if the current bounding rectangle can be expanded in any direction (line 10). To do this, we examine each cell neighboring the given boundary, and if all of them are a part of the considered raw region, the boundary can be shifted in that direction. If at least one border of the bounding rectangle can be expanded, we select a random boundary from this subset and expand it outwards by a single column or row. Once no boundaries can grow further, the loop is broken, and cells within the bounding rectangle are extracted from the raw region (line 12). The newly generated sub-region is then pushed onto the output queue as the new convex region (line 13). Lines 8–14 repeats until no other cells are considered as a part of the analyzed raw region.

This approach exploits the shape of the original raw region by relying on the fact that specific cells are more likely to be absorbed by the growing boundaries of cells in their proximity, even if they are not directly connected. At the same time, as the raw concave regions tend to have curved boundaries, expansion in one direction simultaneously enforces growth limits on the second axis. Thus, we are more likely to obtain a shorter list of sub-regions that vary in size instead of a longer one dominated by small sub-regions of similar size.

We evaluate the range of the possible results of Algorithm 2. To do this, we adjusted the CRSD procedure as shown in the Algorithm 3.

Algorithm 3. Minimum and Maximum length of CRSD output

1: **procedure** MINMAXCRSD(*raw_region*)
2:     *bmin* ← list of all *raw_region* cells
3:     *bmax* ← empty list
4:     **if** isConvex(*raw_region*) **then**
5:         **send** (*raw_region, raw_region*) **to** *output*
6:     **else**
7:         **for** *cell* in *raw_region* **do**
8:             **for** *bounds* in generateAllBounds(*raw_region, cell*) **do**
9:                 *cmin, cmax*   ←   MINMAXCRSD(outsideBounds(*raw_region, bounds*))
10:                *bmin* ← min(*bmin, cmin*)
11:                *bmax* ← max(*bmax, cmax*)
12:         **send** (*bmin, bmax*) **to** *output*

The recursive implementation of MINMAXCRSD in Algorithm 3 is not a part of the usual pipeline and does not corrupt the input vector for PBPPA. Instead, injecting MINMAXCRSD into the previous CRSD implementation allowed us to generate two vastly different input vectors simultaneously. Once again, if the considered raw region is convex, it is immediately pushed onto the output queue (line 5). This time we return two copies of this sub-region to signal that it is present in both the shortest and the longest input vector for this problem.

If the raw region is concave (lines 7–12), we also consider all of its cells, but their order gets irrelevant. Instead, we generate all possible rectangles enclosing each cell, one cell at a time (line 8). To do this, we consider all combinations of the growth vectors that could be generated starting from that cell and replace them with the versions expanded in all directions as long as they exist.

For every generated bounding rectangle, we sift out all of the raw region's cells inside the given bounds and recursively call the algorithm (line 9) using the remaining cells as the definition of a new abstract raw region to subdivide. Every iteration returns the shortest and the longest list of possible sub-regions for this region and is compared to the currently stored versions (lines 10, 11).

Because of the exponential nature of this task, and the pruning introduced to handle this issue, we do not keep track of all similar-in-length vectors. We also do not allow any such vector to replace the old one, as the exact shape of obtained sub-regions is not our concern in the presented research.

5   Experiments with TCG-CCPP

5.1   Methodology of Experimental Research

We selected four areas in Poland with differently spread population densities for our experiments: 1. Gdansk Bay area, 2. Lodz area, 3. Gliwice area, 4. Warsaw suburbs area. Each area is a square. For every area, we conducted four series of experiments in which the areas were represented as 15×15, 30×30, 45×45, and 60×60 grids. Grid cells were labeled according to their population density. We performed computations for 7 to 10 density levels. The range of labels started at 0 and ended at 6–9, depending on the test case.

In every case, we were interested in the relation between the number of convex and concave raw regions and how the number of convex regions increased after dividing concave raw regions into convex sub-regions. Since a concave region can be divided in multiple ways, we kept track of the minimum and maximum number of the resulting sub-regions.

Our computations were conducted on a machine with Intel®Xeon® Processor E5-2660 v3. In some cases, with grid sizes bigger than 45×45 and smaller numbers of population density levels, we did not get any results in a reasonable time of 10 days. These cases proved computationally too expensive for our equipment.

5.2   Outcome of the Simulations

Tables 1 and 2 present the numbers of convex and concave regions in the four test areas for all sizes and selected numbers of density levels (from 7 to 10). One can see that the number of regions differs between these four areas. This difference follows from different patterns of population distribution. However, in all four areas, most raw regions are convex. The percentage of concave raw regions gets lower when the number of density levels grows. For ten density levels, their share is always below 20%. It is obvious that the total number of regions is greater for larger grids. It is also usually greater for a larger number of density levels. However, in the Warsaw suburbs area, using a grid 15×15 with eight density levels results in more raw regions than in the case of nine levels. In the Gdansk Bay area, a grid 45×45 with eight density levels gives more raw regions than in the case of nine levels. In the Lodz area, using grids 45×45 and 60×60, we get more regions with nine density levels than with ten levels. One would expect that with more density levels, the number of regions of a particular density will be smaller, but this is not always the case. The number of regions of the highest density is usually smaller than those of a lower-density class.

Since dividing concave raw regions can be done in multiple ways, the number of resulting convex sub-regions can vary. Table 3 shows the minimal and maximal number of convex sub-regions remaining after CRSD, that is, splitting each of concave regions into a few convex ones. One can see that the differences between the maximum and minimum are usually bigger for a smaller number of levels. It is probably connected to the fact that concave raw regions are larger for a

Table 1. The numbers of regions in the areas of Gdansk Bay and Lodz for all sizes and selected numbers of density levels: ◇—convex regions, ⋆—concave regions

r	the Gdansk Bay area								the Lodz area							
	15 × 15		30 × 30		45 × 45		60 × 60		15 × 15		30 × 30		45 × 45		60 × 60	
	◇	⋆	◇	⋆	◇	⋆	◇	⋆	◇	⋆	◇	⋆	◇	⋆	◇	⋆
0	1	3	7	6	6	7	6	4	5	5	14	9	13	3	14	3
1	12	1	30	5	62	4	89	3	14	3	48	2	66	3	79	3
2	12	1	38	3	62	4	94	1	15	2	47	1	63	2	71	3
3	10	2	38	1	56	3	76	7	12	3	38	3	65	2	75	2
4	9	2	34	3	56	4	66	6	12	3	28	6	42	7	57	4
5	14	0	26	4	39	7	53	9	11	1	23	6	29	7	31	9
6	5	1	17	2	15	6	15	10	3	2	7	4	8	5	8	5
0	3	3	6	6	6	6	8	4	5	4	13	9	14	3	13	3
1	11	1	27	4	58	2	79	1	14	2	43	2	66	0	77	0
2	10	1	36	1	59	1	80	1	15	2	39	1	58	1	72	0
3	12	1	29	3	48	4	69	4	13	2	46	1	52	4	62	3
4	8	1	34	2	50	2	67	3	10	2	34	2	47	2	57	1
5	8	1	30	3	46	5	61	4	18	0	23	4	36	7	44	6
6	11	1	20	5	33	8	40	8	13	1	23	3	29	6	29	9
7	3	1	17	2	22	2	15	7	2	2	6	3	8	3	10	3
0	3	3	6	6	5	7	6	4	7	5	16	9	14	3	13	3
1	12	0	22	4	52	1	70	1	16	1	45	0	60	0	70	0
2	7	1	35	0	52	1	72	1	14	1	35	2	56	1	60	2
3	12	0	29	1	43	3	72	1	11	2	38	2	48	1	56	2
4	9	1	26	2	44	2	65	1	11	1	32	1	51	0	59	1
5	8	1	26	2	45	2	58	3	12	1	28	3	41	3	55	0
6	8	1	26	3	38	5	56	4	11	1	23	2	31	5	39	4
7	7	1	24	4	24	6	33	11	9	2	23	4	26	5	31	5
8	5	0	15	2	18	2	18	5	3	1	7	2	8	3	8	3
0	3	3	7	6	6	6	6	4	11	4	15	7	13	3	14	3
1	10	0	21	4	45	1	64	1	13	1	39	0	55	0	61	0
2	9	0	31	1	46	1	63	1	15	0	30	2	40	3	56	3
3	11	0	29	1	50	0	66	0	11	1	34	1	42	2	52	2
4	8	1	29	1	41	1	59	3	14	1	34	0	46	1	52	1
5	8	1	29	1	43	1	59	1	8	1	27	2	46	0	46	1
6	5	2	27	2	47	2	55	3	15	0	24	2	31	4	34	5
7	8	1	19	4	37	3	48	4	7	1	26	1	25	5	28	7
8	5	1	23	3	26	4	30	8	11	1	15	5	25	4	28	4
9	4	0	13	2	19	2	20	2	4	0	7	2	5	4	6	3

Table 2. The numbers of regions in the areas of Gliwice and Warsaw for all sizes and selected numbers of density levels: ◊—convex regions, ★—concave regions

r	the Gliwice area								the Warsaw suburbs area							
	15 × 15		30 × 30		45 × 45		60 × 60		15 × 15		30 × 30		45 × 45		60 × 60	
	◊	★	◊	★	◊	★	◊	★	◊	★	◊	★	◊	★	◊	★
0	20	5	40	20	52	27	55	23	8	5	20	15	26	19	—	—
1	21	1	63	4	121	7	188	7	15	2	50	10	89	16	—	—
2	22	1	55	8	122	5	187	6	10	4	55	10	118	7	—	—
3	21	1	59	7	124	7	183	6	14	2	42	10	91	11	—	—
4	22	0	59	6	108	7	146	17	18	1	38	10	83	13	—	—
5	12	4	49	7	76	17	124	18	6	3	34	7	53	13	—	—
6	9	2	23	9	40	15	45	21	4	3	3	7	10	8	—	—
0	20	5	42	20	50	26	54	24	9	5	21	15	26	19	—	—
1	18	1	53	4	100	7	165	6	14	1	43	8	77	14	—	—
2	19	1	52	4	105	6	163	6	16	1	60	5	103	5	—	—
3	23	0	57	5	112	4	161	7	21	0	55	4	98	7	—	—
4	12	2	55	3	101	9	168	4	22	0	51	5	87	9	—	—
5	18	1	41	7	101	6	137	8	15	2	33	9	70	11	—	—
6	9	4	51	5	83	11	99	18	8	1	33	8	53	10	—	—
7	9	2	24	7	36	15	47	17	1	3	6	9	5	9	—	—
0	19	5	41	20	48	27	55	24	7	5	20	15	28	19	32	23
1	18	0	47	4	93	6	145	5	11	1	36	8	75	10	125	8
2	16	1	50	3	101	4	153	3	12	1	56	2	94	2	134	2
3	19	0	50	2	96	6	148	5	14	2	48	4	89	5	126	6
4	14	1	50	2	107	3	152	2	15	1	39	6	84	5	115	8
5	16	0	58	1	93	3	121	11	15	1	42	4	73	8	115	11
6	15	1	41	6	74	10	131	7	11	1	32	6	60	11	84	14
7	9	2	51	3	81	8	93	17	5	3	31	7	44	12	65	13
8	7	2	22	6	34	12	42	18	1	3	8	10	8	8	15	9
0	19	4	42	20	51	27	54	24	8	5	21	15	25	19	33	23
1	16	0	42	4	85	5	135	4	9	1	36	6	73	7	117	5
2	18	0	49	3	96	2	136	3	13	0	48	1	87	0	126	3
3	16	0	48	2	96	1	136	3	13	1	46	3	90	2	126	2
4	18	0	42	5	95	2	140	2	15	0	47	2	84	3	115	6
5	9	1	47	2	87	4	141	1	19	0	43	5	77	6	116	5
6	18	0	40	4	85	3	120	4	15	1	35	6	68	5	94	10
7	11	2	40	3	68	8	110	8	8	2	30	4	56	8	74	15
8	8	2	42	3	76	6	86	13	6	2	29	5	45	10	61	12
9	6	1	18	5	32	12	41	15	1	2	9	9	11	8	9	10

smaller number of levels. Thus, there are more possibilities to divide them into convex sub-regions. However, there are exceptions; that is, a greater number of levels does not always mean a smaller difference between the maximum and minimum. For example, in the Lodz area, for the grid 60 × 60, for ten density levels, this difference is smaller than for nine levels.

Table 3. Minimal and maximal numbers of regions obtained by the CRSD procedure: [1]—number of ranks; [2]—length of CRSD input; [3]—length of the shortest CRSD output; [4] — length of the longest CRSD output

	[1]	15 × 15			30 × 30			45 × 45			60 × 60		
		[2]	[3]	[4]	[2]	[3]	[4]	[2]	[3]	[4]	[2]	[3]	[4]
Gd.B.	7	69	78	79	201	225	233	318	354	366	429	474	488
	8	70	78	79	213	239	244	340	370	378	439	474	485
	9	73	78	78	221	243	247	338	367	373	471	505	514
	10	74	82	82	240	263	267	369	391	393	487	516	522
Lodz	7	81	102	107	213	247	258	299	336	346	347	386	401
	8	96	109	113	230	256	264	319	355	364	373	403	417
	9	97	111	115	247	273	281	339	366	374	395	426	434
	10	104	113	114	251	274	282	338	371	379	389	423	432
Gliwice	7	116	126	127	349	403	414	649	732	752	948	1062	1084
	8	119	130	130	368	416	423	696	772	790	1006	1097	1117
	9	121	130	131	396	430	433	731	800	809	1053	1139	1157
	10	126	133	133	399	437	441	763	819	832	1098	1164	1178
Waw.	7	82	104	111	276	366	393	512	631	675	—	—	—
	8	105	115	117	329	399	417	558	663	689	—	—	—
	9	97	111	113	339	410	428	588	682	707	850	964	998
	10	108	118	119	364	423	433	640	718	737	906	1013	1046

6   Summary

In this paper, we propose a Test Case Generator for Problems of Complete Coverage and Path Planning (TCG-CCPP), generating benchmarks for the algorithms optimizing the work of a swarm of UAVs. These algorithms are identified in the text under the common name of Prediction Based Path Planning Algorithms for Victim Detection Optimization (PBPPA). The structure of PBPPA is not specified and does not influence the design of TCG-CCPP. However, the goals, assumptions, and constraints of PBPPA define its class of optimized problems and, consequently, the construction of test tasks generated on the output of TCG-CCPP. The generator starts with data concerning the population density distribution over the considered area. The area is represented as a rectangular grid. Its cells are labeled according to their population density level. Cells with the same density levels are joined to form larger raw regions. Since PBPPA requires convex regions, concave ones are divided into sets of convex sub-regions. PBPPA can then use the resulting list of convex regions.

We experimented with TCG-CCPP using Population and Housing Census Dataset's data published in 2021. For experiments, we selected four areas with differently spread population densities.

We investigated the numbers of raw regions concerning their population density. Our experiments showed that most obtained raw regions are convex in all cases—their percentage varies depending on the size of the grid and the number of density levels. Moreover, we observed the maximum and minimum number of convex sub-regions obtained from concave raw ones.

In experimental comparisons, benchmark users want to determine the algorithm performance for various problems. The proposed generator is parameterized and can create multiple problem instances for a given source data about population density in the area. They represent diverse UAV working environments and could be non-trivial test beds for optimization algorithms.

References

1. Basilico, N., Carpin, S.: Deploying teams of heterogeneous UAVs in cooperative two-level surveillance missions. In: 2015 IEEE/RSJ International Conference on Intelligent Robots and Systems (IROS), pp. 610–615. IEEE, September 2015. https://doi.org/10.1109/iros.2015.7353435
2. Cabreira, T., Brisolara, L., Ferreira Jr., P.R.: Survey on coverage path planning with unmanned aerial vehicles. Drones **3**(1), 4 (2019). https://doi.org/10.3390/drones3010004
3. Galceran, E., Carreras, M.: A survey on coverage path planning for robotics. Robot. Auton. Syst. **61**(12), 1258–1276 (2013). https://doi.org/10.1016/j.robot.2013.09.004. https://linkinghub.elsevier.com/retrieve/pii/S092188901300167X
4. Kapanoglu, M., Alikalfa, M., Ozkan, M., Yazici, A., Parlaktuna, O.: A pattern-based genetic algorithm for multi-robot coverage path planning minimizing completion time. J. Intell. Manuf. **23**(4), 1035–1045 (2010). https://doi.org/10.1007/s10845-010-0404-5
5. Khan, A., Noreen, I., Habib, Z.: On complete coverage path planning algorithms for non-holonomic mobile robots: survey and challenges. J. Inf. Sci. Eng. **33**(1), 101–121 (2017). https://jise.iis.sinica.edu.tw/JISESearch/pages/View/PaperView.jsf?keyId=154_1997
6. Li, L., et al.: Complete coverage problem of multiple robots with different velocities. Int. J. Adv. Robot. Syst. **19**(2), 172988062210916 (2022). https://doi.org/10.1177/17298806221091685
7. Lin, H.Y., Huang, Y.C.: Collaborative complete coverage and path planning for multi-robot exploration. Sensors **21**(11), 3709 (2021). https://doi.org/10.3390/s21113709

8. Nasirian, B., Mehrandezh, M., Janabi-Sharifi, F.: Efficient coverage path planning for mobile disinfecting robots using graph-based representation of environment. Front. Robot. AI **8**, 1–19 (2021). https://doi.org/10.3389/frobt.2021.624333
9. Tan, C.S., Mohd-Mokhtar, R., Arshad, M.R.: A comprehensive review of coverage path planning in robotics using classical and heuristic algorithms. IEEE Access **9**, 119310–119342 (2021). https://doi.org/10.1109/access.2021.3108177. https://ieeexplore.ieee.org/document/9523743/

Application of Artificial Neural Networks in Electric Arc Furnace Modeling

Maciej Klimas$^{(\boxtimes)}$ and Dariusz Grabowski

Department of Electrical Engineering and Computer Science, Silesian University of Technology, Gliwice, Poland
{maciej.klimas,dariusz.grabowski}@polsl.pl

Abstract. Electric arc furnaces (EAF) can cause various power quality problems in power systems. Because of that, it is important to investigate the electric arc phenomena and deepen the knowledge related to the modeling of such loads. This paper presents an overview of both shallow and deep neural networks applied for the purpose of EAF modeling. Namely, Multilayer Perceptron (MLP), dual MLP, Modified Nonlinear Autoregressive Exogenous model (NARX), and Long Short-Term Memory (LSTM) networks. Their topologies, advantages, and disadvantages are described and compared. The overall performance of the proposed models is analyzed and compared using some statistical measures.

Keywords: Electric arc furnace (EAF) · Multilayer Perceptron (MLP) · Nonlinear Autoregressive Exogenous model (NARX) · Long Short-Term Memory (LSTM) · stochastic modeling

1 Introduction

Electric arc furnaces (EAFs) are among the most important and widely used devices used for steel production and recycling. The principle of operation of the EAF is based on the electric arc phenomenon, which because of its extremely high temperature is used as a heat source for melting the scrap steel. Both ignition and later continuous burning of the arc are accompanied by random variations, and maintaining a steadily burning arc is virtually impossible. The electric arc itself is a strongly nonlinear phenomenon, which causes randomly changing distortions of voltage and current waveforms. These aspects of EAF operation cause various power quality (PQ) problems such as harmonics, voltage sags and swells, flickering, or unbalances. The aforementioned PQ problems can worsen their operating conditions by increasing costs, reducing service life, or causing serious faults. Therefore, it is important to mitigate such problems. Among PQ improvement methods there are Static Var Compensators [8], STATCOMs [6], Active Power Filters [23], and passive or hybrid filters [3]. However,

Research co-financed from government funds for science for years 2019–2023 as part of the "Diamond Grant" program and co-financed by the European Union through the European Social Fund (grant POWR.03.05.00-00-Z305).

L. Rutkowski et al. (Eds.): ICAISC 2023, LNAI 14125, pp. 510–521, 2023.
https://doi.org/10.1007/978-3-031-42505-9_43

their appropriate selection, placement, or even design and control require knowledge of the nature of the phenomena that occur in the power system, based, for example, on an accurate electric arc model.

As stated in the previous paragraph, it is necessary to investigate the EAF behavior in order to develop accurate models of such a load. Among the simplest methods there are characteristic approximations with linear piecewise, hyperbolic, exponential, hybrid hyperbolic-exponential functions [3,10] and others, e.g., cubic spline interpolation model [15]. More accurate models that include the dynamic behavior of the arc are most often based on Cassie, Mayr, and hybrid Cassie-Mayr models [22,24] or power balance equation models [17]. In order to further refine the models, it is important to include stochastic components similar to those observable in the real measurement data. In order to do so, various methods are applied, i.e. chaotic components [16], stochastic processes (e.g. white noise, ARIMA models, Markov models) [21] or [24]. The application of machine learning methods can make it easier to develop an accurate model without the need to use complicated statistical analysis. Artificial neural networks (ANNs) have been successfully applied to EAF modeling in the past. For example, in [20] authors used ANN with the hyperbolic tangent sigmoid transfer function to represent the arc length in the arc model, while in [4] the authors applied the radial basis function network combined with the lookup table. Deep learning methods are also applied in the field of EAF modeling, although most often not for the direct representation of the EAF characteristic. For example, deep learning can be applied to predictive compensation in power quality studies, as shown in [2].

This paper is a continuation and extension of the work related to the application of various ANNs for EAF modeling. Methods based on shallow ANNs have been the subject of previous work [12] and [13]. Among them, there are two solutions based on Multilayer Perceptron (MLP) model and one based on Nonlinear Autoregressive Exogenous (NARX) model. The deep ANN approach, based on Long Short-Term Memory (LSTM) neural networks, has also been applied for this purpose and its primary description is included in previous work [11] and [14]. In this paper, we summarize the proposed ANN-based approaches, compared them using an appropriate statistical measure, and provided an overview of the advantages and disadvantages related to their application in EAF modeling.

2   Artificial Neural Network EAF Models

The application of artificial neural networks in signal processing has many advantages. The high universality of ANNs facilitates modeling procedures and often simplifies the reflection of complex phenomena. However, the structure of the used ANN should be selected according to the problem considered. The wide range of available topologies and their complexity make it especially important to review methods for the modeling process, particularly in the case of phenomena as complex as the electric arc. The measurement data used for the

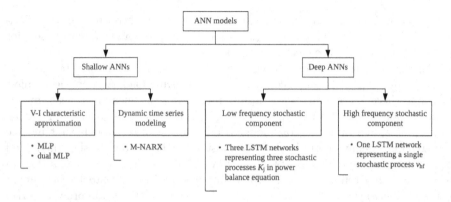

Fig. 1. Diagram presenting all ANN-based solutions described in the paper and their classification.

development of models presented in this paper consist of recordings of phase current and voltage waveforms from the melting stage of the EAF work cycle. We focus on this particular stage as the worst-case scenario in terms of the PQ problems. The details of measurement data have been described in [9]. Two kinds of stochastic components can be observed in the presented data. The first, a low-frequency stochastic component, is related to the changes in the general shape of the V-I characteristic. The second, high-frequency component, consists of high-frequency ripples visible in the measured voltage waveform, especially around its peak values.

Due to the issues described in the previous paragraph, we have proposed the application of several different ANNs to the modeling of the EAF. Proposed solutions vary in complexity and precision. We have applied three shallow ANNs, two for the implementation of the EAF model based on characteristic approximation and one for the dynamic modeling of time series. However, in order to include the stochastic components in the proposed models for better accuracy, we have also applied deep ANNs, for modeling of the low- and high-frequency components separately. A diagram presenting the ANN-based solutions described in this paper is shown in Fig. 1.

2.1   Shallow ANNs

Multilayer Perceptron
The first model from the group of shallow ANNs is a simple Multilayer Perceptron. It is a universal approximator, which is capable of reflecting nonlinear functions, however, more complex relationships can be too complicated for this network. The accuracy is limited especially in cases such as EAF modeling, in which the V-I characteristic, apart from stochastic properties, also contains a hysteresis loop. The MLP consists of an input layer, a hidden layer containing a selected number of units, and an output layer. Several different transfer functions have been tested during the development stage, which finally lead to the

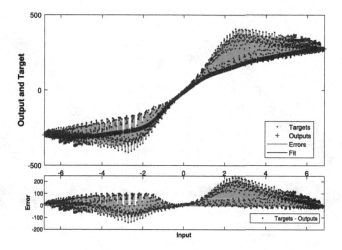

Fig. 2. Output and target data along with the error of the training set of MLP model.

selection of the hyperbolic tangent sigmoid transfer function. A final number of 10 hidden units has been chosen based on repetitive tests conducted with different sizes of the network. The knee point of the error plot has been found for 10 hidden units. Adding more units leads only to an increase in network complexity without performance improvement. Training has been performed using the Levenberg-Marquardt backpropagation. Measurement data have been randomly divided by samples into training (70%), validation (15%), and testing (15%) groups. The model structure remains as described in [13].

The MLP model is a single input, single output (SISO) system, which in this case uses the measured current data as input and voltage as output. Because of the simple structure of the MLP model, it is not particularly suitable for reflecting complex input-output relationships, such as the EAF characteristic. The fitting and error of the points obtained through the training procedure are shown in Fig. 2. As presented, the highest errors are related to the lack of reflection of the hysteresis loop in the approximated function.

Dual MLP

Due to high errors that occur especially around the widest fragments of the V-I characteristic loop, we have proposed an extension of the MLP model, namely two MLP networks, which were trained using the data divided into two parts. Due to the relatively low distortions of the arc current waveform, the current acts as a data division criterion. Samples that correspond to the rising edge of the current belong to the first category, while samples related to the falling edge belong to the second. The training, validation, and testing procedure for the dual MLP model remains the same as for a single MLP network. The only difference

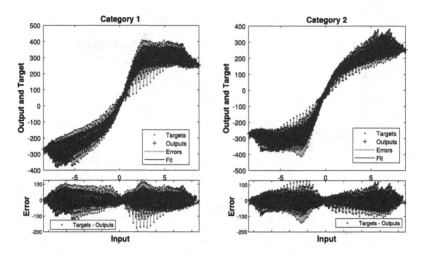

Fig. 3. Output and target data, along with the error of the training set of the dual MLP model, for data sets selected on the base of criterion (1).

is related to the division of the measurement data. The division criterion is as follows:

$$
\begin{aligned}
v_1 &= v\big|_{\frac{di}{dt} \geq 0}, \quad i_1 = i\big|_{\frac{di}{dt} \geq 0}, \\
v_2 &= v\big|_{\frac{di}{dt} < 0}, \quad i_2 = i\big|_{\frac{di}{dt} < 0}.
\end{aligned}
\tag{1}
$$

The fitting and error of the points obtained through the training procedure for both networks have been shown in Fig. 3. Division of the data allowed for separate reflection of two individual parts of the EAF V-I characteristic. As shown in the case of some samples, the error was reduced compared to the single MLP model, however, the overall performance is not significantly better.

Modified NARX

Both MLP-based models presented above lack the reflection of the dynamic changes in the EAF characteristic. In order to include such changes using shallow ANN, we have proposed a solution based on the NARX model. To do so, we have developed a grey-box version of the model which uses a differential equation describing the instantaneous power balance of the arc column. The power balance-based model has been proposed in the past in [1] and is implemented in many simulation programs. The power balance model is described by the following equation:

$$
k_1 r^n(t) + k_2 r(t) \frac{dr(t)}{dt} = \frac{k_3}{r^{m+2}(t)} i^2(t),
\tag{2}
$$

$$v(t) = \frac{k_3}{r^{m+2}(t)} i(t). \tag{3}$$

where:

$r(t)$ – arc radius,
$i(t)$ – arc current,
k_j – proportionality coefficients, $j = 1, 2, 3$,
n, m – parameters, $n = 0, 1, 2$, $m = 0, 1, 2$.

To use the above model for the purpose of the NARX-based model, we have applied a transformation of the equation proposed in [9]. It leads to a form in which the current can be considered as an input and the arc conductance as an output. That kind of modification allows for the separation of static nonlinear components from another linear dynamic one. Thanks to this procedure, the equation can be interpreted as an example of the Hammerstein-Wiener (HW) model, characterized by two nonlinear static blocks on both sides of the linear dynamic block, as presented in [9].

Both static nonlinear components present in the HW model can be implemented directly with mathematical expressions. Our proposal of application of the NARX network assumes that the linear dynamic block in the middle can be represented with this type of ANN. In order to better reflect the actual HW model based on the power balance equation, we modified the NARX network. The delays remained, however, we replaced the default sigmoid tangent transfer function with a linear one. In this way, the hidden layer output would only be a linear combination of the signals from the input and feedback loop. Next, due to the final output interpretation as an arc conductance, we added a rectified linear unit (ReLU) to the output layer to ensure that the final values are positive. This modified NARX network, which will be further referred to as M-NARX, has been presented in [13].

Due to the above procedure for model preparation, the training data had to be preprocessed. The arc conductance has been calculated based on Ohm's law, which, due to numerical accuracy, resulted in some outliers. The conductance waveform has been analyzed, and the outliers have been identified and removed using the Hampel filter [19]. Figure 4 presents exemplary data fed to the M-NARX network for training, validation, and testing. Data have been divided into blocks with proportions of 70%, 15%, and 15%, respectively. Training has been done using the Levenberg-Marquardt backpropagation in the open-loop configuration. As shown, the conductance waveform itself is accurately reflected with the M-NARX network.

2.2   Deep ANNs

The shallow models presented in previous subsections are either limited to the reflection of a single characteristic approximated from measurement data or to the reflection of some of its changes, with no stochastic aspects. In order to

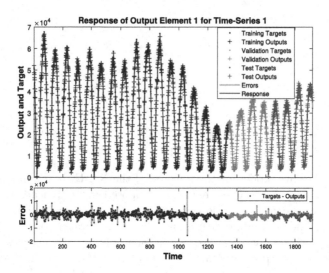

Fig. 4. Exemplary times series response of the M-NARX network for training, validation, and test datasets.

include stochastic components in the model, we have proposed the application of deep ANNs. Their features allow for the replication of complex relationships, which makes them especially useful for modeling the EAF.

We have developed a model based on the LSTM networks, focused on the incorporation of stochastic components into the model. The previous work [7], describes a method of analysis that assumes that the k_j coefficients present in the power balance equation can be represented with discrete time stochastic processes. In this case, we have applied three separate LSTM networks, which have been independently trained to replicate each of the k_j time sequences. After the training procedure, a standalone LSTM-based EAF model uses the current input to the power balance equation to calculate the arc voltage, while for every appropriate time step the values of k_j change according to the sequences generated with three trained LSTM networks. In this way, the V-I characteristic reflects low-frequency stochastic changes.

In addition to the LSTM layer itself, each of the networks also consists of a sequence input layer, then the LSTM layer, a fully connected layer, and a regression output layer. Each of the three LSTM networks has the same topology, however, they have been trained with different datasets. During the development of the model, we tested various sizes of the networks and eventually fitted them with 300 hidden units in the LSTM layer. The training process applied Adam optimizer with a learning rate that changed from the starting point of 0.005. The number of training epochs was also subject to tests and the best results were obtained with a stopping point at 500 epochs. The batch size was equal to 128. The measurement data have additionally been preprocessed by normalizing with standard deviation and mean value.

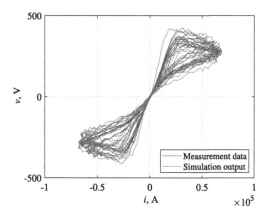

Fig. 5. Overall output V-I characteristic of the combined LSTM model of the EAF.

The first described LSTM model is only capable of reflecting the low-frequency stochastic component. In order to include the high-frequency component, we have added a second LSTM model, which is oriented only at the reflection of the high-frequency signal. First, the low-frequency components were filtered directly from the voltage signal using the high-pass filter with a cutoff frequency of 600 Hz. This high-frequency voltage signal has been used to train another, the fourth, LSTM network to replicate it. Various sizes of the fourth LSTM network have been tested, eventually it was fit with 250 hidden units. The training process applied Adam optimizer with learning rate that changed from the starting point of 0.005. The best results were obtained with a stopping point at 500 epochs. The batch size was equal to 128.

The overall output of a complete EAF LSTM model with low- and high-frequency stochastic components is calculated as the sum of the voltage obtained from the power balance equation supported with stochastic signals generated by the first three LSTM networks and a high-frequency signal generated with the fourth LSTM network. The addition is done with the assumption of linearization of the V-I characteristic around the operating point. The exemplary output of the complete LSTM-based model is shown in Fig. 5.

3   Comparative Analysis

Based on the outputs of all models presented in the previous section, we performed a comparative analysis. Because the models vary not only in their structure but also in the type of output signals, we have proposed a comparison based on the accuracy of reflection of the final output in the form of an arc voltage waveform. Moreover, because of the stochastic components included in some of the models, it was necessary to compute an objective statistical measure that would describe the accuracy with respect to the random variations of the signals. This measure is based on Cramer-von Misés statistic and has been described in

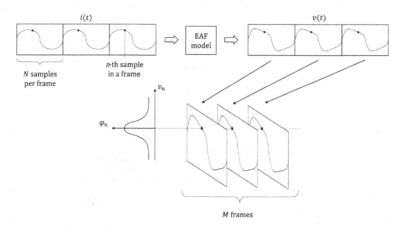

Fig. 6. Diagram presenting data preparation for the purpose of Cramer-von Misés-based statistical measure comparative analysis.

[14]. For the calculation of this measure, we have generated 10 s long voltage waveforms from each of the compared models. The data were then divided into periods and imposed on a single period. A diagram presenting the way to pre-process calculated voltage waveforms is shown in Fig. 6. For each of the n-th corresponding samples taken from every frame, a distribution ϕ_n is obtained. A set of N distributions characterizes every random variable contained in the voltage realization. Distributions ϕ_n have been calculated for measurement data, as well as for every EAF model considered in this paper. For each pair of distributions ϕ_n taken from measurement data and a chosen model, a Cramér-von Mises statistic has been calculated [5]:

$$W^2(n) = CM(\phi_n^{meas}, \phi_n^{sim}), \tag{4}$$

where:

$W^2(n)$ – Cramér-von Mises statistic for distributions of n-th sample taken from the measurement data and the selected model,

ϕ_n^{meas} – distribution of n-th sample taken from the measurement data,

ϕ_n^{sim} – distribution of n-th sample taken from data simulated by the selected model.

The calculations of this measure were repeated for each of the N samples in the frame. In this way, a series of statistics W^2 has been obtained, representing the quality of reflection of the modeled voltage variability with respect to the real measurement data. Lower values of W^2 indicate better conformity between measurement and simulated distributions. Additionally, a single value measure has been proposed as a median of the W^2 statistical time sequence, calculated for each model. A bar plot with the values obtained is presented in Fig. 7. In addition to the models described in this paper, we have also compared them with the constant coefficient models proposed by Ozgun and Abur in [18] and

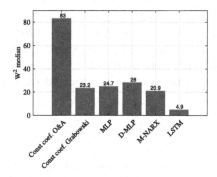
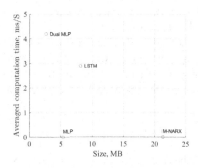

Fig. 7. Comparison of median of W^2 measure between proposed models and models with constant k coefficients (left) and the averaged computation time and size of the proposed models (right).

Grabowski in [9]. As shown, the LSTM-based approach outperforms the rest of the models. The MLP and dual MLP models have slightly worse accuracy than the constant coefficient model improved by Grabowski, however, the M-NARX model is slightly better.

We have also tested the size of the models as well as the average time needed for the calculation of a single output signal sample. All models have been designed and evaluated in Matlab software, and the computing infrastructure included a portable computer with an Intel Core i7 processor (4 cores, 1.8 GHz), 16 GB RAM, and the Windows 10 operating system. The results have also been presented in Fig. 7. The longest computational time of the dual MLP model seems counterintuitive, but is related to the need to check the criterion of the current derivative, whether to use the first or the second MLP model. The lowest memory size and computation time were obtained for the MLP model, however, its accuracy is unsatisfactory. Due to many auxiliary variables and additional data preprocessing stages, M-NARX model takes up the most memory. The LSTM model places itself in the middle of the remaining models.

4   Conclusions

In this paper, we have described several ANN-based models with different complexity for the purpose of EAF modeling. Three of the proposed solutions are based on shallow ANNs, that is, MLP, dual MLP, and M-NARX models, while two others are based on deep ANNs, that is, LSTM networks. The shallow models are characterized by the lowest accuracy, however, far better than in the case of the constant coefficient model proposed by Ozgun and Abur. Although their accuracy is similar to the accuracy of the constant coefficient model proposed by Grabowski. The incorporation of low- and high-frequency components into the model using LSTM networks resulted in a significant improvement in model accuracy. Despite the relatively complex topology of the LSTM model, its computation time and size remain better than those of individual shallow ANN models.

The results provided suggest that the best accuracy can be obtained with deep learning methods. The reflection of real measurement data can be further improved by analyzing the correlation between the power balance equation coefficients represented with LSTM networks. Investigation of such correlations is planned for future research. In addition, investigations are conducted on the usefulness of other shallow ANN topologies.

References

1. Acha, E., Semlyen, A., Rajakovic, N.: A harmonic domain computational package for nonlinear problems and its application to electric arcs. IEEE Trans. Power Deliv. **5**(3), 1390–1397 (1990). https://doi.org/10.1109/61.57981
2. Balouji, E., Salor, Ö., McKelvey, T.: Deep learning based predictive compensation of flicker, voltage dips, harmonics and interharmonics in electric arc furnaces. IEEE Trans. Ind. Appl. **58**(3), 4214–4224 (2022). https://doi.org/10.1109/TIA.2022.3160135
3. Bhonsle, D.C., Kelkar, R.B.: Design and analysis of composite filter for power quality improvement of electric arc furnace. In: 2013 3rd International Conference on Electric Power and Energy Conversion Systems, pp. 1–10 (2013). https://doi.org/10.1109/EPECS.2013.6713091
4. Chang, G.W., Chen, C.I., Liu, Y.J.: A neural-network-based method of modeling electric arc furnace load for power engineering study. IEEE Trans. Power Syst. **25**(1), 138–146 (2010). https://doi.org/10.1109/TPWRS.2009.2036711
5. Cramér, H.: On the composition of elementary errors. Scand. Actuar. J. **1928**(1), 13–74 (1928). https://doi.org/10.1080/03461238.1928.10416862
6. Dheepanchakkravarthy, A., Selvan, M.P., Moorthi, S.: Alleviation of power quality issues caused by electric arc furnace load in power distribution system using 3-phase four-leg DSTATCOM. J. Inst. Eng. (India) Ser. B **100**(1), 9–22 (2019). https://doi.org/10.1007/s40031-018-0351-7
7. Dietz, M., Grabowski, D., Klimas, M., Starkloff, H.J.: Estimation and analysis of the electric arc furnace model coefficients. IEEE Trans. Power Deliv. **37**(6), 4956–4967 (2022). https://doi.org/10.1109/TPWRD.2022.3163815
8. Čerňan, M., Müller, Z., Tlustý, J., Valouch, V.: An improved SVC control for electric arc furnace voltage flicker mitigation. Int. J. Electr. Power Energy Syst. **129**, 106831 (2021). https://doi.org/10.1016/j.ijepes.2021.106831
9. Grabowski, D.: Selected applications of stochastic approach in circuit theory. Publishing House of the Silesian University of Technology (2015)
10. Jebaraj, B.S., et al.: Power quality enhancement in electric arc furnace using matrix converter and Static VAR Compensator. Electronics **10**(9), 1125 (2021). https://doi.org/10.3390/electronics10091125
11. Klimas, M., Grabowski, D.: Application of long short-term memory neural networks for electric arc furnace modelling. In: Yin, H., et al. (eds.) IDEAL 2021. LNCS, vol. 13113, pp. 166–175. Springer, Cham (2021). https://doi.org/10.1007/978-3-030-91608-4_17
12. Klimas, M., Grabowski, D.: Application of shallow neural networks in electric arc furnace modelling. In: 2021 IEEE International Conference on Environment and Electrical Engineering and 2021 IEEE Industrial and Commercial Power Systems Europe (EEEIC/I&CPS Europe), pp. 1–6 (2021). https://doi.org/10.1109/EEEIC/ICPSEurope51590.2021.9584512

13. Klimas, M., Grabowski, D.: Application of shallow neural networks in electric arc furnace modeling. IEEE Trans. Ind. Appl. **58**(5), 6814–6823 (2022). https://doi.org/10.1109/TIA.2022.3180004

14. Klimas, M., Grabowski, D.: Application of long short-term memory neural networks for electric arc furnace modeling. Appl. Soft Comput. **145**, 110574 (2023)

15. Liu, Y.J., Chang, G.W., Hong, R.C.: Curve-fitting-based method for modeling voltage-current characteristic of an ac electric arc furnace. Electric Power Syst. Res. **80**(5), 572–581 (2010). https://doi.org/10.1016/j.epsr.2009.10.015

16. Marulanda-Durango, J., Escobar-Mejía, A., Alzate-Gómez, A., Álvarez-López, M.: A support vector machine-based method for parameter estimation of an electric arc furnace model. Electric Power Syst. Res. **196**, 107228 (2021). https://doi.org/10.1016/j.epsr.2021.107228

17. Marulanda-Durango, J., Zuluaga-Ríos, C.: A meta-heuristic optimization-based method for parameter estimation of an electric arc furnace model. Results Eng. **17**, 100850 (2023). https://doi.org/10.1016/j.rineng.2022.100850

18. Ozgun, O., Abur, A.: Development of an arc furnace model for power quality studies. In: 1999 IEEE Power Engineering Society Summer Meeting. Conference Proceedings (Cat. No. 99CH36364), vol. 1, pp. 507–511 (1999). https://doi.org/10.1109/PESS.1999.784402

19. Pearson, R.K., Neuvo, Y., Astola, J., Gabbouj, M.: Generalized Hampel filters. EURASIP J. Adv. Signal Process. **2016**(1), 87 (2016). https://doi.org/10.1186/s13634-016-0383-6

20. Samet, H., Mojallal, A., Ghanbari, T., Farhadi, M.R.: Enhancement of SVC performance in electric arc furnace for flicker suppression using a gray-ANN based prediction method. Int. Trans. Electr. Energy Syst. **29**(4), e2811 (2019). https://doi.org/10.1002/etep.2811

21. Torabian Esfahani, M., Vahidi, B.: A new stochastic model of electric arc furnace based on hidden Markov model: a study of its effects on the power system. IEEE Trans. Power Deliv. **27**(4), 1893–1901 (2012). https://doi.org/10.1109/TPWRD.2012.2206408

22. Ustariz-Farfan, A.J., Diaz-Cadavid, L.F., Cano-Plata, E.A.: Modeling and simulation of the electric arc furnace: the issues. In: 2021 IEEE Industry Applications Society Annual Meeting (IAS), pp. 1–8 (2021). https://doi.org/10.1109/IAS48185.2021.9677174

23. Vinayaka, K.U., Puttaswamy, P.S.: Improvement of power quality in an electric arc furnace using shunt active filter. In: Sridhar, V., Padma, M.C., Rao, K.A.R. (eds.) Emerging Research in Electronics, Computer Science and Technology. LNEE, vol. 545, pp. 1255–1269. Springer, Singapore (2019). https://doi.org/10.1007/978-981-13-5802-9_107

24. Xu, R., Ma, S., Zhang, M.: Modeling of electric arc furnace for power quality analysis. In: 2022 IEEE 3rd China International Youth Conference on Electrical Engineering (CIYCEE), pp. 1–5 (2022). https://doi.org/10.1109/CIYCEE55749.2022.9958980

Profiling of Webshop Users in Terms of Price Sensitivity

Eliza Kocić[1], Marcin Gabryel[1,2(✉)], and Milan Kocić[1]

[1] Spark Digitup, Plac Wolnica 13 lok. 10, 31-060 Kraków, Poland
marcin.gabryel@sparkdigitup.com
[2] Institute of Computational Intelligence, Czestochowa University of Technology,
Al. Armii Krajowej 36, 42-200 Częstochowa, Poland

Abstract. In this paper we present the results of our study on the possibilities of profiling online store users in terms of price sensitivity. As a result of the study, a model was developed to define three groups of users with a low, medium and high probability of making a repeat purchase. The model was developed on the basis of data derived from monitoring user behaviour when using the web pages of an online shop. During their subsequent visits to the website, information was collected to anonymously identify the user in order to register subsequent visits, the origin of the source of the visits, behaviour on the website and the fact of making a purchase. The results of the conducted study may provide useful information to webshop owners in order to better understand the behaviour of their customers and to adapt their offers, including discounts, according to the price sensitivity of a given user.

Keywords: Profiling users · Price sensitivity · neural network

1 Introduction

Over recent years, the development of online technologies has resulted in a significant increase in the popularity of online shops as a sales channel. With this growth, companies are increasingly turning to advanced technologies to monitor user behaviour in order to better understand user needs and preferences regarding purchases which users make. One method that has gained popularity in this context is user profiling.

User profiling is the process of creating a virtual representation of a user based on their behaviour and preferences. Profiling can be done on different levels, such as customer satisfaction, maintaining customer loyalty, demographic or contextual data. Profiling users in terms of price sensitivity is also an important issue for online shop owners [6]. It allows for a better understanding of customers' needs and expectations and tailoring the offer to their preferences. One of the applications of determining the likelihood of an online shop visitor making a purchase is the possibility of giving them relevant discounts. Webshops offer discounts to their customers, but it does not necessarily mean that all users have the same level of product price discounts. Here, the retailer is able to adapt a strategy that is suitable for them. One possibility is to assume that users who make frequent purchases can expect greater discounts. Another approach may consist in incentivising undecided customers to make a purchase with a larger amount of the discount offered to them.

Pricing decisions are not an easy task for a retailer. Price is not only the amount that customers pay to buy a product. According to consumers, price has the greatest influence on their purchasing decision. Most often, they make rational decisions taking into account their limited income and budget. The seller, on the other hand, will be able to stay in business if and only if they make a profit, which depends entirely on the price. When the seller needs to set the price of a product, they need to think about setting the right price, which should include the quality of the product, availability of its alternatives in the market and different types of product. If the price is not set adequately, consumers will show their negative sensitivity to the product by not buying at all or by buying the product in small volume. Different consumers behave differently when companies raise or lower the current price. Consumer pricing sensitivity is the most important thing that should be highly considered by sellers [6]. Therefore, understanding the consumer's degree of price sensitivity can help manipulate the price in such a way (for example, by setting discount levels) as to encourage purchase of the product and thus increase profits. User profiling also allows companies to employ better targeted marketing activities, such as offering personalised product recommendations and tailoring the product to individual customer needs.

In this article, we present the results of a study on profiling online store users in terms of price sensitivity. For the purpose of the experiments carried out, user behaviour during visits to one of the major Polish online shops was monitored. Information was collected on the number of previous visits by the user, data on the origin of the visit (e.g. from external advertisements), duration of the visit, time since the last visit, type of device (desktop/mobile), number of clicks on the website, change of tab in the web browser and information on scrolling through the page with the selected product and the purchase made. Users remained anonymous and were recognised by a random identifier found in a cookie/in cookies. Based on the collected data, a model was developed to identify three groups with different cent/pricing sensitivity, i.e. low, medium and high. Each group shows a different willingness to make another purchase. The profiles obtained were verified during subsequent shop visits of the surveyed users.

The following chapters discuss the details of data collection, information processing and implementation of the model built from artificial neural networks. The presented user profiling model uses artificial neural networks that return a certain level of probability with which a user will make a repeat purchase. We present a review of the literature that addresses a similar problem. In the paper, we also discuss methods for collecting and analysing user behaviour data, and describe the results of our model's experiments on real data. The results of our research show that user profiling can be a very effective tool for online businesses, allowing for a more efficient and personalised approach to customers. At the same time, our algorithm takes into account issues related to user privacy, which is becoming an increasingly important aspect at this time and age when we are observing a growing consumer awareness.

2　Literature Review

Literature mainly offers analyses of customer behaviour and the practices that online shops need to follow to persuade customers to make a purchasing decision. The paper [3] describes various features of an online shop that influence customer satisfaction when shopping online. These are mainly the promptness of complaint handling, photographs of products on offer, and various payment options. In [2] it was indicated that the satisfaction of online shoppers depends on product delivery, perceived safety, quality of information and product variety.

A description of customer behaviour was presented in [5] where the authors examined the importance that insurance customers give to premiums, insurers, recommendations of intermediaries and bundling strategies. The relationship between attributes and consumer price sensitivity was also investigated. Price sensitivity is influenced by the level of purchase commitment, package discounts and brand loyalty. Furthermore, brand loyalty has a strong influence on customers accepting bundled discounts.

Overview paper [1] collects the most important information on user profiling. The types of profiles obtained (static, dynamic), ways of user modelling (behavioural, interests, intentions), collecting user information with possible data sources and technical ways of user modelling are presented.

In paper [4], the authors provide an overview of user profiling techniques, including the use of demographic, behavioural and contextual data. The paper also discusses the challenges of user profiling, such as data privacy, data quality and scalability. The paper also presents solutions to these challenges, such as the use of machine learning algorithms and data anonymisation techniques.

Paper [6] reviews the literature focusing on answering the question of how consumers show price sensitivity when making product purchase decisions. Consumer price sensitivity has a significant impact on product popularity, as most product purchasing decisions are made based on price rather than brand or availability.

The authors in [7] describe how profiling users and understanding their browsing behaviour is key to improving shopping experience and maximising sales revenue. In the paper, the authors, based on a monthly compilation of data from 2 million users and 67 million purchase and browsing logs, seek to understand how users browse and purchase products and how these behaviours are different.

In paper [8], a neural network model was proposed to predict purchases in active user sessions in an online shop. The training and evaluation of the neural network was carried out using a set of user sessions reconstructed from server log data at the level of HTTP requests: the number of web pages opened by a given user, the duration of the session (in seconds), the average time per page (in seconds), or the activity in terms of operations such as logging in, adding an item to the shopping cart, and finalising the purchase transaction (i.e. confirming the order). In addition, information on the source of the visit is included, corresponding to how the user reached the shop's website. This solution is the closest to our proposed approach.

Despite such an extensive literature, it is difficult to find practical issues directly related to price sensitivity in terms of customer profiling.

3 Description of the Study

The research was carried out by monitoring user behaviour on the websites of a Polish online shop. A total of 562,750 complete user visits were recorded. Each visit recorded sixteen different parameter values, which included information on:

- the number of customer visits (inputs from the same user were taken to be inputs from the same IP) and which of these visits were from advertising and which were internal:

  - over a period of 7 days ['visits_from_last_7_days', 'not_from_ad_last_7_days', 'from_ad_last_7_days'],
  - over a period of one month ['visits_from_last_month', 'not_from_ad_last_month', 'from_ad_last_month'],
  - on a particular day ['visits_today', 'not_from_ad_today', 'from_ad_today'],

- the duration of the customer's last visit ['first_req_st2_close_seconds'],
- time since the customer's last visit ['diff_time_1_seconds'],
- type of the device ['is_mobile'],
- the number of clicks on the website ['mouse_clicks'],
- changing the card ['card_changed'],
- the number of scrolling events and the difference between the highest and lowest points of presence on the page ['scroll_dist_diff', 'scroll_num']
- the fact of making a sale, which was extracted from sales pixels and was used to try to predict the probability for two classes: "is going to buy" – 1, "is not going to buy" – 0.

The data was preprocessed. Empty (null) values were replaced with zeros and duplicate records were removed. They were then adjusted to even out the number of records for both classes (0 and 1). Finally, 83178 records with an equal split for each class (is going to buy/is not going to buy) were selected for further study. The data were standardised. The next step was to divide them into training, testing and validation sets. The number of records in each set was respectively: 67374, 7486, 8318. The data which are categories were converted into zero-one form by the one-hot-encoding process.

The model that was chosen to determine the price sensitivity profiles of users was one-way artificial multilayer networks. The most optimal architecture turned out to be a structure consisting of: a dense input layer consisting of 16 neurons with a 'relu' activation function, a dense hidden layer with 32 neurons with a 'relu' activation function and an output layer with two neurons with a 'sigmoid' activation function.

The model was optimised using the ADAM algorithm with loss function binary cross-entropy. When tested, the following values of the hyperparameters proved to be the best: number of epochs - 100, batch size - 32, learning rate - 0.001. The graph showing the accuracy changes obtained from one of the example network learning processes can be seen in Fig. 1. The model was finally evaluated using the F1-score metric, which finally reached 0.74 on the validation set. The resulting confusion matrix for the test data can be seen in Fig. 2. The network response was obtained in less than 700 ms. It was possible to extract two thresholds for the probability of a subsequent purchase by the customer. Three profiles were thus determined:

- low (threshold <= 0.08),
- medium (0.08 < threshold < 0.8),
- high (threshold >= 0.8).

Figure 3 shows a graph of changes in the probability values obtained for the test data. The horizontal axis shows the numbers of consecutive records from the dataset for which the prediction was made. The vertical axis shows the value of the probability that the customer will make a purchasing decision again (class "1"). The data were sorted by the probability value.

The effectiveness of the model for the test data is shown in Table 1. The test data, according to the obtained probability value, were divided into three profiles. The behaviour of the e-shop users during their subsequent visits to the given e-shop was examined. The next columns show, correspondingly, the number of tested users allocated to the respective group, the percentage of the total, the number of users who made a subsequent purchase and the percentage of these users from the respective group. As can be seen, the assigned profile largely corresponds to making subsequent purchases/purchases later. It should be noted at this point that it is very difficult to test the effectiveness of this model due to the nature of the data. This is because there are a large number of users who visit the shop only to browse the products or who make a purchase only once.

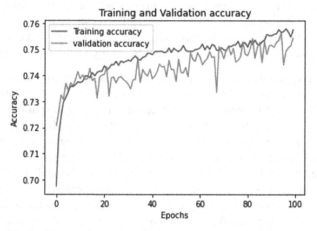

Fig. 1. The accuracy value obtained during the learning process.

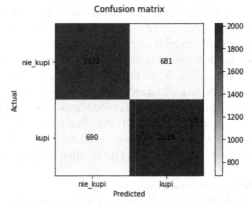

Fig. 2. Confusion matrix obtained for the test data.

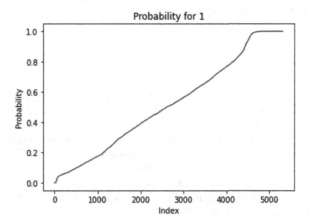

Fig. 3. Probability obtained for the test data.

Table 1. Model performance results for the test data.

Profile	No. of customers	% of customers	Customers who have made a purchase	% of customers who have made a purchase
Low	555	15.07	19	3.42
Medium	2710	73.60	153	5.65
High	417	11.33	30	7.19

4 Conclusions

The paper presented here addresses the possibility of profiling users in e-commerce using a model that allows us to determine the likelihood of a customer making a subsequent purchase based on their past behaviour in an online shop. The model uses a variety of data such as the number of past visits, information on visits coming from external advertising, duration of the visit, device type and number of clicks. The results of the study show that the proposed model is effective in predicting customer behaviour and can help online shops make business decisions, such as personalising product offers and adjusting discount levels. The model provides valuable guidance for entrepreneurs and marketers who want to better understand e-commerce customer behaviour and better align their strategies with customer needs and expectations. The research can be extended by creating other models using fast neural networks that allow for rapid model response [9, 13, 14], the ability to use device fingerprints to identify users [11], autoencoders to detect anomalies [12], clustering algorithms [10] or other models [15, 16].

Acknowledgments. The presented results are obtained within the realization of the project "Sales Bot 2.0 - development of an innovative sales system for e-commerce based on individual user price profiling with a dynamic product recommendation system based on ma-chine learning and device fingerprint" financed by the National Center for Research and Development; grant number POIR.01.01.01-00-0241/19-00.

References

1. Eke, C.I., Norman, A.A., Shuib, L., Nweke, H.F.: A survey of user profiling: state-of-the-art, challenges, and solutions. IEEE Access **7**, 144907–144924 (2019). https://doi.org/10.1109/ACCESS.2019.2944243
2. Mofokeng, T.E.: The impact of online shopping attributes on customer satisfaction and loyalty: moderating effects of e-commerce experience. Cogent Bus. Manage. **8**(1), 1968206 (2021). https://doi.org/10.1080/23311975.2021.1968206
3. Bucko, J., Kakalejčík, L., Ferencová, M., Wright, L.T. (Reviewing editor): Online shopping: factors that affect consumer purchasing behaviour. Cogent Bus. Manage. **5**, 1 (2018). https://doi.org/10.1080/23311975.2018.1535751
4. Vakulenko, Y., Shams, P., Hellström, D., Hjort, K.: Online retail experience and customer satisfaction: the mediating role of last mile delivery. Int. Rev. Retail Distrib. Consum. Res. **29**(3), 306–320 (2019). https://doi.org/10.1080/09593969.2019.1598466
5. Dominique-Ferreira, S., Vasconcelos, H., Proença, J.F.: Determinants of customer price sensitivity: an empirical analysis. J. Serv. Mark. **30**(3), 327–340 (2016). https://doi.org/10.1108/JSM-12-2014-0409
6. Abdullah-Al-Mamun, Rahman, M.K., Robel, S.D.: A critical review of consumers' sensitivity to price: managerial and theoretical issues. J. Int. Bus. Econ. **2**(2), 01–09 (2014)
7. Yan, H., Wang, Z., Lin, T.H., et al.: Profiling users by online shopping behaviors. Multimed. Tools Appl. **77**, 21935–21945 (2018). https://doi.org/10.1007/s11042-017-5365-7
8. Suchacka, G., Stemplewski, S.: Application of neural network to predict purchases in online store. In: Wilimowska, Z., Borzemski, L., Grzech, A., Świątek, J. (eds.) Information Systems Architecture and Technology: Proceedings of 37th International Conference on Information Systems Architecture and Technology – ISAT 2016 – Part IV. Advances in Intelligent Systems and Computing, vol. 524, pp. 221–231. Springer, Cham (2017). https://doi.org/10.1007/978-3-319-46592-0_19
9. Bilski, J., Kowalczyk, B., Kisiel-Dorohinicki, M., Siwocha, A., Żurada, J.: Towards a very fast feedforward multilayer neural networks training algorithm. J. Artif. Intell. Soft Comput. Res. **12**(3), 181–195 (2022). https://doi.org/10.2478/jaiscr-2022-0012

10. Starczewski, A., Scherer, M.M., Książek, W., Dębski, M., Wang, L.: A novel grid-based clustering algorithm. J. Artif. Intell. Soft Comput. Res. **11**(4), 319–330 (2021). https://doi.org/10.2478/jaiscr-2021-0019

11. Gabryel, M., Grzanek, K., Hayashi, Y.: Browser fingerprint coding methods increasing the effectiveness of user identification in the web traffic. J. Artif. Intell. Soft Comput. Res. **10**(4), 243–253 (2020). https://doi.org/10.2478/jaiscr-2020-0016

12. Brunner, C., Kő, A., Fodor, S.: An autoencoder-enhanced stacking neural network model for increasing the performance of intrusion detection. J. Artif. Intell. Soft Comput. Res. **12**(2), 149–163 (2021). https://doi.org/10.2478/jaiscr-2022-0010

13. Korytkowski, M., Scherer, R., Szajerman, D., Połap, D., Woźniak, M.: Efficient visual classification by fuzzy rules. In: 2020 IEEE International Conference on Fuzzy Systems (FUZZ-IEEE), Glasgow, UK, pp. 1–6 (2020). https://doi.org/10.1109/FUZZ48607.2020.9177777

14. Bilski, J., et al.: Fast computational approach to the Levenberg-Marquardt algorithm for training feedforward neural networks. J. Artif. Intell. Soft Comput. Res. **13**(2), 45–61 (2023)

15. Gałkowski, T., Krzyżak, A., Dziwiński, P.: Fast estimation of multidimensional regression functions. In: 2022 17th International Conference on Control, Automation, Robotics and Vision (ICARCV). IEEE (2022)

16. Dziwiński, P., et al.: Hardware implementation of a Takagi-Sugeno neuro-fuzzy system optimized by a population algorithm. J. Artif. Intell. Soft Comput. Res. **11**(3), 243–266 (2021)

Learning Bezier-Durrmeyer Type Descriptors for Classifying Curves – Preliminary Studies

Adam Krzyżak[1,2] , Wojciech Rafajłowicz[3] , and Ewaryst Rafajłowicz[3(✉)]

[1] Department of Computer Science, Concordia University,
1455 De Maisonneuve West, Montreal, QC H3G 1M8, Canada
`krzyzak@cs.concordia.ca`
[2] Department of Electrical Engineering,
Westpomeranian University of Technology (WUT), Szczecin, Poland
[3] Faculty of Information and Comunication Technology,
Wroclaw University of Science and Technology, Wrocław, Poland
`{wojciech.rafajlowicz,ewaryst.rafajlowicz}@pwr.edu.pl`

Abstract. We aim to propose a new approach for generating descriptors for functional data that are represented by curves that may not be functions but rather parametrically described curves in 2D, 3D, etc. The idea of generating these descriptors is based on the Bezier curves, but instead of using classical control points, we propose to generalize the Durrmeyer approach for parametrically defined vector curves. The Durrmeyer-type descriptors are then estimated from noisy samples of the underlying curve and serve as input vectors to a selected classifier that is learned to recognize from which class of curves noisy observations come.

The Bezier curves are not rapidly convergent. However, our aim is not to reconstruct functions but to recognize them, maintaining the shape-preserving and variation-diminishing properties of these curves that increase the classification accuracy in the presence of noise without invoking pre-filtering procedures. For more complicated curves, one can directly apply our approach to their parts in a similar way as polynomial splines are used.

The proposed algorithm for learning descriptors of the Bezier-Durrmeyer type and training classifiers on them was tested on synthetic, but interesting per se, data from two families of the Lissajous curves observed with high amplitude noise.

Keywords: Bezier curves · Durrmeyer type · Shape-preservation · Bernstein-Durrmeyer polynomials · Nonparametric estimation · Descriptors · Learning classifiers · Functional data

1 Introduction

We propose a new class of descriptors for noisy samples of curves to use them as features of classifiers. We admit curves that cannot be described as functions, e.g., S-like curves or closed ones.

© The Author(s), under exclusive license to Springer Nature Switzerland AG 2023
L. Rutkowski et al. (Eds.): ICAISC 2023, LNAI 14125, pp. 530–541, 2023.
https://doi.org/10.1007/978-3-031-42505-9_45

The range of possible applications is relatively high, including classifying signatures of tanks and airplanes, recognizing items on images from their contours, and paths of autonomous vehicles and mechanical tools in 2D and 3D space. More recent applications of classifying curves comprise paths of laser cutting and additive manufacturing, training surgeons in laparoscopic operations, operating drones, and practicing artistic gymnastics and other types of sports. More applications can be found in science and engineering, where distinguishing classes of orbits of dynamic systems and hysteretic curves depending on material properties is essential.

The classic approach to designing descriptors for classifying closed curves from their samples is based on expressing them in polar coordinates and applying the fast Fourier transform. This approach was proved to be successful in many applications, however it may fail if large errors are present in the curve samples, as it is demonstrated in Sect. 2.

Besides fast Fourier transforms, many other boundary descriptors were introduced in the literature [17,33]. They include boundary encodings in the form of Freeman chain codes [16] and slope chain codes [6]. Fourier descriptors derived from shape signatures were introduced by Zahn and Roskies [42] and Granlund [19] and further analyzed in [11]. They are invariant to scale, rotation, and choice of the starting point on the boundary and were applied in the classification of hand-drawn shapes and drawings in [31] and in [26]. Stochastic models of boundaries were proposed and analyzed by Kashyap and Chelappa in [23] and by Dubois and Glanz [13].

Indirect shape representations called skeletons or medial axis transforms were attributed to Blum in [4,38]. They played a significant role in handwritten characters classification. Statistical moments are popular shape descriptors.

Besides Bezier curves, B-splines played significant roles in representing shapes and curves in computer graphics and other domains [2,5].

Many techniques were developed for representing clouds of points by means of curves. Among many approaches, principal curves (and manifolds) deserve attention [12,14,20,24]. They were applied to the skeletonization of handwritten character classification in [25]. Further extensions of principal curves and their applications to fitting the clouds of points were presented in [29].

And finally, in a case when we are interested not only in representing boundaries but also shapes enclosed by them, then the representation of choice are statistical moments. The best known moments are invariant moments introduced by Hu [21], but many others became popular, e.g. Zernike moments. For a comprehensive survey on moment invariants we refer the reader to [15] and to [41] for the reconstruction of images from polar Zernike moments.

For constructing the proposed descriptors, we start with the well-known Bezier curves that are well suited for describing closed shapes. As is known, for specifying the Bezier curves, one has to define the so-called control points, which determine the shape of the curve. This way of designing them is convenient in the computer-aided geometric design area from which they emanated. However, when a curve is represented by its noisy samples, as in most applications mentioned above, there is no algorithmic way of specifying control points. For this reason, the proposed descriptors, in their theoretical version, are based on the Durrmeyer idea of computing integrals of a curve multiplied by the Bernstein polynomials. Such descriptors preserve the shape characteristics of the underlying curve, as explained in Sect. 3. It is of crucial importance for our goal of constructing descriptors of curves, namely, for classifying them.

The next step toward designing our descriptors is to estimate the Bernstein-Durrmeyer descriptors by replacing an unknown curve by its noisy samples. As pointed out at the end of Sect. 3, these empirical descriptors are consistent estimates of their theoretical counterparts. As illustrated in Fig. 1, they also preserve the shape characteristics of the underlying curve, although they are unknown and buried in the intensive noise.

Section 3 discusses an interplay between the descriptors and curve classifiers. The main point is selecting the number of descriptors used as input features of the classifier. To this end, we propose a heuristic criterion and provide the results of its testing. These tests and tests of cooperation between learning descriptors and a classifier were made on synthetic data generated from two families of the Lissajous curves with high-intensity noises.

It should be stressed that combinations of the Bezier idea and the Durrmeyer one also appear in a series of papers in quite a different context than here. We refer the reader to [1], and the bibliography cited therein for this stream of research that concentrates on modifying Bezier-Durrmeyer polynomials to speed up their convergence rate, frequently at the expense of their shape-preserving properties.

To the best of our knowledge, shape-preserving vector descriptors based on the Bezier-Durrmeyer curves were not yet proposed. The closest one is paper [37] in which the Bernstein-Durrmeyer descriptors for functions are proposed. However, the generalization proposed is not only formal since here we are able to describe and to classify curves that are multidimensional and close.

Approximating shapes by the Bezier (but not the Bezier-Durrmeyer) curves in a quite different way than ours was proposed in [9] where the authors say: "we want mainly to approximate segments of the shape by using the Bezier cubic curves which best interpolate the endpoints of the contour shape segments". By the way, we emphasise that in our simulation experiments we have applied the Bezier-Durrmeyer descriptors that are based on the Bernstein polynomials of orders 30–40 or even higher (see Sects. 3 and 4 and [28] for computational aspects). An interesting aspect that is outside the scope of our paper is discussed in [22]. Namely, the authors state the problem of sampling regular curves in such a way that it is possible to select control points along the length of a curve.

We refer the reader to [3,7,10,18,27,32] for basic facts concerning the Bernstein-Bézier methods and the Durrmeyer approach needed here. Further references are provided later at appropriate places.

Other applications in which shape-preserving properties of the Bernstein polynomials are important include [30,34,36], where they are used as a model for COVID-19 growth.

To illustrate further advantages of the proposed descriptors, a 3D curve is plotted in Fig. 1 (left panel). The middle panel in this figure contains 900 samples of this curve corrupted by random noise uniformly distributed in $[-2.5, 2.5]$ interval. In Fig. 1 (right panel) 101 descriptors are plotted, illustrating a proper reproduction of the curve shape.

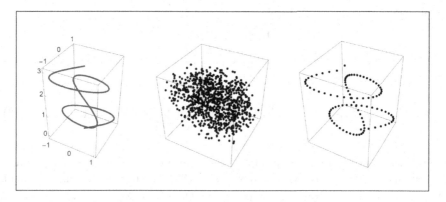

Fig. 1. Example of applying the proposed descriptors (right panel) to noisy samples (middle panel) of an original curve (left panel).

2   Proposed Curve Descriptors

As already mentioned, the proposed descriptors are based on the idea of the Bezier curves that are generalized by replacing classic control points with the estimates of the Durrmeyer moments related to the Bernstein polynomials.

The Bezier Curves. As is well-known, see, e.g., [18], in d-dimensional Euclidean space the Bezier curve $\mathbf{b}_N(t) \in R^d$, $t \in [0, 1]$ that is spanned by $(N + 1)$ control points $\mathbf{p}_k \in R^d$, $k = 0, 1, \ldots, N$ has the following form:

$$\mathbf{b}_N(t) = \sum_{k=0}^{N} \mathbf{p}_k B_k^{(N)}(t), \quad t \in [0, 1], \tag{1}$$

where $B_k^{(N)}(t)$ are the Bersnstein polynomials: $B_k^{(N)}(t) = \binom{N}{k}t^k(1 - t)^{N-k}$, $t \in [0, 1]$ $k = 0, 1, \ldots, N$. To have compact formulas it is customary to set $B_k^{(N)}(t) \equiv 0$, if $k < 0$ or $k > N$. Notice also that $B_0^{(N)}(0) = 1$ and $B_N^{(N)}(1) = 1$. Thus, the Bezier curve starts exactly at $\mathbf{p}_0$ and ends at $\mathbf{p}_N$ when parameter t runs from 0 to 1. A piecewise linear curve joining all control points $\mathbf{p}_k$'s is called the control polygon.

Shape-Preserving Properties of the Bezier Curves. The following well-known shape-preserving properties of the Bezier curves (see, e.g., [10]) are important for our purposes.

Convex Hull Property. Consider the convex hull $\mathcal{C}(\mathbf{p}_0, \ldots, \mathbf{p}_N) \subset R^d$ of all the control points. Then, the convex hull property of the Bezier curve $\mathbf{b}_N(.)$ means that it is a subset of $\mathcal{C}$, i.e.,

$$\forall_{t \in [0, 1]} \quad \mathbf{b}_N(t) \in \mathcal{C}(\mathbf{p}_0, \ldots, \mathbf{p}_N). \tag{2}$$

This fact follows from the direct relationships between the Bernstein polynomials and the binomial distribution, namely:

$$\forall_{t \in [0, 1]} \quad 0 \le B_k^{(N)}(t) \le 1 \quad \text{and} \quad \sum_{k=0}^{N} B_k^{(N)}(t) = 1. \tag{3}$$

Variation Diminishing Property. The variation diminishing property of any Bezier curve can be phrased as follows (see [18]). Let $\mathbf{l}(t)$ be any line segment that crosses $\mathbf{b}_N(.)$ and the control polygon spanned by $\mathbf{p}_0, \ldots, \mathbf{p}_N$). Then, the number of crossings of $\mathbf{b}_N(.)$ by $\mathbf{l}(.)$ is smaller or equal to the number of crossings of the control polygon by $\mathbf{l}(.)$.

The proof of the variation diminishing property is not trivial (see [18] and the bibliography there in) and it follows from the fact the Bernstein basis is totally positive which means that the following matrix

$$\mathbf{B}_N \stackrel{def}{=} \left[B_k^{(N)}(t_i) \right], \quad k = 0, 1, \ldots N, \quad i = 1, 2, \ldots, n \tag{4}$$

has all its minor nonnegative for arbitrary sequence $t_1 < t_2, \ldots, < t_n, t_i \in [0, 1]$ and any $n > 1$.

The variation diminishing property explains why the proposed descriptors can be quite well estimated from noisy samples of curves without applying a pre-filtering. This property also implies the monotonicity- and convexity-preserving properties of the Bezier curves. We stress that these shape-preserving properties of the Bezier curves manifest themselves only when they are present in control points. We do not need to know about that or impose additional constraints.

Proposed Descriptors and Algorithm of their Learning

At the end of this subsection, we describe our algorithm for learning the proposed descriptors. Earlier, we shall provide their intuitive derivation and state the problem of their estimation.

Descriptors – Basic Version. Let $\mathbf{f}(t) \in R^d$, $t \in [0, 1]$ be the parametric description of a continuous curve, where $\mathbf{f}(t) = [f^{(1)}(t), f^{(2)}(t), \ldots, f^{(d)}(t)]^T$. Its basic descriptors, denoted further as $\mathbf{d_k} \in R^d$, are defined as follows:

$$\mathbf{d_k} = (N+1) \int_0^1 \mathbf{f}(t) B_k^{(N)}(t) \, dt, \quad k = 0, 1, \ldots, N. \tag{5}$$

Their elements $d_k^{(j)}$, considered as sequences of $k = 0, 1, \ldots, N$, share all the shape-preserving properties of the descriptors considered in [37], $j = 1, 2, \ldots, d$. Descriptors (5) are later interpreted as the reference points when properties of their empirical counterparts are considered.

To explain the choice (5) as descriptors, consider the following approximation $\mathbf{f}_N(.)$ of $\mathbf{f}(.)$ curve:

$$\mathbf{f}_N(t) = \sum_{k=0}^{N} \mathbf{d}_k B_k^{(N)}(t), \quad t \in [0, 1]. \tag{6}$$

One can interpret it as the Bezier curve, but as the control polygon we take $\mathbf{d}_k$'s that generalizes the Durrmeyer coefficients to curves. Thus, (6) can be called the Bezier curve of the Durrmeyer type. It generalizes the Bernstein-Durrmeyer polynomials. The multiplier $(N + 1)$ in (5) is an important normalizing factor introduced in order to ensure that $\mathbf{f}_N(.)$ correctly reproduces constant vectors, since $\int_0^1 B_k^{(N)}(t)\, dt = 1/(N + 1)$. One can expect that $\mathbf{f}_N(.)$ is the shape-preserving approximation at the expense of a slower convergence rate with N. However, if one needs more exact approximation, the expressions like $\mathbf{f}_N(.)$ can be used as parts of the Bezier spline basis. We shall not use this interpretaion later on since classfiers of curves will work on the descriptors only.

Descriptors – Empirical Version. In practice, we usually do not have an access to $\mathbf{f}(.)$ and (5) can not be directly used. We adopt the following classic sampling scheme, containing n observations,

$$\mathbf{y}_i = \mathbf{f}(t_i) + \mathbf{e}_i, \quad t_i \in [0, 1], \quad i = 1, 2, \ldots, n, \tag{7}$$

where $\mathbf{y}_i \in R^d$, $i = 1, 2, \ldots, n$ are vectors observed at equidistant points t_i's. Concerning errors $\mathbf{e}_i$, we also impose standard assumptions: they are zero mean, mutually independent random vectors with diagonal covariance matrices and finite variances.

According to (7), one curve is represented by $d \times n$ matrix $\mathbf{Y}$ having $\mathbf{y}_i$'s as its columns, tacitly assuming that t_i's are fixed, i.e.,

$$\mathbf{Y} = [\mathbf{y}_1, \mathbf{y}_2, \ldots, \mathbf{y}_n] \tag{8}$$

The number n of observations has to be reasonable large so as to ensure sufficiently accurate approximations of integrals over $[0, 1]$ on the equidistant grid with the step size $\Delta_n = 1/n$. The discussion on selecting t_i's, if possible, according to the rules of the optimal experiment design is outside the scope of this paper. We refer the reader to [35] and the bibliography cited therein.

As estimates $\hat{\mathbf{d}}_k(n, N, \mathbf{Y})$'s of $\mathbf{d}_k$'s we take:

$$\hat{\mathbf{d}}_k(n, N, \mathbf{Y}) = (N + 1)\, \Delta_n \sum_{i=1}^{n} \mathbf{y}_i B_k^{(N)}(t_i), \quad k = 0, 1, \ldots, N. \tag{9}$$

These are descriptors of one curve that is originally represented by $\mathbf{Y}$. We shall use simpler notation $\hat{\mathbf{d}}_k(n, N)$ or even $\hat{\mathbf{d}}_k(N)$ when other arguments are fixed.

It is convenient to rewrite this formula in a recurrent form typical for learning:

$$\hat{\mathbf{d}}_k(i, N) = (N+1) \left[\frac{i-1}{i} \hat{\mathbf{d}}_k(i-1, N) + \frac{1}{i} \mathbf{y}_i B_k^{(N)}(t_i) \right] \quad i = 2, 3, \ldots, n,$$
(10)

where $\hat{\mathbf{d}}_k(1, N) = \mathbf{y}_1 B_k^{(N)}(t_1)$, $k = 0, 1, \ldots, N$ and to compute the Bernstein polynomials according to well-known recurrence:

$$B_k^{(N)}(t) = (1-t) B_k^{(N-1)}(t) + t B_{k-1}^{(N-1)}(t), \quad k = 1, 2, \ldots, N.$$
(11)

From the results presented in [37] it easily follows that if all the elements of $\mathbf{f}(t)$ are have continuous derivatives in $[0, 1]$, then, for fixed N, the mean square error $\mathbb{E}\|\mathbf{d}_k - \hat{\mathbf{d}}_k(n, N)\|^2$ converges to zero as $n \to \infty$, where $\|.\|$ is the Euclidean norm in R^d and $\mathbb{E}$ denotes the expectation.

3   Proposed Descriptors as Inputs of Curve Classifiers

After computing descriptors according to (9) or (10), they can serve as inputs (features) of virtually any standard classifier in the phase of its learning and application. However, it is expedient to sketch an interplay between learning the descriptors and a classifier.

Learning and Testing Sequences. We consider the problem of classifying curve $\mathbf{f}$, represented only by its samples $\mathbf{Y}$ of the form (8), to class A or B, say. We confine to two classes for simplicity. Prior probabilities p_A, p_B, $p_A + p_B = 1$ of drawing $\mathbf{f}$ at random exists, but they are unknown.

The only information for estimating the descriptors of curves and classifying them is contained in the sequence

$$[(\mathbf{Y}_1, l_1), (\mathbf{Y}_2, l_2), \ldots, (\mathbf{Y}_L, l_L)]$$
(12)

of curves samples $\mathbf{Y}_l$'s and their proper classifications that are represented by labels $l_j \in \{A, B\}$, $j = 1, 2, \ldots, L$. Learning $\mathcal{L}$ and testing $\mathcal{L}$ sequences are drawn at random, without replacements, from sequence (12).

Selecting N. The only ingredient of (9) that still has not been discussed is the choice of the number of descriptors $(N+1)$. Notice that we do not state the problem of selecting particular descriptors which is highly time-consuming. However, here the choice of N does not have the structure of nested models since for a larger N all the previous descriptors have to be re-computed since the Bernstein basis is not an orthogonal one. Thus, the problem remains difficult. We refer the reader to [39] for the results on nonparametric estimation when spanning functions are orthogonal.

There are two commonly used approaches for selecting the number of inputs to a classifier, namely,

cross-validation that allows estimating the dependence of the classifier accuracy on N by testing the classifier on randomly selected subsets of data that were not used for training the classifier,

indirect quality indicators that are based on quality measures that are easier to estimate vs. N than the classification accuracy.

The cross-validation (CV) methodology is widely accepted by researchers, but its proper application requires long validation sequences, drawn at random multiple times, subject significant computational burden. The indirect quality indicators, in turn, are less time-consuming, but their relationships to the classifier accuracy are indirect and frequently only intuitively explained.

For these reasons, we propose a heuristic criterion for selecting N that uses the estimated probability of the classifier error $\widetilde{err}(N, \mathcal{C})$ as the main component, where $\mathcal{C}$ is a classifier selected from a predefined list.

Error $\widetilde{err}(N, \mathcal{C})$ can be estimated using the simple version of the CV with 1–3 validation sequences. The second ingredient, denoted as $pen(n, N)$, is a penalty for applying a too large number of descriptors. Inspired by our simulations, we propose to define the penalty as follows: $pen(n, N) = \frac{N}{n} \log_{10}(N)$. For $N \ll n$ multiplier $\frac{N}{n}$ is less than $1/2$. For reasonable N of the order 10^2 the second term $\log_{10}(N)$ does not exceeds 2. Thus, $pen(n, N)$ is less than 1. The probability of error $\widetilde{err}(N)$ is also less than 1. Hence, these two terms are reasonably balanced and as the descriptors error criterion (DEC) we propose to minimize the following expression:

$$DEC(N, \mathcal{C}) = \widetilde{err}(N+1, \mathcal{C}) + \frac{N+1}{n} \log_{10}(N+1), \quad 1 \leq N \leq n/2 \quad (13)$$

with respect to N. Clearly, the result of the minimization depends not only on the number of descriptors but also on the classifier used. However, as we shall demonstrate by example, good classifiers yield very similar plots of $DEC(N, \mathcal{C})$.

At first sight, the DEC looks similar to the well-known Bayesian Information Criterion (BIC). Nevertheless, there are two important differences. The error term $\widetilde{err}(N, \mathcal{C})$ estimates the probability of errors committed by a classifier with $(N + 1)$ descriptors, while in the BIC the error is related the averaged distance between a model output and observations. The second difference is in the dependence of $pen(n, N)$ on N and n. Namely, the BIC penalty term grows with the logarithm of the number of observations. Here, it is decreasing with n, while increasing as $N \log_{10}(N)$ when the number of descriptors used is growing.

Algorithms and Their Testing. The main steps of computational algorithms can be sketched as follows.

Step 1 Select the smallest and the largest number of descriptors N_0, N_{max} to be considered. Compute the sequences of descriptors (9) for $N = N_0, N_0 + 1, \ldots N_{max}$ using $\mathbf{Y}_j$'s from learning sequence $\mathcal{L}$.

Step 2 Select classifier $\mathcal{C}$. Compute $DEC(N, \mathcal{C})$ according to (13) for $N = N_0, N_0 + 1, \ldots N_{max}$ and find $\hat{N}$ for which $DEC(N, \mathcal{C})$ is minimal.

Step 3 Examine classifier $\mathcal{C}$ on testing data $\mathcal{T}$ with $(\hat{N}+1)$ descriptors and obtain $\widetilde{err}(\hat{N}+1, \mathcal{C})$ and other quality indicators (precision, recall, specificity) for them. If they are satisfactory, denote this classifier by $\hat{\mathcal{C}}$ and go to Step 4, otherwise return to Step 2 to select the next classifier for checking.

Step 4 Application phase: acquire samples $\mathbf{Y}$ of a new curve to be classified. Compute descriptors $\hat{\mathbf{d}}_k(n, \hat{N}, \mathbf{Y})$, $k = 0, 1, \ldots, \hat{N}$ and fed them as the input of classifier $\hat{\mathcal{C}}$ and consider its output as the decision.

These algorithms were tested on synthetic data that were generated from two families of the Lissajos curves shown in Fig. 2.

The basic data for simulations were the following: each curve was sampled at $n = 200$ points, 8 curves from class A were extended by the augmentation to 960 curves by adding sampling errors uniformly distributed on $[-2.5, 2.5]$ and analogously for curves and samples from class B. Notice that in the worst case sampling errors are 2.5 larger than the unit amplitudes of the Lissajous curves. Additionally, large errors are more probable than for comparable Gaussians'.

Two popular classifiers were selected as a vehicle for testing the proposed descriptors, namely, the logistic regression (LogR) and the support vector machine (SVM), implemented in *Mathematica*. Their accuracy vs the number of descriptors is shown in Fig. 3 (left panel). Plots of $DEC(N, \mathcal{C})$ (Step 2) for these classifiers are shown in the same figure (right panel) and $\hat{N} = 35$ is selected for further studies. Then, both classifiers with 36 descriptors were verified on the

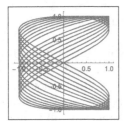
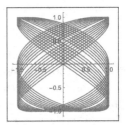

Fig. 2. Two families (class A – left panel, class B – right panel) of the Lissajos curves. Their noisy samples were used for learning descriptors and classifiers.

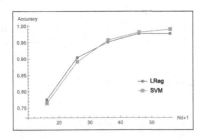
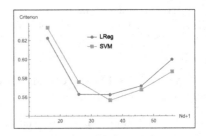

Fig. 3. Right panel – the classification accuracy of two families of curves Fig. 2 obtained by applying the SVM and LogR classifiers to varying number of the descriptors. Right panel – criterion $DEC(N)$ for the SVM and LogR classifiers.

testing data (Step 3). The results are summarized in Tab. 1, leading to the conclusion that 36 descriptors provide satisfactory classification quality, taking into account how large sampling errors were simulated. Notice that $\hat{N} = 35$ means that we used the Bernstein polynomials of that degree.

Table 1. Comparison of the basic classification quality measures obtained by the Logistic Regression (LReg) and the Support Vector Machine (SVM) classifiers on 36 descriptors (see the text for details).

Classifier	LReg	SVM
Accuracy	0.951	0.957
Precision	0.952	0.948
Recall	0.944	0.968
Specificity	0.953	0.947

Concluding Remarks. The proposed descriptors documented their shape-preserving properties when applied to classify rather complicated curves, sampled with large errors. They were stable in computations, even when high order Bernstein polynomials were used. For even more complicated curves, one can apply the proposed descriptors to their parts.

In addition to direct applications of the proposed descriptors for curve recognition, one may hope that they can be useful as a tool for deeper understanding of signals in the spirit of the ideas proposed in [8, 40].

References

1. Agrawal, P.N., Araci, S., Bohner, M., Lipi, K.: Approximation degree of Durrmeyer-Bezier operators of blending type. J. Inequal. Appl., 29 (2018)
2. Ballard, D.H., Brown, C.M.: Computer Vision. Prentice Hall, Englewood Cliffs (1982)
3. Bezier, P.: Numerical Control: Mathematics and Applications. Wiley and Sons, London (1972)
4. Blum, H.: A transformation for extracting new descriptors of shape. In: Wathen-Dunn, W. (ed.) Models for the Perception of Speech and Visual Form, pp. 362–380. MIT Press, Cambridge (1967)
5. de Boor, C.A.: Practical Guide to Splines. Springer, Heidelberg (1978)
6. Bribiesca, E., Guzman, A.: How to describe pure form and how to measure differences in shape using shape numbers. Pattern Recogn. **12**(2), 101–112 (1980)
7. Chen, W., Ditzian, Z.: Best polynomial and Durrmeyer approximation in $L_p(S)$. Indagationes Mathematicae **2**, 437–452 (1991)
8. Chen, G.Y., Krzyżak, A., Duda, P., Cader, A.: Noise robust illumination invariant face recognition via bivariate wavelet shrinkage in logarithm domain. J. Artif. Intell. Soft Comput. Res. **12**(3), 169–180 (2022)

9. Cinque, L., Levialdi, S., Malizia, A.: Shape description using cubic polynomial Bezier curves. Pattern Recogn. Lett. **19**(9), 821–828 (1998)
10. Dahmen, W.: Convexity and Bernstein-Bézier polynomials. In: Curves and Surfaces, pp. 107–134. Academic Press (1991)
11. Dekking, F.M., Van Otterloo, P.J.: Fourier coding and reconstruction of complicated contours. IEEE Trans. Syst. Man Cybern. SMC **16**(3), 395–404 (1986)
12. Delicado, P.: Another look at principal curves and surfaces. J. Multivariate Anal. **77**(1), 84–116 (2001)
13. Dubois, S.R., Glanz, F.H.: An autoregressive model approach to 2-D shape classification. IEEE Trans. Pattern Anal. Pattern Mach. Intell. PAMI **8**, 55–66 (1986)
14. Duchamp, T., Stuetzle, W.: Extremal properties of principal curves in the plane. Ann. Statist. **24**, 1511–1520 (1996)
15. Flusser, J., Zitova, B., Suk, T.: Moments and Moment Invariants in Pattern Recognition. John Wiley Sons, Hoboken (2009)
16. Freeman, H.: On the encoding of arbitrary geometric configurations. IEEE Trans. Elec. Comput. EC **10**, 260–268 (1961)
17. Gonzales, R.C., Woods, R.E.: Digital Image Processing, 4th edn. Pearson, Hoboken (2018)
18. Gordon, W.J., Riesenfeld, R.F.: Bernstein-Bezier methods for the computer-aided design of free-form curves and surfaces. J. ACM (JACM) **21**(2), 293–310 (1974)
19. Granlund, G.H.: Fourier preprocessing for hand printed character recognition. IEEE Trans. Comput. C **21**, 195–201 (1972)
20. Hastie, T., Stuetzle, W.: Principal curves. J. Am. Stat. Assoc. **84**(406), 502–516 (1989)
21. Hu, M.K.: Visual pattern recognition by moment invariants. IRE Trans. Inf. Theory IT **8**, 179–187 (1962)
22. Hernández-Mederos, V., Estrada-Sarlabous, J.: Sampling points on regular parametric curves with control of their distribution. Comput. Aided Geom. Des. **20**(6), 363–382 (2003)
23. Kashyap, R.L., Chellappa, R.: Stochastic models for closed boundary analysis: representation and reconstruction. IEEE Trans. Inf. Theory IT **27**, 627–637 (1981)
24. Kegl, B., Krzyzak, A., Linder, T., Zeger, K.: Learning and design of principal curves. IEEE Trans. Pattern Anal. Mach. Intell. **22**(3), 281–297 (2000)
25. Kegl, B., Krzyzak, A.: Piecewise linear skeletonization using principal curves. IEEE Trans. Pattern Anal. Mach. Intell. **24**(1), 59–74 (2002)
26. Krzyżak, A., Leung, S.Y., Suen, C.Y.: Reconstruction of two-dimensional patterns from Fourier descriptors. Mach. Vision Appl. **3**, 123–140 (1989)
27. Lorentz, G.G.: Bernstein Polynomials. American Mathematical Society (2013)
28. Mainar, E., Peña, J.M.: Evaluation algorithms for multivariate polynomials in Bernstein-Bézier form. J. Approx. Theory **143**(1), 44–61 (2006)
29. Ozertem, U., Erdogmus, D.: Locally defined principal curves and surfaces. J. Mach. Learn. Res. **12**, 1249–1286 (2011)
30. Pepelyshev, A., Rafajłowicz, E., Steland, A.: Estimation of the quantile function using Bernstein-Durrmeyer polynomials. J. Nonparametric Stat. **26**(1), 1–20 (2014)
31. Persoon, E., Fu, K.S.: Shape discrimination using Fourier descriptors. IEEE Trans. Syst. Man Cybern. SMC **7**, 170–179 (1977)
32. Phillips, G.M.: A survey of results on the q-Bernstein polynomials. IMA J. Numer. Anal. **30**(1), 277–288 (2010)
33. Pratt, W.K.: Introduction to Digital Image Processing. CRC Press, Boca Raton (2013)

34. Rafajłowicz, E., Skubalska-Rafajłowicz, E.: Nonparametric regression estimation by Bernstein-Durrmeyer polynomials. Tatra Mt. Math. Publ. **17**, 227–239 (1999)
35. Rafajłowicz, E.: Optimal input signals for parameter estimation. In: Linear Systems with Spatio-Temporal Dynamics, De Gruyter, Berlin, Boston (2022)
36. Rafajłowicz, W.: Learning Decision Sequences For Repetitive Processes—Selected Algorithms. SSDC, vol. 401. Springer, Cham (2022). https://doi.org/10.1007/978-3-030-88396-6
37. Rafajłowicz, W. and Rafajłowicz, E., Więckowski J.: Learning functional descriptors based on the bernstein polynomials - preliminary studies. In: International Conference on Artificial Intelligence and Soft Computing ICAISC 2022, Zakopane, Poland (2022)
38. Rosenfeld, A., Kak, A.C.: Digital Picture Processing. Academic Press, New York (1976)
39. Rutkowski, L., Rafajłowicz, E.: On optimal global rate of convergence of some nonparametric identification procedures. IEEE Trans. Autom. Control AC **34**, 1089–1091 (1989)
40. Tadeusiewicz, R.: Automatic understanding of signals. In: Intelligent Information Processing and Web Mining, pp. 577–590. Springer, Heidelberg (2004). https://doi.org/10.1007/978-3-540-39985-8_66
41. Xin, Y., Pawlak, M., Liao, S.: Image reconstruction with polar zernike moments. In: Singh, S., Singh, M., Apte, C., Perner, P. (eds.) ICAPR 2005. LNCS, vol. 3687, pp. 394–403. Springer, Heidelberg (2005). https://doi.org/10.1007/11552499_45
42. Zahn, C.T., Roskies, R.Z.: Fourier descriptors for plane closed curves. IEEE Trans. Comput. C **21**(3), 269–281 (1972)

Prediction Accuracy of Direction Changes with ELM, MLP and LSTM on the Example of Exchange Rates

Jakub Morkowski[✉]

Poznan University of Economics and Business, Poznan, Poland
jakub.morkowski@ue.poznan.pl

Abstract. This paper aims to test the accuracy of neural network forecasts depending on the hyperparameters used, using selected exchange rates as an example. The empirical study is based on forecasts by three different neural networks - ELM, MLP, and LSTM. Three important currency pairs were selected for forecasting: the Swiss franc, the British pound, and the dollar against the euro. Forecast horizons range from 1 to 10 days, and forecasts are direct. The neural networks use historical data in forecasting, and the network learns at price levels. Based on the research carried out, I conclude that forecasts for selected currency pairs (USD/EUR, GBP/EUR, CHF/EUR) and using three types of neural networks (ELM, MLP, and LSTM) are, in many cases, characterized by forecast accuracy of more than 50% and that there are relationships between forecast accuracy and the hyperparameters used.

Keywords: Neural networks · Currency · Forecasting

1 Introduction

Neural networks are presented in the scientific literature as a tool that manages forecasting on many grounds. The continuous development of the computational capabilities of computers enables them to keep evolving and makes them take on an increasingly crucial role in forecasting, among other things, financial assets. Numerous articles can be found in the literature comparing the forecasting accuracy of neural networks with the forecasting accuracy of, e.g., econometric models. Examples of such articles can already be found at the end of the 20th century, e.g. [1], and in many current works, e.g. [2].

It is also difficult to disagree with the statement that exchange rate quotations play a vital role, whether for individual customers, businesses, or countries as a whole. The relevance of this issue in today's globalized world is the subject of research by both practitioners and theorists in risk management [3,4].

The development of neural networks causes a constant increase in the types of neural networks and hybrid networks by combining different types of neural networks [5,6]. The basic division of neural networks [7] can be made into:

L. Rutkowski et al. (Eds.): ICAISC 2023, LNAI 14125, pp. 542–559, 2023.
https://doi.org/10.1007/978-3-031-42505-9_46

- Artificial Neural Networks (ANN),
- Convolutional Neural Networks (CNN),
- Recursive Neural Networks (RNN).

A literature review identifies many articles for which studies have been carried out on the accuracy of exchange rate forecasting using different types of neural networks. Examples include, for example, a hybrid model using three types of networks [[8]], numerous examples of using LSTM networks for this purpose [9–11] Cao et al. 2020, Zhang, 2018], and MLP networks [12,13].

This article focuses on presenting the accuracy of predictions obtained using three neural networks Extreme Learning Machines (ELM), Multilayer Perceptrons (MLP), and Long Short-term Memory (LSTM) when investing in the three currency pairs of the US dollar (USD), British pound (GBP) and the Swiss franc (CHF) to the euro (EUR). One hundred forty combinations of the two hyperparameters were used for all neural network types. Forecast accuracy is the number of correctly predicted exchange rate directions of a currency pair relative to all forecasts made. In the study, the ability of neural networks to correctly predict the direction of exchange rate changes is of utmost importance. Therefore, the paper's main objectives are to indicate whether there are relationships between the selected hyperparameters and their accuracy and forecast horizon.

The layout of the rest of the article is as follows. The next section describes the data and selected characteristics used in the empirical study. Next, the methodology used in the study is presented, followed by presenting the empirical results - the forecasting accuracy using three neural networks for three currency pairs with different hyperparametrisation. The last section presents the conclusions.

2   Data Description

The empirical study was conducted on three currency pairs: CHF/EUR, GBP/EUR, and USD/EUR. The exchange rates of the currency pairs were selected such that the quoted currency is always the euro, and the base currencies are CHF, GBP, and USD. The study period includes five years, from 1.01.2015 to 31.12.2019. The period was selected so that a similar number of increases characterizes it and decreases over the study period. Table 1 shows the percentage of increases and decreases over the study period for forecast horizons from 1 (t+1) to 3 (t+3).

Table 1. Percentages of increases and decreases from 2014 to 2019 for the three currency pairs (in %)

Currency pairs	USD			GBP			CHF		
Horizon	t+1	t+2	t+3	t+1	t+2	t+3	t+1	t+2	t+3
Increase	49,97	52,26	53,32	51,06	50,87	49,94	50,74	51,07	50,52
Decrease	50,03	47,74	46,68	48,94	49,13	50,06	49,26	48,93	49,48

The data is divided into learning and test sets in neural network forecasting. The test is done at price levels, and the forecast horizon is between 1 and 10 days. The learning set is always a hundred days before the forecast day, which means that the learning set always contains an equal number of observations, but the range depends on the forecast day. In order to indicate the characteristics of the individual currency pairs for the returns of the selected currency pairs, the essential characteristics, i.e., mean, deviation, skewness, and kurtosis, were calculated. These characteristics are presented in Table 2.

Table 2. Descriptive statistics for the currency pairs analyzed

Currency pairs	Arithmetic mean	Standard deviation	Skewness	Kurtosis
CHF/EUR	−0,00011	0,00492	0,07852	2,38802
GBP/EUR	−0,00007	0,00558	−1,26697	15,24767
USD/EUR	0,00006	0,00515	−0,02394	2,70457

A KPSS test was applied to all currency pairs, the null hypothesis of which is that the time series is stationary. The test showed that returns are stationary for all three currency pairs.

3 Methodology

As previously mentioned, forecasting of currency prices is based on historical data price levels using three types of neural networks:

- ELM [14]
- MLP
- LSTM [15]

The study was divided into less complicated (ELM and MLP) and more complicated (LSTM) neural network types. The study used 49 different combinations of neural network settings for ELM, MLP, and LSTM, for 147 different forecast series for each day and ten forecast horizons from 1 to 10 days. The parameters included in the settings were chosen to be equal for all three network types and the number of lags (lags) and hidden nodes (hd). Both parameters can have seven different values. The number of hidden nodes takes the values (2,5,10,15,20,25,50), and the number of lags used in the neural network takes the values (1,2,3,4,5,6,7). [16]. The number of hidden nodes was taken not as sequential natural numbers but with some intervals to search for the optimal order of magnitude of the nodes and to study the dependence of the prediction results on this parameter. The number of lags in the study was selected due to the literature review and the nature of research on financial markets - the rationale for this choice can be found in many academic papers [17]. The empirical study constructed in this way aims to answer the questions posed in the introduction:

- Does increasing the number of hidden nodes positively affect the performance of neural networks, and if so, to what level is it worth increasing the number of hidden nodes so that the benefit of improved performance is greater than the computational burden of using multiple hidden nodes?
- What effect the use of many delays ranging from one to seven has on the accuracy of the predictions? In the case of the LSTM network, setting the hidden nodes to five was omitted due to its complexity. Each day the forecast is made for ten different horizons (from one to 10 days).

The accuracy for all possible combinations of hyperparameters, currency pairs, and forecast horizons will be presented to answer the questions in the next section.

4   Research

In order to clearly show the accuracy of the forecasts obtained in the empirical study, several labels were adopted:

- Green cell filling indicates the highest accuracy for a specific forecast horizon within the studied neural network and currency pair.
- Red cell filling indicates the lowest accuracy for a specific forecast horizon across the studied neural network and currency pair.

In the tables, the first column denotes the combinations of hyperparameters adopted, e.g., hd1lags1 means that it is a neural network with one delay in the network and two hidden nodes. The number of delays is a consecutive natural number, while the number of hidden nodes follows directly from the assumptions presented in the study description. As a reminder:

- hd = (2,5,10,15,20,25,50)

Presentation of the results will be carried out for the following network types. First, tables containing the accuracy of the predictions for an ELM and three different currency pairs will be presented. Afterward, the conclusions for the accuracy of a specific neural network due to the currency pair, the forecast horizon, and the hyperparameters used will be indicated. After the conclusions for the ELM network, the accuracy tables for the MLP network will be demonstrated, followed by the conclusions for this network. Finally, the accuracy and conclusions for the LSTM network will be shown.

Tables 3, 4 and 5 show the forecast accuracy results for the ELM network and the GBP/EUR, CHF/EUR, and USD/EUR currency pairs (in order of presentation).

From the tables, we can formulate the following conclusions for the forecasts obtained with the ELM network:

- For CHF/EUR and USD/EUR, the network's forecasts with all parameters achieved an accuracy of more than 50%, while for GBP/EUR, the accuracy of 50% was not reached even once.

Table 3. Forecast accuracy results for the ELM network and the GBP/EUR currency pair at price levels [%]

	t+1	t+2	t+3	t+4	t+5	t+6	t+7	t+8	t+9	t+10
hd1lags1	49,79	48,75	48,34	48,27	47,09	47,71	46,05	46,53	46,53	45,91
hd1lags2	49,51	48,54	48,54	47,92	47,50	47,36	47,23	46,19	46,67	45,70
hd1lags3	49,38	49,03	47,92	47,43	47,99	47,85	46,95	47,64	46,39	46,26
hd1lags4	49,51	47,30	48,47	47,30	46,74	47,16	46,88	46,53	46,26	45,77
hd1lags5	49,10	47,57	47,50	48,75	46,81	47,36	46,60	46,60	46,26	45,63
hd1lags6	49,03	47,57	47,57	47,64	48,47	47,78	46,74	46,32	45,63	45,70
hd1lags7	49,51	47,36	47,85	48,06	47,71	48,68	46,74	47,36	46,60	45,84
hd2lags1	49,86	48,89	48,54	48,61	47,43	47,78	46,67	46,74	46,67	46,39
hd2lags2	49,79	48,68	48,96	48,40	47,99	47,71	47,23	46,53	46,74	46,32
hd2lags3	49,72	48,96	48,13	47,71	47,92	47,92	47,02	47,50	46,81	46,53
hd2lags4	49,93	47,16	48,54	47,64	46,88	47,64	47,02	46,46	46,39	46,32
hd2lags5	48,75	47,78	47,57	48,89	46,81	46,95	46,46	46,60	45,49	45,63
hd2lags6	49,24	47,16	47,99	47,92	48,40	47,57	46,88	46,26	45,63	45,70
hd2lags7	49,31	47,16	47,43	47,36	47,30	47,99	46,95	47,09	46,39	45,56
hd3lags1	49,79	48,96	48,47	48,54	47,50	47,57	46,46	46,81	46,60	46,60
hd3lags2	49,38	48,89	49,03	48,20	48,27	47,92	47,30	46,88	46,26	46,67
hd3lags3	49,51	48,47	48,27	47,78	48,47	48,13	47,09	47,09	47,02	46,39
hd3lags4	49,93	47,57	48,82	48,20	47,71	47,78	47,36	46,88	46,67	46,39
hd3lags5	48,61	47,36	48,34	48,75	46,88	47,23	47,02	46,88	45,70	45,77
hd3lags6	49,24	47,36	47,64	47,64	48,27	47,02	46,81	46,32	46,26	45,91
hd3lags7	49,51	47,30	47,50	47,09	47,50	48,75	47,23	47,57	46,88	46,26
hd4lags1	49,93	48,96	48,75	48,54	47,78	47,71	46,60	46,95	46,88	46,88
hd4lags2	49,45	48,96	49,51	48,27	48,54	47,57	47,23	46,95	46,39	46,74
hd4lags3	49,45	48,61	48,27	48,34	48,40	48,20	47,02	46,88	47,09	46,46
hd4lags4	49,72	47,57	48,89	47,99	47,57	47,99	47,30	47,23	46,67	46,26
hd4lags5	48,96	47,30	48,34	48,47	47,09	47,50	47,16	46,74	45,49	46,19
hd4lags6	49,58	47,30	47,36	47,78	48,27	47,09	47,02	46,39	46,19	45,98
hd4lags7	49,79	47,09	47,30	47,09	47,36	49,10	47,50	47,92	47,30	46,67
hd5lags1	49,72	49,03	48,96	48,89	47,71	47,64	46,95	47,02	46,95	46,95
hd5lags2	49,58	49,24	49,58	48,27	48,54	47,85	47,30	47,09	46,53	46,74
hd5lags3	49,65	48,40	48,54	48,13	48,40	48,34	46,95	47,02	47,09	46,39
hd5lags4	49,58	47,78	49,31	48,40	47,78	48,27	47,71	47,16	46,88	46,53
hd5lags5	49,03	47,43	48,13	48,47	46,95	47,50	47,02	46,88	45,84	45,84
hd5lags6	49,65	47,30	47,09	47,78	48,47	46,88	47,30	46,39	46,12	45,84
hd5lags7	49,31	47,43	47,16	47,23	47,36	48,96	47,50	47,92	47,43	46,53
hd6lags1	49,65	48,82	49,03	48,68	47,78	47,85	47,16	47,36	47,30	47,16
hd6lags2	49,65	48,89	49,45	48,20	48,61	47,64	46,95	47,02	46,74	46,81
hd6lags3	49,51	48,82	48,54	48,20	48,27	48,47	47,09	47,02	47,09	46,53
hd6lags4	49,65	47,64	49,17	48,20	47,50	48,34	47,43	47,23	46,81	46,32
hd6lags5	48,75	47,50	48,27	48,13	46,74	47,64	46,74	46,81	45,42	45,98
hd6lags6	49,65	47,23	47,09	47,78	48,40	46,95	47,02	46,53	46,32	45,84
hd6lags7	49,24	47,43	47,16	46,81	47,64	48,54	47,09	47,78	47,43	46,39
hd7lags1	49,93	48,96	49,31	48,68	47,92	47,99	47,30	47,64	47,43	47,43
hd7lags2	49,79	49,17	49,31	47,92	48,68	47,92	47,30	47,43	47,02	46,95
hd7lags3	49,86	48,61	48,68	48,89	48,54	48,61	47,43	47,16	47,23	46,81
hd7lags4	49,79	47,57	49,24	48,34	47,71	48,27	47,71	47,02	46,67	46,32
hd7lags5	49,03	47,30	48,54	48,75	46,67	47,78	46,60	46,60	45,84	45,77
hd7lags6	49,58	47,50	47,09	47,36	48,13	46,19	47,02	46,74	46,46	46,12
hd7lags7	49,24	47,50	47,43	47,02	47,36	48,75	46,74	47,64	47,30	46,39

Table 4. Forecast accuracy results for the ELM network and the CHF/EUR currency pair at price levels [%]

	t+1	t+2	t+3	t+4	t+5	t+6	t+7	t+8	t+9	t+10
hd1lags1	51,04	50,49	52,08	52,77	53,33	54,85	54,37	54,58	54,09	53,95
hd1lags2	52,29	50,42	51,94	52,43	54,30	54,51	54,85	54,23	54,23	53,61
hd1lags3	51,46	50,69	51,87	54,09	54,51	54,65	54,23	54,72	54,09	53,61
hd1lags4	51,66	49,72	52,01	52,64	53,81	54,99	54,51	54,16	54,16	53,68
hd1lags5	52,77	51,73	53,19	54,37	53,12	55,69	55,20	54,58	54,30	53,61
hd1lags6	51,53	52,43	52,84	53,74	53,74	54,16	53,95	54,23	54,30	53,54
hd1lags7	51,87	51,60	53,19	53,81	54,09	54,16	53,88	53,33	54,09	53,88
hd2lags1	50,97	50,69	52,29	53,12	53,54	54,92	54,44	54,51	53,88	53,47
hd2lags2	52,15	50,69	51,94	52,98	54,16	54,65	54,58	54,09	53,88	53,33
hd2lags3	51,53	50,90	52,57	54,23	54,79	55,20	54,85	54,58	54,16	53,88
hd2lags4	51,39	49,58	51,39	53,40	53,40	54,65	53,88	53,81	53,47	53,33
hd2lags5	52,22	51,60	52,43	53,74	53,54	54,30	54,37	53,95	53,88	53,12
hd2lags6	51,18	51,73	52,29	52,43	53,47	53,40	53,19	53,05	53,74	52,70
hd2lags7	52,01	50,90	52,57	53,19	53,40	53,40	53,54	52,98	53,47	53,47
hd3lags1	51,04	50,76	52,36	53,19	53,47	54,85	54,37	54,44	53,81	53,40
hd3lags2	52,70	50,69	52,29	52,98	54,23	54,79	54,51	54,09	53,95	53,05
hd3lags3	51,73	51,46	52,70	53,95	54,37	55,34	55,06	54,51	54,16	53,81
hd3lags4	51,87	50,14	51,32	52,84	53,33	54,23	53,74	52,84	52,98	53,05
hd3lags5	52,36	51,87	52,57	53,74	53,68	54,23	53,88	54,23	54,23	53,47
hd3lags6	51,39	51,32	52,29	52,84	53,47	53,54	52,77	52,64	53,54	52,29
hd3lags7	52,22	50,62	51,80	52,98	52,91	53,19	53,26	53,05	53,81	53,40
hd4lags1	50,97	50,83	52,43	53,26	53,40	54,79	54,30	54,37	53,88	53,47
hd4lags2	52,84	50,90	51,87	53,05	54,37	54,58	54,58	54,16	53,61	53,12
hd4lags3	51,60	51,39	53,12	54,09	54,44	55,20	55,41	54,72	54,16	53,61
hd4lags4	51,94	50,21	51,18	53,26	53,33	54,09	54,09	53,12	53,26	53,33
hd4lags5	52,15	51,87	52,57	53,81	53,88	54,23	54,30	53,74	53,95	53,54
hd4lags6	51,46	51,53	52,50	52,01	53,19	53,61	52,77	52,57	53,61	52,36
hd4lags7	52,01	50,42	52,29	52,91	52,91	53,26	53,33	53,47	53,74	53,47
hd5lags1	51,11	50,97	52,43	53,12	53,26	54,51	54,16	54,23	54,02	53,47
hd5lags2	52,43	50,83	51,94	53,26	54,58	54,92	54,51	54,37	53,40	53,19
hd5lags3	52,08	51,53	52,98	54,30	54,72	55,06	55,13	54,65	54,30	53,88
hd5lags4	52,15	49,93	51,60	53,54	52,98	53,68	53,74	53,26	53,19	53,19
hd5lags5	52,57	51,73	52,64	53,61	54,09	53,88	54,37	53,40	53,88	53,74
hd5lags6	51,32	50,97	51,94	52,57	52,77	53,12	52,08	52,01	52,77	51,11
hd5lags7	52,08	50,07	51,87	52,57	52,98	53,12	53,40	53,12	53,81	53,05
hd6lags1	50,97	50,83	52,29	52,98	53,26	54,65	54,16	54,51	54,02	53,61
hd6lags2	53,05	51,11	51,94	53,12	54,58	54,92	54,65	54,09	53,68	53,05
hd6lags3	51,53	51,60	52,70	54,02	54,16	54,79	54,65	54,02	54,16	53,81
hd6lags4	52,22	50,00	51,46	53,47	53,05	53,95	53,95	53,33	53,61	53,26
hd6lags5	52,29	51,60	52,15	53,26	54,16	53,95	53,68	52,70	53,68	53,54
hd6lags6	51,60	51,32	52,01	52,36	52,91	53,05	52,29	52,22	53,19	51,60
hd6lags7	51,94	50,55	51,53	53,05	52,70	52,98	52,98	53,05	53,88	53,12
hd7lags1	51,11	50,83	52,43	52,70	53,12	54,37	53,88	54,09	53,88	53,33
hd7lags2	52,77	51,18	51,87	53,33	54,51	54,99	54,44	54,44	53,61	53,40
hd7lags3	52,15	51,66	53,12	54,30	54,65	55,06	54,85	54,23	54,44	54,23
hd7lags4	52,15	50,14	51,53	53,74	53,26	53,68	53,88	53,47	53,47	52,98
hd7lags5	51,73	51,60	52,08	52,77	53,26	53,40	53,47	52,01	53,12	52,64
hd7lags6	51,73	50,76	51,94	51,73	52,08	52,43	51,87	51,11	52,01	50,62
hd7lags7	51,39	50,35	51,94	51,94	51,87	52,50	53,12	52,15	53,68	52,84

Table 5. Forecast accuracy results for the ELM network and the USD/EUR currency pair at price levels [%]

	t+1	t+2	t+3	t+4	t+5	t+6	t+7	t+8	t+9	t+10
hd1lags1	52,22	52,22	54,09	54,65	54,85	55,76	54,92	54,58	54,23	53,26
hd1lags2	51,80	51,94	54,02	54,51	54,79	55,76	55,06	54,99	54,23	53,54
hd1lags3	52,98	52,22	54,30	53,81	54,65	55,83	54,99	54,51	54,30	53,26
hd1lags4	52,91	52,57	53,81	54,44	54,44	54,92	54,99	54,65	54,30	53,33
hd1lags5	52,36	51,39	54,79	53,81	55,34	55,83	54,72	55,27	55,06	53,74
hd1lags6	52,91	52,08	54,72	54,23	54,85	56,31	55,69	55,34	55,62	54,16
hd1lags7	52,77	52,70	54,85	53,54	54,65	55,62	55,27	56,24	56,38	54,51
hd2lags1	52,36	52,50	54,09	54,65	54,99	55,89	55,20	54,99	54,65	53,81
hd2lags2	51,73	52,29	54,09	54,85	54,65	56,10	55,20	55,20	54,37	54,02
hd2lags3	53,05	52,29	54,02	53,68	54,65	56,24	54,85	54,51	55,13	53,54
hd2lags4	52,77	52,98	53,81	54,09	54,79	54,79	55,48	54,58	54,37	53,40
hd2lags5	52,15	51,80	55,13	54,02	55,06	55,76	55,62	55,27	55,34	53,74
hd2lags6	52,91	52,22	54,85	54,37	55,06	56,38	55,76	55,76	56,10	54,72
hd2lags7	53,33	52,29	55,34	54,23	54,85	56,31	55,27	56,66	56,66	55,06
hd3lags1	52,08	52,08	53,95	54,23	54,72	55,76	55,06	54,85	54,51	53,54
hd3lags2	52,22	51,94	54,16	54,51	54,79	55,89	55,48	55,13	54,51	54,09
hd3lags3	52,98	52,15	53,54	53,68	54,51	55,89	55,06	54,65	54,85	53,40
hd3lags4	52,29	52,91	53,40	54,09	54,79	55,06	55,96	54,72	54,72	53,68
hd3lags5	52,01	51,94	55,06	53,88	55,83	55,89	55,69	55,69	55,69	54,09
hd3lags6	52,84	52,15	54,92	54,85	55,20	56,66	56,45	56,52	56,66	55,41
hd3lags7	53,81	52,64	55,20	54,58	54,72	56,93	56,03	56,87	57,49	55,62
hd4lags1	51,94	52,36	54,09	54,51	54,99	56,03	55,34	55,13	54,79	53,81
hd4lags2	51,94	51,94	54,02	54,65	54,65	56,03	54,99	55,13	54,37	54,09
hd4lags3	52,98	51,73	53,81	54,23	54,85	55,89	54,99	54,58	54,79	53,68
hd4lags4	52,57	53,05	53,81	54,23	54,99	54,85	55,55	54,72	54,92	53,74
hd4lags5	52,22	52,08	55,34	54,02	55,69	55,83	55,62	55,76	55,48	54,37
hd4lags6	53,19	52,70	55,41	54,79	54,99	56,66	56,59	56,73	56,93	55,13
hd4lags7	53,54	52,98	55,55	54,99	55,20	57,00	56,17	57,00	57,21	56,03
hd5lags1	52,29	52,43	54,30	54,72	55,20	56,10	55,41	55,20	54,85	53,74
hd5lags2	52,29	51,94	53,74	54,51	54,79	55,89	55,55	55,27	54,51	54,23
hd5lags3	52,70	52,08	53,74	53,95	54,79	55,96	55,13	54,85	54,99	53,40
hd5lags4	52,36	53,05	53,81	54,09	54,58	54,92	55,83	54,99	55,34	53,95
hd5lags5	52,36	52,01	54,92	54,30	55,55	56,31	55,89	56,24	56,10	54,51
hd5lags6	53,33	52,64	55,34	55,06	55,27	57,42	56,31	57,14	57,21	55,76
hd5lags7	54,30	53,26	55,55	54,65	55,06	56,80	56,31	57,35	57,28	56,03
hd6lags1	52,15	52,43	54,16	54,58	54,92	55,96	55,41	55,20	54,85	53,88
hd6lags2	52,70	51,73	54,09	54,44	54,79	55,83	55,62	55,20	54,30	54,02
hd6lags3	52,70	52,01	54,30	54,09	54,79	56,10	54,99	54,72	55,13	53,88
hd6lags4	52,29	52,91	53,54	54,16	54,85	54,92	55,69	55,06	55,41	53,74
hd6lags5	52,36	52,01	55,48	54,44	56,10	56,45	55,89	56,31	56,03	54,79
hd6lags6	52,98	52,84	55,34	54,99	55,06	57,35	56,93	57,00	57,14	55,83
hd6lags7	53,88	53,19	55,83	54,92	55,41	57,07	56,73	57,07	57,28	55,89
hd7lags1	52,01	52,43	54,30	54,72	55,20	56,24	55,69	55,48	55,13	54,02
hd7lags2	52,36	51,94	53,74	54,51	54,58	55,76	55,41	55,13	54,44	54,09
hd7lags3	52,91	51,94	54,30	54,37	54,65	55,96	55,13	54,99	54,99	53,68
hd7lags4	52,29	52,84	53,54	54,30	54,92	55,06	55,62	55,34	55,76	53,95
hd7lags5	52,43	52,36	54,99	54,65	55,27	56,38	55,96	56,52	56,38	54,92
hd7lags6	53,40	52,98	55,48	54,92	55,27	57,00	57,28	57,56	57,35	55,76
hd7lags7	53,74	53,33	55,83	54,92	55,34	56,87	56,59	57,00	57,42	55,96

– For the currency pairs that achieved good results (CHF/EUR and USD/EUR), higher accuracy was achieved for forecasts at a horizon of 4–9 days (maximum for a forecast six days ahead) and the worst for 1–3 days. In the case of USD/EUR, where the results are worse, the trend is reversed, and the forecasts for a shorter period are more accurate.
– Significant differences in results within the same forecast horizon but for different network settings can be observed. However, in the case of the ELM network, it is difficult to show a relationship between the number of hidden nodes and delays and the results.
– It is impossible to demonstrate a relationship between an increase in the number of hidden nodes and an improvement in forecast accuracy for the analyzed currency pairs forecast using the ELM network.

Tables 6, 7 and 8 contain the forecast accuracy results for the MLP network and the GBP/EUR, CHF/EUR ,and USD/EUR currency pairs (in order of presentation).

In the tables representing the results for the MLP network, the results have different characteristics than for the ELM network. The accuracy of USD/EUR for all settings and forecast horizons exceeds 50%. For CHF/EUR, the significant majority is below 50%, while for GBP/EUR, the results oscillate around 50%. The MLP obtained the best results for the USD/EUR currency pair (Table 8.). Similar correlations can be observed to those of the ELM network, which obtained relatively good results. The worst results for USD/EUR when forecasting with the MLP USD/EUR network were obtained for a forecast horizon of 1–3 days and the best for a horizon of 6–8 days. For the MLP network and the USD/EUR currency pair, the effect of the network's hyperparameter settings on the accuracy can also be observed. In many cases, the networks behave analogously, regardless of the horizon. The most prominent examples in Fig. 1. are:

– Improved results for MLP networks for USD/EUR with settings: two hidden nodes and two delays (hd1lags2) compared to results with the same number of hidden nodes but for delays equal to one (hd1lags1) and three (hd1lags3).
– Improved results for MLP networks for USD/EUR with settings: two hidden nodes and five delays (hd1lags5) compared to results with the same number of hidden nodes but for delays equal to four (hd1lags4) and six (hd1lags6).
– Improved results for MLP networks for USD/EUR with settings of five hidden nodes and three delays (hd2lags3) compared to results with the same number of hidden nodes but for delays equal to two (hd2lags2) and four (hd2lags4).
– Improved results for MLP networks for USD/EUR with settings of ten hidden nodes and one delay (hd3lags2) relative to results with the same number of hidden nodes but for delays equal to two (hd3lags2) and relative to settings with five hidden nodes and seven delays (hd2lags7).

The above relationships are clearly seen in the radar graph - Fig. 1. This graph shows the accuracy of the forecasts depending on the MLP network settings. One can see the individual forecast horizons 'following' in the same direction for the

Table 6. Forecast accuracy results for the MLP network and the GBP/EUR currency pair at price levels [%]

	t+1	t+2	t+3	t+4	t+5	t+6	t+7	t+8	t+9	t+10
hd1lags1	50,28	50,76	51,94	51,80	50,69	49,86	50,14	51,18	51,46	52,01
hd1lags2	50,76	49,24	48,89	50,90	50,28	48,75	48,06	49,65	49,31	50,35
hd1lags3	50,21	49,17	50,76	50,28	49,86	48,89	49,03	48,82	49,51	48,89
hd1lags4	50,83	50,21	48,13	50,28	48,06	47,92	48,34	49,17	49,31	49,10
hd1lags5	51,25	49,17	50,14	49,31	50,35	49,65	48,89	50,42	50,14	51,39
hd1lags6	50,83	49,58	48,89	49,45	50,42	49,65	49,38	50,21	49,93	49,72
hd1lags7	50,00	49,38	49,10	49,72	49,24	50,97	49,51	49,79	49,93	49,79
hd2lags1	50,35	50,28	52,15	51,80	50,62	49,38	49,86	50,55	51,46	51,73
hd2lags2	50,42	49,58	48,96	49,86	50,21	48,27	48,06	49,17	49,03	49,45
hd2lags3	50,28	50,14	51,53	50,76	50,55	48,89	49,65	49,03	50,14	49,51
hd2lags4	50,69	50,14	49,38	51,18	48,89	48,54	48,89	49,65	50,07	49,24
hd2lags5	51,46	49,31	49,93	49,38	50,00	49,79	49,10	49,93	49,86	50,83
hd2lags6	50,69	49,51	48,96	49,86	49,93	50,07	49,31	50,35	50,07	49,17
hd2lags7	50,35	49,65	49,45	49,45	49,65	50,83	49,93	49,58	49,45	49,38
hd3lags1	49,45	49,10	50,62	50,76	49,79	49,10	49,10	49,86	51,32	50,90
hd3lags2	50,07	49,31	48,34	49,51	49,03	47,71	47,71	48,89	49,10	49,31
hd3lags3	50,83	50,42	52,08	51,53	50,76	50,07	49,93	49,24	50,07	49,45
hd3lags4	50,90	51,04	49,24	51,73	49,79	48,82	49,93	50,28	50,28	49,45
hd3lags5	51,18	49,51	49,45	49,51	50,42	49,24	49,31	49,79	50,28	51,18
hd3lags6	50,83	50,28	49,03	49,79	49,79	49,58	49,65	50,49	50,21	49,51
hd3lags7	50,62	50,35	48,89	49,51	49,72	50,97	49,58	50,14	49,72	48,96
hd4lags1	50,76	50,00	51,73	51,53	49,86	48,89	49,17	49,58	50,62	50,90
hd4lags2	50,69	49,10	48,34	49,86	49,31	47,50	47,71	48,40	48,96	49,31
hd4lags3	50,55	49,86	52,08	51,66	50,69	50,35	50,21	49,45	50,49	50,00
hd4lags4	50,62	50,62	48,89	51,32	49,31	48,75	49,24	49,79	49,86	49,31
hd4lags5	51,39	49,72	49,65	49,65	49,93	49,65	49,10	49,45	49,79	51,04
hd4lags6	50,97	49,72	48,61	49,58	49,86	49,10	48,96	50,55	49,93	49,17
hd4lags7	50,07	49,65	49,03	49,10	49,31	50,35	49,58	49,45	49,24	49,24
hd5lags1	50,69	50,07	51,11	50,97	50,21	49,31	49,03	49,58	50,97	50,49
hd5lags2	50,49	49,24	48,61	50,21	49,17	47,92	48,06	48,82	49,24	49,72
hd5lags3	50,49	49,93	51,46	51,32	50,55	49,72	49,10	48,96	49,51	49,17
hd5lags4	51,04	50,55	48,82	51,39	49,17	48,40	48,82	49,72	49,65	49,24
hd5lags5	51,18	49,31	49,65	49,93	49,58	49,10	48,96	49,24	49,65	50,69
hd5lags6	51,46	50,28	49,86	50,07	49,86	49,93	49,17	49,86	49,51	48,82
hd5lags7	49,93	50,35	49,51	50,28	49,65	50,69	49,79	50,14	49,72	49,45
hd6lags1	50,42	50,21	51,60	51,25	49,45	48,20	48,13	48,75	49,93	50,00
hd6lags2	50,00	49,45	48,89	50,21	48,82	47,92	47,36	48,75	48,54	49,17
hd6lags3	50,69	50,21	51,53	50,97	50,07	49,38	49,72	48,82	49,79	49,45
hd6lags4	50,90	51,04	49,10	51,11	48,96	48,13	48,68	49,38	49,58	48,75
hd6lags5	51,18	49,10	49,51	49,51	50,07	49,03	48,47	49,10	49,51	50,49
hd6lags6	51,32	50,49	49,17	49,51	49,45	49,17	48,96	50,21	50,00	49,45
hd6lags7	49,86	50,28	49,38	49,45	49,31	50,97	49,45	49,79	49,79	49,51
hd7lags1	50,14	50,07	51,39	51,11	49,79	47,85	47,71	48,20	49,58	49,51
hd7lags2	50,62	48,89	48,61	49,93	49,24	47,78	47,30	48,34	48,68	49,17
hd7lags3	50,97	51,04	51,73	51,39	50,35	49,51	49,72	48,89	50,21	49,03
hd7lags4	50,97	51,03	49,93	51,60	49,03	48,47	48,89	49,65	49,51	48,96
hd7lags5	50,76	49,17	49,72	49,31	49,65	49,31	48,34	48,61	49,24	50,35
hd7lags6	50,55	49,93	48,82	49,79	49,03	48,54	48,61	49,79	49,51	49,31
hd7lags7	50,21	50,42	48,68	49,24	49,65	50,42	48,89	49,93	50,07	49,10

Table 7. Forecast accuracy results for the MLP network and the CHF/EUR currency pair at price levels [%]

	t+1	t+2	t+3	t+4	t+5	t+6	t+7	t+8	t+9	t+10
hd1lags1	50,49	47,85	47,92	48,61	48,27	49,79	50,42	50,07	51,46	50,42
hd1lags2	51,11	48,96	48,27	50,00	50,07	50,55	50,97	50,62	51,60	51,04
hd1lags3	49,51	48,06	47,78	48,34	48,13	50,07	50,49	50,28	51,32	50,00
hd1lags4	50,35	47,64	47,78	48,13	47,78	49,45	49,93	49,58	50,69	49,65
hd1lags5	50,07	48,13	48,06	48,75	48,54	50,28	51,04	50,83	51,80	50,62
hd1lags6	49,79	47,78	47,92	48,20	47,92	49,65	50,28	49,93	51,04	50,28
hd1lags7	48,82	47,43	46,88	47,50	47,36	48,47	49,51	49,03	50,69	49,17
hd2lags1	48,20	47,09	46,67	47,71	47,85	48,82	49,86	49,51	50,69	48,96
hd2lags2	48,82	47,02	46,81	47,71	47,09	47,92	48,96	47,92	49,17	47,57
hd2lags3	49,17	48,40	47,36	48,61	47,71	49,03	49,79	49,24	50,35	48,54
hd2lags4	49,03	47,57	46,81	47,78	47,57	48,06	48,96	48,40	49,51	47,78
hd2lags5	49,03	47,78	47,71	48,20	47,43	48,13	49,38	48,68	49,93	48,34
hd2lags6	49,03	48,06	47,43	48,54	48,06	48,61	49,10	48,75	50,21	48,40
hd2lags7	48,54	47,64	46,67	46,81	46,74	47,64	48,47	47,78	49,24	47,36
hd3lags1	48,89	47,23	46,32	47,99	47,71	48,82	49,72	48,68	50,49	49,10
hd3lags2	48,89	47,30	46,60	47,71	46,95	47,85	48,75	47,71	49,17	47,23
hd3lags3	48,54	47,43	47,36	48,34	48,27	48,61	49,58	48,89	50,00	48,47
hd3lags4	49,24	48,27	47,71	48,27	47,71	48,54	49,31	48,40	49,72	47,92
hd3lags5	49,17	48,40	47,50	48,06	47,43	48,27	49,86	49,38	50,14	48,75
hd3lags6	48,82	47,36	47,23	48,27	47,85	48,20	49,51	48,89	49,79	48,13
hd3lags7	49,17	47,64	47,64	48,20	47,92	48,82	49,65	49,17	50,21	48,27
hd4lags1	48,61	47,78	47,23	48,34	47,71	48,13	49,17	48,34	49,72	48,13
hd4lags2	48,34	47,78	47,43	48,20	47,43	48,13	48,89	48,68	50,14	48,20
hd4lags3	49,58	48,54	47,99	48,89	48,06	48,75	49,38	48,75	50,28	48,61
hd4lags4	49,45	48,47	48,40	48,47	48,54	48,68	49,45	48,96	50,42	48,75
hd4lags5	48,96	47,36	46,67	47,92	47,23	47,92	48,68	48,06	49,45	47,64
hd4lags6	49,03	47,64	46,88	48,13	47,85	48,40	49,03	48,54	50,00	48,20
hd4lags7	48,68	47,43	46,88	47,64	47,16	48,06	48,68	48,34	49,38	47,85
hd5lags1	48,96	47,99	47,50	48,82	48,06	48,75	49,24	48,47	49,93	48,40
hd5lags2	48,96	47,92	47,78	48,54	47,78	48,20	49,24	48,34	49,79	48,27
hd5lags3	48,75	47,78	47,57	48,34	47,57	48,34	49,03	48,47	50,00	48,40
hd5lags4	48,89	47,50	47,02	47,71	47,16	47,71	48,89	48,40	49,58	48,13
hd5lags5	48,34	46,95	46,12	47,36	46,74	47,71	48,75	47,71	49,17	47,64
hd5lags6	49,24	47,92	47,57	48,82	47,78	48,61	48,82	48,61	49,79	48,20
hd5lags7	48,54	47,71	46,95	48,13	47,43	47,99	48,89	48,54	49,72	47,78
hd6lags1	49,03	48,27	47,50	48,40	47,50	48,47	49,10	48,89	50,35	48,68
hd6lags2	49,51	47,99	47,23	48,34	47,64	48,34	49,24	48,61	49,93	47,85
hd6lags3	49,17	47,99	47,30	48,13	47,57	48,13	48,89	48,40	49,72	48,20
hd6lags4	48,96	47,78	47,02	48,34	47,92	48,61	49,03	48,68	50,14	48,47
hd6lags5	48,61	47,23	46,60	47,78	47,43	48,27	49,03	48,54	49,72	48,06
hd6lags6	49,03	47,23	46,60	47,78	47,36	47,92	48,96	48,20	49,38	47,71
hd6lags7	49,24	47,99	47,36	48,13	47,57	48,27	49,03	48,54	49,58	47,92
hd7lags1	48,61	47,78	47,92	48,61	48,20	48,40	49,51	48,54	50,14	48,61
hd7lags2	48,61	46,95	47,23	47,64	47,36	47,78	48,82	48,27	49,17	47,64
hd7lags3	49,10	47,92	47,64	48,40	47,85	48,54	49,17	48,54	49,72	48,20
hd7lags4	49,38	47,99	48,20	48,68	48,61	49,17	49,79	49,03	50,21	48,75
hd7lags5	48,96	47,99	47,78	48,06	47,71	48,06	48,82	48,27	49,65	48,13
hd7lags6	48,75	47,43	47,50	48,27	47,78	48,54	49,31	48,75	50,28	48,75
hd7lags7	48,96	47,78	47,78	48,06	47,85	48,54	49,51	48,96	50,35	48,89

Table 8. Forecast accuracy results for the MLP network and the USD/EUR currency pair at price levels [%]

	t+1	t+2	t+3	t+4	t+5	t+6	t+7	t+8	t+9	t+10
hd1lags1	53,19	53,95	54,51	53,12	53,95	55,96	55,96	55,48	55,76	55,27
hd1lags2	53,33	54,58	53,40	53,68	53,95	56,10	57,07	56,10	57,07	55,62
hd1lags3	52,29	52,22	54,79	53,47	54,16	56,87	56,73	56,24	57,77	56,31
hd1lags4	54,79	52,70	53,05	53,54	54,44	55,41	56,38	56,31	56,66	55,96
hd1lags5	53,19	53,68	54,44	54,23	56,03	56,17	56,45	56,17	57,14	56,03
hd1lags6	53,68	53,95	55,48	54,37	55,06	57,07	56,31	55,96	57,21	56,03
hd1lags7	53,68	53,95	54,09	53,88	54,92	56,59	56,80	56,24	57,98	56,17
hd2lags1	53,74	54,37	54,85	53,61	54,23	55,96	56,38	56,38	56,59	55,48
hd2lags2	53,68	54,99	52,84	54,16	54,44	56,73	57,28	56,80	57,77	56,03
hd2lags3	52,98	52,98	54,44	53,95	54,79	56,80	57,14	57,49	57,63	56,87
hd2lags4	55,20	53,88	53,47	54,37	54,65	56,38	57,42	56,87	58,04	56,87
hd2lags5	53,47	54,16	54,44	55,20	56,24	55,89	56,59	56,10	57,91	56,73
hd2lags6	53,74	53,81	55,20	55,76	55,83	57,84	56,24	56,03	57,63	56,52
hd2lags7	53,81	54,16	55,20	54,65	55,62	57,49	57,35	56,59	57,63	55,76
hd3lags1	54,44	54,37	55,13	54,02	54,30	55,83	56,17	55,76	56,17	55,13
hd3lags2	54,02	55,20	53,19	54,09	54,72	56,45	57,70	56,73	57,42	56,31
hd3lags3	53,26	53,05	54,92	53,68	54,02	55,96	56,59	57,00	57,21	56,17
hd3lags4	54,85	53,40	54,09	54,99	54,23	55,27	57,56	56,10	57,42	56,87
hd3lags5	54,09	54,16	54,44	56,31	56,45	55,27	56,59	55,96	57,07	55,62
hd3lags6	53,54	53,68	55,20	55,76	56,03	58,46	56,17	56,52	57,77	57,07
hd3lags7	53,68	53,40	54,92	54,72	55,62	57,00	57,63	56,24	57,77	56,17
hd4lags1	54,02	54,51	54,85	54,30	54,85	55,76	56,52	55,76	56,38	55,20
hd4lags2	53,12	55,41	53,12	54,51	54,79	57,00	57,63	57,00	57,63	56,80
hd4lags3	53,61	52,64	54,16	53,95	54,02	56,24	56,87	57,07	57,07	56,24
hd4lags4	54,85	54,09	54,23	55,41	54,58	55,69	57,35	56,59	57,63	56,52
hd4lags5	53,88	54,09	54,30	55,96	56,80	55,83	56,93	56,17	57,42	55,62
hd4lags6	52,98	53,68	54,72	55,41	56,03	58,32	56,59	56,93	57,91	56,93
hd4lags7	53,68	53,74	54,92	54,37	55,62	57,21	57,77	56,31	57,91	56,03
hd5lags1	53,95	54,37	55,27	54,37	54,92	56,45	56,93	56,31	57,07	55,89
hd5lags2	53,74	54,72	53,19	54,51	54,92	56,73	57,63	56,45	57,28	56,31
hd5lags3	52,98	52,29	54,44	53,88	53,81	56,38	57,21	56,73	57,42	56,59
hd5lags4	55,06	53,54	53,88	54,99	54,44	55,27	57,63	56,80	57,91	56,24
hd5lags5	54,44	54,30	54,30	55,69	56,73	55,76	56,73	56,03	57,21	56,03
hd5lags6	53,12	53,61	54,65	54,85	56,10	58,11	55,83	56,31	57,28	57,00
hd5lags7	53,47	53,68	55,62	54,79	56,17	57,84	58,04	56,73	57,56	56,24
hd6lags1	54,16	54,58	55,20	54,16	55,13	56,24	56,87	56,17	57,07	56,17
hd6lags2	53,40	55,06	53,26	54,65	55,06	56,87	57,56	56,66	56,93	56,38
hd6lags3	52,91	52,70	54,30	53,81	53,68	55,69	56,66	56,73	56,45	56,38
hd6lags4	54,79	53,61	54,16	55,34	54,58	55,13	57,35	56,80	57,84	56,31
hd6lags5	53,95	54,16	54,79	55,62	57,00	55,89	56,31	56,52	57,77	56,45
hd6lags6	53,47	53,33	54,72	54,92	55,76	58,60	56,59	56,31	57,70	56,87
hd6lags7	53,61	53,95	55,06	54,37	55,62	57,21	57,70	56,52	57,28	56,24
hd7lags1	53,95	55,06	55,55	55,20	55,34	56,59	57,63	56,80	57,14	56,03
hd7lags2	53,19	53,95	53,33	53,74	54,16	55,96	56,52	56,24	56,59	55,55
hd7lags3	52,91	52,50	54,23	53,40	53,81	55,69	56,45	56,45	56,17	55,96
hd7lags4	54,79	53,81	54,09	55,96	54,58	54,99	57,56	57,00	57,42	55,83
hd7lags5	53,88	54,44	54,92	55,62	56,87	55,76	56,17	56,17	56,93	56,38
hd7lags6	52,91	52,84	53,88	54,79	55,62	58,67	56,45	56,45	57,84	56,73
hd7lags7	53,68	53,40	54,92	54,16	55,55	57,49	58,46	56,80	57,49	56,45

same neural network settings. The following conclusions can be formulated by analyzing the accuracy of forecasts of the CHF/EUR currency pair (Fig. 2.) using MLP networks:

- MLPs for CHF/EUR with settings with two delays obtained the best accuracy for the forecast horizon: two days,
- MLPs for CHF/EUR with settings with five delays obtained the best accuracy for forecast horizons of five days and four days, but for the number of hidden nodes greater than three,
- MLPs for CHF/EUR with settings with six delays obtained the best forecast accuracy for six days from now.

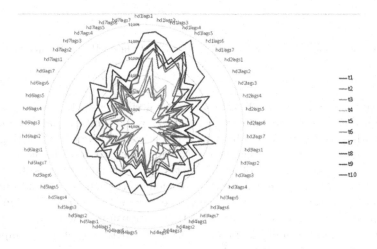

Fig. 1. Relevance results for the MLP network and the USD/EUR currency pair - radar chart

MLPs with a number of delays equal to the forecast horizon do not always give the best results. Such an example is forecasting one day, where the best results were obtained for the CHF/EUR currency with the lags4 hyperparameter. It is also possible to find cases where, at given lags setting and regardless of the settings for the number of hidden nodes, the network produced the worst results compared to other lags settings with the same number of hidden nodes. An example of this is forecasting for two days: the worst results for this network were achieved with a setting with three delays.

Fig. 2. Relevance results for the MLP network and the CHF/EUR currency pair - radar chart

The network obtained the best results is the LSTM network - Tables 9, 10 and 11. The average results for all currency pairs, forecast horizons, and the neural network's hyperparameters are higher than the accuracy when forecasting with the other analyzed network. Therefore, it is important to note the advantage of the LSTM network over the other two networks. This advantage is due to the properties of the LSTM network and, in particular, the retention of information about previous states, which is crucial in the case of time series. For the ELM and MLP networks, it was difficult to see the relationship between an increase in the number of hidden nodes and an increase in prediction accuracy (complexity within the same type of neural network).

For the CHF/EUR accuracy results of the LSTM forecasting, a radar chart was drawn up for all possible combinations of network parameters. In it, it can be seen (except for the 1–2-day forecasting) that the LSTM achieves the best results for all settings with a delay count of 1; after that, as the delay count increases, the accuracy decreases - the situation is the same for all network settings, regardless of the number of hidden layers used in the network. For such settings, the LSTM network achieved more than 70% accuracy for forecasts nine days ahead and nearly 65% for horizons 7,8,10 - as can be seen very well in the radar chart - Fig. 3.

Table 9. Forecast accuracy results for the LSTM network and the GBP/EUR currency pair at price levels [%]

	t+1	t+2	t+3	t+4	t+5	t+6	t+7	t+8	t+9	t+10
hd1lags1	49,93	58,04	61,51	64,70	65,53	64,49	68,24	69,28	70,39	72,19
hd1lags2	50,00	49,45	55,06	57,07	58,95	59,15	60,47	61,65	63,66	61,44
hd1lags3	51,04	49,38	49,24	54,02	54,02	54,51	55,48	59,71	59,02	58,74
hd1lags4	50,90	49,65	50,14	49,58	50,97	51,73	53,61	54,92	55,34	55,89
hd1lags5	51,18	47,99	48,47	47,78	48,34	50,69	51,04	52,43	53,26	52,64
hd1lags6	51,73	49,45	49,65	48,89	48,20	48,89	49,79	51,25	51,66	51,04
hd1lags7	50,83	50,07	48,61	49,93	49,51	49,86	48,27	50,83	50,14	50,90
hd2lags1	51,46	59,43	62,97	67,48	67,34	68,93	71,57	72,33	73,51	73,65
hd2lags2	51,39	49,79	56,52	58,74	60,82	60,06	63,52	65,40	66,37	66,85
hd2lags3	50,83	49,45	49,65	53,26	54,23	55,34	56,73	60,19	62,00	61,79
hd2lags4	51,18	50,14	48,68	48,89	50,55	52,22	54,02	55,69	57,63	57,14
hd2lags5	51,39	49,58	49,65	48,47	48,47	49,65	52,22	53,54	54,65	53,95
hd2lags6	51,53	49,31	49,93	47,85	49,79	49,79	51,25	50,90	51,87	52,29
hd2lags7	50,35	49,93	50,49	51,32	51,32	51,60	51,11	51,94	52,15	52,77
hd3lags1	50,07	59,92	63,52	66,37	68,86	68,72	70,32	72,88	74,20	75,38
hd3lags2	49,51	48,89	56,03	57,07	60,26	60,68	64,49	64,49	67,75	67,34
hd3lags3	51,04	49,93	49,86	54,51	54,37	54,65	57,63	59,57	61,86	61,72
hd3lags4	50,97	48,47	49,65	48,27	51,39	52,36	54,44	55,34	57,56	57,98
hd3lags5	51,32	49,86	48,82	48,40	49,24	50,49	51,60	53,88	53,54	53,88
hd3lags6	51,46	50,83	50,35	50,07	48,34	48,96	51,73	51,39	53,12	52,08
hd3lags7	51,11	49,51	49,65	50,55	49,51	50,35	49,38	50,55	52,36	52,64
hd4lags1	51,11	58,11	63,11	66,57	68,86	69,63	70,80	71,22	74,06	74,76
hd4lags2	51,66	48,47	55,20	57,35	59,92	61,58	64,56	66,30	66,71	67,61
hd4lags3	50,00	50,69	49,58	54,23	54,85	53,95	56,93	58,95	61,03	61,10
hd4lags4	50,90	48,61	48,89	47,64	51,11	51,94	55,06	55,55	57,98	58,67
hd4lags5	50,83	48,47	48,75	48,13	47,99	49,38	51,32	53,54	53,19	53,88
hd4lags6	51,04	50,76	49,03	48,89	49,38	50,00	50,14	52,08	52,50	52,70
hd4lags7	50,42	51,04	49,51	50,28	50,07	50,07	48,75	51,32	52,43	53,05
hd5lags1	51,53	56,87	63,31	66,50	68,79	68,79	70,18	71,84	72,05	74,20
hd5lags2	50,62	49,93	55,55	58,39	59,78	61,65	63,66	65,53	66,64	67,20
hd5lags3	49,65	49,93	49,51	53,54	54,51	55,69	58,46	60,19	62,07	61,44
hd5lags4	50,21	48,75	46,95	48,27	50,83	51,66	54,30	54,79	56,66	56,87
hd5lags5	50,35	49,58	47,78	47,99	48,47	50,21	52,15	54,09	54,51	53,95
hd5lags6	51,32	50,07	48,75	49,10	48,96	48,54	50,42	52,36	51,53	52,29
hd5lags7	50,83	51,39	50,55	50,62	50,90	51,32	49,72	51,18	52,01	52,22
hd6lags1	51,53	57,56	62,97	65,95	68,10	69,56	70,53	72,88	75,24	72,95
hd6lags2	49,10	50,35	55,83	57,77	60,26	59,92	63,18	64,63	66,64	67,13
hd6lags3	50,83	50,35	50,28	54,79	55,48	56,10	58,18	59,64	62,07	62,62
hd6lags4	49,86	48,13	49,03	48,75	51,25	51,53	53,88	55,41	57,35	58,39
hd6lags5	50,35	50,35	48,68	48,40	49,51	49,86	52,43	53,05	54,16	54,02
hd6lags6	51,60	50,76	49,10	48,40	48,82	49,93	49,10	52,22	52,84	53,81
hd6lags7	50,07	49,58	49,86	50,90	50,00	49,38	49,93	50,90	51,25	51,39
hd7lags1	53,95	55,06	55,55	55,20	55,34	56,59	57,63	56,80	57,14	56,03
hd7lags2	53,19	53,95	53,33	53,74	54,16	55,96	56,52	56,24	56,59	55,55
hd7lags3	52,91	52,50	54,23	53,40	53,81	55,69	56,45	56,45	56,17	55,96
hd7lags4	54,79	53,81	53,09	55,96	54,58	54,99	57,56	57,00	57,42	55,83
hd7lags5	53,88	54,44	54,92	55,62	56,87	55,76	56,17	56,17	56,93	56,38
hd7lags6	52,91	52,84	53,88	54,79	55,62	58,67	56,45	56,45	57,84	56,73
hd7lags7	53,68	53,40	54,92	54,16	55,55	57,49	58,46	56,80	,57,49	56,49

Table 10. Forecast accuracy results for the LSTM network and the CHF/EUR currency pair at price levels [%]

	t+1	t+2	t+3	t+4	t+5	t+6	t+7	t+8	t+9	t+10
hd1lags1	50,62	59,36	63,31	66,30	70,25	65,40	64,98	69,00	74,13	69,97
hd1lags2	49,65	53,54	56,87	60,19	61,65	60,47	58,81	62,62	67,75	66,30
hd1lags3	50,42	52,29	51,80	54,37	56,17	57,42	57,35	59,36	62,55	60,61
hd1lags4	49,65	52,64	51,39	50,97	53,12	53,81	54,44	56,59	59,64	58,25
hd1lags5	49,58	52,43	50,21	50,97	51,87	51,46	51,11	54,44	56,38	54,85
hd1lags6	49,93	51,87	50,62	50,83	50,76	50,07	50,00	50,55	54,02	53,95
hd1lags7	50,69	53,05	52,36	52,36	52,70	51,25	49,79	50,83	53,26	53,05
hd2lags1	48,13	59,29	64,77	65,60	71,29	66,50	66,23	71,22	76,63	72,26
hd2lags2	48,75	53,19	57,49	62,21	64,77	61,30	60,47	64,49	69,07	66,85
hd2lags3	48,82	53,61	51,04	55,55	55,96	57,42	57,28	59,22	63,52	62,34
hd2lags4	49,72	50,90	50,14	53,40	54,30	54,85	54,65	57,84	59,43	58,53
hd2lags5	50,69	51,46	50,07	52,29	51,73	52,22	50,90	53,12	58,46	57,56
hd2lags6	50,42	52,22	50,49	51,46	51,66	49,65	51,39	51,80	56,24	55,27
hd2lags7	50,76	52,36	50,62	51,80	50,62	50,35	49,79	51,60	53,74	54,58
hd3lags1	49,86	59,08	65,53	67,27	72,05	66,85	67,27	71,29	75,87	72,33
hd3lags2	48,68	51,53	57,35	61,72	63,52	61,72	61,10	64,01	70,67	67,96
hd3lags3	48,96	51,80	51,87	54,85	57,28	57,28	56,80	59,29	63,80	63,11
hd3lags4	51,04	51,25	49,86	52,57	53,81	54,79	54,44	56,17	60,40	58,95
hd3lags5	49,65	50,07	50,90	51,80	50,90	53,33	51,73	54,30	56,45	55,20
hd3lags6	50,55	51,60	51,32	52,08	52,15	52,77	50,83	52,50	57,49	54,23
hd3lags7	50,49	52,91	50,62	51,66	51,04	50,14	49,65	51,39	53,74	53,74
hd4lags1	49,03	59,99	65,05	66,78	73,16	67,27	67,06	71,84	76,84	72,61
hd4lags2	48,75	52,77	57,21	60,54	64,70	62,07	60,89	64,42	71,08	68,10
hd4lags3	48,89	51,53	50,76	55,41	58,04	59,29	58,04	61,37	65,40	63,04
hd4lags4	49,38	51,32	52,43	52,77	53,95	55,20	56,03	57,98	60,89	59,43
hd4lags5	50,28	50,90	50,90	52,08	50,83	53,19	51,39	54,37	57,07	55,62
hd4lags6	51,25	52,36	51,53	51,60	51,32	50,76	50,49	52,57	55,20	55,34
hd4lags7	49,10	51,73	49,31	51,18	50,35	50,69	49,72	51,11	53,95	54,09
hd5lags1	50,42	59,71	64,15	67,61	71,98	65,81	65,81	70,53	77,53	74,20
hd5lags2	49,79	53,61	56,38	62,07	64,29	61,79	60,89	64,49	71,50	69,35
hd5lags3	49,03	51,11	50,76	56,73	57,42	57,56	57,35	59,36	62,97	63,80
hd5lags4	50,35	52,36	50,97	52,70	52,70	54,72	54,16	56,93	58,95	58,39
hd5lags5	50,49	51,25	51,18	51,87	50,35	53,12	51,80	53,47	56,73	55,76
hd5lags6	49,31	51,18	51,25	52,15	49,86	50,35	49,51	51,53	55,96	55,89
hd5lags7	51,60	51,46	50,83	52,77	50,14	50,28	49,86	50,90	53,47	53,26
hd6lags1	49,86	59,15	64,91	68,10	73,30	66,99	66,85	71,36	77,18	73,44
hd6lags2	49,31	52,08	58,60	61,03	64,84	63,04	62,14	65,33	71,98	69,00
hd6lags3	48,89	51,80	51,18	55,13	57,98	58,88	57,98	60,54	64,49	62,34
hd6lags4	50,42	52,77	51,18	53,12	54,79	56,10	54,72	57,63	61,10	59,43
hd6lags5	50,49	52,29	50,21	52,08	51,73	52,77	53,33	53,47	57,56	57,14
hd6lags6	50,62	50,55	50,28	51,87	50,14	51,66	50,55	52,29	56,17	54,72
hd6lags7	50,62	51,11	50,69	51,32	51,39	50,21	50,69	51,32	54,30	53,19
hd7lags1	53,95	55,06	55,55	55,20	55,34	56,59	57,63	56,80	57,14	56,03
hd7lags2	53,19	53,95	53,33	53,74	54,16	55,96	56,52	56,24	56,59	55,55
hd7lags3	52,91	52,50	54,23	53,40	53,81	55,69	56,45	56,45	56,17	55,96
hd7lags4	54,79	53,81	54,09	55,96	54,58	54,99	57,56	57,00	57,42	55,83
hd7lags5	53,88	54,44	54,92	55,62	56,87	55,76	56,17	56,17	56,93	56,38
hd7lags6	52,91	52,84	53,88	54,79	55,62	58,67	56,45	56,45	57,84	56,73
hd7lags7	53,68	53,40	54,92	54,16	55,55	57,49	58,46	56,80	57,49	56,45

Table 11. Forecast accuracy results for the LSTM network and the USD/EUR currency pair at price levels [%]

	t+1	t+2	t+3	t+4	t+5	t+6	t+7	t+8	t+9	t+10
hd1lags1	49,65	56,93	60,12	63,25	63,11	66,02	66,44	69,97	70,18	71,50
hd1lags2	50,76	51,18	55,13	57,63	58,32	60,89	61,30	62,83	63,45	63,87
hd1lags3	50,69	51,53	50,83	53,74	54,51	56,59	58,04	58,81	59,85	59,64
hd1lags4	50,76	49,51	51,25	50,97	53,61	54,58	55,06	55,96	58,04	55,96
hd1lags5	50,76	50,14	52,22	51,73	50,90	52,77	53,88	55,62	56,17	55,96
hd1lags6	50,49	49,17	51,32	51,80	51,32	51,18	52,01	52,84	54,09	53,88
hd1lags7	50,21	49,93	52,08	51,39	51,18	50,76	52,22	53,33	53,61	54,65
hd2lags1	49,45	57,28	60,61	65,46	66,64	66,92	70,53	72,40	73,65	73,16
hd2lags2	50,62	51,32	56,38	58,88	60,06	63,52	64,01	64,77	67,20	68,24
hd2lags3	51,11	51,18	50,28	55,83	56,17	60,47	61,65	61,72	62,55	63,87
hd2lags4	50,76	50,69	51,53	52,50	53,68	56,45	57,77	59,36	59,57	59,92
hd2lags5	50,83	50,21	52,22	53,05	52,64	54,99	55,69	57,07	57,70	60,54
hd2lags6	51,25	51,11	52,36	52,36	52,36	53,26	53,40	54,99	55,34	56,80
hd2lags7	49,72	50,42	52,98	52,57	51,53	51,73	53,95	54,09	55,48	57,14
hd3lags1	50,62	58,88	62,55	67,06	67,89	69,63	71,22	72,82	75,10	74,76
hd3lags2	51,04	49,93	56,80	60,54	60,06	64,22	64,08	66,57	68,17	69,07
hd3lags3	50,07	50,28	50,90	56,31	56,03	60,12	62,00	62,83	63,73	63,87
hd3lags4	50,90	50,69	51,73	53,61	54,44	58,53	58,46	61,17	62,34	62,07
hd3lags5	49,79	49,45	50,49	52,43	51,66	54,51	55,96	57,98	59,78	60,26
hd3lags6	51,04	50,21	51,73	52,77	51,46	52,91	53,54	54,51	55,76	56,10
hd3lags7	49,72	50,97	53,12	52,64	51,94	53,95	54,09	54,16	55,62	57,21
hd4lags1	48,89	59,22	61,37	66,71	66,99	69,56	70,25	72,68	74,90	74,41
hd4lags2	51,18	49,93	56,31	60,12	60,68	62,41	64,70	66,30	69,35	67,13
hd4lags3	50,07	52,15	51,25	57,14	56,24	60,12	61,79	62,55	63,11	63,38
hd4lags4	50,90	51,80	51,94	52,77	54,44	57,77	57,56	58,39	60,26	60,61
hd4lags5	51,53	49,79	52,22	53,68	53,26	55,96	56,52	57,63	60,06	58,32
hd4lags6	51,46	51,80	51,39	52,22	51,80	52,84	51,66	54,99	56,24	55,34
hd4lags7	51,18	51,11	52,91	52,15	52,64	53,05	53,19	54,58	55,62	54,99
hd5lags1	50,21	57,77	61,93	65,88	67,75	68,45	69,69	72,40	73,99	73,65
hd5lags2	50,28	51,18	55,27	59,71	60,12	63,80	62,90	66,09	67,34	68,17
hd5lags3	50,42	52,84	51,80	56,52	57,35	60,54	61,58	62,14	64,08	64,36
hd5lags4	52,15	50,62	52,15	54,30	55,55	57,07	58,04	59,29	61,23	62,55
hd5lags5	49,31	50,90	51,80	53,68	52,98	55,76	55,55	57,70	59,29	60,06
hd5lags6	50,83	51,25	51,32	53,33	51,87	54,79	53,95	55,13	56,66	57,35
hd5lags7	49,58	51,46	52,70	52,15	52,70	53,54	53,95	54,30	55,41	56,80
hd6lags1	49,31	59,15	62,76	66,57	66,71	67,89	69,49	73,16	73,99	73,02
hd6lags2	50,14	51,39	56,80	60,82	61,10	63,04	64,56	65,40	67,34	69,63
hd6lags3	49,93	53,05	50,83	56,17	55,34	60,26	60,89	62,76	63,52	64,29
hd6lags4	50,62	51,39	51,18	53,81	54,58	56,87	58,88	59,99	60,89	61,65
hd6lags5	51,87	51,25	52,91	53,26	51,80	54,79	56,59	57,98	59,02	59,15
hd6lags6	51,04	50,55	52,84	52,47	52,15	52,50	53,33	55,41	55,89	56,45
hd6lags7	51,80	51,53	52,57	52,77	53,47	54,85	53,05	54,85	56,45	57,07
hd7lags1	53,95	55,06	55,55	55,20	55,34	56,59	57,63	56,80	57,14	56,03
hd7lags2	53,19	53,95	53,33	53,74	54,16	55,96	56,52	56,24	56,59	55,55
hd7lags3	52,91	52,50	54,23	53,40	53,81	55,69	56,45	56,45	56,17	55,96
hd7lags4	54,79	53,81	54,09	55,96	54,58	54,99	57,56	57,00	57,42	55,83
hd7lags5	53,88	54,44	54,92	55,62	56,87	55,76	56,17	56,17	56,93	56,38
hd7lags6	52,91	52,84	53,88	54,79	55,62	58,67	56,45	56,45	57,84	56,73
hd7lags7	53,68	53,40	54,92	54,16	55,55	57,49	58,46	56,80	57,49	56,45

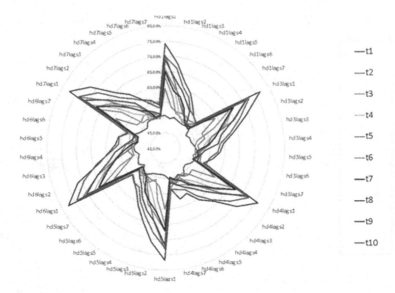

Fig. 3. Forecast accuracy results for the LSTM network and the USD/EUR currency pair at price levels [%]

5   Discussion

The research results confirm the effectiveness of neural networks in forecasting the direction of changes in currency pairs. It is necessary to agree with the statements quoted in the introduction about the difficulty and complexity of forecasting in this market and the many factors that may influence the increase or decrease of forecast accuracy. The study identifies numerous relationships between forecast accuracy and network hyperparameters. This theme can be further developed in subsequent phases of the study by, among other things, changing the asset to be forecast, changing the types of networks, extending the hyperparameterisation (especially for LSTM networks), and extending the period studied in order to find the dependence of forecast accuracy on the current market situation.

6   Conclusions

Summarizing the conclusions obtained for all types of neural networks, it is necessary to point out the highest percentage of correctly predicted directions of change by the LSTM network, especially for settings with one delay (lags1). When forecasting with the MLP network, for some of the currencies and forecast horizons studied, an improvement in accuracy can be observed when the number of lags used in the settings of this network is equal to the forecast horizon. For the MLP network, unique settings were also noted for which the network gave more accurate forecasts than all other settings, regardless of the forecast horizon. For the ELM network, it was most difficult to identify relationships between forecast accuracy and network settings and forecast horizon or forecast currency pair.

References

1. Kuan, C.M., Liu, T.: Forecasting exchange rates using feedforward and recurrent neural networks. J. Appl. Econ. **10**(4), 347–364 (1995)
2. Shobana, G., Umamaheswari, K.: Forecasting by machine learning techniques and econometrics: a review. In 2021 6th International Conference on Inventive Computation Technologies (ICICT), pp. 1010–1016. IEEE (2021)
3. Mishchenko, V., Naumenkova, S., Ivanov, V., Tishchenko, I.: Special aspects of using hybrid financial tools for project risk management in Ukraine. Invest. Manag. Finan. Innov. **15**(2), 257–266 (2018)
4. Bitar, J.: Foreign currency intermediation: systemic risk and macroprudential regulation. Latin Am. J. Central Bank. **2**(2), 100028 (2021)
5. Zhao, R., et al.: A framework for the general design and computation of hybrid neural networks. Nature Commun. **13**(1), 1–12 (2022)
6. Li, Y., Dai, W.: Bitcoin price forecasting method based on CNN? LSTM hybrid neural network model. J. Eng. **2020**(13), 344–347 (2020)
7. Mundt, M., Johnson, W.R., Potthast, W., Markert, B., Mian, A., Alderson, J.: A comparison of three neural network approaches for estimating joint angles and moments from inertial measurement units. Sensors **21**(13), 4535 (2021)
8. Yang, H.L., Lin, H.C.: Applying the hybrid model of EMD, PSR, and ELM to exchange rates forecasting. Comput. Econ. **49**(1), 99–116 (2017)
9. Lin, H., Sun, Q., Chen, S.Q.: Reducing exchange rate risks in international trade: a hybrid forecasting approach of CEEMDAN and multilayer LSTM. Sustainability **12**(6), 2451 (2020)
10. Cao, W., Zhu, W., Wang, W., Demazeau, Y., Zhang, C.: A deep coupled LSTM approach for USD/CNY exchange rate forecasting. IEEE Intell. Syst. **35**(2), 43–53 (2020)
11. Zhang, B.: Foreign exchange rates forecasting with an EMD-LSTM neural networks model. In: Journal of Physics: Conference Series, vol. 1053, no. 1, p. 012005. IOP Publishing (2018)
12. Dhamija, A.K., Bhalla, V.K.: Exchange rate forecasting: comparison of various architectures of neural networks. Neural Comput. Appl. **20**(3), 355–363 (2011)
13. Pandey, T.N., Jagadev, A.K., Dehuri, S., Cho, S.B.: A novel committee machine and reviews of neural network and statistical models for currency exchange rate prediction: An experimental analysis. J. King Saud Univ.-Comput. Inf. Sci. **32**(9), 987–999 (2020)
14. Rumelhart, D.E., Hinton, G.E., Williams, R.J.: Learning internal representations by error propagation. In: Rumelhart, D.E., McCelland, J. (eds.) Parallel Distributed Processing, vol. 1. The MIT Press, Cambridge (1986)
15. Hochreiter, S., Schmidhuber, J.: Long short-term memory. Neural Comput. **9**(8), 1735–1780 (1997)
16. Moghar, A., Hamiche, M.: Stock market prediction using LSTM recurrent neural network. Procedia Comput. Sci. **170**, 1168–1173 (2020)
17. De Myttenaere, A., Golden, B., Le Grand, B., Rossi, F.: Using the mean absolute percentage error for regression models. In: Proceedings, p. 113. Presses universitaires de Louvain (2015)

Child Tracking and Prediction of Violence on Children In Social Media Using Natural Language Processing and Machine Learning

M. K. Nallakaruppan[1](✉), Gautam Srivastava[2], Thippa Reddy Gadekallu[3], Praveen Kumar Reddy[1], Sivarama Krishnan[1], and Dawid Polap[4]

[1] School of Information Technology and Engineering, Vellore Institute of Technology, Vellore, India
{nallakaruppan.mk,praveenkumarreddy,siva.s}@vit.ac.in

[2] Department of Mathematics and Computer Science, Brandon University, Brandon, Canada
srivastavag@brandonu.ca

[3] School of Information Technology and Engineering, Vellore Institute of Technology, Department of Electrical and Computer Engineering, Lebanese American University, Lebanon, Zhongda Group, Jiaxing 314312, Zhejiang, China
thippareddy.g@vit.ac.in

[4] Faculty of Applied Mathematics, Silesian University of Technology, Kaszubska 23, 44-100 Gliwice, Poland
Dawid.Polap@polsl.pl

Abstract. Crimes against children are a direct threat to the world of tomorrow. The future of the world is in the hands of children who are the real wealth of mankind. The challenge for society is to address and handle challenges against children such as sexual abuse, trafficking, child labour, and harassment. Even though measures are taken by several governments globally, violence against children is an evident day-to-day process. This becomes the most challenging issue in the post-Internet era, where organized crime against children takes place around the world through a targeted group of people through virtual private networks and the dark web. What comes next is the emergence of social media, which provides an opportunity for these criminals to harm children globally through powerful social networks [15]. The existing methods focus on classifiers that do not work across multiple keywords [6] to look for sentiment analysis regarding a single classifier. There are only a few works that address the issue and these methods do not employ the multi-classification model [2]. In this paper, we propose a model which includes the Twitter API, the APIFY web scraper framework, as well as the VADER semantic analyzer in Python which possesses Decision tree analysis of sentiment prediction. The proposed work provides 99.6904% accuracy and predicts the classification of sentiment analysis. Our work has novelty in attribute selection, child trade, and violence analysis in social media and prediction of classification accuracy using the Decision Tree algorithm.

Keywords: NLP · Child Safety · Machine Learning

© The Author(s), under exclusive license to Springer Nature Switzerland AG 2023
L. Rutkowski et al. (Eds.): ICAISC 2023, LNAI 14125, pp. 560–569, 2023.
https://doi.org/10.1007/978-3-031-42505-9_47

1   Introduction

Child trafficking is one of the horrible crimes that puts the livelihood of the future under a serious threat. A more worrying factor is that these potential criminals easily gain benefits through available social media and form crime networks across the globe. There are many works done before to predict similar trafficking on Twitter. In [2], the authors deal with the prediction of child trafficking with image processing, however the accuracy of prediction was limited to $80 - 82\%$ and data was acquired from Twitter along with images and text. In [15], the authors have applied text classification in human trafficking however it is not done on social media directly [3]. So, existing systems work around either a single classifier or a lack of real-time social media investigation. The proposed work can be done in real-time, and it works with multiple classifiers and also provides sentiment analysis of neutral data items with numeric quantification.

Social media is one of the places where youth can post or request help in case of an emergency [16,19]. Our proposed system works around a framework that performs sentiment analysis on the Twitter social platform and looks for sensitive messages that are communicated through a targeted community or when anyone is requesting help based on the API interface through the APIFY web scraper with sentiment analysis performed by the VADER sentiment analyzer which is part of the Python Library. The results predict the sentiment in three such classes: positive, negative and neutral, where the positive class indicates an alert message where intervention may be required. Further, these classes develop a dataset and through feature selection, essential features are extracted and subjected to further classification through the Decision Tree (DT) algorithm which predicts the accuracy of the text classification process [8]. This trains the system with $66/34\%$ of training/test data and provides the opportunity to match the incoming text stream to be classified in an appropriate order. Therefore, the proposed system provides novelty with not only text classification of multiple attributes, but also provides an accuracy check using the VADER sentiment analyzer library. Our proposed system is unique in the problem domain where not much research has been conducted to date to the best of our knowledge.

1.1   Contributions of the Paper

Our contributions can be summarized as follows:

- The prescribed work performs a multi-classification model for finding the sentiment of words
- Works in real-time and results are also predicted for classification accuracy.
- Provides sentiment analysis of neutral samples which was not addressed in the existing systems
- The API deployed in the prescribed work is social site independent.

2   Recent Works

In this section, we discuss some of the recent works on the application of Machine Learning/Natural Language Processing (ML/NLP) for child tracking and violence prediction.

Child trafficking is one of the major offenses happening across the world. In many cases, child trafficking is done to exploit children sexually. For tracking children who are abducted, the authors in [13] developed a pipeline based on ML techniques to identify children from images that are intercepted by nonprofit organizations that focus on the prevention of child abuse. In this work, the authors proposed to identify schools of children through images of children with uniforms through a tool called Mark-RCNN that is used for object recognition. Automating the identification of the school of the children, this work can significantly sped up the identification of children.

The authors in [17] leveraged a large deep web dataset that has been consolidated from prominent sex websites along with a framework that is based on ML for uncovering pathways which are suspected of recruiting abducted children for sale. Through this framework, the authors intended to provide a view of the commercial supply chain network that may be spreading globally. The proposed work helps in inferring routes of alleged criminal child trafficking, identifies several approaches used to lure children to abduct them and also highlights the variations in recruitment versus sales across several regions. The insights provided by the proposed methodology can be used by law enforcement agencies to infer the trafficking routes in a coordinated way.

In [14], the authors have applied ML algorithms to incorporate reporting and international human rights law. The authors proposed a novel framework for analyzing how the interpretation of statutory compliance is done and also responses to ambiguity in statutory laws that can improve disclosures of child trafficking in the global supply chain.

The authors in [11] investigated domestic abuse of children and women in families in Bangladesh during the COVID-19 pandemic. The authors have used several ML algorithms such as the Naïve Bayes classifier, Random Forest, and Logistic Regression to predict domestic violence on a dataset collected from several families in Bangladesh during the pandemic.

In other interesting work, the authors in [12] discussed how violence and the bad relationship between parents may lead to child abuse. In another work, the authors in [20] have used several ML models to predict future violence against women and children. The authors have proposed a web-based system, in which data related to violence against children and women is stored in a database, and the prediction results regarding these crimes are generated using ML algorithms. The system also helps victims to get adequate information regarding their rights through a developed web application. From statistical analysis of a few datasets, it was found that the XG Boost machine learning model performed better than other considered algorithms. Hence, the authors have used the XG Boost algorithm for generating predicted crime reports that can help in reducing crime in the first place. Several law enforcement agencies and Governments can predict future crimes against women and children to help potential victims to get appropriate settlement/justice.

In [10], the authors have discussed the potential risks of violence against children due to parental violence and the effects it can have on the mental health of refugee children who live in resource-poor camps. The authors analyzed the risk factors mentioned above by collecting a sample of 226 Burundian families who lived in refugee camps in Tanzania.

Our prescribed work here is unique in the area of child tracking and violence detection in social media. Our novel methodology combines the efforts of NLP and ML which have been rarely implemented in the area of child abuse in social media. The uniqueness of the prescribed work also includes a dataset which is developed in real-time.

3   System Architecture

Child criticality data is detected on Twitter, using the Twitter API and the APIFY web scraping application which collects sensitive information regarding child abuse, kidnapping, child trafficking or any other scenarios based on the target attributes. This data is converted to CSV format which is processed by the NLP [1,5] library in Python for cleaning and integration. Later, the system is subjected to Vader sentimental analysis [4,7] which provides three target word classifiers based on the sentiments received from system data such as positive, negative, and neutral. A positive sentiment indicates an occurrence of a crime against a child, a negative sentiment is non-critical data and final neutral sentiment defines neither positive nor negative which needs further investigation based on the weights of the word vector. Then, this data is plotted and transformed into a dataset. Finally, this dataset is investigated by a Decision Tree which checks the accuracy of the NLP process and classification of the target attributes. The overall system architecture is presented in Fig. 1. It shows the Twitter Server to the end system with the direction of data flow. The NLP part is a critical aspect of the complete architecture as shown in Fig. 1.

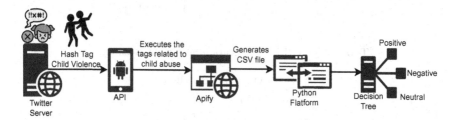

Fig. 1. Overall System Architecture

4   Results and Discussion

The child trafficking framework is designed with social media integration using the Python Deep Learning (DL) library through the Twiter API and a Web scraper interface called APIFY[1]. This web scraper interface allows the Twitter API to interact with the DL Python library. The data which is extracted through the Twitter API is presented to APIFY using the attributes shown in Table 1. The accuracy of VADER sentiment Analyzer is calculated using Eq. 4.1.

$$\text{Accuracy} = \frac{(TP + TN)}{(TP + FP + TN + FN)} \tag{4.1}$$

Table 1. Attributes for Child Trafficking

S.No	Name of the Feature	Criticality
1	Child abuse	High
2	kidnap	Medium
3	Child trade	High
4	Paedophile	High
5	Violence	Medium
6	Harassment	Medium
7	Sex abuse	High

These features are classified through various tweets (posts on Twitter) classified from 1st October to the present date on Twitter, however, you can extract data for less than six months with a sample size of 3200-row instances. The results provide a table-like structure with these 3 value indicators. This data is plotted in a box plot shown in Fig. 2. A Rule base method is applied for the positive, negative and neutral data to present the dataset in a categorical order shown in Fig. 2. The results of the sentiment analysis with three categories such as positive, negative, and neutral are represented in Table 2.

Table 2. VADER classification Sentiment Results

S. No.	Sentiment	Instances
1	Positive	531
2	Negative	281
3	Neutral	138

---

[1] https://apify.com/.

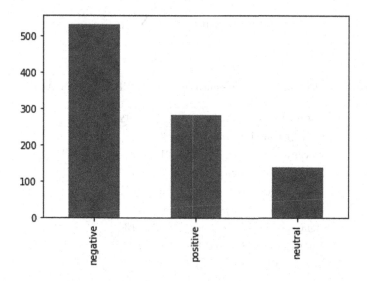

Fig. 2. Box Plot

Finally, the Python dataset is extracted to a dataset which is further applied with a Decision Tree to determine the accuracy of the overall process. The size of the sentiment analyzer is represented in Table 3. The Decision Tree approximation and results are shown in Fig. 3. The Decision Tree applies the CART model which predicts the target classes through classification and uses a regression analysis. The prescribed work performs feature selection through the k-Nearest Neighbors algorithm (kNN) which selects the features that are mapped closer to the target variable. Then, the Decision Tree is run on these features to predict the target variable for accuracy and error rates. The impurity of the given sample values are calculated using Eq. 4.2. Entropy values range from 0 to 1.

$$\text{Entropy}(E) = \sum_{b \in B} p(b) \log_2 p(b) \qquad (4.2)$$

where E denotes the dataset that entropy is measured, b denotes the number of classes in the given set, $p(b)$ denotes the proportion of data points for the given class b to the total data points in set, E. The information gain is the difference of entropy value before split and after the split which is calculated using Eq. 4.3.

$$\text{Information Gain } (E, x) = \text{Entropy}(E) - \sum_{vevcalues\ (x)} \frac{|E_v|}{|E|} \text{Entropy} (S_v) \quad (4.3)$$

Gini Impurity is used to build the decision trees by the use of splitting nodes. If the set is pure the impurity values are considered to be zero which is denoted using Eq. 4.4.

$$\text{Gini Impurity } = 1 - \sum_i (p_i)^2 \tag{4.4}$$

Table 3. Decision Tree Classification of VADER sentiment Analyzer

Parameter	Quantity	Accuracy
Correct Classification	322	99.6904 %
Deviation	1	0.3096 %
Statistics of Kappa	0.9948	
Mean Error(Absolute)	0.0021	
RMSE Error	0.0454	
Relative Absolute Error	0.5289%	
Root Relative Squared Error	10.1408%	
Total test samples	323	

Fig. 3. Decision Tree prediction on VADER sentiment Results

The Decision Tree provides a result of 99.6904% for 950 instances of training against 322 instances of the test samples with a low root-mean-square error (RMSE) value of 0.0454. Thus, the classification accuracy of the Vader Sentiment Analyzer is verified and target classes are mapped with the input attributes. The results are shown in Table 3.

5   Compartive Analaysis with Existing Systems

We make the following observations about the results and analysis of this paper:

- The model provides 99.064% of accuracy in sentiment analysis
- The model also detects neutral sentiments along with positive and negative
- The API is a cross-platform and common gateway for similar social media networks.

6   Conclusion and Future Work

This paper provides a solution for violence against children through social media through an integrated framework. This work provides the integration of social media with a developer perspective, and APIs such as APIFY for web scraping and data extraction from the server, VADER sentiment analysis and the Waikato Environment for Knowledge Analysis (WEKA) platform to perform Decision Tree classification on the categorical data. We tested for the best possible accuracy during the training and validation of sentiment analysis processes. Our work here can be extended through multiple social platforms and comparative analysis can be made across multiple social platforms through sentiment analysis and classification processes. Our research provides opportunities for further research on different social media platforms, understanding which platform is more vulnerable and exploitable. We also provide a framework that can also be applied to similar problem domains such as women trafficking, smuggling of national treasures, or the illegal trade of rare species through the implementation of a similar framework. Therefore, we provide an opportunity for upcoming research in similar or relevant domains and provide a roadmap for researchers. The proposed work is a common gateway model for multi-source sentiment analysis using NLP with machine learning. The APIFY web scraper allows the integration of multiple social media platforms and thus enables a thorough comparative analysis of crime indexers across various social media platforms. The training of the model can be enhanced through detailed segmentation of the sentiment analysis and exhaustive training of the target machine learning models with added features for comprehensive prediction of the results on cross-platform social media predictive analysis. Moreover, several pre-processing techniques can be used to reduce the feature space and remove insignificant features to be considered for classification/NLP [9,18].

References

1. Akram, M.W., Salman, M., Bashir, M.F., Salman, S.M.S., Gadekallu, T.R., Javed, A.R.: A novel deep auto-encoder based linguistics clustering model for social text. Transactions on Asian and Low-Resource Language Information Processing (2022)
2. Hernández-Álvarez, M., Granizo, S.L.: Detection of human trafficking ads in twitter using natural language processing and image processing. In: Ahram, T. (ed.) AHFE 2020. AISC, vol. 1213, pp. 77–83. Springer, Cham (2021). https://doi.org/10.1007/978-3-030-51328-3_12

3. Amrit, C., Paauw, T., Aly, R., Lavric, M.: Identifying child abuse through text mining and machine learning. Expert Syst. Appl. **88**, October 2017
4. Asghar, M.Z., et al..: Senti-esystem: a sentiment-based esystem-using hybridized fuzzy and deep neural network for measuring customer satisfaction. Softw. Practice Exp. **51**(3), 571–594 (2021)
5. Ashokkumar, P., Shankar, S., Srivastava, G., Maddikunta, P., Gadekallu, T.: A two-stage text feature selection algorithm for improving text classification. ACM Trans. Asian Low-Resource Lang. Inf. Process. **20**(3), 1–19 (2021)
6. Bibi, M., et al.: A novel unsupervised ensemble framework using concept-based linguistic methods and machine learning for twitter sentiment analysis. Pattern Recogn. Lett. **158**, 80–86 (2022)
7. Fu, W., Liu, S., Srivastava, G.: Optimization of big data scheduling in social networks. Entropy **21**(9), 902 (2019)
8. Gadekallu, T.R., Srivastava, G., Liyanage, M., Iyapparaja, M., Chowdhary, C.L., Koppu, S., Maddikunta, P.K.R.: Hand gesture recognition based on a harris hawks optimized convolution neural network. Comput. Electr. Eng. **100**, 107836 (2022)
9. Hakak, S., Alazab, M., Khan, S., Gadekallu, T.R., Maddikunta, P.K.R., Khan, W.Z.: An ensemble machine learning approach through effective feature extraction to classify fake news. Futur. Gener. Comput. Syst. **117**, 47–58 (2021)
10. Hecker, T., Kyaruzi, E., Borchardt, J., Scharpf, F.: Factors contributing to violence against children: insights from a multi-informant study among family-triads from three east-african refugee camps. J. Interpersonal Violence **37**(15–16), NP14507-NP14537 (2022)
11. Hossain, M.M., Asadullah, M., Rahaman, A., Miah, M.S., Hasan, M.Z., Paul, T., Hossain, M.A.: Prediction on domestic violence in bangladesh during the covid-19 outbreak using machine learning methods. Appl. Syst. Innov. **4**(4), 77 (2021)
12. Liel, C., Eickhorst, A., Zimmermann, P., Stemmler, M., Walper, S.: Fathers, mothers and family violence: Which risk factors contribute to the occurrence of child maltreatment and exposure to intimate partner violence in early childhood? findings in a german longitudinal in-depth study. Child Abuse & Neglect **123**, 105373 (2022)
13. Mukherjee, S., Sederholm, T., Roman, A.C., Sankar, R., Caltagirone, S., Ferres, J.L.: A machine learning pipeline for aiding school identification from child trafficking images. In: Proceedings of the Conference on Information Technology for Social Good. pp. 297–300 (2021)
14. Nersessian, D., Pachamanova, D.: Human trafficking in the global supply chain: Using machine learning to understand corporate disclosures under the uk modern slavery act. Harvard Human Rights Journal 35 (2022)
15. Pandey, A.: Text classification for human trafficking using advanced transformers. Acta Sci. Comput. Sci. **3**, 21–26 (10 2021)
16. Połap, D.: Human-machine interaction in intelligent technologies using the augmented reality. Inf. Technol. Control **47**(4), 691–703 (2018)
17. Ramchandani, P., Bastani, H., Wyatt, E.: Unmasking human trafficking risk in commercial sex supply chains with machine learning. Available at SSRN 3866259 (2021)
18. Reddy, G.T., Reddy, M.P.K., Lakshmanna, K., Kaluri, R., Rajput, D.S., Srivastava, G., Baker, T.: Analysis of dimensionality reduction techniques on big data. IEEE Access **8**, 54776–54788 (2020)

19. Reddy Maddikunta, P.K., Srivastava, G., Reddy Gadekallu, T., Deepa, N., Boopa-thy, P.: Predictive model for battery life in IoT networks. IET Intel. Transport Syst. **14**(11), 1388–1395 (2020)
20. Reza, M.R., Mannan, F.M.B., Barua, D., Islam, S., Khan, N.I., Mahmud, S.R.: Developing a machine learning based support system for mitigating the suppression against women and children. In: 2021 5th International Conference on Electrical Engineering and Information & Communication Technology (ICEEICT), pp. 1–6. IEEE (2021)

Adequate Basis for the Data-Driven and Machine-Learning-Based Identification

Marcel Rojahn[1]([✉]) [iD], Maximilian Ambros[2] [iD], Tibebu Biru[2],
Hermann Krallmann[2], Norbert Gronau[1] [iD], and Marcus Grum[1] [iD]

[1] University of Potsdam, Potsdam, Germany
marcel.rojahn@wi.uni-potsdam.de
[2] Krallmann AG, Berlin, Germany

Abstract. Process mining (PM) has established itself in recent years as a main method for visualizing and analyzing processes. However, the identification of knowledge has not been addressed adequately because PM aims solely at data-driven discovering, monitoring, and improving real-world processes from event logs available in various information systems. The following paper, therefore, outlines a novel systematic analysis view on tools for data-driven and machine learning (ML)-based identification of knowledge-intensive target processes. To support the effectiveness of the identification process, the main contributions of this study are (1) to design a procedure for a systematic review and analysis for the selection of relevant dimensions, (2) to identify different categories of dimensions as evaluation metrics to select source systems, algorithms, and tools for PM and ML as well as include them in a multi-dimensional grid box model, (3) to select and assess the most relevant dimensions of the model, (4) to identify and assess source systems, algorithms, and tools in order to find evidence for the selected dimensions, and (5) to assess the relevance and applicability of the conceptualization and design procedure for tool selection in data-driven and ML-based process mining research.

Keywords: Data mining · Knowledge engineering · Various applications

1 Introduction

Process management is a central discipline that has been discussed and practiced in companies and research institutions for years. The initial process survey, the process improvement, the process maintenance, and the continuous process optimization are time-consuming. During the process survey especially, a close exchange with the departments and employees involved is necessary to bring together the distributed knowledge and obtain a holistic picture of the process. The time horizon depends on the availability of the departments and

L. Rutkowski et al. (Eds.): ICAISC 2023, LNAI 14125, pp. 570–588, 2023.
https://doi.org/10.1007/978-3-031-42505-9_48

employees. PM meets this challenge by replacing time-consuming experiments and interviews with data-driven analyses. As a result, data-driven analyses not only reduce the time required but also create an objective picture of the business processes that are not shaped by the subjective process thinking of the participants involved in the process. The market for PM systems and tools is relatively young but has already developed into a widespread and perceived commercial niche. In this market environment, vendors specialize in core competencies for which they see a distinct value proposition. For example, some vendors focus on extract-transform-load tools, which are the precursors to PM analytics tools. Others enrich their business intelligence suites with PM tools and/or create a unique selling proposition by extending their tools with, for example, Robotic Process Automation (RPA) or chatbots. However, a PM tool that is based on sophisticated Artificial Intelligence (AI) techniques, has not been realized yet.

In order to be able to use AI performance in PM and identify a novel adequate tool selection for creating AI-based PM, a mechanism for the comparison of different systems and tools is required. This selection and comparison represent the novelty of this contribution. The tools are therefore analyzed by the following four categories: (1) source systems, e.g. in silos of Enterprise Resource Planning (ERP) systems and databases, (2) knowledge-based AI systems (tools, applications, and libraries), (3) machine learning tools (algorithms and applications), and (4) PM tools (algorithms and applications). A specific definition of the categories and the justification of the selection decision is explained in Sect. 3.1.

This paper does not intend to draw a comprehensive description of concrete technical realization of this novel mining approach. It is intended as a first step towards clarifying the preparation of a novel adequate data foundation. Accordingly, the research question is: *"How can an adequate basis for the data-driven, machine-learning-based identification of as-is processes be systematically identified?"*

In this paper, therefore, a novel systematic analysis of tools for data-driven identification of knowledge-intensive target processes is established as follows: (1) a procedure and (2) a selection tool design for the adequate design of source systems, AI-based and ML-based systems, as well as PM systems. In the selection tool demonstration, a ranking of representative candidates is derived (3). The tool is validated empirically by expert experiments (4), so that candidates selected can serve as the basis for the creation of a ML-based and data-driven identification of knowledge in processes.

By following a design-oriented research approach [1], the remainder of this paper is organized as follows. The first section is used for a general introduction, showing the motivation, and the research question. The second section presents the theoretical foundations of PM and an adequate ML foundation. The third section identifies requirements for the intelligent systems modeling problem and a methodological approach. These are realized through a design that aims to cope with the modeling problem. It also demonstrates the operation of the design, which is evaluated in the fourth section by argumentation. The final section summarizes the extent to which the initial modeling problem has been solved and the research questions have been answered.

2   Theoretical Foundations and Basic Concepts

In the first subsection, the goal of PM is explained and fields of application are given so that an interpretation of the tools for data-driven identification of target processes can be created. Subsequently, knowledge modeling approaches are compiled as a basis for the design of the meta-model. In the second subsection an adequate foundation for a data-based knowledge identification is explained.

2.1   Contemporary Process Mining and Artifical Intelligence Foundation

PM has established itself in recent years as a central method for visualizing and analyzing processes and is becoming the go-to solution in the industry to quickly uncover manual business processes. In PM, the fields of business process management and data mining are combined. Conventionally, PM aims at discovering, monitoring, and improving real processes by extracting knowledge from event logs available in different information systems. Accordingly, PM is a data-driven method in which the process flows lived in the company are identified in an automated way.

PM usually pursues different objectives. On the one hand, transparency is created about the business processes existing in the company in order to uncover weaknesses and optimization potentials. This objective can, for example, lower process costs and reduce throughput times i.e., by identifying loops. On the other hand, a conformity check can be performed in which deviations can be identified and analyzed by comparing the predefined reference process (target process) with the actual process variants. PM can also be used as a tool in conjunction with process automation through RPA to discover automation opportunities and processes suitable for RPA or to validate and analyze already implemented RPA initiatives. This opportunity refers to process automation approaches in which repetitive, manual, time-consuming or error-prone activities can be learned and automated by so-called software robots. PM can also boost digital transformation by linking strategy and operations, in which processes are standardized and harmonized on the basis of the analysis.

In principle, PM can be used wherever the activities of a process leave a digital trace in information technology (IT) systems in which the relationship and sequence of the steps can be traced. Since most business processes in companies today are supported by IT systems, PM can be used in numerous industries and company divisions. These include, for example, business processes in the areas of production, logistics, human resource management, accounting, finance, health care, etc.

The three main methods of PM are as follows: (1) process discovery, (2) conformance check, and (3) process enhancement [2]. It is therefore worth explicating the key terminologies of the main PM methods.

(1) Process discovery. In process discovery, event logs and mining algorithms are used to automatically construct process models that provide an unbiased view of process structures without the use of additional information. This step can be applied, for example, to gain insight into the process complexity which allows one to make statements about process variants and their frequency. It is therefore a visualization of the event logs.

(2) Conformance check. The goal of this step is to compare different process models with each other and to check the actual reality documented in event logs against given target models. By applying this step, possible deviations between the logged and the modeled behavior can be identified, visualized and measured. Moreover, it must be emphasized that the target processes must be defined before applying conformance check as automated processing is not state of the art.

(3) Process enhancement. Process enhancement can also be used to either improve or further develop existing a priori process models by taking into account additional aspects and perspectives. This includes, for example, the explicit inclusion of process performance, throughput times or other data attributes in order to perform performance investigations and deeper analyses.

While PM helps to identify as-is processes, the challenge remains in the ability to derive the ideal path from a large number of lived process variants. In contemporary PM approaches, target processes are usually elicited through time-consuming interviews and experiments. Various PM software vendors recommend deriving the target process based on the first X process variants that cover most business transactions as best practice. However, this approach is misleading in many cases as it can lead to process variants that are run less often being marked as not conforming to the target process, even though they are conforming in reality. For this reason, the use of AI and ML is attractive to enable data-driven identification of the target process.

2.2   Adeqaute Foundation for Data-Based Knowledge Identification

The rapid growth of event data highly influences the business process management practice [3]. The focus towards only model-based analysis and model-based implementation without using valuable information hidden in information systems will lead to loss of competitive advantage. This accounts particularly for those kinds of organizations that are competing to use the vast amount of available data intelligently for analytics and ML [4,5]. In order to set up a novel adequate foundation for data-based knowledge identification, a data-driven approach needs to capture the following procedure steps: (1) collecting, (2) organizing, and (3) extracting process data that is distributed across organizations [6]. In addition, this needs to be (4) visualized and managed [7]. The following therefore outlines each proceeding steps individually.

(1) Collection of data. Process data is typically extracted from different knowledge sources, such as ERP systems, Customer Relationship Management (CRM) systems, Business Process Management (BPM) systems, and Knowledge

Management (KM) systems. A selection tool therefore needs to consider different kinds of knowledge source systems.

(2) Organization of data. Although the adoption of PM techniques grew rapidly in recent years, a large portion of time and effort is spent in data extraction and transformation to prepare event logs from different data sources [8]. In general, the preparation of data sources for PM should consider not only specific systems and platforms of organizations but also data types (Comma-Separated Values (CSV), eXtensible Event Stream (XES), Structured Query Language (SQL), Excel, etc.) used in organizations. For PM, the flexibility to take data in multiple formats and across multiple systems will help derive valuable knowledge from different data sources to mine the process flow.

To extract events from existing data sources (e.g., *SAP*, *Oracle*, ERP-systems, and CRM-systems) and to transform them into the so-called "event logs", specialized import modules are used that offer cross-vendor functionalities and can thus be flexibly connected to the specific customer systems. The source systems represent the data basis for training the ML algorithms. In the next step, a transformation is applied to the extracted data to convert it into the standard PM format supported by many PM tools. XES and CSV files are standard formats for logging events. Once the relevant data is extracted and converted, an event log is created in which each event refers to a case, activity, and timestamp. An event log can be considered as a collection of cases and a case as a trace/sequence of events [2].

(3) Extraction of knowledge from data. Different techniques are used to extract knowledge from event logs to discover, monitor, and improve processes [4]. PM involves importing and exporting IEEE XES or CSV files (event logs) and process discovery using various algorithms (alpha miner, genetic miner, inductive miner, and correlation miner). Conformance checking can then be used to evaluate the performance of the so-called process discovery [3]. Token-based replay, alignment-based replay, decomposition of alignments and footprints techniques are used to check the conformance and thus all process deviations from the actual to the target process [9]. In addition, anomaly detection and root-cause analysis algorithms can be performed to better understand the process. The calculation of different statistics in addition to the classical event logs and graphical representations help to understand different aspects (throughput time, case arrival, lead time, and cycle time) of event logs.

(4) Visualization for management of knowledge. Process-oriented knowledge modeling aims to visually model knowledge, its creation as well as its use along knowledge-intensive processes [8]. Even though it has its strength in visualization, it lacks the provision of object information. A novel adequate basis therefore will capture a combination of PM and process-oriented description languages and making them accessible by means of the tools.

3   Objectives and Methodoly

Following the Design Science Research Methodology (DSRM) approach [1], this section establishes objectives independent of a design. A methodology is then presented that satisfies the methodological objectives. These are separated from the design and its demonstration so that artifacts can be created and then evaluated for meeting the requirements. After a methodological foundation, the designed artifacts give evidence of their functionality in a demonstration.

3.1 Objectives

Based on the research goal of constructing a data-driven and ML-based PM to realize the identification of knowledge-based target processes, this section presents a set of requirements that must be considered in the realization of a tool that is adequate for identifying the best basis of a data-driven and ML-based PM. Thus, the following requirements have been identified as consensus within experiments of expert circles of 17 practitioners and ten researchers.

1. An adequate base of tools needed for the design must be identified systematically and methodically.
2. Different organizational sources of knowledge must be considered. In this context, we find source systems that are silos of ERP-systems and databases.
3. Different AI systems (e.g., at AI-based tools, applications, and libraries) must be considered.
4. Different ML tools must be considered. This refers to different algorithmic approaches and applications.
5. Different PM tools (algorithmic and applications) must be considered.
6. The tool analysis needs to be based on the evaluation of twelve experts within experiments to control subjective tendencies.
7. The tool identification needs to be based on a ranking to realize a comprehensible tool selection. Based on these requirements, a methodological foundation focusing on a morphological analysis and design-oriented artifact creation is sought.

Based on these requirements, a methodological foundation focusing on a morphological analysis and design-oriented artifact creation is sought.

3.2 Morphological Analysis

For designing an artefact according to DSRM, the steps of Zwicky is followed. In order to investigate all possible solutions of a multidimensional and non-quantified complex problem for different domains, morphological analysis is a suitable tool [10]. It is recognized in various fields such as anatomy, geology, botany, and biology, and consists of different morphological methods [11].

Starting from the general morphological analysis, the morphological box called the Zwicky box is constructed in five iterative steps [12]:

Phase 1: First, the problem dimensions are properly defined. Since these are likely to relate to relevant facts, practical applicability is supported.

Phase 2: Then, parameters are defined as a spectrum of values for the dimensions. These usually refer to different approaches to solving the problem for each dimension.

Phase 3: Third, the morphological box is constructed by juxtaposing the parameters in an n-dimensional matrix. Since each cell of the n-dimensional box represents a parameter of the problem, the selection of one parameter per dimension marks a particular state or condition of the problem complex. The selection is called a configuration and represents a solution to the problem complex. In our case, an empirical investigation was conducted to determine the best configuration with the highest acceptance.

Phase 4: A fourth step examines and evaluates possible solutions with respect to the intended purpose. In our context, this is to identify an optimal basis for the design. In experiment sessions with twelve research and consulting experts of the domains of KM, AI, PM, and business applications, the guidance questions were answered individually for the software tools that were identified by the experiment participants. In total, 41 tools were divided into four clusters, namely three source systems, 14 knowledge-based AI systems, ten ML tools and 14 PM tools. After domain experts evaluation based on selected dimensions, the best tools for each cluster were determined in the final stage.

Phase 5: A fifth step is the practical application of the optimal solution, namely the morphological box. If the need arises, findings from the application in the previous steps are taken into account.

3.3   Design

In accordance with the DSRM [1], this section presents artifacts designed to address the modeling problem. In doing so, the design of the systematic selection of tools relevant to the implementation is explained. Then, the design is presented which is used to describe the technical understanding. Finally, a human-readable form of visualization is designed. In order to systematically capture the requirements in different dimensions, a morphological box was constructed. The dimensions examined in this process were: (1) PM Relevance, including the supported control-flow constructs (e.g. sequence, parallelism or duplicate tasks), the completeness of the information logs (event and trace significance), the abstraction levels (each transaction refers to a single event class) [13,14] and under-fitting vs. over-fitting [15,16]. (2) Technology, contains live access to systems (real-time data), ability of systems to communicate, sense, carry out actions and process. (3) Knowledge, described by the availability of data, explicit knowledge, tacit knowledge, competence, and experience. (4) AI, characterized by the availability of input, output, state, action, reward, punishment data. (5) Customers, contains the perceptibility, usefulness of data and expected relevance. (6) Vendors, stands out by the system costs, paid access, vendor market share and reputation. (7) Finance, described by the presence of data structure. (8) Policy, including the limitations by laws. (9) Ethics, contains the limitations by labor unions. [17]

For each dimension, corresponding attributes were compiled and substantiated by appropriate guiding questions (as follows: "Does the supported control-flow constructs include sequences?" or "Does the system support unsupervised learning?"). Then, different scales (e.g. yes/no and explicitly indicated/implicitly indicated/indicated not at all) per dimension were collected and evaluated using a consensus to determine if there were any conditions that were mutually exclusive. Finally, the possible scales were examined for the broadest acceptance in each case by means of expert experiments. The best configuration of the morphological box is shown in Fig. 1.

3.4   Demonstration

This section applies the artifact designed to demonstrate its use and evaluate if the initial research problem has been answered and demonstrates the morphological box to identify a novel adequate basis for the data-driven, ML-based identification of as-is processes. In accordance with the fifth step of the morphological analysis described in Sect. 3.2, the previously established best configuration of the morphological box has been applied for the identification of a novel adequate basis for the data-driven, ML-based identification of as-is processes. The better a parameter of a tool performs at a certain dimension, the more suitable the tool is for being a novel adequate basis. The preferred tools are those that are closest to the previously determined optimum and the detailed analysis can be seen from (Fig. 3) to (Fig. 6) at the appendices in which the suitability has been visualized by the color range from red (poor choice) over yellow (In between poor and best choice) to green (best choice).

AI Cluster. In the knowledge-based AI systems cluster (Fig. 3), the *domain-specific language (DSL) modeling standard* as a tool was chosen because it supports the knowledge modeling best [12]. As an application, the *DSL Chat-Bot* was chosen because it builds on the *DSL modeling standard* [16] and provides a chatbot that is able to generate event logs for the ML-based PM algorithm. The libraries *TensorFlow, PyTorch, PyBrain*, and *PM4PY* have been chosen because of the possibility to explicitly consider data with different learning approaches. All these systems thus serve as ML implementation frameworks for the PM algorithm or support the basic functioning of the algorithm. Furthermore, these systems have a technique advantage compared to their competitors and their business model is unique. According to the selected AI dimension, these systems support reinforced learning (Action data availability, reward data availability, and reinforced functional approaches).

ML Cluster. In the ML cluster (Fig. 4), the algorithms *Automatic Relevance Determination regression (ARD), Random Forest (RF), Neural Network (NN)*, and *Long Short-Term Memory (LSTM)* will be used to derive actionable knowledge. *ARD* is an automatic feature selection algorithm that is easy to implement and computationally fast. From the family of tree-based ML algorithms, *RF* is chosen as it is a more robust model and prevents over-fitting and gives accurate results. *NN* is chosen to investigate the predictive performance of simple *NN* architecture and to compare the result to those of more complex *NN* architecture. *LSTM*, recurrent *NN*, handles sequential data better and it captures long and short-term dependencies.

PM-Tools Cluster. In the PM tools cluster (Fig. 5 and Fig. 6), *alpha miner* and *genetic miner* are chosen as algorithms because of their high coverage of the selected PM relevant dimensions. The *alpha miner* fulfills in the dimension of the "supported control-flow constructs a sequence", parallelism, choices, and loops. For the dimension of completeness of the information logs, the *alpha miner* includes a completeness of direct succession. At least in the log, direct succession of two transitions is possible. Within the dimension of the abstraction levels, each transition refers to a single event class and a direct correspondence exists between the event classes in the log and the transitions in the model. The *genetic miner* fulfills in the dimension of the "supported control-flow constructs a sequence", parallelism, choices, loops, non-free-choices, and invisible tasks. Besides, the *genetic miner* includes a trace significance in the dimension of completeness of the information logs. Therefore, the most relevant behavior in terms of cases appears most frequently in the log. When the dimension of the vendor market share is considered, both algorithms have a very high acceptance. For the application category, *Celonis*, and *Pafnow* are chosen because of their price model. *Celonis* also provides a comprehensive approach for process enhancement which includes a python-based ML workbench for predictive insights and Application Programming Interface (API)-powered action engine for intelligent process recommendations. On the other hand, *Pafnow* possesses intelligent and fully automated process analysis engine that adds a new dimension to critical path detection efficiency.

4   Evaluation

In the first subsection, based on the evaluation of the demonstration, the requirements of a tool that is adequate for identifying the best basis of a data-driven and ML based PM the goal of PM are checked for their fulfillment. In the second subsection, the collected experiences of the demonstration, in the context of the experts are explained.

4.1   Requirement Fulfillment

In accordance with the DSRM of Peffers [1], this section evaluates the demonstration issued in the previous section if requirements, that have been presented at Sect. 3.1, are fulfilled.

Req. 1 has been satisfied because the methodology of a morphological analysis has served to create a tool for analyzing different kinds of tools for their suitability to act as a foundation for an algorithm. By applying the empirically verified morphological box and identifying a consensus on the evaluation of attractive tools from the viewpoint of domain experts, a novel adequate basis of tools has been systematically and methodically identified. In addition, subjectivity has been reduced (cf. Req. 6) because the evaluation has been based on the knowledgeable assessment of different domain experts.

Req. 2–5 have been satisfied because representatives, that have been identified in literature and by expert consensus, have been considered for analysis in each category as follows: First, the silos *MS-Dynamics* and *Oracle* have been considered as source systems, the *DSL* modeling standard has been considered as knowledge-based AI system, although the *CoNM* outperformed all. Second, the *DSL Chat Bot* application has been considered as organizational knowledge sources. Third, at the algorithm section, the ML libraries *TensorFlow* and *PyBrain* were considered. The ML algorithm referred to *ARD*, *RF*, *NN*, and *LSTM*. Fourth, for PM algorithm representatives, *alpha miner* and *genetic miner* have been chosen, as well as *Celonis* and *Pafnow*, which refer to applications.

Since a ranking of tools has been derived per cluster (each ranking was based on the best dimension and parameter fulfillment), best tool candidates have been identified per cluster (source system/AI systems/ML tools/PM tools). Therefore, the tool selection is comprehensible, and Req. 7 has been satisfied.

Interim-conclusion: Since all requirements have been satisfied, it can be stated that the artifact creation of a selection and analysis tool has been realized successfully in the sense of DSRM.

4.2   Demonstration Experiences

Facing experts in experiments and panels with the selection and analysis tool, the usefulness of the tool has been confirmed by them. Notably, experts were supported in discussions about the selection of tools for creating an AI-based PM because most attractive candidates have been identifiable per category. So, experts have been enabled for selecting tools in relevant categories. If different preferences have become transparent, strengths and weaknesses of tools have been compared easily. Further, alternatives of a category have been ranked spontaneously by experts in conflict situations, so that experts could agree on the best compromise. In order to nevertheless visualize the ratio of all decisions of the twelve experts transparently, the summarized percentages were given in brackets for the respective answers in Table 2 to 6. Considering all the tools analyzed, the analysis and selection tool was supportive for identifying a research gap of AI-based PM. Obviously, there was no representative identified that showed good performances over all categories. The best over-all performance has shown the *CoNM* tool. However, by selecting the most attractive tool per category, experts came up with a set of tools, which seems most promising for creating an AI-based PM approach. On-building research will be based on this selection.

Dim. Category	Dimension		Scale	Source
Process Mining relevant Dimensions	Supported Control-Flow Constructs	Sequences (seq)	Does the supported control-flow constructs include sequences?	yes / no	[13] [14]
		parallelism (par)	Does the supported control-flow constructs include parallelism?	yes / no	
		choices (cho)	Does the supported control-flow constructs include choices?	yes / no	
		loops (lo)	Does the supported control-flow constructs include loops?	yes / no	
		non-free-choices (nfc)	Does the supported control-flow constructs include non-free-choices?	yes / no	
		invisible tasks (it)	Does the supported control-flow constructs include invisible tasks?	yes / no	
		duplicate tasks (df)	Does the supported control-flow constructs include duplicate tasks?	yes / no	
	Completeness of Information in Logs	Completeness of direct succession (DS)	If two transitions can follow each other directly, has this occurred at least once in the log?	yes / no	[13]
		Event significance (ES)	For one, if there is a causal dependency between two transitions, does the direct successions of these transitions reflect that?	yes / no	
		Trace significance (TS)	Does the most relevant behavior in terms of cases appears most frequently in the log?	yes / no	
	Abstraction Levels	Each transition refers to a single event class (1:1)	Does a direct correspondence between the events-classes in the log and the transitions in the model occurs?	yes / no	[13]
		Transitions do not refer to any event in the log (1:0..1)	Doesn't the transitions refer to any event in the log?	yes / no	
	Underfitting vs Overfitting	Underfitting	Does the model allows for "too much behavior" that is not supported by log?	yes / no	[13] [15] [16]
		Overfitting	Doesn't the model generalize and is sensitive to particularities in log?	yes / no	
Technical Dimensions	Presence of digital representation of systems		Does the system provide a digital representation?	...	[17]
	Live access to systems (real-time data)		Is the system able to deal with real-time-data?	yes / no	
	Ability of systems to communicate (technique)		Is the system able to communicate?	yes / no	
	Ability of systems to communicate (standard)		Is the system able to communicate?	yes / no	
	Ability of systems to communicate (interfaces)		Is the system able to communicate?	yes / no	
	Ability of systems to sense		Is the system able to sense its environment?	yes / no	
	Ability of systems to carry out actions		Is the system able to interact with its environment?	yes / no	
	Ability of systems to process		Is the system able to process data?	yes / no	
	Requirement of additional setup		Do we need any additional setup (e.g. client application, third-party connections, etc.)?	yes / no	
	Presence of API		Can we access the data via an API?	yes / no	
Knowledge Dimensions	Availability of data		Is the system able to interact with its environment?	yes / no	[17]
	Availability of explicit knowledge		Is the data easily available?	yes / no	
	Availability of tacit knowledge		Hard to identify? Structured form?	yes / no	
	Role as knowledge carrier in process		Does the system participate in the process, so that it uses its knowledge? Does it have a role in the process?	yes / no	
	Degree of articulation		Is it hard to explain the function?	yes / no	
	Degree of generality		How general is the knowledge? Can it be used in multiple dialogues?	yes / no	
	Competence		Does the system address competences for the dialog?	yes / no	
	Experience		Does the system address experience for the dialog?	yes / no	
	Documentation availability		Is the product completed by a great documentation?	public Wiki / vendor documentation / no	
	Sample data availability		Can we access sample data?	yes / no	
AI Dimensions	Input data availability		Does the system support unsupervised learning?	explicitly indicated / implicitly indicated / indicated not at all	[17]
	Unsupervised functional approaches		Does the system support unsupervised learning?	available / not available	
	Output data availability		Does the system support supervised learning?	explicitly indicated / implicitly indicated / indicated not at all	
	Supervised functional approaches		Does the system support supervised learning?	available / not available	
	State data availability		Does the system support supervised learning?	explicitly indicated / implicitly indicated / indicated not at all	
	Action data availability		Does the system support reinforced learning?	explicitly indicated / implicitly indicated / indicated not at all	
	Reward data availability		Does the system support reinforced learning?	explicitly indicated / implicitly indicated / indicated not at all	
	Punishment data availability		Does the system support reinforced learning?	explicitly indicated / implicitly indicated / indicated not at all	
	Reinforced functional approaches		Does the system support reinforced learning?	available / not available	
Customer Dimensions	Perceptability		How can data be perceived in the dialog system?	obvious / questionable	[17]
	Usefulness of data		How might this data be useful?	yes / no	
	SME relevance		How relevant is this software for SMEs (KMUs)?	yes / no	
	Expected relevance		What future relevance for this software do we predict?	yes / no	
Vendor Dimensions	System costs		What is the cost the system (license, consulting, maintenance, infrastructure)?	$/period in months (per user)	[17]
	Paid access		Do we need to pay for (API) access?	$/period in months (per user)	
	Vendor market share		What is the market share of the vendor? How many of the clients are SMEs in Germany? How many companies use this kind of software?	amount (in %)	
	Vendor reputation		What is the vendor reputation?	target group fit / not fitting to target group	
	Vendor business model uniqueness		How is the vendor's business model unique?	small / medium / huge	
	Trial version		Is there a trial developer account?	no / period in days / Open Source	
	Technical support		What is the level of tech support by the vendor?	paid vendor / community / not at all	
	Vendor technique advantage		What is vendor's technological advantage?	small / medium / huge	
Financial Dimensions	Presence of data structure		Does the system provide a data structure, so that the implementation is not expensive?	yes / no	[17]
Political Dimensions	Limitations by laws		Does the use os system-specific data correspond to contemporary laws?	yes / no	[17]
Ethical Dimensions	Limitations by labor unions		Does the use of system-specific data correspond to contemporary ethical understanding?	yes / no	[17]

Fig. 1. Morphologic box with best parameters.

Dim. Category	Dimension		Scales	Selection of systems and algorithms									
				Source Systems			Knowledge-based AI Systems							
				ERP-Systems		Database	Tools		Applications					
				SAP	Microsoft-Dynamics	Oracle	CoNM	DBL Modeling Standard	DBL Chat-Bot	International evaluation of an AI system for breast cancer screening [18]	Automated detection of COVID-19 cases using deep neural networks with X-ray images [19]	A review on artificial intelligence based load demand forecasting techniques for smart grid and buildings [20]	LSTM network: a deep learning approach for short-term traffic forecast [21]
Process Mining relevant Dimensions	Supported Control-Flow Constructs	Sequences (seq)	yes / no	no	no	no	no	no	no	no	no	no	no
		parallelism (par)	yes / no	no	no	no	no	no	no	no	no	no	no
		choices (cho)	yes / no	no	no	no	no	no	no	no	no	no	no
		loops (lo)	yes / no	no	no	no	no	no	no	no	no	no	no
		non-free-choices (nfc)	yes / no	no	no	no	no	no	no	no	no	no	no
		invisible tasks (it)	yes / no	no	no	no	no	no	no	no	no	no	no
		duplicate tasks (dt)	yes / no	no	no	no	no	no	no	no	no	no	no
	Completeness of Information in Logs	DS	yes / no	no	no	no	no	no	no	no	no	no	no
		ES	yes / no	no	no	no	no	no	no	no	no	no	no
		TS	yes / no	no	no	no	no	no	no	no	no	no	no
	Abstraction Levels	... (1:1)	yes / no	no	no	no	no	no	no	no	no	no	no
		... (1:0..1)	yes / no	no	no	no	no	no	no	no	no	no	no
	Underfitting vs. Overfitting	Underfitting	yes / no	no	no	no	yes	no	yes	no	no	no	no
		Overfitting	yes / no	no	no	no	no	no	no	no	no	no	no
Technical Dimensions	Presence of digital representation of systems		yes / no	yes	yes	yes	yes	no	no	yes	yes	yes	yes
	Live access to systems (real-time data)		yes / no	yes	yes	yes	yes	no	yes	yes	yes	yes	yes
	Ability of systems to communicate (techniques)		yes / no	yes	yes	yes	yes	no	yes	yes	yes	yes	yes
	Ability of systems to communicate (standard)		yes / no	yes	yes	yes	yes	no	yes	yes	yes	yes	yes
	Ability of systems to communicate (interfaces)		yes / no	yes	yes	yes	yes	no	yes	yes	yes	yes	yes
	Ability of systems to sense		yes / no	yes	yes	yes	yes	no	no	no	no	no	no
	Ability of systems to carry out actions		yes / no	yes	yes	yes	yes	no	no	no	no	no	no
	Ability of systems to process		yes / no	yes	yes	yes	yes	no	yes	yes	yes	yes	yes
	Requirement of additional setup		yes / no	yes	yes	yes	yes	no	yes	yes	yes	yes	yes
	Presence of API		yes / no	yes	yes	no	yes	yes	no	yes	no	no	no
Knowledge Dimensions	Availability of data		yes / no	yes	yes	yes	yes	no	yes	yes	yes	yes	yes
	Availability of explicit knowledge		yes / no	yes	yes	yes	yes	yes	yes	yes	yes	yes	yes
	Availability of tacit knowledge		yes / no	no	no	no	yes	yes	yes	no	no	no	no
	Role as knowledge carrier in process		yes / no	yes	yes	yes	yes	yes	yes	no	no	no	no
	Degree of articulation		yes / no	no	no	no	yes	no	no	no	no	no	no
	Degree of generality		yes / no	no	no	no	yes	no	no	no	no	no	no
	Competence		yes / no	yes	yes	yes	yes	yes	yes	no	no	no	no
	Experience		yes / no	yes	yes	yes	yes	yes	yes	no	no	no	no
	Documentation availability		public Wiki / vendor documentation / no	vendor documentation	vendor documentation	vendor documentation	public wiki	no	no	vendor documentation	vendor documentation	vendor documentation	vendor documentation
	Sample data availability		yes / no	yes	yes	yes	yes	no	no	yes	no	no	no
AI Dimensions	Input data availability		explicitly indicated / implicitly indicated	implicitly indicated	implicitly indicated	implicitly indicated	explicitly indicated	implicitly indicated	implicitly indicated	explicitly indicated	explicitly indicated	explicitly indicated	explicitly indicated
	Unsupervised functional approaches		available / not available	not available	not available	not available	available	not available	not available	available	available	available	available
	Output data availability		explicitly indicated / implicitly indicated	implicitly indicated	implicitly indicated	implicitly indicated	explicitly indicated	implicitly indicated	implicitly indicated	explicitly indicated	explicitly indicated	explicitly indicated	explicitly indicated
	Supervised functional approaches		available / not available	not available	not available	not available	available	not available	available	available	available	available	available
	State data availability		explicitly indicated / indicated not at all	indicated not at all	indicated not at all	indicated not at all	explicitly indicated	indicated not at all	indicated not at all	indicated not at all	indicated not at all	indicated not at all	indicated not at all
	Action data availability		explicitly indicated / indicated not at all	indicated not at all	indicated not at all	indicated not at all	explicitly indicated	indicated not at all	indicated not at all	indicated not at all	indicated not at all	indicated not at all	indicated not at all
	Reward data availability		explicitly indicated / indicated not at all	indicated not at all	indicated not at all	indicated not at all	explicitly indicated	indicated not at all	indicated not at all	indicated not at all	indicated not at all	indicated not at all	indicated not at all
	Punishment data availability		explicitly indicated / indicated not at all	indicated not at all	indicated not at all	indicated not at all	explicitly indicated	indicated not at all	indicated not at all	indicated not at all	indicated not at all	indicated not at all	indicated not at all
	Reinforced functional approaches		available / not available	not available	not available	not available	available	not available	not available	not available	not available	not available	not available
Customer Dimensions	Perceptability		obvious	obvious	obvious	obvious	obvious	obvious	obvious	obvious	obvious	obvious	obvious
	Usefulness of data		yes / no	yes	yes	yes	yes	yes	yes	yes	yes	yes	yes
	SME relevance		yes / no	yes	yes	yes	yes	yes	yes	yes	yes	yes	yes
	Expected relevance		yes / no	yes	yes	yes	yes	yes	yes	yes	yes	yes	yes
Vendor Dimensions	System costs		$/period in months (per user)	$3,213 - Professional $1,666 - Limited $1,357 - Starter	$1500 - Essentials $2100 - Premium	$1000	0	0	0	0	0	0	0
	Paid access		$/period in months (per user)	$108 - Knowledgeable license $56 - Restricted license	$59 - Business Central Essentials $84 - Business Central Premium $42 - Customer Service Pro $54 - Sales Professional	$176 - Financial reporting plan $90 - Advanced Financial control plan $130 - Advance access control package	0	0	0	0	0	0	0
	Vendor market share		amount (in %)	6%	19%	12%	1%	2%	1%	10%	10%	30%	30%
	Vendor reputation		target group fit	target group fit	target group fit	target group fit	target group fit	target group fit	target group fit	target group fit	target group fit	target group fit	target group fit
	Vendor business model uniqueness		small / medium / huge	huge	huge	huge	huge	huge	huge	huge	huge	huge	huge
	Trial version		no / period in days / open source	30	30	14	open source	open source	no	open source	open source	open source	open source
	Technical support		paid vendor / community	vendor	vendor	community	community	community	community	community	community	community	community
	Vendor technique advantage		small / medium / huge	huge	huge	huge	huge	huge	huge	huge	huge	huge	huge
Financial Dimensions	Presence of data structure		yes / no	yes	yes	yes	no	no	no	yes	yes	yes	yes
Political Dimensions	Limitations by laws		yes / no	yes	yes	yes	no	no	no	yes	yes	yes	yes
Ethical Dimensions	Limitations by labor unions		yes / no	yes	yes	yes	no	no	no	yes	yes	yes	yes
Evaluation	Final selection with sum of choices		yes / no (amount in %)	no (75%)	yes (100%)	yes (75%)	no (100%)	yes (100%)	yes (100%)	no (100%)	no (100%)	no (100%)	no (100%)

Fig. 2. Tool analysis and evaluation for data-driven, ML-based identification of as-is processes (part 1).

Dim. Category	Dimension	Scales	Tensor Flow	PyTorch	Google Dialog Flow	Amazon LEX	PyBrain	PM4Py	BupaR and processmapR (both in R)
			Knowledge-based AI Systems		**Libraries**				
Process Mining relevant Dimensions	Supported Control-Flow Constructs — Sequences (seq)	yes / no	no	no	no	no	no	no	no
	parallelism (par)	yes / no	no	no	no	no	no	no	no
	choices (cho)	yes / no	no	no	no	no	no	no	no
	loops (lo)	yes / no	no	no	no	no	no	no	no
	non-free-choices (nfc)	yes / no	no	no	no	no	no	no	no
	invisible tasks (it)	yes / no	no	no	no	no	no	no	no
	duplicate tasks (dt)	yes / no	no	no	no	no	no	no	no
	Completeness of Information in Logs — DS	yes / no	no	no	no	no	no	no	no
	ES	yes / no	no	no	no	no	no	no	no
	TS	yes / no	no	no	no	no	no	no	no
	Abstraction Levels ...(1:1)	yes / no	no	no	no	no	no	no	no
	...(1:0..1)	yes / no	no	no	no	no	no	no	no
	Underfitting vs Overfitting — Underfitting	yes / no	no	no	no	no	no	no	no
	Overfitting	yes / no	no	no	no	no	no	no	no
Technical Dimensions	Presence of digital representation of systems	yes / no	no	no	yes	yes	no	no	no
	Live access to systems (real-time data)	yes / no	yes	yes	yes	yes	yes	yes	yes
	Ability of systems to communicate (technique)	yes / no	no	no	yes	yes	no	no	no
	Ability of systems to communicate (standard)	yes / no	no	no	yes	yes	no	no	no
	Ability of systems to communicate (interfaces)	yes / no	no	no	yes	yes	no	no	no
	Ability of systems to sense	yes / no	yes	yes	yes	no	yes	yes	yes
	Ability of systems to carry out actions	yes / no	no	no	no	no	no	no	no
	Ability of systems to process	yes / no	yes	yes	yes	yes	yes	yes	yes
	Requirement of additional setup	yes / no	yes	yes	yes	yes	yes	yes	yes
	Presence of API	yes / no	yes	yes	yes	yes	yes	no	no
Knowledge Dimensions	Availability of data	yes / no	yes	yes	yes	yes	yes	yes	yes
	Availability of explicit knowledge	yes / no	no	no	no	no	no	no	no
	Availability of tacit knowledge	yes / no	no	no	no	no	no	no	no
	Role as knowledge carrier in process	yes / no	no	no	no	no	no	no	no
	Degree of articulation	yes / no	no	no	no	no	no	no	no
	Degree of generality	yes / no	no	no	no	no	no	no	no
	Competence	yes / no	no	no	yes	yes	no	yes	yes
	Experience	yes / no	no	no	yes	yes	no	yes	yes
	Documentation availability	public Wiki / vendor documentation / no	vendor documentation	vendor documentation	vendor documentation	vendor documentation	vendor documentation	vendor documentation	vendor documentation
	Sample data availability	yes / no	yes	yes	yes	yes	yes	yes	yes
AI Dimensions	Input data availability	explicitly indicated	explicitly indicated	explicitly indicated	explicitly indicated	explicitly indicated	explicitly indicated	explicitly indicated	explicitly indicated
	Unsupervised functional approaches	available / not available	available	available	available	available	available	not available	not available
	Output data availability	explicitly indicated	explicitly indicated	explicitly indicated	explicitly indicated	explicitly indicated	explicitly indicated	explicitly indicated	explicitly indicated
	Supervised functional approaches	available	available	available	available	available	available	available	available
	State data availability	explicitly indicated / indicated not at all	explicitly indicated	explicitly indicated	explicitly indicated	explicitly indicated	explicitly indicated	indicated not at all	indicated not at all
	Action data availability	explicitly indicated / indicated not at all	explicitly indicated	explicitly indicated	indicated not at all	indicated not at all	explicitly indicated	indicated not at all	indicated not at all
	Reward data availability	explicitly indicated / indicated not at all	explicitly indicated	explicitly indicated	indicated not at all	indicated not at all	explicitly indicated	indicated not at all	indicated not at all
	Punishment data availability	indicated not at all	indicated not at all	indicated not at all	indicated not at all	indicated not at all	indicated not at all	indicated not at all	indicated not at all
	Reinforced functional approaches	available / not available	available	available	not available	not available	available	not available	not available
Customer Dimensions	Perceptability	obvious / questionable	questionable	questionable	obvious	obvious	questionable	questionable	questionable
	Usefulness of data	yes / no	no	no	yes	yes	no	yes	yes
	SME relevance	yes / no	no	no	yes	yes	no	yes	yes
	Expected relevance	yes / no	yes	yes	yes	yes	no	yes	yes
Vendor Dimensions	System costs	$/period in months (per user)	0	0	0	$80	0	0	0
	Paid access	$/period in months (per user)	0	0	$2	$80	0	0	0
	Vendor market share	amount (in %)	30%	2%	10%	10%	5%	1%	1%
	Vendor reputation	target group fit	target group fit	target group fit	target group fit	target group fit	target group fit	target group fit	target group fit
	Vendor business model uniqueness	small / medium / huge	huge	huge	medium	medium	small	huge	medium
	Trial version	open source	open source	open source	open source	open source	open source	open source	open source
	Technical support	community	community	community	community	community	community	community	community
	Vendor technique advantage	small / medium / huge	huge	huge	medium	medium	medium	huge	medium
Financial Dimensions	Presence of data structure	yes / no	yes	yes	yes	yes	yes	yes	yes
Political Dimensions	Limitations by laws	yes / no	no	no	no	no	no	no	no
Ethical Dimensions	Limitations by labor unions	yes / no	no	no	no	no	no	no	no
Evaluation	Final selection with sum of choices	yes / no (amount in %)	yes	yes (100%)	no (100%)	no (100%)	yes (75%)	yes (100%)	no (100%)

Fig. 3. Tool analysis and evaluation for data-driven, ML-based identification of as-is processes (part 2).

Dim. Category	Dimension		Scales	Automatic Relevance Determination regression (ARD)	k-means Clustering	Hierarchical Clustering	k-Nearest Neighbors (kNN)	Random Forest (RF)	Neuronale Netze (NN)	Long Short-Term Memory (LSTM)	GPT-2/3	BERT	ELMo
				ML-Tools / Algorithms							**Applications**		
Process Mining relevant Dimensions	Supported Control-Flow Constructs	Sequences (seq)	yes / no	no	no	no	no	no	no	no	no	no	no
		parallelism (par)	yes / no	no	no	no	no	no	no	no	no	no	no
		choices (cho)	yes / no	no	no	no	no	no	no	no	no	no	no
		loops (lo)	yes / no	no	no	no	no	no	no	no	no	no	no
		non-free-choices (nfc)	yes / no	no	no	no	no	no	no	no	no	no	no
		invisible tasks (it)	yes / no	no	no	no	no	no	no	no	no	no	no
		duplicate tasks (dt)	yes / no	no	no	no	no	no	no	no	no	no	no
	Completeness of Information in Logs	DB	yes / no	no	no	no	no	no	no	no	no	no	no
		ES	yes / no	no	no	no	no	no	no	no	no	no	no
		TS	yes / no	no	no	no	no	no	no	no	no	no	no
	Abstraction Levels	...(1:1)	yes / no	no	no	no	no	no	no	no	no	no	no
		...(1:0..1)	yes / no	no	no	no	no	no	no	no	no	no	no
	Underfitting vs Overfitting	Underfitting	yes / no	no	no	no	no	no	no	no	no	no	no
		Overfitting	yes / no	no	no	no	no	no	no	no	no	no	no
Technical Dimensions	Presence of digital representation of systems		yes / no	no	no	no	no	no	no	no	no	no	no
	Live access to systems (real-time data)		yes / no	no	no	no	no	no	no	no	no	no	no
	Ability of systems to communicate (technique)		yes / no	no	no	no	no	no	no	no	no	no	no
	Ability of systems to communicate (standard)		yes / no	no	no	no	no	no	no	no	no	no	no
	Ability of systems to communicate (interfaces)		yes / no	no	no	no	no	no	no	no	no	no	no
	Ability of systems to sense		yes / no	yes	yes	yes	yes	yes	yes	yes	yes	yes	yes
	Ability of systems to carry out actions		yes / no	yes	yes	yes	yes	yes	yes	yes	yes	yes	yes
	Ability of systems to process		yes / no	yes	yes	yes	yes	yes	yes	yes	yes	yes	yes
	Requirement of additional setup		yes / no	no	no	no	no	no	no	no	no	no	no
	Presence of API		yes / no	no	no	no	no	no	no	no	no	no	no
Knowledge Dimensions	Availability of data		yes / no	no	no	no	no	no	no	no	no	no	no
	Availability of explicit knowledge		yes / no	no	no	no	no	no	no	no	no	no	no
	Availability of tacit knowledge		yes / no	no	no	no	no	no	no	no	no	no	no
	Role as knowledge carrier in process		yes / no	no	no	no	no	no	no	no	no	no	no
	Degree of articulation		yes / no	no	no	no	no	no	no	no	no	no	no
	Degree of generality		yes / no	no	no	no	no	no	no	no	no	no	no
	Competence		yes / no	no	no	no	no	no	no	no	no	no	no
	Experience		yes / no	yes	yes	yes	yes	yes	yes	yes	yes	yes	yes
	Documentation availability		public Wiki	public wiki	public wiki	public wiki	public wiki	public wiki	public wiki	public wiki	public wiki	public wiki	public wiki
	Sample data availability		yes / no	no	no	no	no	no	no	no	no	no	no
AI Dimensions	Input data availability		explicitly indicated / indicated not at all	indicated not at all	indicated not at all	indicated not at all	indicated not at all	indicated not at all	indicated not at all	indicated not at all	indicated not at all	indicated not at all	indicated not at all
	Unsupervised functional approaches		available / not available	not available	available	available	not available	not available	available	available	available	available	available
	Output data availability		explicitly indicated	explicitly indicated	explicitly indicated	explicitly indicated	explicitly indicated	explicitly indicated	explicitly indicated	explicitly indicated	explicitly indicated	explicitly indicated	explicitly indicated
	Supervised functional approaches		available / not available	available	not available	not available	available	available	available	available	available	available	available
	State data availability		indicated not at all	indicated not at all	indicated not at all	indicated not at all	indicated not at all	indicated not at all	indicated not at all	indicated not at all	indicated not at all	indicated not at all	indicated not at all
	Action data availability		indicated not at all	indicated not at all	indicated not at all	indicated not at all	indicated not at all	indicated not at all	indicated not at all	indicated not at all	indicated not at all	indicated not at all	indicated not at all
	Reward data availability		indicated not at all	indicated not at all	indicated not at all	indicated not at all	indicated not at all	indicated not at all	indicated not at all	indicated not at all	indicated not at all	indicated not at all	indicated not at all
	Punishment data availability		indicated not at all	indicated not at all	indicated not at all	indicated not at all	indicated not at all	indicated not at all	indicated not at all	indicated not at all	indicated not at all	indicated not at all	indicated not at all
	Reinforced functional approaches		not available	not available	not available	not available	not available	not available	not available	not available	not available	not available	not available
Customer Dimensions	Perceptability		obvious / questionable	obvious	obvious	obvious	obvious	obvious	obvious	obvious	obvious	obvious	obvious
	Usefulness of data		yes / no	no	no	no	no	no	no	no	no	no	no
	SME relevance		yes / no	yes	yes	yes	yes	yes	yes	yes	yes	yes	yes
	Expected relevance		yes / no	yes	yes	yes	yes	yes	yes	yes	yes	yes	yes
Vendor Dimensions	System costs		$/period in months (per user)	0	0	0	0	0	0	0	0	0	0
	Paid access		$/period in months (per user)	0	0	0	0	0	0	0	0	0	0
	Vendor market share		amount (in %)	2%	70%	20%	50%	50%	70%	90%	25%	70%	35%
	Vendor reputation		target group fit	target group fit	target group fit	target group fit	target group fit	target group fit	target group fit	target group fit	target group fit	target group fit	target group fit
	Vendor business model uniqueness		small / medium / huge	small	small	small	small	small	small	small	small	small	small
	Trial version		open source	open source	open source	open source	open source	open source	open source	open source	open source	open source	open source
	Technical support		community	community	community	community	community	community	community	community	community	community	community
	Vendor technique advantage		small / medium / huge	small	small	small	small	small	small	small	small	small	small
Financial Dimensions	Presence of data structure		yes / no	yes	yes	yes	yes	yes	yes	yes	yes	yes	yes
Political Dimensions	Limitations by laws		yes / no	no	no	no	no	no	no	no	no	no	no
Ethical Dimensions	Limitations by labor unions		yes / no	no	no	no	no	no	no	no	no	no	no
Evaluation	Final selection with sum of choices		yes / no (amount in %)	yes (100%)	no (75%)	no (75%)	no (75%)	yes (100%)	yes (100%)	yes (100%)	no (100%)	no (100%)	no (100%)

Fig. 4. Tool analysis and evaluation for data-driven, ML-based identification of as-is processes (part 3).

Dim. Category	Dimension		Scales	Selection of systems and algorithms					
				PM-Tools					
				Algorithms					
				Alpha miner [22]	Heuristic miner [23] [24]	Genetic miner [16] [25]	Fuzzy miner [26]	Inductive miner [27]	Correlation miner [28]
Process Mining relevant Dimensions	Supported Control-Flow Constructs	Sequences (seq)	yes / no	yes	yes	yes	yes	yes	yes
		parallelism (par)	yes / no	yes	yes	yes	yes	yes	yes
		choices (cho)	yes / no	yes	yes	yes	yes	yes	yes
		loops (lo)	yes / no	yes	yes	yes	yes	yes	no
		non-free-choices (nfc)	yes / no	no	yes	yes	no	no	no
		invisible tasks (it)	yes / no	no	no	yes	no	yes	no
		duplicate tasks (dt)	yes / no	no	no	no	no	no	no
	Completeness of Information in Logs	DS	yes / no	yes	no	no	no	no	no
		EB	yes / no	no	yes	no	no	no	no
		TB	yes / no	no	no	yes	no	no	no
	Abstraction Levels	... (1:1)	yes / no	yes	no	no	no	no	no
		... (1:0..1)	yes / no	no	yes	yes	no	no	no
	Underfitting vs Overfitting	Underfitting	yes / no	no	yes	yes	no	no	no
		Overfitting	yes / no	yes	no	yes	no	no	no
	...		...	...	...	...	...	...	...
Technical Dimensions	Presence of digital representation of systems		yes / no	no	no	no	no	no	no
	Live access to systems (real-time data)		yes / no	no	no	no	no	no	no
	Ability of systems to communicate (technique)		yes / no	no	no	no	no	no	no
	Ability of systems to communicate (standard)		yes / no	no	no	no	no	no	no
	Ability of systems to communicate (interfaces)		yes / no	no	no	no	no	no	no
	Ability of systems to sense		yes / no	no	no	no	no	no	no
	Ability of systems to carry out actions		yes / no	no	no	no	no	no	no
	Ability of systems to process		yes / no	no	no	no	no	no	no
	Requirement of additional setup		yes / no	no	no	no	no	no	no
	Presence of API		yes / no	no	no	no	no	no	no
	...		...	...	...	...	...	...	...
Knowledge Dimensions	Availability of data		yes / no	no	no	no	no	no	no
	Availability of explicit knowledge		yes / no	no	no	no	no	no	no
	Availability of tacit knowledge		yes / no	no	no	no	no	no	no
	Role as knowledge carrier in process		yes / no	no	no	no	no	no	no
	Degree of articulation		yes / no	no	no	no	no	no	no
	Degree of generality		yes / no	no	no	no	no	no	no
	Competence		yes / no	no	no	no	no	no	no
	Experience		yes / no	no	no	no	no	no	no
	Documentation availability		no	no	no	no	no	no	no
	Sample data availability		yes / no	no	no	no	no	no	no
	...		...	...	...	...	...	...	...
AI Dimensions	Input data availability		indicated not at all	indicated not at all	indicated not at all	indicated not at all	indicated not at all	indicated not at all	indicated not at all
	Unsupervised functional approaches		not available	not available	not available	not available	not available	not available	not available
	Supervised functional approaches		indicated not at all	indicated not at all	indicated not at all	indicated not at all	indicated not at all	indicated not at all	indicated not at all
	Output data availability		not available	not available	not available	not available	not available	not available	not available
	Static data availability		indicated not at all	indicated not at all	indicated not at all	indicated not at all	indicated not at all	indicated not at all	indicated not at all
	Action data availability		indicated not at all	indicated not at all	indicated not at all	indicated not at all	indicated not at all	indicated not at all	indicated not at all
	Reward data availability		indicated not at all	indicated not at all	indicated not at all	indicated not at all	indicated not at all	indicated not at all	indicated not at all
	Punishment data availability		indicated not at all	indicated not at all	indicated not at all	indicated not at all	indicated not at all	indicated not at all	indicated not at all
	Reinforced functional approaches		not available	not available	not available	not available	not available	not available	not available
	...		...	...	...	...	...	...	...
Customer Dimensions	Perceptability		obvious / questionable	questionable	questionable	questionable	questionable	questionable	questionable
	Usefulness of data		yes / no	no	no	no	no	no	no
	SME relevance		yes / no	no	no	no	no	no	no
	Expected relevance		yes / no	no	no	no	no	no	no
	...		...	...	...	...	...	...	...
Vendor Dimensions	System costs		$/period in months (per user)	0	0	0	0	0	0
	Paid access		$/period in months (per user)	0	0	0	0	0	0
	Vendor market share		amount (in %)	70%	50%	50%	10%	10%	5%
	Vendor reputation		target group fit	target group fit	target group fit	target group fit	target group fit	target group fit	target group fit
	Vendor business model uniqueness		small / medium / huge	small	small	small	small	small	small
	Trial version		open source	open source	open source	open source	open source	open source	open source
	Technical support		community	community	community	community	community	community	community
	Vendor technique advantage		small / medium / huge	small	small	small	small	small	small
	...		...	...	...	...	...	...	...
Financial Dimensions	Presence of data structure		yes / no	no	no	no	no	no	no
	...		...	...	...	...	...	...	...
Political Dimensions	Limitations by laws		yes / no	no	no	no	no	no	no
	...		...	...	...	...	...	...	...
Ethical Dimensions	Limitations by labor unions		yes / no	no	no	no	no	no	no
	...		...	...	...	...	...	...	...
Evaluation	Final selection with sum of choices		yes / no (amount in %)	yes (75%)	no (100%)	yes (75%)	no (100%)	no (100%)	no (100%)

Fig. 5. Tool analysis and evaluation for data-driven, ML-based identification of as-is processes (part 4).

Fig. 6. Tool analysis and evaluation for data-driven, ML-based identification of as-is processes (part 5).

5   Conclusion

The research question (*"How can an adequate basis for the data-driven, machine-learning-based identification of as-is processes be systematically identified?"*) can be answered by the realization of a novel morphological analysis as follows. Based on literature research and expert experiments, relevant parameters have been identified, that are required for the identification of a novel adequate basis for the data-driven, ML-based identification of as-is processes. Based on empirical research, their relevance has been estimated. So, a best dimension configuration has been identified and a morphological box was constructed. By demonstrating the morphological box constructed, a selected set of tools has been analyzed. Finally, the best tools have been identified category-wise. These candidates refer to *MS-Dynamics* and *Oracle* as source systems, *DSL Modeling Standard* as knowledge-based AI system, *DSL Chatbot* as application, ML libraries (*TensorFlow*, and *PyBrain*), ML algorithms (*ARD*, *RF*, *NN* and *LSTM*), as well as PM algorithms (*alpha miner* and *genetic miner*). In addition, *Celonis* and *Pafnow* are selected as applications. All the selected algorithms, libraries, and tools can stand as a novel adequate basis for the development of a ML-based PM. Future research should focus on the following:

(1) Although the principle of integration has been considered in a practical validation, the technical proof and its validation in everyday situations has not been presented here.

(2) Further, only key dimensions have been chosen (e.g. Supported Control-Flow Constructs, Completeness of Information in Logs, Abstraction Levels and Undercutting vs. Over-fitting). A greater set of dimensions would present a more versatile picture on the tool identification. This also includes further developed systems and algorithms.

(3) Furthermore, only the morphological box and the interviews were used as the primary research method. To increase the robustness of the evaluation results, further research methods will be applied in the future. The resulting findings can be used to validate the already elaborated results or allow further interpretations of the results.

(4) The extent to which morphological boxes can be further developed is an interesting field of scientific research. Our morphological box can make a scientific contribution to this from a practical point of view in the context of PM.

(5) The algorithm performance and the training with the algorithms are therefore interesting fields of future research. Hence, next steps of the future research endeavor will focus on the implementation and the examination of the algorithm for industrial use cases.

References

1. Peffers, K., et al.: The design science research process: a model for producing and presenting information systems research. In: 1st International Conference on Design Science in Information Systems and Technology (DESRIST), vol. 24, no. 3, pp. 83–106 (2006)
2. van der Aalst, W.M.P.: Data science in action. in Process Mining. Springer, Berlin, Heidelberg, pp. 3–23 (2016). https://doi.org/10.1007/978-3-662-49851-4
3. van der Aalst, W.M.P.: Business process management: a comprehensive survey. ISRN Software Engineering, pp. 1–37 (2013). https://doi.org/10.1155/2013/507984
4. van der Aalst, W.M.P.: Process Mining: Discovery. Conformance and Enhancement of Business Processes. Springer-Verlag, Berlin (2011). https://doi.org/10.1007/978-3-642-19345-3
5. van der Aalst, W.M.P.: Data Scientist: The Engineer of the Future. In: Mertins, K., Benaben, F., Poler, R., Bourrieres, J., editors, Proceedings of the I-ESA Conference, volume 7 of Enterprise Interoperability, pp. 13–28. Springer-Verlag, Berlin (2014). https://doi.org/10.1007/978-3-319-04948-9_2

6. Aalst, W.M.P.: Extracting event data from databases to unleash process mining. In: vom Brocke, J., Schmiedel, T. (eds.) BPM - Driving Innovation in a Digital World. MP, pp. 105–128. Springer, Cham (2015). https://doi.org/10.1007/978-3-319-14430-6_8

7. Grum, M.: Managing human and artificial knowledge bearers. In: Shishkov, B. (ed.) BMSD 2020. LNBIP, vol. 391, pp. 182–201. Springer, Cham (2020). https://doi.org/10.1007/978-3-030-52306-0_12

8. Gronau, N.: Modeling and analyzing knowledge intensive business processes with KMDL: comprehensive insights into theory and practice, p. 7. GITOmbh, Berlin (2012)

9. Allesandro, B., van der Aalst, W.M.P.: A novel token-based replay technique to speed up conformance checking and process enhancement (2020)

10. Zwicky, F.: Discovery, Invention, Research - Through the Morphological Approach. The Macmillan Company, Toronto (1969)

11. Ritchey, T.: Problem structuring using computer-aided morphological analysis. J. Oper. Res. Soc., Special Issue Probl. Struct. Methods 57(7), 792–801 (2006)

12. Zwicky, F.: Entdecken, Erfinden, Forschen im morphologischen Weltbild. D. Knaur, California (1966)

13. van Dongen, B.F., Alves de Medeiros, A.K., Wen, L.: Process mining: overview and outlook of petri net discovery algorithms. In: Jensen, K., van der Aalst, W.M.P. (eds.) Transactions on Petri Nets and Other Models of Concurrency II. LNCS, vol. 5460, pp. 225–242. Springer, Heidelberg (2009). https://doi.org/10.1007/978-3-642-00899-3_13

14. van der Aalst, W.M.P., Weijters, A.J.M.M., Eds.: Process Mining, Special Issue of Computers in Industry, vol. 53(3). Elsevier Science Publishers, Amsterdam (2004)

15. can der Aalst, W.M.P., Rubin, V., can Dongen, B.F., Kindler, E., Günther, C.W.: Process mining: a two-step approach using transition systems and regions. BPM Center Report BPM-06-30, BPMcenter.org (2006)

16. Alves de Medeiros, A.K., Weijters, A.J.M.M., van der Aalst, W.M.P.: Genetic process mining: an experimental evaluation. Data Mining Knowl. Discov. 14(2), 245–304 (2007)

17. M. Grum, D. Kotarski, M. Ambros, T. Biru, H. Krallmann, N. Gronau. "Managing Knowledge of Intelligent Systems - The Design of a Chatbot Using Domain-Specific Knowledge". in: Business Modeling and Software Design. Springer International Publishing, 2021

18. McKinney, S.M., et al.: International evaluation of an AI system for breast cancer screening. In: Nature, vol. 577, issue 7788, p. 89 (2020). https://doi.org/10.1038/s41586-019-1799-6

19. Ozturk, T., Talo, M., Yildirim, E.A., Baloglu, U.B., Yildirim, O., Acharya, U.R.: Automated detection of COVID-19 cases using deep neural networks with X-ray images. In: Computers in Biology and Medicine, vol. 121, Article Number 103792 (2020). https://doi.org/10.1016/j.compbiomed.2020.103792

20. Raza, M.Q., Khosravi, A.: A review on artificial intelligence based load demand forecasting techniques for smart grid and buildings. Renew. Sustain. Energy Rev. 50, 1352–1372 (2015). https://doi.org/10.1016/j.rser.2015.04.065

21. Zhao, Z., Chen, W.H., Wu, X.M., Chen, P.C.Y., Liu, J.M.: LSTM network: a deep learning approach for short-term traffic forecast. IET Intell. Transport Syst. 11(2), 68–75 (2017). https://doi.org/10.1049/iet-its.2016.0208

22. Weijters, A.J.M.M., van der Aalst, W.M.P.: Rediscovering workflow models from event-based data using little thumb. Integr. Comput.-Aid. Eng. 10(2), 151–162 (2003)

23. Günther, C.W., van der Aalst, W.M.P.: Fuzzy mining - adaptive process simplification based on multi-perspective metrics. In: Alonso, G., et al., Eds., BPM, vol. 4714 of Lecture Notes in Computer Science, pp. 328–343. Springer (2007). https://doi.org/10.1007/978-3-540-75183-0_24

24. Color, J., Desel. J.: Application and theory of petri nets and concurrency. In: 34th International Conference, PETRI NETS 2013 Milan, Italy, Proceedings, pp. 311–329 (2013)

25. Pourmirza, S., Dijkman, R., Grefen, P.: Correlation mining: mining process orchestratoins without case identifiers. In: Eindhoven University of Technology, The Netherlands, Springer-Verlag, Berlin Heidelberg, pp. 237–252 (2015)

26. van der Aalst, W.M.P., et al.: Business process mining: an industrial application. Inf. Syst. **32**(5), 713–732 (2007). https://doi.org/10.1016/j.is.2006.05.003

27. Weijters, A.J.M.M., van der Aalst, W.M.P., Alves de Medeiros, A.K.: Process mining with heurisitics miner algorithm. In: BETA Working Paper Series, WP 166, Eindhoven University of Technology, Eindhoven (2006)

28. van der Aalst, W.M.P., Weijters, A.J.M.M., Maruster, L.: Workflow mining: discovering process models from event logs. IEEE Trans. Knowl. Data Eng. **16**(9), 1128–1142 (2004)

29. Alves de Medeiros, A.K.: Genetic process mining. PhD thesis, Eindhoven University of Technology, Eindhoven, The Netherlands (2006)

30. van Dongen, B.F., de Medeiros, A.K.A., Verbeek, H.M.W., Weijters, A.J.M.M., van der Aalst, W.M.P.: The ProM framework: a new era in process mining tool support in applications and theory of petri nets 2005. Proceedings **3536**, 444–454 (2005)

Author Index

Printed in the United States
by Baker & Taylor Publisher Services